AWS® Certified Advanced Networking

Official Study Guide

AWS®

Certified Advanced Networking

Official Study Guide Specialty Exam

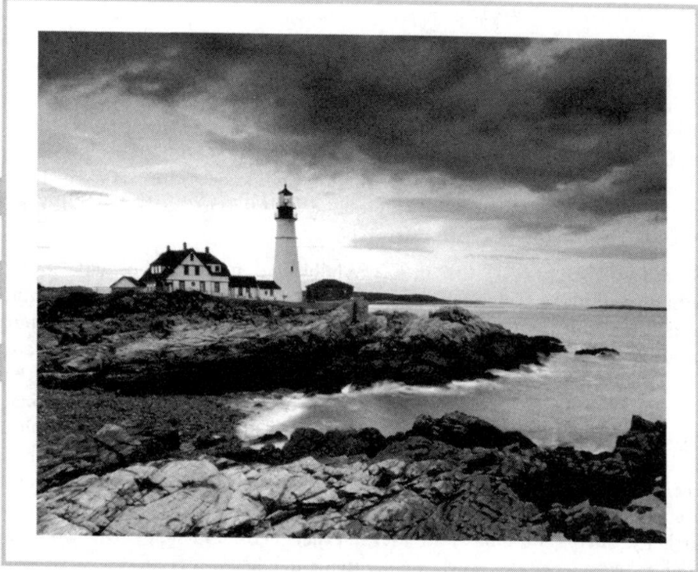

Sidhartha Chauhan, James Devine, Alan Halachmi, Matt Lehwess, Nick Matthews, Steve Morad, Steve Seymour

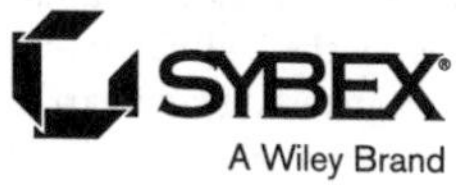

Senior Acquisitions Editor: Kenyon Brown
Project Editor: Gary Schwartz
Copy Editor: Kezia Endsley
Editorial Manager: Pete Gaughan and Mary Beth Wakefield
Production Manager: Kathleen Wisor
Executive Editor: Jim Minatel
Book Designers: Judy Fung and Bill Gibson
Proofreader: Nancy Carrasco
Indexer: Johnna VanHoose Dinse
Project Coordinator, Cover: Brent Savage
Cover Designer: Wiley
Cover Image: ©Jeremy Woodhouse/Getty Images, Inc.

Published by John Wiley & Sons, Inc., Indianapolis, Indiana

Published simultaneously in Canada

ISBN: 978-1-119-43983-7
ISBN: 978-1-119-43988-2 (ebk.)
ISBN: 978-1-119-43990-5 (ebk.)

Library of Congress Control Number: 2017962409

10 9 8 7 6 5 4 3 2 1

To those who designed and built what we explain herein.

Acknowledgments

The authors would like to thank a few people who helped us develop and write this AWS Certified Advanced Networking – Specialty Official Study Guide.

First, thanks to all of our families for supporting us in our seemingly endless efforts to produce this book. We know the hours away from home were only possible because of you. The readers of this book owe you a debt of gratitude, as well.

A huge thanks to our colleagues, Dave Cuthbert and Dave Walker, who guest authored the chapters on automation and risk and compliance, respectively. Many thanks to James Hamilton for the Foreword and to Mark Ryland and Camil Samaha for their cover-to-cover contributions.

When we wrote this book, many of the features and services described were only on the drawing board. Thanks to the product and engineering teams for taking the time to provide us with insight into new and exciting capabilities. Our readers thank you, too!

Of course, we must thank all of the supporting team members who helped shepherd us to the finish line: Nathan Bower and Victoria Steidel, our thoughtful technical editors, who reviewed and edited all of the content; Mary Kay Sondecker, who answered our call for project help; and Sharon Saternus, our project manager, who had the task of herding cats – the authors.

About the Authors

Sidhartha Chauhan, Solutions Architect, Amazon Web Services

Sid works with enterprise customers to design highly-scalable cloud architectures. He has a special inclination toward computer networking technologies and holds a master's degree in computer networking from North Carolina State University, along with various leading industry certifications. Before joining Amazon, Sid worked with a large telecommunications organization designing large-scale Local Area Network (LAN)/Wide Area Network (WAN) networks. In his free time, Sid plays guitar for an award-winning New York City-based Indian band called "Rhythm Tolee." He also enjoys photography and fitness.

James Devine, Solutions Architect, Amazon Web Services

Using AWS to help design solutions for nonprofit customers who are making a difference in the world is what keeps James motivated. He holds a bachelor's degree in computer science from Allegheny College and a master's degree in computer science from the Stevens Institute of Technology. Prior to joining AWS, James was a senior infrastructure engineer at MITRE Corporation, a nonprofit government contractor, where he used his skills in infrastructure to help various government organizations solve some of their toughest problems and realize the value of cloud computing.

Alan Halachmi, Senior Manager, Solutions Architecture, Amazon Web Services

Alan leads a team of specialist solutions architects supporting public sector customers. These specialists provide deep expertise in domains such as Geospatial Information Systems (GIS), High Performance Computing (HPC), and machine learning. Alan supports public sector organizations across the globe in the areas of networking and security. He holds a Certified Information Systems Security Professional (CISSP®) certification as well as a half-dozen AWS certifications. He participated in the development of the Solutions Architect – Associate, Solutions Architect – Professional, and Advanced Networking – Specialty exams. Additionally, Alan has authored multiple AWS whitepapers that focus on the intersection of networking and security. Prior to joining Amazon, he worked in various leadership positions focused on homeland protection and identity systems at both established and startup companies in the private sector. Alan holds a bachelor's degree in network communication and information security from Duke University. In his free time, Alan enjoys family and tinkering with new toys.

Matt Lehwess, Principal Solutions Architect, Amazon Web Services

Matt has spent many years working as a network engineer in the network service provider space, building large-scale WAN networks in the Asia Pacific region and North America, as well as deploying data center technologies and their related network infrastructure. As a result, he is most at home working with Amazon VPC, AWS Direct Connect, and Amazon's other infrastructure-focused products and services. Matt is also a public speaker for AWS, and he enjoys spending time helping customers solve large-scale problems using the AWS Cloud platform. Outside of work, Matt is an avid rock climber, both indoor and outdoor, and a keen surfer. When he misses the waves of his hometown back in Australia, a trip to Santa Cruz, California from his home in San Francisco soon alleviates any homesick feelings.

Nick Matthews, Senior Solutions Architect, Amazon Web Services

Nick Matthews leads the networking segment of AWS partner support organization. He helps AWS partners create new networking solutions and make traditional networking products work on AWS. He enjoys assisting AWS customers to architect their networks for scalability and security. Nick also speaks at industry events on networking and security best practices. Before joining Amazon, Nick spent 10 years at Cisco working on Voice over IP (VoIP), Software-Defined Networking (SDN), and routing (Cisco Certified Internetwork Expert [CCIE] #23560). He founded the Network Programmability Users Group (`npug.net`) to help users with SDN and programming network equipment. In his free time, he enjoys eating, drinking, and playing beach volleyball.

Steve Morad, Senior Manager, Solutions Builders, Amazon Web Services

Steve Morad holds a BA in computer science from Wheaton College (IL), and an MBA from Virginia Tech. He started his career by graduating from college and running off to join the circus. Since then, he gained systems administration, development, and architecture experience in the entertainment, financial services, and technology industries. Steve spent five years as a principal solutions architect supporting customers of all sizes and maturity levels, with a sub-specialty in AWS networking and security. He helped develop the Solutions Architect Associate, Developer Associate, SysOps Associate, Solutions Architect Professional, DevOps Professional, and Network Specialty exams. Steve is also an AWS public speaker and has developed network-related technical articles, whitepapers, and reference implementations. Steve is currently a senior manager of solutions builders at AWS. Outside of work, Steve enjoys helping coach soccer goalies and watching his kids perform in various musical ensembles.

Steve Seymour, Principal Solutions Architect, Amazon Web Services

Steve is a principal solutions architect and networking specialist within the AWS team covering Europe, the Middle East, and Africa. He uses his networking expertise to help customers of all sizes—from fast growing startups to the world's largest enterprises—use AWS networking technologies to meet and exceed their business requirements. Steve has more than 15 years of experience working with enterprise infrastructure, data center implementations, and migration projects with complex IP communications requirements. He is passionate about applying this experience to a broad range of industries to support customer success on AWS. Steve enjoys the outdoors, regularly coaches canoeing, and goes geocaching whenever traveling.

Contents at a Glance

Contents

Table of Exercises

Foreword

Cloud computing is fundamentally disrupting most aspects of the information technology business. Users no longer buy hardware, storage, or databases. Instead, they rent what they need in a consumption-based model—by the gigabyte per day or hour for storage, by the hour, minute, or even millisecond for compute. For example, as of this writing, users of Amazon Web Service's Lambda event-driven functional compute service pay $0.0000002 per request, and $0.000000208 per 100 milliseconds of compute time for functions when using 128 MB of RAM, but only after first using up one million requests and 3,200,000 compute-seconds that are provided free of charge each month.

A critical part of this disruption is the radical changes happening in the networking market. For years, networking was the last bastion of the mainframe computing model: vertically integrated, incredibly complex, very slow to evolve, and with ridiculously high margins. Networking has been completely different from the server world, where competition has emerged at every level: the component level, the finished server level, the operating system level, and of course the application stack, which has literally thousands of competitors. Networking has been like a step backwards in time, where one company produced everything from the core ASIC, to the finish router, through to the control software and protocol stack.

FIGURE 1 Comparison of networking equipment and general-purpose servers

Central Logic Manufacture
• Proprietary & closely guarded
• Single source
Finished Hardware Supply
• Proprietary & closely guarded
• Single source
System Software Supply
• Proprietary & closely guarded
• Single source
Application Stack
• Not supported
• No programming tools
• No 3rd party ecosystem
Net Equipment
Central Logic Manufacture
• Standard design (x86)
• Multiple source
• AMD, Intel, Via, ...
Finished Hardware Supply
• Standard design
• Multiple source
• Dell, SGI, HP, IBM, ...
System Software Supply
• Linux (many distros/support)
• Windows & other proprietary offerings
Application Stack
• Public/published APIs
• High quality programming tools
• Rich 3rd party ecosystem
X86 Server

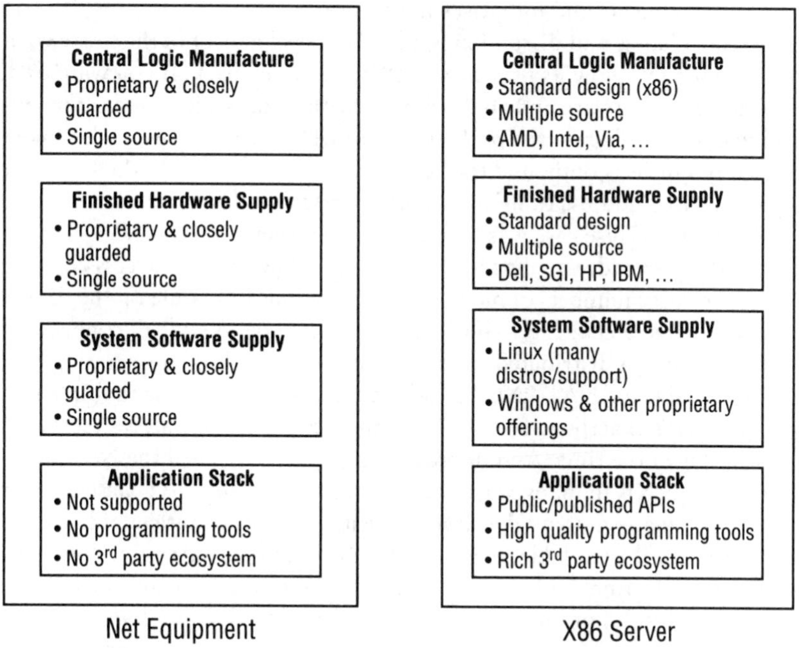

What's changing in the networking world is that there is now a variety of competitors emerging for all components in a networking device, and cloud computing providers have the scale to be able to justify investing in a very well-staffed network engineering team. There now is another way and, consequently, networking costs are falling fast while bandwidth is escalating and latency is improving.

Building networks using custom-designed routers running custom control software and protocol stacks is a substantial undertaking, and only the largest operators have the scale to justify the investment. Those that can support the research and development effort of going to a fully-customized hardware and software networking stack are rewarded with far lower costs and much higher availability. The biggest availability improvements come from focusing the complexity on exactly what is needed to support a single homogeneous but massive world-wide networking plant rather than having to support simultaneously a hodge-podge of diverse networks implemented by generations of networking engineers over decades at enterprises throughout the world.

How does the rest of the world take advantage of this first level of disruption at the physical network level? Primarily at the next level. The second level of change and disruption is loosely described as "software defined networking" or SDN. At this level, a cooperating set of components (networking devices, Hypervisors, network coprocessors on hosts, and so forth) conspire to create networking constructs—CIDR ranges and subnets, IP addresses, LANs, routes, and so on—dynamically and under software control as exposed through APIs. In this area, Amazon Virtual Private Cloud technology is one of the largest and most mature SDN technologies in the industry, but there are many other interesting and important developments and initiatives in this area.

The third level of change and disruption is a further development of the first two, and it is just now beginning to show its presence in AWS. Let's step back. If you want to define networking behavior in software and you're dealing with cloud-scale systems, then you're going to need to dynamically re-write packets in parallel flows at massive scale. Take something as apparently simple as outbound traffic from a private network to the Internet that flows through a network address translation/port address translation (NAT/PAT) gateway. Historically, the NAT/PAT use case was limited to a single networking device because there is a shared state (the port/address mapping table) that all flows need to access constantly. The only way to support large numbers of high-speed connections is to scale up the device, and then availability becomes a challenge—if that single device goes down, all connectivity is lost.

Suppose that we build a distributed state machine—hundreds of cooperating hosts that have a shared state table for NAT/PAT, but one that can operate on the multiple network flows in parallel. That's exactly what AWS has done with its NAT Gateway service, as I discussed on my blog at the time. And, more recently, AWS launched the Network Load Balancing service, which is in many ways the mirror image of the NAT Gateway service. In those services and many more under development, we take advantage of the scale of the AWS cloud to build highly-available, massively-parallel networking engines on Amazon Elastic Compute Cloud (Amazon EC2) itself with customized hardware assist. These engines appear to both sides of the connection as a single IP address—like a giant switch or router. In between the "inner" and "outer" single IP addresses could be dozens or hundreds of powerful hosts pumping packets at their maximum per-host rate, potentially rewriting those packets at line rate, all the while participating in a distributed state machine that has the high availability and massive scalability of parallel and distributed cloud architecture.

Using these and a range of other new technologies, AWS is able to provide a set of powerful networking and security features, dynamically defined by software, supported by hardware assist and delivered very inexpensively. The beneficiaries are every kind of IT consumer, all the way from national governments and large enterprises, to start-ups, non-profits, and small businesses.

I've mostly been talking about the guts of our cloud networking system: How it's built and what's inside. But the most important thing is not how (which can and will change dynamically under the hood as we constantly iterate and advance our technology) but the what; that is, what you as an IT professional can do with the features that these advanced technologies expose.

In this book, AWS experts will take you through that what. In the following chapters, you'll begin with the basics and then advance through the most sophisticated networking features that the AWS cloud has to offer. When you complete this study guide, you will have the fundamental knowledge required to succeed on the AWS Certified Advanced Networking – Specialty certification.

The best thing about networking in the cloud is that networking is no longer a static, expensive, and labor-intensive domain managed only by experts and evolved only at great expense in labor and hardware. Networking is now an integral part of developing, deploying, and managing powerful and highly-secure software using modern secure dev/ops approaches. Networking is now open to builders. Now go build!

James Hamilton
Vice President and Distinguished Engineer
Amazon Web Services

Introduction

There's a lot to know if you want to provide highly available, scalable, performant, and flexible architectures. This study guide is designed to help you develop appropriate networking solutions using AWS and to provide you with the knowledge required to achieve the AWS Certified Advanced Networking – Specialty certification.

This study guide covers relevant topics on the exam, with additional context to help further your understanding. By referencing the exam blueprint, this study guide provides a comprehensive view of the knowledge required to pass the exam. While Chapter 2, Amazon Virtual Private Cloud (Amazon VPC) and Networking Fundamentals, provides a review of key networking fundamentals for Amazon Virtual Private Cloud (Amazon VPC), this study guide does not include many of the concepts covered by the prerequisite exams. It is also expected that you have hands-on experience architecting and implementing network solutions.

This study guide begins with an introduction to AWS networking, which is then followed by chapters on the topics covered in the exam. Chapters include specific information on services or topics, followed by an Exam Essentials section that contains key information needed for your exam preparation.

Each chapter includes an Exercise section with activities designed to help reinforce the topic of the chapter with hands-on learning. Each chapter then contains Review Questions to assess your knowledge. Note that the actual exam questions will require you to combine multiple concepts to determine the correct answer. The Review Questions in this study guide focus specifically on the topics and concepts of a given chapter.

The guide also contains a self-assessment exam with 25 questions. Two practice exams with 50 questions each are also included to help you gauge your readiness to take the exam, as well as flashcards to help you learn and retain key facts needed to prepare for the exam.

What Does this Book Cover?

This book covers topics that you need to know to prepare for the Amazon Web Services (AWS) Certified Advanced Networking – Specialty exam:

Chapter 1: Introduction to Advanced Networking This chapter provides an overview of the AWS Global Infrastructure, Amazon Virtual Private Cloud, and other AWS networking services. The chapter provides a baseline understanding of concepts like AWS Regions and Availability Zones. It also characterizes where various network capabilities reside within the overall AWS infrastructure.

Chapter 2: Amazon Virtual Private Cloud (Amazon VPC) and Networking Fundamentals This chapter reviews the basics of Amazon VPC and the components within it. The content covers the foundational knowledge required for operating both IPv4 and IPv6 in an Amazon VPC. Subsequent chapters build on the information provided in this chapter.

Chapter 3: Advanced Amazon Virtual Private Cloud (Amazon VPC) In this chapter, you will learn advanced Amazon VPC concepts such as AWS PrivateLink, VPC endpoints, and transitive routing. There is a review of a few of the ways to connect services privately in different VPCs. In addition, there are some advanced IP address features, such as reclaiming elastic IP addresses.

Chapter 4: Virtual Private Networks This chapter is intended to provide you with an understanding of how to design Virtual Private Networks (VPNs) on AWS. We go into detail on the various options available for VPN termination in AWS. We evaluate the options in terms of ease of VPN creation and management, high availability, scalability, and additional features. We sum up the chapter by talking about various design patters around VPN use in AWS including transitive routing.

Chapter 5: AWS Direct Connect In this chapter, we will expand on the elements involved in deploying AWS Direct Connect, beginning with Physical Connectivity at Direct Connect Locations, the provisioning process, and finally covering the logical configuration of Virtual Interfaces. Both hosted connections and dedicated connections are covered along with Public and Private Virtual Interfaces including integration with Direct Connect Gateway.

Chapter 6: Domain Name System and Load Balancing This chapter begins with an overview of Domain Name System and Amazon EC2 DNS. It then describes Amazon Route 53, including domain registration and routing policies. This chapter then dives into Elastic Load Balancing and each of the three types of Load Balancers: CLB, ALB, and NLB.

Chapter 7: Amazon CloudFront This chapter describes the Amazon CloudFront service, its components, and how Amazon CloudFront distributions can be uses to serve static, dynamic, and streaming objects.

Chapter 8: Network Security This chapter focuses on the network security capabilities provided by or enabled through AWS services. You will learn about the spectrum of network security options available from the edge of the network through to individual Amazon EC2 instances. This chapter also discussed new AWS offerings that leverage Artificial Intelligence and Machine Learning to protect information regarding your network infrastructure.

Chapter 9: Network Performance This chapter discusses network performance. There is a brief review of the components of network performance, how they are implemented in AWS, and how to configure your applications for better network performance. The chapter also reviews some example use cases where network performance is important for applications.

Chapter 10: Automation This chapter describes how to automate the deployment and configuration of networks on AWS. You'll start by learning how to maintain the network infrastructure as code by creating AWS CloudFormation templates and stacks, and how to use AWS CodePipeline to enable the continuous deployment of this infrastructure at scale. The chapter finishes by covering Amazon CloudWatch to monitor the health and performance of your network and how to create alarms that alert you when an issue arises.

Chapter 11: Service Requirements This chapter discusses AWS services that can be launched within a VPC. It maps the service requirements of each service to the corresponding network requirements. Knowledge of network requirements for each service will help you design and assess appropriate network architectures on the exam.

Chapter 12: Hybrid Architectures This chapter explains how to design hybrid architectures using the technologies and AWS Cloud services. We go into detail on how AWS Direct Connect and Virtual Private Networks (VPNs) can be leveraged to enable common hybrid IT application architectures. We also dive deep into the transit VPC architecture, discussing the various design elements of the architecture and the various use cases where it can be leveraged.

Chapter 13: Network Troubleshooting This chapter begins with a discussion of both traditional and AWS-provided network troubleshooting tools. It then addresses common troubleshooting scenarios and the steps to take in each scenario.

Chapter 14: Billing In this chapter, we will cover the elements involved in AWS billing as it relates to Networking. The content considers factors such as data processing fees, data transfer fees, and hourly service charges in relation to Amazon EC2, VPN, AWS Direct Connect, and Elastic Load Balancing. The chapter also discusses data transfer specifically between Availability Zones and AWS Regions.

Chapter 15: Risk and Compliance In this chapter, you will learn about a range of risk and compliance considerations when leveraging the cloud. The chapter begins with a review of threat modeling, access control, and encryption. The chapter then discusses network monitoring and malicious activity detection. Finally, you will learn about executing penetration and vulnerability assessment on your AWS workloads.

Chapter 16: Scenarios and Reference Architectures This chapter covers scenarios and reference architectures for combining different AWS network components to meet common customer requirements. These scenarios include implementing networks that span multiple regions and locations, connecting to enterprise shared services, and creating hybrid networks.

Interactive Online Learning Environment and Test Bank

The authors have worked hard to provide you with some really great tools to help you with your certification process. The interactive online learning environment that accompanies the *AWS Certified Advanced Networking – Specialty Official Study Guide* provides a test bank with study tools to help you prepare for the certification exam. This will help you increase your chances of passing it the first time! The test bank includes the following:

Sample Tests All of the questions in this book, including the 25-question Assessment Test at the end of this introductory section and the Review Questions are provided at the end of each chapter. In addition, there are two Practice Exams online with 50 questions each. Use these questions to test your knowledge of the study guide material. The online test bank runs on multiple devices.

Flashcards The online test banks include 100 Flashcards specifically written to quiz your knowledge of AWS operations. After completing all of the exercises, Review Questions, Practice Exams, and Flashcards, you should be more than ready to take the exam. The flashcard questions are provided in a digital flashcard format (a question followed by a single correct answer). You can use the Flashcards to reinforce your learning and provide last-minute test prep before the exam.

Glossary A Glossary of key terms from this book is available as a fully-searchable PDF.

Go to `http://www.wiley.com/go/sybextestprep` to register and gain access to this interactive online learning environment and test bank with study tools.

Exam Objectives

The *AWS Certified Advanced Networking – Specialty Exam* is intended for people who have experience designing and implementing scalable network infrastructures. Exam concepts that you should understand for this exam include the following:

- Designing, developing, and deploying cloud-based solutions using AWS
- Implementing core AWS services according to basic architectural best practices
- Designing and maintaining network architecture for all AWS services
- Leveraging tools to automate AWS networking tasks

In general, certification candidates should understand the following:

- AWS networking nuances and how they relate to the integration of AWS services
- Advanced networking architectures and interconnectivity options (for example, IP VPN, and MPLS/VPLS)
- Networking technologies within the OSI model and how they affect implementation decisions
- Development of automation scripts and tools
- Design, implementation, and optimization of the following:
  - Routing architectures
  - Multi-region solutions for a global enterprise
  - Highly-available connectivity solutions
- CIDR and subnetting (IPv4 and IPv6)
- IPv6 transition challenges

- Generic solutions for network security features, including WAF, IDS, IPS, DDoS protection, and Economic Denial of Service/Sustainability (EDoS)
- Professional experience using AWS technology
- Experience implementing AWS security best practices
- Knowledge of AWS storage options and their underlying consistency models

The exam covers six different domains, with each domain broken down into objectives and subobjectives.

Objective Map

The following table lists each domain and its weighting in the exam, along with the chapters in the book where that domain's objectives and subobjectives are covered.

Domain	Percentage of Exam	Chapter
Domain 1.0: Design and implement hybrid IT network architectures at scale	23%	1, 3, 4, 5 12, 16
1.1 Implement connectivity for hybrid IT		4, 12
1.2 Given a scenario, derive an appropriate hybrid IT architecture connectivity solution		3, 4, 12, 16
1.3 Explain the process to extend connectivity using AWS Direct Connect		5
1.4 Evaluate design alternatives that leverage AWS Direct Connect		1, 4, 5, 12
1.5 Define routing policies for hybrid IT architectures		3, 4, 5, 12
Domain 2.0: Design and implement AWS networks	29%	1, 2, 3, 6, 7, 8, 9, 10, 13, 14, 16
2.1 Apply AWS networking concepts		1, 2, 3, 10, 13
2.2 Given customer requirements, define network architectures on AWS		8, 10, 16
2.3 Propose optimized designs based on the evaluation of an existing implementation		10, 16

Domain	Percentage of Exam	Chapter
2.4 Determine network requirements for a specialized workload		6, 7, 9
2.5 Derive an appropriate architecture based on customer and application requirements		3, 6, 7, 8, 9, 10
2.6 Evaluate and optimize cost allocations given a network design and application data flow		14
Domain 3.0: Automate AWS tasks	8%	8, 10
3.1 Evaluate automation alternatives within AWS for network deployments		10
3.2 Evaluate tool-based alternatives within AWS for network operations and management		8, 10
Domain 4.0: Configure network integration with application services	15%	1, 2, 6, 7, 11, 12
4.1 Leverage the capabilities of Amazon Route 53		1, 6
4.2 Evaluate DNS solutions in a hybrid IT architecture		6, 12
4.3 Determine the appropriate configuration of DHCP within AWS		2
4.4 Given a scenario, determine an appropriate load balancing strategy within the AWS ecosystem		1, 6
4.5 Determine a content distribution strategy to optimize for performance		1, 6, 7
4.6 Reconcile AWS service requirements with network requirements		11

Domain	Percentage of Exam	Chapter
Domain 5.0: Design and implement for security and compliance	12%	1, 3, 4, 5, 8, 12, 15
5.1 Evaluate design requirements for alignment with security and compliance objectives		3, 8, 15
5.2 Evaluate monitoring strategies in support of security and compliance objectives		8, 15
5.3 Evaluate AWS security features for managing network traffic		1, 8, 15
5.4 Utilize encryption technologies to secure network communications		4, 5, 8, 12, 15
Domain 6.0: Manage, optimize, and troubleshoot the network	13%	13
6.1 Given a scenario, troubleshoot and resolve a network issue		13

Assessment Test

1. Which Virtual Private Network (VPN) protocols are supported under the AWS managed VPN connection option?

   A. Internet Protocol Security (IPsec)

   B. Generic Routing Encapsulation (GRE)

   C. Dynamic Multipoint VPN (DMVPN)

   D. Layer 2 Tunneling Protocol (L2TP)

2. How will you vertically-scale Virtual Private Network (VPN) throughput in a Virtual Private Cloud (VPC) when terminating the VPN on Amazon Elastic Compute Cloud (Amazon EC2) with minimal downtime?

   A. Attach multiple elastic network interfaces to the existing Amazon EC2 instance responsible for VPN termination.

   B. Stop the Amazon EC2 instance and change the instance type to a larger instance type. Start the instance.

   C. Take a snapshot of the instance. Launch a new, larger instance using this snapshot, and move the Elastic IP address from the existing instance to the new instance.

   D. Launch a new Amazon EC2 instance of a larger instance type. Move the Amazon Elastic Block Store (Amazon EBS) disk from the existing instance to the new instance.

3. Which of the following is required to create a 1 Gbps AWS Direct Connect connection?

   A. Open Shortest Path First (OSPF)

   B. 802.1Q Virtual Local Area Network (VLAN)

   C. Bidirectional Forwarding Detection (BFD)

   D. Single-mode fiber

4. The Letter of Authorization – Connecting Facility Assignment (LOA-CFA) document downloaded via the AWS Management Console provides the AWS Direct Connect location provider with which of the following?

   A. The cross-connect port detail for the AWS end of the connection

   B. The cross-connect port detail for the customer end of the connection

   C. The cross-connect's assigned AWS Region

   D. The billing address for the cross-connect

5. You have a three-tier web application. You have to move this application to AWS. As a first step, you decide to move the web layer to AWS while keeping the application and database layer on-premises. During initial phases of this migration, the web layer will have servers both in AWS and on-premises. How will you architect this setup? (Choose two.)

   A. Set up an AWS Direct Connect private Virtual Interface (VIF).

   B. Use Network Load Balancer to distribute traffic to the web layer on-premises and in the Virtual Private Cloud (VPC).

C. Set up an AWS Direct Connect public VIF.

D. Set up an IP Security (IPsec) Virtual Private Network (VPN) from on-premises to AWS, terminating at the Virtual Private Gateway (VGW).

E. Use Classic Load Balancer to distribute traffic to the web layer on-premises and in the VPC.

6. You have set up a transit Virtual Private Cloud (VPC) architecture. You are connected to the hub VPC using AWS Direct Connect and a detached Virtual Private Gateway (VGW). You want all hybrid IT traffic to the production spoke VPC to pass through the transit hub VPC. You also want on-premises traffic to the test VPC to bypassing the transit VPC, reaching the test spoke VPC directly. How will you architect this solution, considering least latency and maximum security?

   A. Set up an AWS Direct Connect private Virtual Interface (VIF) to an AWS Direct Connect Gateway. Attach the VGW of the test VPC to the AWS Direct Connect Gateway.

   B. Assign public IP addresses to the Amazon Elastic Compute Cloud (Amazon EC2) instance in the test VPC, and access these resources using the public IP addresses over AWS Direct Connect public VIF.

   C. Set up a VPN from a detached VGW to an Amazon EC2 instance in the test VPC.

   D. Set up a VPN from the detached VGW to the VGW of the test VPC.

7. You have created a Virtual Private Cloud (VPC) with an IPv4 CIDR of 10.0.0.0/27. What is the maximum number of IPv4 subnets that you can create?

   A. 1

   B. 2

   C. 3

   D. 4

8. You create a new Virtual Private Cloud (VPC) in us-east-1 and provision three subnets inside this VPC. Which of the following statements is true?

   A. By default, these subnets will not be able to communicate with each other; you will need to create routes.

   B. All subnets are public by default.

   C. All subnets will have a route to one another.

   D. Each subnet will have identical Classless Inter-Domain Routing (CIDR) blocks.

9. Your networking group has decided to migrate all of the 192.168.0.0/16 Virtual Private Cloud (VPC) instances to 10.0.0.0/16. Which of the following is a valid option?

   A. Add a new 10.0.0.0/16 Classless Inter-Domain Routing (CIDR) range to the 192.168.0.0/16 VPC. Change the existing addresses of instances to the 10.0.0.0/16 space.

   B. Change the initial VPC CIDR range to the 10.0.0.0/16 CIDR.

   C. Create a new 10.0.0.0/16 VPC. Use VPC peering to migrate workloads to the new VPC.

   D. Use Network Address Translation (NAT) in the 192.168.0.0/16 space to the 10.0.0.0/16 space using NAT Gateways.

10. What do Amazon CloudFront Origin Access Identities (OAIs) do?
    A. Increase the performance of Amazon CloudFront by preloading video streams.
    B. Allow the use of Network Load Balancer as an origin server.
    C. Restrict access to Amazon Elastic Compute Cloud (Amazon EC2) web instances.
    D. Restrict access to an Amazon Simple Storage Service (Amazon S3) bucket to only special Amazon CloudFront users.

11. Which types of distributions are required to support Amazon CloudFront Real-Time Messaging Protocol (RTMP) media streaming? (Choose two.)
    A. An RTMP distribution for the media files
    B. A web distribution for the media player
    C. A web distribution for the media files
    D. An RTMP distribution for media files and the media player
    E. Amazon CloudFront does not support RTMP streaming.

12. Voice calls to international numbers from inside your company must go through an open-source Session Border Controller (SBC) installed on a custom Linux Amazon Machine Image (AMI) in your Virtual Private Cloud (VPC) public subnet. The SBC handles the real-time media and voice signaling. International calls often have garbled voice, and it is difficult to understand what people are saying. What may increase the quality of international voice calls?
    A. Place the SBC in a placement group to reduce latency.
    B. Add additional network interfaces to the instance.
    C. Use an Application Load Balancer to distribute load to multiple SBCs.
    D. Enable enhanced networking on the instance.

13. Your big data team is trying to determine why their proof of concept is running slowly. For the demo, they are trying to ingest 100 TB of data from Amazon Simple Storage Service (Amazon S3) on their c4.8xl instance. They have already enabled enhanced networking. What should they do to increase Amazon S3 ingest rates?
    A. Run the demo on premises, and access Amazon S3 from AWS Direct Connect to reduce latency.
    B. Split the data ingest on more than one instance, such as two c4.4xl instances.
    C. Place the instance in a placement group, and use an Amazon S3 endpoint.
    D. Place a Network Load Balancer between the instance and Amazon S3 for more efficient load balancing and better performance.

14. An AWS CloudFormation change set can be used for which of the following purposes? (Choose two.)
    A. Checking if an existing resource has been altered outside of AWS CloudFormation.
    B. Examining the differences between the current stack and a new template.
    C. Specifying which changes are to be applied to a stack from a new template by editing the change set.

D. Rolling back a previous update to an existing stack.

E. Executing a stack update after changes are approved in a continuous delivery pipeline.

15. You have created an AWS CloudFormation stack to manage network resources in an account with the intent of allowing unprivileged users to make changes to the stack. When a user attempts to make a change and update the stack, however, the user gets a permission denied error when a resource is updated. What might be the cause?

A. The stack does not have a stack policy attached to it that allows updates.

B. The user does not have permission to invoke the CloudFormation:UpdateStack Application Programming Interface (API).

C. The template does not have a stack policy attached to it that allows updates.

D. The stack does not have an AWS Identity and Access Management (IAM) service role attached to it that allows updates.

16. You are trying to resolve host names from an instance in VPC A for instances that resides in VPC B. The two VPCs are peered within the same region. What action must be taken to enable this?

A. Disable DNS host names by setting the `enableDnsHostnames` value to false in VPC B, the peered VPC.

B. Enable the value for Allow DNS Resolution from Peer VPC for the VPC peering connection.

C. Build an IP Security (IPsec) tunnel from an instance in the VPC A to the VGW of VPC B to allow DNS resolution between the VPCs.

D. Build your own DNS resolver in VPC B, and point VPC A's instances to this resolver.

17. When using Amazon Route 53, the EDNS0 extension is used when you want to do which of the following?

A. Adjust the Time To Live (TTL) of Domain Name System (DNS) records.

B. Increase the accuracy of geolocation routing by adding optional extensions to the DNS protocol.

C. Increase the accuracy of geolocation routing by removing unneeded extensions to the DNS protocol.

D. Create a geolocation resource record set in a private hosted zone.

18. What happens when you associate an Amazon CloudFront distribution with an AWS Lambda@Edge function?

A. AWS Lambda is deployed in your Virtual Private Cloud (VPC).

B. AWS Lambda@Edge will create an Amazon Simple Notification Service (Amazon SNS) topic for email notification.

C. Amazon CloudFront intercepts requests and responses at Amazon CloudFront Regional Edge Caches.

D. Amazon CloudFront intercepts requests and responses at Amazon CloudFront edge locations.

19. After deploying Amazon RDS in a new subnet within a VPC, application developers report that they cannot connect to the database from another subnet within the VPC. What action must be taken?

A. Create a VPC peering connection to the Amazon RDS subnets.

B. Enable Multi-AZ deployment.

C. Create a route to the Amazon RDS instance subnets.

D. Add the application server security group to the Amazon RDS inbound security group.

20. Which of the following techniques is used to mitigate the impact on Amazon Route 53 of malicious actors?

A. Classifying and prioritizing requests from users who are known to be reliable

B. Leveraging customer-provided whitelist/blacklist IP addresses

C. Blocking traffic using customer-defined Amazon Route 53 security groups

D. Redirecting suspicious DNS requests to honeypot responders

21. You are responsible for your company's AWS resources, and you notice a significant amount of traffic from an IP address in a foreign country in which your company does not have customers. Further investigation of the traffic indicates that the source of the traffic is scanning for open ports on your Amazon Elastic Compute Cloud (Amazon EC2) instances. Which one of the following resources can deny the IP address from reaching the instances in your VPC?

A. Security group

B. Internet gateway (IGW)

C. Network Access Control List (ACL)

D. AWS PrivateLink

22. AWS uses what framework to provide independent confirmation around the efficacy of guest-to-guest separation on Amazon Elastic Compute Cloud (Amazon EC2) hypervisors?

A. Health Insurance Portability and Accountability Act (HIPAA)

B. International Organization for Standardization (ISO) 27001

C. Service Organization Controls (SOC) 2

D. Payment Card Industry Data Security Standard (PCI DSS)

23. You place an application load balancer in front of two web servers that are stateful. Users begin to report intermittent connectivity issues when accessing the website. Why is the site not responding?

A. The website needs to have port 443 open.

B. Sticky sessions must be enabled on the application load balancer.

C. The web servers need to have their security group set to allow all Transmission Control Protocol (TCP) traffic from 0.0.0.0/0.

D. The network Access Control List (ACL) on the subnet needs to allow a stateful connection.

24. You create a new instance, and you are able connect over Secure Shell (SSH) to its private IP address from your corporate network. The instance does not have Internet access, however. Your internal policies forbid direct access to the Internet. What is required to enable access to the Internet?

    A. Assign a public IP address to the instance.

    B. Ensure that port 80 and port 443 are not set to DENY in the instance security group.

    C. Deploy a Network Address Translation (NAT) gateway in the private subnet.

    D. Make sure that there is a default route in the subnet route table that goes to your on-premises network.

25. You create Virtual Private Cloud (VPC) peering connections between VPC A and VPC B and between VPC B and VPC C. You can communicate between VPC A and VPC B and communicate between VPC B and VPC C, but not between VPC A and VPC C. What must be done to allow traffic between VPC A and VPC C?

    A. Create a network Access Control List (ACL) to allow the traffic.

    B. Create an additional peering connection between VPC A and VPC C.

    C. Update the route tables in VPC A and VPC C.

    D. Add a rule to the security groups on VPC A and VPC C.

Answers to Assessment Test

1. A. Only IPsec is a supported VPN protocol.

2. C. To vertically-scale, you need to change the instance type to a larger instance. Setting up a standby instance and moving the IP to this instance will result in the least amount of downtime. The downtime will be equal to the time required for the instance to re-create Internet Protocol Security (IPsec) tunnels and establish Border Gateway Protocol (BGP) neighbor relationships. This will be done automatically, or it will have to be initiated manually by you depending on the software on the Amazon EC2 instance. If you stop an existing instance and change its instance type, you also suffer the additional downtime required to boot an instance.

3. D. AWS Direct Connect supports 1000BASE-LX or 10GBASE-LR connections over single mode fiber using Ethernet transport. Your device must support 802.1Q VLANs; however, the use of 802.1Q is required for creating the virtual interface. It is not required for creating the connection.

4. A. A LOA-CFA provides details of the port assignment on the AWS side of the cross-connect with full demarcation and interface details. It is the customer's responsibility to provide details for their end of the cross-connect. No other region or customer information is provided on the document.

5. A, B. Setting up AWS Direct Connect private VIF will enable connectivity to the VPC. Using the connectivity Network Load Balancer will load balance traffic to servers in the VPC and those on-premises.

6. A. The test VPC can be accessed directly over private VIF. It is not a good practice to access Amazon EC2 instances using public IPs when a more secure alternative exists. Option C is possible, but it induces additional latencies.

7. B. The minimum size subnet that you can have in a VPC is /28. A /27 Classless Inter-Domain Routing (CIDR) may contain two /28 subnets.

8. C. When you provision a VPC, each route table has an immutable local route that allows all subnets to route traffic to one another.

9. C. You cannot add different RFC1918 CIDR ranges to an existing VPC, and you also cannot use new CIDR ranges on existing subnets. In addition, NAT Gateways will not support custom NAT. The only option presented that works is peering to a new VPC.

10. D. This is the easiest way to ensure that content in an Amazon S3 bucket is only accessed by Amazon CloudFront.

11. A, B. When using an RTMP distribution for Amazon CloudFront, you need to provide both your media files and a media player to your end users with your distribution. You need two types of distributions: a web distribution to serve the media player and an RTMP distribution for the media files.

12. D. Enhanced networking can help reduce jitter and network performance. Placement groups and lower latency will not assist with flows leaving the VPC. Network interfaces do not affect network performance. An Application Load Balancer will not assist with performance issues.

13. B. Using more than one instance will increase the performance because any given flow to Amazon S3 will be limited to 25 Gbps. Moving the instance will not increase Amazon S3 bandwidth. Placement groups will not increase Amazon S3 bandwidth either. Amazon S3 cannot be natively placed behind a Network Load Balancer.

14. B, E. AWS CloudFormation change sets are computed from the differences between an existing stack and a new template. This can be subsequently applied to update the stack. AWS CloudFormation does not inspect the underlying resources to see if they have been altered. Change sets cannot be edited or reversed.

15. D. A stack can have an IAM service role attached to it that specifies the actions that AWS CloudFormation is allowed to perform while managing the stack. If the stack does not have an attached IAM service role, then the stack uses the caller's credentials—those of the unprivileged user in this case. Stack policies can also allow resources to be preserved, but all actions are permitted without a policy. If the user did not have permission to call CloudFormation:UpdateStack, then the error would have occurred before any resource updates were attempted.

16. B. DNS resolution is supported over VPC peering connections; however, DNS resolution must be enabled for the peering connection.

17. B. To improve the accuracy of geolocation routing, Amazon Route 53 supports the edns-client-subnet extension of EDNS0.

18. D. When you associate an Amazon CloudFront distribution with an AWS Lambda@Edge function, Amazon CloudFront intercepts requests and responses at Amazon CloudFront edge locations. Lambda@Edge functions execute in response to Amazon CloudFront events in the region or edge location that is closest to your customer.

19. D. Security groups control access to Amazon RDS.

20. A. AWS edge locations classify and prioritize traffic to mitigate the impact of malicious actors.

21. C. Network ACL rules can deny traffic.

22. D. The PCI DSS audit report contains statements about guest-to-guest separation in the AWS hypervisor. If this guest-to-guest separation assurance is insufficient for your own threat model, Amazon Elastic Compute Cloud (Amazon EC2) Dedicated Instances are also available.

23. B. Sticky sessions will enable a session to be kept with the same web server to facilitate stateful connections.

24. D. Because you can access the instance but not the Internet, there is not a default route to the Internet through the on-premises network.

25. B. VPC peering connections are not transitive.

AWS®

Certified Advanced Networking

Official Study Guide

Introduction to Advanced Networking

THE AWS CERTIFIED ADVANCED NETWORKING – SPECIALTY EXAM OBJECTIVES COVERED IN THIS CHAPTER MAY INCLUDE, BUT ARE NOT LIMITED TO, THE FOLLOWING:

Domain 1.0: Design and implement hybrid IT network architectures at scale

- ✓ **1.4 Evaluate design alternatives that leverage AWS Direct Connect**

Domain 2.0: Design and Implement AWS Networks

- ✓ **2.1 Advanced knowledge of AWS networking concepts**

Domain 4.0: Configure network integration with application services

- ✓ **4.1 Leverage the capabilities of Route 53**
- ✓ **4.4 Given a scenario, determine an appropriate load balancing strategy within the AWS ecosystem**
- ✓ **4.5 Determine a content distribution strategy to optimize for performance**

Domain 5.0: Design and implement for security and compliance

- ✓ **5.3 Evaluate AWS security features for managing network traffic**

Networks are foundational in our connected world. They are simultaneously critical to our everyday lives and frequently overlooked. Although network infrastructures, like the Internet, are likely the most distributed systems on Earth, they are not noticed unless they are operating poorly. This contrast makes networks quite interesting, both to learn about and to work with.

In addition to its distributed characteristics, modern networks are also a combination of new and old. The Internet Protocol (IP) and Transmission Control Protocol (TCP) were created in the 1970s, and though they have been updated over time, they still run the Internet. Meanwhile, new innovations, including advanced encapsulations, automation, and improved security mechanisms, continue to push the capabilities of the network forward. AWS has driven innovation in cloud networking with capabilities like Amazon Virtual Private Cloud (Amazon VPC), which provides customers with their own logical segment of the Amazon network—on demand and in minutes.

This study guide covers the breadth and depth of AWS networking in scope for the AWS Certified Advanced Networking – Specialty exam. The study guide reviews a broad array of topics relevant to the Amazon global infrastructure, various regional AWS networking features, on-premises hybrid networking, and AWS edge networking. The study guide's contents assume that you have a strong understanding of networking concepts and that you have successfully completed the AWS Certified Solutions Architect – Associate exam.

AWS Global Infrastructure

AWS operates a global infrastructure. This network is operated by one company, Amazon, and it spans the continents where AWS has a presence. This infrastructure enables traffic to flow between AWS Regions, Availability Zones, edge locations, and customer cross-connect facilities. Traffic between nodes on this network uses the AWS global infrastructure, with the exception of AWS GovCloud (US) and China. A representation of the global infrastructure is shown in Figure 1.1.

Regions

A *region* is a geographic area in the world where AWS operates cloud services (for example, Amazon Elastic Compute Cloud, also known as Amazon EC2).

FIGURE 1.1 AWS global infrastructure

AWS Regions are designed to be completely independent from other regions. This approach provides fault isolation, fault tolerance, and stability.

Most AWS Cloud services operate within a region. Since these regions are separated, you only see the resources tied to the region that you have specified. This design also means that customer content that you put into a region stays in that region unless you take an explicit action to move it.

Availability Zones

Each region is composed of two or more *Availability Zones*. Each Availability Zone contains one or more data centers. The zones are engineered such that they have different risk profiles. That is, AWS considers factors like power distribution, floodplains, and tectonics when placing Availability Zones within a region. The zones are connected to one another by low-latency, high-bandwidth fiber optics. Availability Zones are typically less than 2 milliseconds apart.

Amazon operates state-of-the-art, highly-available data centers. Although rare, failures can occur that affect the availability of resources that are in the same location. If you host all of your Amazon EC2 instances in a single location that is affected by such a failure, for example, none of your instances would be available. When you launch an Amazon EC2 instance, you can select an Availability Zone or let AWS choose one for you. If you distribute your instances across multiple Availability Zones and then one instance fails, you can design your application so that an instance in another zone can handle requests.

Edge Locations

To deliver content to end users with low latency, AWS provides a global network of edge locations. This content distribution network is called *Amazon CloudFront.* As end users make requests, the AWS Domain Name System (DNS), Amazon Route 53, routes requests to the Amazon CloudFront edge location that can best serve the user's request, typically the nearest edge location in terms of latency.

In the edge location, Amazon CloudFront checks its cache for the requested content. If the data is locally cached, Amazon CloudFront returns the content to the user. If the data is not in the cache, Amazon CloudFront forwards the request for the files to the applicable origin server for the corresponding file type. The origin servers then send the files back to the Amazon CloudFront edge location.

Amazon Virtual Private Cloud

Amazon Virtual Private Cloud (Amazon VPC) lets you provision a logically-isolated section of the AWS Cloud. You can launch AWS resources like Amazon EC2 instances in a virtual network that you define. You have complete control over your virtual networking environment, including selection of your own IP address range, creation of subnets, and configuration of route tables and network gateways. You can use both IPv4 and IPv6 in your Amazon VPC for secure and easy access to resources and applications.

VPC Mechanics

Amazon VPC enables you to launch resources into a logical network that you define. This network closely resembles the traditional networks that you operate in your own data centers, with the additional scalability and capability benefits of AWS. Amazon VPC uses many traditional concepts, like subnets, IP addresses, and stateful firewalls.

The underlying Amazon VPC mechanics differ, however, from the composition of standard, on-premises networking infrastructures. AWS built a custom network environment that satisfies the scale, performance, flexibility, and security requirements of the millions of active customers who use AWS each day. Consider that each customer has their own isolated network, and many customers are making thousands of changes per day. While the technology underlying Amazon VPC is not within the scope of the exam, understanding how it works will help you reason about its operation and functionality.

The Amazon VPC infrastructure is composed of various support components (such as the Amazon DNS server, instance metadata, and the Dynamic Host Configuration Protocol [DHCP] server) and the underlying physical servers onto which customers launch their Amazon EC2 instances. Each of these physical servers has its own IP address. As customers launch Amazon EC2 instances into their VPCs, AWS determines the physical server on which the instance will run. This decision is based on multiple factors, including the desired Availability Zone, instance type, instance tenancy, and whether the instance is part of a placement group. When different AWS accounts launch instances using Amazon VPC, these instances are not visible to each other.

Tenant isolation is a core function of Amazon VPC. In order to understand which resources are part of a given VPC, Amazon VPC uses a mapping service. The mapping service abstracts your VPC from the underlying AWS infrastructure. For any given VPC, the mapping service maintains information about all of its resources, their VPC IP addresses, and the IP addresses of the underlying physical server on which the resource is running. It is the definitive source of topology information for each VPC.

When an Amazon EC2 instance, say Instance A, in your VPC initiates communication with another Amazon EC2 instance, say Instance B, over IPv4, Instance A will broadcast an Address Resolution Protocol (ARP) packet to obtain the Instance B's Media Access Control (MAC) address. The ARP packet leaving Instance A is intercepted by the server Hypervisor. The Hypervisor queries the mapping service to identify whether Instance B exists in the VPC and, if so, obtains its MAC address. The Hypervisor returns a synthetic ARP response to Instance A containing Instance B's MAC address.

Instance A is now ready to send an IP packet to Instance B. The IP packet has Instance A's source IP and Instance B's destination IP. The IP packet is encapsulated in an Ethernet header with Instance A's MAC as the source address and Instance B's MAC as the destination address. The Ethernet packet is then transmitted from Instance A's network interface.

As Instance A emits the packet, it is intercepted by the server Hypervisor. The Hypervisor queries the mapping service to learn the IPv4 address of the physical server on which Instance B is running. Once the mapping service provides this data, the packet emitted by Instance A is encapsulated in a VPC header that identifies this specific VPC and then encapsulated again in an IP packet with a source IP address of Instance A's physical server and a destination IPv4 address of Instance B's physical server. The packet is then placed on to the AWS network.

When the packet arrives at Instance B's physical server, the outer IPv4 header and VPC header are inspected. The instance Hypervisor queries the mapping service to confirm that Instance A exists on the specific source physical server and in the specific VPC identified in the received packet. When the mapping service confirms that the mapping is correct, the Hypervisor strips off the outer encapsulation and delivers the packet that Instance A emitted to the Instance B network interface.

The details of packet exchange in Amazon VPC should provide you clarity on why, for example, Amazon VPC does not support broadcast and multicast. These same reasons explain why packet sniffing does not work. As you reason about Amazon VPC operation and functionality, consider this example.

Services Outside Your VPC

Many AWS Cloud services are provided from locations outside of your own VPC. These services are delivered from the following:

- Edge locations (for example, Amazon Route 53 and Amazon CloudFront)
- Directly inside your VPC (for example, Amazon Relational Database Service [Amazon RDS] and Amazon Workspaces)
- VPC Endpoints in your VPC (for example, Amazon DynamoDB and Amazon Simple Storage Service [Amazon S3])
- Public service endpoints outside your VPC (for example, Amazon S3 and Amazon Simple Queue Service [Amazon SQS])

AWS Cloud services use the same global infrastructure described earlier in this chapter. When you use services that are delivered directly on the Internet, such as edge locations and public service endpoints, you control network behaviors using service-specific mechanisms like policies and whitelists. When you use services that are exposed directly to your VPC, typically through a network interface or a VPC endpoint in your VPC, you may also use Amazon VPC features like security groups, network Access Control Lists (ACLs), and route tables in addition to service-specific mechanisms.

For the exam, you should understand how AWS Cloud services integrate into your overall network architecture and allow you to control network behavior. You do not need to understand the specific mechanisms that AWS uses to deliver services. However, understanding these delivery models will aid you in the development of scalable, performant, and highly-available architectures.

An overview of service locations can be seen in Figure 1.2.

FIGURE 1.2 Overview of the AWS service locations

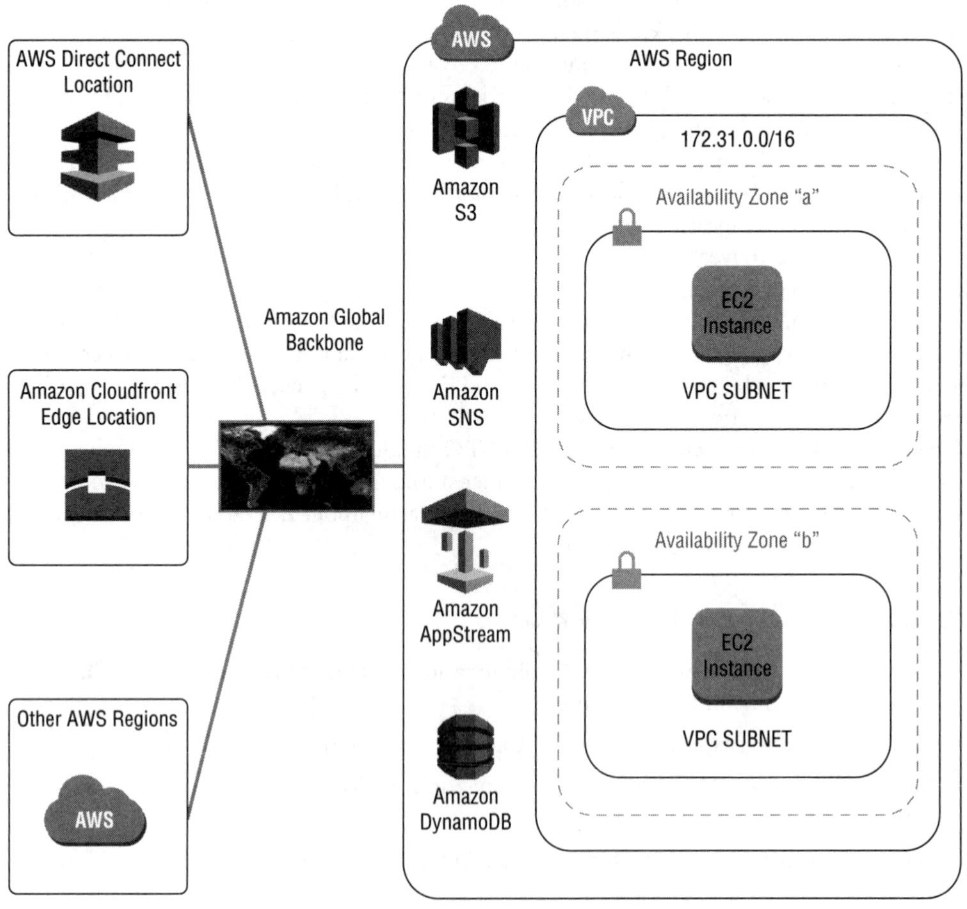

AWS Networking Services

AWS provides many services that you can combine to meet business or organizational needs. This section introduces the AWS Cloud services specifically related to networking. Later chapters provide a deeper view of the services pertinent to the exam.

Amazon Elastic Compute Cloud

Amazon Elastic Compute Cloud (Amazon EC2) is a web service that provides resizable compute capacity in the cloud. It allows organizations to obtain and configure virtual servers in Amazon's data centers and to harness those resources to build and host software systems. Organizations can select from a variety of operating systems and resource configurations (for example, memory, CPU, and storage) that are optimal for the application profile of each workload. Amazon EC2 presents a true virtual computing environment, allowing organizations to launch compute resources with a variety of operating systems, load them with custom applications, and manage network access permissions while maintaining complete control.

Amazon Virtual Private Cloud

Amazon Virtual Private Cloud (Amazon VPC) lets organizations provision a logically-isolated section of the AWS Cloud where they can launch AWS resources in a virtual network that they define. Organizations have complete control over the virtual environment, including selection of the IP address range, creation of subnets, and configuration of route tables and network gateways. In addition, organizations can extend their corporate data center networks to AWS by using hardware or software *Virtual Private Network (VPN)* connections or dedicated circuits by using AWS Direct Connect. Amazon VPC is covered in depth in Chapter 2, "Amazon Virtual Private Cloud (Amazon VPC) and Networking Fundamentals," and Chapter 3, "Advanced Amazon Virtual Private Cloud."

AWS Direct Connect

AWS Direct Connect allows organizations to establish a dedicated network connection from their data center to AWS. Using AWS Direct Connect, organizations can establish private connectivity between AWS and their data center, office, or colocation (AWS) environment, which in many cases can reduce network costs, increase bandwidth throughput, and provide a more consistent network experience than Internet-based VPN connections. AWS Direct Connect is covered in depth in Chapter 5, "AWS Direct Connect."

Elastic Load Balancing

Elastic Load Balancing automatically distributes incoming application traffic across multiple Amazon EC2 instances in the cloud. It enables organizations to achieve greater levels of fault tolerance in their applications, seamlessly providing the required amount of load balancing capacity needed to distribute application traffic. Elastic Load Balancing is covered in depth in Chapter 6, "Domain Name System and Load Balancing."

Amazon Route 53

Amazon Route 53 is a highly available and scalable DNS service. It is designed to give developers and businesses an extremely reliable and cost-effective way to route end users to Internet applications by translating human-readable names, such as `www.example.com`, into the numeric IP addresses, such as 192.0.2.1, which computers use to connect to each other. Amazon Route 53 also serves as a domain registrar, allowing customers to purchase and manage domains directly from AWS. Amazon Route 53 is covered in depth in Chapter 6.

Amazon CloudFront

Amazon CloudFront is a global Content Delivery Network (CDN) service that securely delivers data, videos, applications, and Application Programming Interfaces (APIs) to an organization's viewers with low latency and high transfer speeds. Amazon CloudFront is integrated with AWS, both with physical locations that are directly connected to the AWS global infrastructure and software that works seamlessly with other AWS Cloud services. These include AWS Shield for Distributed Denial of Service (DDoS) mitigation, Amazon S3, Elastic Load Balancing, or Amazon EC2 as origins for applications, as well as AWS Lambda to run custom code close to the content viewers. Amazon CloudFront is covered in depth in Chapter 7, "Amazon CloudFront."

GuardDuty

GuardDuty is a continuous security monitoring, threat detection solution that gives customers visibility into malicious or unauthorized activity across their AWS accounts and the applications and services running within them. GuardDuty is capable of detecting threats such as reconnaissance by attackers (for example, port probes, port scans, and attempts to obtain account credentials), Amazon EC2 instances that have been compromised (such as instances serving malware, bitcoin mining, and outbound DDoS attacks), and compromised accounts (for example, unauthorized infrastructure deployments, AWS CloudTrail tampering, and unusual API calls). When a threat is detected, the solution delivers a security finding. Each finding includes a severity level, detailed evidence for the finding, and recommended actions. GuardDuty is covered in depth in Chapter 8, "Network Security."

AWS WAF

AWS WAF helps protect web applications from common attacks and exploits that could affect application availability, compromise security, or consume excessive resources. AWS WAF gives organizations control over which traffic to allow or block to their web applications by defining customizable web security rules. AWS WAF is covered in depth in Chapter 8.

AWS Shield

AWS Shield is a managed DDoS protection service that safeguards web applications running on AWS. AWS Shield provides always-on detection and automatic inline mitigations that minimize application downtime and latency. There are two tiers of AWS Shield: Standard and Advanced. All AWS customers benefit from the automatic protections of AWS Shield Standard at no additional charge. AWS Shield Standard defends against the most common, frequently occurring network and transport layer DDoS attacks that target websites or applications. AWS Shield is covered in depth in Chapter 8.

Summary

AWS provides highly-available technology infrastructure services with multiple locations worldwide. These locations are composed of regions and Availability Zones. AWS provides networks and network features spanning edge locations, VPCs, and hybrid networks. AWS operates a global network connecting these locations.

Amazon VPC provides complete control over a virtual networking environment, enabling secure and easy access to resources and applications.

This chapter introduced the primary services related to networking on AWS. This chapter also provided the background and context so that you can understand more advanced networking introduced later in this study guide.

Resources to Review

For further review, check out the following URLs:

AWS Global Infrastructure:

`https://aws.amazon.com/about-aws/global-infrastructure/`

Amazon EC2:

`https://aws.amazon.com/ec2/`

Amazon VPC:

`https://aws.amazon.com/vpc/`

AWS Direct Connect:

`https://aws.amazon.com/directconnect/`

Elastic Load Balancing:

`https://aws.amazon.com/ elasticloadbalancing/`

Amazon Route 53:

`https://aws.amazon.com/route53/`

Amazon CloudFront:

`https://aws.amazon.com/cloudfront/`

AWS WAF:

`https://aws.amazon.com/waf/`

AWS Shield:

`https://aws.amazon.com/shield/`

Exam Essentials

Understand the global infrastructure. AWS operates a global infrastructure. This network is operated by one company, Amazon. This infrastructure enables traffic to flow between regions, Availability Zones, edge locations, and customer cross-connect facilities. Traffic between nodes on this network uses the AWS global infrastructure.

Understand regions. A region is a geographic area in the world where AWS operates cloud services such as Amazon EC2. AWS Regions are designed to be completely independent from other regions. Most AWS Cloud services operate within a region. Since these regions are separated, content you put into a region stays in that region, unless you take an explicit action to move it.

Understand Availability Zones. An Availability Zone consists of one or more data centers within a region, which are designed to be isolated from failures in other Availability Zones. Availability Zones provide inexpensive, low-latency, high-bandwidth network connectivity to other zones in the same region. By placing resources in separate Availability Zones, you can protect your website or application from a service disruption affecting a single location.

Understand Amazon VPC. Amazon VPC is an isolated, logical network in the AWS infrastructure. A VPC contains resources, such as Amazon EC2 instances. There is a VPC mapping service that enables the routing capability inside a VPC.

Understand how AWS Cloud service integration works. You should understand how AWS Cloud services integrate into your overall network architecture and how to control network behavior. You do not need to understand the specific mechanisms that AWS uses to deliver services. Understanding these delivery models, however, will aid you in the development of scalable, performant, and highly-available architectures.

Test Taking Tip

Manage your time wisely when taking this exam. Don't waste time on questions where you are stumped. Mark it for later review and move on. Plan on leaving time at the end of the exam for review. Go through each marked question to answer any that you may have skipped or to make sure that you are still happy with previously-marked answers.

Exercise

EXERCISE 1.1

Review Network Service Documentation

Navigate to all of the URLs in the resources to review the section above and review the network service product material.

1. Navigate to the AWS Global Infrastructure website. Review the information provided about AWS Regions and Availability Zones. Become familiar with the AWS Global Infrastructure.
2. Navigate to the Amazon VPC product documentation. Review the product details and FAQs. Become familiar with the additional product documentation in the related links section.
3. Navigate to the AWS Direct Connect product documentation. Review the product details and FAQs. Become familiar with the additional product documentation in the related links section.
4. Navigate to the Elastic Load Balancing product documentation. Review the product details and FAQs. Become familiar with the additional product documentation section.
5. Navigate to the Amazon Route53 product documentation. Review the product details and FAQs. Become familiar with the additional product documentation section.
6. Navigate to the Amazon CloudFront product documentation. Review the product details and FAQs. Become familiar with the additional product documentation section.
7. Navigate to the AWS WAF product documentation. Review the product details and FAQs. Become familiar with the additional product documentation section.
8. Navigate to the AWS Shield product documentation. Review the product details and FAQs. Become familiar with the additional product documentation section.

After completing this exercise, you will be familiar with AWS network-related products, where to find related documentation, and the different types of additional documentation that AWS provides.

Review Questions

1. Which of the following services provides private connectivity between AWS and your data center, office, or colocation environment?
   A. Amazon Route 53
   B. AWS Direct Connect
   C. AWS WAF
   D. Amazon Virtual Private Cloud (Amazon VPC)

2. Which AWS Cloud service uses edge locations to deliver content to end users?
   A. Amazon Virtual Private Cloud (Amazon VPC)
   B. AWS Shield
   C. Amazon CloudFront
   D. Amazon Elastic Compute Cloud (Amazon EC2)

3. Which of the following statements is true?
   A. AWS Regions consist of multiple edge locations.
   B. Edge locations consist of multiple Availability Zones.
   C. Availability Zones consist of multiple AWS Regions.
   D. AWS Regions consist of multiple Availability Zones.

4. Which of the following describes a physical location around the world where AWS clusters data centers?
   A. Endpoint
   B. Collection
   C. Fleet
   D. Region

5. What feature of AWS Regions allows you to operate production systems that are more highly available, fault-tolerant, and scalable than is possible using a single data center?
   A. Availability Zones
   B. Replication areas
   C. Geographic districts
   D. Compute centers

6. What AWS Cloud service provides a logically-isolated section of the AWS Cloud where you can launch AWS resources in a logical network that you define?
   A. Amazon Simple Workflow Service (Amazon SWF)
   B. Amazon Route 53
   C. Amazon Virtual Private Cloud (Amazon VPC)
   D. AWS CloudFormation

7. Which AWS Cloud service provides Distributed Denial of Service (DDoS) mitigation?
   A. AWS Shield
   B. Amazon Route 53
   C. AWS Direct Connect
   D. Amazon Elastic Compute Cloud (Amazon EC2)
8. How many companies operate the AWS global infrastructure?
   A. 1
   B. 2
   C. 3
   D. 4
9. Amazon Virtual Private Cloud (Amazon VPC) enables which one of the following?
   A. Connectivity from your on-premises network
   B. Creation of a logical network defined by you
   C. Edge caching of user content
   D. Network threshold alarms
10. Which Amazon Virtual Private Cloud (Amazon VPC) component maintains a current topology map of the customer environment?
    A. Route table
    B. Mapping service
    C. Border Gateway Protocol (BGP)
    D. Interior Gateway Protocol (IGP)
11. You may specify which of the following when creating a Virtual Private Cloud (VPC)?
    A. AWS data centers to use
    B. 802.1x authentication methods
    C. Virtual Local Area Network (VLAN) tags
    D. IPv4 address range
12. Amazon Route 53 allows you to perform which one of the following actions?
    A. Create subnets
    B. Register domains
    C. Define route tables
    D. Modify stateful firewalls

13. Which service provides a more consistent network experience when connecting to AWS from your corporate network?
    A. AWS Direct Connect
    B. Amazon CloudFront
    C. Internet-based Virtual Private Network (VPN)
    D. Amazon Route 53

14. Which AWS Cloud service enables you to define customizable web security rules?
    A. Amazon Route 53
    B. AWS Shield
    C. AWS WAF
    D. GuardDuty

15. Which service increases the fault tolerance of your Amazon Elastic Compute Cloud (Amazon EC2) applications on AWS?
    A. AWS Direct Connect
    B. Elastic Load Balancing
    C. AWS Shield
    D. AWS WAF

Amazon Virtual Private Cloud (Amazon VPC) and Networking Fundamentals

THE AWS CERTIFIED ADVANCED NETWORKING – SPECIALTY EXAM OBJECTIVES COVERED IN THIS CHAPTER MAY INCLUDE, BUT ARE NOT LIMITED TO, THE FOLLOWING:

Domain 2.0: Design and implement AWS networks

- ✓ **2.1 Apply AWS networking concepts**

Domain 4.0: Configure network integration with application services

- ✓ **4.3 Determine the appropriate configuration of DHCP within AWS**

Amazon Virtual Private Cloud (Amazon VPC) allows customers to define a virtual network within the AWS Cloud. You can provision your own logically-isolated section of AWS, similar to designing and implementing a separate, independent network that would operate in an on-premises data center.

This chapter will review the core components of Amazon VPC that you learned by studying for the prerequisite exam. The exercises at the end of this chapter will refresh the skills required to build your own Amazon VPC in the cloud. A strong understanding of Amazon VPC technologies and troubleshooting is required to pass the AWS Certified Advanced Networking - Specialty exam, and we highly recommend that you complete the exercises in this chapter.

Introduction to Amazon Virtual Private Cloud (Amazon VPC)

Amazon VPC is the networking layer for Amazon Elastic Compute Cloud (Amazon EC2), and it allows you to build your own virtual network within an AWS Region. You control various aspects of your VPC, including selecting your own IP address range, creating your own subnets, and configuring your own route tables, network gateways, and security settings. You can create multiple VPCs within a region, and each VPC is logically isolated, even if it overlaps or shares IP address space with another VPC. You can launch AWS resources, such as Amazon EC2 instances, into your VPC.

When you create a VPC, you must assign an IPv4 address range by choosing a *Classless Inter-Domain Routing (CIDR)* block, such as 10.0.0.0/16. You may select any IPv4 address range, but Amazon VPC treats the CIDR block as private. Amazon will not advertise the network to the Internet. To connect with the Internet, or to enable communication between your resources and other AWS Cloud services that have Internet endpoints, you can assign a globally unique, public IPv4 address to your resource. The initially-assigned IPv4 address range of the VPC cannot be changed after the VPC is created. A VPC IPv4 address range may be as large as /16 (65,536 addresses) or as small as /28 (16 addresses), and it should not overlap any other network to which the VPC is to be connected.

You may optionally associate an IPv6 address range to your VPC. The IPv6 address range is a fixed size of /56 (4,722,366,482,869,645,213,696 addresses) and is assigned to your VPC from Amazon's own IPv6 allocation. The IPv6 addresses that you receive from Amazon are *Global Unicast Address (GUA)* space. Amazon advertises GUAs to the Internet, so these IPv6 addresses are public. If an Internet gateway (discussed later in this chapter) is attached to your VPC, then the VPCs are reachable over the Internet.

An IPv4 CIDR block is required to create a VPC. IPv4 addresses are assigned to every resource in your VPC, regardless of whether you use IPv4 for communication. Therefore, the number of usable IPv6 addresses in your VPC is constrained by the pool of available IPv4 addresses.

The current list of IP address ranges used by AWS is available in JSON format at `https://ip-ranges.amazonaws.com/ip-ranges.json`.

Your VPC can operate in *dual-stack mode*. This means that resources in your VPC can communicate over IPv4, IPv6, or both. Because Amazon VPC is dual-stack, however, IPv4 and IPv6 operate independently. You will need to configure the routing and security components of your VPC for each address family. Table 2.1 provides a comparison of IPv4 and IPv6 for Amazon VPC.

TABLE 2.1 IPv4 and IPv6 Comparison

IPv4	IPv6
The address is 32-bit, dotted-decimal notation.	The address is 128-bit, colon-separated hextet notation.
Default and required for all Amazon VPCs; cannot be removed.	Opt-in only.
The Amazon VPC CIDR block size can be from /16 to /28.	The Amazon VPC CIDR block size is fixed at /56.
You can choose the private IPv4 CIDR block for your VPC.	Amazon assigns the IPv6 CIDR block for your VPC from Amazon's pool of IPv6 addresses. You cannot select your own range.
There is a distinction between private and public IP addresses. To enable communication with the Internet, a public IPv4 address is required.	There is no distinction between public and private IP addresses. IPv6 addresses are GUAs. Security is controlled with routing and security policies.

Prior to Amazon VPC, users launched Amazon EC2 instances in a single, flat network shared with other AWS users. This Amazon EC2 environment is now called *EC2-Classic*. AWS accounts created after December 2013 only support Amazon VPC. EC2-Classic does not appear on the exam, and we do not discuss EC2-Classic further in this study guide.

To simplify the initial user experience with Amazon VPC, AWS accounts have a default VPC created in each region with a default subnet created in each Availability Zone. The assigned CIDR block of the VPC will be 172.31.0.0/16. IPv6 is not enabled on the default VPC.

Figure 2.1 illustrates a VPC with an address space of 10.0.0.0/16, two subnets with different address ranges (10.0.0.0/24 and 10.0.1.0/24) placed in different Availability Zones, and a route table with the local route specified.

FIGURE 2.1 VPC, subnets, and a route table

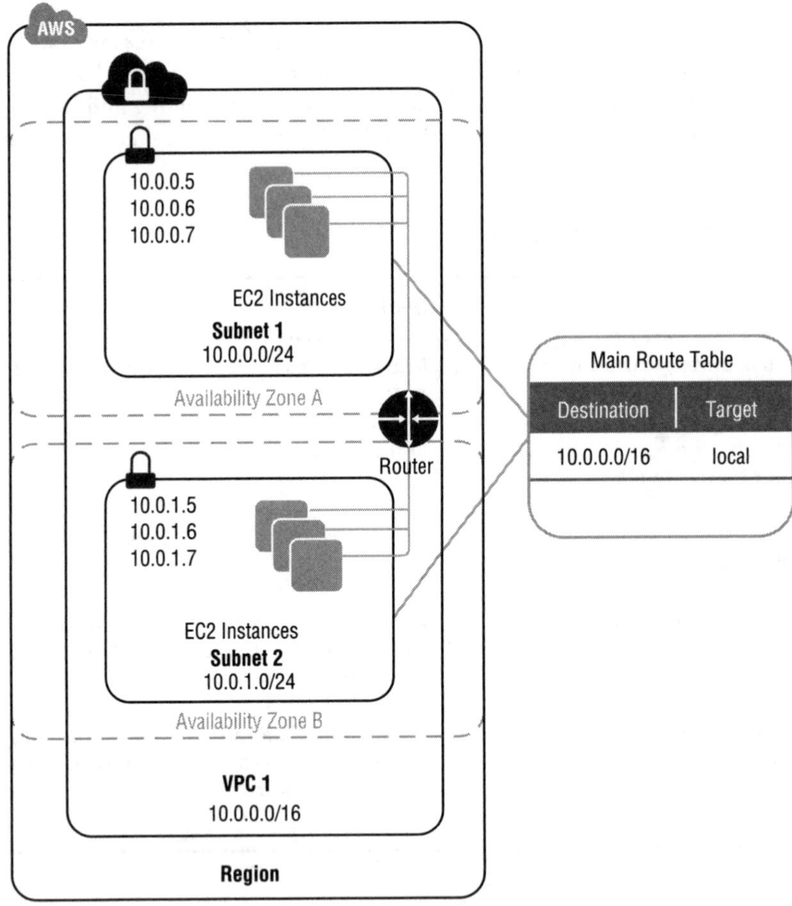

An Amazon VPC consists of the following concepts and components:

- Subnets
- Route Tables
- IP Addressing
- Security Groups
- Network Access Control Lists (ACLs)

- Internet Gateways
- Network Address Translation (NAT) Instances and NAT Gateways
- Egress Only Internet Gateways (EIGWs)
- Virtual Private Gateways (VGWs), Customer Gateways, and Virtual Private Networks (VPNs)
- VPC Endpoints
- VPC Peering
- Placement Groups
- Elastic Network Interfaces
- Dynamic Host Configuration Protocol (DHCP) Option Sets
- Amazon Domain Name Service (DNS) Server
- VPC Flow Logs

Subnets

A *subnet* is a segment of a VPC that resides entirely within a single Availability Zone. While a VPC spans all Availability Zones in a region, a subnet cannot span more than one Availability Zone. You may create zero, one, or more subnets in each Availability Zone. When creating a subnet, you specify the target Availability Zone and allocate a contiguous block of IPv4 addresses from the VPC CIDR block. You launch Amazon EC2 resources, like Amazon Relational Database Service (Amazon RDS), into one or more subnets.

The maximum size of a subnet is determined by the size of the VPC IPv4 CIDR range. The smallest subnet that you can create is a /28 (16 IPv4 addresses). For example, if you created a VPC with IPv4 CIDR 10.0.0.0/16, you could create multiple subnets of /28. You could also create a single subnet in a single Availability Zone of size /16. AWS reserves the first four IPv4 addresses and the last IPv4 address of every subnet for internal networking purposes. For example, a subnet defined as a /28 has 16 available IPv4 addresses; subtract the 5 IPs needed by AWS to yield 11 IPv4 addresses for your use within the subnet.

Within Amazon VPC, broadcast and multicast traffic is not forwarded. Subnets can be as large as you like without impacting performance and traffic forwarding.

If an IPv6 address block is associated with your Amazon VPC, you may optionally associate an IPv6 CIDR block to an existing subnet. Each IPv6 subnet is a fixed prefix length of /64, and the CIDR range is allocated from the VPC's /56 CIDR block. When you specify the IPv6 subnet address range, you control the last 8 bits of the subnet's IPv6 prefix, called the subnet identifier. Figure 2.2 shows how the hexadecimal (Hex) and binary (Bin) representations align with their use (Use). For example, if your VPC is assigned 2001:0db8:1234:1a00::/56, you specify the value of the low order 8 bits.

FIGURE 2.2 Subnet identifier

```
Hex :|   2    0    0    1:   0    d    b    8:   1    2    3    4:   1    a|   0    0|::/64
Bin :| 0010 0000 0000 0001 0000 1101 1011 1000 0001 0010 0011 0100 0001 1010| 0000 0000|
Use :|                            VPC CIDR ID                               |Subnet  ID|
```

In Figure 2.2, Subnet 1 uses a subnet identifier of 00, which yields the CIDR 2001:db8:1234:1a00::/64. Note that IPv6 notation does not require that leading zeros are shown, so 2001:0db8::/56 and 2001:db8::/56 are equivalent. Additionally, any single, contiguous section of the address that is consecutive zeros can be notated with double colons (::).

You can disassociate an IPv6 CIDR block from a subnet if no IPv6 addresses are in use. If no subnets have an assigned IPv6 CIDR, you can also disassociate the IPv6 CIDR from your Amazon VPC. You can request a new IPv6 CIDR from Amazon at a later time.

If you disassociate an IPv6 CIDR from your VPC, you cannot expect to receive the same CIDR if you subsequently request an IPv6 block from Amazon.

For both IPv4 and IPv6, subnets can be classified as public, private, or VPN-only. Table 2.2 shows how these distinctions compare, using Figure 2.3 as an example. Regardless of the type of subnet, the internal IPv4 address range of the subnet is always private (namely, not announced by AWS on the Internet), and the internal IPv6 address range is always a GUA (that is, announced by AWS on the Internet).

TABLE 2.2 IPv4 and IPv6 Subnets

	IPv4	IPv6
Public subnet (Subnet 1)	Associated route table (discussed later in this chapter) contains a route entry targeting an Internet gateway.	
Private subnet (Subnet 2)	Associated route table does not contain a route to an Internet gateway. May contain a route to a NAT instance or a NAT gateway (discussed later in this chapter).	Associated route table does not contain a route to an Internet gateway. May contain a route to an Egress-Only Internet gateway (discussed later in this chapter).
VPN-only subnet (Subnet 3)	Associated route tables direct traffic to the VPC's VGW (discussed later in this chapter) or an Amazon EC2 instance running a software VPN.	Associated route tables direct traffic to an Amazon EC2 instance running a software VPN.

FIGURE 2.3 Public, private, and VPC-only subnets

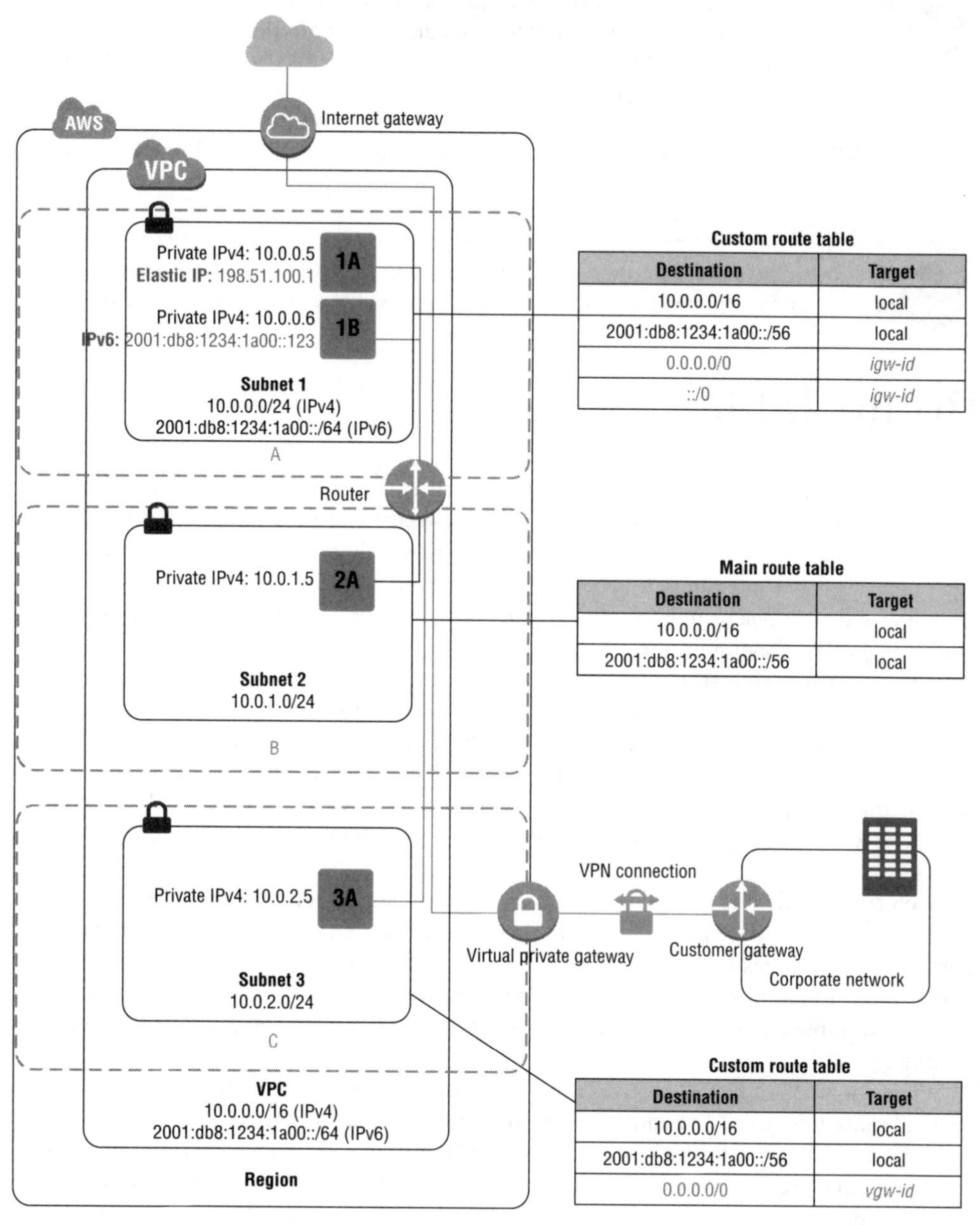

While subnets are often referred to as "public" or "private" in AWS documentation, their underlying capabilities are the same. The defining distinction between a private subnet and a public subnet is a route to an attached Internet gateway.

Default VPCs contain one public subnet in every Availability Zone within the region, with a netmask of /20.

Users are cautioned not to delete the default VPC. It can have unintended consequences for other services that expect a default VPC to exist.

Route Tables

Each subnet within a VPC contains a logical construct called an *implicit router*. The implicit router is the next hop gateway on a subnet where routing decisions are made. These routing decisions are governed by a *route table*, which includes a set of route entries. You can create custom route tables to define specific routing policies. Custom route tables may be associated with one or more subnets. Your VPC also contains a "main" route table that you can modify. The main route table is used for all subnets that are not explicitly associated with a custom route table.

Each route table entry, or *route*, consists of a destination and a target. The destinations for your route tables are either CIDR blocks or, in the case of VPC gateway endpoints (discussed later in this chapter), prefix lists. Targets of your route table can include Internet gateways, NAT gateways, egress-only Internet gateways (EIGWs), virtual private gateways (VGW), VPC gateway endpoints, VPC peers, and elastic network interfaces.

Each route table has one or more local route entries associated with the IPv4 and IPv6 CIDR blocks configured for your VPC. Every route table has an entry for the defined CIDR ranges with a target of "Local," and these entries cannot be removed. You cannot add a more specific route to your route table than the local route. The local route table entries ensure that all resources in your VPC have a route to one another.

When the implicit router receives a packet, the next hop target is determined by a specific route priority. The route table includes local, static, and dynamic routes. The route for the VPC CIDR block is local. Explicitly configured routes are static. Dynamic routes originate through route propagation from a VGW (discussed later in this chapter). Table 2.3 describes the route priority order. Recall that Amazon VPC operates IPv6 in a dual-stack mode, meaning that routing evaluations are executed independently for IPv4 and IPv6.

TABLE 2.3 Route Priority

Priority	Description
1	Local route, even if a more specific route exists for the CIDR
2	Most specific route (longest-prefix match)
3	Static routes are preferred over dynamic routes for equivalent prefixes
4	Dynamic routes propagated from AWS Direct Connect (discussed later)
5	Static routes configured on a VGW VPN connection (discussed later)
6	Dynamic routes propagated from a VPN (discussed later)

You should remember the following points about route tables:

- Your VPC has an implicit router.
- Your VPC automatically comes with a main route table that you can modify.
- You can create additional custom route tables for your VPC.
- Each subnet is associated with a route table, which controls the routing for the subnet. If you don't explicitly associate a subnet with a particular route table, the subnet uses the main route table.
- You can set a custom route table as the main route table so that new subnets are automatically associated with it.
- Each route in a table specifies a destination CIDR and a target; for example, traffic destined for 172.16.0.0/12 is targeted for the VGW.
- AWS uses a predefined route priority process to determine how to route the traffic.

IP Addressing

Resources in your VPC use IP addresses to communicate with each other and with resources over the Internet. Amazon EC2 and Amazon VPC support both IPv4 and IPv6 addressing protocols.

Amazon EC2 and Amazon VPC require you to use the IPv4 addressing protocol. When you create a VPC, you must assign it an IPv4 CIDR block. Amazon EC2 features like *instance metadata* and the Amazon DNS Server require the use of IPv4.

The IPv4 CIDR block that you allocate to your VPC is considered a private IPv4 address range by Amazon, regardless of whether or not the address block is routable on the

Internet. To connect your instance to the Internet, or to enable communication between your instances and other AWS Cloud services that have public endpoints, assign public IPv4 addresses. There are multiple ways to assign public IPv4 addresses, and these methods are covered in this section.

You can optionally associate an IPv6 CIDR block with your VPC and subnets and assign IPv6 addresses from that block to the resources in your VPC. IPv6 addresses are public and reachable over the Internet. There are multiple types of IPv6 addresses. This section of the guide covers the types of IPv6 addresses and the methods used to assign IPv6 addresses to your Amazon EC2 instances.

IPv4 Addresses

IPv4 addresses in your VPC are broadly categorized as private and public IP addresses. Private IP addresses are IPv4 addresses assigned from the CIDR block of your VPC. These addresses are assigned either automatically or manually at launch. Public IP addresses are assigned from a pool of routable IPv4 addresses administered by Amazon. The assignment of public IPv4 addresses to an instance occurs either automatically at launch or dynamically after launch using an IPv4 Elastic IP address.

The primary interface of an Amazon EC2 instance is assigned an IPv4 private address at launch. You can specify the private IP address if it is unused and is within the target subnet address range. If a manually defined IP address is not provided at launch, Amazon automatically assigns a private IP address from the available address pool of the subnet. The private IP address on the primary interface is retained until it is terminated. It is possible to launch Amazon EC2 instances with multiple elastic network interfaces (discussed later in this chapter) and secondary private IP addresses. The private IP addresses on additional elastic network interfaces are retained until the interface is deleted.

Amazon EC2 instances may also receive public IPv4 addresses, either automatically at launch or dynamically after launch. All VPC subnets have a modifiable attribute that determines whether elastic network interfaces created in the subnet will automatically receive public IPv4 addresses. Regardless of this attribute, you can override it either to assign or withhold automatic public IPv4 address assignment.

You cannot manually disassociate the automatically-assigned public IP address from your instance after launch. It is automatically released in certain cases, for example when you stop or terminate your instance, after which you cannot reuse it.

An *Elastic IP address* is a static, public IPv4 address that you can allocate to your account (pull from the pool) and release from your account (return to the pool). The address comes from a pool of regional IPv4 addresses that Amazon manages. Elastic IP addresses allow you to maintain a set of IPv4 addresses that remain fixed, while the underlying infrastructure may change over time.

In AWS documentation, and in this book, the phrase "public IP" has two meanings. Even though Elastic IP addresses are always publicly routable addresses, you may see phrases such as "a public IP address" or "Elastic IP address." Depending on the context, a public IP address may refer to any publicly-routable address, or it may refer to the first dynamically-assigned public address to an instance, which is not an Elastic IP address.

Here are the important points to understand about Elastic IP addresses for the exam:

- You must first allocate an Elastic IP address within a VPC and then assign it to an instance.
- Elastic IP addresses are specific to a region. An Elastic IP address in one region cannot be assigned to an instance within a VPC in a different region.
- There is a one-to-one relationship between private IPv4 addresses and Elastic IP addresses. Your instance will receive traffic destined to the private address mapping for your Elastic IP address.
- You can map Elastic IP addresses from one private IPv4 address to another, either in the same VPC or a different VPC, within the same region and account.
- Elastic IP addresses remain associated with your AWS account until you explicitly release them.
- You are not charged for the first Elastic IP address assigned to an instance, provided that the instance is running. Additional Elastic IP addresses per instance and Elastic IP addresses not associated with a running instance incur a small hourly charge.

IPv6 Addresses

The IPv6 protocol uses a variety of addresses for operation. For the exam, you should understand *Link-Local Addresses (LLAs)* and GUAs. LLAs are addresses from the reserved fe80::/10 IPv6 CIDR block. The LLA is a required "on-link" address used for a variety of IPv6 processes, including DHCPv6 and Neighbor Discovery Protocol. Think of the latter as the IPv6 version of IPv4's Address Resolution Protocol.

The implicit router in your VPC is accessible through its LLA. Amazon VPC expects the LLA of a given interface to conform with the modified EUI-64 format in which the 48-bit MAC address of the elastic network interface is converted into a 64-bit interface ID. As shown in Figure 2.4, the modified EUI-64 address is created by flipping the seventh-most significant bit and inserting FF:FE into the address. The LLA is significant only to the link, or VPC subnet, on which the elastic network interface resides. LLA packet processing is enabled on your elastic network interface when you assign it a GUA.

FIGURE 2.4 48-bit MAC to 64-bit modified EUI-64

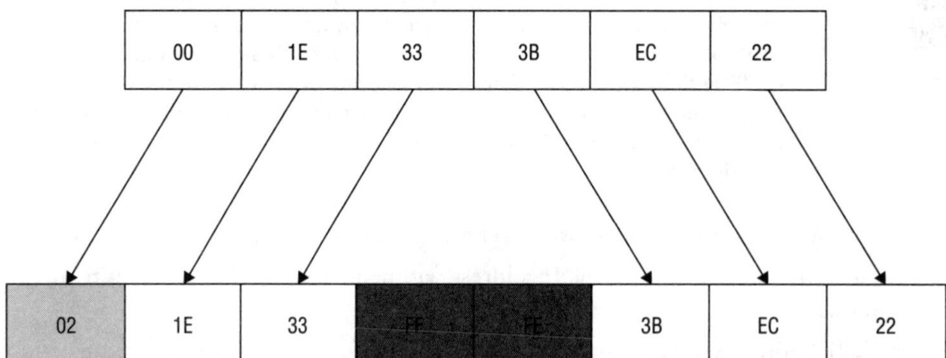

Amazon maintains large IPv6 GUA allocations from Regional Internet Registries (RIRs). To communicate with the Internet over IPv6, your instance must use an Amazon GUA. To receive a GUA, associate an IPv6 block from Amazon's public IPv6 pool with your VPC. Amazon will allocate to you a fixed-size /56 CIDR block for your VPC. Then, associate a fixed-size /64 IPv6 CIDR block to each subnet that requires IPv6. While you have no control over the /56 address allocation to your VPC, you assign the low-order byte of /64 IPv6 subnets. In subnets with IPv6 addresses, you can assign IPv6 addresses to your elastic network interfaces.

There are two ways to assign IPv6 addresses to your elastic network interface. You may assign the addresses automatically or manually at launch or after launch. Similar to IPv4, you can configure an attribute on your subnet to assign an IPv6 address automatically to new elastic network interfaces created in a given subnet. This attribute has the effect of automatically assigning an IPv6 GUA to your instance at launch. As with IPv4, you are able to override this attribute at launch. If you prefer to assign the value of the IPv6 GUA manually, you may specify the IPv6 address at launch to override automatic address assignment. Running instances may receive IPv6 addresses as well. When you assign an IPv6 address to a running instance, you can specify the IPv6 address or allow Amazon VPC to select an IPv6 address automatically for you.

Security Groups

A *security group* is a stateful virtual firewall that controls inbound and outbound network traffic to AWS resources and Amazon EC2 instances. All Amazon EC2 instances are launched with a security group. If a security group is not specified at launch, then the instance will be launched with the default security group for the VPC in which it is launched. An unmodified, default security group allows communication between all resources within the security group, and it allows all outbound traffic; all other traffic is denied implicitly. You may change the rules for the default security group, but you may not delete the default security group. Table 2.4 describes the settings of the default security group.

TABLE 2.4 Security Group Rules

Inbound			
Source	**Protocol**	**Port Range**	**Comments**
sg-xxxxxxxx	All	All	Allow inbound traffic from instances within the same security group.
Outbound			
Destination	**Protocol**	**Port Range**	**Comments**
0.0.0.0/0	All	All	Allow all outbound traffic.
::/0	All	All	Allow all outbound IPv6 traffic. This rule is added if an IPv6 CIDR block is associated with your VPC.

If you modify the outbound rules for the default security group, AWS does not automatically add an outbound rule for IPv6 when you associate an IPv6 CIDR with your VPC.

For each security group, you add rules that control the inbound traffic to instances and a separate set of rules that control the outbound traffic. For example, Table 2.5 describes a security group for web servers.

TABLE 2.5 Security Group Rules for a Web Server

Inbound			
Source	**Protocol**	**Port Range**	**Comments**
0.0.0.0/0	TCP	80	Allow all inbound traffic to port 80.
Your network's public IP address range	TCP	22	Allow Secure Shell (SSH) traffic from your company network.
Your network's public IP address range	TCP	3389	Allow Remote Desktop Protocol (RDP) traffic from your company network.

TABLE 2.5 Security Group Rules for a Web Server *(continued)*

Outbound			
Destination	**Protocol**	**Port Range**	**Comments**
The security group ID associated with your MySQL database servers (sg-xxxxxxxx)	TCP	3306	Allow outbound MySQL access to instances in the specified security group.
The security group ID associated with your Microsoft SQL Server database servers (sg-xxxxxxxx)	TCP	1433	Allow outbound Microsoft SQL Server access to instances in the specified security group.

If your VPC has a peering connection with another VPC in the same region, you can reference security group IDs from the peer VPC. This allows you to create security groups that automatically accommodate changes in the peer network, including Auto Scaling events. If the peer VPC deletes a referenced security group, the rule in your security group is marked as `stale`.

When applying a security group to an instance, the changes are applied to the primary network interface.

Here are the important points to understand about security groups for the exam:

- You can create up to 500 security groups for each VPC.
- You can add up to 50 inbound and 50 outbound rules to each security group.
- You can associate up to five security groups with each network interface.
- You can specify allow rules but not deny rules. This is an important difference between security groups and network ACLs.
- You can specify separate rules for inbound and outbound traffic.
- By default, no inbound traffic is allowed until you add inbound rules to the security group.
- By default, new security groups have an outbound rule that allows all outbound traffic. You can remove the rule and add outbound rules that allow specific outbound traffic only.
- Security groups are *stateful*. This means that responses to allowed inbound traffic are allowed to flow outbound regardless of outbound rules and vice versa. This is an important difference between security groups and network ACLs.

- Instances associated with the same security group cannot communicate with each other unless you add rules to the security group allowing the security group to communicate within itself.
- You can change which security groups an instance is associated with after launch, and the changes will take effect in seconds.

Network Access Control Lists (ACLs)

A *network ACL* is another layer of security that acts as a stateless firewall on a subnet level. A network ACL is an ordered list of rules that AWS evaluates, starting with the lowest numbered rule, to determine whether traffic is allowed in or out of any subnet associated with the network ACL. Each network ACL has a final deny all rule that you cannot change. VPCs are created with a modifiable default network ACL associated with every subnet. The default network ACL allows all inbound and outbound traffic for IPv4. When you create a custom network ACL, its initial configuration will deny all inbound and outbound traffic until you create rules that allow otherwise. You may set up network ACLs with rules similar to your security groups in order to add another layer of security to your VPC, or you may choose to use the default network ACL that does not filter traffic traversing the subnet boundary. Every subnet must be associated with a network ACL. If you associate an IPv6 CIDR block with your VPC, Amazon automatically adds rules that allow all inbound and outbound IPv6 traffic.

If you modify the inbound rules for the default network ACL, AWS does not automatically add an allow rule for IPv6 if you subsequently associate an IPv6 CIDR with your VPC. The same behavior applies to changes in the outbound rules of the default network ACL.

Table 2.6 explains the differences between a security group and a network ACL. You should remember the following differences for the exam.

TABLE 2.6 Comparison of Security Groups and Network ACLs

Security Group	Network ACL
Operates at the network interface level.	Operates at the subnet level.
Supports allow rules only.	Supports allow rules and deny rules.
Stateful: Return traffic is automatically allowed, regardless of any rules.	*Stateless*: Return traffic must be explicitly allowed by rules.
AWS evaluates all rules to decide whether to allow traffic.	Evaluates rules in number order to decide whether to allow traffic.

Internet Gateways

An *Internet gateway* is a horizontally-scaled, redundant, and highly available Amazon VPC component that allows communication between instances in your VPC and the Internet. An Internet gateway is a target in your VPC route tables for Internet-routable traffic.

In the case of IPv4, when traffic is sent from the instance to the Internet, the Internet gateway translates any private source IPv4 address to the associated public IPv4 address. An Amazon EC2 instance can receive a public IPv4 address either automatically at launch or dynamically using an IPv4 Elastic IP address. The Internet gateway maintains the one-to-one mapping of the instance's private IPv4 address and public IPv4 address. When an instance receives traffic from the Internet, the Internet gateway translates the destination address (public IPv4 address) to the instance's private IPv4 address, as appropriate, and forwards the traffic to the VPC.

Because your IPv6 addresses are allocated from Amazon's GUA blocks, Amazon EC2 instances within a VPC are aware of their public IPv6 addresses. When traffic is sent from the instance to the Internet, the Internet gateway forwards the instance's source IPv6 address unchanged. When an instance receives traffic from the Internet, the Internet gateway forwards the traffic to the Amazon EC2 destination instance with the matching GUA.

You must do the following to create a public subnet with Internet access:

- Create and attach an Internet gateway to your VPC.
- Create a route in the associated subnet route table to send non-local traffic (0.0.0.0/0 for IPv4 or ::/0 for IPv6) to the Internet gateway.
- Configure your network ACLs and security group rules to allow relevant traffic to flow to and from your instance.

You must do the following to enable an Amazon EC2 instance to send and receive traffic from the Internet:

- Assign a public IPv4 or Elastic IP address.
- Assign an IPv6 GUA.

You can specify a default route (0.0.0.0/0 for IPv4 or ::/0 for IPv6), or you can scope the route to a specific range of IP addresses. For example, you can define a route limited to the public IP addresses of your company's endpoints outside of AWS.

Figure 2.5 illustrates a VPC with an IPv4 CIDR of 10.0.0.0/16, one subnet with an address range of 10.0.0.0/24, a route table, an attached Internet gateway, and a single Amazon EC2 instance with a private IPv4 address and an Elastic IP address. The route table contains two routes: the local route that permits intra-VPC communication and a default route that sends all non-local traffic to the Internet gateway (`igw-id`). Note that the Amazon EC2 instance has a public IPv4 address (Elastic IP address = 198.51.100.2); this instance can be accessed from the Internet, and traffic may originate from and return to this instance.

FIGURE 2.5 VPC, subnet, route table, and Internet gateway

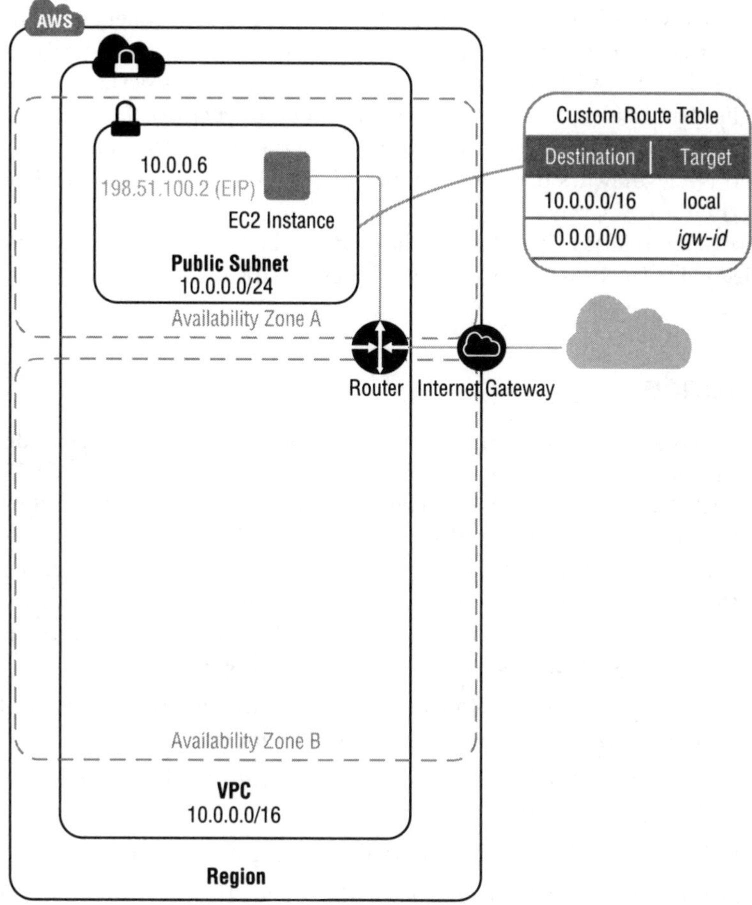

Network Address Translation (NAT) Instances and NAT Gateways

By definition, any instance that you launch into a private subnet in a VPC is not able to communicate directly with the Internet through an Internet gateway. That is, the subnet route table includes no routes to an Internet gateway. More importantly, connections originating from outside your VPC cannot reach instances inside your private subnet. IPv4 instances within private subnets may require outbound access to the Internet in order to apply security patches, update application software, or make Application Programming Interface (API) calls to Internet endpoints. AWS provides *NAT instances* and *NAT gateways* to allow IPv4 instances deployed in private subnets to gain outbound Internet access. For common use cases, we recommend that you use a NAT gateway rather than a NAT instance. The NAT gateway provides better availability, provides higher bandwidth, and requires less administrative effort than NAT instances. Note that although we use the term NAT to describe these two offerings, both NAT instances and NAT gateways perform many-to-one IPv4 translation, called *Port Address Translation (PAT)*.

NAT is not supported for IPv6. One of the goals of the IPv6 protocol is to provide end-to-end connectivity. To create a private IPv6 subnet, see the section on the egress-only Internet gateway.

NAT Instance

A NAT instance is an Amazon Linux Amazon Machine Image (AMI) that is designed to accept traffic from instances within a private subnet, translate the source IPv4 addresses to the private IPv4 address of the NAT instance, and forward the traffic to the Internet gateway where one-to-one NAT is performed to a public IPv4 address. The NAT instance maintains a translation table with the state of the forwarded traffic in order to return response traffic from the Internet to the proper instance in the private subnet.

To allow instances within a private subnet to access Internet resources through the Internet gateway via a NAT instance, you must do the following:

- Create a security group for the NAT instance with outbound rules that specify the needed Internet resources by port, protocol, and IP address.
- Launch an Amazon Linux NAT AMI as an instance in a public subnet and associate it with the NAT security group.
- Disable the Source/Destination Check attribute of the NAT instance.
- If you did not launch your NAT instance with a public IPv4 address, allocate an Elastic IP address and associate it with the NAT instance.
- Configure the route table associated with the private subnet to direct Internet-bound traffic to the NAT instance (for example, `i-1a2b3c4d`).

Amazon provides Amazon Linux AMIs that are preconfigured to run as NAT instances. These AMIs include the string `amzn-ami-vpc-nat` in their names so that you can search for them in the Amazon EC2 console.

This configuration allows instances in private subnets to send outbound Internet communication, but it prevents the instances from receiving inbound traffic initiated by someone on the Internet.

NAT Gateway

A *NAT gateway* is an AWS-managed resource that is designed to operate just like a NAT instance but is simpler to manage and highly available within an Availability Zone.

To allow instances within a private subnet to access Internet resources via a NAT gateway, you must do the following:

- Create a NAT gateway in a public subnet.
- Allocate and associate an IPv4 Elastic IP address with a NAT gateway.
- Configure the route table associated with the private subnet to direct Internet-bound traffic to the NAT gateway (for example, `nat-1a2b3c4d`).

Like a NAT instance, this managed service allows outbound Internet communication and prevents the instances from receiving inbound traffic initiated by someone on the Internet.

To create an Availability Zone-independent architecture, create a NAT gateway in each Availability Zone and configure your subnet route tables such that resources use the NAT gateway in the same Availability Zone.

PAT overloads a single IP address by using multiple, different User Datagram Protocol (UDP) or Transport Control Protocol (TCP) ports. This limits a single NAT gateway to roughly 65,000 simultaneous flows to a single destination IP, port, and protocol tuple.

Egress-Only Internet Gateways (EIGWs)

One of the goals of the IPv6 protocol is to provide end-to-end connectivity. As such, Amazon does not support NAT, or Network Prefix Translation, for IPv6. Each instance that is enabled for IPv6 packet processing has at least one GUA. As the name implies, these addresses are unique and global in scope and are public, routable IPv6 addresses.

You probably have Amazon EC2 instances that should not be accessible from the Internet. With IPv4, this protection is accomplished in your VPC by creating a private subnet with a NAT instance or NAT gateway.

In order to provide a semantically similar experience to NAT for IPv6, Amazon created the *egress-only Internet gateway (EIGW)*. The EIGW is a horizontally-scaled, redundant, and highly-available VPC component that allows outbound communication over IPv6 from your instances to the Internet. It prevents traffic originating on the Internet from connecting to your instances, however. Unlike a NAT instance or a NAT gateway, the EIGW performs no address translation function. The instance IPv6 address is visible end to end.

For the exam, you must understand the dual-stack nature of the Amazon VPC IPv6 implementation. When configuring a private subnet where instances need to communicate with the Internet, the IPv4 default route (destination) in the subnet's associated route table will point to (target) a NAT instance or NAT gateway. In turn, the NAT instance or NAT gateway will reside within a public subnet with a default route pointing to an Internet gateway. For IPv6, that same route table for your private subnet will include a default route pointing to an EIGW attached to the VPC. Figure 2.6 shows a private subnet where IPv4 traffic is confined to the VPC but IPv6 traffic originating from within the VPC may access the Internet.

FIGURE 2.6 Egress-Only Internet gateway

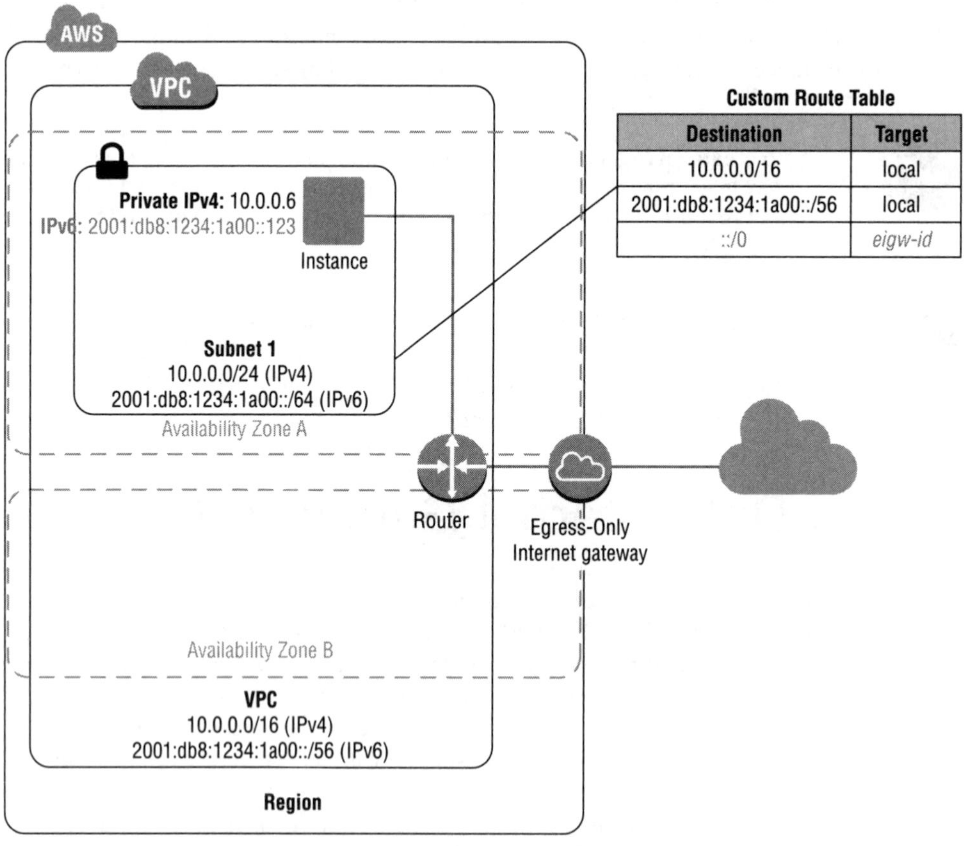

Virtual Private Gateways (VGWs), Customer Gateways, and Virtual Private Networks (VPNs)

You can connect an existing data center to your VPC using either hardware or software VPN connections. Both options make the VPC an extension of your data center. To create a VPN using AWS-provided VPN hardware, configure a virtual private gateway, a customer gateway, and a VPN connection.

The *virtual private gateway (VGW)* is a logical construct in your VPC that provides edge routing for AWS managed VPN connections and AWS Direct Connect (discussed later). For the exam, it is important that you understand that the VGW manages edge routing information that is separate from your VPC route tables. It is conceptually a next-hop router. To use AWS managed VPN connections, you must create and attach a VGW to your VPC.

A *customer gateway* represents the physical device or software application on the remote end of the VPN connection. The customer gateway must have a static IPv4 address. The customer gateway may reside behind a device performing NAT. You define the customer gateway in your VPC.

Once the VGW and the customer gateway have been created, the last step is to create a *VPN connection*. VPN tunnel negotiation must be initiated by the customer gateway. After the tunnel is negotiated and established, traffic can route over the tunnel. Figure 2.7 illustrates a single VPN connection between a corporate network and a VPC.

FIGURE 2.7 VPC with a VPN connection to a customer network

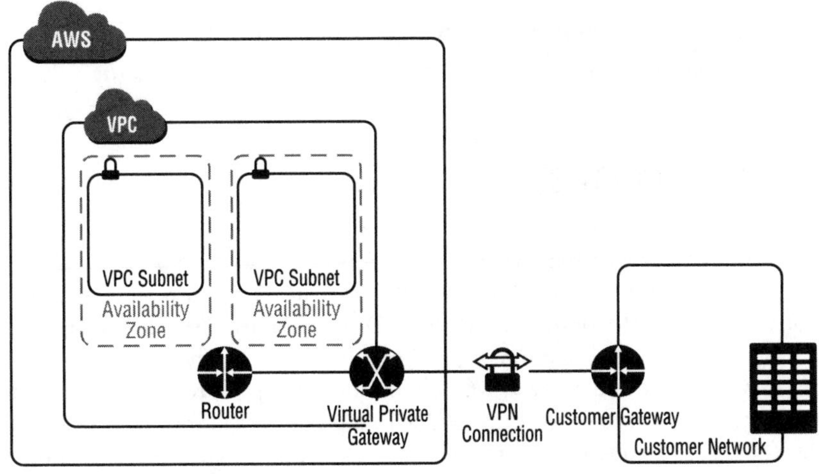

A single VPN connection consists of two *Internet Protocol Security (IPsec)* tunnels for high availability to the VPC. Amazon performs maintenance on the VPN from time to time. This maintenance may disable one of the two tunnels briefly.

You must specify the type of routing that you plan to use when you create a VPN connection. If the customer gateway supports *Border Gateway Protocol (BGP)*, configure the VPN connection for dynamic routing. Otherwise, configure the connections for static routing. If you will be using static routing, you must enter the routes for your network that should be communicated to the VGW. To allow your resources to route traffic back to the corporate network through the VGW and across the VPN tunnel, you configure route propagation from or static routes to the VGW. There is further discussion of VPN options in Chapter 4, "Virtual Private Networks."

Amazon will provide the information needed by the network administrator to configure the customer gateway and establish the VPN connection with the VGW.

A software VPN connection is established with your VPC when you launch an Amazon EC2 instance running VPN software. In this scenario, your instance must have a public IPv4 address, be accessible from the Internet, and have the correct ports and protocols enabled in the security group. You must also disable the Source/Destination Check attribute on the Amazon EC2 instance. Once configured, you update the relevant route tables to forward the appropriate destination networks to the target instance's elastic network interface. When using an instance-based, software VPN endpoint, you are responsible for scalability, availability, and performance.

Here are the important points to understand about VGWs, customer gateways, and VPNs for the exam:

- The VGW is the AWS end of the VPN connection.
- The customer gateway is a hardware or software application on the remote end of the VPN connection.
- You must initiate the VPN tunnel from the customer gateway to the VGW.
- VGWs support both dynamic routing with BGP and static routing.
- The VPN connection consists of two tunnels for high availability to the VPC.

VPC Endpoints

A *VPC endpoint* enables you to connect your VPC privately to supported AWS services and VPC endpoint services (powered by *AWS PrivateLink*) without requiring an Internet gateway, NAT device, VPN connection, or AWS Direct Connect connection. VPC endpoints are horizontally-scaled, redundant, and highly available. There are two types of VPC endpoints: interface and gateway. Interface endpoints (powered by AWS PrivateLink) use an elastic network interface in your VPC with a private IP address that serves as an entry point for traffic destined to a supported service. Gateway endpoints use a route table target for a specified route in your route table for supported services. Endpoints allow resources in your VPC to use their private IPv4 addresses to communicate with resources outside of their VPC. Resources in your VPC do not need public IPv4 addresses. Moreover, traffic between your VPC and the endpoint does not leave the Amazon network.

Gateway endpoints currently support communication with Amazon Simple Storage Service (Amazon S3) and Amazon DynamoDB. Interface endpoints support Amazon Kinesis Streams, Elastic Load Balancing API, Amazon EC2 API, Amazon EC2 Systems Manager (SSM), AWS Service Catalog, Endpoint services hosted by other accounts, and supported Marketplace partner services. Chapter 3, "Advanced Amazon Virtual Private Cloud (Amazon VPC)," covers endpoints services in more detail. Additional AWS Cloud services are expected to be added in the future.

VPC endpoints are supported for IPv4 traffic only.

You must do the following when creating a gateway endpoint:

- Specify the VPC.
- Specify the service. An Amazon service is identified by a *prefix list* of the form `com.amazonaws.<region>.<service>`.
- Specify the policy. You can allow full access or create a custom policy. This policy can be changed at any time.
- Specify the route tables. A route will be added to each specified route table, which will state the service prefix list as the destination and the endpoint as the target.

You can use prefix lists in your VPC outbound security group rules.

Figure 2.8 shows an example route table (Subnet 1) that routes all Internet traffic (0.0.0.0/0) to an Internet gateway. Any traffic from the subnet that is destined for another AWS Cloud service (for example, Amazon S3 or Amazon DynamoDB) will be sent to the Internet gateway in order to reach that service.

Figure 2.8 also shows an example route table (Subnet 2) that directs traffic from the subnet that is destined for Amazon S3 in the same region to the gateway endpoint.

When using gateway endpoints for Amazon S3, you can further refine access control by creating bucket policies that use the VPC endpoint data. Using a VPC endpoint, your Amazon S3 bucket policy can allow access based on a VPC identifier or on a specific VPC endpoint identifier. Amazon S3 bucket policies do not, however, support policies based on IP addresses when using a VPC endpoint. Since you can create multiple VPCs with overlapping IP addresses, an IP-based bucket policy for evaluating VPC endpoints does not add any real measure of security.

FIGURE 2.8 Route table for a VPC endpoint

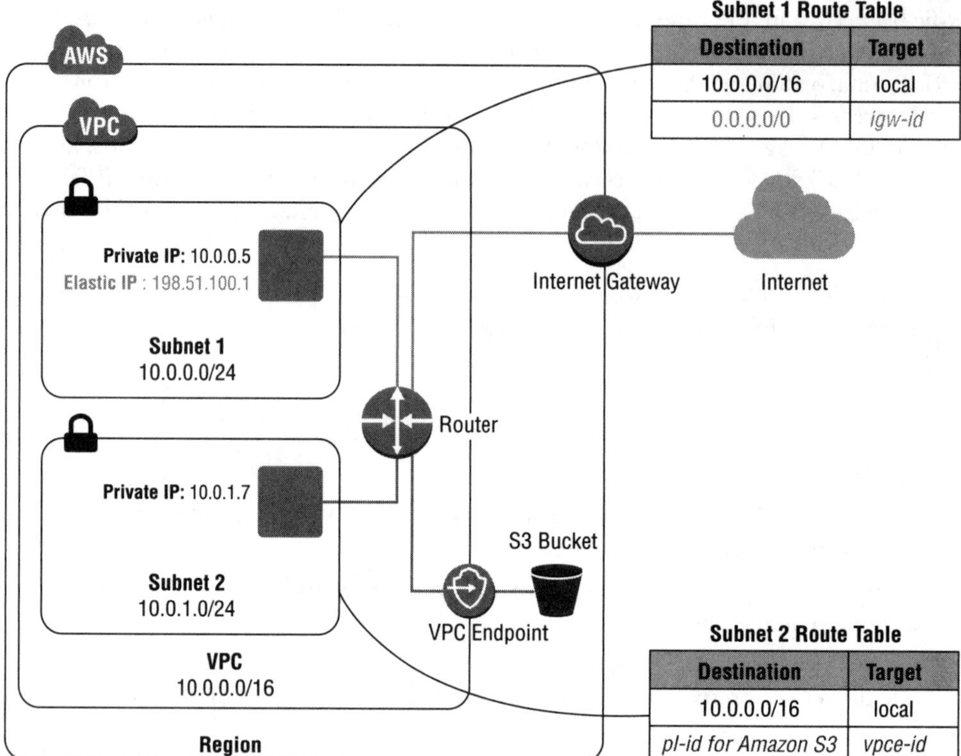

VPC Peering

A *VPC peering* connection is a networking connection between two VPCs that enables instances in either VPC to communicate with each other as if they were within the same network. You can create a VPC peering connection between your own VPCs or with a VPC in another AWS account. VPC peering is supported in the same region or to another region within the same Amazon partition. Amazon provides encryption for VPC peer traffic between regions. A peering connection is neither a gateway nor an Amazon VPN connection, and it does not introduce a single point of failure for communication.

Resources within the AWS Cloud are each given a unique Amazon Resource Name (ARN). These ARNs are used in various ways, including the construction of Identity and Access Management (IAM) policies. The first element of an ARN is the partition. Partitions allow Amazon to group regions with common, but distinct, operational requirements into isolated administrative domains. Standard AWS Regions use the partition `aws`. Resources in China use the partition `aws-cn`. Resources in the AWS GovCloud (US) Regions use `aws-us-gov`.

Peering connections are created through a request/accept protocol. The owner of the initiating VPC sends a request to peer to the owner of the peer VPC. If the peer VPC is within the same account, it is identified by its VPC ID. If the peer VPC is within a different account, it is identified by account ID and VPC ID. The owner of the peer VPC has seven days either to accept or reject the request to peer with the requesting VPC before the peering request expires.

Once a VPC peer is established, both sides of the peer must add routes for the respective peer. Each route entry will use the peer connection ID (`pcx-xxxxxxxx`) as the target. If routes are not added, the VPC implicit router will not pass traffic across the peer. In Figure 2.9, VPC A would add routes to 10.0.0.0/16 through the peer connection. VPC B would add routes to 172.16.0.0/16 through the peer connection.

FIGURE 2.9 VPC peering connections do not support transitive routing

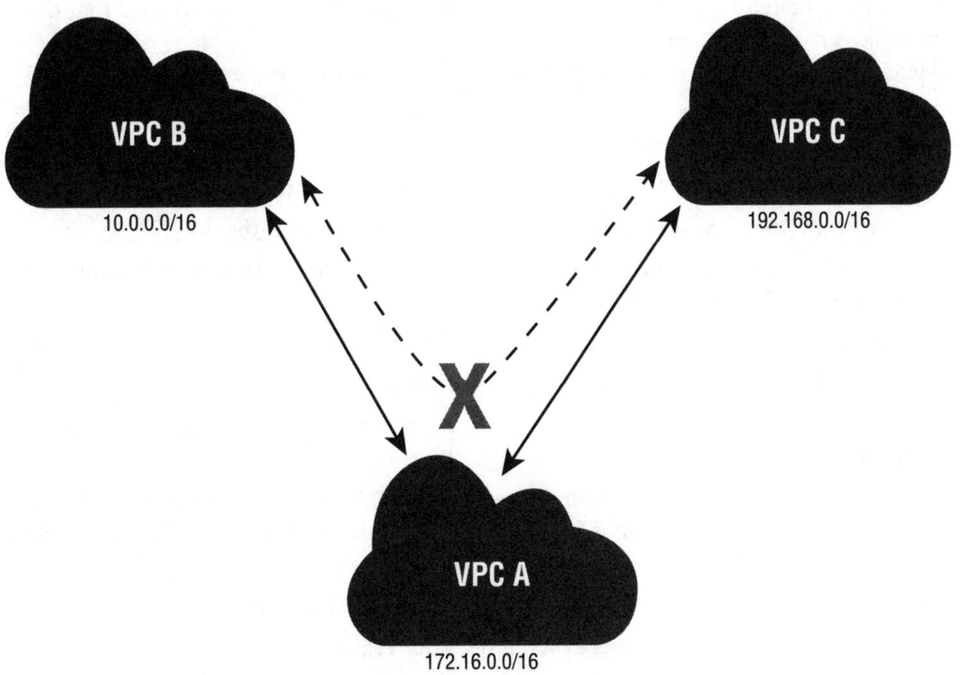

You can also use partial prefixes in the route table for peering. This approach is helpful when a peered VPC doesn't require full access to the entire CIDR range.

A VPC may have multiple peering connections. Peering is a one-to-one relationship between VPCs, meaning that two VPCs cannot have two peering agreements between them. In addition, peering connections do not support transitive routing, as depicted in Figure 2.9.

In Figure 2.9, VPC A has two peering connections with two different VPCs: VPC B and VPC C. Therefore, VPC A can communicate directly with VPC B and VPC C. Because peering connections do not support transitive routing, VPC A cannot be a transit point for traffic between VPC B and VPC C. In order for VPC B and VPC C to communicate with each other, a peering connection must be explicitly created between them.

If a peer is established within the same region, you can reference security groups in the peer VPC. Similarly, if a peer is established within the same region, you can enable DNS hostname resolution for the peer VPC. By default, if instances use the public DNS hostname of an instance in a peer VPC, the public IPv4 address is returned. Traffic to the instance flows over an Internet gateway. When DNS resolution is enabled on the peer, the private IPv4 address of the instance is returned instead. Traffic flows over the peer connection. Each VPC must enable DNS hostnames, local DNS resolution, and allow DNS resolution from the peering VPC. For IPv6, only public GUAs are used by Amazon VPC and Amazon EC2; therefore, traffic will flow through the peer connection, provided that the route tables are properly configured.

Here are the important points to understand about peering for the exam:

- You cannot create a peering connection between VPCs that have matching or overlapping CIDR blocks.
- Peering connections are confined to the same Amazon partition.
- Peers within the same region may reference security groups in the peer VPC.
- Peers within the same region may enable hostname resolution to receive private IPv4 addresses for peer instances.
- Amazon encrypts traffic between peers in different regions.
- VPC peering connections do not support transitive routing.
- You cannot have more than one peering connection between the same two VPCs at the same time.
- For certain applications (for example, web services), it may be more beneficial to use VPC endpoints. VPC peering will generally offer wider access to subnets and CIDR ranges. VPC endpoints allow connectivity between VPCs for specific applications.
- Jumbo frames are supported only between peers in the same region.
- IPv6 is supported only between peers in the same region.

Placement Groups

Placement groups are logical groupings of instances within a single Availability Zone. Instances in the placement group are proximate in the Amazon network infrastructure, delivering low-latency, high packet-per-second performance, and high network throughput. Placement groups are appropriate for workloads like High Performance Computing (HPC) when internode network performance is important. We recommend that you use instance types with enhanced networking (discussed later in Chapter 9, "Network Performance") in your placement group.

Since a placement group causes instances to colocate in a section of the Amazon infrastructure, it is recommended that you start the number of instances that you need in a single launch. While it is possible to add and remove instances from a placement group, you run the risk that additional capacity may not be available in the section of the Amazon network where the placement group resides.

Here are important points to understand about placement groups for the exam:

- Placement groups are confined to a single Availability Zone.
- Maximum network throughput between any two instances is limited to the slowest instance.
- Network traffic outside of the placement group is limited to 25 Gbps for Amazon EC2 and Amazon S3 in the same region. Other traffic is limited to 5 Gbps.
- Placement groups support both IPv4 and IPv6.

Further information about placement groups is available in Chapter 9.

Elastic Network Interfaces

An *elastic network interface* is a virtual network interface that you can attach to an instance in a VPC. Elastic network interfaces are only available within a VPC and are associated with a subnet upon creation. Each elastic network interface has a primary IPv4 private address, a MAC address, and at least one security group. An elastic network interface may optionally have secondary private IPv4 addresses, one or more Elastic IP addresses, one public IPv4 address, and one or more IPv6 addresses. Attaching a second elastic network interface to an Amazon EC2 instance allows it to have network presence in different subnets. An elastic network interface created independently of a particular instance persists regardless of the lifetime of the instance to which it is attached; if an underlying instance fails, the IP address may be preserved by attaching the elastic network interface to a replacement instance. You cannot, however, detach the primary network interface of an Amazon EC2 instance.

Multiple elastic network interfaces allow you to use network and security appliances in your VPC, create dual-homed instances with workloads/roles on distinct subnets, or create a low-budget, high-availability solution. Elastic network interfaces can be attached to an instance while running (hot attach), when stopped (warm attach), or at launch (cold attach). However, multiple elastic network interfaces cannot be used for NIC teaming.

Auto Scaling only supports launch configurations with a single interface. For solutions that require multiple interfaces and Auto Scaling, you can use automation to attach multiple interfaces after instances are launched.

The maximum number of elastic network interfaces per instance and the number of IPv4 or IPv6 addresses supported on the elastic network interface vary based on the Amazon EC2 instance type.

Here are some important items to know about elastic network interfaces for the exam:

- Elastic network interfaces must have a primary, private IPv4 address and are always associated with at least one security group.
- Elastic network interfaces can be attached to an instance while running (hot attach), when stopped (warm attach), or at launch (cold attach).
- You cannot detach the primary network interface.
- An elastic network interface is confined to a single Availability Zone. When attaching multiple elastic network interfaces to an Amazon EC2 instance, the instance and the elastic network interfaces must all be in the same Availability Zone.
- NIC teaming cannot be used to increase bandwidth to or from an Amazon EC2 instance.

Dynamic Host Configuration Protocol (DHCP) Option Sets

Dynamic Host Configuration Protocol (DHCP) is a standard for passing configuration information to hosts on an IP network. The options field of a DHCP message contains the configuration parameters. Some of those parameters are the domain name, domain name server, and the NetBIOS node type.

AWS automatically creates and associates a DHCP option set for your VPC upon creation and sets two options:

domain-name-servers: This defaults to AmazonProvidedDNS.

domain-name: This defaults to the internal Amazon domain name for your region.

AmazonProvidedDNS is the Amazon DNS server. Amazon DNS, when enabled, allows Amazon EC2 instances to resolve domain names for destinations on the Internet and in a VPC peer in the same region.

The DHCP option sets of a VPC allow you to change how host and domain names are assigned to your Amazon EC2 resources. To assign your own domain name to your instances, create a custom DHCP option set and assign it to your VPC. You can configure the following values within a DHCP option set:

domain-name-servers: The IP addresses of up to four domain name servers, separated by commas.

domain-name: Specify the desired domain name (for example, `mycompany.com`).

ntp-servers: The IP addresses of up to four Network Time Protocol (NTP) servers, separated by commas.

netbios-name-servers: The IP addresses of up to four NetBIOS name servers, separated by commas.

netbios-node-type: Set this value to 2.

Each VPC must have exactly one DHCP option set assigned to it.

Amazon Domain Name Service (DNS) Server

The *Domain Name Service* provides a standard mechanism to resolve a hostname to an IP address. Amazon VPC provides an integrated *DNS server.* DNS service and Amazon EC2 hostname resolution for instances within your VPC are enabled by default when your VPC is created using the console wizard. The Amazon VPC attribute `enableDnsSupport` determines whether or not the Amazon DNS server is enabled for your VPC. The Amazon VPC attribute `enableDnsHostnames` determines whether Amazon EC2 instances receive hostnames.

The Amazon DNS server runs on a reserved IP address at the base of the VPC IPv4 CIDR range, plus two. For example, the DNS server for a VPC using 172.16.0.0/16 is available from 172.16.0.2. The Amazon DNS server is also available at 169.254.169.253. The Amazon DNS server can integrate with Amazon Route 53 private hosted zones and AWS Directory Service (both described in Chapter 6, "Domain Name System and Load Balancing."

If the `domain-name-servers` in your DHCP options is set to use the Amazon DNS server, your Amazon EC2 instance is assigned a private Fully Qualified Domain Name (FQDN) for the instance IPv4 address. If a public IPv4 address is assigned to the instance, a public FQDN is assigned as well. When instances within the VPC query the Amazon DNS server using the public FQDN of another instance within the VPC, the Amazon DNS server returns in the private IPv4 address. You can enable this same behavior between VPC peers in the same region.

Note that some AWS Cloud services, including Amazon EMR, require instances to resolve their own FQDN.

VPC Flow Logs

VPC Flow Logs is a feature of Amazon VPC that captures IP traffic flow information in your VPC. The flow data is stored in Amazon CloudWatch Logs. VPC Flow Logs can be enabled at the VPC, subnet, or network interface level. The logs are published approximately every 10 minutes. Table 2.7 indicates the information collected in the logs.

TABLE 2.7 VPC Flow Log Data Elements

Field	Description
`version`	The VPC Flow Logs version.
`account-id`	The AWS account ID for the flow log.

TABLE 2.7 VPC Flow Log Data Elements *(continued)*

Field	Description
`interface-id`	The ID of the network interface for which the log stream applies.
`srcaddr`	The source IPv4 or IPv6 address. The IPv4 address of the network interface is always its private IPv4 address.
`dstaddr`	The destination IPv4 or IPv6 address. The IPv4 address of the network interface is always its primary, private IPv4 address.
`srcport`	The source port of the traffic.
`dstport`	The destination port of the traffic.
`protocol`	The Internet Assigned Numbers Authority (IANA) protocol number of the traffic. For more information, go to Assigned Internet Protocol Numbers.
`packets`	The number of packets transferred during the capture window.
`bytes`	The number of bytes transferred during the capture window.
`start`	The time, in Unix seconds, of the start of the capture window.
`end`	The time, in Unix seconds, of the end of the capture window.
`action`	The action associated with the traffic: ▪ `ACCEPT`: The recorded traffic was permitted by the security groups or network ACLs. ▪ `REJECT`: The recorded traffic was not permitted by the security groups or network ACLs.
`log-status`	The logging status of the flow log: ▪ `OK`: Data is logging normally to Amazon CloudWatch Logs. ▪ `NODATA`: There was no network traffic to or from the network interface during the capture window. ▪ `SKIPDATA`: Some flow log records were skipped during the capture window. This may be because of an internal capacity constraint or an internal error.

VPC Flow Logs are useful for a number of reasons, including anomaly detection and troubleshooting. Anomaly detection is covered in Chapter 8, "Network Security." Logs are useful for troubleshooting as well. For example, when a record appears twice in the log for a packet inbound from the Internet to an Amazon EC2 instance, once with an `ACCEPT` action and once with a `REJECT` action, you will know that the network ACL was passed but the security group failed. The log shows this behavior because network ACLs are evaluated for traffic into a subnet before the security group of the target instance is evaluated.

VPC Flow Logs do not collect information in certain cases:

- Amazon EC2 instances communicating with the Amazon DNS server.
- Windows instances communicating with the Amazon Windows license activation server.
- Traffic to and from 169.254.169.254 for instance metadata.
- DHCP traffic.
- Traffic destined to the implicit router.

Summary

In this chapter, you reviewed core concepts of Amazon VPC and Amazon EC2. In its simplest form, Amazon VPC allows you to create your own private virtual network within the AWS Cloud. You can provision your own logically-isolated section of AWS in a way that is similar to designing and implementing a separate, independent network in a physical data center. Once your VPC is created, you can launch resources into your private network.

The core components of a VPC are as follows:

- Dynamic Host Configuration Protocol (DHCP) option sets
- IPv4
- Network access control lists (ACLs)
- Route tables
- Security groups
- Subnets

A VPC has the following optional components:

- Amazon Domain Name Service (DNS) server
- Elastic network interfaces
- Gateways (Internet gateway, EIGW, NAT gateway, VGW, and customer gateway)
- Virtual Private Networks (VPNs)
- IPv6
- NAT instances
- Placement groups
- VPC endpoints
- VPC Flow Logs
- VPC peering

Subnets can be public, private, or VPN-only. A public subnet is one in which the associated route table directs the subnet's traffic to the VPC's Internet gateway. A private subnet is one in which the associated route table does not direct the subnet's traffic to the VPC's Internet gateway. A VPN-only subnet is one in which the associated route table directs the subnet's traffic to the VPC's VGW and does not have a route to the Internet. Regardless of the type of subnet, the internal IPv4 address range of the subnet is private, and the internal IPv6 address range is an AWS-provided GUA.

Each subnet within a VPC contains a logical construct called an implicit router. The implicit router is the next hop gateway on a subnet where routing decisions are made. These routing decisions are governed by a route table. You can create custom route tables to define specific routing policies. Custom route tables may be associated with one or more subnets. Your VPC also contains a "main" route table that you can modify. The main route table is used for all subnets that are not explicitly associated with a custom route table. Each route table has one or more local routes that specify the IPv4 and IPv6 CIDR blocks associated with your VPC.

An Internet gateway provides a VPC gateway to the Internet. Internet gateways allow traffic originating from the Internet to reach Amazon EC2 instances with public IPv4 or IPv6 addresses. NAT gateways and NAT instances allow IPv4 traffic originating from within a subnet to reach the Internet. Traffic from the Internet cannot reach the Amazon EC2 instances behind a NAT gateway or NAT instance. Similarly, EIGWs allow IPv6 traffic originating from within a subnet to reach the Internet without allowing traffic inbound that originates from the Internet.

A VGW connects to the VPN endpoints on the AWS side of a VPN connection. A customer gateway is a physical device or a software application on the customer's side of the VPN connection. Once these two elements of a VPC have been created, the last step is to create a VPN connection. Each Amazon VPN connection consists of two tunnels for high availability. A tunnel is established after traffic is generated from the remote end of the VPN connection the tunnel is negotiated.

A VPC endpoint enables you to create a private connection between your VPC and another AWS Cloud service or VPC without requiring access over the Internet or through a NAT instance, VPN connection, or AWS Direct Connect.

A VPC peering connection is a networking connection between two VPCs that enables instances in either VPC to communicate with each other as if they were within the same network. You can create a VPC peering connection between your own VPCs or with an VPC in another AWS account within an Amazon partition. VPC peering can also be used across regions. A peering connection is neither a gateway nor a VPN connection and does not introduce a single point of failure for communication. Peering connections in the same region can share security groups and DNS hostname resolution.

A security group is a virtual stateful firewall that controls inbound and outbound traffic to Amazon EC2 instances. When you first launch an Amazon EC2 instance into a VPC, you will specify the security group with which it will be associated or the default security group that will be applied. The default security group allows all instances associated with the default security group to communicate with each other and allow all outbound traffic. You may change the rules for the default security group, but you may not delete the default security group.

A network ACL is another layer of security that acts as a stateless firewall on a subnet level. VPCs are created with a modifiable default network ACL that is associated with every subnet, and it allows all inbound and outbound traffic. The default network ACL allows all inbound and outbound traffic. If you want to create a custom network ACL, its initial configuration will deny all inbound and outbound traffic until you create a rule that states otherwise.

Placement groups allow you to launch Amazon EC2 instances that are close to one another on the Amazon infrastructure. This network proximity allows for high-bandwidth, high packet-per-second, and high-throughput performance. Placement groups are particularly relevant for workloads with strict performance tolerances, like HPC.

An elastic network interface is a virtual network interface that you attach to an instance in a VPC. Each elastic network interface has a primary IPv4 private address, a MAC address, and at least one security group. Attaching a second elastic network interface to an Amazon EC2 instance allows it to be dual-homed. An elastic network interface created independently of a particular instance persists regardless of the lifetime of the attached instance; if an underlying instance fails, the IP address may be preserved by attaching the elastic network interface to a replacement instance. You cannot detach the primary network interface of an Amazon EC2 instance.

Amazon VPC supports both IPv4 and IPv6 addresses. You select an IPv4 CIDR between /16 and /28 when you create your VPC. An Elastic IP address is a static, public IPv4 address that you can allocate to your account from a regional IPv4 pool and release back into the regional IPv4 pool. Elastic IP addresses allow you to maintain a set of IP addresses that remain fixed while the underlying infrastructure may change over time. You may optionally associate an IPv6 CIDR of size /56 from Amazon's GUA space to your Amazon VPC. You must enable IPv6 on your VPC, subnet, and Amazon EC2 instance to use the protocol.

The DHCP option sets element of a VPC allows you to direct Amazon EC2 hostname assignment to your own resources. In order for you to assign your own domain name to your instances, you create a custom DHCP option set and assign it to your VPC.

The Amazon DNS server provides DNS resolution within the Amazon VPC. Amazon DNS integrates with Amazon Route 53 and AWS Directory Service. When two VPCs within the same region are peered, you can enable DNS resolution for Amazon EC2 instances across the peering.

VPC Flow Logs provide a periodic view of network flow information. Log data is pushed to Amazon CloudWatch Logs approximately every 10 minutes. VPC Flow Logs are useful for understanding network traffic, including anomaly detection and troubleshooting.

Resources to Review

For further review, check out the following URLs:

Amazon EC2:

`https://aws.amazon.com/documentation/ec2/`

Amazon VPC:

`https://aws.amazon.com/documentation/vpc/`

Exam Essentials

Understand what a VPC is and its core and optional components. A VPC is a logically isolated network in the AWS Cloud. A VPC is made up of the following core elements: subnets (public, private, and VPN-only), route tables, security groups, network ACLs, IPv4, and DHCP option sets. Optional elements include gateways (Internet gateways, EIGW, NAT gateway, VGW, and customer gateway), Virtual Private Networks (VPNs), Elastic IP addresses, endpoints, peering connections, NAT instances, placement groups, elastic network interfaces, Amazon DNS, VPC Flow Logs, and IPv6.

Understand the purpose of a subnet. A subnet is a segment of a VPC's IP address range where you can place groups of isolated resources. Subnets are defined by CIDR blocks—for example, 10.0.1.0/24, 10.0.2.0/24—and are contained within an Availability Zone.

Identify the difference between a public subnet, a private subnet, and a VPN-only subnet. If a subnet's traffic is routed to an Internet gateway, the subnet is known as a public subnet. If a subnet doesn't have a route to the Internet gateway, or if it does have a route to an EIGW, the subnet is known as a private subnet. If a subnet doesn't have a route to the Internet gateway or EIGW but has its traffic routed to a VGW, the subnet is known as a VPN-only subnet.

Understand the purpose of a route table. Route tables contain routing rules that determine where network traffic is directed. Each subnet can have its own route table. These routing rules are executed by the implicit router using a route priority process. An unmodifiable local route exists in all route tables within the VPC, and it allows Amazon EC2 instances within different subnets of the same VPC to communicate with each other.

Understand the purpose of an Internet gateway. An Internet gateway is a horizontally-scaled, redundant, and highly-available Amazon VPC component that allows communication between instances in your VPC and the Internet. Internet gateways are fully redundant and have no bandwidth constraints. An Internet gateway provides a target in your VPC route tables for Internet-routable traffic and performs NAT for instances that have a private IPv4 to public IPv4 address mapping.

Understand what a NAT provides to a VPC. A NAT instance or NAT gateway enables instances in a private subnet to initiate outbound traffic to the Internet. This allows outbound Internet communication to download patches and updates, for example, but it prevents the instances from receiving inbound traffic initiated by nodes on the Internet.

Understand what an EIGW provides to a VPC. The IPv6 protocol was designed to provide end-to-end connectivity. As such, Amazon does not support NAT for IPv6. The EIGW enables instances in a private subnet to initiate outbound traffic to the Internet, but it prevents the instances from receiving inbound traffic initiated on the Internet.

Understand the role of a VGW. The VGW is a logical construct in your VPC that provides edge routing for AWS managed VPN connections and AWS Direct Connect (discussed in Chapter 5, "AWS Direct Connect"). The VGW maintains edge routing information that is separate from your VPC route tables. It is a next-hop router that makes routing decisions based on information received from the VPC and from the attached VPN or AWS Direct Connect connections.

Understand the components needed to establish a VPN connection from a network to a VPC. A VGW is attached to the VPN endpoints on the AWS side of the VPN connection between the Amazon network and the customer network. A customer gateway represents a physical device or a software application on the customer's side of the VPN connection. The VPN connection consists of two IPsec tunnels, and the tunnel must be initiated from the customer gateway side.

Understand what benefits endpoints provide to a VPC. A VPC endpoint enables you to create a private connection between your VPC and another AWS Cloud service or VPC without requiring access over the Internet or through a NAT instance, a VPN connection, or AWS Direct Connect. Endpoints only support services within the local region.

Understand VPC peering. A VPC peering connection is a networking connection between two VPCs that enables resources in either VPC to communicate with each other as if they were within the same network. Peering connections are created through a request/accept protocol. Transitive peering is not supported, and peering is only available between VPCs within the same Amazon partition. Peers within the same region can share security group and Amazon DNS information. It's also possible to peer between VPCs in different regions.

Know the difference between a security group and a network ACL. A security group applies at the network interface level. You can have multiple instances in multiple subnets that are members of the same security groups. Security groups are stateful, which means that outbound return traffic is automatically allowed, regardless of any outbound rules. A network ACL is applied on a subnet level, and traffic is stateless. You need to allow both inbound and outbound traffic on the network ACL in order for resources in a subnet to be able to communicate over a particular protocol. Traffic between instances in the same subnet are not evaluated by network ACLs.

Know what a placement group provides and why it is used. A placement group ensures that Amazon EC2 instances are launched in proximity to one another in the Amazon network. Placement groups are confined to a single Availability Zone. The result is low-latency, high packet-per-second performance, and high network throughput. Amazon EC2 instances used in placement groups should enable enhanced networking. Placement groups are used for applications that have strict network performance requirements.

Understand how elastic network interfaces are configured and used in a VPC. An elastic network interface is a virtual network interface that you can attach to an instance in a VPC. Elastic network interfaces are associated with a subnet. Each elastic network interface has a primary IPv4 private address, a MAC address, and at least one security group. An elastic network interface may optionally have secondary private IPv4 addresses, one or more Elastic IP addresses, one public IPv4 address, and one or more IPv6 addresses. Attaching multiple elastic network interfaces to an Amazon EC2 instance allows it to be multi-homed. Elastic network interfaces allow for the movement of network adapters in case of an underlying failure. The IP address may be preserved by attaching the elastic network interface to a replacement instance. You cannot detach the primary network interface of an Amazon EC2 instance.

Know the difference between a VPC public IP address and an IPv4 Elastic IP address. A public IP address is an AWS-provided IPv4 or IPv6 that is automatically assigned at launch to instances within a subnet. An Elastic IP address is an AWS-provided public IPv4 address that you allocate to your account and assign to instances or network interfaces on demand.

Understand what DHCP option sets provide to a VPC. The DHCP option sets element of an VPC allows you to direct Amazon EC2 hostname assignment to your own resources. You can specify the domain name for instances within an Amazon VPC and identify the IP addresses of custom DNS servers, NTP servers, and NetBIOS servers.

Understand the features of the Amazon DNS server. The Amazon DNS server is integrated into the VPC. It provides name resolution for both internal Amazon EC2 instances and for Internet DNS. The Amazon DNS server is located at both VPC CIDR+2 (for example, 10.0.0.2 for 10.0.0.0/16) and 169.254.169.253. When two peered VPCs within the same region enable the feature, Amazon DNS resolves internal Amazon EC2 hostnames across the peer connection. Amazon DNS integrates with Amazon Route 53 private hosted zones and AWS Directory Service.

Understand the capabilities and uses for VPC Flow Logs. VPC Flow Logs provide visibility into the network traffic flows in your VPC. The logs are stored in Amazon CloudWatch Logs approximately every 10 minutes. The logs can be enabled at the VPC, subnet, and network interface level. Log data is useful for determining anomalies in the network and for troubleshooting connectivity problems. When a secondary IP address on an elastic network interface is used as a destination, the logs capture the primary IP address of the interface in the log.

Test Taking Tip

Questions on the exam are typically either multiple choice, where one of the answers is correct, or multiple response, where a specified number of answers are correct. In both cases, the incorrect responses are plausible. As a result, you might second-guess yourself or question your knowledge. In most cases, your initial answer is correct.

Exercises

The best way to become familiar with Amazon VPC is to build your own custom VPC and then deploy Amazon EC2 instances into it, which is what you'll be doing in this section. You should repeat these exercises until you can create and decommission VPCs with confidence.

For assistance completing these exercises, refer to the Amazon VPC User Guide located at `http://aws.amazon.com/documentation/vpc/`.

EXERCISE 2.1

Create a Custom VPC

In this exercise, you will manually create a VPC with IPv4 and IPv6 enabled.

1. Sign in to the AWS Management Console as Administrator or Power User.
2. Select the Amazon VPC icon to launch the Amazon VPC Dashboard.
3. Create a VPC with an IPv4 CIDR block equal to 192.168.0.0/16, an AWS-provided IPv6 CIDR block, a name tag **My First VPC**, and default tenancy.

You have created your first custom VPC.

EXERCISE 2.2

Create Two Subnets for Your Custom VPC

In this exercise, you will manually add two subnets to your VPC with IPv4 and IPv6 addresses.

1. Create a subnet in the VPC from Exercise 2.1 and specify an Availability Zone for the subnet (for example, `us-east-1a`). Set the subnet IPv4 CIDR block equal to 192.168.1.0/24 and IPv6 CIDR block to subnet ID 01. Use a name tag of **My First Public Subnet**.

EXERCISE 2.2 *(continued)*

2. Create a second subnet in the same VPC from Exercise 2.1 and specify a different Availability Zone from the first subnet (for example, `us-east-1b`). Set the subnet IPv4 CIDR block equal to 192.168.2.0/24 and the IPv6 CIDR block to subnet ID 02. Use a name tag of **My First Private Subnet**.

You have now created two new subnets, each in its own Availability Zone. It's important to remember that one subnet equals one Availability Zone. You cannot stretch a subnet across multiple Availability Zones.

EXERCISE 2.3

Connect Your Custom VPC to the Internet and Establish Routing

In this exercise, you will enable Internet access over IPv4 and IPv6. You will use Internet gateways, egress-only Internet gateways, NAT gateways, and route tables.

For assistance with this exercise, refer to the Amazon EC2 key-pair documentation at `http://docs.aws.amazon.com/AWSEC2/latest/UserGuide/ec2-key-pairs.html`.

For assistance with this exercise, refer to the NAT instances documentation at `http://docs.aws.amazon.com/AmazonVPC/latest/UserGuide/VPC_NAT_Instance.html#NATInstanc`.

1. Create an Amazon EC2 key-pair in the same region as your custom VPC.
2. Create an Internet gateway with a name tag of **My First Internet gateway** and attach it to your custom VPC.
3. Add IPv4 and IPv6 routes to the main route table for your custom VPC that directs Internet traffic (0.0.0.0/0 and ::/0) to the Internet gateway.
4. Create a NAT gateway, place it in the public subnet of your custom VPC, and assign it an Elastic IP address.
5. Create an EIGW for your custom VPC.
6. Create a new route table with a name tag of **My First Private Route Table** and place it within your custom VPC. Add a route to it that directs IPv4 Internet traffic (0.0.0.0/0) to the NAT gateway and IPv6 Internet traffic (::/0) to the EIGW. Associate the route table with the private subnet.

You have now created a connection to the Internet for resources within your VPC.

EXERCISE 2.4

Launch a Public Amazon EC2 Instance and Test the Connection to the Internet

In this exercise, you will launch an Amazon EC2 instance in a public subnet and confirm Internet connectivity.

1. Launch a t2.micro Amazon Linux AMI as an Amazon EC2 instance into the public subnet of your custom VPC. Enable Amazon EC2 to auto-assign a public IPv4 address and an IPv6 address. Give your instance a name tag of **My First Public Instance**, allow SSH (TCP/22) in the associated security group, and select the newly-created key-pair for secure access to the instance.
2. Securely access the Amazon EC2 instance in the public subnet via SSH with the newly-created key-pair.
3. Execute an update to the operating system instance libraries by executing the following command:

```
# sudo yum update -y
```

You should see output showing the instance downloading software from the Internet and installing it.

You have now provisioned an Amazon EC2 instance in a public subnet. You are able to apply patches to the Amazon EC2 instance in the public subnet, and you have demonstrated connectivity to the Internet.

Notice the IP address assigned to the instance. You should see both a private and public address.

4. Execute the following command:

```
# ip address show
```

Notice that the instance is only aware of its private address because the Internet gateway will perform NAT for any traffic destined to the public address.

EXERCISE 2.5

Launch a Private Amazon EC2 Instance and Test the Connection to the Internet

In this exercise, you will launch an Amazon EC2 instance in a private subnet and confirm that traffic is only allowed outbound from the subnet.

EXERCISE 2.5 ***(continued)***

1. Launch a t2.micro Amazon Linux AMI as an Amazon EC2 instance into the private subnet of your custom VPC. Enable Amazon EC2 to auto-assign a public IPv4 address and an IPv6 address. Give your instance a name tag of **My First Private Instance** and select the newly-created key-pair for secure access to the instance.
2. Confirm that you are unable to SSH into the instance over IPv4 or IPv6 from the Internet.
3. Securely access your Amazon EC2 instance in the public subnet via SSH with the newly-created key-pair. Use the SSH client on this instance to access your private Amazon EC2 instance.
4. Execute an update to the operating system instance libraries by executing the following command:

```
# sudo yum update -y
```

You should see output showing the instance downloading software from the Internet and installing it. If so, your instance is able to originate traffic to the Internet, but traffic on the Internet cannot initiate a connection with your private Amazon EC2 instance.

You have now provisioned an Amazon EC2 instance in a private subnet. You are able to apply patches to the Amazon EC2 instance in the private subnet, and you have demonstrated connectivity to the Internet.

Review Questions

1. You are a solutions architect working for a large travel company that is migrating its existing server estate to AWS. You have recommended that they use a custom Virtual Private Cloud (VPC), and they have agreed to proceed. They will need a public subnet for their web servers and a private subnet for their databases. They also require the web servers and database servers to be highly available, and there is a minimum of two web servers and two database servers each. How many subnets should you have to maintain high availability?

   A. 2

   B. 3

   C. 4

   D. 1

2. You launch multiple Amazon Elastic Compute Cloud (Amazon EC2) instances into a private subnet. These instances need to access the Internet to download patches. You decide to create a Network Address Translation (NAT) gateway. Where in the VPC should the NAT gateway reside?

   A. In the private subnet

   B. In the public subnet

   C. In the Virtual Private Gateway (VGW)

   D. In the Internet gateway

3. You are supporting a customer that executes tightly coupled High Performance Computing (HPC) workloads. What Virtual Private Cloud (VPC) option provides high-throughput, low-latency, and high packet-per-second performance?

   A. NIC Teaming

   B. 25 Gbps Ethernet

   C. IPv6 addressing

   D. Placement groups

4. What happens when you create a new Virtual Private Cloud (VPC)?

   A. A main route table is created by default.

   B. Three subnets are created by default, one for each Availability Zone.

   C. Three subnets are created by default in one Availability Zone.

   D. An Internet gateway is created by default.

5. How many Internet gateways can you attach to an Virtual Private Cloud (VPC) at any one time?

   A. 1

   B. 2

   C. 3

   D. 4

6. What aspect of a Virtual Private Cloud (VPC) is stateful?

   A. Network Access Control Lists (ACLs)

   B. Security groups

   C. VPC Flow Logs

   D. Prefix list

7. Which of the following exposes the Amazon side of a Virtual Private Network (VPN) connection?

   A. An Elastic IP address

   B. A customer gateway

   C. An Internet gateway

   D. A Virtual Private Gateway (VGW)

8. Which Amazon Virtual Private Cloud (Amazon VPC) feature allows you to create a dual-homed instance?

   A. Elastic IP address

   B. Customer gateways

   C. Security groups

   D. Elastic network interface

9. How many Internet Protocol Security (IPsec) tunnels are available for a single Virtual Private Network (VPN) connection?

   A. 4

   B. 3

   C. 2

   D. 1

Advanced Amazon Virtual Private Cloud (Amazon VPC)

THE AWS CERTIFIED ADVANCED NETWORKING – SPECIALTY EXAM OBJECTIVES COVERED IN THIS CHAPTER MAY INCLUDE, BUT ARE NOT LIMITED TO, THE FOLLOWING:

Domain 1.0: Design and Implement Hybrid IT Network Architectures at Scale

- ✓ **1.2 Given a scenario, derive an appropriate hybrid IT architecture connectivity solution**
- ✓ **1.5 Define routing policies for hybrid IT architectures**

Domain 2.0: Design and Implement AWS Networks

- ✓ **2.1 Apply AWS networking concepts**
- ✓ **2.5 Derive an appropriate architecture based on customer and application requirements**

Domain 5.0: Design and Implement for Security and Compliance

- ✓ **5.1 Evaluate design requirements for alignment with security and compliance objectives**

In the previous chapter, you reviewed the core components of Amazon Virtual Private Cloud (Amazon VPC). In this chapter, we go deeper into the more advanced features of Amazon VPC. The core components from the previous chapter meet the requirements of most designs, but some environments demand greater security, flexibility, and scalability from the network.

We review Amazon VPC endpoints, IP address features, and some elastic network interface features. We also review some of the design considerations that are important as you start to use and combine these features with other concepts like VPC peering. Some design scenarios include how you would create private access to services over a Virtual Private Network (VPN) with VPC endpoints.

VPC Endpoints

The idea behind the *principle of least privilege* is that users and services should only have the minimum access required to perform their function. If a user needs read-only access, they should not have permissions that allow modifications. From a networking perspective, if your Amazon EC2 instances only need access to other instances in the same Amazon VPC, they should not have Internet access. How does this concept apply when internal instances need to access public AWS Application Programming Interfaces (APIs) such as Amazon Elastic Compute Cloud (Amazon EC2) or Amazon Redshift? In these scenarios, *VPC endpoints* can allow instances to access shared resources through a private endpoint in a VPC.

A VPC endpoint lets you privately connect your VPC to an AWS Cloud service without requiring an Internet gateway, a Network Address Translation (NAT) device, a VPN connection, or AWS Direct Connect. Instances in your VPC do not require public IP addresses to communicate with AWS resources when using VPC endpoints. Traffic between your VPC and the AWS Cloud service does not leave the Amazon network.

Endpoints are virtual devices. They are horizontally scaled, redundant, and highly available VPC components that allow communication from resources in your VPC without imposing availability risks or bandwidth constraints on your network traffic.

VPC endpoints only support IPv4.

VPC Endpoints and Security

Beyond the principle of least privilege, there are additional use cases for VPC endpoints. For some customers, security and compliance impose strict requirements on resources with access to the Internet. VPC endpoints allow access to public AWS APIs without requiring access to the Internet. VPC endpoints also allow you to define granular access control to services between VPCs or accounts without allowing the broad access provided by VPC peering. The principle of least privilege and controlling Internet access is covered in more detail in Chapter 15, "Risk and Compliance." Reducing the number of instances or subnets that have Internet access can make security operations simpler, avoiding the complexity involved with NAT and routing policies and reducing the scope of certain audits and compliance checks.

Services such as Amazon Simple Storage Service (Amazon S3) allow more granular access when they are accessed over VPC endpoints using bucket policies and endpoint policies. It is possible to limit Amazon S3 bucket access to specific VPC endpoints, which can be configured for specific subnets and instances through routing and security groups.

It is also possible to reduce or eliminate the need for an AWS Direct Connect public Virtual Interface (VIF) if all of the AWS Cloud services that you need to access are available through VPC endpoints. This is another method to reduce public exposure. Details on how to access endpoints over AWS Direct Connect are provided later in this chapter.

VPC Endpoint Policy

VPC endpoints may support a *VPC endpoint policy*. A VPC endpoint policy is an AWS Identity and Access Management (IAM) resource policy that you attach to an endpoint when you create or modify the endpoint. If you do not attach a policy when you create an endpoint, AWS attaches a default policy for you that allows full access to the service. An endpoint policy does not override or replace IAM user policies or service-specific policies (such as Amazon S3 bucket policies). It is a separate policy for controlling access from the endpoint to the specified service.

VPC Endpoint Overview

There are two types of VPC endpoints that you can use to access services privately. We compare them briefly and then review each endpoint type in more detail.

Gateway VPC Endpoints

A *gateway VPC endpoint* is a gateway that serves as a target for a route in your route table for traffic destined to an AWS Cloud service. This type of endpoint supports Amazon S3 and Amazon DynamoDB. Gateway VPC endpoints use routes and prefix lists to route privately to AWS Cloud services. Instances using gateway VPC endpoints will resolve the service's Domain Name System (DNS) to a public address. The route to those public addresses uses the gateway VPC endpoint to access the service.

Interface VPC Endpoints

Interface VPC endpoints (powered by AWS PrivateLink) are implemented as special elastic network interfaces in Amazon VPC. When you create an interface VPC endpoint, AWS generates endpoint network interfaces in the subnets that you specify. Each interface VPC endpoint is specific to a single VPC and uses IPv4 addresses from the local subnets. When you create an interface VPC endpoint, AWS generates endpoint-specific DNS hostnames that you can use to communicate with the service. For AWS services and AWS Marketplace partner services, you can optionally enable private DNS for the endpoint. This option associates a private hosted zone with your VPC. The hosted zone contains a record set for the default DNS name for the service, which resolves to the private IP addresses of the endpoint network interfaces in your VPC. This enables you to make requests to the service using its default DNS hostname instead of the endpoint-specific DNS hostnames.

AWS PrivateLink

AWS PrivateLink is a type of interface VPC endpoint for AWS in addition to customer and partner services. AWS provides access to services such as the Amazon EC2 API and Elastic Load Balancing API with AWS PrivateLink. AWS PrivateLink is a newer and different way to access AWS Cloud services compared to gateway VPC endpoints.

AWS PrivateLink also enables building your own *VPC endpoint services*. AWS PrivateLink customers and service providers can create private endpoints to resources or services in their own VPC. You can access services in another VPC or account, including service providers and partners that support AWS PrivateLink. Each AWS PrivateLink connection is a relationship between a *service consumer* and a *service provider*. Example use cases for AWS PrivateLink include accessing a shared enterprise-provided API across many VPCs or accessing a Software as a Service (SaaS) logging provider's services with a private connection.

Gateway VPC Endpoints

A gateway VPC endpoint enables you to create a private connection between your VPC and AWS Cloud services without requiring access over the Internet or through a NAT device, a VPN connection, or AWS Direct Connect. Amazon S3 and Amazon DynamoDB have gateway VPC endpoints.

Amazon S3 Endpoints

An *Amazon S3 endpoint* allows private access to Amazon S3 from your VPC. As shown in Figure 3.1, instances in subnet 2 can access Amazon S3 through the VPC endpoint.

FIGURE 3.1 Amazon S3 endpoint

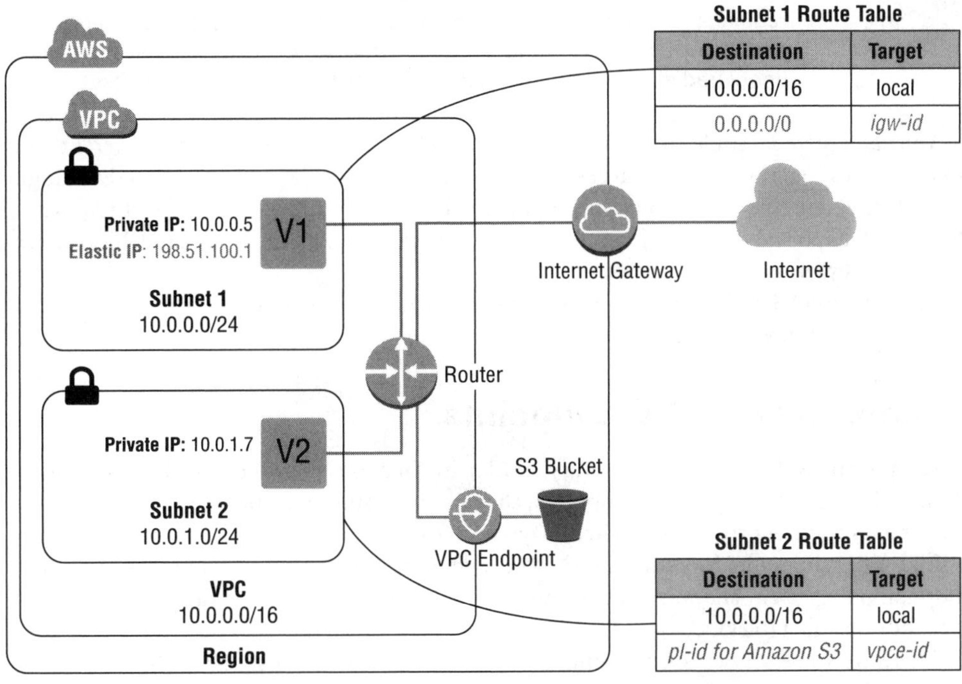

When you create an Amazon S3 endpoint, a *prefix list* and a VPC endpoint are created in your VPC. The prefix list is the collection of IP addresses that Amazon S3 uses. It is formatted as `pl-xxxxxxxx` and becomes an available option in both subnet routing tables and security groups.

You can get the current list of IP addresses in the prefix lists with the DescribePrefixLists API.

The VPC endpoint uses the format of `vpce-xxxxxxxx`, and it appears as a route destination in your route tables. The subnets that you select when you create the Amazon S3 endpoint will receive a new route for the prefix list directed toward the new gateway VPC endpoint. Table 3.1 shows a sample routing table using gateway VPC endpoints.

TABLE 3.1 Sample Routing Table Using Gateway VPC Endpoints

Prefix	Destination
10.0.0.0/16	local
pl-xxxxxxxx	vpce-xxxxxxxx

You cannot use the `aws:SourceIp` condition in your bucket policies for requests to Amazon S3 through a VPC endpoint. The condition fails to match any specified IP address or IP address range, and it may have an undesired effect when you make requests to an Amazon S3 bucket.

You can create multiple endpoints in the same VPC. This is used to apply different endpoint policies to allow different access. Because each route table may contain only a single prefix list, you are limited to one endpoint per subnet. If instances in the subnet require different Amazon S3 access policies, consider alternative subnet designs that achieve your desired policy or control outcomes.

The Amazon S3 endpoint uses DNS to direct traffic to the endpoint. You must enable DNS resolution in your VPC.

Amazon DynamoDB Endpoints

Amazon DynamoDB endpoints are very similar to Amazon S3 endpoints. Because Amazon DynamoDB uses gateway VPC endpoints, they use the same concepts of prefix lists and route tables to direct traffic to Amazon DynamoDB.

Like VPC endpoints for Amazon S3, VPC endpoints for Amazon DynamoDB support endpoint policies. An endpoint policy can restrict access to operations such as writes or access to specific tables.

There are some service-specific limitations that endpoints impose that, while out of the scope of this exam, may be important for design. One example is that you cannot access Amazon DynamoDB Streams through an endpoint.

Accessing Gateway Endpoints Over Remote Networks

Gateway VPC endpoints use AWS route table entries and DNS to route traffic privately to AWS Cloud services. These mechanisms only work within a VPC and prevent access to gateway endpoints from outside the VPC. Connections that originate from Amazon VPN or AWS Direct Connect through a Virtual Private Gateway (VGW) cannot directly access gateway endpoints. You also cannot access a gateway endpoint over VPC peering.

This restriction is related to *transitive routing*, which is not supported within a VPC. If the source of a packet is not an interface in the local VPC, the destination of the connection must be a network interface IP address local to the VPC. Either the destination or source of the packet must be an interface local to the VPC.

In order to overcome transitive routing limitations, you can modify DNS resolution and use a proxy fleet to reach VPC endpoints. Figure 3.2 shows a DNS-based proxy solution that directs traffic from a corporate network to a VPC endpoint for Amazon S3.

FIGURE 3.2 A proxy fleet is configured to access an Amazon S3 endpoint over AWS VPN.

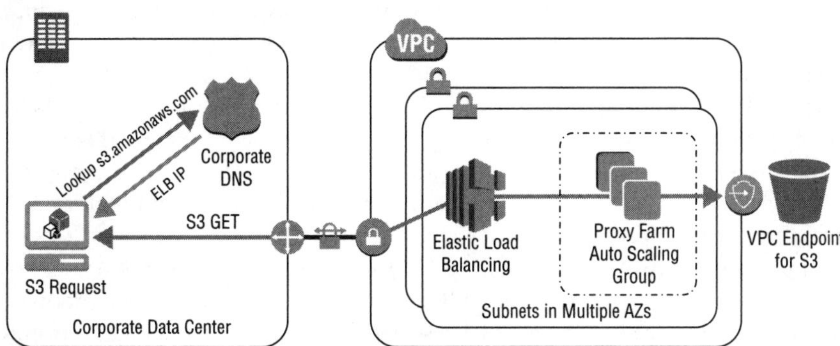

Core components of the solution are Elastic Load Balancing, a proxy farm, and the corporate DNS. The corporate DNS is configured to direct Amazon S3 requests to the CNAME of the load balancer. In this scenario, the destination IP address is a load balancer interface in the VPC. This configuration resolves the transitive routing scenario. The load balancer forwards the traffic to an Auto Scaling group of proxy instances. The proxy instances are placed in a subnet with access to an Amazon S3 endpoint. The proxies can be configured with an additional policy to allow or disallow certain requests, which can augment the level of control that the endpoint policy and Amazon S3 bucket policy provide.

This solution applies to both Amazon S3 and Amazon DynamoDB. The solution will work for VPN and AWS Direct Connect traffic sources.

Securing Gateway VPC Endpoints

VPC endpoint policies can limit what resources, such as buckets or tables, are accessible using the endpoint. When using endpoints for Amazon S3, bucket policies can allow incoming requests from either public connections or specific Amazon S3 endpoints.

Inside the VPC, you can control endpoint access by limiting the subnets with routes to the VPC endpoint. To provide granular access per instance, you can specify the prefix list in an outbound security group rule. The prefix list is not available in a network Access Control List (ACL).

Amazon S3 bucket policies can be configured to allow traffic from only VPC endpoints. These policies have the effect of preventing Internet access to a bucket.

Interface VPC Endpoints

Interface VPC endpoints are a different and more recently added approach to service endpoints. As opposed to gateway VPC endpoints that use routing and prefix lists, interface endpoints are local IP addresses in your VPC. The interface approach simplifies routing and allows for more flexibility. AWS Cloud services supported by interface endpoints include the Amazon EC2 API, Amazon EC2 Systems Manager (SSM), Amazon Kinesis, and the Elastic Load Balancing API.

Interface VPC endpoints appear as an elastic network interface in your VPC. When the interface endpoint is created, AWS creates regional and zonal DNS entries that resolve to local IP addresses within your VPC. This design allows you to switch your connections gracefully from public AWS endpoints to your private VPC endpoints without causing any downtime. Interface VPC endpoints also support connectivity over AWS Direct Connect, enabling applications outside AWS to access AWS Cloud services via the Amazon private network. Interface VPC endpoints are highly available, can deliver high network performance, and are managed by Amazon. These endpoints are powered by a distributed networking architecture called *AWS Hyperplane*. Hyperplane is not on the exam, but it is an internal AWS architecture used to build services such as NAT gateway, Network Load Balancer, and AWS PrivateLink.

Interface VPC Endpoints

Interface VPC endpoints allow you to access specific AWS Cloud services. This access method is also called AWS PrivateLink for AWS Services. In Figure 3.3, instances in subnet 1 can communicate with Amazon Kinesis through the interface VPC endpoint. Instances in subnet 2 communicate over the Internet through an Internet gateway.

The following are some considerations that you should take into account when accessing services over an interface VPC endpoint.

- You can access a VPC endpoint from AWS Direct Connect; however, you cannot access a VPC endpoint from across an AWS managed VPN connection or a VPC peering connection.
- For each AWS Cloud service, you can create one interface endpoint in each Availability Zone within your VPC.
- AWS Cloud services may not be available in all Availability Zones through an interface endpoint.
- Each endpoint can support a bandwidth of up to 10 Gbps per Availability Zone. Additional capacity may be added automatically based on your usage.
- Endpoints support IPv4 traffic only.
- AWS Cloud services cannot initiate requests to resources in your VPC through the endpoint. An endpoint can only return responses to traffic initiated from resources in the VPC.

FIGURE 3.3 An Amazon Kinesis endpoint interface is created using AWS PrivateLink.

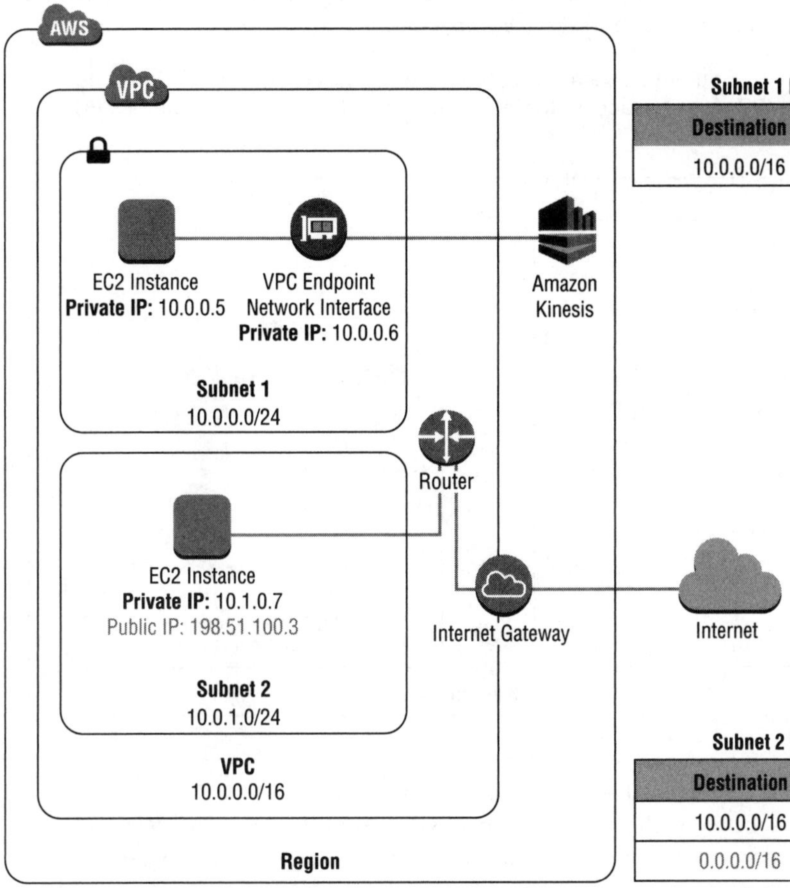

Subnet 1 Route Table

Destination	Target
10.0.0.0/16	local

Subnet 2 Route Table

Destination	Target
10.0.0.0/16	local
0.0.0.0/16	*igw-id*

AWS PrivateLink for Customer and Partner Services

So far, this chapter has discussed how to access AWS Cloud services privately through VPC endpoints, but you may also want to access your own or someone else's services privately. AWS PrivateLink allows you to access or share a service securely between VPCs or accounts using the Network Load Balancer to create *VPC endpoint services*. A VPC endpoint service is an interface VPC endpoint that you control and that keeps traffic within Amazon's private network.

Customers can build microservices architectures and share applications between VPCs, though these use cases may create complex networking challenges that involve many VPCs, granular security requirements, and overlapping addresses. In addition, many hosted services and SaaS offerings are provided on AWS. It is possible to increase the security of accessing these services with the VPC endpoint service.

VPC endpoint service uses private and public DNS, Network Load Balancer, and elastic network interfaces to operate between VPCs. In Figure 3.4, VPC endpoint service is configured between a *service provider* and *service consumer.*

FIGURE 3.4 An endpoint service is created from the service provider VPC to the service consumer VPC. An interface endpoint is created in the service consumer VPC.

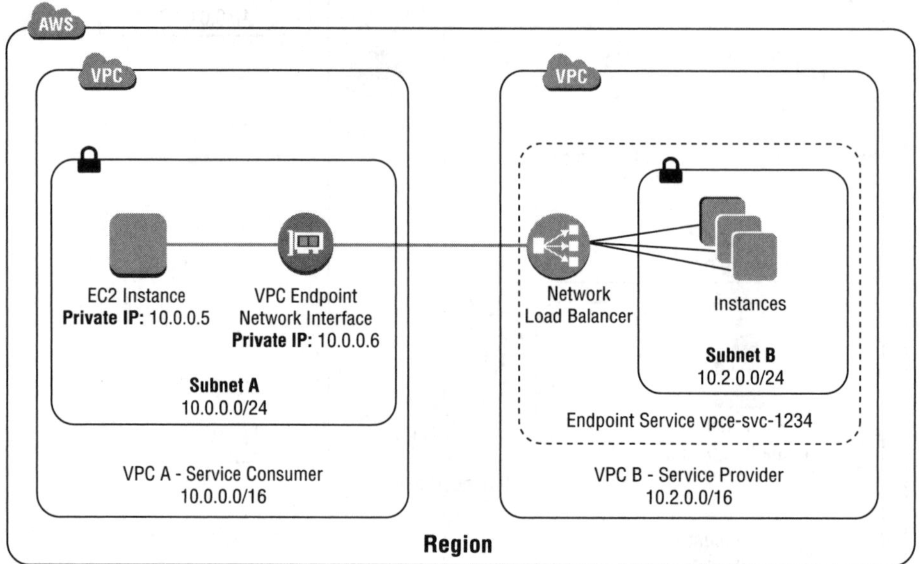

The provider has a service that is registered as something like `vpce-svc-0569c51ce317ddfdb.us-east-2.vpce.amazonaws.com`.

This name is associated with a Network Load Balancer in the provider's VPC. The interfaces and IP addresses for this Network Load Balancer are in the consumer's VPC. DNS will resolve `vpce-svc-0569c51ce317ddfdb.us-east-2.vpce.amazonaws.com` in the consumer VPC to the local IP addresses, which will forward the traffic to the provider's Network Load Balancer in another VPC. It is recommended to treat this name in a similar manner as Elastic Load Balancing DNS names and to use an alias record to make the endpoint easier to use, such as `vpce.example.com`. The Network Load Balancer will perform source NAT using the source IP of the Network Load Balancer. The source NAT allows for providers to connect consumers with overlapping addresses. Providers can determine the source of traffic by enabling proxy protocol on the load balancer or by using application-level identification.

VPC endpoint service functionality is useful for connecting applications across VPCs. Use cases include shared services VPCs, connecting with business partners and customers, and enabling more granular access between applications in different VPCs. The shared services VPC concept is explained in greater depth in Chapter 16 on Scenarios and Reference Architectures.

Comparing AWS PrivateLink and VPC Peering

As discussed in Chapter 2 on Amazon VPC and Networking Fundamentals, VPC peering allows for two Amazon VPCs to communicate. Peering requires the requested VPC to accept the peering request and for both VPCs to configure routing over the peering connection in the applicable subnets.

VPC peering is appropriate when there are many resources that should communicate between the peered VPCs. If there is a high degree of inter-VPC communication and the security and trust levels are similar, VPC peering is a good choice for connectivity.

You can use AWS PrivateLink to simplify multi-VPC network configurations in a variety of scenarios. First, VPC peering allows access to the full VPC. To limit traffic across VPC peers, you can use route table entries and security groups. Even with the availability to reference security groups in a peered VPC in the same region, there is ample room for errors. Moreover, if you are providing a service to multiple VPCs, there are scalability challenges in managing the volume routes and security groups. If you only need to share one application, even across multiple VPCs, AWS PrivateLink significantly reduces overall complexity. AWS PrivateLink allows one-way access on a per-application basis, from the consumer to the provider, solving connectivity between multiple VPCs in a simple way.

Second, peering requires non-overlapping VPC Classless Inter-Domain Routing (CIDR) ranges. If multiple VPCs use a common IP range, then they cannot peer directly together. A hub VPC can peer with multiple spoke VPCs that use the same address range, but the hub will only be able to route any particular portion of the overlapping address range to a single peered VPC. AWS PrivateLink supports overlapping CIDR ranges by applying source NAT from the consumer to the provider of the AWS PrivateLink.

Third, there are scale limits associated with VPC peering. A VPC can only peer with 125 other VPCs. AWS PrivateLink scales to thousands of consumers per VPC. The amount of services provided by a single VPC is limited by the amount of Network Load Balancers supported. Providing services can be split into multiple VPCs if they do not have dependencies on each other.

AWS PrivateLink has its own design considerations. AWS PrivateLink only allows the consumer to originate connections to the provider. If bidirectional communication is needed, VPC peering or a reciprocal AWS PrivateLink between the consumer and provider may be required. In addition, traffic to AWS PrivateLink is load balanced, and it inherits the design considerations of Network Load Balancer. For example, Network Load Balancer only supports Transmission Control Protocol (TCP) (more about Network Load Balancer design considerations are covered in Chapter 6 on Domain Name System and Load Balancing). In addition, connections from the consumer to the provider go through source NAT, which may prevent applications from identifying the consumer IP address. This behavior is different than the standard Network Load Balancer behavior, where the source IP is preserved.

AWS PrivateLink Service Provider Considerations

This section reviews what is involved with configuring the provider side of a VPC endpoint service (powered by AWS PrivateLink). You may choose to configure a provider endpoint to offer services publicly, to a business partner, or privately within a trusted set of accounts or VPCs.

The first step is to associate a Network Load Balancer with your service. You will need to select the Availability Zones applicable for your service. The Network Load Balancer is responsible for the load balancing, exposing a single address per Availability Zone, and performing source NAT on incoming connections.

You can create an endpoint service after the Network Load Balancer is configured. You will receive the DNS name of your endpoint after creating the endpoint, such as `vpce-svc-0569c51ce317ddfdb.us-east-2.vpce.amazonaws.com`. You will also receive the service name that consumers will reference, such as `com.amazonaws.vpce.us-east-2.vpce-svc-0569c51ce317ddfdb`.

The consumer will receive multiple endpoint DNS names to allow for a regional name and names for each Availability Zone in which the service operates.

The next step is to allow access to the endpoint. You can whitelist IAM principals such as account or choose to offer the service to all AWS accounts.

AWS PrivateLink Service Consumer Considerations

To consume a VPC endpoint (powered by AWS PrivateLink), you can start by requesting access to a private service with the service name. You may also choose to consume available public endpoints from AWS Marketplace and AWS Cloud services. There may be multiple endpoints available, depending on the service and Availability Zones chosen.

There are multiple ways to reach a VPC endpoint. You may want to enable split-horizon DNS with the private DNS name, available for AWS Cloud services and AWS Marketplace endpoints. *Split-horizon DNS* configures a private hosted zone with the appropriate DNS entries to map the service name to the created endpoints. This will map a DNS entry such as `api.example.com` to `vpce-svc-0569c51ce217fffdb.us-east-2.vpce.amazonaws.com`. You may also choose to do this yourself or use your own DNS solution for your own endpoint services using Amazon Route 53 private hosted zones.

Each VPC endpoint will have both a regional DNS name and a DNS name for each Availability Zone. The consumer has the choice of using the services local to each Availability Zone to increase performance. If DNS is not supported or causes application issues, it is possible to hardcode endpoint IP addresses into applications. Similar to Elastic Load Balancing, you are not charged for traffic crossing Availability Zones.

Just because you can hardcode IP addresses doesn't mean that you should. It is possible for IP addresses to become unavailable or the address to change by deleting and creating a new endpoint.

Security of the VPC endpoint is the consumer's responsibility. Traffic can only connect from the consumer to the provider. Only responses to connections originating from the consumer are possible.

Accessing a Shared Services VPC

There are multiple scenarios where you may need to access services that are in a different VPC. You can use interface VPC endpoints, for example, to access AWS Cloud services. You can also access services provided by third parties or partners. If your organization has common access requirements across many VPCs, it is helpful to centralize common or shared services. You can use AWS PrivateLink to access privately shared central services, which may be called "Services VPC," "Shared Services VPC," "Administrator VPC," or similar names. These common resources may include authentication, provisioning, or security services.

Figure 3.5 illustrates what a shared services VPC may look like.

FIGURE 3.5 A shared service uses a Network Load Balancer and AWS PrivateLink to provide endpoint services into spoke VPCs.

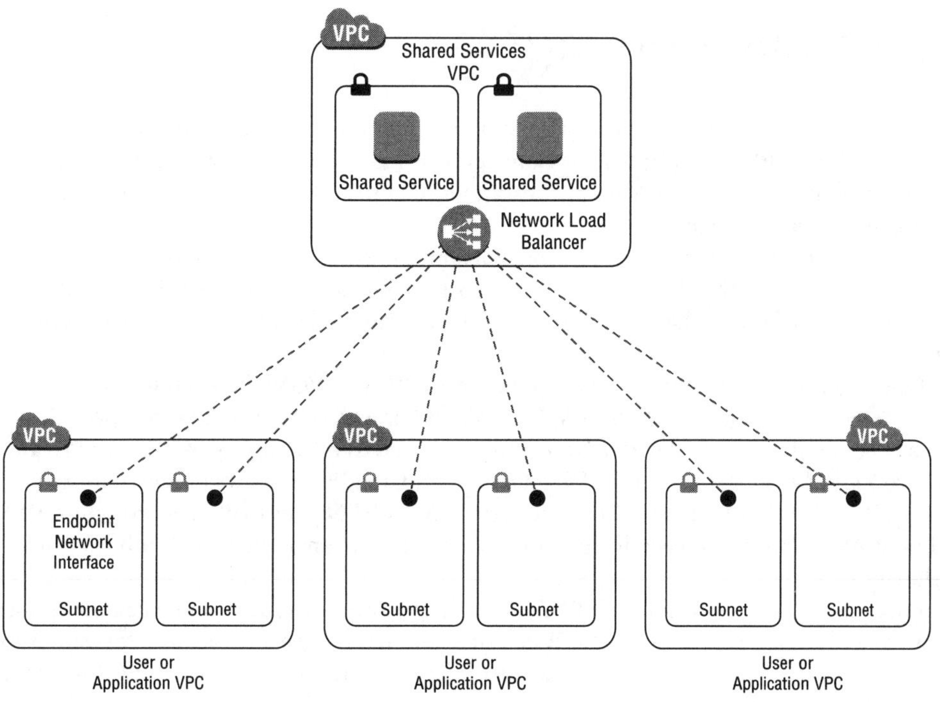

In Figure 3.5, there is a dedicated VPC for shared services. There are two instances running in two subnets that are targets for a Network Load Balancer. There is a single service in the shared services VPC in this example, but in practice there could be many other services. The service is shared to three consumer VPCs that have private access to the shared service. Each can use the VPC endpoint DNS name to access the service. This design pattern allows the organization to deploy and operate core services centrally, such as authentication, logging, monitoring, code pipeline tools, and other administrative and security services.

Depending on organizational requirements, there could be multiple "services VPCs," or they may be segmented further by function such as security, networking, administrative tools, incident response, and more. VPC endpoints offers greater scale and address flexibility than VPC peering. This model scales to thousands of consumer VPCs, and it allows for the consumer VPCs to have overlapping IP addresses. VPC endpoint connectivity originates from consumers toward the provider services. Provider services cannot initiate connections to the consumer resources. VPC peering or other connectivity methods are needed for provider-initiated communication.

Transitive Routing

Transitive routing was briefly mentioned earlier in the context of accessing gateway VPC endpoints over VPN and AWS Direct Connect. It is important that you understand transitive routing in the context of AWS network functionality. It is worth repeating the VPC routing requirements again.

If the source of a packet is not an interface in the local VPC, the destination of the connection must be the IP address of a network interface local to the VPC. The destination or source of the packet must be an interface local to the VPC or the traffic will be dropped.

One exception to this guideline involves the VGW. The VGW, by default, will re-advertise any routes it receives over VPN or AWS Direct Connect to all other peers. This functionality is called *CloudHub*, and it is covered in Chapter 4 on Virtual Private Networks and Chapter 5 on AWS Direct Connect. CloudHub allows traffic that arrives at the VGW from an AWS Direct Connect peer or AWS VPN peer to connect to other AWS VPN or AWS Direct Connect destinations. You cannot change the CloudHub routing behavior of a VGW.

Proxies, routers, Amazon EC2 VPN, and NAT instances can enable more flexible connectivity to and from external networks. When these devices receive a packet and forward it to the next hop, the retransmitted packet will then have a source of the Amazon EC2 instance instead of the external network. This behavior requires disabling the source/destination check.

Security Benefits of VPC

One of the security benefits of VPC is that there are forwarding mechanisms that check the validity of source and destination IP addresses to prevent address spoofing. The source/destination check will not allow an instance to receive a packet if the destination does not match one of the assigned IP addresses. It also will not allow an instance to send a packet with a source IP address that it has not been assigned. Instances that perform routing, proxy, and other network functions often need to disable the source/destination check because they send and receive packets that are not associated with their assigned addresses.

Transitive Routing Examples

This section reviews use cases that transitive routing influences.

- When peering multiple VPCs together, full VPC connectivity requires all VPCs to be peered together directly. As shown in the following graphic, a peered VPC cannot use another VPC's peers to access VPCs to which it does not have direct connectivity. In this case, the source of the packet comes in from a peering connection and is destined for another VPC peer that is not a local network interface, and so it is dropped. This is covered in Chapter 2, in the section on VPC peering.

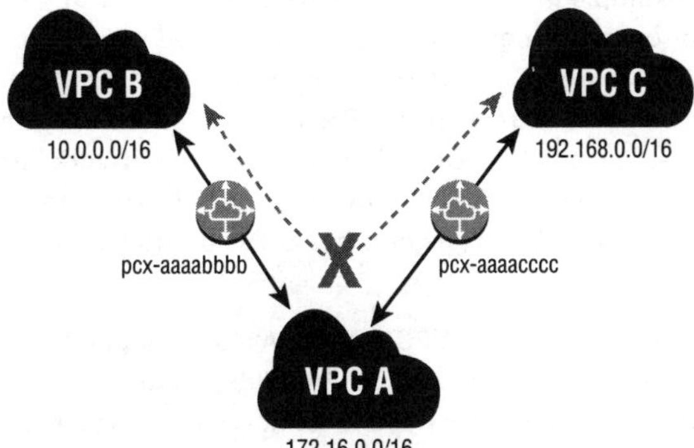

- In the Amazon S3 endpoint example earlier in this chapter, we showed how to use a DNS proxy to access gateway VPC endpoints over AWS Direct Connect or VPN. If you natively try to connect to an Amazon S3 endpoint over AWS VPN, the source packet comes from outside the VPC, and the destination address is an Amazon S3 address. This means that the packet will be dropped. If the destination is a proxy instead, the destination is a local network interface.
- In the graphic that follows, there are two VPCs peered together and an Internet gateway attached to one of the VPCs. The VPC without an Internet gateway has a default route pointing to the peering connection. The peered VPC without an Internet

gateway will not be able to access the Internet through the peering connection. When traffic arrives at the Internet-connected VPC, the source is outside the VPC, and the destination is not a local network interface. This is another scenario where using an Internet proxy in the Internet-connected VPC can resolve the transitive routing problem. Alternatively, a new Internet gateway could be attached to the other VPC.

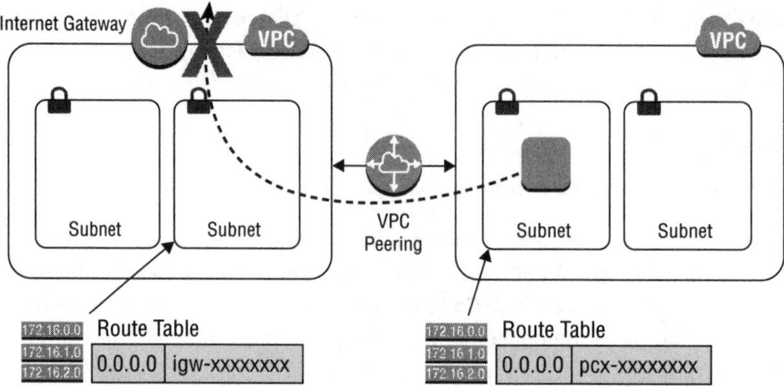

- A more nuanced example is accessing AWS DNS services from AWS VPN, AWS Direct Connect, or over VPC peering. If you have defined private hosted zones with Amazon Route 53 in your VPC, those DNS names are only accessible via the local VPC by default. If a request comes over VPN, then the source will be external. The destination IP address is the VPC DNS IP, which is not a network interface IP address. This means that the traffic will not be natively routed. To solve this issue, you can use other instances such as DNS proxies or other DNS solutions. This is covered in more depth in Chapter 6.
- In the following graphic, there is a VPC with an AWS managed VPN connection to a customer gateway. If traffic arrives to the VGW destined to the Internet, it will be dropped because the destination is not a local network interface. Similarly, if Internet traffic arrives destined for the VPN network, it will be dropped when the traffic is evaluated at the VPC because the destination is not a local network interface. The same applies for any traffic arriving from the VPN network where the destination is an address in a peered VPC. This scenario can be solved by using an Internet proxy instance in the VPC and requiring that connections arriving from the VPN connection have that instance as a destination. Alternatively, an Amazon EC2 instance running as a VPN endpoint can forward traffic to external sources. The Amazon EC2 instance terminates the VPN tunnel, de-encapsulates the inner packet, and creates a new connection where the source is now an internal network interface. This is covered in more depth in Chapter 4.

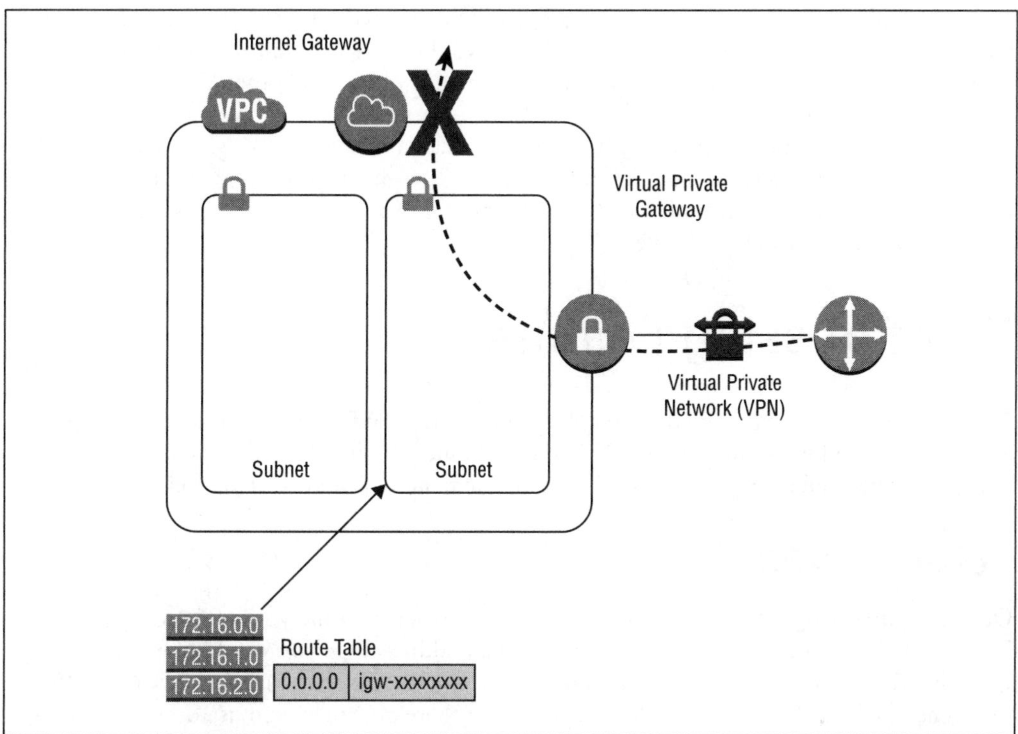

Amazon VPC route tables only influence outgoing traffic. Route tables do not influence inbound traffic arriving from sources such as Internet gateways, VPC peering, VPN, or AWS Direct Connect. If the traffic enters a VPC from an Internet gateway, NAT Gateway, or VPC peering connection, then the destination IP address needs to belong to a local network interface. If the traffic arrives on a VGW, then the destination can be a local network interface or another route advertised to the VGW.

Routing Across Peered VPCs

A common pattern to solve transitive routing scenarios is to use instances in each VPC to proxy or forward the traffic by providing a local network interface as the destination for remote networks. Inside a VPC, it is common for route tables to target firewalls, proxies, and caching servers to process or inspect network traffic.

This routing design changes when VPC peering is used. As typically defined in the route table, traffic destined to the remote VPC CIDR range uses the peering connection (`pcx-xxxxxxxx`) as its target. It is not possible to route traffic to a network interface in the peered VPC.

An example of this behavior would be a firewall in a shared services VPC. If all Internet-bound traffic must pass through the firewall, you would configure subnet route tables to forward Internet-bound traffic to the instance. If the firewall is in another VPC, you cannot configure a route to a network interface over VPC peering. To provide these types of architectures, there is a detailed review with approaches such as the *transit VPC* in Chapter 16 and other architectures reviewed later in this book. There are also routing options involving cross-account elastic network interfaces that provide a solution in limited scenarios, which is covered later in this chapter.

IP Addressing Features

There is a review of Elastic IP addresses, IPv6 addressing, and the different options for private and public addresses in Chapter 2. There are some additional IP addressing features that you should understand, such as resizing an Amazon VPC and NAT options.

Resizing a VPC

One of the first design decisions that you must make when creating your VPCs on AWS is the IPv4 CIDR range. There are options for what address type you would like to use, including RFC1918 addresses, public addresses, and other addresses such as RFC6598. We recommend RFC1918 addresses when possible, but there are reasons to use other ranges. The second choice is how large the CIDR range should be.

Historically, AWS has recommended starting with a large CIDR range so that you avoid the work of redesigning connectivity associated with exhausting the available IPv4 addresses. Allocating large blocks of IPv4 addresses to multiple VPCs can be challenging if you are constrained on available IPv4 address space.

The *resize VPC* feature allows you to add up to five additional IPv4 CIDR ranges to your VPC. You can submit a request to increase the limit higher than five. This feature allows for IPv4 expansion in VPCs that have exhausted their addresses and reduces the design tradeoffs involved with starting with smaller CIDR ranges.

Resizing VPC Considerations

New VPC CIDR ranges cannot overlap with the existing CIDR range or the CIDR range of any current VPC peer. In addition, the new ranges must be more specific than any currently-defined static route in the VPC route tables. Dynamic routes propagated by the VGW do not cause a conflict, and any new CIDR ranges will be automatically preferred because they are local routes. There are also restrictions on which CIDR ranges can be defined, depending on the original CIDR range configured for the VPC.

Figure 3.6 illustrates the changes to the local routing table when you add a new CIDR range. A new local route was added in this case for 10.2.0.0/16. You must have space for additional route entries in your route tables, since new local routes are added. In addition, the VGW will begin advertising the new address range. You can define a new CIDR range ranging from a /16 to a /28. This means that you can effectively create ranges up to a /14 or /15 using individual /16 ranges. Advertisements from the VGW will not summarize contiguous address ranges.

FIGURE 3.6 An example of adding a CIDR range to an existing VPC. New subnets can use the new CIDR addresses.

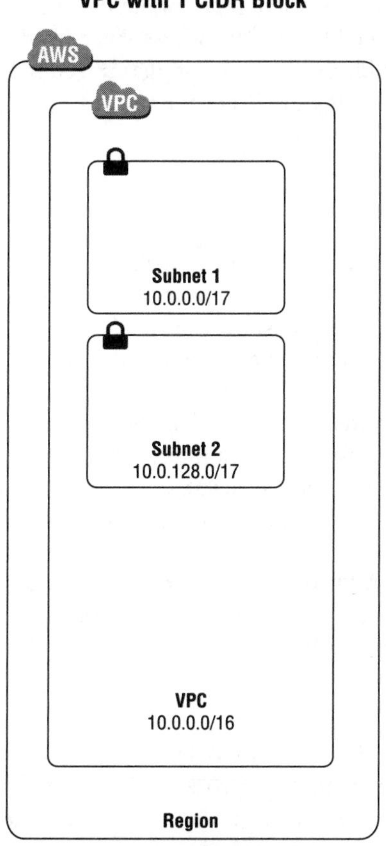

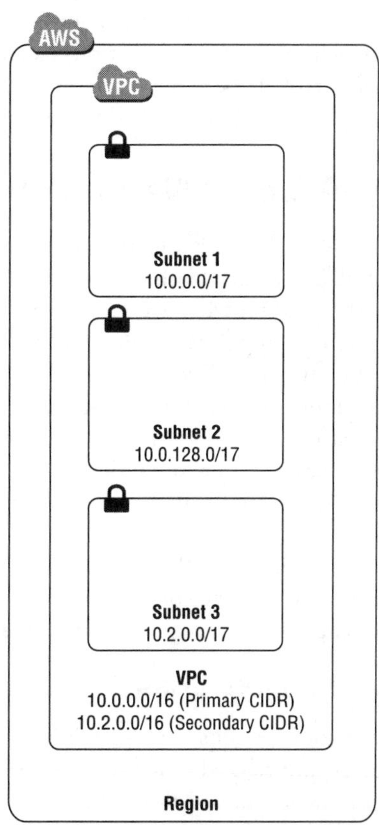

Main Route Table

Destination	Target
10.0.0.0/16	local

Main Route Table

Destination	Target
10.0.0.0/16	local
10.2.0.0/16	local

Only new subnets can use the new address space; subnets created before the added CIDR ranges cannot use the new addresses.

IP Address Features

IP addresses are typically simple, but there are a few edge cases which you can control.

Reclaiming Elastic IP Addresses

There may be a scenario where you have accidentally released an Elastic IP address when you still have dependencies on the public address. Human error and automation errors can both cause this issue. There is a method through the AWS Command Line Interface (AWS CLI) to make a request to reclaim a previously-owned Elastic IP address. Success is best-effort, which means AWS will try to reclaim the address, but it is not guaranteed if another customer is already be using the public address. This feature is not for auto-assigned public IP addresses—only Elastic IP addresses.

Cross-Account Network Interfaces

There are some network scenarios that benefit from extending a networking interface from an instance into another account. The *cross-account network permission* grants an AWS-authorized provider account permission to attach a customer network interface to an instance in the provider account. The provider account must be whitelisted by AWS to provide this functionality.

An example use case for this feature is Amazon Relational Database Service (Amazon RDS). Customers want to modify and control the elastic network interface of the Amazon RDS instances, but they should not have access to the instance itself. In the Amazon RDS scenario, the instance is in a VPC managed by AWS, and the elastic network interface is in the customer VPC.

This capability also allows customers to define VPC route table entries pointing to the elastic network interface of an instance in another account. This makes the elastic network interface capable of routing to an instance in another VPC or account.

Design Considerations

There are good reasons why AWS has widely used Elastic Load Balancing to provide availability and reliability for services as opposed to single network interfaces. The cross-account network interface does not provide high availability or fault tolerance. When a cross-account network interface is used, such as in the case of Amazon RDS, it is important that there is fault tolerance built in at the application level. It is also important to understand that a network interface is specific to a subnet and Availability Zone, which means that the cross-account interface must reside in the same Availability Zone as the provider's instance.

Other design factors are scalability and cost effectiveness. Instances have a fixed number of interfaces, generally between 2 and 15. If a provider uses cross-account network interface functionality to more endpoints than there are interfaces, the provider must create additional instances to support the volume. Moreover, the number of interfaces available to a given instance is typically proportional to the amount of memory and CPU. It may not be cost effective to use high-end instance types simply for the density of network interfaces.

In summary, a cross-account network interface is a useful feature if you are interacting with a low level of abstraction. That said, this type of low-level control can cause architectural problems if used improperly, which is why it requires whitelisting.

Comparison with VPC Peering and VPC Endpoints

Cross-account network interfaces effectively move the instance out of the VPC while maintaining a network interface for communication. In that perspective, you are dealing with a single instance for each network interface. The benefits of cross-account network interfaces are the simplicity of the connectivity and the ability to treat the connectivity like any other network interface. The challenge is that network interfaces by themselves do not scale well or have any built-in availability.

VPC peering and VPC endpoints are both designed to allow many instances to communicate to many instances over VPC boundaries. One large difference is that VPC peering is generally available for anyone to use, while cross-account network interfaces are limited to whitelisted provider accounts. You can't point a route entry to a network interface that exists on the other side of a VPC peering connection. VPC peering allows more broad access between the two VPCs.

VPC endpoints (powered by AWS PrivateLink) are unidirectional and apply source NAT to incoming traffic. There may be use cases that require routing, require bidirectional communication, are not compatible with load balancing, or are not compatible with NAT.

Summary

In this chapter, you learned about advanced VPC components, VPC endpoints, transitive routing, and IP address features. These features may not be used by all customers, but they are important to understand for use cases that require additional security, agility, or scale, or for specific application architectures.

We reviewed VPC endpoints that come in both interface and gateway types. Gateway VPC endpoints allow you to connect to services but do not exist as a networking component in your VPC. Interface VPC endpoints are elastic network interfaces, private IP addresses, and DNS names that allow you to access AWS Cloud services privately from within your VPC.

AWS PrivateLink is an extension of interface VPC endpoints, and it allows you to create your own endpoints or consume endpoints that others have created. The endpoints use Network Load Balancer and DNS to provide private access.

We also reviewed the way that routing works within a VPC in the transitive VPC section. This section has examples to illustrate the ways that you can make complex routing work in AWS.

Overall, this chapter sets up the platform for the more advanced architectures and concepts in the rest of the book. Every service on AWS uses networking in some way, and understanding the core mechanics will allow you to conceptualize more complex architectures better.

Exam Essentials

Understand the security benefits of VPC endpoints. The principle of least privilege means that you should offer as little access as needed. Restricting access to resources over private connections limits the overall attack and vulnerability surface. Endpoints simplify connectivity and make it easier to create granular access.

Understand the different types of VPC endpoints. There are gateway and interface endpoints. Gateway endpoints are reached through a route table entry and use a prefix list to define access to public IP addresses. Interface endpoints are network interfaces inside the VPC with private IP addresses and use DNS names to direct traffic to the network interfaces. Gateway and interface endpoints provide different features to restrict access.

Understand how to access VPC endpoints from external networks. Different design patterns are used for accessing VPC endpoints from external networks. Gateway endpoints require a proxy for access originating outside the VPC. Interface endpoints are accessible over AWS Direct Connect but not over VPN or VPC peering.

Understand how to secure VPC endpoints. VPC endpoint policy allows more granular access for specific resources or actions. VPC endpoint policy extends what is possible with route entries, prefix lists, security group rules, and network ACLs. Additional policies such as Amazon S3 bucket policies can also be used to restrict access.

Understand how AWS PrivateLink works. AWS PrivateLink is a type of interface VPC endpoint. It uses a Network Load Balancer to distribute traffic to a shared resource. The endpoint has multiple DNS names for regional and zonal access.

Understand the difference between AWS PrivateLink and VPC peering. VPC peering is a coarser method of providing access for two VPCs. AWS PrivateLink is a scalable way to provide access to a single service for many VPCs. VPC peering does not support overlapping addresses, and it is more difficult to use to create specific access at an instance level. VPC endpoints are also more suited for VPC relationships that have different trust levels.

Understand the difference between consumer and provider requirements for VPC endpoints (powered by AWS PrivateLink). Providers must define a set of attributes for their endpoint and associate a Network Load Balancer. The consumer is responsible for securing the endpoint. The consumer can also choose among the regional DNS name, zonal DNS name, or a direct IP address.

Understand transitive routing and the limitations of VPC routing. If traffic arrives externally from a VPC, the destination must be a network interface in the local VPC. The exception is that traffic arriving on a VGW may leave via another VGW route. Transitive routing affects traffic that arrives or leaves via an Internet gateway, NAT Gateway, VPC peering, gateway VPC endpoint, DNS services, AWS Direct Connect, or AWS VPN. There are many permutations of this routing behavior that are important to understand for the exam.

Understand how to add IPv4 CIDR ranges to a VPC. There are some caveats around what types of addresses you can add, prefix lengths (/16 to /28), and how adding CIDR ranges works. Each new prefix adds a local route, and the new prefix cannot overlap or conflict with existing VPC routes.

Understand Elastic IP features. It is possible to reclaim an accidentally-released Elastic IP address in some circumstances, such as if another customer has not used a released address.

Understand cross-account network interfaces. Cross-account network interfaces are for whitelisted partner accounts to use. Using cross-account network interfaces requires understanding of the availability and scalability tradeoffs of network interfaces and which types of applications are appropriate for this feature. Additionally, you should understand the benefits and design tradeoffs versus VPC peering and VPC endpoints.

Test Taking Tip

Transitive routing applies across many AWS networking scenarios, including AWS Direct Connect, VPN, endpoints, and Internet connectivity. It is critical to understand the different applications and implications of transitive routing on AWS for the exam.

Resources to Review

For further review, visit the following URLs:

Adding new CIDR blocks:

http://docs.aws.amazon.com/AmazonVPC/latest/UserGuide/VPC_Subnets.html#add-cidr-block-restrictions

VPC endpoints:

http://docs.aws.amazon.com/AmazonVPC/latest/UserGuide/vpc-endpoints.html

VPC limits:

http://docs.aws.amazon.com/AmazonVPC/latest/UserGuide/VPC_Appendix_Limits.html

Exercises

In this section, you will configure some more advanced VPC features that will help solidify the concepts introduced in this chapter.

For assistance completing these exercises, refer to the Amazon VPC User Guide located at http://aws.amazon.com/documentation/vpc/ and the Amazon EC2 User Guide located at https://aws.amazon.com/documentation/ec2/.

EXERCISE 3.1

Create a Gateway VPC Endpoint for Amazon S3

In this exercise, you will create an Amazon S3 endpoint and access data privately. The graphic shows the topology that you will be creating.

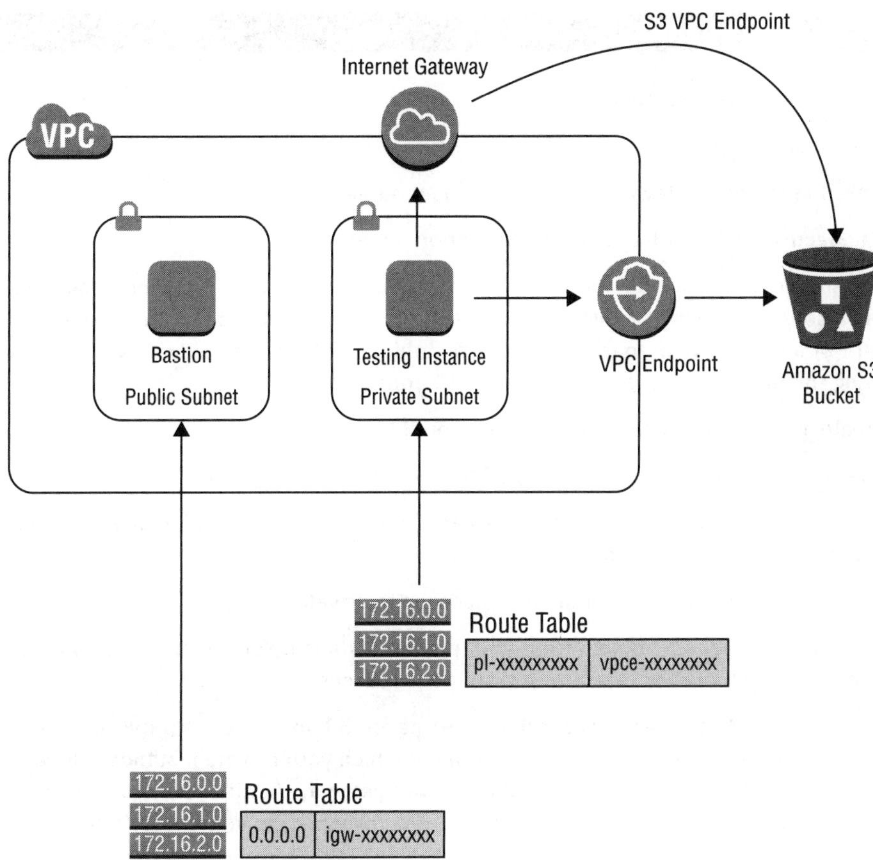

1. Create a new VPC.
2. Create two subnets in your VPC: one private and one public.
3. Launch one instance, the bastion instance, in the public subnet. Launch another instance, the private instance, in the private subnet. The instances can be any type or size. You will use the bastion instance to reach the private instance. The private instance will be used to access Amazon S3.
4. Configure security groups such that the bastion instance is accessible over TCP port 22 from your IP address. The private instance should be accessible over TCP port 22 from the bastion instance.
5. Create an Internet gateway and attach it to your VPC.
6. Create a route table for both the private and public subnet. Associate the route tables with their respective subnets.
7. Create a 0.0.0.0/0 route to the Internet gateway in the route table associated with the public subnet.

EXERCISE 3.1 *(continued)*

8. Create an Amazon S3 bucket.
9. Upload an object such as a text file into the bucket.
10. Make the Internet gateway Amazon S3 object public.
11. Use Secure Shell (SSH) to access the bastion instance.
12. You should not be able to access the Amazon S3 file from the private instance. You can also try accessing the file from the bastion instance. You can use a tool such as `curl` or a web browser to test access to the object. This test should show that you are using the Internet to access the Amazon S3 endpoint.
13. Create a Gateway VPC Endpoint for Amazon S3.
14. Specify the private subnet in your VPC that will use the endpoint.
15. Check the route table entries for the private subnet. It should now include a route to the endpoint for the Amazon S3 prefix list.
16. Use SSH from the bastion instance to access the private instance.
17. Access the Amazon S3 object from your private instance. You can use a browser on Windows or a tool such as `curl` on Linux to test access.
18. To confirm that you are not accessing the Amazon S3 object over a public interface, check the route table for the private subnet in which your private instance is located. Confirm that there are no routes to the Internet gateway. Additionally, you can check the Amazon S3 access logs and look for access from private addresses from within your VPC.

If you wish to secure the Amazon S3 object further, you can make the bucket accessible to requests only from the VPC endpoint that you created with an Amazon S3 bucket policy.

EXERCISE 3.2

Create a VPC Endpoint Service

In this exercise, you will create a VPC endpoint service. You will start by creating the provider side of the AWS PrivateLink endpoint.

1. Create two new VPCs. You can also reuse existing VPCs. Name your VPCs **`consumer`** and **`provider`** for clarity.

2. Create a public subnet in the same Availability Zone in both VPCs.
3. In the provider VPC, create a web server in the public subnet. A t2.micro or similar instance will work. Configure the web server to receive a public IP address. This will act as your shared service.
4. The inbound security group should allow TCP port 80 from all IP addresses.
5. The inbound security group should also allow SSH so that you can configure a web server. It's recommended to choose the My IP Address option as the IP source for TCP port 22.
6. SSH to the public IP address of the instance.
7. Install the HTTP web server package.

```
$ sudo yum install -y httpd
$ sudo service httpd start
```

The default Apache web server page doesn't respond 200 OK to health checks. This example will work as outlined, but to see health checks pass with a Network Load Balancer, you should put a dummy HTML file in the `/var/www/html/` directory. A plaintext file works for this purpose.

8. You should be able to check the webpage at `http://<public-ip>/` for your web server now. If not, check your security group configuration.
9. In the Amazon EC2 Console, click on Load Balancers and create a new Network Load Balancer.
10. The Network Load Balancer should be internal and listen on port 80. Choose your public VPC and the Availability Zone in which your public subnet and web server are located.
11. Create a new target group on TCP port 80, and choose instance for the target type.
12. Choose your newly-created web server as a target.
13. Finish launching the Network Load Balancer. It may take a few minutes to create.
14. After the load balancer is available, go into the Amazon VPC configuration console. Click on Endpoint Services.
15. Click on Create Endpoint Service.
16. Associate the newly-created load balancer to the endpoint service. Confirm that acceptance is required for the endpoint.
17. You will receive a "Service Name". Copy the name for the next exercise.

EXERCISE 3.3

Create VPC endpoint

In this exercise, you will consume the AWS PrivateLink endpoint that you created in the previous exercise. In this exercise, we're choosing a VPC in the same account. The consumer side also works for any VPC or account within the same AWS Region. You will finish connectivity by creating the consumer side of the AWS PrivateLink endpoint.

1. In the consumer VPC, launch another instance. You will use this instance to test access to the endpoint. Choose a t2.micro or equivalent instance type. Launch it in the public subnet of the consumer VPC. Allow incoming SSH access from your IP address.
2. While the instance is launching, request access to the provider endpoint that was just created. In the VPC configuration console, click on Endpoints. Click on Create Endpoint.
3. Choose Find service by name, and enter or paste the Service Name from the last exercise and press Verify.
4. Select the consumer VPC for the VPC selection, and select the public subnet in which the testing instance is located.
5. At the bottom of the screen, create a new security group that allows TCP port 80 in and apply it to the endpoint.
6. Click Create endpoint.
7. Go back to Endpoint Services in the Amazon VPC console, and select the endpoint you created. On the Endpoint Connections tab, you should now see a Pending Acceptance request. In the Actions, you can accept the request.
8. Your endpoint should now be functional in the public subnet of the consumer VPC. To test this, SSH to the public address of the test instance in the consumer VPC.
9. On the test instance, connect to the endpoint service. From the Endpoints page in the Amazon VPC console, you can select the first DNS name listed in the Details tab. This will be different than the service name that was used to find and create the endpoint.

   ```
   $ curl <endpoint name>
   ```

   ```
   Example: $ curl vpce-01847ae84f118942c-xvi8p3vm.vpce-svc-0d669f84acd4283ee
   .us-east-2.vpce.amazonaws.com
   ```

10. You may also want to check the IP address in your VPC that you're using for this connectivity.

   ```
   $ curl <endpoint name>
   ```

11. If you wanted to extend this further, you could create another consumer VPC with the same CIDR range to prove that the endpoint works with VPCs with overlapping or duplicate CIDR ranges. You can also test AWS PrivateLink for AWS Services with an Amazon EC2 endpoint or an endpoint from the AWS Marketplace.

EXERCISE 3.4

Working with Transitive Routing

While we covered transitive routing in this chapter, it is good practice to see it in your own environment. Complete this exercise to do so.

You will configure the environment in the graphic shown here. There are three VPCs: 10.0.0.0/16, 10.1.0.0/16, and 10.2.0.0/16. 10.1.0.0 is peered with the other two VPCs. Each VPC has an Internet gateway so that you can use SSH to access the instances. The route table for each VPC has a route to the Internet and routes to the other two VPCs over the peering connection.

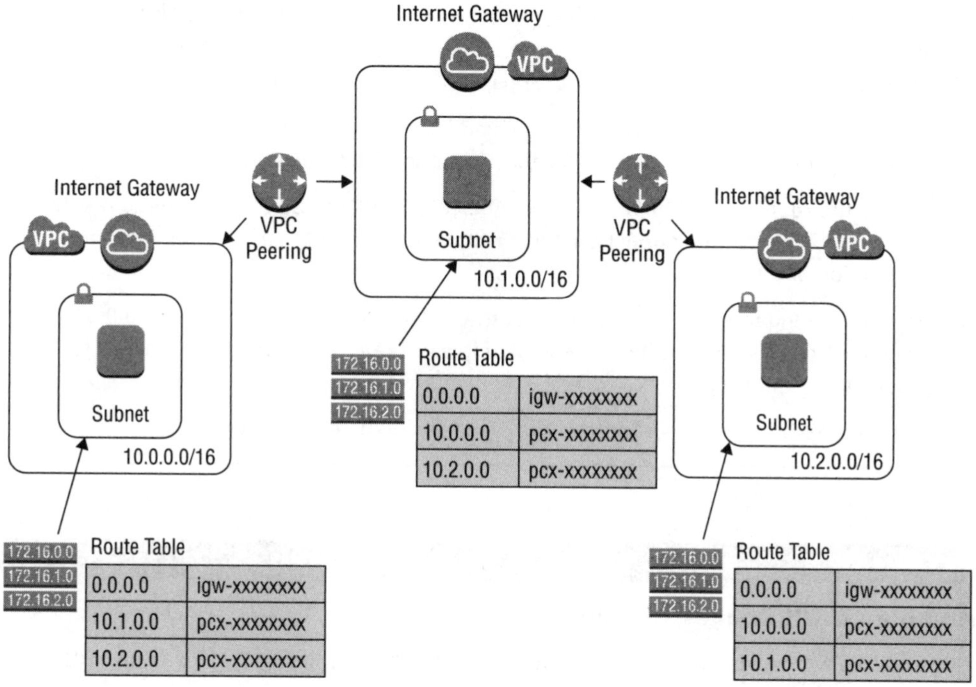

1. Create three VPCs with the assigned CIDR ranges.
2. Create a subnet in each VPC.
3. Create an Internet gateway. Attach the Internet gateway to each VPC.
4. Create an instance in each VPC with a public address. The instance can be any size and use any operating system. You will be using these instances to attempt pings between VPCs.
5. Modify the security group for each instance to allow incoming SSH access from your IP address. Enable all Internet Control Message Protocol (ICMP) traffic from 10.0.0.0/14.

EXERCISE 3.4 *(continued)*

6. Create a VPC peering connection from the 10.0.0.0/16 VPC to the 10.1.0.0/16 VPC.
7. Create a VPC peering connection from the 10.1.0.0/16 VPC to the 10.2.0.0/16 VPC.
8. Identify the route table for your instances, depending on the subnet in which the instance was deployed. In the route table, configure the routes as defined in the graphic. Routes to the other two CIDR ranges should be directed over the peering link (`pcx-xxxxxxxx`). All three subnets should have three routes, in addition to the local route(s): one to the Internet and two to the other VPCs.
9. Use SSH to access the instance in the 10.0.0.0/16 VPC.
10. Attempt to ping the private IP addresses of instances in both the 10.1.0.0/16 and 10.2.0.0/16 VPCs. Only the 10.1.0.0/16 instance should be reachable. If 10.1.0.0/16 is not reachable, check your security groups for ICMP and route tables in both VPCs.
11. To fix the transitive routing issue, you will add a peering connection. Create a new peering connection between the 10.0.0.0/16 and the 10.2.0.0/16 VPCs.
12. Modify the routes in the 10.0.0.0/16 and 10.2.0.0/16 VPCs to point the route to the new `pcx-xxxxxxxx` peering connection. Each route should point to a different peering connection at this point.
13. Attempt to ping the private IP address of the 10.2.0.0/16 instance from the 10.0.0.0/16 instance. The ping should be successful. If it is not reachable, check your security groups and routes again.

You now can see how transitive routing works in your own environment.

EXERCISE 3.5

Add IPv4 CIDR Ranges to a VPC

This exercise will review the mechanics of adding IPv4 CIDR ranges to an existing VPC.

1. Choose a VPC to add CIDR ranges or create a new one if you wish.
2. Create a subnet if there is not one already.
3. Check the assigned CIDR ranges in the CIDR Blocks tab of the VPC.
4. In the actions or right-click menu, choose Edit CIDRs.
5. If there is not an IPv6 CIDR, add one.
6. Attempt to add a new IPv4 CIDR range.

7. Try other ranges such as 10.0.0.0/16, 192.168.0.0/16, 172.16.0.0/16, 100.64.0.0/16, and 198.19.0.0/16. Did they work? Why not?
8. Return to the CIDR Blocks tab. How different is it now?
9. In one of the route tables, create a route to a /24 subnet that is within your RFC1918 space but not currently assigned. Point the route to an elastic network interface, NAT Gateway, peering connection, or Internet gateway. You may need to delete one of the added CIDR ranges.
10. Try adding a CIDR block less than a /24 to your VPC.
11. Delete the /24 route and try adding the CIDR again.
12. Create a new subnet in your VPC and use the address range of the CIDR range added in Step 11. Which address ranges are available?
13. Can you try to change the address range of the existing subnet? (Answer: No.)
14. Can you delete the original CIDR block? (Answer: No.)
15. Delete the added CIDR blocks.

In this exercise, you reviewed the mechanics of adding CIDR ranges to an existing VPC.

Review Questions

1. Which of the following is a security benefit of Amazon Virtual Private Cloud (Amazon VPC) endpoints?

   A. VPC endpoints provide private connectivity that increases performance to AWS Cloud services.

   B. VPC endpoints limit access to services from the Internet, reducing who can access the Application Programming Interfaces (APIs) and services that AWS provides.

   C. VPC endpoints provide greater availability and reliability than public endpoints, which increases security by limiting access for Distributed Denial of Service (DDoS) and other attacks.

   D. VPC endpoints provide private access, limiting the number of instances that require Internet access.

2. You are configuring a secure access policy for your Amazon Simple Storage Service (Amazon S3) bucket. There is a Virtual Private Cloud (VPC) endpoint and Amazon S3 bucket policy that restricts access to the VPC endpoint. When browsing the bucket through the AWS Management Console, you do not have access to the buckets. Which statement is NOT true?

   A. This is expected behavior.

   B. Your corporate web proxy may be blocking access to downloading objects.

   C. The objects are still available via the Amazon S3 VPC endpoint.

   D. You must specifically enable AWS Management Console access as part of the Amazon S3 VPC endpoint policy.

3. You have created a centralized, shared service Virtual Private Cloud (VPC) for your organization. It uses VPC peering, and you have been asked to evaluate AWS PrivateLink to optimize connectivity. Which of the following design considerations are true? (Choose two.)

   A. Applications that require the source IP address will have access to the source IP through AWS PrivateLink.

   B. The scalability of VPC peering is higher for high-bandwidth applications. This allows for faster transfers and more spoke VPCs.

   C. AWS PrivateLink is only appropriate for solutions that originate requests to the services VPC. Services in the shared VPC cannot initiate connections to spoke VPCs.

   D. AWS PrivateLink supports more connected VPCs than VPC peering.

   E. AWS PrivateLink will increase the overall performance capability of the shared services by using a Network Load Balancer.

4. You have configured an AWS PrivateLink connection between your Virtual Private Cloud (VPC) and the VPC of a business partner's hospital. The hospital has specialized applications that staff developed in-house; some were developed more than 10 years ago. The hospital is trying to enable access to your private service but is having problems connecting to your service. Which of the following are possible solutions? (Choose two.)

   A. The hospital is sending traffic over User Datagram Protocol (UDP). They must find a way to send traffic over Transmission Control Protocol (TCP).

   B. The hospital application does not support Domain Name System (DNS). They can manually specify the IP address of the VPC endpoint.

   C. VPC endpoints are not supported by applications that do not support DNS names.

   D. It is possible that the hospital applications need to support the appropriate authentication methods to use VPC endpoints in their VPC.

   E. Create an IP Security (IPsec) Virtual Private Network (VPN) through the VPC endpoint to enable tunneling of all traffic types for better compatibility.

5. You have configured a new Amazon Simple Storage Service (Amazon S3) endpoint in your Virtual Private Cloud (VPC). You have created a public Amazon S3 bucket so that you can test connectivity. You can download objects from your laptop but not from instances in the VPC. Which of the following could be the problem? (Choose two.)

   A. Domain Name System (DNS) was not enabled for the subnets, so you must enable DNS.

   B. There are not enough free IP addresses in your subnet, so you must choose a larger subnet or remove unused interfaces and IP addresses.

   C. The VPC endpoint is attached to a public subnet, and you must configure the endpoint for a private subnet.

   D. The route to the Amazon S3 prefix list is not in the routing table for the instance's subnet.

6. You have configured private subnets so that applications can download security updates. You have a Network Address Translation (NAT) instance in each Availability Zone as the default gateway to the Internet for each private subnet. You find that you cannot reach port 8080 of a server on the Internet from any of your private subnets. Which are the most likely causes of the problem? (Choose two.)

   A. The inbound security group does not allow port 8080 outbound.

   B. The NAT instances are blocking traffic to port 8080.

   C. The NAT instances have run out of ports to NAT traffic.

   D. The inbound network Access Control List (ACL) blocks traffic to port 8080.

   E. The remote server is blocking access from your instances.

7. You have created three Virtual Private Clouds (VPCs) named A, B, and C. VPC A is peered with VPC B. VPC B is peered with VPC C. Which statement is true about this peering arrangement?

   A. Instances in VPC A can reach instances in VPC C by default.

   B. Instances in VPC A can reach instances in VPC C if the correct routes are configured.

   C. Instances in VPC A can reach instances in VPC C if they use a proxy instance in VPC B.

   D. Instances in VPC A can reach instances in VPC C if they set their routes to an instance in VPC B.

8. You have configured a consumer Virtual Private Cloud (VPC) endpoint for a remote authentication service hosted by a business partner using AWS PrivateLink. The endpoints have been whitelisted and configured on the consumer and provider. Some instances are not able to access the private authentication service. Which of the following could cause this issue? (Choose two.)

   A. The prefix list to the VPC endpoint is not configured in all subnets.

   B. The instances do not have enough network interfaces to connect to the provider endpoint.

   C. The instances are not using the correct Domain Name System (DNS) entry to reach the VPC endpoint.

   D. The outbound security group of the instances does not allow the authentication port.

   E. The route to the endpoint does not include all of the provider's IP addresses.

9. You are trying to create a new Virtual Private Cloud (VPC). You try to add a Classless Inter-Domain Routing (CIDR) range, but the additional CIDR range is not being applied. Which of the following could solve this issue? (Choose two.)

   A. Delete unused routes if you are at the maximum allowed routes.

   B. Delete unused subnets if you are at the maximum allowed subnets.

   C. Delete unused, additional VPCs if you are at the maximum allowed VPCs.

   D. Define a valid CIDR range based on the original VPC CIDR.

   E. The additional CIDR range is currently being used by another VPC.

10. You have defined your original Virtual Private Cloud (VPC) Classless Inter-Domain Routing (CIDR) as 192.168.20.0/24. Your on-premises infrastructure is defined as 192.168.128.0/17. You have configured a route to on-premises as 192.168.0.0/16 in your VPC route table. You have added a new CIDR range of 192.168.100.0/24 to your VPC. Users on-premises say that they can no longer reach the original 192.168.20.0/24 addresses. Which of the following is true?

    A. The route should be defined for 192.168.128.0/17 to allow more granular routing to on-premises devices.

    B. The new CIDR range should be contiguous to the existing VPC CIDR range.

    C. New CIDR ranges cannot be more specific than existing routes.

    D. This is a valid configuration, so the issue is not related to the CIDR configuration.

11. You run a hosted service on AWS. Each copy of your hosted service is in a separate Virtual Private Cloud (VPC) and is dedicated to a single customer. Your hosted service has thousands of customers. The services in the dedicated VPCs require access to central provisioning and update services. Which connectivity methods can enable this architecture? (Choose two.)

    A. Use VPC peering between the dedicated VPCs and the central service.

    B. Reference security groups across VPCs but use Network Address Translation (NAT) Gateways for inter-VPC access.

    C. Use AWS PrivateLink to access central services from the dedicated VPCs.

    D. Make the central services public. Access the central services over the Internet using strong encryption and authentication.

    E. Create a VPN from the Virtual Private Gateway (VGW) in each hosted VPC to the VGW in the provisioning VPC.

12. Your networking group has decided to migrate all of the 192.168.0.0/16 Virtual Private Cloud (VPC) instances to 10.0.0.0/16. Which of the following is a valid option?

    A. Add a new 10.0.0.0/16 Classless Inter-Domain Routing (CIDR) range to the 192.168.0.0/16 VPC. Change the existing addresses of instances to the 10.0.0.0/16 space.

    B. Change the initial VPC CIDR range to the 10.0.0.0/16 CIDR.

    C. Create a new 10.0.0.0/16 VPC. Use VPC peering to migrate workloads to the new VPC.

    D. Perform Network Address Translation (NAT) on everything in the 192.168.0.0/16 space to the 10.0.0.0/16 space using NAT Gateways.

13. Your organization has a single Virtual Private Cloud (VPC) for development workloads. An open source Virtual Private Network (VPN) running on an Amazon Elastic Compute Cloud (Amazon EC2) instance is configured to provide developers with remote access. The VPN instance gives users IP addresses from a Classless Inter-Domain Routing (CIDR) range outside the VPC and performs a source Network Address Translation (NAT) on received traffic to the private address of the instance. Your organization acquired a company that also uses AWS with their own VPC. You have configured VPC peering between the two VPCs and instances can communicate without issue. Which of the following flows will fail?

    A. An incoming connection from one user on the VPN to another user on the VPN.

    B. A virus scan from an instance in the acquired VPC to a user connected through VPN.

    C. An Application Programming Interface (API) request from a VPN user to an instance in the acquired VPC.

    D. A web request to the Internet from a user connected through VPN.

14. Which of the following services can you access over AWS Direct Connect? (Choose two.)

    A. Interface Virtual Private Cloud (VPC) endpoints

    B. Gateway VPC endpoints

    C. Amazon Elastic Compute Cloud (Amazon EC2) instance metadata

    D. Network Load Balancer

15. Some people in your company have created a very complicated and management-intensive workflow for automating development builds and testing. They have requested those involved in creating it not to repeat this workflow more than once. The security organization, however, wants every developer to have their own account to reduce the blast radius of development issues. What is the best design for providing access to the development system?

A. Provide one large Virtual Private Cloud (VPC). Configure network Access Control Lists (ACLs) and security groups so that the blast radius for developers is limited.

B. Ask the developers simply to automate the deployment of their build system and make it a distributed system. Deploy a copy of this in each developer VPC to prevent any blast radius or complexity problems.

C. Deploy the development system in a central VPC. Allow developers to access the system through AWS PrivateLink.

D. Deploy the development system in a central VPC. Extend network interfaces with cross-account permissions so that developers can route their code to the development system.

16. An administrator was using an Elastic IP address to perform Application Programming Interface (API) calls with a business partner. The business partner whitelisted that IP in their firewalls. Unfortunately, the administrator ran a script that they did not understand which deleted the instance; the public address is no longer available. The administrator has submitted an API call to recall the Elastic IP address, but the address is not being returned. What could be the cause of this issue? (Choose two.)

A. The IP was auto-assigned rather than an assigned Elastic IP address.

B. The Elastic IP address was not tagged correctly for recall.

C. The IP was never owned by the account.

D. It is not possible to recall an Elastic IP address after it has been released.

E. The associated instance has the maximum number of assigned Elastic IP addresses.

Virtual Private Networks

THE AWS CERTIFIED ADVANCED NETWORKING – SPECIALTY EXAM OBJECTIVES COVERED IN THIS CHAPTER MAY INCLUDE, BUT ARE NOT LIMITED TO, THE FOLLOWING:

Domain 1.0: Design and Implement Hybrid IT Network Architectures at Scale

- ✓ **1.1 Apply procedural concepts for the implementation of connectivity for hybrid IT architecture**
- ✓ **1.2 Given a scenario, derive an appropriate hybrid IT architecture connectivity solution**
- ✓ **1.4 Evaluate design alternatives leveraging AWS Direct Connect**
- ✓ **1.5 Define routing policies for hybrid IT architectures**

Domain 5.0: Design and Implement for Security and Compliance

- ✓ **5.4 Utilize encryption technologies to secure network communications**

Introduction to Virtual Private Networks

This chapter is intended to provide you with an understanding of how to design *Virtual Private Networks (VPNs)* on AWS. We will go into detail on the various options available and various scenarios for VPN creation.

A *VPN* is a network that allows hosts to communicate privately over an untrusted intermediary network like the Internet as if they were all colocated in an isolated private network. A common reason for creating a VPN is to allow on-premises servers to communicate with servers in a Virtual Private Cloud (VPC) over the public Internet in a private and secure manner. In this scenario, we create what is called a *site-to-site VPN* connection. Another type of VPN, called a *client-to-site VPN*, or remote access VPN, can be created when individual remote users want to connect to the server resources inside a VPC from their client devices (like laptops) in a secure manner. As we go through this chapter, we will explore how to architect an approach for each of these scenarios.

A VPN can be set up using different protocols and technologies, each with its own advantages. The most widely-used VPN technology is a set of protocols called the *Internet Protocol Security (IPsec)* protocols, often referred to as an IPsec VPN. According to RFC 6071, *IPsec* is a suite of protocols that provides security to Internet communications at the IP layer. Some other VPN technologies are *Generic Routing Encapsulation (GRE)* and *Dynamic Multipoint Virtual Private Network (DMVPN).*

Site-to-Site VPN

A *site-to-site VPN* connection allows two networking domains, referred to as sites, to communicate securely with each other over an untrusted intermediary network, such as the public Internet. These two sites can be a VPC and an on-premises data center, or two different VPCs in different or the same AWS Regions. In order for the two sites to set up a VPN connection, a VPN termination endpoint is required at each site. This endpoint is responsible for running the VPN protocols and the associated packet processing, including *encapsulation* and *encryption.* All the traffic flow between the two sites is passed via these endpoints, and hence it is important to think about the availability and scalability of these endpoints in hybrid architectures.

A VPN connection to AWS can only be used to access resources inside a VPC. This excludes services such as Amazon S3 that sit outside the boundaries of a VPC. Since every VPC is its own isolated network, you will require a VPN connection per VPC.

Let's discuss the VPN termination endpoint options available in the context of creating a site-to-site VPN between AWS and an on-premises data center (customer network). There are two ways to terminate a VPN connection to a VPC: a Virtual Private Gateway and an Amazon Elastic Compute Cloud (Amazon EC2) instance.

Virtual Private Gateway as a VPN Termination Endpoint

The *Virtual Private Gateway (VGW)* is a managed gateway endpoint for your VPC. It is responsible for hybrid IT connectivity leveraging VPN and AWS Direct Connect. The VGW is a self-sustainable entity, and it can be created without the requirement of a pre-existing VPC. Once created, it then can be attached to any VPC in the same account and region. A key point to remember here is that each VPC can have only one VGW attached to it at any given point in time, but you have the ability to detach one VGW and attach another one to a VPC. You can create a VGW by navigating to the Amazon VPC dashboard in the AWS Management Console or by making an Application Programming Interface (API) call.

When creating a VGW, you will have an option to define an *Autonomous System Number (ASN)* for the AWS side of the external *Border Gateway Protocol (BGP)* session. You can choose any private ASN. Ranges for 16-bit private ASNs include 64512 to 65534. You can also provide 32-bit ASNs between 4200000000 and 4294967294. AWS will provide a default ASN for a VGW if you don't choose one.

Once defined, the ASN cannot be changed at a later stage. You will have to delete and re-create the VGW with a new ASN.

Once a VGW is created, you can terminate a VPN connection on it. The VGW supports only IPsec VPN in the *Encapsulating Security Payload (ESP)* mode. Figure 4.1 depicts this connection architecture.

FIGURE 4.1 VPN termination at VGW

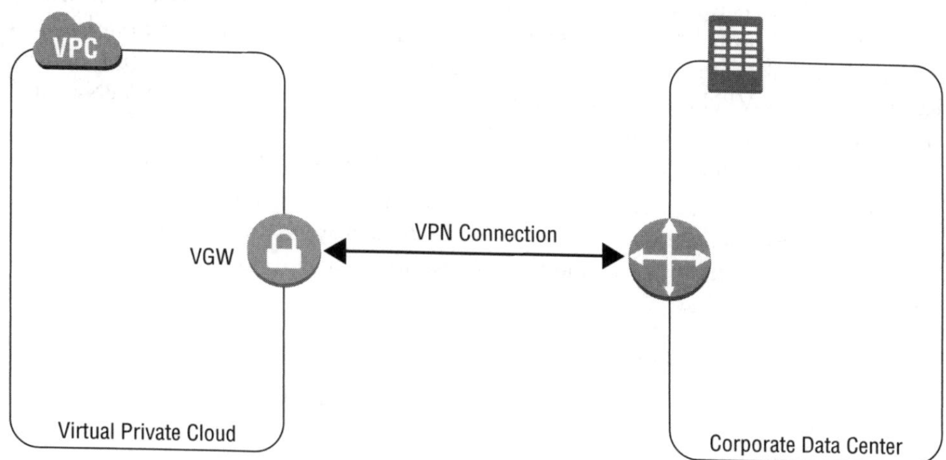

Availability and Redundancy

The VGW has built-in high availability and redundancy for VPN connectivity. Upon VPN creation, AWS automatically creates two highly available endpoints, each in a different Availability Zone. As shown in Figure 4.2, each endpoint has an IP address associated with it that will be used to terminate the VPN at the AWS end. Both of these endpoints are available and can be used to set up VPN tunnels in Active/Active mode. These two tunnels are collectively denoted as a Single VPN connection in AWS terminology.

FIGURE 4.2 VGW HA endpoints

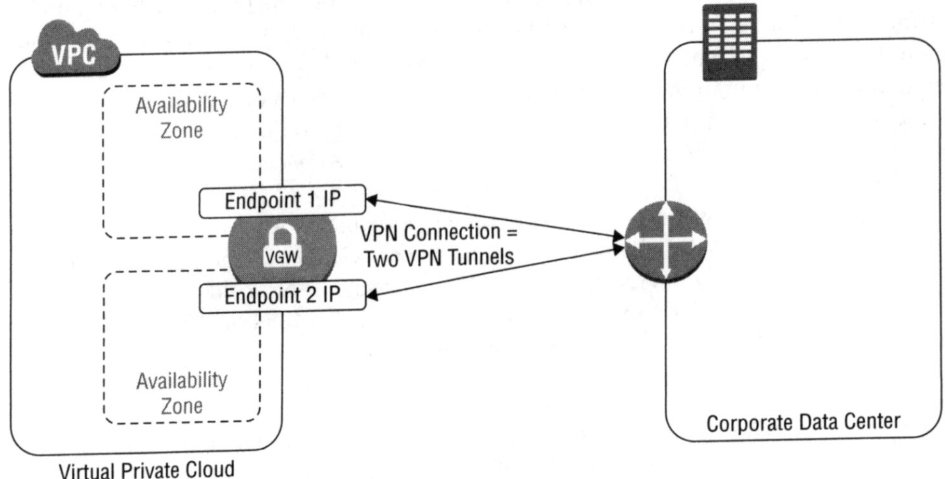

Each tunnel contains an *Internet Key Exchange (IKE) Security Association (SA)*, an IPsec SA, and a BGP Peering (optional, used in route-based VPNs). You are limited to one unique SA pair per tunnel (one inbound and one outbound) and therefore two unique SA pairs in total for two tunnels (four SAs). Some devices use policy-based VPNs and will create as many SAs as there are Access Control List (ACL) entries.

Policy-based VPNs that are configured with more than one security association will drop existing VPN tunnel connections when initiating a VPN tunnel connection that uses a different SA. This problem will be perceived as intermittent packet loss or connectivity failure because new VPN connections with one security association interrupt VPN tunnel connections established with a different security association.

You can overcome this problem by considering either of these two approaches:

- Limit the number of encryption domains (networks) that are allowed access to the VPC and consolidate. If there are more than two encryption domains (networks) behind your VPN termination endpoint, consolidate them to use a single security association.

- Configure the policy to allow "any" network (0.0.0.0/0) from behind your VPN termination endpoint to the VPC Classless Inter-Domain Routing (CIDR). Essentially, this allows any network behind your VPN termination endpoint that is destined to the VPC to pass through the tunnel. This will only create a single security association. This improves the stability of the tunnel and allows future networks not defined in the policy to have access to the AWS VPC. This is the generally-recommended best approach.

Route-based VPN leveraging BGP for routing doesn't have this problem.

VPN Features

The VPN features discussed in this chapter refer to the new AWS VPN service.

Security

From a security standpoint, VGW supports the following cryptography suites:

- Advanced Encryption Standard (AES) 256
- Secure Hash Algorithm (SHA) 2
- Phase 1 Diffie Hellman(DH) groups: 2, 14-18, 22, 23, and 24
- Phase 2 DH groups: 1, 2, 5, 14-18, 22, 23, and 24

VGW also has backward compatibility for older cryptography protocols. The cryptography used in Internet Key Exchange (IKE) Phase 1 and 2 is automatically determined at the time of IPsec negotiations. It is important to make sure that your VPN termination endpoint is enabled/configured for using these cryptography standards. Otherwise, the tunnel might be negotiated using older standards.

Routing

The VGW supports both static route VPNs and those based on the BGP dynamic routing protocol. The BGP routing protocol allows your on-premises device to advertise multiple IP prefixes dynamically to the VGW using BGP route advertisements. The VGW advertises the IP ranges of the VPC to which it is attached via BGP route advertisements to your VPN termination endpoint. A VGW runs the standard BGP protocol over Transmission Control Protocol (TCP) port 179 and honors common BGP parameters like AS (Autonomous System) prepends and BGP MED (Multi-Exit Discriminator).

You can have up to 100 propagated routes per VPC subnet route table. This is a hard limit, and it cannot be raised; therefore, you should limit the number of routes that you are advertising to VGW using BGP route advertisements to less than 100 total. In the event that you have more than 100 prefixes, it is recommended that you summarize your routes or even advertise a default route if that fits your use case. Within a VPC, you can enable VGW route propagation, which will allow the VPC subnet route table to ingest routes learned by the VGW automatically via BGP.

Note that VGW is a managed entity, so you will not have access to the BGP console of the VGW and cannot make any changes to the actual BGP configuration running in VGW once the VPN is created.

Two tunnels are created per VPN connection by default, and you can establish multiple VPN connections for high-availability purposes. These conditions can increase the probability of asymmetric routing for a given prefix (that is, inbound traffic from on-premises to AWS flows through one tunnel while return traffic flows through the other tunnel). To mitigate this, we recommend that you use VPN tunnels in Active/Standby mode using as-path prepends or MED BGP parameters as shown in Figure 4.3.

FIGURE 4.3 Avoiding asymmetric routing by using BGP parameters

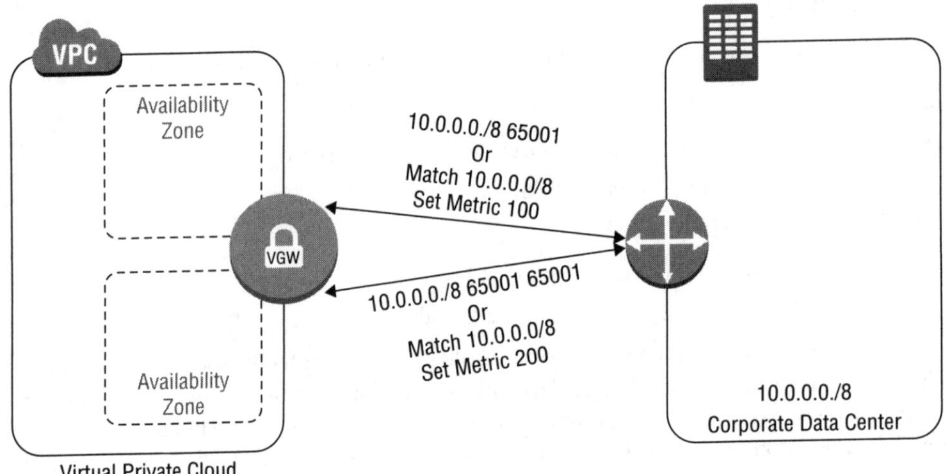

Network Address Translation (NAT) Traversal (NAT-T) Support

AWS VGWs also have support for *Network Address Translation (NAT) Traversal (NAT-T)*. Traditionally, the IPsec protocol does not work very well when traversing a *NAT* device. Due to the encrypted nature of the ESP header, NAT translations fail. NAT-T solves this problem by encapsulating the packet in a User Datagram Protocol (UDP) header using port 4500. By enabling this option, IPsec traffic can pass through a NAT device with successful port/IP translations.

In order to create a VPN from behind a NAT device, the IPsec gateway behind the NAT device and the gateway in the non-NAT environment must support NAT-T (that is, both VPN endpoints must support NAT-T).

AWS VPN CloudHub

An AWS VGW supports functionality called *AWS VPN CloudHub*, which acts as a hub router connecting multiple remote networks. A VGW supports this functionality irrespective of whether it is attached to a VPC, or if it is running in a detached mode. This design is suitable for customers with multiple branch offices and existing Internet connections who want to implement a convenient, potentially low-cost hub-and-spoke model for primary or backup connectivity between these remote offices.

To use the AWS VPN CloudHub, you must create a VGW and set up a VPN connection to all of the sites to which you want to connect via the CloudHub. You can use different or the same BGP ASNs for each site based on your preference and use case. Customer gateways advertise the appropriate routes (BGP prefixes) over their VPN connections. These routing advertisements are received and re-advertised to each BGP peer, enabling each site to send data to and receive data from the other sites. The sites must not have overlapping IP ranges. If the VGW is attached to a VPC, each site can also send and receive data from the VPC as if they were using a standard VPN connection. Figure 4.4 depicts this functionality.

FIGURE 4.4 AWS VPN CloudHub functionality

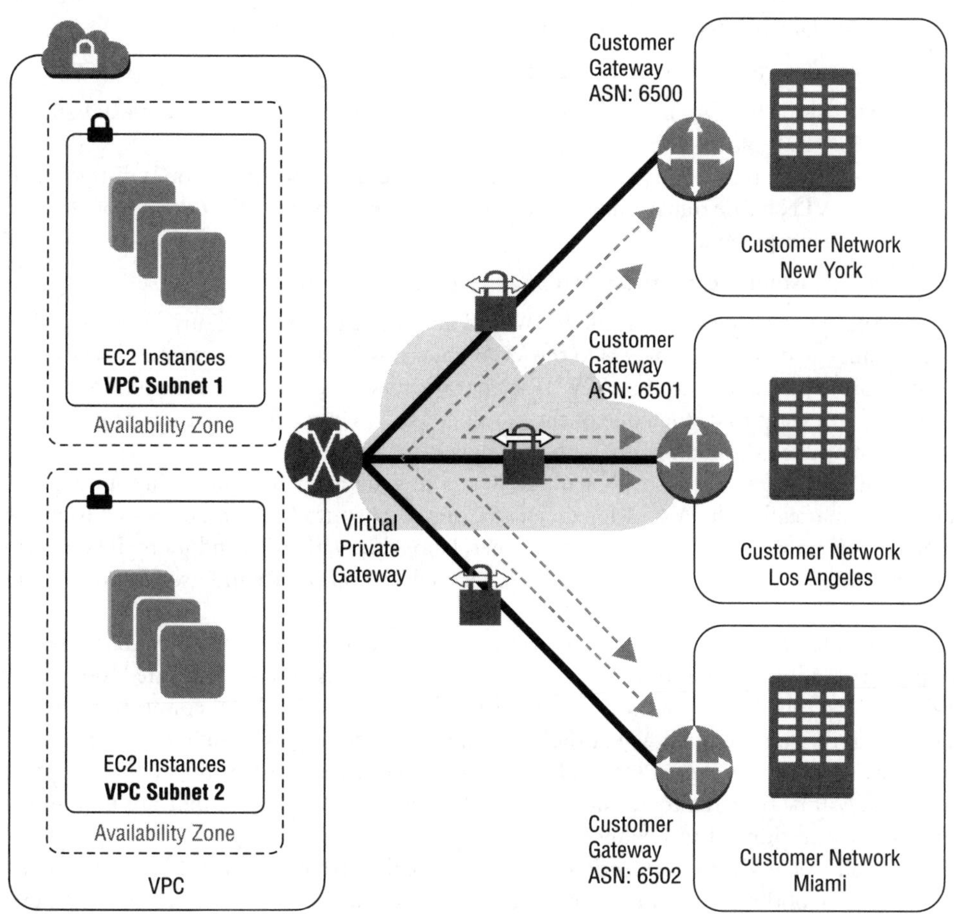

VPN Creation Process

It is simple and quick to set up a VPN connection. You'll use the AWS Management Console or make an API call to create a VPN connection. You will have to specify the following details during this step:

- The VGW to which you want to set up the VPN connection
- A customer gateway (the IP address of the VPN termination endpoint at your end)—more details on the customer gateway are provided later in this chapter.
- Routing Method
  - **Option 1:** Static Tunnel (routing via static routes). Specify routes that you want to advertise to AWS.
  - **Option 2:** Dynamic Tunnel (routing via BGP). Specify BGP ASN.
- Tunnel Configurations
  - **AWS Default:** Values shown below will be automatically generated.
  - **Custom:** Manually specify the below values.
    - **Inside IPv4 Addresses for the Tunnels:** (2 x /30 range within 169.254.0.0/16 CIDR block). When creating multiple VPN connections to a single VGW, ensure that the inside tunnel IP address for each VPN connection is distinct. The VPN inside tunnel addresses can be the same as the peer IP addresses on AWS Direct Connect.
    - **Custom Pre-Shared Key (PSK).**

Based on the values you enter, the VGW will automatically be configured for this VPN connection. You do not have access to the VGW internals because it is a managed service—you cannot make changes to the VGW IPsec parameters once the VPN connection is created. If you want to change one of the parameters, you must delete the existing VPN connection and create a new VPN with new parameters.

The AWS Management Console will allow you to generate a configuration for your device automatically. The AWS Management Console has information pertaining to many VPN vendors, including Cisco, Juniper, Fortinet, Palo Alto Networks, and more. If your vendor is not listed there, you can download a generic configuration file and use that to configure your device.

Once you have created the VPN connection at the AWS end, use the AWS-generated configuration file to configure your device. Two VPN tunnels should be created: one to each of the VGW public IP endpoints. This completes the creation of a VPN connection with high availability and redundancy at the AWS end. We encourage you to have redundancy at your end as well by having multiple VPN termination devices. A separate VPN connection per device will be required to accomplish this. We will explore this configuration in more detail in later sections of this chapter.

After you create a VPN connection, the VPN tunnel activates when traffic is generated from your side of the VPN connection. The VGW is not the initiator; your customer gateway must initiate the tunnels. If your VPN connection experiences a period of idle time (usually 10 seconds, depending on your configuration), the tunnel may go down. This is because AWS uses an on-demand DPD mechanism. If AWS receives no traffic from a VPN peer for 10 seconds, AWS sends a DPD "R-U-THERE" message. If the VPN peer does not respond to three successive DPDs, the VPN peer is considered dead and AWS closes the tunnel.

Monitoring

As shown in Figure 4.5, you can monitor the status of the VPN tunnels using Amazon CloudWatch metrics. Amazon CloudWatch is a monitoring service for AWS Cloud resources and the applications that you run on AWS. The supported Amazon CloudWatch metrics for VPN connections are as follows:

TunnelState: The state of the tunnel. 0 indicates DOWN and 1 indicates UP.

TunnelDataIn: The bytes received through the VPN tunnel.

TunnelDataOut: The bytes sent through the VPN tunnel.

FIGURE 4.5 Graphical representation of VPN metrics in the Amazon CloudWatch dashboard

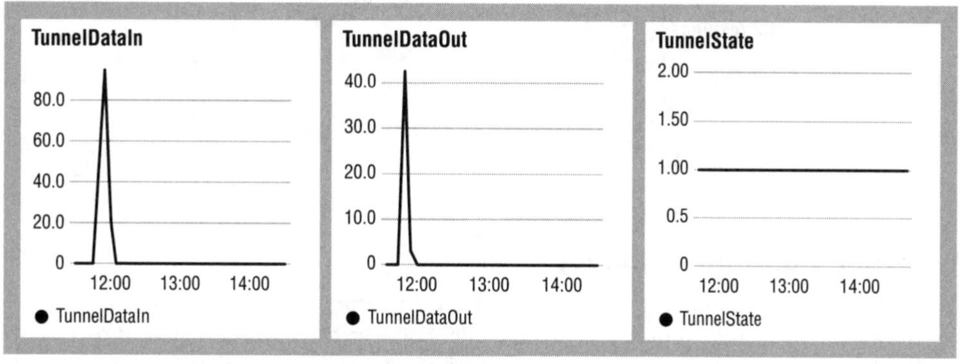

Check the AWS documentation for the latest and complete list of Amazon CloudWatch metrics for VPN.

Amazon Elastic Compute Cloud (Amazon EC2) Instance as a VPN Termination Endpoint

An alternative to using a VGW as a VPN termination endpoint at the AWS end is to terminate the VPN on an Amazon Elastic Compute Cloud (Amazon EC2) instance running VPN software. There are a few special scenarios in which you may choose to do this. They are as follows:

- You require a special set of features on your VPN termination endpoint, such as advanced threat protection or transitive routing capabilities.

- Your on-premises device is not compatible with running IPsec VPN, and you want to run a different VPN protocol, such as DMVPN or GRE VPN.
- You want to support complex networking requirements, such as connecting two networks with an overlapping CIDR range, setting up multicast between Amazon EC2 instances, or enabling transitive routing.

As shown in Figure 4.6, there is no VGW involved, and VPN is terminated directly on the Amazon EC2 instance.

FIGURE 4.6 VPN termination in an Amazon EC2 instance

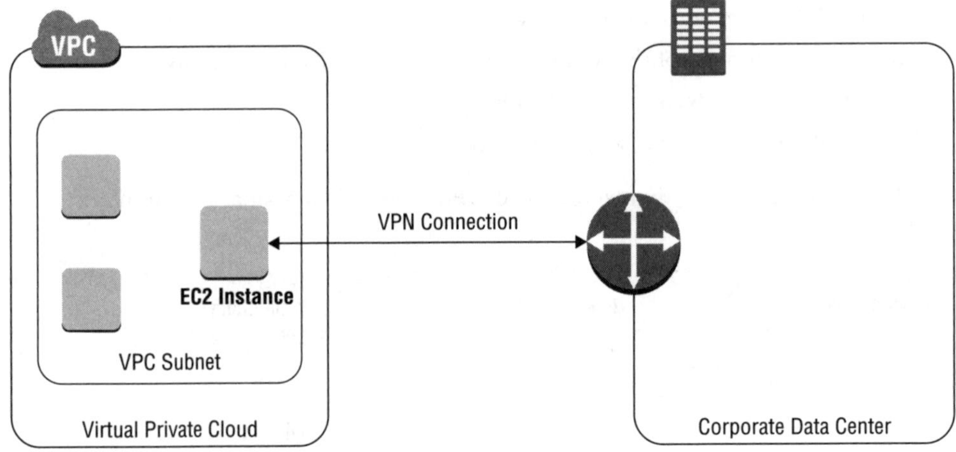

Availability and Redundancy

The availability and redundancy of this option is your responsibility. There are four ways that the availability and redundancy of your VPN connection can be affected. It can be due to a VPN configuration error, a problem with the VPN software that you are using, an operating system error, or the Amazon EC2 instance becoming unhealthy. The first three causes are within your control, and you should have checks in place to rectify them. An Amazon EC2 instance failure can be rectified by the Amazon EC2 auto recovery feature.

In any case, it is recommended to have two Amazon EC2 instances active at any given time for VPN termination in an Active/Standby mode.

As shown in Figure 4.7, only one Amazon EC2 instance can be used for VPN traffic at any given time for a given destination prefix per VPC subnet. This is due to the way that subnet route tables work. Within a subnet route table, you can have only one next hop for a given prefix.

FIGURE 4.7 High availability when terminating VPN on an Amazon EC2 instance

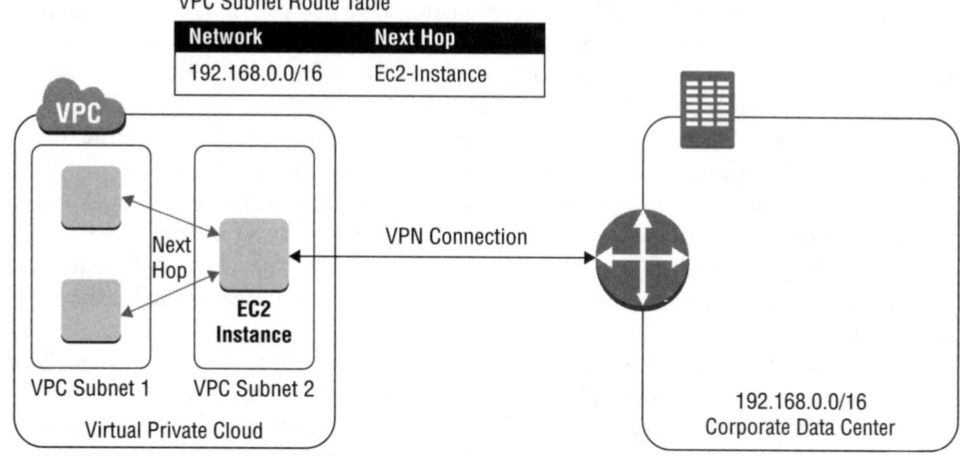

In order to achieve failover from the primary Amazon EC2 instance to the secondary, you will have to set up a monitoring script. This script will detect the failure of a VPN tunnel and then make changes to the subnet route table to point to the secondary instance wherever the primary instance was initially referenced. This automated failover configuration is depicted in Figure 4.8.

FIGURE 4.8 High availability when terminating VPN on an Amazon EC2 instance—automated failover

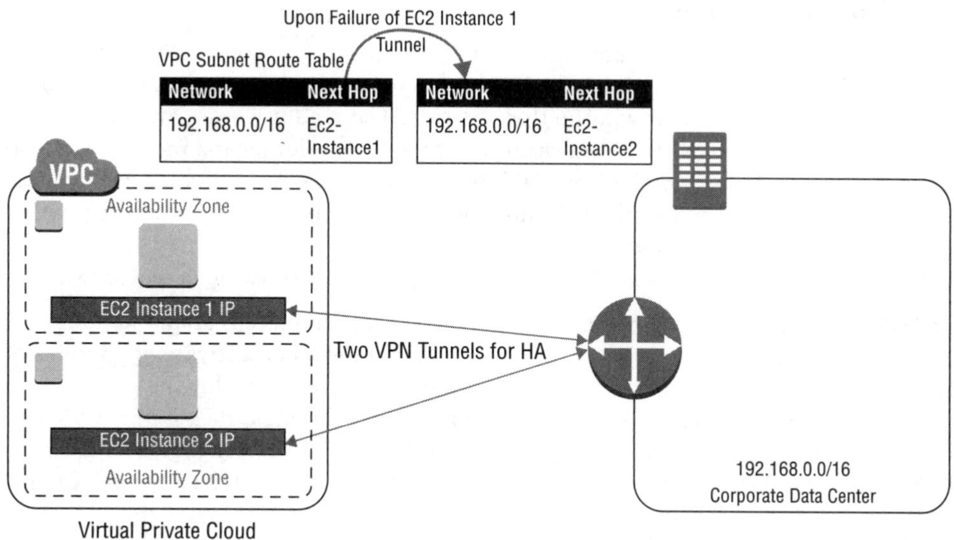

Once the route table entry is changed and the data path has been shifted to the secondary Amazon EC2 instance, the next step is to get the failed Amazon EC2 instance back to a healthy state. If the hardware that hosts a particular Amazon EC2 instance becomes impaired, Amazon EC2 auto recovery will reboot your instance into a healthy state. If your instance is configured to store the VPN configuration on persistent Amazon Elastic Block Store (Amazon EBS) storage, and you have enabled automated restart of the IPsec process at boot, your VPN connection should come up without manual effort. If the problem was at the VPN software level because of an incorrect configuration or software crash, it is your responsibility to fix the problem. Because creating new instances is easy, it might be easier to terminate the old instance and launch a new instance to recover from failure. In the event that the Amazon EC2 instance was public facing with an Elastic IP mapped to it, make sure that the failed instance and recovered instance have the same Elastic IP mapped to them.

If you are using a partner VPN solution from the *AWS Marketplace* (for example, Cisco, Aviatrix, Riverbed, Juniper, Sophos, Palo Alto, or Checkpoint), many of the automation and failover efforts described here are already built into the solution, and so no manual effort or scripting would be required to achieve high availability and recovery from failure scenarios. Note that features will vary by vendor.

Amazon EC2 Features

One of the biggest advantages of VPN termination on an Amazon EC2 instance over a VGW is the capability to have additional feature sets on top of just VPN termination and routing. The actual features offered are dependent on the VPN software that you are using on the Amazon EC2 instance.

VPN Creation Process

Because this option is based on running VPN software on an Amazon EC2 instance, the first step in VPN creation is choosing the VPN software you wish to run and the size of the Amazon EC2 instance that will run this software. The vendor whose software you choose for VPN creation dictates the feature set of the VPN solution and the out-of-the-box automation around failure and high availability. The size of the Amazon EC2 instance will determine the network bandwidth of the instance as well as the compute power required for packet encapsulation and encryption.

Once you have decided on a vendor, you can set up the VPN software in one of two ways:

Use AWS Marketplace As shown in Figure 4.9, AWS Marketplace is an online store where you can sell or buy software that runs on AWS. If the VPN software of your liking is available as an AWS Marketplace offering, you can directly deploy the software on an Amazon EC2 instance type that fits your needs using a single click in the AWS Marketplace console. An Amazon EC2 instance will be launched from an Amazon Machine Image (AMI) with the VPN software preinstalled and optimized by the vendor. Depending on the license model, you can use an AWS-provided license or Bring Your Own License (BYOL).

FIGURE 4.9 AWS Marketplace

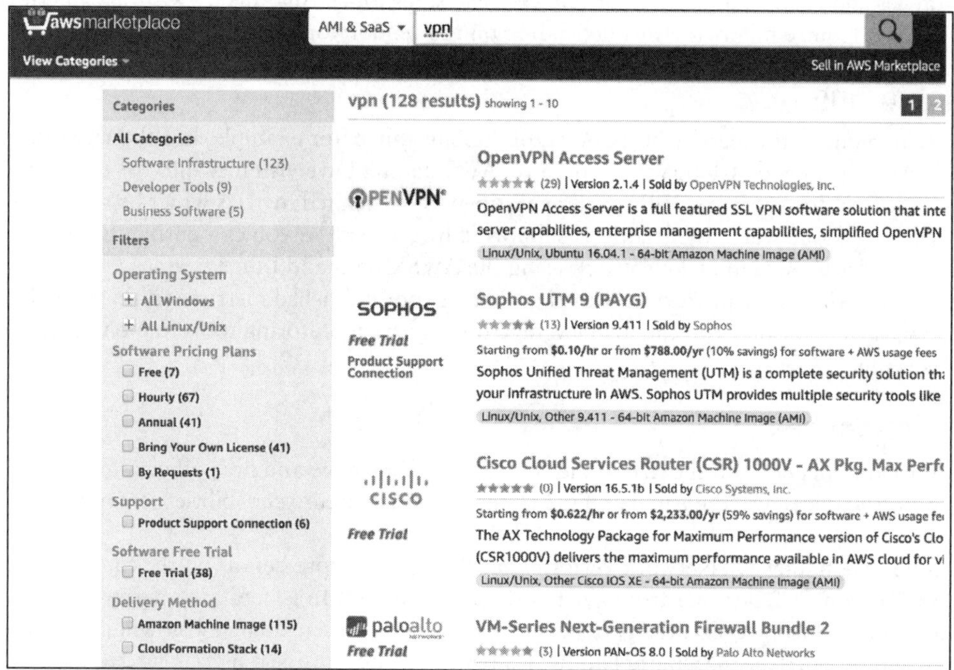

Manual Install on an Amazon EC2 Instance If the software is not available on AWS Marketplace, you can manually install it. First launch an Amazon EC2 instance of a type and size that meets your needs, which is loaded with an operating system that is recommended for the VPN software. Then install the VPN software directly from the vendor's repository. You will have to interact directly with the vendor regarding any licensing contracts for their VPN software.

You need to make sure that the Amazon EC2 instance has the right connectivity to reach the VPN termination device at your end. If this requires Internet access, assign an Elastic IP address to the Amazon EC2 instance and make sure that a route to the Internet gateway exists in the subnet route table. Ideally, you would also have the right ports opened in the instance security group for inbound IPsec traffic to pass from the on-premises device to the Amazon EC2 instance, but you can skip this if the Amazon EC2 instance initiates the IPsec negotiation. Due to the stateful nature of security groups, return traffic for an existing stateful connection is automatically allowed.

Once the Amazon EC2 instance is set up with proper connectivity and loaded with the VPN software, you will have to configure IPsec parameters and the associated routing on both the Amazon EC2 instance and the VPN device at the remote end (on-premises data center) to bring up the VPN tunnel. To enable routing of traffic, make sure that the source/destination check is disabled on the Amazon EC2 instance and IP forwarding is enabled at the operating system level.

For high-availability configurations, you will need to launch multiple Amazon EC2 instances and set up automation for failover. The steps for setting this up will vary in effort and might require minimal effort depending on the vendor you choose.

Monitoring

You can monitor the metrics of the Amazon EC2 instance (for example, health, network in/out) using Amazon CloudWatch. Because AWS doesn't have visibility into the operating system or vendor software, VPN- and operating system-related metrics won't be visible in Amazon CloudWatch by default. If supported by the vendor, you can push custom VPN metrics to Amazon CloudWatch using the AWS Command Line Interface (AWS CLI) or an API. You can view statistical graphs of your published metrics within the AWS Management Console. You can also leverage third-party monitoring tools to monitor the VPN setup.

Performance

Performance depends on the size of the Amazon EC2 instance and how efficiently the VPN software can use the Amazon EC2 instance infrastructure capabilities (compute and memory).

Refer to Chapter 9, "Network Performance," to gather more details on the capabilities of an Amazon EC2 instance from a networking standpoint. In general, the bigger the Amazon EC2 instance size, the better average networking performance you will get from the instance, with the maximum bandwidth being 25 Gbps inside a placement group and 5 Gbps outside the placement group.

Vertical Scaling

You should establish the correct instance type needed for the Amazon EC2 instance running the VPN software through testing. You can use the agility of the Amazon EC2 to scale vertically by changing the instance to a larger size in the event that you need more network throughput.

Vertical scaling may require downtime, typically a few minutes, because an Amazon EC2 instance being scaled up has to be restarted. If you have designed your system for high availability (Active/Backup), you should be able to avoid downtime or minimize it by first upgrading the secondary (Backup) instance, promoting it to master (Active), and then upgrading the primary which then becomes the backup.

Note that after a certain threshold, the VPN throughput becomes fairly constant even with an increase in the Amazon EC2 instance size. This is due to the limits on the speed at which IPsec packet processing can be performed in software. One way to increase the VPN throughput above this threshold is to offload the encryption to multiple Amazon EC2 instances. In this scenario, you will have one Amazon EC2 instance configured as the next hop for all VPN traffic. This Amazon EC2 instance will not provide VPN termination but is instead responsible for load balancing traffic to a fleet of Amazon EC2 instances that are responsible for VPN termination. Since the intermediary Amazon EC2 instance is not responsible for IPsec encryption, it can transmit packets at a much faster rate. There are two ways to set this up as follows:

Single Availability Zone Within the same subnet, the intermediary Amazon EC2 instance runs BGP (or a similar protocol that can used for L3 load balancing of traffic) with a fleet of Amazon EC2 VPN instances to keep track of routing information and to insert the VPN instances as the next hop for remote networks in its host routing table. BGP multipath can be used for load balancing traffic. This architecture is depicted in Figure 4.10.

FIGURE 4.10 Vertical scaling with load balancing—single Availability Zone

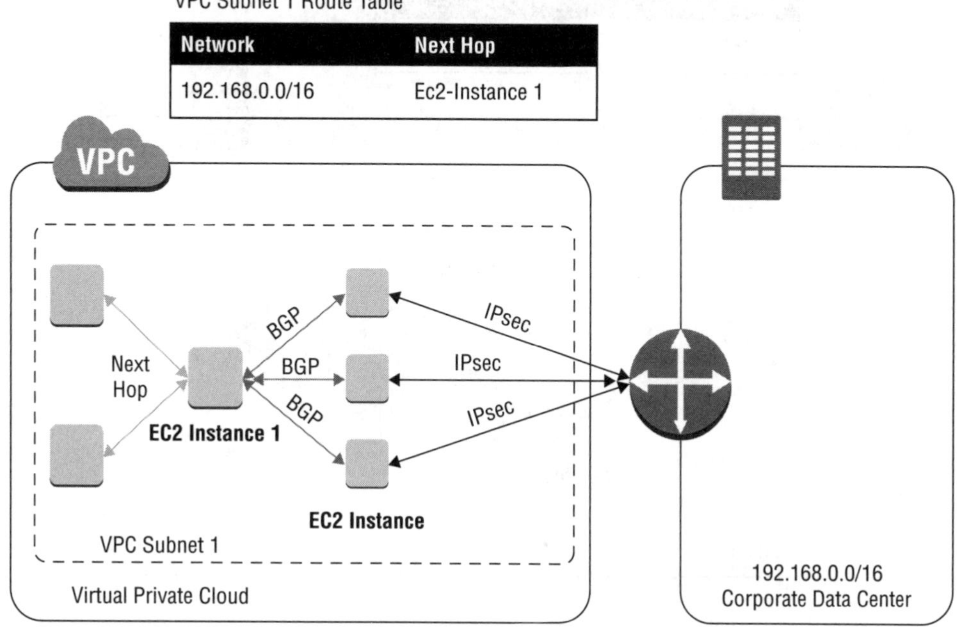

In the single Availability Zone solution, return traffic will not flow via the intermediary Amazon EC2 instance. If that is a requirement, you can establish NAT on this instance or implement the multiple Availability Zone option.

Multiple Availability Zones Place the VPN Amazon EC2 instances in different Availability Zones and establish GRE tunnels from the intermediary instance to the VPN instances. GRE tunnels are used as EC2 instances cannot establish BGP peering with an instance in a different subnet. This is a limitation of the way BGP neighbor relationships are established. A GRE tunnel creates a virtual network connecting the two instances in the same virtual network. If you are using your own load balancing protocol, then you might be able to load balance traffic to instances in a different subnet without the need to use a GRE. Like the previous option, this intermediary Amazon EC2 instance runs BGP with the VPN instances to keep track of routing information and to insert the VPN instances as the next hop for the remote network in its routing table. BGP multipath can be used for load balancing traffic. This architecture is depicted in Figure 4.11.

FIGURE 4.11 Vertical scaling with load balancing—multiple Availability Zones

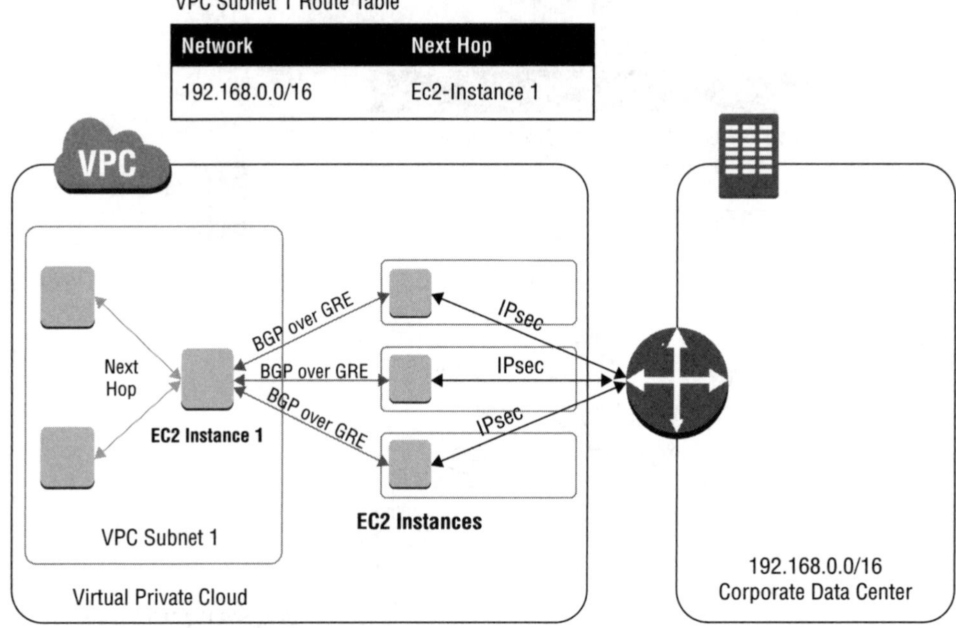

BGP multipath is used in the above two vertical scaling options as a mechanism to load balance traffic from the intermediary instance to the fleet of VPN Amazon EC2 instances. It is not an absolute requirement. If BGP multipath is not supported by the software you choose to deploy on the intermediary instance, you will have to choose some other way of performing load balancing.

Horizontal Scaling

From a horizontal scaling point of view, you can launch multiple Amazon EC2 instances and use them simultaneously (Active/Active) for VPN traffic. Due to the way VPC routing tables work, only one Amazon EC2 instance can be used as a next hop for a given prefix. You will have to design the way you want to distribute outgoing VPN traffic carefully among multiple Amazon EC2 VPN gateway instances. As shown in Figure 4.12, one approach is to have one Amazon EC2 instance VPN gateway per VPC subnet.

FIGURE 4.12 Horizontal Scaling based on VPC Subnets

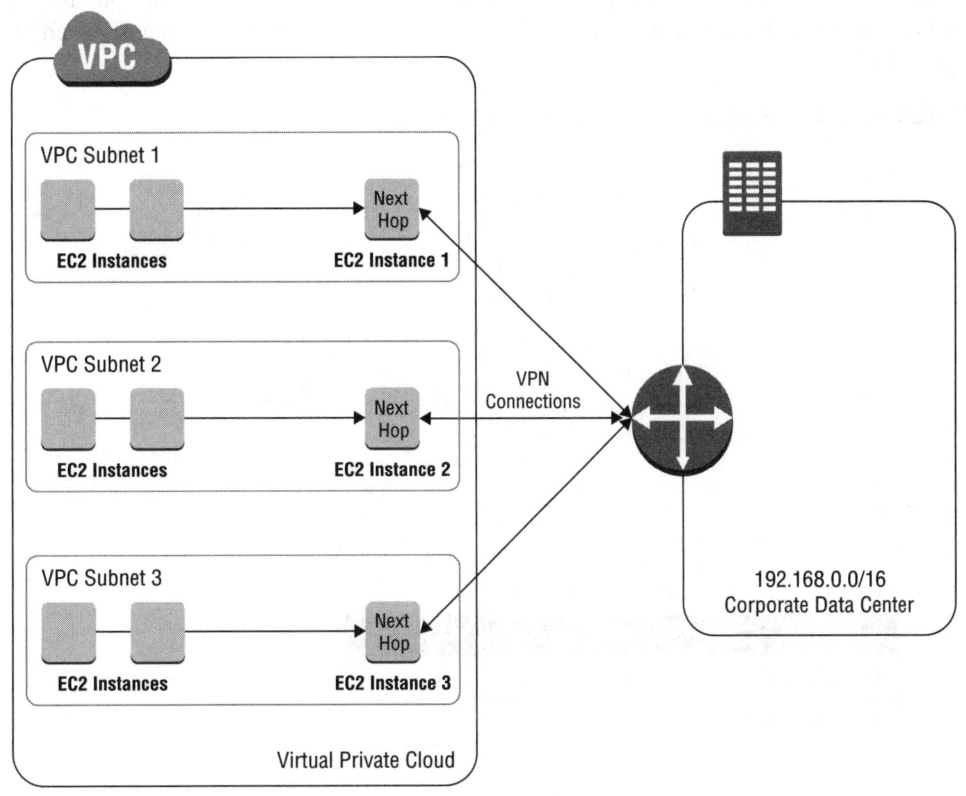

VPC Subnet 1 Route Table

Network	Next Hop
192.168.0.0/16	Ec2-Instance 1

VPC Subnet 2 Route Table

Network	Next Hop
192.168.0.0/16	Ec2-Instance 2

VPC Subnet 3 Route Table

Network	Next Hop
192.168.0.0/16	Ec2-Instance 3

Another way to distribute traffic across multiple Amazon EC2 instances is based on the destination prefix. The idea is to split the on-premises network prefix into multiple sub-prefixes and use a different Amazon EC2 instance to reach each prefix. This is depicted in Figure 4.13.

FIGURE 4.13 Horizontal Scaling based on destination prefix

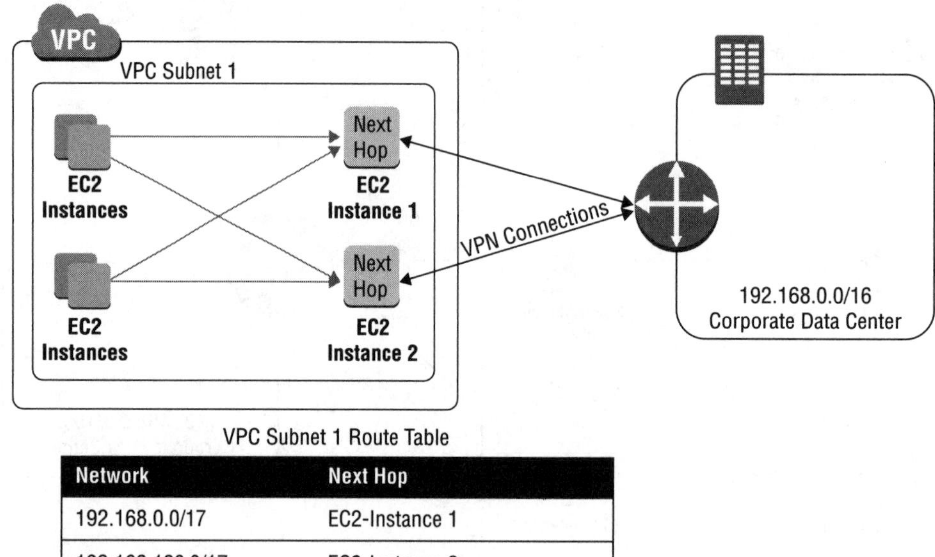

Network	Next Hop
192.168.0.0/17	EC2-Instance 1
192.168.128.0/17	EC2-Instance 2

VPN Termination Endpoint for On-Premises Networks (Customer Gateways)

At the non-AWS end of a VPN connection, the VPN is terminated on a customer gateway. A customer gateway is the AWS term for the VPN termination device at the customer's on-premises end. A customer gateway can also be hosted in AWS as an EC2 instance running VPN software that meets the requirements given in the next section.

Most customers don't require the purchase of an additional device and can reuse an existing on-premises VPN termination device to create a tunnel to a VPC.

Figure 4.14 shows an architectural representation of a customer gateway.

FIGURE 4.14 Customer gateway

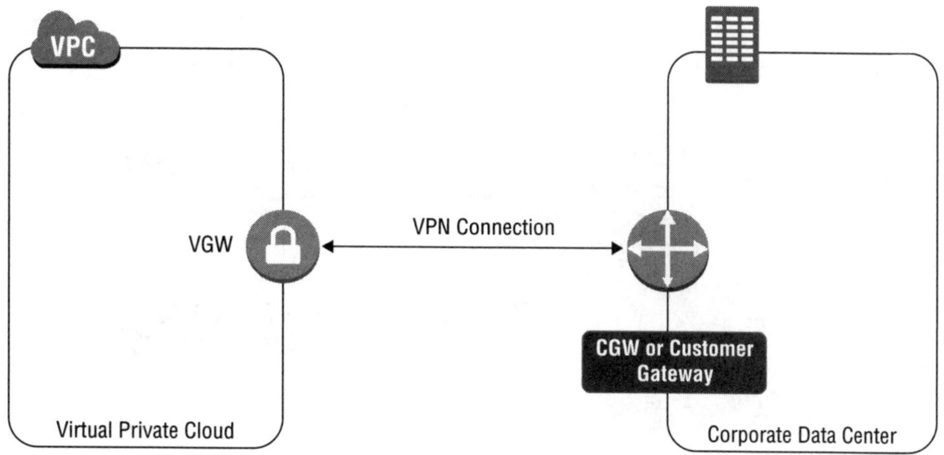

Third-Party VPN Device

You can use any third-party VPN device that supports Layer 3 VPN technologies. AWS does not support Layer 2 VPN technologies.

IPsec is used for the VGW at the AWS end of VPN termination, and so the IPsec protocol must be supported by your VPN device. You will set up two VPN tunnels per VGW. Support for BGP routing protocol is optional but recommended for advanced routing capabilities. Other routing protocols like Open Shortest Path First (OSPF) are not supported by AWS. You must ensure that you have opened the right ports in your on-premises firewall for the IPsec traffic to flow.

When using the Amazon EC2 instance-based VPN termination option, the choice of VPN protocol is dependent on the VPN software that you install on the Amazon EC2 instance. Common protocols like GRE, DMVPN, and others can be used as an alternative to IPsec. The routing protocols that are supported again depend on the VPN software running on the Amazon EC2 instance.

You are responsible for the availability and redundancy of the third-party device. As depicted in Figure 4.15, we recommend using multiple VPN termination devices at your end. If possible, these devices should be located in different physical data centers for a higher level of redundancy. You can use BGP parameters like local preference to designate primary/secondary exit points for the VPN traffic destined to AWS. For return traffic from AWS to your data center, use as-path prepends or MED to influence traffic path.

FIGURE 4.15 Customer gateway high availability

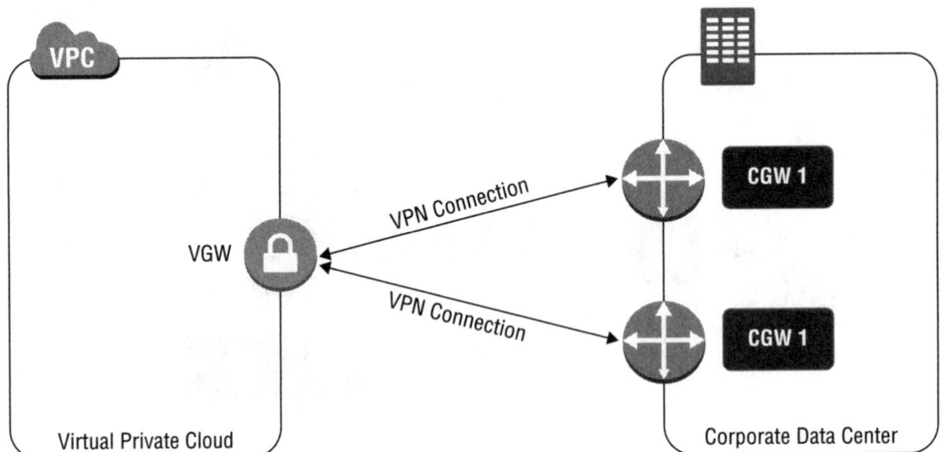

Client-to-Site VPN

A *client-to-site VPN* (also referred to as a remote access VPN) allows single hosts to gain access to resources inside a given network in a secure and private manner across an untrusted intermediary network. This is typically useful in the case of remote workers who are trying to gain access to corporate resources. In an AWS Cloud scenario, this can be useful for a remote laptop or PC to gain access to Amazon EC2 instances inside an Amazon VPC over the public Internet. Note that every end host will have to set up a VPN tunnel to the VPN gateway. If you have a remote office/site that consists of multiple end-user hosts/devices on their own internal network that all require access to VPC resources, you should set up a site-to-site tunnel between the remote site and the VPC.

As shown in Figure 4.16, to set this up, you need a gateway inside of the VPC that will be responsible for accepting VPN connections from remote hosts. Unlike site-to-site VPN, AWS currently does not offer a managed gateway endpoint for this type of VPN setup. You will have to use an Amazon EC2 instance as a client-to-site VPN gateway.

Similar to the Amazon EC2 instance-based VPN termination option for site-to-site VPN, setting up client-to-site VPN termination on an Amazon EC2 instance can be done in one of two ways:

Use AWS Marketplace You can use a pre-baked AMI with both software and license preinstalled to launch an Amazon EC2 instance and configure it as a VPN termination endpoint for remote clients. OpenVPN, Cisco CSR (with Cisco AnyConnect clients), Aviatrix, Sophos, and Palo Alto are examples of client-to-site VPN products on AWS Marketplace.

Manual install on an Amazon EC2 instance If the software is not available on AWS Marketplace, you can manually install it on an Amazon EC2 instance.

FIGURE 4.16 Client-to-site VPN

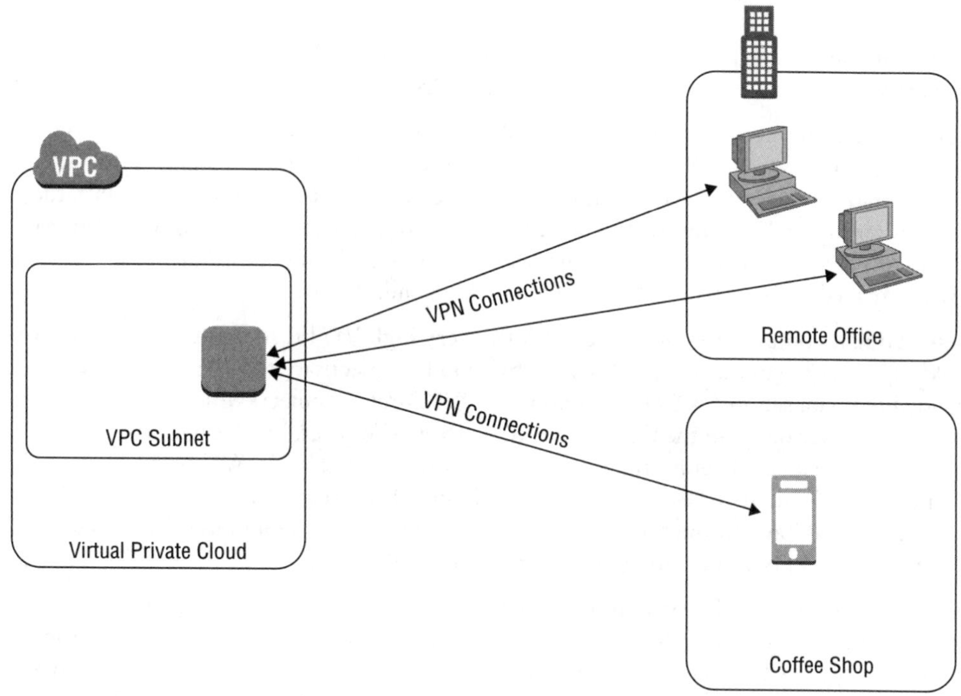

The arguments made regarding the availability, redundancy, and performance of the Amazon EC2 instance-based VPN termination option for site-to-site VPNs hold true for client-to-site VPN as well. Many client-to-site VPN solutions, like Cisco AnyConnect or Aviatrix, support load balancing client VPN connections to multiple VPN servers. This can be done by either using Network Load Balancer to send VPN traffic to multiple EC2 instances (for example, OpenVPN in TCP mode), DNS based load balancing (client DNS queries resolve to different VPN servers), or just specifying multiple VPN server IP addresses in the client.

When hosting multiple Amazon EC2 VPN servers in Active/Active setup for load balancing, it is advised to use Transit VPC architecture with the client tunnels terminating on the transit EC2 instances. This is explained in greater detail in Chapter 12, "Hybrid Architectures."

Additional features like split tunneling, threat protection, endpoint compliance, profile based authentication, and so forth can be implemented, but that depends on the software vendor you choose for the client-to-site VPN solution.

Design Patterns

Now that you are aware of the various options for setting up VPN connections on AWS, let's look at some scenarios requiring the use of VPN.

Connecting an on-premises network to a VPC This is the standard and the most common scenario for which VPN is used. In their journey to AWS, most customers operate in a hybrid mode, where on-premises applications need to be able to communicate with the applications in the VPC. By creating a VPN connection, you can enable this communication in a secure way without much setup lead time. It is recommended that you use AWS-managed VPN endpoints (VGWs) at the AWS end.

Connecting an on-premises network to a VPC: very high VPN throughput If you are looking for very high throughput for your hybrid IT connectivity to AWS, it is recommended that you set up AWS Direct Connect. AWS Direct Connect, which will be discussed in greater detail in the Chapter 5, "AWS Direct Connect," is a service that allows you to set up dedicated connectivity between your data center and AWS, providing you with bandwidths up to 10 Gbps over a single circuit. If you require a high-speed VPN over the Internet and have an Internet connection to support it, you should use the Amazon EC2 instance-based VPN connection option with horizontal scaling.

Connecting an on-premises network to a VPC: non-IPsec protocol If you have set up an existing VPN infrastructure for your remote sites using a different Layer 3 VPN protocol like DMVPN or GRE, you can use the same protocol to connect a VPC to your network. This connection can be achieved using the VPN termination on an Amazon EC2 instance option. The VPN software running on the Amazon EC2 instance should support this protocol.

Connecting an on-premises network to a VPC: advanced threat protection Under some scenarios, you may want to enable advanced threat protection on your VPN termination endpoint in the VPC. For example, you want a third-party vendor to have access to resources inside your VPC using VPN, but you want to run threat analysis on every packet that comes from the remote site because you consider the third-party vendor network an untrusted zone. In this scenario, you will want to terminate the VPN on an Amazon EC2 instance and load the Amazon EC2 instance with software that can perform this threat analysis.

Layer 3 encryption between Amazon EC2 instances A VPC is a private network, and traffic within a customer's VPC is completely isolated and not visible to any other customer. Some compliance requirements might dictate that all traffic between Amazon EC2 virtual machines should be encrypted, however. The ideal way to do this is to enable

TLS communication between Amazon EC2 instances in the VPC. In the event that Layer 3 encryption is desired, a VPN mesh will have to be set up between all Amazon EC2 instances. Every instance will have an inside tunnel IP address that will belong to the overlay VPN network. You will have to use this IP address for data flow between instances. For this implementation, VPN software will have to be installed on each Amazon EC2 instance. The VPN software can be open source software or third-party software of your choice. You are responsible for the set up and maintenance of the solution.

Enable multicast in Amazon VPC The Amazon VPC service doesn't presently permit multicast or broadcast traffic. In the event that you have an application that uses multicast to function, you can leverage GRE tunnels to create a mesh VPN overlay network between your Amazon EC2 instances. Multicast traffic can flow over this overlay network. Multicast is simulated by leveraging many unicast flows. This can be easily achieved using the available IP_GRE tunnel module or built into the kernel when using Linux operating systems. This is also a customer-managed solution. You are responsible for the set up and maintenance of the solution.

L3 encryption over AWS Direct Connect Traffic over AWS Direct Connect is not encrypted by default because the link is completely private and isolated. There are some compliance standards that might require data to be encrypted, however. As mentioned earlier, a common way to solve this problem is to use Layer 4 encryption protocols like Transport Layer Security (TLS). In the event that Layer 3 encryption is desirable, an IPsec VPN can help. An IPsec VPN connection can be easily set up over AWS Direct Connect. You will create an IPsec connection to the VGW as explained in the AWS-managed VPN option, but the actual traffic flow will be over AWS Direct Connect. A VIF has to be created over AWS Direct Connect for accessing resources inside AWS. VGW endpoints can be accessed over public VIF. Chapter 5 provides more details on how VIFs work. Further details on encryption over Direct Connect can be found in Chapter 5, "AWS Direct Connect" and Chapter 12, "Hybrid Architectures."

Transitive routing Transit is a word most commonly used to describe scenarios where traffic originating from network A reaches network C by crossing, or "transiting," through network B. This scenario is useful in cases where you want network B to have visibility into all communications between networks A and C for security reasons. As shown in Figure 4.17, such functionality doesn't natively exist in AWS as of this writing. Traffic from VPC A destined to VPC C cannot flow via VPC B. This is due to the non-transitive functionality of AWS networking endpoints like VPC Peering, VGW, VPC Endpoints, and Internet gateway. In general, these endpoints allow traffic to flow only to VPCs to which they are directly connected (and in the case of VGW, also to the remote networks for which it has routes). Any other VPC traffic will be automatically dropped.

FIGURE 4.17 Transitive routing

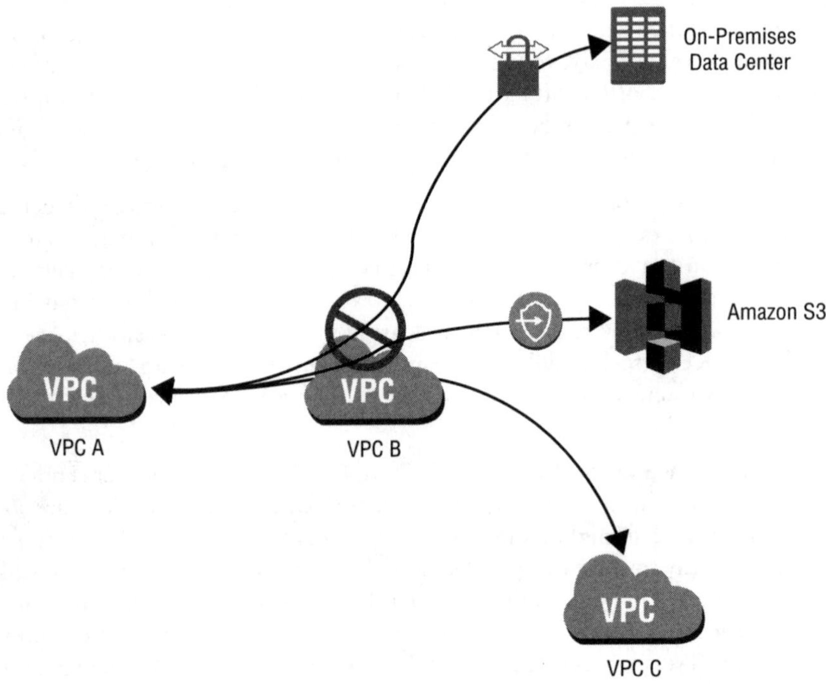

As shown in Figure 4.18, one way to overcome this is to set up an overlay network using VPNs. Let's take the scenario where VPC A wants to communicate with VPC C but all traffic must pass through VPC B for traffic monitoring and threat assessment. In order to enable this flow, an Amazon EC2 instance-based VPN termination endpoint in VPC B will act as the transit point. Traffic originating in VPC A will be tunneled to this Amazon EC2 instance in VPC B, where it will then be tunneled to VPC C.

Within VPCs A and C, you can use either a VGW or an Amazon EC2 instance as the VPN endpoints. This transitive flow is made possible because the actual destination of the packet (VPC C) in this case is hidden and encapsulated inside an outer VPN header that contains VPC B as its destination. This outer header is allowed to pass via the AWS gateway endpoints like VGW or a peering gateway.

Note that although VGW is used as a VPN termination endpoint, it is a non-transitive endpoint, hence the transit point has to be an Amazon EC2 instance. This Amazon EC2 instance can also be your security and threat protection endpoint. You should consider high availability and scalability when designing such a solution because this transit point will be the weakest link in your architecture with regard to throughput and availability. Additional details on the transit VPC architecture is covered in Chapter 12.

FIGURE 4.18 Enabling transitive routing in AWS

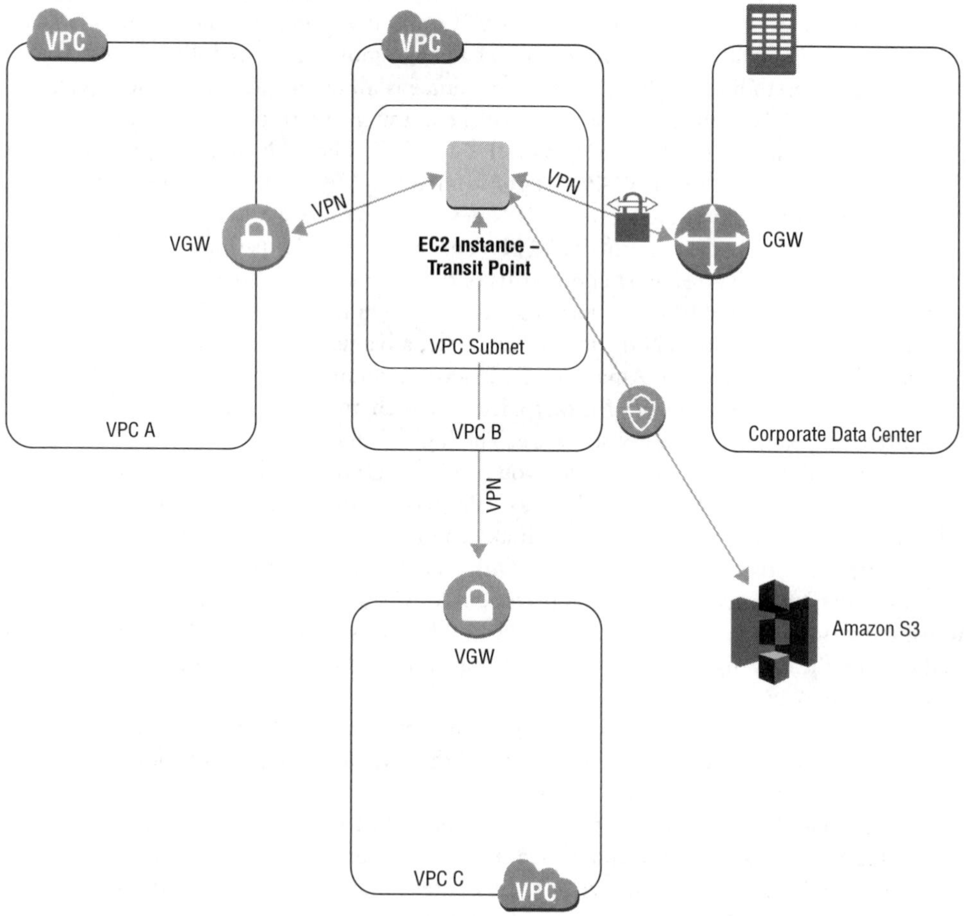

Summary

There are two kinds of VPN architectures discussed in this chapter. The first is site-to-site VPN, which allows you to set up a VPN connection between a VPC and your data center. Any resources inside your data center should then be able to access resources inside the VPC. There are two general ways to terminate a site-to-site VPN connection on AWS. The first is by using an AWS-managed VPN endpoint called a VGW. The second is by using an Amazon EC2 instance-based VPN termination.

A VGW is a managed gateway endpoint for your VPC, and it is responsible for all hybrid IT connectivity involving VPN and AWS Direct Connect. You can create a standalone (detached) VGW without a preexisting VPC, and it will behave like a router/gateway. VGW has high availability built into it, and it can span multiple Availability Zones. Uptime, high availability, patching, and maintenance is all taken care of by AWS. AWS VPN leveraging VGW comes with support for the latest cryptography suite. It also supports both static and dynamic (BGP) routing as well as NAT-T. The VPN creation process is very simple and requires no IPsec or BGP configuration at the AWS end. You can download a prepopulated configuration file for your VPN device from the AWS Management Console.

You can also terminate a site-to-site VPN on an Amazon EC2 instance rather than use an AWS-managed VPN. You may choose this option if you are looking to leverage a different VPN technology than IPsec for your tunnels, or if you have a requirement demanding additional features on the VPN device (for example, advanced threat protection). To set this up, you will have to launch an Amazon EC2 instance and manually install the VPN software. You can also leverage AWS Marketplace to launch an Amazon EC2 instance automatically with pre-deployed VPN software. The high availability and scaling of this option is your responsibility. Using automation, you can build a failover cluster consisting of multiple Amazon EC2 instances that will act as VPN termination endpoints. If one instance fails, automated scripts should be able to make changes to the VPC route table to point the VPN traffic to the secondary instance. Only one Amazon EC2 instance can be used as a VPN gateway for a given destination prefix per VPC subnet. When planning for Active/Active setup or when horizontally scaling the number of Amazon EC2 VPN instances, you need to plan a traffic distribution strategy by splitting traffic bound for multiple prefixes among the Amazon EC2 instances.

At the customer end, you can leverage your on-premises VPN termination device to terminate a VPN connection. It is recommended that you use two physical devices spread across multiple data centers for redundancy.

The second VPN architecture we discussed was client-to-site or remote access VPN. This architecture allows remote end devices to access resources inside your VPC. You will have to use an Amazon EC2 instance as the VPN termination endpoint for this option. Deployment, high availability, and scaling for this option are similar to the site-to-site VPN termination for an Amazon EC2 scenario.

There are several design patterns relevant to the usage of VPN in the cloud, which vary by use case and customer requirements. For the standard use case of connecting your on-premises data center to a VPC, it is recommended to use the AWS-managed VPN option. If you require the same connectivity but with support for very high VPN throughput, you should leverage Amazon EC2-based VPN termination. For scenarios requiring the use of non-IPsec VPN protocol or advanced features on the VPN device, you should leverage an Amazon EC2-based VPN termination endpoint as well. If encryption or multicast is required inside a given VPC between Amazon EC2 instances, an overlay network will be required using Amazon EC2-based VPN termination. Amazon VPC does not natively allow transitive routing (that is, VPC A cannot communicate to a different network by transiting an intermediary VPC B), though a VPN overlay can be used to enable it. An Amazon EC2 instance will act as a transit point for the transitive routing. The high availability and scalability of this Amazon EC2 instance is your responsibility, although it can be automated using scripts.

Exam Essentials

Know the different VPN termination options available. You can terminate VPN on a VGW or on an Amazon EC2 instance. An AWS VPN terminating on a VGW is a managed solution; AWS takes care of IPsec and BGP configuration as well as uptime, availability, and patching/maintenance of the VPN termination endpoint. When terminating a VPN on an Amazon EC2 instance, you are responsible for deploying the software, VPN configuration, routing, high availability, and scaling.

Know the features of an AWS-managed VPN. An AWS-managed VPN offers a strong cryptography suite, including AES 256. It also supports BGP protocol and NAT-T. It can act as a hub router for connecting multiple remote networks, a configuration known as AWS VPN CloudHub.

Know the high-availability model of an AWS-managed VPN. An AWS-managed VPN comes with built-in redundancy across two Availability Zones. When you create a VPN connection, two endpoints on the VGW are made available. VPN tunnels to both of these endpoints should be created for high availability. Failover is automatic and taken care of by AWS behind the scenes.

Know the steps required to establish a VPN connection to VGW. Creating an AWS-managed VPN is quick and easy. You navigate to the AWS Management Console or use an API to create a VPN connection. You will be prompted to enter various IPsec and routing parameters. You can also download a configuration file for your on-premises device from the AWS Management Console.

Know the steps required to terminate a VPN on an Amazon EC2 instance. VPN connection termination on an Amazon EC2 instance option requires you to create an Amazon EC2 instance and install the VPN software on it. This can be done manually or by using AWS Marketplace. You will have to configure IPsec and routing on the instance.

Know the failover architecture for Amazon EC2-based VPN termination. You will have to set up multiple Amazon EC2 instances for the purpose of high availability. Only one Amazon EC2 instance can be used per subnet for a given destination prefix. For that destination prefix, you have to set up Amazon EC2 instances in Active/Standby mode with a monitoring script to detect failure and perform failover steps.

Know the scaling architectures for Amazon EC2-based VPN termination. Vertical scaling can be achieved by stopping the Amazon EC2 instance and changing its size. For horizontal scaling, you have to decide on a strategy to divide traffic among multiple Amazon EC2 instances. You can also use architectures where your next hop is a single Amazon EC2 instance, which then sends all traffic over GRE to multiple Amazon EC2 instances for actual IPsec encryption.

Know the advantages and disadvantages of Amazon EC2-based VPN termination. You may choose to terminate a VPN on Amazon EC2 if you desire to use a non-IPsec VPN protocol (such as GRE) or if you want additional features on the VPN device (for example, advanced threat protection). The Amazon EC2-based VPN option is also applicable when very high VPN throughput is required or transitive routing architectures will be built.

Know the details of how to set up VPN on the customer side. VPN setup on the customer's on-premises side can be achieved using an existing VPN termination device.

Know the options available to set up a client-to-site VPN. A client-to-site VPN can be set up by terminating a VPN on an Amazon EC2 instance.

Know the various scenarios in which a VPN can be leveraged. A VPN is used to connect on-premises networks to AWS. It can also be leveraged when encryption is required over AWS Direct Connect or for all traffic between Amazon EC2 instances. A VPN mesh overlay can enable multicast. You can also leverage a VPN to enable transitive routing on the Amazon VPC service.

Know the transitive routing restrictions within a VPC. Amazon VPC does not natively allow transitive routing (for example, VPC A cannot talk to VPC C or another remote network by transiting VPC B). Transitive routing is blocked at all gateway endpoints (for example, peering gateway, VGW, VPC, and Internet gateway).

Know how to create a VPN overlay to enable transitive routing functionality. To enable transitive routing, you will have to set up VPN connections between VPCs and use an Amazon EC2 instance as a transit point.

Test Taking Tip

You have notepaper, so make sure to use it. You can't take the paper out of the room, but you can use it to draw the scenarios presented in the questions into actual architectures, which will help you visualize the answers.

Resources to Review

VPN Sections of the Amazon VPC User Guide:

`http://docs.aws.amazon.com/AmazonVPC/latest/UserGuide/vpc-ug.pdf`

VPN Connections Documentation:

`http://docs.aws.amazon.com/AmazonVPC/latest/UserGuide/vpn-connections.html`

Multiple-VPC VPN Connection Sharing:

`https://aws.amazon.com/answers/networking/aws-multiple-vpc-vpn-connection-sharing/`

AWS Global Transit Network:

`https://aws.amazon.com/answers/networking/aws-global-transit-network/`

Single Region Multi-VPC Connectivity:

`https://aws.amazon.com/answers/networking/aws-single-region-multi-vpc-connectivity/`

You can follow these re:Invent networking talks on the AWS YouTube channel:

AWS re:Invent 2017: Deep Dive: AWS Direct Connect and VPNs (NET403):

`https://www.youtube.com/watch?v=eNxPhHTN8gY`

AWS re:Invent 2017: Extending Data Centers to the Cloud: Connectivity Options and Co (NET301):

`https://www.youtube.com/watch?v=lN2RybC9Vbk`

Exercises

The best way to learn about Virtual Private Network (VPN) connectivity options in AWS and how they compare to each other is to set them up and perform various tests against them. As part of the exercises in this chapter, we will set up the various VPN connectivity options that we discussed in this chapter.

EXERCISE 4.1

Create a VPN Connection Using the AWS-Managed VPN Option

In this exercise, you will create a VPN connection from a customer gateway located on-premises to a VPC, terminating on the VGW. This will allow on-premises resources access to EC2 instances inside the VPC. You will verify this by doing a ping test at the end of the exercise.

1. Navigate to the Amazon VPC dashboard of the AWS Management Console and create a new VGW.
2. Attach the VGW to an existing VPC.
3. In the Amazon VPC dashboard, navigate to Customer Gateways and create a new customer gateway. You will need to enter the IP address of the VPN endpoint at your end. If you are using an on-premises device, this will be the public-facing IP addresses of that device. If you are using an Amazon EC2 instance as the customer gateway, this will be the Elastic IP of the instance.
4. In the Amazon VPC dashboard, navigate to VPN Connections and create a new VPN connection. Provide the customer gateway, the routing type, and other required information.

EXERCISE 4.1 *(continued)*

5. Download the configuration file from the AWS Management Console and use this file to configure the customer gateway.
6. Enable VGW route propagation in the VPC subnet route tables.
7. Test ping connectivity between an Amazon EC2 instance in the VPC and a server behind the customer gateway. (Make sure ICMP echo traffic is permitted by the relevant VPC Security Groups and operating system firewalls.)

You have now successfully created a VPN connection terminating on a VGW, allowing access to EC2 instances inside the VPC from on-premises environments. The ping test in step 7 verifies this connectivity.

EXERCISE 4.2

Create a VPN Connection Using an Amazon EC2 Instance as the VPN Termination Endpoint

Prior to starting this exercise, browse through the various software options you have for provisioning a VPN solution on an Amazon EC2 instance. You can look at the AWS Marketplace for third-party vendor software or research open source VPN software on the Internet. Both Windows and Linux operating systems are supported. In this exercise, we will use the strongSwan open source software.

Look at the various Amazon EC2 instance types and choose the instance that you want to use for VPN termination. In this example, we will use a c4.large instance.

1. Navigate to the Amazon VPC dashboard, and create a VPC with public and private subnets. Launch a t2.nano EC2 instance in the private subnet. We will use this EC2 instance to test connectivity from an on-premises network at the end of this exercise.
2. Navigate to the Amazon EC2 dashboard of the AWS Management Console and launch an Amazon Linux AMI in a VPC. Choose c4.large as the Amazon EC2 instance type. Make sure that the instance is launched in a public subnet so that it has a route to the Internet gateway for Internet traffic. Associate an Elastic IP with the instance.
3. Disable source destination check on the instance from the Amazon EC2 instance dashboard and make sure that IP forwarding is enabled at the operating system level.
4. Use Secure Shell (SSH) to access the instance and install the strongSwan software.
5. Configure the strongSwan software with the right IPsec parameters in accordance with your on-premises VPN termination device. If you are using a VGW at the other end of the VPN tunnel, download a generic configuration file from the AWS Management Console for the VGW and use that to configure the Amazon EC2 instance.

6. Configure the VPC private subnet route table to point traffic toward the elastic network interface of the Amazon EC2 instance for the remote subnet.
7. Test ping connectivity from an on-premises server to the EC2 instance in the private subnet. (Make sure ICMP echo traffic is permitted by the relevant VPC Security Groups and operating system firewalls.)

You have now successfully created a VPN connection terminating on an EC2 instance allowing access to EC2 instances inside the VPC from on-premises environments. The ping test in step 7 verifies this connectivity.

EXERCISE 4.3

Connect Two Remote Networks Using a Detached VGW and VPN Connections Leveraging AWS VPN CloudHub

In this exercise, you will set up the architecture shown in the following graphic.

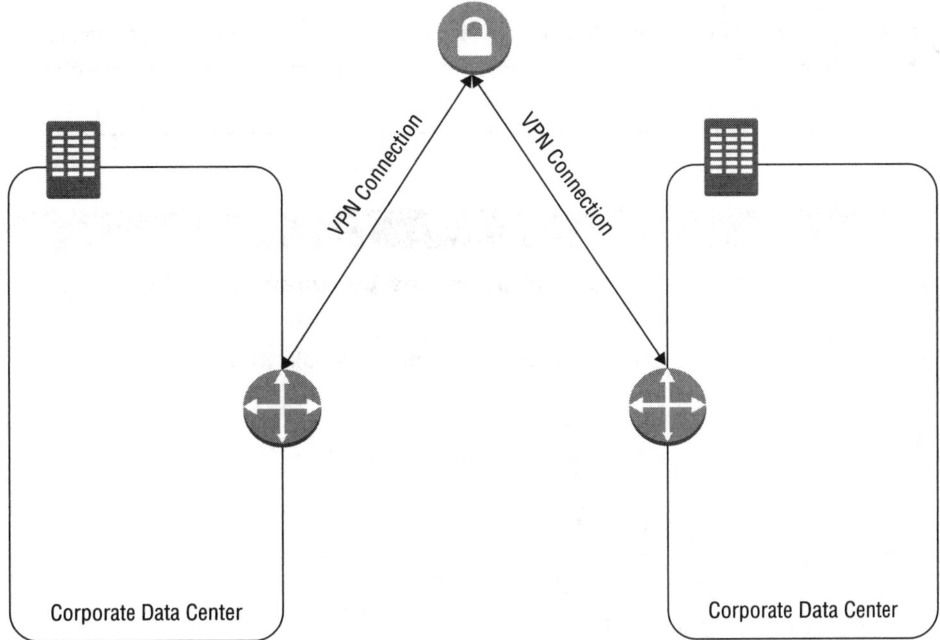

By building this architecture, you will learn how the CloudHub feature of the VGW can be used to connect two remote networks.

1. Navigate to the Amazon VPC dashboard in the AWS Management Console and create a new VGW.

EXERCISE 4.3 *(continued)*

2. In the Amazon VPC dashboard, navigate to Customer Gateways and create two new customer gateways. These customer gateways are the VPN termination endpoints at the remote networks.
3. In the Amazon VPC dashboard, navigate to VPN Connections and create a new VPN connection. Provide the customer gateway, the routing type, and other required information. Repeat this process for both of the customer gateways. A total of two VPN connections will be created—one per customer gateway.
4. Download the configuration file from the AWS Management Console and use this file to configure the two customer gateways.
5. VGW will automatically advertise routes learned from one customer gateway to the other customer gateway. Verify this functionality by looking at the route advertisements at any of the customer gateways.
6. Test connectivity between the two remote networks. A server behind one customer gateway should be able to ping another server behind the second customer gateway.

You have now successfully connected two remote networks using VGW. The connectivity test in step 6 should validate the setup. Any resources in these two remote networks should now be able to communicate.

EXERCISE 4.4

Create a VPN Overlay to Allow Connections Between Two VPCs via a Transit Point

In this exercise, you will set up the architecture shown in the following graphic.

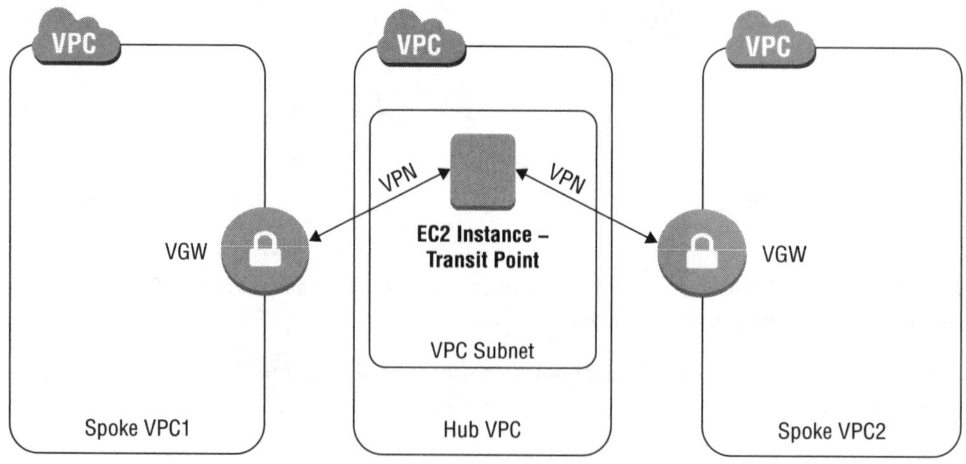

1. Navigate to the Amazon VPC dashboard in the AWS Management Console and create three VPCs: Spoke VPC1 and Spoke VPC2, and Hub VPC.
2. Navigate to the Amazon EC2 dashboard and launch an Amazon Linux AMI in the Hub VPC. Choose c4.large as the Amazon EC2 instance type. Make sure that the instance is launched in a public subnet that has a route to the Internet gateway for Internet traffic. Associate an Elastic IP with the instance.
3. Disable source destination check on the instance from the Amazon EC2 instance dashboard and make sure that IP forwarding is enabled at the operating system level.
4. Use SSH to access the instance and install VPN software that supports BGP routing. You can install Quagga for actual BGP routing. You will perform the actual IPsec and BGP configuration in a later step.
5. Configure the VPC route table so that traffic destined for the CIDR ranges of the two spoke VPCs is pointed toward the elastic network interface of the Amazon EC2 instance.
6. Repeat the following steps for Spoke VPC1 and Spoke VPC2.
7. Navigate to the Amazon VPC dashboard and create a new VGW.
8. Attach the VGW to Spoke VPC1 or Spoke VPC2.
9. In the Amazon VPC dashboard, navigate to Customer Gateways and create a new customer gateway. Enter the Elastic IP of the Amazon EC2 instance that you created earlier.
10. In the Amazon VPC dashboard, navigate to VPN connections and create a new VPN connection. Provide the customer gateway, the routing type, and other required information.
11. Download the configuration file from the AWS Management Console.
12. Enable VGW route propagation in the VPC subnet route tables.
13. Use SSH to access the Amazon EC2 instance and configure IPsec and BGP using the configuration files that you downloaded in the earlier step. Perform this configuration for both Spoke VPC1 and Spoke VPC2.
14. Launch two Amazon EC2 instances in the spoke VPC subnets and test connectivity between them.

You have now successfully set up a transitive routing architecture leveraging VPN overlay connectivity. This is verified in step 14. All traffic that is sent between VPC 1 and VPC 2 will now flow via the transit EC2 instances.

Review Questions

1. What are the two endpoints that can be used to terminate a Virtual Private Network (VPN) on AWS? (Choose two.)
   - **A.** Amazon Elastic Compute Cloud (Amazon EC2) instance
   - **B.** AWS VPN CloudHub
   - **C.** Amazon Virtual Private Cloud (Amazon VPC)
   - **D.** Internet gateway
   - **E.** Virtual Private Gateway (VGW)

2. How many Virtual Private Network (VPN) tunnels have to be established to use the out-of-the-box high availability of an AWS-managed VPN option?
   - **A.** 1
   - **B.** 2
   - **C.** 3
   - **D.** 4

3. What are the routing mechanisms supported by a Virtual Private Gateway (VGW)? (Choose two.)
   - **A.** Open Shortest Path First (OSPF)
   - **B.** Border Gateway Protocol (BGP)
   - **C.** Static Routes
   - **D.** Routing Information Protocol Version 2 (RIPv2)
   - **E.** Enhanced Interior Gateway Routing Protocol (EIGRP)

4. Which of the following is the responsibility of AWS when you terminate a Virtual Private Network (VPN) on an Amazon Elastic Compute Cloud (Amazon EC2) instance?
   - **A.** Configure Internet Protocol Security (IPsec) parameters.
   - **B.** Manage redundancy and high availability of the VPN tunnel.
   - **C.** Manage scaling of the VPN tunnel.
   - **D.** Manage the underlying Amazon EC2 host health.

5. Which of the following steps is necessary to ensure proper routing when terminating a Virtual Private Network (VPN) on an Amazon Elastic Compute Cloud (Amazon EC2) instance?
   - **A.** Disable source destination check on the Amazon EC2 instance.
   - **B.** Enable source destination check on the Amazon EC2 instance.
   - **C.** Enable route propagation in a Virtual Private Cloud (VPC) subnet route table.
   - **D.** Enable enhanced networking mode on the Amazon EC2 instance.

6. You are tasked with setting up a VPN connection to a VPC from your on-premises data center. You have to purchase a new VPN termination device to be used as customer gateway. You are leveraging a Virtual Private Gateway at the AWS end. Which of the following must be supported by the hardware you choose to deploy on-premises for setting up the VPN connection?
   - **A.** BGP routing protocol
   - **B.** 802.1Q encapsulation standard
   - **C.** IPsec protocol
   - **D.** GRE protocol
7. When setting up a client-to-site Virtual Private Network (VPN) to access AWS resources, how can you achieve highest availability with least management overhead?
   - **A.** Leverage the high availability built into Virtual Private Gateway (VGW).
   - **B.** Configure client software to use a DNS name as a VPN termination endpoint. Map the DNS name to multiple IP addresses using Amazon Route 53 and set up health checks.
   - **C.** Configure client software to use an EC2 elastic IP as the VPN termination endpoint. Build in automation to detect failure, and move Elastic IP from the primary to the secondary EC2 instance.
   - **D.** Configure the client software to use an EC2 elastic IP as the VPN termination endpoint. Turn on EC2 auto-recovery on this instance.
8. Which AWS Cloud service is used for a client-to-site Virtual Private Network (VPN) considering minimum management overhead?
   - **A.** Virtual Private Gateway (VGW)
   - **B.** Amazon Elastic Compute Cloud (Amazon EC2)
   - **C.** AWS VPN CloudHub
   - **D.** Virtual Private Cloud (VPC) private endpoint
9. You are deploying an application on multiple Amazon Elastic Compute Cloud (Amazon EC2) instances. The application must be U.S. Health Insurance Portability and Accountability Act (HIPAA) compliant and requires end-to-end encryption in motion. The application runs on Transmission Control Protocol (TCP) port 7128. What is the most effective way to deploy the application?
   - **A.** Navigate to the Amazon EC2 instance's properties and check the encryption box.
   - **B.** Set up an Internet Protocol Security (IPsec) Virtual Private Network (VPN) between all Amazon EC2 instances in a mesh.
   - **C.** Use Secure Sockets Layer (SSL) to encrypt traffic at the application layer.
   - **D.** Enable encryption using an AWS KMS key for all Amazon EBS volumes.
10. Which of the following parameters are automatically generated when you create a Virtual Private Network (VPN) connection to a Virtual Private Gateway (VGW)?
    - **A.** VGW public IP
    - **B.** VGW Border Gateway Protocol (BGP) Autonomous System Number (ASN)
    - **C.** Inside tunnel IP addresses
    - **D.** Internet Protocol Security (IPsec) Pre-Shared Key (PSK)

AWS Direct Connect

THE AWS CERTIFIED ADVANCED NETWORKING – SPECIALTY EXAM OBJECTIVES COVERED IN THIS CHAPTER MAY INCLUDE, BUT ARE NOT LIMITED TO, THE FOLLOWING:

Domain 1.0: Design and Implement Hybrid IT Network Architectures at Scale

✓ **1.3 Explain the process to extend connectivity using AWS Direct Connect**

✓ **1.4 Evaluate design alternatives leveraging AWS Direct Connect**

✓ **1.5 Define routing policies for hybrid IT architectures**

Content may include the following:

- How to provision AWS Direct Connect connections
- Differences between private and public Virtual Interfaces (VIFs)
- Implementation of resilient connectivity

Domain 5: Design and Implement for Security and Compliance

✓ **5.4 Utilize encryption technologies to secure network communications**

Content may include the following:

- Implement encrypted Virtual Private Networks (VPNs)

What Is AWS Direct Connect?

AWS Direct Connect is a service that enables you to establish a dedicated network connection from sites—such as data centers, offices, or colocation environments—to AWS. In many cases, this service can reduce network costs, increase bandwidth throughput, and provide a more consistent network experience than Internet-based connections. AWS provides dedicated connections for this service at bandwidths of 1 Gbps and 10 Gbps. You are also able to use sub-1 Gbps hosted connections via AWS Direct Connect partners that have already established an interconnect with AWS.

Core Concepts

You must support 802.1Q VLANs across 1 Gbps or 10 Gbps Ethernet connections. Your network must also support Border Gateway Protocol (BGP) and BGP MD5 authentication. You can optionally configure Bidirectional Forwarding Detection (BFD) on your network.

802.1Q Virtual Local Area Networks (VLANs)

802.1Q is an Ethernet standard as defined by the Institute of Electrical and Electronics Engineers (IEEE) that enables Virtual Local Area Networks (VLANs) on an Ethernet network. It uses the addition of a VLAN tag to the header of an Ethernet frame to define membership of a particular VLAN. Networking equipment that supports this standard is then able to maintain separation for the associated traffic at Layer 2.

Border Gateway Protocol

Border Gateway Protocol (BGP) is a routing protocol used to exchange network routing and reachability information, either within the same or a different autonomous system. This is known as Internal BGP (iBGP) and External BGP (eBGP), respectively. BGP is defined by RFC 4271 - A Border Gateway Protocol 4 (BGP-4).

Bidirectional Forwarding Detection

Bidirectional Forwarding Detection (BFD) is a mechanism used to support fast failover of connections in the event of a failure in the forwarding path between two routers. If a failure occurs, then BFD notifies the associated routing protocols to cause a recalculation of available routes, which reduces convergence time.

Physical Connectivity

Physical connectivity to AWS Direct Connect is established either at an AWS Direct Location or via a Partner.

AWS Direct Connect Locations

All AWS Regions have associated AWS Direct Connect locations. The locations are provided by third-party colocation providers, also known as *Carrier Neutral Facilities (CNFs)* or *Carrier Hotels*. An authoritative list of these locations is maintained on the AWS website within the AWS Direct Connect Product Details page.

These locations host multiple devices used to provide the physical connectivity from your location to AWS. This equipment is connected to the AWS global backbone network and provides you with fully diverse and resilient connectivity to all AWS Regions (with the exception of China).

You can establish multiple physical connections to AWS via the same location. AWS will make its best efforts to provision each additional connection automatically for an account on an independent AWS device. If different accounts are used for each connection, then the AWS Management Console can help to identify on which AWS device a connection terminates. AWS support can change this assignment if requested via a support case. An AWS Direct Connect location always has two AWS devices at a minimum.

You can also establish multiple physical connections to multiple AWS Direct Connect locations. This option provides you with geographical diversity for your connections, providing the highest level of redundancy.

Dedicated Connections

Within the AWS Direct Connect location, AWS devices provide dedicated connections with a bandwidth capability of 1 Gbps and 10 Gbps. These are presented as Single-Mode Optical Fiber (SMF) ports using a wavelength of 1310 nm on the AWS equipment.

The port type used for 1 Gbps connections is 1000base-LX. The port type used for 10 Gbps connections is 10Gbase-LR.

To use a dedicated connection, the equipment that is connected to these ports must support these same capabilities. Depending on the overall solution, this may be equipment you own within the location or equipment that is being used by your AWS Direct Connect partner.

Provisioning Process

You can set up an AWS Direct Connect connection in one of the following ways:

- At an AWS Direct Connect location.
- Through a member of the AWS Partner Network (APN) or a network carrier.
- Through a hosted connection provided by a member of the APN.

A partner in the APN can help you establish network circuits between an AWS Direct Connect location and your data center, office, or colocation environment.

Requesting a Connection

The process to request a connection is self-service and fully documented in the AWS Direct Connect User Guide. You must first identify the AWS Region to which you wish to connect and the specific AWS Direct Connect location. You can then use any of the supported methods—AWS Management Console, Application Programming Interface (API), or AWS Command Line Interface (AWS CLI)—to request a new connection. AWS may require additional information at this stage, so you should monitor the primary email address for your AWS account for such an email and provide an appropriate reply.

Download Your Letter of Authorization

AWS will provision your port within 72 hours, after which you will be able to download the Letter of Authorization – Connecting Facility Assignment (LOA-CFA or simply LOA). This document provides specific demarcation details for your assigned port within the facility that will provide connectivity to AWS.

Cross-Connect to the AWS Port

The AWS Direct Connect locations each use their own defined process for arranging physical connectivity between different organizations within their facilities. These connections are known as *cross-connects*, and they are typically passive-fiber connections between the AWS equipment and either your equipment or that of your AWS Direct Connect partner. In some cases, the AWS Direct Connect location is listed as a campus of buildings. In that case, a cross-connect can provide connectivity from any site on the campus back to the AWS equipment. Note that a campus site does not imply that AWS has equipment within every building in the campus, so the campus should be viewed as a single "location" from an architectural and risk- assessment perspective.

Cross-connects must typically be ordered by an organization that has a physical presence within the AWS Direct Connect location and a commercial agreement with the location provider. If you are using an AWS Direct Connect partner to provide this remote connectivity, it will be the partner that places the order for the cross-connect. You will need to provide them with a copy of the LOA-CFA document to enable them to place the order.

Once the connection is in place, you should see a "link up" and good light levels being received at your equipment. The AWS Management Console will also reflect the status of the connection as either down or available. The AWS Direct Connect monitoring tools in the AWS Management Console can be used to validate the appropriate transmit and receive light levels for 10 Gbps connections. Figure 5.1 illustrates the components involved in establishing the physical connection to AWS.

FIGURE 5.1 Physical components of AWS Direct Connect

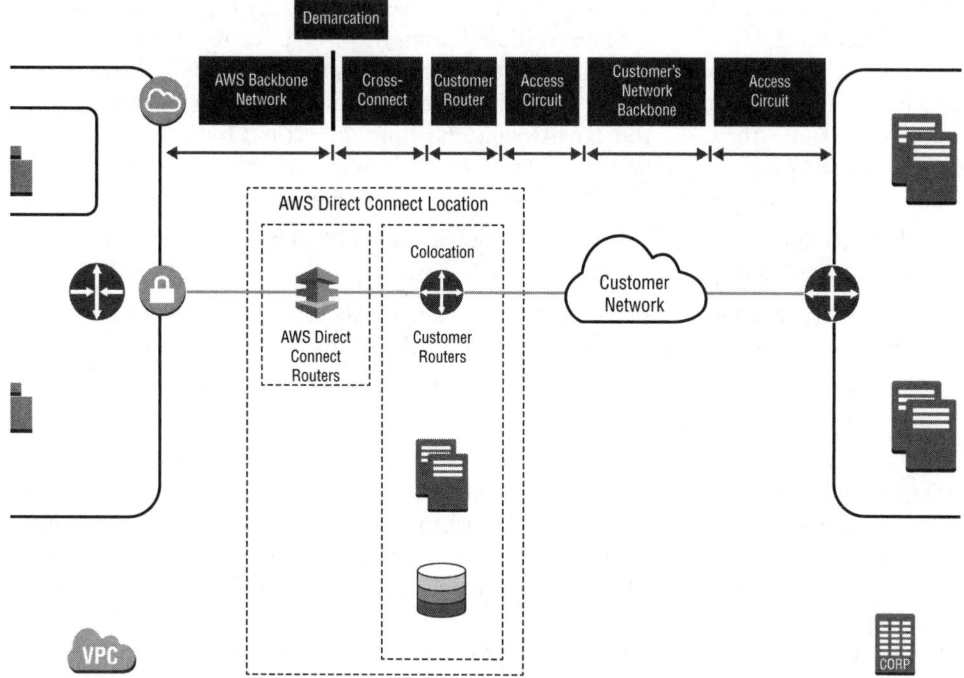

Multiple Connections

You may choose to use multiple AWS Direct Connect connections to increase the resilience and bandwidth of your environment. These connections can be one of the following:

- At the same location, on the same AWS device
- At the same location, on a different AWS device
- At a different location

When provisioning multiple connections at the same AWS Direct Connect location, AWS will automatically provision these additional ports on different devices where possible. This enables a level of resilience to interface failure, device failure, or planned maintenance. You may also choose the "Associate with Link Aggregation Group" (LAG) option when creating the additional connections. This will ensure that the connection is allocated on the same AWS device such that it can be used with a LAG.

When additional connections are provisioned on different AWS devices or in different AWS Direct Connection locations, multiple connections provide a level of resilience against a potential location-level failure in addition to the benefits of connecting via different devices.

Link Aggregation Groups

A *Link Aggregation Group (LAG)* is a logical interface that uses the Link Aggregation Control Protocol (LACP) to aggregate multiple 1 Gbps or 10 Gbps connections at a single AWS Direct Connect location, allowing you to treat them as a single, managed connection. You can create a LAG from existing connections, or you can provision new connections. After you've created the LAG, you can associate existing connections (whether standalone or part of another LAG) with the LAG.

The following rules apply to LAGs:

- All connections in the LAG must use the same bandwidth. The following bandwidths are supported: 1 Gbps and 10 Gbps.
- You can have a maximum of four connections in a LAG. Each connection in the LAG counts toward your overall connection limit for the region.
- All connections in the LAG must terminate at the same AWS Direct Connect location and on the same AWS device.

All LAGs have an attribute that determines the minimum number of connections in the LAG that must be operational for the LAG itself to be operational. By default, new LAGs have this attribute set to 0. You can update your LAG to specify a different value. Doing so means that your entire LAG becomes non-operational if the number of operational connections falls below this threshold. This attribute can be used to prevent overutilization of the remaining connections.

For example, if you provision a LAG with four connections and you configure the minimum number of connections to be two, should there be a failure on two of the connections, the overall LAG operation status remains "Up" and passing traffic. Should a third connection fail, then the operational status will be changed to "Down," even though a single connection remains available. This will enable any failover paths that you have in place to take over, avoiding the potential of the single remaining circuit becoming congested and impacting performance.

AWS Direct Connect Partners

AWS Direct Connect partners are members of the AWS Partner Network (APN) that can provide connectivity to an AWS Direct Connect location within the geographies they service. The method by which they deliver this service can vary in terms of the technologies used. Their core capability is to extend the Ethernet ports presented at the AWS Direct Connect location to your on-premises infrastructure.

Some AWS Direct Connect partners specialize in local telecoms-style delivery, while others focus on delivery of colocation facilities or data centers.

Beyond extending Ethernet ports from an AWS Direct Connect location, these partners have an additional capability to provide hosted connections at bandwidth increments less than those available from a dedicated connection (1 Gb/10 Gb). Multiple hosted connections are combined and delivered to the partner using a physical partner *interconnect*. The interconnect is shared between those customers with hosted connections configured and allocated specific bandwidths by the partner.

Hosted Connections

A hosted connection is available via AWS Direct Connect partners at bandwidth increments less than those available from a dedicated 1 Gbps or 10 Gbps connection. These are provided using a physical partner interconnect on which these hosted connections are provisioned. Partner interconnects have similar characteristics to dedicated connections; however, they can only be ordered by approved partners using a specifically-enabled partner console.

Hosted connections can be provided at bandwidths of 50 Mbps, 100 Mbps, 200 Mbps, 300 Mbps, 400 Mbps, and 500 Mbps. The provisioning process differs from dedicated connections. Because the physical interconnect is already in place, there is no need for you to download the LOA-CFA or arrange for cross-connects to AWS. The partner interconnects are shared and support multiple AWS customers' hosted connections.

The process for ordering a hosted connection begins with speaking to an AWS Direct Connect partner. They will establish how the hosted connection will be delivered to your own location and with the appropriate interface types. Hosted connections are often used by AWS Direct Connect partners to enable rapid delivery of AWS connectivity to existing Multiprotocol Label Switching (MPLS) Virtual Private Network (VPN)-based solutions.

Once the method of delivery has been agreed on, you must provide your 12-digit AWS account number to the AWS Direct Connect partner, who will use this to provision the hosted connection on their interconnect. The hosted connection will be presented in your AWS account for the appropriate AWS Region in preparation for you to accept it. As part of the provisioning process, the AWS Direct Connect partner will have chosen an 802.1Q VLAN identifier on the interconnect. This may not be relevant depending on how you are consuming the service, and some partners may translate this VLAN to a different one at the point of service presentation to customers.

Accepting the hosted connection in your AWS account enables the billing for the associated port-hours and any data transfer to commence. This is charged on your monthly AWS bill and may be in addition to any fees the AWS Direct Connect partner charges for the service they are providing.

Logical Connectivity

You must create a virtual interface to begin using your AWS Direct Connect connection.

Virtual Interfaces

In order to access AWS resources over an AWS Direct Connect connection, a BGP peering relationship must be established between the AWS device and your customer router and then appropriate routes exchanged. In order to enable these actions, you need to create a *Virtual Interface (VIF)*. A VIF is a configuration consisting primarily of an 802.1Q VLAN and the options for an associated BGP session. It contains all of the configuration parameters required for both the AWS end of a connection and your end of the connection. AWS Direct Connect supports two types of VIFs:

- Public VIFs
- Private VIFs

A *public VIF* enables your network to reach all of the AWS public IP addresses on the AWS global backbone network in all regions (with the exception of China).

A *private VIF* enables your network to reach resources that have been provisioned within your Virtual Private Cloud (VPC) via their private IP address.

Both types of VIFs require the following to be specified as configuration parameters:

Type (public or private) Here you choose whether you want to create a public VIF or private VIF.

VIF name You can specify any arbitrary name. It is a good practice to have a naming strategy that will allow easy identification of resources.

VIF owner (my AWS account or another AWS account) For private VIFs (when choosing the owner to be "My AWS Account"), you will be prompted to choose the Virtual Private Gateway (VGW) or Direct Connect Gateway.

When choosing "Another AWS Account," you will be prompted to enter the AWS account ID.

VLAN You can select any VLAN ID. On a given AWS Direct Connect connection, the same VLAN ID cannot be reused for two different VIFs.

For hosted connections, this has already been selected by your AWS Direct Connect partner and will therefore be grayed out.

Address family (IPv4 or IPv6) When choosing IPv4 or IPv6, you will be prompted for additional information specific to that address family. This establishes a peering for that particular address family. A second peering can be added after the VIF has been created for the other address family.

For Private VIFs, you can specify private IP addresses.

For public VIFs, you need to specify public IP addresses you own or that have been obtained by opening an AWS support case.

The BGP Autonomous System Number (ASN) for your network Any ASN can be chosen; however, it is recommended that you use either an ASN that you own or a private ASN

(64512 – 65535). If you are using a public ASN on a public VIF, you must own it; ownership will be verified as part of the creation process.

BGP MD5 key (can be auto-generated) MD5 authentication is configured between two BGP peers, which causes each segment sent on the TCP connection between the peers to be validated. The password on both BGP peers must be the same, otherwise a connection will not be established.

For public VIFs, you will also be prompted to provide the prefixes that you want to advertise.

You can create multiple VIFs on a dedicated AWS Direct Connect connection. If you are using a hosted connection from an AWS Direct Connect partner, you can only create a single VIF and may need to request additional hosted connections for future requirements. Each VIF is associated with a single VGW (which is attached to a single VPC or a Direct Connect Gateway).

AWS Direct Connect supports a Maximum Transmission Unit (MTU) of up to 1,500 bytes at the IP layer and 1,522 bytes at the physical connection layer (14 bytes Ethernet header + 4 bytes VLAN tag + 1,500 bytes IP datagram + 4 bytes Frame Check Sequence [FCS]).

Public Virtual Interfaces

Public Virtual Interfaces (VIFs) enable your network to reach all of the AWS public IP addresses for the AWS Region with which your AWS Direct Connect connection is associated. In addition, public VIFs are also enabled for "Global" capabilities, which allows you to receive BGP announcements for all AWS public IPs globally. BGP communities are then used both to identify the source of the AWS prefix announcements and for you to control where your announcements are propagated within the AWS backbone network.

Public VIFs are typically used to enable direct network access to services that are not reachable via a private IP address within your own VPC. These include, but are not limited to, Amazon Simple Storage Service (Amazon S3), Amazon DynamoDB, Amazon Simple Queue Services (Amazon SQS), and the public endpoints used to provide AWS-managed VPN services.

When creating a public VIF with an address family type of IPv4, you must specify public IP addresses for both the Amazon router peer IP and your router peer IP. When creating (or adding a peering) to your VIF for the address family IPv6, AWS will always auto-generate the peering IP addresses using Amazon-owned IPv6 address space.

You must also specify the IP address prefixes you plan to announce to AWS over this type of VIF. This enables AWS to verify that you are the owner of these IP addresses and that you are authorized to announce them. If the IP addresses are listed in the regional Internet registries as belonging to another entity, then you will receive an email to the primary email address on your AWS account with further instructions. If you do not have your own public IP addresses to use for the peering and to announce, you should raise a case with AWS support.

The number of prefixes that AWS will announce to you can vary by region and whether your account is enabled for inter-region capabilities. In return, AWS will accept up to 1,000 prefixes from you.

Once AWS receives a BGP announcement from you, all network traffic from AWS destined to the announced prefix will be routed via AWS Direct Connect. This includes traffic from other AWS customers using public or Elastic IP addresses on their Amazon Elastic Compute Cloud (Amazon EC2) instances, traffic routed via Network Address Translation (NAT) gateways, AWS Lambda functions that make outbound connections, and more. You should configure your routers and firewalls appropriately to accept or reject this traffic per your own routing policies. AWS does not re-advertise customer prefixes to other customers that have been received over AWS Direct Connect public VIFs. The prefixes that AWS announces do change, and a current list can be obtained using the public `ip-ranges.json` file maintained and available at `https://ip-ranges.amazonaws.com/ip-ranges.json`.

You could use the `ip-ranges.json` file to build filters on your routers and only install routes for particular services or regions.

Private Virtual Interfaces

Private Virtual Interfaces (VIFs) enable your network to reach resources that have been provisioned within your VPC via their private IP address. A private VIF is associated with the VGW for your VPC to enable this connectivity. Because this is a private VIF, the BGP peer IP addresses do not need to be public and therefore can be defined by you at the time of creation for IPv4 or automatically generated for both IPv4 and IPv6.

Private VIFs are used to enable direct network access to services that are reachable via an IP address within your own VPC. These include, but are not limited to, Amazon EC2, Amazon Relational Database Service (Amazon RDS), and Amazon Redshift.

When the BGP session comes up, your peer router will receive announcements for all Classless Inter-Domain Routing (CIDR) address ranges associated with your VPC. You are able to announce up to 100 prefixes to AWS over a private VIF, including a default (0.0.0.0/0) route. These routes are used by the VGW and can optionally be propagated into route tables within your VPC. The routes also contribute to CloudHub within the VGW, which enables you to route between multiple AWS Direct Connect private VIFs, VPN connections, and the attached VPC.

Because this is a private VIF, it is acceptable to announce any prefix regardless of whether it is considered public or private address space and irrespective of IP ownership. In a VPC, more specific routes always take preference over default routes, hence propagation or use of these routes in your VPC will take precedence over the default route to the

Internet via the Internet gateway. Take care if you're using non-RFC1918 (or other private address space) that might otherwise also exist somewhere on the Internet.

If you need to advertise more than 100 prefixes, then you should either summarize your routes to reduce the total number of prefixes or advertise a default route. You can then apply more specific routes within the route tables for your VPC with a target of the VGW.

Direct Connect Gateway

A *Direct Connect Gateway* enables you to combine Private VIFs with multiple VGWs in the local or in remote regions. You can use this feature to establish connectivity from an AWS Direct Connect location in one geographical zone to an AWS Region in a different geographical zone. This is in addition to being able to use a single private VIF to access multiple VPCs in multiple AWS Regions (in the same account). Your router will establish a single BGP session with the Direct Connect Gateway and, from there, receive announcements for all associated VPCs. Note that the Direct Connect Gateway does not enable CloudHub between the associated private VIFs and VGWs. This is shown in Figure 5.2.

FIGURE 5.2 Direct Connect Gateway

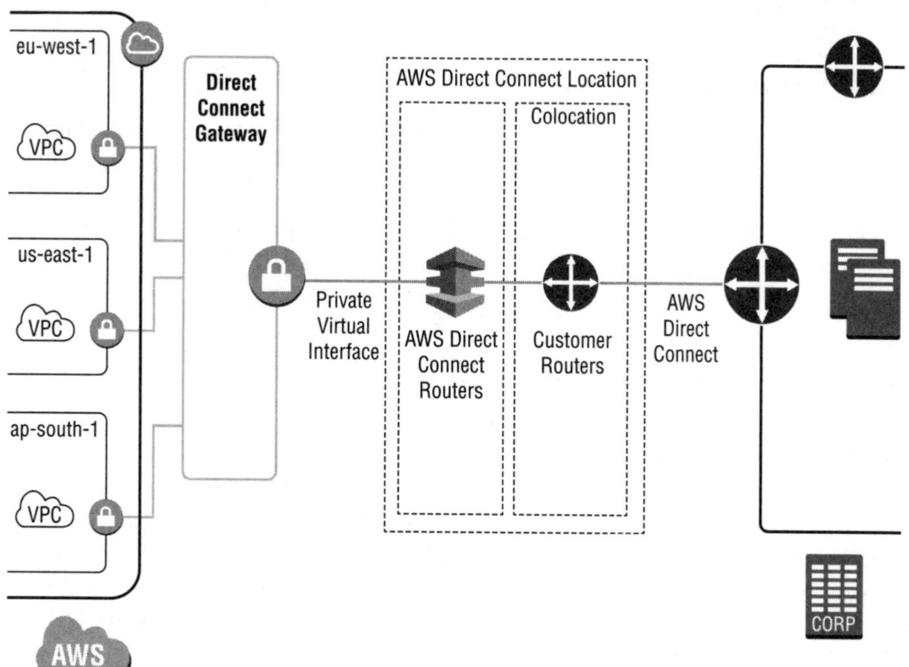

Hosted Virtual Interfaces

When creating a VIF (both public and private) you are able to choose the VIF owner. This can be "My AWS Account" or "Another AWS Account." When choosing "Another AWS Account," you are prompted to provide a 12-digit account number. All of the BGP configuration is still completed in the account that owns the AWS Direct Connect connection; however, when choosing another account, that VIF becomes a *hosted VIF*. The recipient of the hosted VIF must choose to accept it and, in the case of a private VIF, choose which VGW to associate it with. A hosted VIF results in all related data transfer charges being charged to the recipient account holder's AWS bill. Note that the port-hour charges are always charged to the owner of the AWS Direct Connect connections.

Resilient Connectivity

Each AWS Direct Connect location has diverse and resilient connectivity paths to the associated AWS Region. This connectivity uses the AWS global backbone network that enables the various inter-region features previously discussed. It is your responsibility as an AWS customer to decide how much resilience is appropriate regarding how you reach AWS Direct Connect locations and the devices within them. When architecting a solution to cope with failure, it's important to plan for maximum 50 percent usage of available bandwidth such that any failover to secondary paths can carry the full load.

Single Connection

A *single physical connection* will provide high bandwidth and consistent latency. It does not provide, however, resilience to circuit, hardware or device failure, or alternative traffic paths when AWS undertakes planned or emergency maintenance on the associated device. If your architecture consists of a single AWS Direct Connect connection, AWS would always recommend using a VPN connection as a backup path for network traffic to your VPC. An example deployment using a single connection is shown in Figure 5.3.

Dual Connection: Single Location

Dual connections at a single location can be configured in two different ways: as a LAG or as independent connections.

When used as a LAG, multiple connections are combined and behave as a connection of their aggregated bandwidth. Depending on your minimum link configuration, the LAG will continue to function at reduced bandwidth even if one or more individual connections fail. Because all connections within a LAG must terminate on the same AWS Direct Connect device, however, this is still subject to the risk of device failure or maintenance activities.

FIGURE 5.3 Single connection with VPN backup

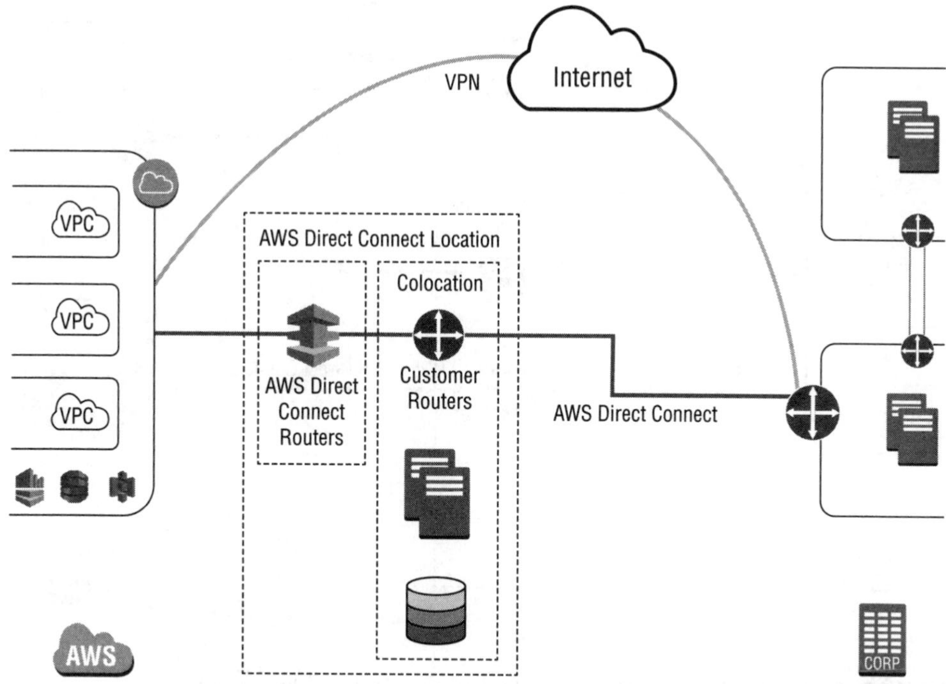

When used as independent connections located on different AWS Direct Connect devices, dual connections increase the level of resilience to failure. Single interfaces, device failures, or maintenance activities pose less of an outage risk to your connectivity in this scenario. AWS would still recommend that you implement a backup VPN connection to provide a backup in the event of a complete location-impacting event. A solution implementing dual connections in the same location with VPN backup is shown in Figure 5.4.

Single Connections: Dual Locations

When a connection is created at multiple AWS Direct Connect locations, you benefit from location diversity and resilience from local hardware failures. Because each location has its own independent and diverse connectivity to the AWS backbone, this scenario provides a good level of resilience. Depending on your overall risk assessment for connectivity, you may want to consider an additional backup VPN connection. This is illustrated in Figure 5.5.

FIGURE 5.4 Dual connections: single location—VPN backup

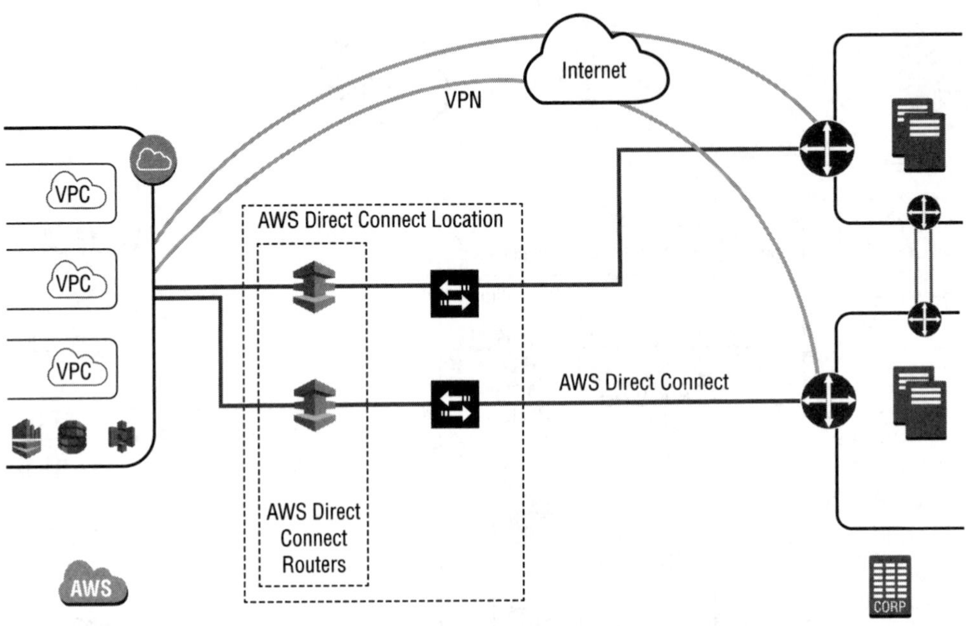

FIGURE 5.5 Single connections: dual locations—VPN Backup

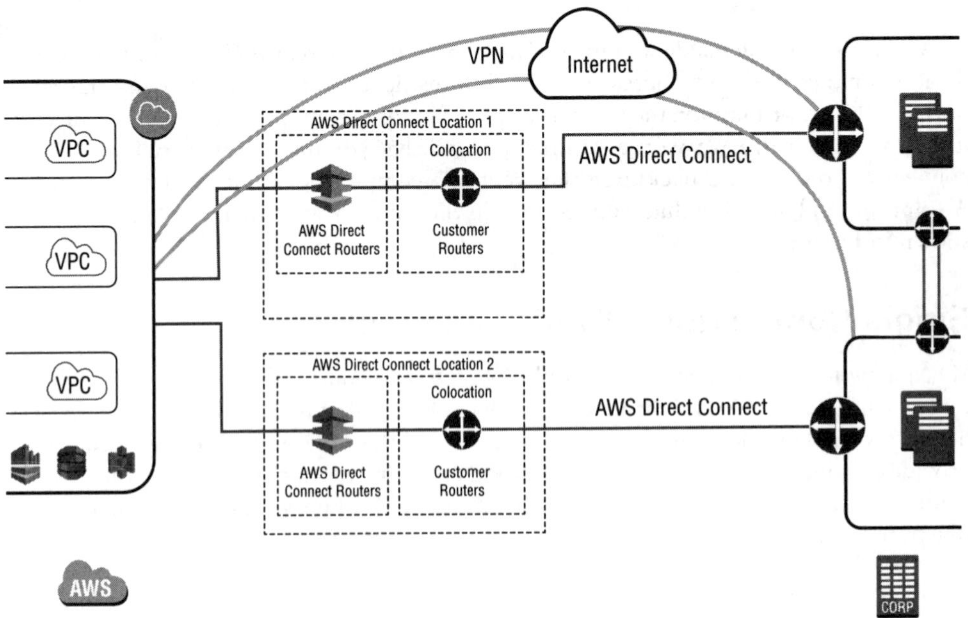

Dual Connections: Dual Locations

This solution provides the highest level of resilience currently available, particularly when combined with a backup VPN connection. When designed for 25 percent total utilization, it can withstand a number of potential outages caused by different events and still provide full connectivity.

Virtual Interface Configuration

When configuring multiple AWS Direct Connect connections for resilience, you will need to also configure a VIF on each connection.

Public Virtual Interface Configuration

For public VIFs, each one will have unique peer IP addresses but be configured to announce the same prefixes from your router. Depending on your network architecture, you may want AWS to prefer one connection for a specific range of IPs over the other for traffic flowing from AWS toward your routers. You can influence this using standard BGP configurations such as announcing a more specific prefix or by using AS_PATH prepending (if you are using a public ASN). More specific prefixes are preferred on the Amazon network as longest prefix match is the first criteria examined when processing a packet for path selection. A common configuration is to announce a supernet (such as /23) on both public VIFs and then a more specific subnet (for example, /24) on each individual VIF, depending on where that particular connection terminates on your network.

AS_PATH prepending is a mechanism where you artificially make the AS_PATH longer on one connection compared to the other by adding your own ASN multiple times to the path. AWS will always prefer the shortest path for a prefix if there are multiple options.

Private Virtual Interface Configuration

The same configuration options can be applied on private VIFs to influence how network traffic flows from a VPC to your network. You will create two or more private VIFs (one VIF per AWS Direct Connect connection) and associate them with the same VGW or Direct Connect Gateway to enable the different paths to the VPC. You can then use AS_PATH prepending or announcements of more specific prefixes to influence which path traffic will take traffic flowing from AWS to your network. On a private VIF, you are not required to use a public ASN to use AS_PATH prepending.

For influencing traffic flowing from your routers toward AWS within your own network, you will need to configure the routing appropriately using either local preference or similar options.

The options described all lead to an active/passive setup of some kind where one of the connections is chosen specifically for the network traffic from AWS. An alternative option is to run an active/active setup where both connections are used to carry network traffic. To enable this, you should ensure that the BGP configuration on both VIFs is the same. Within AWS, if the same prefix is seen with multiple identical paths via the same location,

Equal-Cost Multi-Path (ECMP) is performed and individual traffic flows are hashed to one particular connection in turn. The result, given a reasonable mix of source and destination IPs or ports, is an effective method of load balancing across the various paths available.

Bidirectional Forwarding Detection

Bidirectional Forwarding Detection (BFD) is a network fault detection protocol that provides fast failure detection times, which facilitates faster re-convergence time for dynamic routing protocols. It is independent of media, routing protocol, and data.

We recommend enabling BFD when configuring multiple AWS Direct Connect connections or when configuring a single AWS Direct Connect connection and a VPN connection as a backup to ensure fast detection and failover. You can configure BFD to detect link or path failures and update dynamic routing because AWS Direct Connect quickly terminates BGP peering so that backup routes can activate. This ensures that the BGP neighbor relationship is quickly torn down instead of waiting for three keepalives to fail at a hold-down time of 90 seconds.

Asynchronous BFD is automatically enabled for each AWS Direct Connect VIF on the AWS side, but it does not take effect until it is configured on your router. The AWS Direct Connect default sets the BFD liveness detection minimum interval to 300 ms and the BFD liveness detection multiplier to 3.

Virtual Private Network with AWS Direct Connect

VPN's can be used with AWS Direct Connect, either as a backup connectivity solution or to provide encryption for the transport of data over AWS Direct Connect.

Backup Virtual Private Network (VPN)

Backup VPN is covered in more detail in Chapter 4, "Virtual Private Networks," but it is often used as a backup for AWS Direct Connect connections that use a private VIF. A VPN connection provides encrypted access over the Internet to resources within your VPC using their private IP address. Both AWS Direct Connect and VPN connections terminate on the VGW for your VPC.

When combining a VPN connection as a backup for AWS Direct Connect, AWS recommends that you use a dynamic BGP-based VPN to enable the most flexible and consistent behavior for all network traffic flows.

Routes received via AWS Direct Connect and a VPN are consolidated within the VGW. From here, path selection is applied to an outbound packet with AWS Direct Connect always prioritized over a VPN for any given prefix that is advertised over both connections.

It is possible to prioritize the VPN by advertising a more specific prefix over the VPN and a supernet over AWS Direct Connect. For example, you want to use a VPN for traffic destined to non-production servers in your data center that belong to a /27 range, but you want to have AWS Direct Connect as a backup. You can advertise the /27 over a VPN while advertising a supernet such as a /24 on AWS Direct Connect. In this scenario, VPN will be the primary and AWS Direct Connect will be the backup.

Virtual Private Network Over AWS Direct Connect

For some customers, there is an additional need to encrypt their network traffic over AWS Direct Connect due to their applications not natively encrypting in transit. The preferred way to do this is to enable encryption at Layer 4, for example, using Transport Layer Security (TLS). If you want to implement encryption at Layer 3, the simplest way to do this is to combine a public VIF with a managed VPN connection.

Public VIFs enable announcements of all Amazon public IPs. Within those public IPs are the endpoints that are provisioned when you create a VPN connection. Within your network, the public VIF over AWS Direct Connect provides you with an optimal path to those AWS endpoints (compared to routing over the Internet) and enables your VPN customer gateway to establish a connection using that path. In the event of an outage on AWS Direct Connect, your customer gateway should use an alternative path to reach the VPN endpoints such as over the Internet. This solution is illustrated in Figure 5.6, which shows the public VIF and two VPN tunnels.

FIGURE 5.6 VPN over Direct Connect public VIF

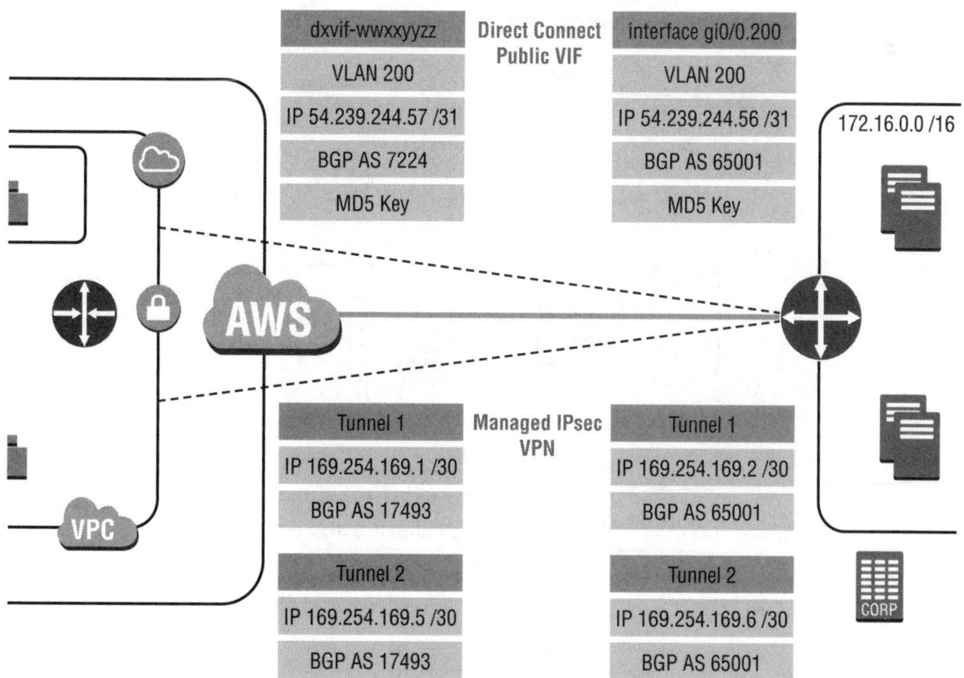

VPN over AWS Direct Connect can also be used over inter-region public VIFs. A single public VIF created on an AWS Direct Connect connection in one region can provide connectivity to VPN endpoints in a remote region.

Integration with the Transit Virtual Private Cloud Solution

AWS Direct Connect can be used with the Transit VPC Solution most easily by using a detached VGW. This is a VGW that has been created but not attached to a specific VPC. Within the VGW, CloudHub provides the ability to receive routes via BGP from both VPN and AWS Direct Connect and then re-advertise/reflect them back to each other. This enables the VGW to form the hub for your connectivity. Tagging the detached VGW appropriately enables it to be added automatically to the Transit VPC Solution configuration, and appropriate VPN tunnels are configured from the Amazon EC2 software routers.

Once these VPN tunnels are established, you should attach one or multiple private VIFs to the same VGW, which will cause the routes received from the Amazon EC2-based software routers to be reflected to your remote network over AWS Direct Connect. Conversely, your routes advertised over AWS Direct Connect will be reflected by CloudHub into the transit VPC Amazon EC2-based software routers via the VPN tunnels. An example deployment is shown in Figure 5.7.

FIGURE 5.7 Transit VPC with detached VGW

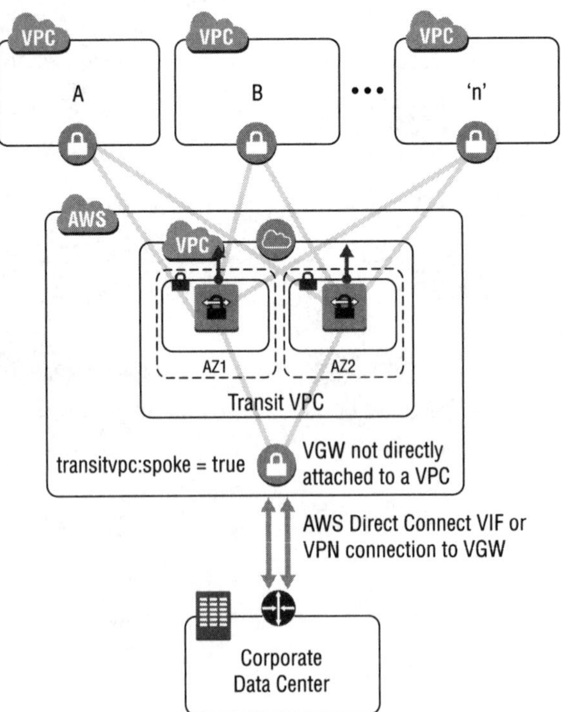

Border Gateway Protocol Path Selection

Routing decisions for network traffic leaving your VPC occur first within the VPC based on entries in your route tables and then within the VGW. The VGW consolidates the available paths from all of the associated private VIFs and VPN connections before making a selection.

The path selection order is as follows:

1. Local routes to the VPC (no override with more specific routing)
2. Longest prefix match first
3. Static route table entries preferred over dynamic
4. Dynamic routes:
    a. Prefer AWS Direct Connect BGP routes
        i. Shorter AS_PATH
        ii. Considered equivalent and will balance traffic per flow
    b. VPN static routes (defined on VPN connection)
    c. BGP routes from VPN
        i. Shorter AS_PATH

Billing

AWS Direct Connect pricing has two main cost components: (1) Pricing per port-hour for all AWS Direct Connect locations and (2) data transfer-out fees by AWS Direct Connect locations and AWS region.

Port-Hours

Whether you are using a dedicated 1 Gbps or 10 Gbps AWS Direct Connect connection or a sub-1 Gbps hosted connection via an AWS Direct Connect partner, you will incur port-hour charges. These are charged by AWS on your monthly bill and consist of a simple hourly charge applied from the first time your connection showed as available. For dedicated 1 Gbps or 10 Gbps connections, AWS will automatically start billing for port-hours after 90 days if the connection is not showing as available during that time. The 90-day window allows for your partner or carrier to provision the associated connectivity that may be required to deliver a service to your location.

In the case of hosted connections, billing for port-hours commences immediately after accepting the hosted connection in your account. Therefore, you should confirm with your AWS Direct Connect partner that any other dependencies for the solution are delivered and that you will be able to use the service before accepting the hosted connection in your AWS account.

Port-hours are always charged to the AWS account that owns the connection which, as discussed earlier, is not necessarily the same as the account that owns the (hosted) VIF.

Billing for port-hours stops when the connection or hosted connection is deleted from your AWS account. Being in a "down" state does not cause the charges to stop.

Pricing for the different bandwidth connections available for AWS Direct Connect is shown at `http://aws.amazon.com/directconnect/pricing`.

Data Transfer

AWS Direct Connect enables you to benefit from reduced data transfer charges relative to those applied to data transfer over the Internet. There is no charge for inbound data transfer to AWS over either AWS Direct Connect or the Internet. All charges are related to data transfer out of AWS.

Private Virtual Interface Data Transfer

A private VIF is always associated with a Direct Connect Gateway or a VGW, which is then attached to a VPC. As a result, when network traffic flows from an Amazon EC2 instance in your VPC via the VGW, you are charged at the reduced AWS Direct Connect data transfer rate. This can be viewed as simply being metered on the VIF itself and the charges applied to the AWS account that owns the VPC and VIF. In the case of a hosted VIF, the ownership of the private VIF is separate from the ownership of the actual AWS Direct Connect connection. Hence, the data transfer charges are charged to the owner of the VPC/VIF while the port fees are charged to the owner of the AWS Direct Connect connection. The rate charged for this data transfer is calculated by referencing the pricing matrix on the AWS Website. It is a combination of the AWS Region and the AWS Direct Connect location being used.

Public Virtual Interface Data Transfer

Public VIFs on AWS Direct Connect provide a network path that applies to all network traffic that leaves the AWS non-VPC network. This will include both your network traffic as well as traffic potentially flowing from other AWS resources that you do not own. For example, if you browse a website that is hosted on AWS by a third party, the traffic from your network to and from that website will flow over your public VIF. In this situation, you will not be charged for any data transfer—the owner of the website will receive any related charges.

If your public VIF is used to access AWS resources that are owned by you, then the reduced data transfer charge is applied. This is applicable to any resources owned by the same account as the public VIF as well as to any linked accounts within the same billing family or AWS organization structure. In this way, a single public VIF can provide reduced data transfer pricing benefits to all of your related AWS accounts.

Consider the following example:

- Account A is the payer account for your organization.
- Account B is the owner of a public VIF.
- Account C has an Amazon S3 bucket containing a large volume of objects available for download.
- Account D retrieves those objects from your company network routing over the public VIF.

Assuming that Accounts B, C, and D are all linked to the payer Account A or are in the same AWS organization, Account C will observe data transfer charges at the AWS Direct Connect rate on their monthly bill.

Summary

AWS Direct Connect provides the ability to establish a dedicated network connection from sites—such as data centers, offices, or colocation environments—to AWS. It provides a more consistent network experience than Internet-based connections at bandwidths ranging from 50 Mbps to 10 Gbps on a single connection.

AWS Direct Connect allows customers to connect to AWS from multiple global locations. These locations are typically in colocation or carrier-neutral facilities. If you do not have a presence in one of these locations, AWS Direct Connect partners can provide connectivity to you.

AWS Direct Connect provides both public VIFs and private VIFs. Public VIFs provide global connectivity to public AWS resources, including AWS public service endpoints, public Amazon EC2 IP addresses, and public Elastic Load Balancing addresses. Private virtual interfaces provide global connectivity through Direct Connect Gateways and VGWs to your VPC. When you use private VIFs, your VPC is a logical extension of your network. VPN connections can be established over AWS Direct Connect to provide additional encryption if required.

A LAG is a logical interface that uses the LACP to aggregate multiple 1 Gbps or 10 Gbps connections at a single AWS Direct Connect location, allowing you to treat them as a single, managed connection. You can create a LAG from existing connections, or you can provision new connections.

BGP is used to exchange routing information between a customer network and AWS. 802.1Q VLANs are used to separate virtual interfaces on the same connection. BFD can be used to increase the speed at which connection failures are detected and cause failover to alternative routes.

AWS Direct Connect is billed based on port-hours for the connection and data transfer outbound from AWS. The data transfer rates are less than standard Internet-out rates.

Exam Essentials

Understand the physical elements of AWS Direct Connect. AWS provides AWS Direct Connect at port speeds of 1 Gbps and 10 Gbps. Using an interconnect, AWS Direct Connect partners can provide lower bandwidth connections.

Understand the process to establish connectivity. AWS Direct Connect requires physical connectivity between the AWS network and your network. This process involves ordering connections, receiving LOA-CFA documentation, ordering cross-connects, and configuring VLANs and BGP.

Understand BGP and path selection. AWS Direct Connect uses BGP to exchange routing information between AWS and customer networks. ASNs, BGP configuration parameters, and BGP path selection all affect routing in your architecture.

Understand the interaction of AWS Direct Connect with the AWS VPN solution. A hybrid deployment model using AWS Direct Connect with a VPN as backup is a common architectural pattern. The two services interact with each other to provide resilience for connectivity to the AWS Cloud.

Test Taking Tip

When reviewing questions involving AWS Direct Connect, you should always consider the direction of the network traffic flow and the options available to influence it.

Resources to Review

AWS Direct Connect:

`https://aws.amazon.com/directconnect/`

AWS Direct Connect User Guide:

`https://aws.amazon.com/documentation/direct-connect/`

AWS re:Invent presentations on YouTube and SlideShare covering AWS Direct Connect and VPN

Exercises

The best way to become familiar with AWS Direct Connect is to configure your own connections and VIFs, which is what you'll be doing in this section.

For assistance completing these exercises, refer to the AWS Direct Connect User Guide located at `https://aws.amazon.com/documentation/direct-connect/`.

EXERCISE 5.1

Create a Public VIF

In this exercise, you will create an AWS Direct Connect Public VIF and configure your router appropriately.

1. Sign in to the AWS Management Console as Administrator or Power User.
2. Select the AWS Direct Connect icon to launch the AWS Direct Connect dashboard.

3. Using an existing AWS Direct Connect connection, create a public VIF for an IPv4 peering session by specifying a range of public IP addresses that you own or that have been provided by AWS support.
4. Configure your router to match the VLAN and BGP parameters specified when creating the VIF. Verify that a BGP session is established.
5. Test connectivity to an AWS public IP address using the connection.

A suggestion is to retrieve a file from S3 and verify that the path taken is via AWS Direct Connect.

EXERCISE 5.2

Create a Private VIF

In this exercise, you will create an AWS Direct Connect Private VIF and configure your router appropriately.

1. Sign in to the AWS Management Console as Administrator or Power User.
2. Select the AWS Direct Connect icon to launch the AWS Direct Connect dashboard.
3. Using an existing AWS Direct Connect Connection, create a Private Virtual Interface for an IPv4 peering session by choosing a VGW associated with a VPC.
4. Configure your router to match the VLAN and BGP parameters specified when creating the virtual interface and verify that a BGP session has been established.
5. Test connectivity to an Amazon EC2 instance in your VPC.

You should be able to ping an EC2 instance if the associated security group is configured appropriately.

EXERCISE 5.3

Add IPv6 to a Private VIF

In this exercise, you will create an additional peering for IPv6 on your AWS Direct Connect Private VIF and configure your router appropriately.

1. Sign in to the AWS Management Console as Administrator or Power User.
2. Select the AWS Direct Connect icon to launch the AWS Direct Connect dashboard.
3. Using an existing private VIF, add an IPv6 peering to the existing IPv4 peering.
4. Configure your router with the additional IPv6 peering. Verify that a BGP session is established.

EXERCISE 5.3 *(continued)*

5. Test connectivity to an Amazon EC2 instance in your VPC using its IPv6 address.

You should be able to ping an EC2 instance if the associated security group is configured appropriately.

EXERCISE 5.4

Create a Private Hosted VIF

In this exercise, you will create an AWS Direct Connect Private VIF that is then shared with another AWS Account.

1. Sign in to the AWS Management Console as Administrator or Power User.
2. Select the AWS Direct Connect icon to launch the AWS Direct Connect dashboard.
3. Using an existing AWS Direct Connect Connection, create a private VIF and share it with a second AWS account.
4. Log in to the second AWS account and accept the private VIF. From the second account, choose a VGW to associate with a VPC in that account.
5. Configure your router to match the VLAN and BGP parameters specified when creating the virtual interface. Verify that a BGP session is established.
6. Test connectivity to an Amazon EC2 instance in the VPC of the second AWS account.

You should be able to ping an EC2 instance if the associated security group is configured appropriately.

EXERCISE 5.5

Create a LAG

In this exercise, you will combine multiple Direct Connect Connections to create a Link Aggregation Group.

1. Sign in to the AWS Management Console as Administrator or Power User.
2. Select the AWS Direct Connect icon to launch the AWS Direct Connect dashboard.
3. Using an existing AWS Direct Connect connection, create a LAG and set the Minimum Links to 1.
4. Add a second connection to the newly-created LAG, and ensure that this is reflected in the console.

Review Questions

1. A private Virtual Interface (VIF) on AWS Direct Connect attaches to your Virtual Private Cloud (VPC) using which of the following?
   - **A.** Internet gateway
   - **B.** VPC endpoint
   - **C.** Virtual Private Gateway (VGW)
   - **D.** Peering connection
2. Which routing protocol is supported by AWS Direct Connect Virtual Interfaces (VIFs)?
   - **A.** Border Gateway Protocol (BGP)
   - **B.** Routing Information Protocol (RIP)
   - **C.** Open Shortest Path First (OSPF)
   - **D.** Intermediate System to Intermediate System (IS-IS)
3. What is the minimum number of connections supported in a Link Aggregation Group (LAG)?
   - **A.** 4
   - **B.** 3
   - **C.** 2
   - **D.** 1
4. Which of the following is a type of Virtual Interface (VIF) that is supported on AWS Direct Connect?
   - **A.** Global
   - **B.** Virtual Private Network (VPN)
   - **C.** Local
   - **D.** Public
5. A resilient AWS Direct Connect connection requires you to connect at what number of AWS Direct Connect locations?
   - **A.** 1
   - **B.** 2
   - **C.** 3
   - **D.** 4
6. How many prefixes can be announced from a customer to AWS over an AWS Direct Connect Private Virtual Interface (VIF)?
   - **A.** 10
   - **B.** 50
   - **C.** 100
   - **D.** 1,000

7. When using a Link Aggregation Group (LAG) composed of two AWS Direct Connect connections, how many IPv4 Border Gateway Protocol (BGP) sessions are required per Virtual Interface (VIF)?

   A. 1

   B. 2

   C. 3

   D. 4

8. Which of the following has the highest route priority in the Border Gateway Protocol (BGP) path selection algorithm used by AWS?

   A. Static routes

   B. Local routes to the Virtual Private Cloud (VPC)

   C. Shortest AS path

   D. BGP routes from a Virtual Private Network (VPN)

9. Hosted Virtual Interfaces (VIFs) on AWS Direct Connect describe which of the following scenarios?

   A. A partner providing a new connection on their interconnect to a customer

   B. A customer providing a Virtual Interface (VIF) to another customer on their connection

   C. A partner providing a VIF on their interconnect to a customer

   D. A customer providing a new connection on their connection to another customer

10. All billing for AWS Direct Connect ceases when which of the following occurs?

   A. The last Virtual Interface (VIF) on a connection is deleted.

   B. The port on the customer equipment is disabled.

   C. The cross-connect is removed.

   D. The connection is deleted.

Domain Name System and Load Balancing

THE AWS CERTIFIED ADVANCED NETWORKING – SPECIALTY EXAM OBJECTIVES COVERED IN THIS CHAPTER MAY INCLUDE, BUT ARE NOT LIMITED TO, THE FOLLOWING:

Domain 2.0: Design and Implement AWS Networks

✓ 2.4 Determine network requirements for a specialized workload

✓ 2.5 Derive an appropriate architecture based on customer and application requirements

Domain 4.0: Configure Network Integration with Application Services

✓ 4.1 Leverage the capabilities of Amazon Route 53

✓ 4.2 Evaluate DNS solutions in a hybrid IT architecture

✓ 4.4 Given a scenario, determine an appropriate load balancing strategy within the AWS ecosystem

✓ 4.5 Determine a content distribution strategy to optimize for performance

Introduction to Domain Name System and Load Balancing

Amazon Route 53 is a highly available and scalable cloud Domain Name System (DNS) service. It is designed to give you the ability to route end users to Internet applications by translating domain names such as `www.example.com` into numeric IP addresses such as `192.0.2.122`. Elastic Load Balancing gives you the capability to distribute incoming application traffic automatically across multiple targets, such as Amazon Elastic Compute Cloud (Amazon EC2) instances, containers, and IP addresses. Amazon Route 53 and Elastic Load Balancing can work together to provide you with a scalable and fault-tolerant architecture for your applications.

This chapter reviews the core components of DNS, comparing and contrasting Amazon EC2 DNS with Amazon Route 53. We review the components that make up Amazon Route 53, including the architectural features that make Amazon Route 53 so reliable. We then dive into Elastic Load Balancing and the three types of load balancers that are available in AWS.

The exercises at the end of this chapter reinforce how to use Amazon Route 53 and Elastic Load Balancing. The exercises help provide an understanding of the building blocks that make up Amazon Route 53 and Elastic Load Balancing, as well as their advanced use cases. You are expected to have a strong understanding of these concepts to pass the exam.

Domain Name System

To begin our discussion on *Domain Name System (DNS)*, we'll start with a simple analogy. The IP address of your website is like a phone number in the contacts on your mobile device. Without a name identifier such as Harry or Sue, it would be difficult to distinguish between phone numbers or even remember which number is Harry's or Sue's.

Similarly, when a visitor wants to access your website, their computer takes the domain name typed in (`www.amazon.com`, for example) and looks up the IP address for that domain using DNS.

DNS is a globally distributed service that is foundational to the way people use the Internet. It uses a hierarchical name structure, with each level separated with a dot (`.`). Consider the domain names `www.amazon.com` and `aws.amazon.com`. In both of these examples, `com` is the Top-Level Domain (TLD) and `amazon` is the Second-Level Domain (SLD). There can be any number of lower levels (for example, `www` or `aws`) below the SLD.

Computers use the DNS hierarchy to translate human-readable names (for example, `www.amazon.com`) into the IP addresses (such as `192.0.2.1`) that computers use to connect to one another. Every time you use a domain name, a DNS service must translate the name into the corresponding IP address. In short, if you have used the Internet, you've used DNS.

Amazon Route 53 is an *authoritative DNS system*. An authoritative DNS system provides a direct update mechanism that developers use to manage their public DNS names. It then answers DNS queries, translating domain names into IP addresses so that computers can communicate with each other.

Domain Name System Concepts

This section of the chapter defines DNS terms, describes how DNS works, and explains commonly used *record types*.

Top-Level Domains

A *Top-Level Domain (TLD)* is the most general part of the domain. The TLD is the farthest portion to the right (as separated by a dot).

TLDs are at the top of the hierarchy in terms of domain names. Certain parties are given management control over TLDs by the *Internet Corporation for Assigned Names and Numbers (ICANN)*. These parties can then distribute domain names under the TLD, usually through a domain registrar. These domains are registered with the *Network Information Center (InterNIC)*, a service of ICANN that enforces the uniqueness of domain names across the Internet. Each domain name becomes registered in a central database, known as the *WHOIS database*.

There are two types of top-level domains:

1. *Generic TLDs* are global in nature and recognized across the globe. Some of the more common are `.com`, `.net`, and `.org`. Generic TLDs also include specialty domains, such as `.auction`, `.coffee`, and `.cloud`. It is worth noting that not all Generic TLDs support *Internationalized Domain Names (IDN)*. An IDN is one that includes non-ASCII characters, such as accented Latin, Chinese, and Russian. It is worth checking whether a TLD supports IDNs if they are needed before registering a domain with Amazon Route 53.

2. *Geographic TLDs* are associated with areas such as countries or cities and include country-specific extensions, known as *country code Top-Level Domains (ccTLDs)*. Examples include `.be` (Belgium), `.in` (India), and `.mx` (Mexico). The naming and registration rules vary for each ccTLD.

Domain Names, Subdomains, and Hosts

A *domain name* is the human-friendly name associated with an Internet resource. For instance, amazon.com is a domain name.

A *subdomain* is a domain name within a larger hierarchy. Every domain name except the root domain name is a subdomain: com is a subdomain of the root domain, amazon.com is a subdomain of com, and aws.amazon.com is a subdomain of amazon.com associated with systems operated by AWS.

The root domain does not have a name. Depending on the application or protocol, it is represented either as an empty string or a single dot (.). A *host* is a label within a subdomain that has one or more IP addresses associated with it.

IP Addresses

An IP address is a number that is assigned to a host. Each IP address must be unique within its network. For public websites, this network is the entire Internet. IP addresses will be in either an IPv4 format, such as 192.0.2.44, or IPv6 format, such as 2001:0db8:85a3:0000:0000:abcd:0001:2345. DNS provides IPv4 addresses in response to a type A query and IPv6 addresses in response to a type AAAA query. Amazon Route 53 supports both type A and type AAAA resource record sets.

Fully Qualified Domain Names

A *Fully Qualified Domain Name (FQDN)*, also referred to as an *absolute domain name*, specifies a domain or host in relation to the absolute root of the DNS.

This means that the FQDN specifies each parent domain, including the TLD. A proper FQDN ends with a dot, indicating the root of the DNS hierarchy. For example, mail.amazon.com. is an FQDN. Sometimes, software that calls for an FQDN does not require the ending dot, but it is required to conform to ICANN standards.

In Figure 6.1, you can see that the entire string is the FQDN, which is composed of the domain name, subdomain, root, TLD, SLD, and host.

FIGURE 6.1 FQDN components

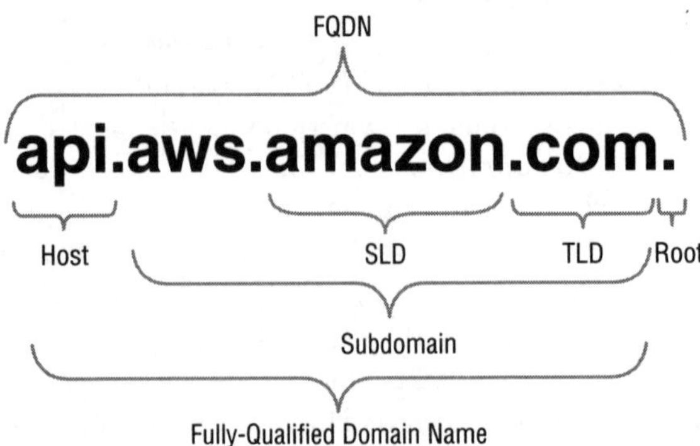

Name Servers

Name Servers are servers in the DNS that translate domain names into IP addresses in response to queries. Name Servers will do most of the work in the DNS. Since the total volume of domain queries are too numerous for any one server, each server may redirect requests to other Name Servers or delegate responsibility for a subset of subdomains for which they are responsible.

Name Servers can be authoritative or non-authoritative for a given domain. *Authoritative servers* provide answers to queries about domains under their control. *Non-authoritative servers* point to other servers or serve cached copies of other Name Servers' data. In almost all cases clients first connect to non-authoritative Name Servers, which keep cached copies of previous lookups to authoritative Name Servers. Thus the entire DNS system is a global distributed cached database, which both allows it to be enormously scalable, but can also cause problems when the cached data becomes stale or is not properly refreshed.

Zones

A *zone* is a container that holds information about how you want to route traffic on the Internet for a domain (`example.com`) and its subdomains (`apex.example.com` and `acme.example.com`).

If you have an existing domain and zone and want to create subdomain records, you can do either of the following:

- Create the records you need inside the existing `example.com` zone.
- Create a new zone to hold the records associated with your subdomain, as well as a delegation set in the parent zone that refers clients to the subdomain hosted zone.

The first method requires fewer zones and fewer queries, while the second method offers more flexibility when managing zones (for example, restricting who may edit the different zones). In addition to containing hosts or subdomains (additional zones), zones themselves can also have IP addresses. These IP addresses are called "zone root" or "zone apex" addresses, and enable scenarios such as the use of `http://example.com` in a user's browser. Compared to host names (like `www.example.com`), they also create some special challenges.

Domain Name Registrars

Because all of the names in a given domain and domains themselves must be unique, there needs to be a way to organize them so that domains are not duplicated. This is where *domain name registrars* come in. A domain name registrar is an organization or commercial entity that manages the reservation of Internet domain names. A domain name registrar must be accredited by the Generic TLD registries and ccTLD registries for which it provides domain name registration services. The management is done in accordance with the guidelines of the designated domain name registries.

Steps Involved in DNS Resolution

When you type a domain name into your browser, your computer first checks it's hosts file to see if it has that domain name stored locally. If it does not, it will check its DNS cache to see if you have visited the site before. If it still does not have a record of that domain name, it will contact a DNS server to resolve the domain name.

DNS is, at its core, a hierarchical system. At the top of this system are root servers. ICANN delegates the control of these servers to various organizations.

As of this writing, there are 13 root servers in operation. Root servers handle requests for information about TLDs. When a request comes in for a domain that a lower-level Name Server cannot resolve, a query is made to the root server for the authoritative Name Servers for that domain.

In order to handle the incredible volume of resolutions that happen every day, these root servers are mirrored and replicated. When requests are made to a certain root server, the request will be routed to the nearest mirror of that root server.

The root servers will not actually know where the domain is hosted. They will, however, be able to direct the requester to the Name Servers that handle the specifically-requested TLD.

For example, if a type A (IPv4 address) request for `www.wikipedia.org` is made to the root server, it will check its resource records for a listing that matches that domain name, but it will not find one in its records. It will instead find a record for the `.org` TLD and refer the requester to the Name Servers responsible for `.org` addresses, providing their domain names and IP addresses.

TLD Servers

After a root server returns the IP addresses of the servers responsible for the TLD of a request, the requester then sends a new request to one of those addresses.

To continue the example from the previous section, the requesting entity would send a request to the Name Server responsible for knowing about `.org` domains to see if it can locate `www.wikipedia.org`.

Once again, when the `.org` TLD Name Server searches its zone records for a `www.wikipedia.org` listing, it will not find one in its records. It will, however, find records for the Name Servers responsible for `wikipedia.org` and return their names and IP addresses.

Domain Level Name Servers

At this point, the requester has the IP address of a Name Server that are authoritative for the `wikipedia.org` domain. It sends a new request to one or more of the Name Servers asking, once again, if it can resolve `www.wikipedia.org`.

The Name Server knows that it is authoritative for the `wikipedia.org` zone and checks its records for a host or subdomain matching the www label within this zone. If found, the Name Server returns the actual IPv4 address or addresses to the requester.

In this example, the requester made an ANY query for the host. The answers returned by the Name Server, therefore, may include additional information. For example, the Wikimedia Name Servers hosting the `wikipedia.org` domain also return AAAA (IPv6) records in response to type ANY queries.

Resolving Name Servers

In the previous scenario, we referred to a *requester*. What is the requester in this situation?

In almost all cases, the requester will be what is called a *resolving Name Server*, which is a server that is configured to ask other servers questions. Its primary function is to act as an intermediary for a user, caching previous query results to improve speed and providing the addresses of appropriate root servers to resolve new requests.

Users will usually have a few resolving Name Servers configured on their computer systems. The resolving Name Servers are typically provided by an Internet Service Provider (ISP) or other organization. There are also several public resolving DNS servers that you can query. These can be configured in your computer either automatically or manually.

When you type a URL in the address bar of your browser, your computer first looks to see if it can find the resource's location locally. It checks the hosts file on the computer and any locally stored cache. If not found, it then sends the request to the resolving Name Server and waits to receive the IP address of the resource.

The resolving Name Server then checks its cache for the answer. If it does not find it, it goes through the steps outlined in the previous sections.

Resolving Name Servers take care of the requesting process for the end user transparently. The clients simply have to know to ask the resolving Name Servers where a resource is located, and the resolving Name Servers will do the work to investigate and return the final answer.

Record Types

Each zone file contains resource records. In its simplest form, a *resource record* is a single mapping between a resource and a name. These can map a domain name to an IP address or define resources for the domain, such as Name Servers or mail servers. This section describes each record type.

Start of Authority Record

A *Start of Authority (SOA)* record is mandatory in all zones, and it identifies the base DNS information about the domain. Each zone contains a single SOA record.

The SOA record stores information about the following:

- The name of the DNS server for that zone
- The administrator of the zone
- The current version of the data file
- The number of seconds that a secondary Name Server should wait before checking for updates

- The number of seconds that a secondary Name Server should wait before retrying a failed zone transfer
- The maximum number of seconds that a secondary Name Server can use data before it must either be refreshed or expire
- The default Time To Live (TTL) value (in seconds) for resource records in the zone

A and AAAA

Both types of address records map a host to an IP address. A *records* are used to map a host to an IPv4 IP address, while *AAAA records* are used to map a host to an IPv6 address.

Certificate Authority Authorization

A *Certificate Authority Authorization (CAA)* record lets you specify which Certificate Authorities (CAs) are allowed to issue certificates for a domain or subdomain. Creating a CAA record helps prevent the wrong CAs from issuing certificates for your domains.

Canonical Name

A *Canonical Name (CNAME)* record is a type of resource record in the DNS that defines an alias for a host. The CNAME record contains a domain name that must have an A or AAAA record.

Mail Exchange

Mail Exchange (MX) records are used to define the mail servers used for a domain and ensure that email messages are routed correctly. The MX record should point to a host defined by an A or AAAA record and not one defined by a CNAME. Again, this may be allowed by some clients but is not allowed by the DNS standards.

Name Authority Pointer

A Name Authority Pointer (NAPTR) is a resource record set type that is used by Dynamic Delegation Discovery System (DDDS) applications to convert one value to another or to replace one value with another. For example, one common use is to convert phone numbers into Session Initiation Protocol (SIP) Uniform Resource Identifiers (URIs).

Name Server

Name Server (NS) records are used by TLD servers to direct traffic to the DNS servers that contain the authoritative DNS records.

Pointer

A *Pointer (PTR)* record is essentially the reverse of an A record. PTR records map an IP address to a DNS name, and they are mainly used to check if the server name is associated with the IP address from where the connection was initiated.

Sender Policy Framework

Sender Policy Framework (SPF) records are used by mail servers to combat spam. An SPF record tells a mail server what IP addresses are authorized to send an email from your domain name. For example, if you wanted to ensure that only your mail server sends emails from your company's domain (`example.com`), you would create an SPF record with the IP address of your mail server. That way, an email sent from your domain (`marketing@example.com`) would need to have an originating IP address of your company mail server in order to be accepted. This prevents people from spoofing emails from your domain. (SPF records are actually not a distinct record type in the DNS specification and system, but rather a defined way of using TXT records; see next item.)

Text

Text (TXT) records are used to hold text information. This record provides the ability to associate some arbitrary and unformatted text with a host or other name, such as human readable information about a server, network, data center, and other accounting information.

This record is sometimes used to provide programmatic data about a name that is not covered by other record types. For example, domain control is sometimes "proven" to a third party by setting a TXT record to a challenge value provided by the third party.

Service

A *Service (SRV)* record is a specification of data defining the location (the hostname and port number) of servers for specified services. The idea behind SRV is that, given a domain name (`example.com`) and a service name (web HTTP) which runs on a protocol (*Transmission Control Protocol [TCP]*), a DNS query may be issued to find the hostname that provides such a service for the domain, which may or may not be within the domain.

A CAA record is not a substitute for the security requirements that are specified by your CA, such as the requirement to validate that you are the owner of a domain.

Amazon EC2 DNS Service

When you launch an Amazon EC2 instance within an Amazon Virtual Private Cloud (Amazon VPC), the Amazon EC2 instance is provided with a private IP address and, optionally, a public IP address. The private IP address resides within the Classless Inter-Domain Routing (CIDR) address block of the VPC. The public IP address, if assigned, is from an Amazon-owned CIDR block and is associated with an instance via a static one-to-one Network Address Translation (NAT) at the Internet gateway. This is illustrated in Figure 6.2.

FIGURE 6.2 NAT at the VPC Internet gateway

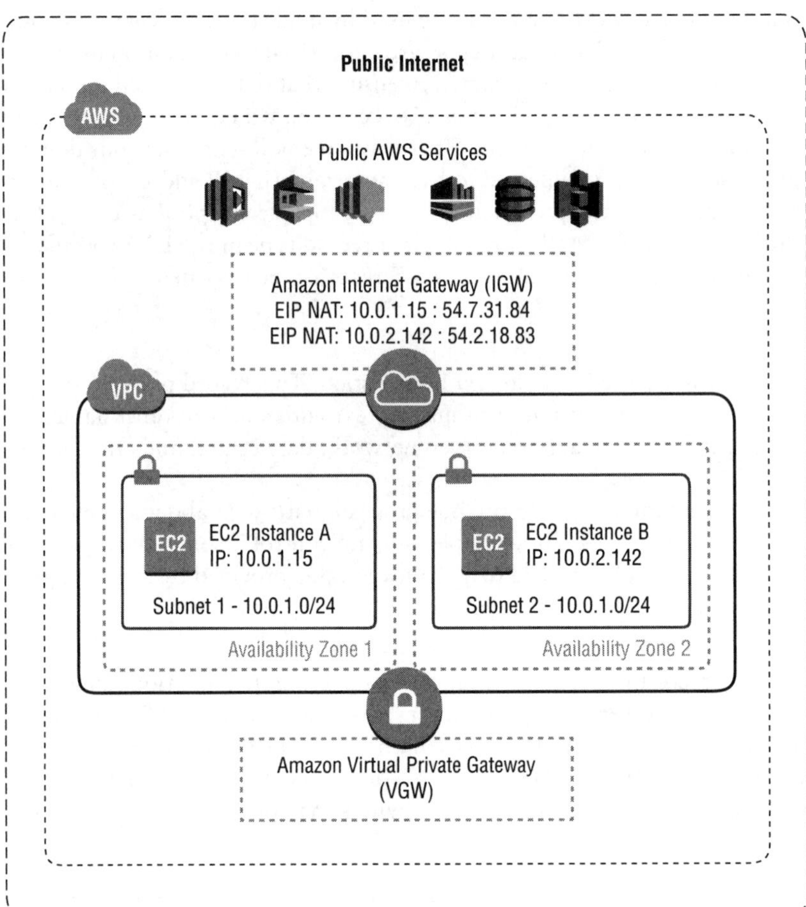

DNS names are provided for both the private and public IP addresses. Internal DNS hostnames for Amazon EC2 are in the form `ip-`*`private-ipv4-address`*`.ec2.internal` for the US-East-1 region and `ip-`*`private-ipv4-address`*`.`*`region`*`.compute.internal` for all other regions (where *`private-ipv4-address`* is the reverse lookup IPv4 address of the instance with dots replaced by dashes, and *region* is replaced by the API name of the AWS regions, for example, "us-west-2"). The private DNS hostname of an Amazon EC2 instance can be used for communication between instances within the VPC. This DNS name is not, however, resolvable outside of the instance's network.

External DNS hostnames for EC2 are in the form `ec2-`*`public-ipv4-address`*`.compute-1.amazonaws.com` for the US-East-1 region and `ec2-`*`public-ipv4-address`*`.`*`region`*`.amazonaws.com` for other regions. Outside of the VPC, the external hostname resolves to the public IPv4 address of the instance outside the instance's VPC. Within the VPC and on peered VPCs, the external hostname resolves to the private IPv4 address of the instance.

Amazon VPCs have configurable attributes, as shown in Table 6.1, which control the behavior of the EC2 DNS service.

TABLE 6.1 Amazon VPC DNS Attributes

Attributes	Description
`enableDnsHostnames`	Indicates whether the instances launched in the VPC will receive a public DNS hostname. If this attribute is true, instances in the VPC will receive public DNS hostnames, but only if the `enableDnsSupport` attribute is also set to true, and only if the instance has a public IP address assigned to it.
`enableDnsSupport`	Indicates whether the DNS resolution is supported for the VPC. If this attribute is false, the Amazon-provided Amazon EC2 DNS service in the VPC that resolves public DNS hostnames to IP addresses is not enabled. If this attribute is true, queries to the Amazon-provided DNS server at the `169.254.169.253` IP address, or the reserved IP address at the base of the VPC IPv4 network range plus two, will succeed.

For most use cases, the Amazon-assigned DNS hostnames are sufficient. If customized DNS names are needed, you can use Amazon Route 53.

Amazon EC2 DNS vs. Amazon Route 53

As shown in Table 6.1, Amazon will auto-assign DNS hostnames to Amazon EC2 instances when the `enableDnsHostname` attribute is set to true. Conversely, if customer-specified hostnames are required, Amazon Route 53 is the service that provides you with the ability to specify either a public DNS hostname through public hosted zones or private hosted zones. More information is provided in the Amazon Route 53 hosted zones section later in this chapter.

With Amazon DNS for Amazon EC2 instances, AWS takes care of the DNS name creation and configuration for EC2 instances, but customization capabilities are limited. Amazon Route 53 is a fully-featured DNS solution where you can control many more aspects of your DNS, including DNS CNAME creation and management.

Amazon EC2 DNS and VPC Peering

DNS resolution is supported over VPC peering connections. You can enable resolution of public DNS hostnames to private IP addresses when queried from the peered VPC. To enable a VPC to resolve public IPv4 DNS hostnames to private IPv4 addresses when queried from instances in the peer VPC, you must modify the peering connection configuration and enable Allow DNS Resolution from Accepter VPC (`vpc-identifier`) to Private IP.

When enabling DNS resolution over VPC peering connections, both VPCs must be enabled for DNS hostnames and DNS resolution.

Using DNS with Simple AD

Simple AD is a Microsoft Active Directory-compatible managed directory powered by Samba 4. Simple AD supports up to 500 users (approximately 2,000 objects, including users, groups, and computers).

Simple AD provides a subset of the features offered by Microsoft Active Directory, including the ability to manage user accounts and group memberships, create and apply group policies, securely connect to Amazon EC2 instances, and provide Kerberos-based Single Sign-On (SSO). Note that Simple AD does not support features such as trust relationships with other domains, Active Directory Administrative Center, PowerShell support, Active Directory recycle bin, group managed service accounts, and schema extensions for POSIX and Microsoft applications.

Simple AD forwards DNS requests to the IP address of the Amazon-provided DNS servers for your VPC. These DNS servers will resolve names configured in your Amazon Route 53 private hosted zones. By pointing your on-premises computers to Simple AD, you can resolve DNS requests to the private hosted zone. This solves the issue of building private applications within your VPC and not having the ability to resolve those private-only DNS hostnames from your on-premises environment.

Simple AD is one of the easiest ways for your on-premises devices to access private hosted zones within your VPC. By pointing DNS queries at Simple AD, it will then forward requests internally within AWS for VPC DNS name resolution.

Custom Amazon EC2 DNS Resolver

In some cases, you may want a custom DNS resolver running on an Amazon EC2 instance within your VPC. This lets you leverage DNS servers that are capable of both conditional forwarding for DNS queries and recursive DNS resolution. This is shown in Figure 6.3.

As shown in Figure 6.3, DNS queries in this scenario work in the following way:

1. DNS queries for public domains are recursively resolved by the custom DNS resolver using the latest root hints available from the Internet Assigned Number Authority (IANA). The names and IP addresses of the authoritative Name Servers for the root zone are provided in the cache hints file so that a recursive DNS server can initiate the DNS resolution process.

2. DNS queries bound for on-premises servers are conditionally forwarded to on-premises DNS servers.
3. All other queries are forwarded to the Amazon DNS server.

FIGURE 6.3 Amazon EC2 DNS instance acting as resolver and forwarder

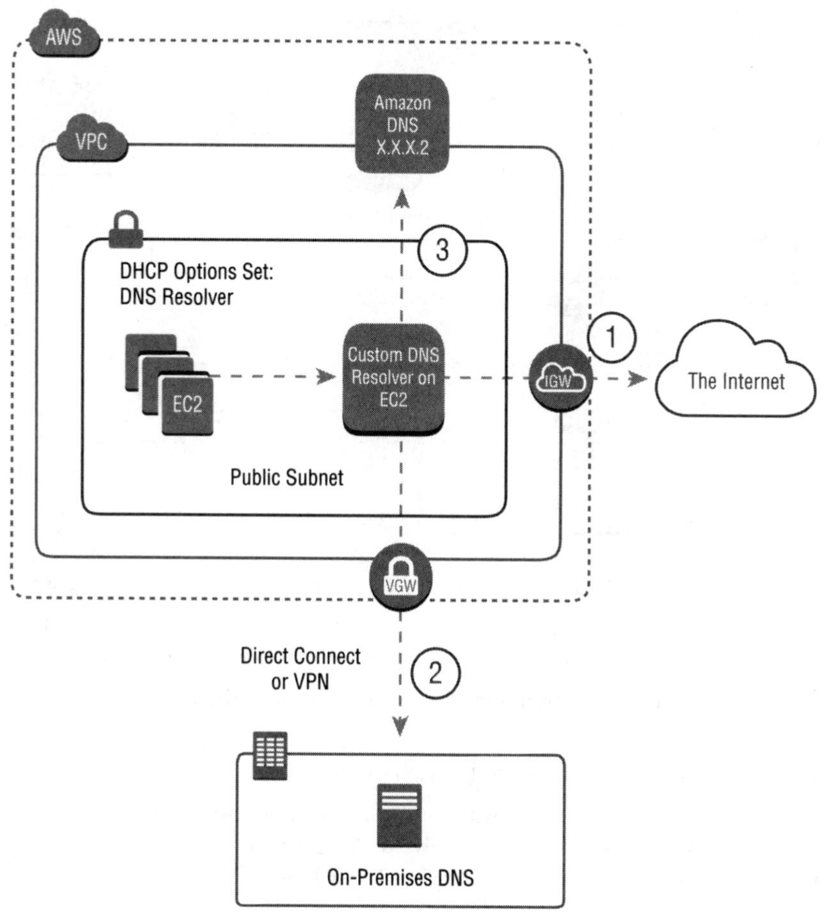

Because the DNS server is running within a public subnet, exposing both forwarding and recursive DNS to the public Internet may not be desirable. In this case, it is possible to run recursion in the public subnet and a forwarder in the private subnet that handles all DNS queries from instances, as shown in Figure 6.4.

FIGURE 6.4 Amazon EC2 DNS instances with segregated resolver and forwarder

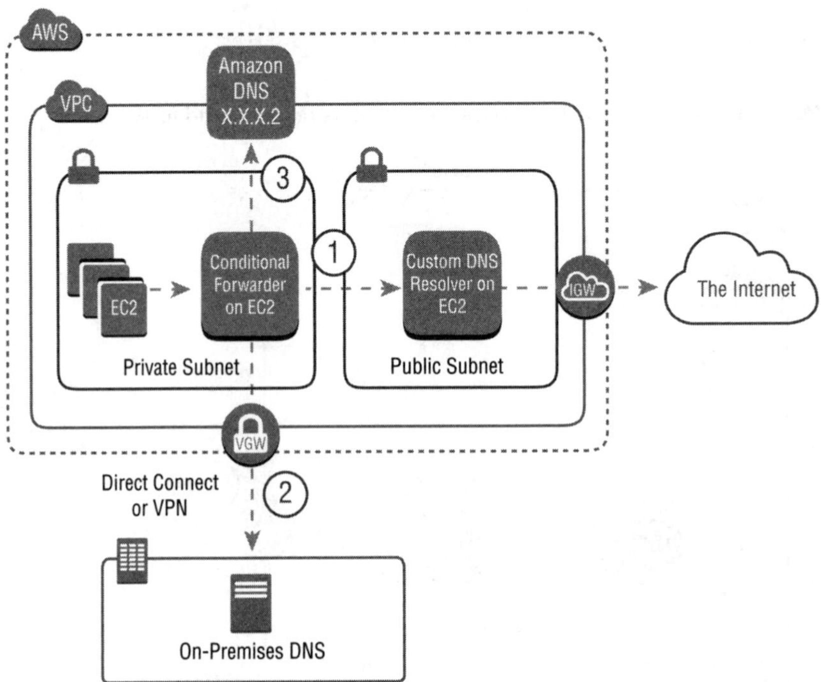

As shown in Figure 6.4, DNS queries in this scenario work in the following way:

1. DNS queries for public domains from instances are conditionally forwarded by the DNS forwarder in the private subnet to the custom DNS resolver in the public subnet.
2. DNS queries bound for on-premises servers are conditionally forwarded to on-premises DNS servers.
3. All other queries are forwarded to the Amazon DNS server.

By having a customer-managed forwarder and resolver running within your VPC on Amazon EC2 instances, it is possible to resolve to Amazon DNS from on-premises in the same way that was achievable by using Simple AD for DNS.

Further DNS hybrid architectures can be found in the AWS whitepaper Hybrid Cloud DNS Solutions for VPC, found at: `https://aws.amazon.com/whitepapers/`.

Amazon Route 53

Now that we have reviewed the foundational components that make up DNS, the different DNS record types, and Amazon EC2 DNS, we can explore Amazon Route 53.

Amazon Route 53 is a highly available and scalable cloud DNS web service that is designed to give developers and organizations an extremely reliable and cost-effective way to route end users to Internet applications. It can also be used to provide much more control over private DNS resolution within customers' VPCs using its private hosted zone feature.

Amazon Route 53 performs three main functions:

1. **Domain registration** Amazon Route 53 lets you register domain names, such as `example.com`.
2. **DNS service** Amazon Route 53 translates friendly domain names like `www.example.com` into IP addresses like `192.0.2.1`. Amazon Route 53 responds to DNS queries using a global network of authoritative DNS servers, which reduces latency. To comply with DNS standards, responses sent over User Datagram Protocol (UDP) are limited to 512 bytes in size. Responses exceeding 512 bytes are truncated, and the resolver must re-issue the request over TCP.
3. **Health checking** Amazon Route 53 sends automated requests over the Internet to your application to verify that it is reachable, available, and functional.

You can use the Domain registration and DNS service together or independently. For example, you can use Amazon Route 53 as both your registrar and your DNS service, or you can use Amazon Route 53 as the DNS service for a domain that you registered with another domain registrar.

In the following sections, we discuss the use of Route 53's graphical user interface within the AWS console. Please note, however, that all functions of Route 53, including the end-to-end flow of domain registration, can also be accomplished using its API or accompanying CLI. That means that all these workflows can be automated and accomplished via software without any human intervention. Especially in the area of domain registration, this makes Route 53 uniquely powerful as compared to most other domain registration services.

Domain Registration

If you want to create a website or any other public-facing service, you first need to register the domain name. If you already registered a domain name with another registrar, you have the option to transfer the domain registration to Amazon Route 53. Transfer is not required, however, to use Amazon Route 53 as your DNS service or to configure health checking for your resources.

The following are the domain registration steps for Amazon Route 53:

1. Choose the domain that you want to register. In the Amazon Route 53 console, navigate to Domain Registration and then Get Started Now. Select Check to find out whether the domain name is available.
2. If the domain is available, choose Add to Cart. The domain name will appear in your shopping cart. Note that related domain name suggestions will show other domains that you might want to register instead of your first choice (if it is not available) or in addition to your first choice, up to a maximum of five domains.
3. Continue and enter the contact details for your domain(s), including domain registrant, administrator, and technical contacts. The values that you enter here are applied for all

of the domains that you are registering. By default, AWS will use the information for all three contacts. To use individual information, change the value of My Registrant, Administrative, and Technical Contacts Are All the Same to No.

4. Some TLDs require that AWS collect additional information. For these TLDs, enter the applicable values after the Postal/ZIP Code field.
5. Some TLDs allow you to hide your contact details from the public WHOIS database. For these TLDs, decide whether this feature should be enabled and select Continue.
6. For generic TLDs, if you specified an email address for the registrant contact that has never been used to register a domain with Amazon Route 53, you need to verify that the address is valid.
7. When your email has been verified (if required) and the domain has been purchased, the next step depends on whether you want to use Amazon Route 53 or another DNS service as the DNS for the domain. Amazon Route 53 automatically creates a public hosted zone for the domain upon creation and sets Name Server records for the domain to point to the Name Servers for this zone. If a different DNS service is desired, update the Name Servers for your domain and delete the Route 53 hosted zone.

Amazon Route 53 supports domain registration for a wide variety of generic TLDs (for example, `.com` and `.org`) and geographic TLDs (such as `.be` and `.us`). For a complete list of supported TLDs, refer to the Amazon Route 53 Developer Guide: `https://docs.aws.amazon.com/Route53/latest/DeveloperGuide/`.

Transferring Domains

You can transfer domain registration from another registrar to Amazon Route 53, from one AWS account to another, or from Amazon Route 53 to another registrar. When transferring a domain to Amazon Route 53, the following steps must be performed. If you skip any of these steps, your domain might become unavailable on the Internet.

1. Confirm that Amazon Route 53 supports the TLD.
2. If necessary, transfer your DNS service to Amazon Route 53 or another DNS service provider.
3. Change settings with the current registrar, including unlocking the domain if necessary.
4. Get the names of your Name Servers.
5. Request the transfer in the Amazon Route 53 console. This will send a confirmation email to the domain owner.
6. Click the link in the authorization email.
7. Update the domain configuration to use the new DNS servers.

Transferring your domain can also affect the current expiration date. When you transfer a domain between registrars, TLD registries may let you keep the same expiration date for your domain, add a year to the expiration date, or change the expiration date to one year after the transfer date. For most TLDs, you can extend the registration period for a domain by up to 10 years after you transfer it to Amazon Route 53.

Costs associated with registering or transferring domains are billed immediately as opposed to the end of the billing period.

Domain Name System Service

Amazon Route 53 is an authoritative *Domain Name System (DNS) Service* that routes Internet traffic to your website by translating friendly domain names into IP addresses. When someone enters your domain name in a browser or sends you an email, a DNS request is forwarded to the nearest Amazon Route 53 DNS server in a global network of authoritative DNS servers. Amazon Route 53 responds with the IP address that you specified.

If you register a new domain name with Amazon Route 53, Amazon Route 53 will be automatically configured as the DNS service for the domain and a hosted zone will be created for your domain. You add resource record sets to the hosted zone that define how you want Amazon Route 53 to respond to DNS queries for your domain. These responses can include, for example, the IP address of a web server, the IP address for the nearest Amazon CloudFront Edge location, or the IP address for an Elastic Load Balancing load balancer.

Amazon Route 53 charges a monthly fee for each hosted zone (separate from charges for domain registration). There is also a fee charged for the DNS queries that are received for your domain.

If you do not want to use your domain directly after creation, you can delete the hosted zone. If you delete it within 12 hours of registering the domain, there will not be any charge for the hosted zone on your AWS bill.

If you registered your domain with another domain registrar, that registrar is probably providing the DNS service for your domain. You are able to transfer the DNS service to Amazon Route 53, with or without transferring registration for the domain.

If you are using Amazon CloudFront, Amazon Simple Storage Service (Amazon S3), or Elastic Load Balancing, you can configure Amazon Route 53 to resolve the IP addresses of these resources directly by using *aliases*. Unlike the alias feature provided by CNAME records, which work by sending a referral message back to the requester, these aliases dynamically look up the current IP addresses in use by the AWS service, and return A or AAAA (IPv4 or IPv6 address records, respectively) directly to the client. This allows you to use these resources as the target of a zone apex record. Note that dynamic resolution of zone apex names to IP addresses won't work with other DNS services, which signficantly restrict the use of CloudFront, S3, or Elastic Load Balancing (ELB) in conjunction with the zone apex hosted by another DNS service. The exception is the Network Load Balancer mode of ELB, which provides fixed and unchanging IP addresses (one per availability zone) for the lifetime of the load balancer. These IP addresses can be added to the zone apex of a domain hosted in another DNS service.

Hosted Zones

A *hosted zone* is a collection of resource record sets hosted by Amazon Route 53. Like a traditional DNS zone file, a hosted zone represents resource record sets that are managed together under a single domain name. Each hosted zone has its own metadata and configuration information. Likewise, a resource record set is an object in a hosted zone that you use to define how you want to route traffic for the domain or subdomain.

There are two types of hosted zones: private and public. A *private hosted zone* is a container that holds information about how you want to route traffic for a domain and its subdomains within one or more VPCs. A *public hosted zone* is a container that holds information about how you want to route traffic on the Internet for a domain (such as `example.com`) and its subdomains (for example, `apex.example.com` and `acme.example.com`).

The resource record sets contained in a hosted zone must share the same suffix. For example, the `example.com` hosted zone can contain resource record sets for the `www.example.com` and `www.aws.example.com` subdomains, but it cannot contain resource record sets for a `www.example.ca` subdomain.

You can use Amazon S3 to host your static website at the hosted zone (for example, `domain.com`) and redirect all requests to a subdomain (such as `www.domain.com`). Then, in Amazon Route 53, you can create an alias resource record that sends requests for the root domain to the Amazon S3 bucket.

Use an alias record, not a CNAME, if you want to provide IP addresses for the zone itself. CNAMEs are not allowed for hosted zones in Amazon Route 53 or any other DNS service.

Supported Record Types

Amazon Route 53 supports the following DNS resource record types. When you access Amazon Route 53 using the Application Programming Interface (API), you will see examples of how to format the `Value` element for each record type.

A

AAAA

CAA

CNAME

MX

NAPTR

NS

PTR

SOA

SPF

SRV

TXT

Additionally, Amazon Route 53 offers Alias records, which are Amazon Route 53-specific virtual records. Alias records are used to map resource record sets in your hosted zone to other AWS Cloud services such as Elastic Load Balancing load balancers, Amazon CloudFront distributions, AWS Elastic Beanstalk environments, or Amazon S3 buckets that are configured as websites.

Alias records work like a CNAME record in that you can map one DNS name (`example.com`) to another target DNS name (`elb1234.elb.amazonaws.com`). Alias records differ from a CNAME record in that they are not visible to resolvers; the dynamic lookup of current IP addresses is handled transparently by Route 53. Resolvers only see the A record and the resulting IP address of the target record.

Routing Policies

When you create a resource record set, you set a *routing policy* that determines how Amazon Route 53 responds to queries. Routing policy options are simple, weighted, latency-based, failover, geolocation, multianswer value, and geoproximity (only through the Amazon Route 53 traffic flow feature). When specified, Amazon Route 53 evaluates a resource's relative weight, the client's network latency to the resource, or the client's geographical location when deciding which resource to send back in a DNS response.

Routing policies can also be associated with health checks. Unhealthy resources are removed from consideration before Amazon Route 53 decides which resource to return. A description of possible routing policies and health check options follows.

Simple Routing Policy

This is the default routing policy when you create a new resource. Use a simple routing policy when you have a single logical resource that performs a given function for your domain (for example, the load balancer on front of the web server that serves content for the `example.com` website). In this case, Amazon Route 53 responds to DNS queries based only on the values in the resource record set (such as the CNAME of a load balancers DNS name, or the IP address of a single server in an A record).

Weighted Routing Policy

With weighted DNS, you can associate multiple resources (such as Amazon EC2 instances or Elastic Load Balancing load balancers) with a single DNS name. Use the weighted routing policy when you have multiple resources that perform the same function (such as web servers that serve the same website) and want Amazon Route 53 to route traffic to those resources in proportions that you specify.

To configure weighted routing, you create resource record sets that have the same name and type for each of your resources. You then assign each record a relative weight that corresponds with how much traffic you want to send to each resource.

When processing a DNS query, Amazon Route 53 searches for a resource record set or a group of resource record sets that have the same name and DNS record type (such as an A record). Amazon Route 53 then selects one record from the group. The probability of any resource record set being selected is governed by the Weighted DNS Formula:

$$\frac{\text{Weight for a Specific Record}}{\text{Sum of the Weights for All Records}}$$

For example, if you want to send a tiny portion of your traffic to a test resource and the rest to a control resource, you might specify weights of 1 and 99. The resource with a weight of 1 gets 1 percent of the traffic [1/(1+99)], and the other resource gets 99 percent [99/(1+99)]. You can gradually change the balance by changing the weights. If you want to stop sending traffic to a resource, you can change the weight for that record to 0.

Latency-Based Routing Policy

Latency-based routing allows you to route your traffic based on the lowest network latency for your end user. You can use a latency-based routing policy when you have resources that perform the same function in multiple Availability Zones or AWS Regions and you want Amazon Route 53 to respond to DNS queries using the resources that provide the lowest latency to the client.

For example, suppose that you have Elastic Load Balancing load balancers in the US-West-2 (Oregon) region and in the AP-Southeast-2 (Singapore) region. You create a latency resource record set in Amazon Route 53 for each load balancer for your domain. A user in London enters the name of your domain in a browser, and DNS routes the request to the nearest Amazon Route 53 Name Server using a technology called Anycasting. Amazon Route 53 refers to its data on latency between London and the Singapore region and between London and the Oregon region. If latency is lower between London and the Oregon region, Amazon Route 53 responds to the user's request with the IP address of your load balancer in Oregon. If latency is lower between London and the Singapore region, Amazon Route 53 responds with the IP address of your load balancer in Singapore.

Latency over the Internet can change over time due to changes in network connectivity and the way packets are routed. Latency-based routing is based on latency measurements that are continually reevaluated by Amazon Route 53. As a result, a request from a given client might be routed to the Oregon region one week and the Ohio region the following week due to routing changes on the Internet.

Failover Routing Policy

Use a failover routing policy to configure active-passive failover, in which one resource takes all of the traffic when it is available and the other resource takes all of the traffic when the first resource fails health checks failover resource record sets are only available for public hosted zones as of this writing.

For example, you might want your primary resource record set to be in US-West-1 (N. California) and a secondary disaster recovery resource to be in US-East-1 (N. Virginia). Amazon Route 53 will monitor the health of your primary resource endpoints using a health check that you have configured.

The health check configuration tells Amazon Route 53 how to send requests to the endpoint whose health you want to check: which protocol to use (HTTP, Hypertext Transfer

Protocol Secure [HTTPS], or TCP), which IP address and port to use, and, for HTTP/HTTPS health checks, a domain name and path.

After you have configured a health check, Amazon will monitor the health of your selected DNS endpoint. If your health check fails, then failover routing policies will be applied and your DNS will fail over to your disaster recovery site.

To configure failover in a private hosted zone by checking the endpoint within a VPC by IP address, you must assign a public IP address to the instance in the VPC. An alternative could be to configure a health checker to check the health of an external resource upon which the instance relies, such as a database server. You could also create an Amazon CloudWatch metric, associate an alarm with the metric, and then create a health check that is based on the state of the alarm.

Geolocation Routing Policy

Geolocation routing lets you choose where Amazon Route 53 will send your traffic based on the geographic location of your users (the location from which DNS queries originate). For example, you might want all queries from Europe to be routed to a fleet of Amazon EC2 instances that are specifically configured for your European customers, with local languages and pricing in Euros.

You can also use geolocation routing to restrict distribution of content only to those locations in which you have distribution rights. Another possible use is for balancing load across endpoints in a predictable, easy-to-manage way so that each user location is consistently routed to the same endpoint.

You can specify geographic locations by continent, by country, or by state in the United States. You can also create separate resource record sets for overlapping geographic regions, with conflicts resolved in favor of the smallest geographic region. This allows you to route some queries for a continent to one resource and to route queries for selected countries on that continent to a different resource. For example, if you have geolocation resource record sets for North America and Canada, users in Canada will be directed to the Canada-specific resources.

Geolocation works by using a database to map IP addresses to locations. Exercise caution, however, because these results are not always accurate. Some IP addresses have no geolocation data associated with them, and an ISP may move an IP block across countries without notification. Even if you create geolocation resource record sets that cover all seven continents, Amazon Route 53 will receive some DNS queries from locations that it cannot identify.

In this case, you can create a default resource record set that handles queries from both unmapped IP addresses and locations lacking geolocation resource record sets. If you omit a default resource record set, Amazon Route 53 returns a "no answer" response for queries from those locations.

Create a default resource record set to prevent Amazon Route 53 from returning a "no answer" response in the case where Amazon Route 53 receives a DNS query from a location that it cannot identify.

You cannot create two geolocation resource record sets that specify the same geographic location. You also cannot create geolocation resource record sets that have the same values for Name and Type as the Name and Type of non-geolocation resource record sets.

To improve the accuracy of geolocation routing, Amazon Route 53 supports the edns-client-subnet extension of EDNS0, which adds several optional extensions to the DNS protocol.

Amazon Route 53 can use edns-client-subnet only when DNS resolvers support it, with the following behavior to be expected:

- When a browser or other viewer uses a DNS resolver that does not support edns-client-subnet, Amazon Route 53 uses the source IP address of the DNS resolver to approximate the location of the user and responds to geolocation queries with the DNS record for the resolver's location.
- When a browser or other viewer uses a DNS resolver that does support edns-client-subnet, the DNS resolver sends Amazon Route 53 a truncated version of the user's IP address. Amazon Route 53 determines the location of the user based on the truncated IP address as opposed to using the source IP address of the DNS resolver, which typically will provide a more accurate estimate of the user's location.

Creating geolocation resource record sets in private hosted zones is not supported.

More information on edns-client-subnet can be found in the IETF EDNS draft at: `https://tools.ietf.org/html/draft-vandergaast-edns-client-subnet-02`.

Multivalue Answer Routing

Multivalue answer routing lets you configure Amazon Route 53 to return multiple values, such as IP addresses for your web servers, in response to DNS queries. Any DNS record type except for NS and CNAME is supported. You can specify multiple values for almost any record, but multivalue answer routing also lets you check the health of each resource, so Amazon Route 53 returns only values for healthy resources. While this is not a substitute for a load balancer, the ability to return multiple health-checkable IP addresses improves availability and load balancing efficiency.

To route traffic in a reasonably random manner to multiple resources, such as web servers, you can create a single multivalue answer record for each resource and optionally associate an Amazon Route 53 health check with each record. Amazon Route 53 will then respond to DNS queries with up to eight healthy records and will give different answers to different requesting DNS resolvers.

If you associate a health check with a multivalue answer record, Amazon Route 53 responds to DNS queries with the corresponding IP address only when the health check is healthy.

If you do not associate a health check with a multivalue answer record, Amazon Route 53 always considers the record to be healthy.

Traffic Flow to Route DNS Traffic

Managing resource record sets for complex Amazon Route 53 configurations can be challenging, especially when using combinations of Amazon Route 53 routing policies.

Through the AWS Management Console, you get access to Amazon Route 53 traffic flow. This provides you with a visual editor that helps you create complex decision trees in a fraction of the time and effort. You can then save the configuration as a traffic policy and associate the traffic policy with one or more domain names in multiple hosted zones. Amazon Route 53 traffic flow then allows you to use the visual editor to find resources that you need to update and apply updates to one or more DNS names. You then have the ability to roll back updates if the new configuration is not performing as you intended. Figure 6.5 shows an example traffic policy using Amazon Route 53 traffic flow.

FIGURE 6.5 Amazon Route 53 traffic flow—an example traffic policy

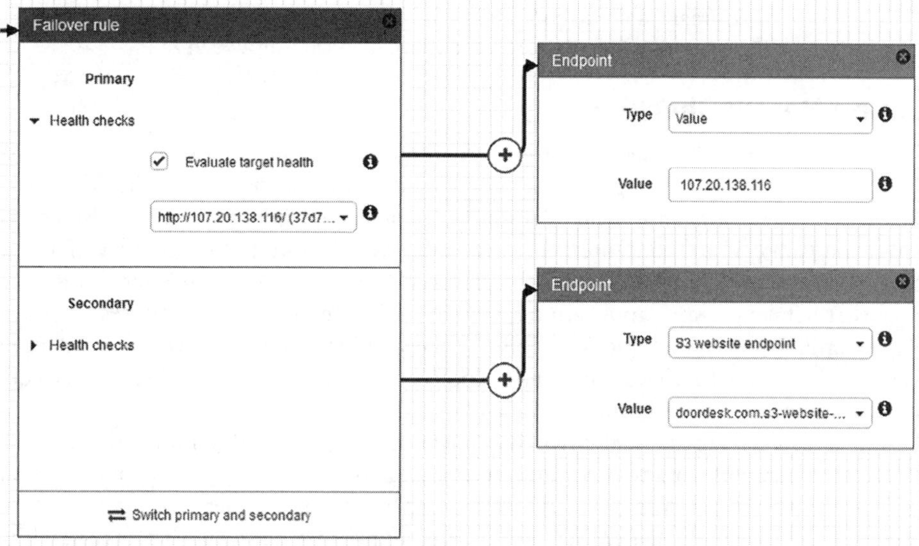

Geoproximity Routing (Traffic Flow Only)

Geoproximity routing lets Amazon Route 53 route traffic to your resources based on the geographic location of your resources. Additionally, geoproximity routing gives you the option to route more traffic or less traffic to a particular resource by specifying the value, *bias*, which will expand or shrink the size of a geographic region to where traffic is currently being routed.

When creating a geoproximity rule for your AWS resources, you must specify the AWS Region in which you created the resource. If you're using non-AWS resources, you must specify the latitude and longitude of the resources.

You can then optionally expand the size of the geographic region from which Amazon Route 53 routes traffic to a resource by specifying a positive integer from 1 to 99 for the bias. When you specify a negative bias of -1 to -99, the opposite is true: Amazon Route 53 will shrink the size of the geographic region to which it routes traffic.

We recommend that you change the bias in small increments to prevent overwhelming your resources due to an unanticipated swing in traffic.

The effect of changing the bias for your resources depends on a number of factors, including the number of resources that you have, how close the resources are to one another, and the number of users that you have near the border area between geographic regions.

If you have resources in Boston and Washington, D.C., and you have a large number of users in New York City (roughly equidistant between your resources), a small change in bias could result in a large swing in traffic from resources in Boston to resources in D.C. or vice versa.

More on Health Checking

Amazon Route 53 health checks monitor the health of your resources such as web servers and email servers. You can configure Amazon CloudWatch alarms for your health checks so that you receive notification when a resource becomes unavailable. You can also configure Amazon Route 53 to route Internet traffic away from resources that are unavailable.

Health checks and DNS failover are the primary tools in the Amazon Route 53 feature set that help make your application highly available and resilient to failures. If you deploy an application in multiple Availability Zones and multiple AWS Regions and attach Amazon Route 53 health checks to every endpoint, Amazon Route 53 will respond to queries with a list of healthy endpoints only.

Health checks can automatically switch to a healthy endpoint with minimal disruption to your clients and without any configuration changes. You can use this automatic recovery scenario in active-active or active-passive setups, depending on whether your additional endpoints are always hit by live traffic or only after all primary endpoints have failed. Using health checks and automatic failovers, Amazon Route 53 improves your service uptime, especially when compared to the traditional monitor-alert-restart approach of addressing failures.

Amazon Route 53 health checks are not triggered by DNS queries; they are run periodically by AWS, and the results are published to all DNS servers. This way, Name Servers can be aware of an unhealthy endpoint and route differently within approximately 30 seconds of a problem (after three failed tests in a row with a request interval of 10 seconds) and new DNS results will be known to clients a minute later (if your TTL is set to 60 seconds), bringing complete recovery time to about a minute and a half in total in this scenario. Beware, however, that DNS TTLs are not always honored by some intermediate Name Servers nor by some client software, so for some clients the ideal failover time might be much longer.

Figure 6.6 shows an overview of how health checking works in the scenario where you want to be notified when resources become unavailable, with the following workflow:

1. Health checks are configured by you to monitor endpoints.
2. Requests are periodically sent to endpoints.
3. If a health check fails to receive a response, it will trigger an action.
4. An Amazon CloudWatch alarm is triggered, and it will then trigger an action with Amazon Simple Notification Service (Amazon SNS).
5. Recipients who are subscribed to an Amazon SNS topic will receive a notification that a health check has failed.

FIGURE 6.6 Amazon Route 53 health checking

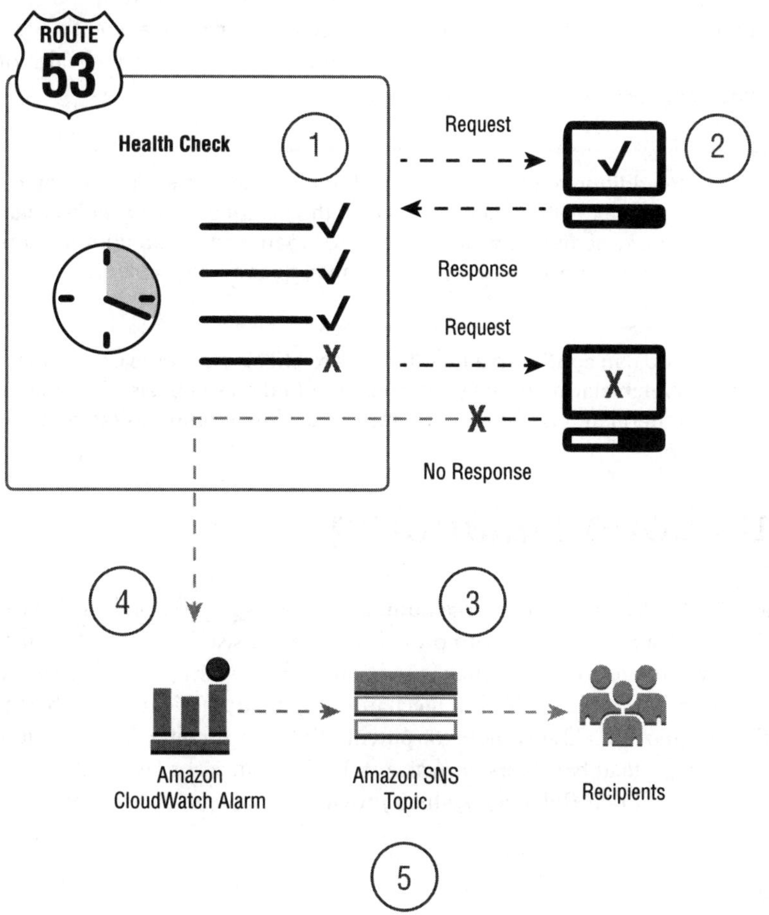

You can create a health check and stipulate values that define how you want the health check to work, specifying the following attributes:

- *IP address* or *domain name* of the endpoint, such as a web server, that you want Amazon Route 53 to monitor. You can also monitor the status of other health checks or the state of an Amazon CloudWatch alarm.
- *Protocol* that you want Amazon Route 53 to use to perform the check: HTTP, HTTPS, or TCP.
- *Request interval* that Amazon Route 53 will use as the time between sending requests to the endpoint.
- *Failure threshold* that Amazon Route 53 will use to track how many consecutive times the endpoint must fail to respond to requests before considering an endpoint unhealthy.

You can additionally set how you want to be notified when Amazon Route 53 detects that an endpoint is unhealthy. When you configure notification, Amazon Route 53 will automatically set an Amazon CloudWatch alarm. Amazon CloudWatch uses Amazon SNS to notify users that an endpoint is unhealthy.

It is important to note that Amazon Route 53 does not check the health of the resource specified in the resource record set, such as the A record for `example.com`. When you associate a health check with a resource record set, it will begin to check the health of the endpoint that you have specified in the health check.

In addition to checking the health of a specified endpoint, you can configure a health check to check on the health of one or more other health checks so that you can be notified when a specified number of resources, such as two web servers out of five, become unavailable.

You can configure a health check to check the status of an Amazon CloudWatch alarm so that you can be notified on the basis of a broad range of criteria, not just whether a resource is responding to requests.

Elastic Load Balancing

An advantage of having access to a large number of servers in the cloud, such as Amazon EC2 instances on AWS, is the ability to provide a more consistent experience for the end user. One way to ensure consistency is to balance the request load across more than one server. A *load balancer* in AWS is a mechanism that automatically distributes traffic across multiple Amazon EC2 instances (or potentially other targets). You can either manage your own virtual load balancers on Amazon EC2 instances or leverage an AWS Cloud service called *Elastic Load Balancing*, which provides a managed load balancer for you. A combination of both virtual managed load balancers on Amazon EC2 instances and Elastic Load Balancing can also be used. This configuration is referred to as the ELB sandwich.

Using Elastic Load Balancing can provide advantages over building a load balancing service based on Amazon EC2 instances. Because Elastic Load Balancing is a managed service, it scales in and out automatically to meet the demands of increased application traffic and is highly available within a region itself as a service. Elastic Load Balancing provides high availability by helping you distribute traffic across healthy instances in multiple Availability Zones. Additionally, Elastic Load Balancing seamlessly integrates with the Auto Scaling service to scale automatically the Amazon EC2 instances behind the load balancer. Lastly, Elastic Load Balancing can offer additional security for your application architecture, working with Amazon VPC to route traffic internally between application tiers. This allows you to expose only Internet-facing public IP addresses of the load balancer.

The Elastic Load Balancing service allows you to distribute traffic across a group of Amazon EC2 instances in one or more *Availability Zones*, enabling you to achieve high availability in your applications. Using multiple Availability Zones is always recommended when using services that do not automatically provide regional fault-tolerance, such as Amazon EC2.

Elastic Load Balancing supports routing and load balancing of Hypertext Transfer Protocol HTTP, HTTPS, TCP, and Transport Layer Security (TLS) traffic to Amazon EC2 instances. Note, Transport Layer Security (TLS) and its predecessor Secure Sockets Layer (SSL) are protocols that are used to encrypt confidential data over insecure networks such as the Internet. The TLS protocol is a newer version of the SSL protocol. In this chapter, we refer to both SSL and TLS protocols as the SSL protocol, with Elastic Load Balancing supporting TLS 1.2, TLS 1.1, TLS 1.0, SSL 3.0.

Elastic Load Balancing provides a stable, single DNS name for DNS configuration and supports both Internet-facing and internal application-facing load balancers. Network Load Balancers also provide a stable set of IP addresses (one per Availability Zone) over their lifetimes. It is still a best practice, however, to use the DNS name of a load balancer as the mechanism for referencing it.

Elastic Load Balancing supports health checks for Amazon EC2 instances to ensure that traffic is not routed to unhealthy or failing instances. Elastic Load Balancing can automatically scale based on collected metrics recorded in Amazon CloudWatch.

Elastic Load Balancing also supports integrated certificate management and SSL termination.

Types of Load Balancers

Elastic Load Balancing provides three different types of load balancers at the time of this writing: Classic Load Balancer, Application Load Balancer, and Network Load Balancer. Each type of Amazon load balancer is suited to a particular use case. The features of each type are shown in Table 6.2. Each type of load balancer can be configured as either internal for use within the Amazon VPC or external for use on the public Internet. Elastic Load Balancing also supports features such as HTTPS and encrypted connections.

TABLE 6.2 Elastic Load Balancer Comparison

Feature	Classic Load Balancer	Application Load Balancer	Network Load Balancer
Protocols	TCP, SSL, HTTP, HTTPS	HTTP, HTTPS	TCP
Platforms	EC2-Classic, VPC	VPC	VPC
Health checks	✓	✓	✓
Amazon CloudWatch metrics	✓	✓	✓
Logging	✓	✓	✓
Availability Zone failover	✓	✓	✓
Connection draining (deregistration delay)	✓	✓	✓
Load balancing to multiple ports on the same instance		✓	✓
WebSockets		✓	✓
IP addresses as targets		✓	✓
Load balancer deletion protection		✓	✓
Path-based routing		✓	
Host-based routing		✓	
Native HTTP/2		✓	
Configurable idle connection timeout	✓	✓	
Cross-zone load balancing	✓	✓	
SSL offloading	✓	✓	
Sticky sessions	✓	✓	
Back-end server encryption	✓	✓	
Static IP			✓
Elastic IP address			✓
Preserve source IP address			✓

Classic Load Balancer

Classic Load Balancer is the original class of Elastic Load Balancing prior to the release of Application Load Balancer and Network Load Balancer. The Classic Load Balancer will distribute incoming application traffic across multiple Amazon EC2 instances in multiple Availability Zones, increasing the fault tolerance of your application. You can configure health checks to monitor the health of the registered targets so that the load balancer can send requests only to the healthy targets.

Classic Load Balancers can be configured to pass TCP traffic directly through (Layer 4 in the Open Systems Interconnect [OSI] model) or to handle HTTP/HTTPS requests (Layer 7) and perform SSL termination and insert HTTP proxy headers.

In most cases, an Application Load Balancer or Network Load Balancer will be the better choice when building your load balancing architecture. For load balancing across Amazon EC2-classic targets, however, using Classic Load Balancers is required. The Classic Load Balancer architecture is shown in Figure 6.7.

FIGURE 6.7 Classic Load Balancer

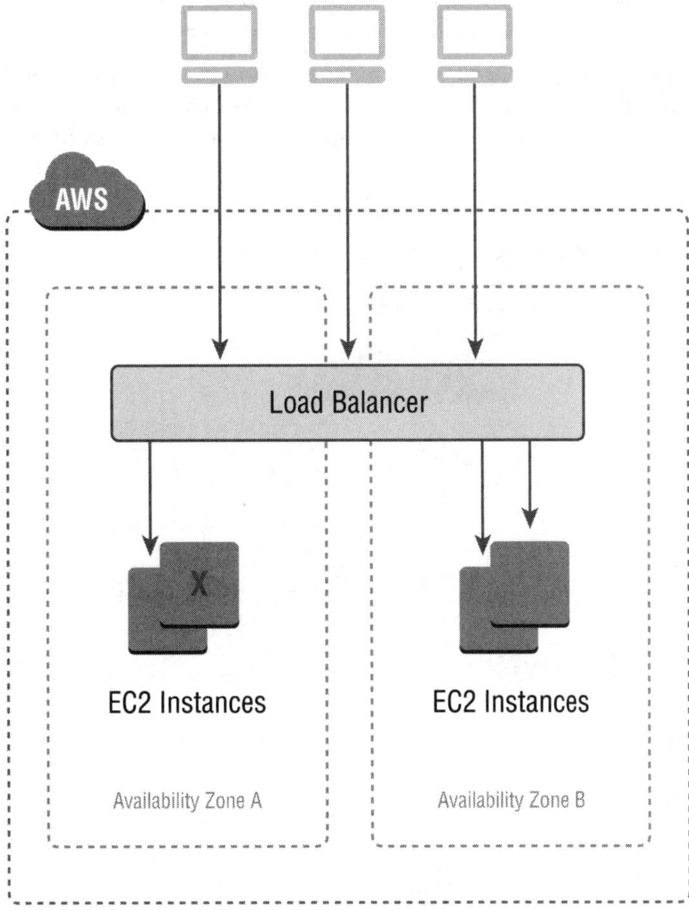

Application Load Balancer

An *Application Load Balancer* operates at the application layer (Layer 7) of the OSI model. After receiving a request, the Application Load Balancer will evaluate the listener rules in a priority order to determine which rule to apply, then select the appropriate target from a target group using the round robin routing algorithm.

The Application Load Balancer serves as a single point of contact for clients, increasing the availability of your application. It also gives you the ability to route requests to different target groups based on the content of the application traffic. As with Classic Load Balancer, you can configure health checks to monitor the health of the registered targets so that the load balancer can send requests only to the healthy targets.

The Application Load Balancer is the ideal choice when you need support for:

- *Path-based routing*, with rules for your listener that forward requests based on the HTTP URL in the request.
- *Routing requests to multiple services on a single EC2 instance* by registering the same instance using multiple ports.
- *Containerized applications* by having the ability to select an unused port when scheduling a task and registering that task with a target group using this port.
- *Monitoring the health of each service independently* because health checks are defined at the target group level and many Amazon CloudWatch metrics are reported at the target group level. Attaching a target group to an Auto Scaling group enables you to scale each service dynamically based on demand.
- *Improved load balancer performance* over the Classic Load Balancer.

The Application Load Balancer architecture is shown in Figure 6.8.

FIGURE 6.8 Application Load Balancer

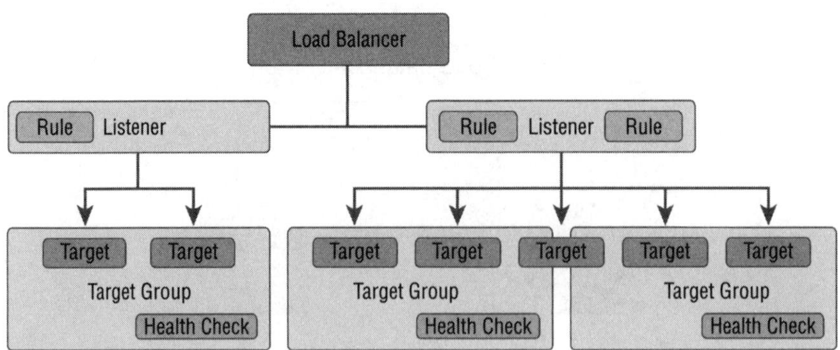

Targets and target groups are discussed later in this chapter.

Network Load Balancer

An Amazon *Network Load Balancer* operates at the transport layer (Layer 4) of the OSI model. Network Load Balancer works by receiving a connection request, selecting a target from the target group associated with the Network Load Balancer, and then attempting to open a TCP connection to the selected target on the port specified in the listener configuration.

The Network Load Balancer architecture is shown in Figure 6.9.

FIGURE 6.9 Network Load Balancer

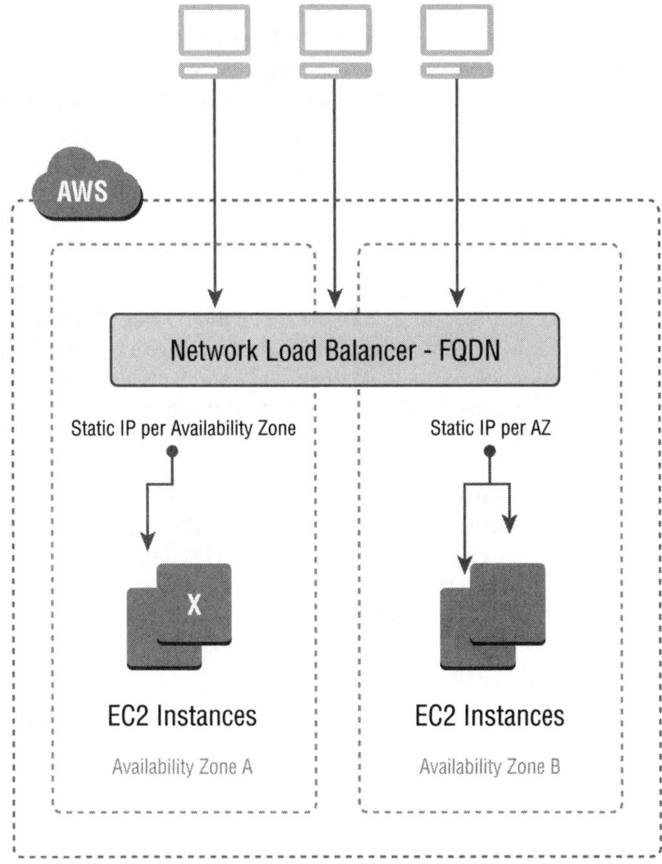

Using a Network Load Balancer instead of a Classic Load Balancer or Application Load Balancer has the following benefits:

- Ability to handle volatile workloads and scale to millions of requests per second.
- Support for static IP addresses for the load balancer. You can also assign one Elastic IP address per Availability Zone enabled for the load balancer.
- Support for registering targets by IP address, including targets outside the VPC for the load balancer.
- Support for routing requests to multiple applications on a single EC2 instance. You can register each instance or IP address with the same target group using multiple ports.
- Support for containerized applications. Amazon EC2 Container Service (Amazon ECS) can select an unused port when scheduling a task and register the task with a target group using this port. This enables you to make efficient use of your clusters.

- Support for monitoring the health of each service independently, as health checks are defined at the target group level and many Amazon CloudWatch metrics are reported at the target group level. Attaching a target group to an Auto Scaling group enables you to scale each service dynamically based on demand.

It is also worth noting that with Network Load Balancers, the load balancer node that receives the connection selects a target from the target group using a flow hash algorithm. This flow hashing algorithm is based on the protocol, source IP address, source port, destination IP address, destination port, and TCP sequence number. As the TCP connections from a client have different source ports and sequence numbers, each connection can be routed to a different target. Each individual TCP connection is also routed to a single target for the life of the connection.

Network Load Balancers can preserve the source IP of the client if you use the instance ID when configuring a target. If you're specifying the target by IP address, the source IP of the client cannot be preserved and proxy protocol must be used to pass the client IP on to the target.

You cannot register instances by instance ID if they have the following instance types: C1, CC1, CC2, CG1, CG2, CR1, G1, G2, HI1, HS1, M1, M2, M3, or T1. You can register instances of these types by IP address. You also cannot register targets in a peered VPC or linked through an AWS Hardware Virtual Private Network (VPN).

Internet-Facing Load Balancers

An *Internet-Facing Load Balancer* is, as the name implies, a load balancer that takes requests from clients over the Internet and distributes them to Amazon EC2 instances or IP addresses that are registered with the load balancer. Each of the three types of Elastic Load Balancer can be configured as Internet-Facing Load Balancers, with publicly reachable endpoints through a public subnet within a VPC.

When you configure a load balancer, it receives a public DNS name that clients can use to send requests to your application. The DNS servers resolve the DNS name to your load balancer's public IP address, which can be visible to client applications.

Classic Load Balancer and Application Load Balancer IP addresses may change as the load balancers scale. Referencing them by their IP addresses instead of DNS names may result in some load balancer endpoints being underutilized or sending traffic to incorrect endpoints.

Because Elastic Load Balancing scales in and out to meet traffic demand, it is not recommended to bind an application to an IP address that may no longer be part of a load balancer's pool of resources. Network Load Balancer has a *static IP* feature, where the load balancer will be represented by a single IP address per Availability Zone regardless of the scale of the Network Load Balancer. Classic Load Balancer and Application Load Balancer do not have this static IP functionality.

Both the Classic Load Balancer and Application Load Balancer support dual stack addressing (IPv4 and IPv6). At the time of this writing, Network Load Balancer only supports IPv4.

Internal Load Balancers

In a multi-tier application, it is often useful to load balance between the tiers of the application. For example, an Internet-Facing Load Balancer might receive and balance external traffic to the presentation or web tier composed of Amazon EC2 instances. These instances then send requests to a load balancer sitting in front of an application tier that should not receive traffic from the Internet. You can use *internal load balancers* to route traffic to your application-tier Amazon EC2 instances in VPCs with private subnets.

HTTPS Load Balancers

Both Application Load Balancer and Classic Load Balancer support HTTPS traffic. You can create an Application Load Balancer or Classic Load Balancer that uses the SSL/Transport Layer Security (TLS) protocol for encrypted connections (also known as *SSL offload*). This feature enables traffic encryption between your load balancer and the clients that initiate HTTPS sessions. It also enables the connection between your load balancer and your back-end Elastic Load Balancing to provide security policies that have predefined SSL negotiation configurations. These can be used to negotiate connections between clients and the load balancer. In order to use SSL, you must install an SSL certificate on the load balancer that it uses to terminate the connection and then decrypt requests from clients before sending requests to the back-end Amazon EC2 instances. You can optionally choose to enable authentication on your back-end instances. If you are performing SSL on your back-end instances, the Network Load Balancer may be a better choice.

Elastic Load Balancing Concepts

A load balancer serves as the single point of contact for clients. Clients can send a request to the load balancer, and the load balancer will send them to targets, such as Amazon EC2 instances, in one or more Availability Zones. Elastic Load Balancing load balancers are made up of the following concepts.

Listeners

Every load balancer must have one or more listeners configured. A *listener* is a process that waits for connection requests. Every listener is configured with a protocol, a port for a front-end connection (client to load balancer) and a protocol, and a port for the back-end (load balancer to Amazon EC2 instance) connection. Application Load Balancer and Classic Load Balancer load balancers both support the following protocols:

- HTTP
- HTTPS
- TCP
- SSL

Classic Load Balancer supports protocols operating at two different OSI layers. In the OSI model, Layer 4 is the transport layer that describes the TCP connection between the client and your back-end instance through the load balancer. Layer 4 is the lowest level that is configurable for your load balancer. Layer 7 is the application layer that describes the use of HTTP and HTTPS connections from clients to the load balancer and from the load balancer to your back-end instance.

The Network Load Balancer supports TCP (Layer 4 of the OSI model). Application Load Balancer supports HTTPS and HTTP (Layer 7 of the OSI model).

Listener Rules

A major advantage of Application Load Balancer is the ability to define listener rules. The rules that you define for your Application Load Balancer will determine how the load balancer routes requests to the targets in one of more target groups for the Application Load Balancer. Listener rules are composed of the following:

A rule priority Rules are evaluated in priority order, from the lowest value to the highest value.

One or more rule actions Each rule action has a type and a target group. Currently, the only supported type is forward, which forwards requests to the target group.

Rule conditions When the conditions for a rule are met, then its action is taken. You can use *host* conditions to define rules that forward requests to different target groups based on the hostname in the host header (also known as *host-based routing*). You can use *path* conditions to define rules that forward requests to different target groups based on the URL in the request (also known as *path-based routing*).

Targets

An Application Load Balancer or Network Load Balancer serves as a single point of contact for clients and distributes traffic across healthy registered targets. *Targets* are selected destinations to which the Application Load Balancer or Network Load Balancer sends traffic. Targets such as Amazon EC2 instances are associated with a target group and can be one of the following:

- An *instance*, where the targets are specified by instance ID.
- An *IP*, where the targets are specified by IP address.

When a target type is IP, you can specify addresses from one of the following CIDR blocks:

- The subnets of the VPC for the target group
- 10.0.0.0/8 (RFC 1918)
- 100.64.0.0/10 (RFC 6598)
- 172.16.0.0/12 (RFC 1918)
- 192.168.0.0/16 (RFC 1918)

These supported CIDR blocks enable you to register the following with a target group: ClassicLink instances, instances in a peered VPC, AWS resources addressable by IP address and port (for example, databases), and on-premises resources that are reachable by either AWS Direct Connect or a VPN connection.

If you specify targets using an instance ID, traffic is routed to instances using the primary private IP address specified in the primary network interface for the instance. If you specify targets using IP addresses, you can route traffic to an instance using any private IP address from one or more network interfaces. This enables multiple applications on an instance to use the same port. Each network interface can also have its own security group assigned.

If demand on your application increases, you can register additional targets with one or more of your target groups, with the load balancer additionally routing requests to newly registered targets, as soon as the registration process completes and the new target passes the initial health checks.

If you are registering targets by instance ID, you can use your load balancer with an Auto Scaling group. After you attach a target group to an Auto Scaling group, Auto Scaling registers your targets with the target group for you when it launches them.

Target Groups

Target groups allow you to group together targets, such as Amazon EC2 instances, for the Application Load Balancer and Network Load Balancer. The target group can be used in listener rules. This makes it easy to specify rules consistently across multiple targets.

You define health check settings for your load balancer on a per-target group basis. After you specify a target group in a rule for a listener, the load balancer continually monitors the health of all targets registered within the target group that are in an Availability Zone that is enabled for the load balancer. The load balancer will then route requests to registered targets within the group that are healthy.

Elastic Load Balancer Configuration

Elastic Load Balancing allows you to configure many aspects of the load balancer, including *idle connection timeout*, *cross-zone load balancing*, *connection draining*, *proxy protocol*, *sticky sessions*, and *health checks*. Configuration settings can be modified using either the AWS Management Console or a Command Line Interface (CLI). Most features are available for Classic Load Balancer, Application Load Balancer, and Network Load Balancer. A few features, like cross-zone load balancing, are only available for Classic Load Balancer and Application Load Balancer.

Idle Connection Timeout

The *Idle Connection Timeout* feature is applicable to the Application Load Balancer and Classic Load Balancer. For each request that a client makes through a load balancer, the load balancer maintains a front-end connection to the client and a back-end connection to the Amazon EC2 instance. For each connection, the load balancer manages an idle timeout that is triggered when no data is sent over the connection for a specified time period. After the idle timeout period has elapsed and no data has been sent or received, the load balancer closes the connection.

By default, Elastic Load Balancing sets the idle timeout to 60 seconds for both connections. If an HTTP request fails to complete within the idle timeout period, the load balancer closes the connection, even if the request is still being processed. You can change the idle timeout setting for the connections to ensure that lengthy operations, such as large file uploads, have time to complete.

If you use HTTP and HTTPS listeners, we recommend that you enable the *TCP keep-alive* option for your Amazon EC2 instances. This is configured either on the application or the operating system running on your Amazon EC2 instances. Enabling keep-alive allows the load balancer to reuse connections to your back-end instance, which reduces CPU utilization.

Cross-Zone Load Balancing

Cross-zone load balancing, available for Classic Load Balancer and Application Load Balancer, ensures that request traffic is routed evenly across all back-end instances for your load balancer, regardless of the Availability Zone in which they are located. Cross-zone load balancing reduces the need to maintain equivalent numbers of back-end instances in each Availability Zone and improves your application's ability to handle the loss of one or more back-end instances. It is still recommended that you maintain approximately equivalent numbers of instances in each Availability Zone for higher fault tolerance.

For environments where clients cache DNS lookups, incoming requests might favor one of the Availability Zones. Using cross-zone load balancing, this imbalance in the request load is spread across all available back-end instances in the region, reducing the impact of misconfigured clients.

Connection Draining (Deregistration Delay)

Available for all load balancer types, *connection draining* ensures that the load balancer stops sending requests to instances that are deregistering or unhealthy while keeping the existing connections open. This enables the load balancer to complete in-flight requests made to these instances.

When you enable connection draining, you can specify a maximum time for the load balancer to keep connections alive before reporting the instance as deregistered. The maximum timeout value can be set between 1 and 3,600 seconds, with the default set to 300 seconds. When the maximum time limit is reached, the load balancer forcibly closes any remaining connections to the deregistering instance.

Proxy Protocol

This option is available for Classic Load Balancer. When you use TCP or SSL for both front-end and back-end connections, your load balancer forwards requests to the back-end instances without modifying the request headers. If you enable *proxy protocol*, connection information, such as the source IP address, destination IP address, and port numbers, is injected into the request before being sent to the back-end instance.

Before enabling proxy protocol, verify that your load balancer is not already behind a proxy server with proxy protocol enabled. If proxy protocol is enabled on both the proxy server and the load balancer, the load balancer injects additional configuration information into the request, interfering with the information from the proxy server. Depending on how your back-end instance is configured, this duplication might result in errors.

Proxy protocol is not needed when using an Application Load Balancer, because the Application Load Balancer already inserts HTTP X-Forwarded-For headers. Network Load Balancer provides client IP pass-through to Amazon EC2 instances (if you use the instance ID when configuring a target).

Sticky Sessions

This feature is applicable to Classic Load Balancer and Application Load Balancer. By default, an Application Load Balancer or Classic Load Balancer load balancer will route each request independently to the registered instance with the smallest load. You can also use the *sticky session* feature (also known as *session affinity*), which enables the load balancer to bind a user's session to a specific instance. This ensures that all requests from the user during the session are sent to the same instance.

The key to managing sticky sessions with the Classic Load Balancer is to determine how long your load balancer should consistently route the user's request to the same instance. If your application has its own session cookie, you can configure Classic Load Balancing so that the session cookie follows the duration specified by the application's session cookie. If your application does not have its own session cookie, you can configure Elastic Load Balancing to create a session cookie by specifying your own stickiness duration. Elastic Load Balancing creates a cookie named AWSELB that is used to map the session to the instance.

Sessions for the Network Load Balancer are inherently sticky due to the flow hashing algorithm used.

Health Checks

Elastic Load Balancing supports *health checks* to test the status of the Amazon EC2 instances behind an Elastic Load Balancing load balancer. For the Classic Load Balancer, the status of the instances that are healthy at the time of the health check is InService, and any instances that are unhealthy at the time of the health check are labeled as OutOfService.

For Network Load Balancer and Application Load Balancer, before the load balancer will send a health check request to the target, you must register it with a target group, specify its target group in a listener rule, and ensure that the Availability Zone of the target is enabled for the load balancer. There are also five health check states for targets:

Initial This state is where the load balancer is in the process of registering the target or performing the initial health checks on the target.

Healthy This state is where the target is healthy.

Unhealthy This state is where the target did not respond to a health check or failed the health check.

Unused This state is where the target is not registered with a target group, the target group is not used in a listener rule for the load balancer, or the target is in an Availability Zone that is not enabled for the load balancer.

Draining This state is where the target is deregistering and connection draining is in process.

In general, the load balancer performs health checks on all registered instances to determine whether the instance is in a healthy state or an unhealthy state. A health check is a ping, a connection attempt, or a page that is checked periodically. You can set the time interval between health checks and also the amount of time to wait to respond in case the health check page includes a computational aspect. Lastly, you can set a threshold for the number of consecutive health check failures before an instance is marked as unhealthy.

Long-running applications will eventually need to be maintained and updated with a newer version of the application. When using Amazon EC2 instances running behind an Elastic Load Balancing load balancer, you may deregister these long-running Amazon EC2 instances associated with a load balancer manually and then register newly-launched Amazon EC2 instances that you have started with the new updates installed.

ELB Sandwich

When you want to deploy virtual load balancers on Amazon EC2 instances, it is up to you to manage the redundancy of these instances. As the Elastic Load Balancing service has native redundancy that is managed by AWS, you can use a combination of Elastic Load Balancing load balancers and virtual load balancers on instances. Virtual load balancers may be used when you want access to vendor-specific features, such as F5 Big-IP iRules. An overview of the ELB sandwich is shown in Figure 6.10.

FIGURE 6.10 ELB sandwich

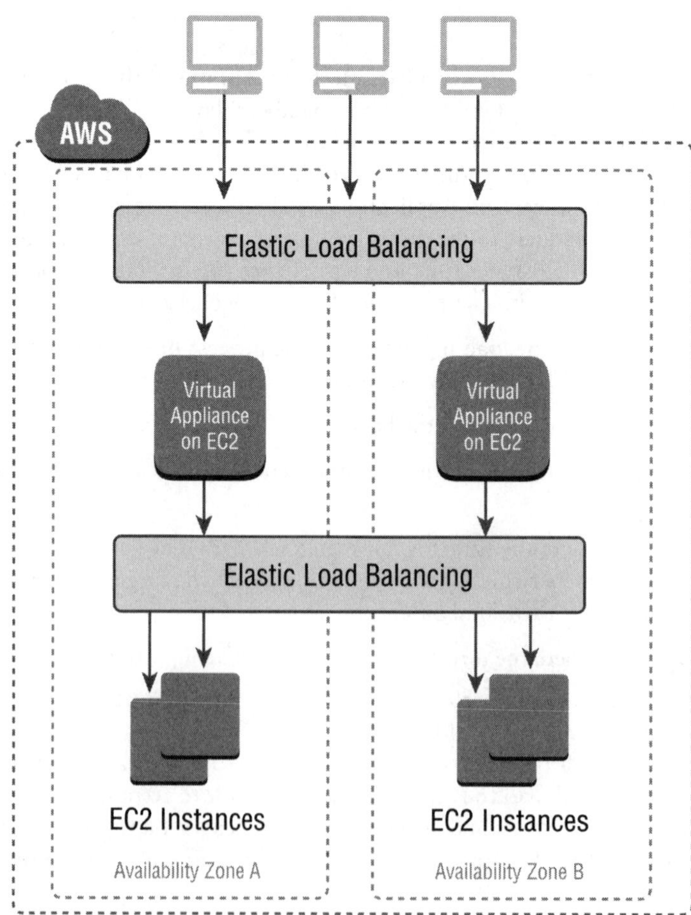

The ELB sandwich uses an Elastic Load Balancing load balancer to serve front-end traffic from users, such as web users wanting to reach a website. The first load balancing layer in the ELB sandwich is made of an Elastic Load Balancing load balancer and is represented by the ELB FQDN. The FQDN of the load balancer could also be referred to by an Amazon Route 53 domain name pointing to the load balancer via an Alias record. The first layer of an ELB sandwich, usually the Classic Load Balancer or Network Load Balancer, will then load balance across your virtual instances such as HAProxy, NGINX, or the F5 LTM Big-IP Virtual Edition. The virtual load balancer layer will then forward traffic on to your second layer of Elastic Load Balancing, which then load balances across your front-end application tier. The *ELB sandwich* is a method of using native high availability that is built into the Elastic Load Balancing product to provide higher availability for Amazon EC2 virtual instances.

Many virtual load balancers that run in AWS cannot natively refer to their next hop via a FQDN. For the traditional ELB sandwich using Classic Load Balancer, it is always a good idea to reference the FQDN of an Elastic Load Balancing load balancer as required to forward traffic to the second layer of load balancers. This is due to the fact that the instances within the Elastic Load Balancing load balancer may change at any point. Pointing directly to IP addresses of the second tier of load balancer could cause traffic loss if the Classic Load Balancer IPs change, similar to what happens during Classic Load Balancer scaling.

Virtual load balancing vendors have, in some cases, implemented solutions that will periodically look up the FQDN of a load balancer and store these IPs as the next hop for traffic. This, however, requires periodic lookups of the Classic Load Balancer's FQDN. An alternate solution is to use the Network Load Balancer as the second tier of load balancers in front of the web tier. This is a better solution because the Network Load Balancer supports having a single static IP per Availability Zone, which the virtual layer of load balancers can point to rather than having to perform periodic lookups of the load balancer's FQDN.

When using an ELB sandwich, using a Network Load Balancer as the second tier of load balancing can help with vendor's devices that do not support referencing an FQDN or CNAME as the next hop because Network Load Balancer can be referenced by the static IP for each Availability Zone in which it is configured to run. Using the Network Load Balancer as the first tier of load balancing and registering the virtual appliance instances by instance ID will provide the instances with the true source IP of the client, allowing for greater visibility into client distribution and security if using a security appliance.

Summary

This chapter reviewed the fundamentals of DNS, which is the methodology that computers use to convert human-friendly domain names (such as `amazon.com`) into IP addresses (for example, `192.0.2.1`).

DNS starts with TLDs (such as `.com` and `.edu`). The IANA controls the TLDs in a root zone database, which is essentially a database of all available TLDs.

DNS names are registered with a domain registrar. A registrar is an authority that can assign domain names directly under one or more TLDs. These domains are registered with InterNIC, a service of ICANN, which enforces the uniqueness of domain names across the Internet. Each domain name becomes registered in a central database, known as the WHOIS database.

DNS consists of a number of different record types, including but not limited to the following:

A

AAAA

CAA

CNAME

MX

NAPTR

NS

PTR

SOA

SPF

SRV

TXT

You also learned about the difference between Amazon DNS and Amazon Route 53, including how to build hybrid DNS architectures between your on-premises environment and AWS.

We covered Amazon Route 53, which is a highly available and highly scalable AWS-provided DNS service, including the registration and creation of domain names. Amazon Route 53 connects user requests to infrastructure running on AWS (for example, Amazon EC2 instances and Elastic Load Balancing load balancers). It can also be used to route users to infrastructure outside of AWS.

With Amazon Route 53, your DNS records are organized into hosted zones that you configure with the Amazon Route 53 API. A hosted zone simply stores records for your domain. These records can consist of A, CNAME, MX, and other supported record types.

Amazon Route 53 allows you to have several different routing policies, including the following:

Simple Most commonly used when you have a single resource that performs a given function for your domain.

Weighted Used when you want to route a percentage of your traffic to one particular resource or group of resources.

Latency-based Used to route your traffic based on the lowest latency, so that your users get the fastest response times.

Failover Used for disaster recovery and to route traffic from your resources in a primary location to a standby location.

Geolocation Used to route traffic based on your end user's location.

Multivalue answer routing Used to configure Amazon Route 53 to return up to eight values, such as IP addresses for your web servers, in response to DNS queries.

Traffic flow Used to manage resource record sets for complex Amazon Route 53 configurations, allowing you visually to edit complex trees that comprise a traffic policy.

Geoproximity routing Used when you want to route traffic based on the location of your resources and, optionally, shift traffic from one resource in one location to resources in another location.

With Amazon Route 53 health checking, you can monitor the health of your resources, such as web servers and email servers. You can also configure Amazon CloudWatch alarms for your health checks so that you receive a notification when a resource becomes unavailable.

We covered the fundamentals of Elastic Load Balancing and the different types of load balancers available on AWS Cloud:—Classic Load Balancer, Application Load Balancer, and Network Load Balancer—each working across a different OSI model layer and having different capabilities and advantages.

Classic Load Balancer Used when you want to load balance for Amazon EC2 Classic.

Application Load Balancer Used when you want to have support for path-based routing and host-based routing.

Network Load Balancer Used when you want support for static IP addresses for the load balancer, target registration by IP addresses, client IP pass-through when registering targets by instance ID, and volatile workloads that require scaling to millions of requests per second.

ELB sandwich Used when you want to take advantage of the automatic scaling of the Elastic Load Balancing load balancer while still using a particular vendor's software on an Amazon EC2 instance to get access to their feature set (for example, F5 Big-IP's iRules)

The chapter also covered various other features of the Elastic Load Balancing product set, such as cross-zone load balancing, connection draining, proxy protocol, sticky sessions, and health checks.

For more information on combining Amazon Route 53 and the Elastic Load Balancing service to build a highly available and resilient network architecture, refer to the case studies in Chapter 16, "Scenarios and Reference Architectures."

Exam Essentials

When using these concepts to build an application that is highly available and resilient to failures, consider the following building blocks.

Understand what DNS is. DNS is the methodology that computers use to convert human-friendly domain names (for example, `amazon.com`) into IP addresses (for example, `192.0.2.1`).

Know how DNS registration works. Domains are registered with domain registrars that in turn register the domain name with InterNIC, a service of ICANN. ICANN enforces uniqueness of domain names across the Internet. Each domain name becomes registered in a central database known as the WHOIS database. Domains are defined by their TLDs. TLDs are controlled by IANA in a root zone database, which is essentially a database of all available TLDs. Familiarize yourself with the steps involved both to register a domain with Amazon Route 53 and to transfer a domain to Amazon Route 53.

Remember the steps involved in DNS resolution. Your browser asks the resolving DNS server what the IP address is for `amazon.com`. The resolving server does not know the address, so it asks a root server the same question. There are 13 root servers around the world, and these are managed by ICANN. The root server replies that it does not know the IP address, but it can give an address to a TLD server that knows about `.com` domain names. The resolving server then contacts the TLD server. The TLD server does not know the address of the domain name either, but it does know the address of the resolving Name Server. The resolving server then queries the resolving Name Server. The resolving Name Server contains the authoritative records and sends these to the resolving server, which then saves these records locally so that it does not have to perform these steps again in the near future. The resolving Name Server returns this information to the user's web browser, which also caches the information.

Remember the different record types. DNS consists of the following different record types: A, AAAA, CNAME, MX, NAPTR, NS, PTR, SOA, SPF, SRV, and TXT. You should know the differences among each record type.

Know the difference between Amazon EC2 DNS and Amazon Route 53. With Amazon EC2 DNS, AWS takes care of the DNS name creation and configuration for Amazon EC2 instances and other services like Elastic Load Balancing. Amazon Route 53 is the fully-featured DNS solution where you can control many more aspects of your DNS in a highly available and scalable way.

Remember the different routing policies. With Amazon Route 53, you can have different routing policies. The simple routing policy is most commonly used when you have a single resource that performs a given function for your domain. Weighted routing is used when you want to route a percentage of your traffic to a particular resource or group of resources. Latency-based routing is used to route your traffic based on the lowest latency so that your users get the fastest response times. Failover routing is used for disaster recovery and to route your traffic from a primary resource to a standby resource. Geolocation routing is used to route your traffic based on your end user's location. Multivalue answer routing is used to configure Amazon Route 53 to return up to eight values, such as IP addresses for your web servers, in response to DNS queries. Traffic flow is the AWS Management Console-based tool to manage resource record sets for complex Amazon Route 53 configurations. Geoproximity routing lets Amazon Route 53 route traffic to your resources based on the geographic location of those resources, with the ability to route more traffic or less traffic to a particular resource by specifying the value bias.

Understand how health checking works and how it can be used with Amazon Route 53. Health checks can monitor the health of your resources, such as web servers and email servers. You can configure Amazon CloudWatch alarms for your health checks so that you receive notification when a resource becomes unavailable.

Know the differences between the three types of Elastic Load Balancing. Use Classic Load Balancer when you need support for load balancing in Amazon EC2 Classic or support for proxy protocol. Use Application Load Balancer when you need path-based routing or host-based routing. Use Network Load Balancer when you need support for static IP addresses, client IP pass-through, and scaling to millions of requests per second.

Understand the different features of Elastic Load Balancing and how they apply to each type of load balancer. You should understand cross-zone load balancing, connection draining or deregistration delay, proxy protocol, sticky sessions, and health checks. You should also understand where each of these features is used and the type of Elastic Load Balancing load balancer to which they apply.

Know when and how to deploy virtual appliances in an ELB sandwich configuration. When you want to build a highly-scalable application using Elastic Load Balancing and also use features or functionality that come with other vendors' virtual appliances, the ELB sandwich can be used. An ELB sandwich uses a front-end Elastic Load Balancing load balancer, a virtual appliance in the middle, and a back-end Elastic Load Balancing load balancer for the downstream applications instances (for example, your web instances).

Understand the different Elastic Load Balancing components. Internet-Facing Load Balancers are accessible to the public Internet. Internal load balancers are accessible only within a VPC. HTTPS load balancers support HTTPS types of traffic. Listener rules determine how the load balancer routes requests to the targets in one or more target groups for the Application Load Balancer. Targets are a selected destination to which the selected Application Load Balancer or Network Load Balancer sends traffic. Target groups provide registration of targets, such as Amazon EC2 instances into a specific group.

Remember the components that can be configured with Elastic Load Balancing. You can configure idle connection timeout, where the load balancing maintains two connections for each request that a client makes through a load balancer. One connection is with the client, and the other connection is to the back-end instance. By default, if the instance does not send some data at least every 60 seconds (this timing is configurable), the load balancer can close the connection. You can configure connection draining or deregistration delay, where the load balancer will stop sending new connections to unhealthy or deregistering instances. You can configure proxy protocol, for the pass-through of client IPs to the Elastic Load Balancing destination instances via a human-readable header. You can configure sticky sessions or session affinity to route sessions consistently to the same back-end instance using cookies for identification of the requester. You can configure health checks to test the status of Amazon EC2 instances behind an Elastic Load Balancing load balancer.

Know how the ELB sandwich works and where you would use it. The ELB sandwich is used to deploy AWS partners' virtual devices, usually from the AWS Marketplace, inside your VPC in a highly scalable and redundant manner. The ELB sandwich uses an Elastic Load Balancing load balancer in front of the virtual appliance to load balance across the virtual appliance Amazon EC2 instances. A second-tier Elastic Load Balancing load balancer in front of the web or application instances is used as a destination by the virtual appliances.

Test Taking Tip

It is always valuable to build out infrastructure on AWS with the products and services that you are trying to learn about. This can help give you a broader context and deeper understanding on a particular service, such as Amazon Route 53. Without using a service in practice, it can be hard for facts to solidify, which means that you might find it harder to recall during the exam. Doing is a great way to learn.

Resources to Review

For further information, review the following URLs:

Amazon Route 53 documentation:

`https://aws.amazon.com/documentation/route53/`

Elastic Load Balancing documentation:

`https://aws.amazon.com/documentation/elastic-load-balancing/`

Hybrid Cloud DNS Solutions for Amazon VPC:

`https://d1.awsstatic.com/whitepapers/hybrid-cloud-dns-options-for-vpc.pdf`

AWS re:Invent 2017: DNS Demystified: Global Traffic Management with Amazon Route 53 (NET302):

`https://www.youtube.com/watch?v=PVBC1gb78r8`

AWS re:Invent 2017: Elastic Load Balancing Deep Dive and Best Practices (NET402):

`https://www.youtube.com/watch?v=9TwkMMogojY`

Exercises

The best way to become familiar with Amazon Route 53 and the various services and features of AWS Elastic Load Balancing load balancers is through direct, hands-on experience. The following exercises provide you with the opportunity to experiment and learn. You should expand beyond the exercises. Exercise 6.1 outlines the steps needed to register your own domain name; you can skip this exercise if you already have a domain name that you want to use. For specific, step-by-step instructions, refer to the Amazon route 53 documentation at:

`https://aws.amazon.com/documentation/route53`,

and the Elastic Load Balancing documentation at: `https://aws.amazon.com/documentation/elastic-load-balancing/`.

EXERCISE 6.1

Register a New Domain Name with Amazon Route 53

In this exercise, you will register a new domain name with Amazon Route 53. To do so, use the following steps.

1. Log in to the AWS Management Console. Navigate to the Amazon Route 53 console.
2. If you are new to Amazon Route 53, navigate to Domain Registration and choose Get Started Now. If you are already using Amazon Route 53, navigate to Registered Domains and choose Register Domain.
3. Enter the domain name that you want to register. Choose Check to find out whether the domain name is available.
4. If the domain is available, add the domain to your shopping cart. Select the number of years for which you want to register the domain and choose Continue.
5. Choose whether you want to hide your contact information from WHOIS queries and choose Continue.
6. For generic TLDs, if you specified an email address for the registrant contact that has never been used to register a domain with Amazon Route 53, you need to verify that the address is valid. If required, follow the verification steps to Verify the Email Address for the Registrant Contact.
7. Once you have verified your email, return to the Amazon Route 53 console. If the status does not automatically update to say that the email address is verified, choose Refresh Status.
8. Review the information that you entered, read the terms of service, and select the checkbox to confirm that you have read the terms of service. Choose Complete Purchase. If you were not able to complete email validation earlier, follow the email verification process now.

EXERCISE 6.1 *(continued)*

9. When the domain registration is complete, your next step depends on whether you want to use Amazon Route 53 or another DNS service as the DNS service for the domain. In Exercise 6.3, we use Amazon Route 53 by creating record sets to tell Amazon Route 53 how we will be routing traffic.

You have now registered your own domain name and have created your first Amazon Route 53 hosted zone for this domain, which you will use in Exercise 6.2.

EXERCISE 6.2

Configuring Elastic Load Balancing

In this exercise, you will configure four separate web instances, with both instance pairs existing in two separate regions. You will then create a Network Load Balancer for each set of instances. You will use the steps from this exercise when setting up Amazon Route 53 to resolve your hostname to your instances in Exercise 6.3.

Create an Amazon EC2 instance

1. Log in to the AWS Management Console. Change your region to US East (N. Virginia).
2. In the Compute section, navigate to the Amazon EC2 dashboard. Launch an instance. Select the first Amazon Linux AMI.
3. Select the instance type (a t2.micro will be sufficient) and configure your instance details. You need this instance to be launched in a public VPC subnet with a public address. Note the VPC and subnets used for each instance.
4. Name the instance **`US-East-01`**. Add a security group that allows HTTP.
5. Launch your new Amazon EC2 instance and verify that it has launched properly.

Configure Your Amazon Instance

6. Navigate to the Amazon EC2 instance in the AWS Management Console. Copy the public IP address to your clipboard.
7. Using a Secure Shell (SSH) client of your choice, connect to your Amazon EC2 instance using the public IP address, the user name **`ec2-user`**, and your private key.
8. When prompted about the authenticity of the host, type **Y** and choose Continue.
9. You should now be connected to your Amazon EC2 instance. Elevate your privileges to root by typing **`sudo su`**.
10. While you are logged in as the root user to your Amazon EC2 instance, run the following command to install Apache httpd: `yum install httpd -y`.
11. After the installation has completed, run the command `service httpd start` followed by `chkconfig httpd on`.

12. In the Amazon EC2 instance, type **`cd /var/www/html`**.
13. Type **`nano index.html`** and press Enter.
14. In Nano, type **`This is the US-East Server 01`** and then press Ctrl+X.
15. Type **`Y`** to confirm that you want to save the changes and then press Enter.
16. Type **`ls`**. You should now see your newly created `index.html` file.
17. In your browser, navigate to `http://yourpublicipaddress/index.html`.
18. Repeat Steps 1-17 to create a second server in the US East (N. Virginia) Region. Name this server **`US-East-01`** and use **`This is the US-East Server 02`** for your home page. Note that you can alternatively create an AMI of the web server to greatly simplify the deployment of the second instance.

You should now see your `This is the US-East Server 01` or `This is the US-East Server 02` home page, depending on which server you navigate to. If you do not see this message, check your security group to make sure that you are allowed to access port 80.

Configure a Network Load Balancer

19. Return to the AWS Management Console. Navigate to the Amazon EC2 Console. Navigate to the Load Balancers section of the console, under Load Balancing.
20. Select Create Load Balancer. Chose Network Load Balancer to create an Internet-Facing Network Load Balancer named US-East-Web. Leave the settings at their default values. Select the VPC and subnets into which you launched your instances in the previous steps.
21. Configure and name your target group as **`US-East-Web-TG`**. Leave the default values.
22. Register your targets by selecting the instances that you created earlier and clicking Add to Registered.
23. Create your Network Load Balancer.

You should now be able to browse to your Network Load Balancer via the Network Load Balancer DNS name and see the response change from `This is the US-East Server 01` to `This is the US-East Server 02` after refreshing the web page (it may take several refreshes to see the switch).

Create these Resources in a Second Region

24. Return to the AWS Management Console. Change your region to South America (Sao Paulo).
25. Repeat the three procedures in this section to add a third and fourth Amazon EC2 instance and load balancer in this new region.

You have now created four web servers in two different regions of the world and placed these regions behind Network Load Balancers.

EXERCISE 6.3

Create an Alias A Record with a Simple Routing Policy

In this exercise, you will create an alias A record with a simple routing policy.

1. Log in to the AWS Management Console. Navigate to the Amazon Route 53 dashboard.
2. Select your newly-created zone domain name. Create a record set, leaving the name blank, and use type A – IPv4 Address.
3. Choose the Alias radio button. From the Alias Target drop-down list that appears, select the US-East Network Load Balancer that you created in Exercise 6.2. Leave your routing policy set to Simple.
4. In your web browser, navigate to your domain name. You should now see a welcome screen for the US East (N. Virginia) Region. If you do not see this, check that your Amazon EC2 instances are attached to your load balancer and that the instances are in service. If the instances are not in service, this means that the load balancer is failing its health check. Check that Apache HTTP Server (HTTPD) is running and that your `index.html` document is accessible on both instances.

You have now created your first Alias A record using the simple routing policy.

EXERCISE 6.4

Create a Weighted Routing Policy

In this exercise, you will create a weighted routing policy.

1. Return to the AWS Management Console. Navigate to the Amazon Route 53 dashboard.
2. Navigate to hosted zones and select your newly-created zone domain name.
3. Create a record set with the name **`developer`** and type A – IPv4 Address. This will create a subdomain of `developer.yourdomainname.com`.
4. Select your US-East network load balancer. Change the routing policy to Weighted with a value of 50 and a type of US-East. Leave the other values at their defaults. Click Create. You will now see your newly-created DNS entry.
5. Create another record set with the name **`developer`** and type A – IPv4 Address. This will add a new record with the same name that you created earlier. Both records will work together.
6. Select your Sao Paulo load balancer. Change the routing policy to Weighted with a value of 50 and type of Sao Paulo. Leave the other values at their defaults. Click Create. You will now see your newly-created DNS entry.

7. Test your DNS by visiting http://developer.yourdomainname.com and refreshing the page. You should be accessing the US-East instances 50 percent of the time and the SA-East instances the other 50 percent of the time.

You have now created a weighted DNS routing policy. You can continue to experiment with other routing policies by following the documentation at http://docs.aws.amazon.com/Route53/latest/DeveloperGuide/routing-policy.html.

EXERCISE 6.5

Deploy a Set of HAProxy Instances in an ELB Sandwich Configuration

In this exercise, you will deploy a set of HAProxy instances in an ELB sandwich configuration. You will use the existing Network Load Balancer for US-East that you created earlier, along with the two web instances for the web tier of the ELB sandwich.

Launch and Configure Your Virtual Appliance Instances

1. Follow the same steps as in Exercise 6.2 to create a new set of instances. These instances will be your HAProxy instances.
2. To configure your instances, use SSH to perform the following on each HAProxy instance:
   a. `sudo yum install haproxy`
   b. Edit the HAProxy configuration file located at: /etc/haproxy/haproxy.cfg.
   c. A sample configuration follows. Note that the Network Load Balancer that you used as a back-end previously can be used as the back-end here.

```
global
daemon
log /dev/log local4
maxconn 40000
ulimit-n 81000

defaults
log global
timeout connect 4000
timeout server 43000
timeout client 42000

listen http1
bind *:80
```

EXERCISE 6.5 *(continued)*

```
mode http
balance roundrobin
server http1_1 <NLB DNS Name>:80 cookie http1_1 check inter 2000 rise 2 fall 3
```

d. `sudo service haproxy start`

Configure Your Outside Network Load Balancer

3. Create an Internet-Facing Network Load Balancer named **US-East-ELB-SW**. Leave the settings at their default values. Select the VPC and subnets into which you launched your instances.
4. Configure and name your target group **US-East-SW-TG**. Leave the default values.
5. Register your targets by selecting your HAProxy instances that you created earlier and selecting Add to Registered.
6. Create your Network Load Balancer.

You have now created a set of virtual appliances in your VPC and a front-end Network Load Balancer. By pointing your Network Load Balancer to each HAProxy instance via their instance ID, your HAProxy instances will see the requesting host's true client IP. You could also replace the HAProxy instances in this example with a vendor's instances from the AWS Marketplace at: `https://aws.amazon.com/marketplace`.

Review Questions

1. What are the two types of Amazon Route 53 hosted zones? (Choose two.)
   - **A.** Public hosted zones
   - **B.** Global hosted zones
   - **C.** NULL hosted zones
   - **D.** Routed hosted zones
   - **E.** Private hosted zones

2. Amazon Route 53 cannot route queries to which AWS resources?
   - **A.** Amazon CloudFront distribution
   - **B.** Elastic Load Balancing load balancer
   - **C.** Amazon Elastic Compute Cloud (Amazon EC2) instance
   - **D.** AWS CloudFormation

3. To stop sending traffic to resources with weighted routing for Amazon Route 53, you must do which one of the following?
   - **A.** Delete the resource record.
   - **B.** Change the resource record weight to 100.
   - **C.** Change the resource record weight to 0.
   - **D.** Switch to a multivalue answer resource record.

4. If you do not associate a health check with an Amazon Route 53 multivalue answer record, which of the following occurs?
   - **A.** Amazon Route 53 always considers the record to be healthy.
   - **B.** Amazon Route 53 always considers the record to be unhealthy.
   - **C.** Amazon Route 53 will give you an error.
   - **D.** You must use a Text (TXT) record instead.

5. How do you access traffic flow for Amazon Route 53?
   - **A.** Using the AWS Command Line Interface (CLI)
   - **B.** Through an Amazon Elastic Compute Cloud (Amazon EC2) instance inside your Amazon Virtual Private Cloud (Amazon VPC)
   - **C.** Through AWS Direct Connect
   - **D.** Using the AWS Management Console

6. What should you use if you want Amazon Route 53 to respond to Domain Name System (DNS) queries with up to eight healthy records selected at random?
   - **A.** Geolocation routing policy
   - **B.** Simple routing policy
   - **C.** Alias record
   - **D.** Multivalue answer routing policy

7. Why is referencing the Application Load Balancer or Classic Load Balancer by its DNS CNAME recommended?

    A. IP addresses may change as the load balancers scale.

    B. DNS CNAMEs provide a lower latency than IP addresses.

    C. You want to preserve the source IP of the client.

    D. IP addresses are public and open to the Internet.

8. With the `enableDnsHostname` attribute set to true, Amazon will do which of the following?

    A. Enable Domain Name System (DNS) resolution for your Amazon Virtual Private Cloud (Amazon VPC).

    B. Auto-assign DNS hostnames to Amazon Elastic Compute Cloud (Amazon EC2) instances.

    C. Assign internal-only DNS hostnames to Amazon EC2 instances.

    D. Allow for the manual configuration of hostnames to Amazon EC2 instances.

9. You have the `enableDnsHostname` attribute set to true for your VPC. Your Amazon Elastic Compute Cloud (Amazon EC2) instances are not receiving DNS hostnames, however. What could be the potential cause?

    A. DNS resolution is not supported over VPC peering.

    B. You need to configure your Amazon Route 53 private hosted zone.

    C. Amazon does not assign DNS hostnames to instances.

    D. `enableDnsSupport` is not set to true.

10. You are assessing load balancer options for your AWS deployment. You want support for static IP addresses for the load balancer. What would be the best choice of Elastic Load Balancing load balancer for this purpose?

    A. Amazon Route 53

    B. Network Load Balancer

    C. Application Load Balancer

    D. Classic Load Balancer

Amazon CloudFront

THE AWS CERTIFIED ADVANCED NETWORKING – SPECIALTY EXAM OBJECTIVES COVERED IN THIS CHAPTER MAY INCLUDE, BUT ARE NOT LIMITED TO, THE FOLLOWING:

Domain 2.0: Design and Implement AWS Networks

- ✓ **2.4. Determine network requirements for a specialized workload**
- ✓ **2.5. Derive an appropriate architecture based on customer and application requirements**

Domain 4.0: Configure Network Integration with Application Services

- ✓ **4.5 Determine a content distribution strategy to optimize for performance**

Introduction to Amazon CloudFront

Amazon CloudFront is a global Content Delivery Network service that speeds up the distribution of your static and dynamic web content. Amazon CloudFront delivers your content through a worldwide network of edge locations. Amazon CloudFront integrates with other AWS products to give developers and organizations an easy way to distribute content to end users with low latency, high data transfer speeds, and no minimum usage commitments. This chapter reviews the components that make up Amazon CloudFront and then examines its advanced features. The chapter concludes with key exercises and questions related to Amazon CloudFront and the AWS Certified Advanced Networking – Specialty Exam.

Content Delivery Network Overview

A *Content Delivery Network (CDN)* is a globally-distributed network of caching servers that accelerate the downloading of web pages, images, videos, and other content. CDNs use Domain Name System (DNS) *geolocation* to determine the geographic location of each request for a web page or other content. They then serve that content from caching servers closest to that location—whether "closest" is measured in distance or time (latency)—instead of the original web server. A CDN allows you to increase the scalability and decrease the latency of a website or mobile application easily in response to traffic spikes. In most cases, using a CDN is completely transparent—end users simply experience better website performance, while the load on your original website is reduced.

CDNs were primarily invented to circumvent a constant that has yet to be overcome in the networking world: the speed of light. In a vacuum, the speed of light is roughly 300,000 kilometers per second; in fiber-optic cables, it can be up to 30 percent slower. When such fiber-optic cables and their associated optical repeaters traverse the vast expanse of the Pacific Ocean, for example, responses from web servers back to clients can take upwards of hundreds of milliseconds. In the networking world, this results in reduced throughput and poor performance for customers. By using a CDN, you can overcome the limitations of serving content over large distances by caching or pre-positioning data at predefined locations. You can also isolate the load on your centralized web servers by having each edge location where your content is cached serve the content for you, therefore increasing your scale immensely on an edge location basis.

The AWS CDN: Amazon CloudFront

Amazon CloudFront is the AWS CDN. It can be used to deliver your web content using Amazon's global network of *edge locations*. When a user requests content that is served with Amazon CloudFront, the user is routed to the edge location that provides the lowest latency (time delay), so content is delivered with the best possible performance. If the content is already in the edge location with the lowest latency, Amazon CloudFront delivers it immediately. If the content is not currently in that edge location, Amazon CloudFront retrieves it from the *origin server*, such as an Amazon Simple Storage Service (Amazon S3) bucket or a web server. The *origin server* stores the original, definitive versions of your content.

Amazon CloudFront is optimized to work with other AWS Cloud services that serve as the origin server, including Amazon S3 buckets, Amazon S3 static websites, Amazon Elastic Compute Cloud (Amazon EC2) instances, and Elastic Load Balancing load balancers. Amazon CloudFront also works seamlessly with non-AWS origin servers, such as an existing on-premises web server. Amazon CloudFront also integrates with Amazon Route 53.

Amazon CloudFront supports all content that can be served over HTTP or HTTPS. This includes any popular static files that are a part of your web application, such as HTML files, images, JavaScript, and CSS files, and also audio, video, media files, or software downloads. Amazon CloudFront also supports serving dynamically generated web pages, so it can be used to deliver your entire website. Lastly, Amazon CloudFront supports *media streaming*, using both HTTP and Real-Time Messaging Protocol (RTMP).

Amazon CloudFront Basics

There are three core concepts that you need to understand in order to start using Amazon CloudFront: distributions, origins, and cache control. With these concepts, you can use Amazon CloudFront to speed up delivery of content from your websites.

Distributions

To use Amazon CloudFront, you start by creating a distribution, which is identified by a DNS domain name such as `d111111abcdef8.cloudfront.net`. To serve files from Amazon CloudFront, you simply use the distribution domain name in place of your website's domain name; the rest of the file paths stay unchanged. You can use the Amazon CloudFront distribution domain name as-is, or more typically you create a user-friendly DNS name in your own domain by creating a Canonical Name Record (CNAME) in Amazon Route 53 or another DNS service that refers to the distribution's domain name. Clients who use the CNAME are automatically redirected to your Amazon CloudFront distribution domain name. If you use Route53 as your DNS service, you can also use a feature called aliases to redirect a zone root address such as "example.com" (which cannot be a CNAME) to your CloudFront distribution.

Origins

When you create a distribution, you must specify the DNS domain name of the origin—the Amazon S3 bucket or HTTP server—from which you want Amazon CloudFront to retrieve the definitive version of your objects (web files). For example, note the following:

- **Amazon S3 bucket:** `myawsbucket.s3.amazonaws.com`
- **Amazon EC2 instance:** `ec2-203-0-113-25.compute-1.amazonaws.com`
- **Elastic Load Balancing Load Balancer:** `my-load-balancer-1234567890.us-west-2.elb.amazonaws.com`
- **Website URL:** `mywebserver.mycompanydomain.com`

Cache Control

Once requested and served from an edge location, objects stay in the cache until they expire or are evicted to make room for more frequently requested content. By default, objects expire from the cache after 24 hours. After an object expires, the next request results in Amazon CloudFront forwarding the request to the origin to verify that the object is unchanged or to fetch a new version if it has changed.

Optionally, you can control how long objects stay in an Amazon CloudFront cache before expiring. To do this, you can choose to use Cache-Control headers set by your origin server, or you can set the minimum, maximum, and default *Time to Live (TTL)* for objects in your Amazon CloudFront distribution.

You can also remove copies of an object from all Amazon CloudFront edge locations at any time by calling the *invalidation Application Programming Interface (API)* or through the Amazon CloudFront console. This feature removes the object from every Amazon CloudFront edge location regardless of the expiration period you set for that object on your origin server. The invalidation feature is designed to be used in unexpected circumstances, such as to correct an error or to make an unanticipated update to a website—not as part of your everyday workflow.

Instead of invalidating objects manually or programmatically, it is a best practice to use a version identifier as part of the object (file) path name. For example, note the following:

- **Old file:** `assets/v1/css/narrow.css`
- **New file:** `assets/v2/css/narrow.css`

When using versioning, users will see the latest content through Amazon CloudFront when you update your site without using invalidation. Old versions will expire from the cache automatically. That said, depending on other settings, you may need to invalidate the base page that includes references to the versioned objects.

How Amazon CloudFront Delivers Content

After some initial setup, Amazon CloudFront works transparently to speed up delivery of your content. This overview provides you with the steps required to set up Amazon CloudFront to serve your content, as well as the process that happens behind the scenes when serving content to your users.

Configuring Amazon CloudFront

The following steps walk you through the process required to configure Amazon CloudFront:

Configure Your Origin Servers

1. CloudFront uses your origin server to retrieve your files for distribution from Amazon CloudFront edge locations.

   An origin server stores the original, definitive version of your objects. If you are serving content over HTTP, your origin server is either an Amazon S3 bucket or an HTTP server, such as a web server. Your HTTP server can run on an Amazon EC2 instance or on a server that you manage; these servers are also known as *custom origins*.

   If you distribute media files on demand using the Adobe RTMP protocol, your origin server is always an Amazon S3 bucket.

Place Your Content on Your Origin Servers

2. Your files, known as objects, typically include web pages, images, and media files, but they can be anything that is served over HTTP or a supported version of Adobe RTMP, the protocol used by Adobe Flash Media Server. Dynamically generated content, such as HTML generated from a database in response to an HTTP GET operation, is also fully supported.

You can make the objects in your bucket publicly readable so that anyone who knows the URLs for your objects can access them. You also have the option of keeping objects private and controlling who accesses them, too. Amazon CloudFront does not require Amazon S3 buckets to be public, and it is a good idea to keep them private.

Create Your Amazon CloudFront Distribution

3. The Amazon CloudFront distribution will tell CloudFront which origin servers to get your content from when users request the content through your website or application. You can also specify details such as whether you want Amazon CloudFront to log all requests, and whether you want the distribution to be enabled as soon as it is created.

Amazon CloudFront Assigns a Domain Name

4. After creating your distribution, Amazon CloudFront will automatically assign a domain name that will be used to reference your distribution.

Amazon CloudFront Configures Its Edge Locations

5. After assigning a domain name, Amazon CloudFront will automatically send your distribution's configuration (but not your content) to all of its edge locations.

As you build your website or application, you can use the domain name that Amazon CloudFront provides for your URLs when referencing objects. For example, if Amazon CloudFront returns the domain `d111111abcdef8.cloudfront.net` for your distribution, the URL for `logo.jpg` in your Amazon S3 bucket or the root directory of your web server would be as follows: `http://d111111abcdef8.cloudfront.net/logo.jpg`. A more typical practice, however, is to use relative paths that do not specify the host part of the URL at all, unless another host name is actually required. This provides more flexibility in terms of site construction and the use of CNAMEs, load balancers, and CloudFront distributions. For example, an image file would be referenced as "/images/website-logo.png", or to take the previous example, "logo.jpg". This allows the reference to work properly whether the web page is accessed directly from the server by its DNS name or IP address, via the CloudFront distribution's DNS name, or via a CNAME such as `www.example.com` that you provide that points to the CloudFront distribution's DNS name.

Optionally, you can configure your origin server to add headers to the files, with a header indicating how long you want the files to stay in the cache in the Amazon CloudFront edge location. By default, each object stays in an edge location for 24 hours before it expires. The minimum expiration time is 0 seconds, with no maximum expiration time limit.

Figure 7.1 shows an overview of the steps required to configure your Amazon CloudFront distribution.

How CloudFront Operates

The following steps outline what happens when users request objects after you've configured Amazon CloudFront to deliver your content.

1. Users access your website or application and request one or more objects, such as an image file and an HTML file.
2. DNS routes the request to the Amazon CloudFront edge location that can best serve the user's request, typically the nearest Amazon CloudFront edge location in terms of network latency.
3. In the edge location, Amazon CloudFront will check its cache for the requested files, returning them to the user if they are found in the cache. If the files are not found in the cache, Amazon CloudFront will perform the following actions:
   a. Amazon CloudFront will compare the request with your distribution configuration and forward the request for the files to the applicable origin server for the corresponding file type (for example, to your Amazon S3 bucket for image files and to your HTTP server for the HTML files).
   b. The origin servers send the files back to the Amazon CloudFront edge location.
   c. As soon as the first byte arrives from the origin, Amazon CloudFront begins to forward the files to the user. Amazon CloudFront also adds the files to the cache in the edge location for the next time someone requests those files.

The process for CloudFront content delivery is shown in Figure 7.2.

FIGURE 7.1 Configuring your Amazon CloudFront distribution

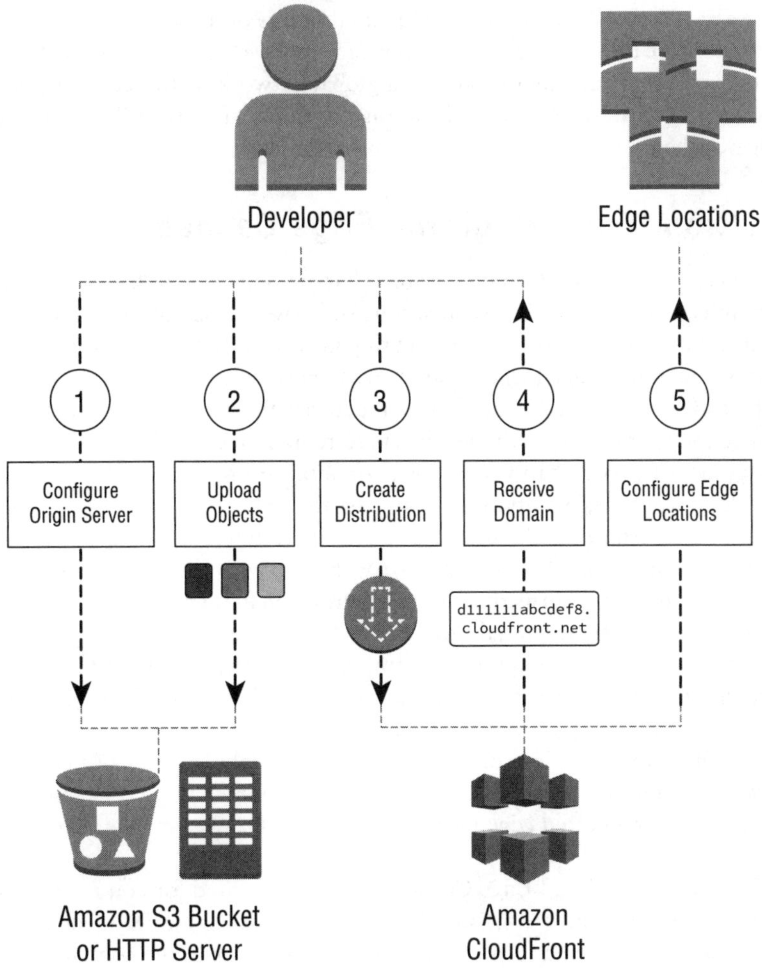

FIGURE 7.2 Amazon CloudFront content delivery

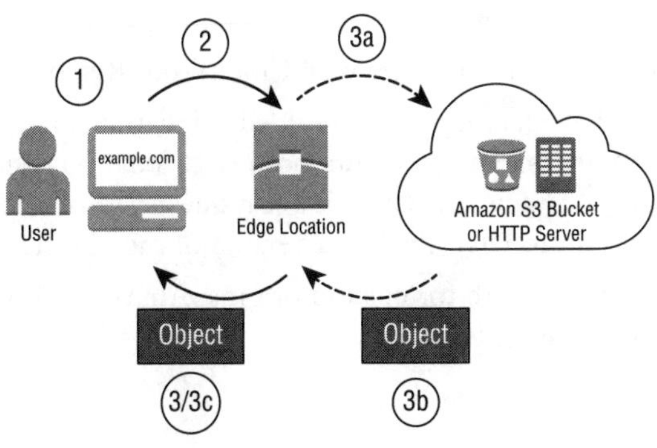

Amazon CloudFront Edge Locations

Amazon CloudFront edge locations are the regional points of presence that are used to cache objects and store these closer to your application or website's end users. As of the time of this writing, Amazon CloudFront has a global network of 100 edge locations in 50 cities across 23 countries. These edge locations include 89 Points of Presence and 11 Regional Edge Caches.

Amazon CloudFront Regional Edge Caches

Regional Edge Caches are CloudFront locations that are deployed globally in AWS regions, at closer proximity to your users. These locations sit between your origin server and the global edge locations that serve traffic directly to your users. As the popularity of your objects declines, individual edge locations may evict those objects to make room for more popular content. Regional Edge Caches have a much larger cache size than their global edge location counterparts, which allows objects to remain in cache longer.

When a user makes a request to your website or application, DNS routes the request to the Amazon CloudFront edge location that can best serve the user's request. This location is typically the nearest Amazon CloudFront edge location in terms of latency. In the edge location, Amazon CloudFront checks its cache for the requested files. If the files are in the cache, Amazon CloudFront returns them to the user. If the files are not in the cache, the edge servers go to the nearest Regional Edge Cache to fetch the object. In the Regional Edge Cache location, Amazon CloudFront again checks its cache for the requested files. If the files are in the cache, Amazon CloudFront forwards the files to the requested edge location.

As soon as the first byte arrives from a Regional Edge Cache location, Amazon CloudFront will begin to forward the files to the user. Amazon CloudFront also adds the files to the cache in the requested edge location for the next time someone requests those files.

Amazon CloudFront Regional Edge Cache locations are suited for content that might not be popular enough to remain consistently within Amazon CloudFront edge locations but still might benefit from being located closer to the requestor of the content.

Some important points to consider for Amazon CloudFront Regional Edge Caches:

- You do not need to make any changes to your Amazon CloudFront distributions that use Regional Edge Caches; they are enabled by default for all Amazon CloudFront distributions.
- There is no additional cost for using Amazon CloudFront Regional Edge Caches.
- Regional Edge Caches have feature parity with edge locations. For example, a cache invalidation request removes an object from both edge locations and Regional Edge Caches before it expires. The next time a viewer requests the object, Amazon CloudFront returns to the origin to fetch the latest version of the object.
- Regional Edge Caches work with for custom origins. Amazon S3 origins are, however, accessed directly from the edge locations.

- Proxy methods `PUT/POST/PATCH/OPTIONS/DELETE` flow directly to the origin from the edge locations and do not proxy through the Regional Edge Caches.
- Dynamic content, as determined at request time (cache behavior configured to forward all headers), does not flow through the Regional Edge Caches but goes directly to the origin.
- You can measure the performance improvements from this feature by using cache-hit ratio metrics available from the Amazon CloudFront console.

Web Distributions

When you want to use Amazon CloudFront to distribute your content, you create a distribution and specify configuration settings such as your origin and whether you want your files to be available to everyone or have restricted access.

You can also configure Amazon CloudFront to require users to use HTTPS to access your content, forward cookies and/or query strings to your origin, prevent users from particular countries from accessing your content, and create access logs.

You can use web distributions to serve the following content over HTTP or HTTPS:

- Static and dynamic content. For example, HTML, CSS, JS, and image files using HTTP or HTTPS.
- Multimedia content on demand using progressive download and Apple HTTP Live Streaming (HLS). You cannot serve Adobe Flash multimedia content over HTTP or HTTPS, but you can serve it using an Amazon CloudFront RTMP distribution.
- A live event, such as a meeting, conference, or concert, in real time. For live streaming, you can create the distribution automatically by using an AWS CloudFormation stack.

Dynamic Content and Advanced Features

Amazon CloudFront can do much more than simply serve static web files. To start using the service's advanced features, you will need to understand how to use cache behaviors and how to restrict access to sensitive content.

Dynamic Content, Multiple Origins, and Cache Behaviors

Serving static assets, as described previously, is a common way to use a CDN. An Amazon CloudFront distribution, however, can easily be set up to also serve dynamic content and to use more than one origin server. You can control which requests are served by which origin and how requests are cached using a feature called *cache behaviors*.

A *cache behavior* lets you configure a variety of Amazon CloudFront functionalities for a given URL path pattern for files on your website, as shown in Figure 7.3. One cache behavior applies to all PHP files in a web server (dynamic content) using the path pattern `*.php`, while another behavior applies to all JPEG images in another origin server (static content) using the path pattern `*.jpg`.

FIGURE 7.3 Amazon CloudFront content delivery

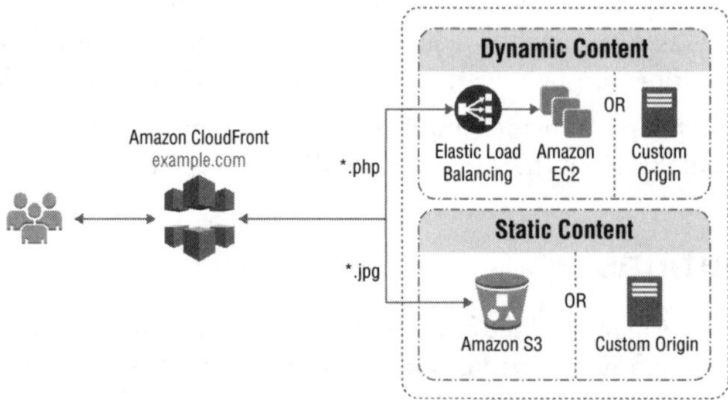

The functionality that you can configure for each cache behavior includes the following:

- The path pattern
- Which origin to forward your requests to
- Whether to forward query strings to your origin
- Whether accessing the specified files requires signed URLs
- Whether to require HTTPS access
- The amount of time that those files stay in the Amazon CloudFront cache (regardless of the value of any cache control headers that your origin adds to the files)

Cache behaviors are applied in order; if a request does not match the first path pattern, it drops down to the next path pattern. Normally, the last path pattern specified is * to match all files.

A Note on Performance: Dynamic Content and HTTP/2

It is very useful that Amazon CloudFront can seamlessly deal with all content, including dynamically-generated content that is not cacheable alongside a wide array of content that can be cached (see previous and following sections). But you may assume that there is no performance benefit in that case. After all, if the Amazon CloudFront edge location needs to reach back to the origin each time it receives a request for a particular URL representing dynamic content, how can it speed up content delivery? You may then assume that if an item is not in the Amazon CloudFront cache, the use of Amazon CloudFront won't speed up access to that content the first time it is requested.

As it turns out, even dynamic or initially uncached content will often be delivered with lower latency to end users. The reason has to do with the time it takes to set up the TCP or TLS connections that underlie the content caching and delivery mechanisms. Each such connection takes a finite amount of time to establish, and if a connection from CloudFront to the origin can be reused, significant latency gains are possible.

For example, let's assume that the round-trip latency between an end user and the Amazon CloudFront edge location is 30 milliseconds, and the round-trip latency between the edge location and the origin is 100 milliseconds. (For context, as of this writing, even over the high performance AWS backbone the roundtrip latency from the Singapore region to the Northern Virginia region was about 240 milliseconds.) In all cases, before any content can be delivered for the very first time, the TCP connection establishment between the three hosts (which require one full round-trip for the SYN/ACK packets from client to edge, and the edge to origin) will take at least 130 milliseconds (ignoring local overhead, which is much higher for TLS connections).

Now, let's assume a new client connects to the edge location and begins requesting content from the same origin, whether dynamic content, or content not yet in the edge cache. The Amazon CloudFront edge server will often be able to re-use an existing connection to the origin server, and avoid the connection setup overhead. This can reduce the first-byte delivery time by 100 milliseconds or more. That may not seem like a lot, but even 1/10 of a second *per TCP connection* can add up quickly. Avoiding the overhead of establishing an encrypted TLS session each time will decrease latency even more. So using Amazon CloudFront is a performance win even in cases where content caching is not playing a role. Your users will be happy to receive the best possible performance in all of these scenarios.

Amazon CloudFront also supports connections from clients via the HTTP/2 protocol. That new protocol, already supported by most modern browsers, provides a significant number of enhancements that improve performance by connection re-use, multiplexing, server push, etc. Even if your origin server does not support HTTP/2 yet, those enhanced features in use between your end-users and the Amazon CloudFront edge servers can significantly improve performance even when Amazon CloudFront is accessing your origin server using HTTP/1.x. Not only can you use Amazon CloudFront to optimize origin access via connection re-use, but content in the edge cache will delivered faster than it could be from your origin servers, even ignoring latency differences between the edge and the origin.

Whole Website

Using cache behaviors and multiple origins, you can easily use Amazon CloudFront to serve your whole website and to support different behaviors for different client devices.

Private Content

In many cases, you may want to restrict access to content in Amazon CloudFront only to selected requestors, such as paid subscribers or to applications or users in your company network. Amazon CloudFront provides several mechanisms to allow you to serve private content:

Signed URLs Use URLs that are valid only between certain times and optionally from certain IP addresses.

Signed cookies Require authentication via public and private key pairs.

Origin Access Identities (OAI) Restrict access to an Amazon S3 bucket only to a special Amazon CloudFront user associated with your distribution. This is the easiest way to ensure that content in a bucket is accessed only by Amazon CloudFront.

RTMP Distributions

RTMP distributions stream media files using Adobe Media Server and the Adobe RTMP. When using an RTMP distribution for Amazon CloudFront, you need to provide both your media files and a media player to your end users. Media player examples include JW Player, Flowplayer, and Adobe Flash.

End users will view your media files using the media player that you provide for them. They do not use the media player (if any) that is already installed on their computer or device. This is due in part to the fact that when the end user streams your media file, the media player begins to play the content of the file while the file is still being downloaded from Amazon CloudFront. The media file is not stored locally on the end user's system.

To use Amazon CloudFront to serve media in this way, you need two types of distributions: a web distribution to serve the media player and an RTMP distribution for the media files. The web distribution will serve files over HTTP, while the RTMP distribution will stream media files over RTMP or a variant of RTMP.

Figure 7.4 shows that the media files and your media player are stored in different buckets in Amazon S3. You could also make the media player available to users in other ways, such as using Amazon CloudFront and a custom origin; however, the media files must use an Amazon S3 bucket at the origin.

FIGURE 7.4 Streaming distributions, web, and RTMP

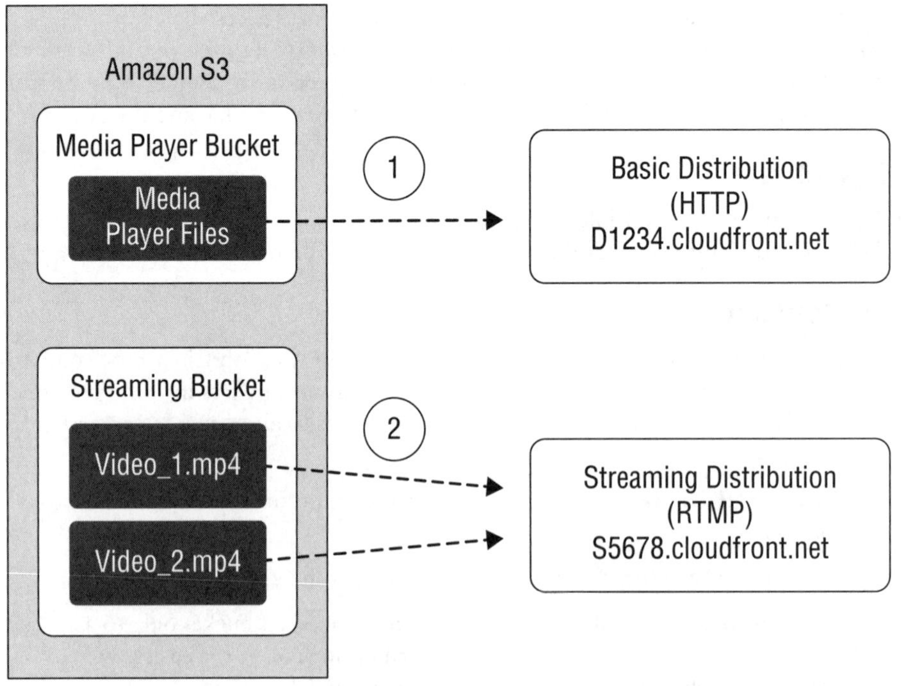

Figure 7.4 also shows two separate buckets being used: one for your media files and the other for your media player. You can also store media files and your media player in the same Amazon S3 bucket (not shown in the figure).

In Figure 7.4, there are two distributions used for Amazon CloudFront streaming:

1. Your media player bucket holds the media player, and it is the origin server for a regular HTTP distribution. In this example, the domain name for the distribution is `d1234.cloudfront.net`. The *d* in `d1234.cloudfront.net` indicates that this is a web distribution.
2. Your streaming media bucket holds your media files, and it is the origin server for an RTMP distribution. In this example, the domain name for the distribution is `s5678.cloudfront.net`. The `s` in `s5678.cloudfront.net` indicates that this is an RTMP distribution.

There are other streaming options available with Amazon CloudFront.

Wowza Streaming Engine 4.2 You can use the Wowza Streaming Engine 4.2 to create live streaming sessions for global delivery using Amazon CloudFront. Wowza Streaming Engine 4.2 supports the following HTTP-based streaming protocols:

- HLS
- HTTP Dynamic Streaming (HDS)
- Smooth Streaming
- MPEG Dynamic Adaptive Streaming over HTTP (DASH)

For these protocols, Amazon CloudFront will break video into smaller chunks that are cached in the Amazon CloudFront network for improved performance and scalability.

Live HTTP streaming using Amazon CloudFront and any HTTP origin Amazon CloudFront supports any live encoder, such as Elemental Live. The encoder must output HTTP-based streams to stream live performances, webinars, and other events.

On-demand video streaming using Amazon CloudFront and other media players When streaming media files using Amazon CloudFront, you provide both the media files and media player that you want end users to utilize to play the media file.

Alternate Domain Names

In Amazon CloudFront, an alternate domain name lets you use your own domain name (for example, `www.example.com`) for links to your objects instead of using the domain name that CloudFront assigns to your distribution. Both web and RTMP distributions support alternate domain names.

When you create a distribution, Amazon CloudFront returns a domain name for the distribution, for example: `d111111abcdef8.cloudfront.net`.

When you use the Amazon CloudFront domain name for your objects, the URL for an object called `/images/image.jpg` would be: `http://d111111abcdef8.cloudfront.net/images/image.jpg`.

If you want to use your own domain name, such as www.example.com, instead of the cloudfront.net domain name that Amazon CloudFront assigned to your distribution, you can add an alternate domain name to your distribution for www.example.com. You can then use the following URL for /images/image.jpg: http://www.example.com/images/image.jpg.

When you add alternate domain names, you can use the wildcard * at the beginning of a domain name instead of specifying subdomains individually. For example, with an alternative domain name of *.example.com, you can use any domain name that ends with example.com in your object URLs, such as www.example.com, product-name.example.com, and marketing.product-name.example.com.

The alternate domain name must begin with an asterisk and a dot (*.). You cannot use a wildcard to replace part of a subdomain name (such as *domain.example.com), and you cannot replace a subdomain in the middle of a domain name (similarly like subdomain.*.example.com).

HTTPS

For web distributions, you can configure Amazon CloudFront to require that viewers use HTTPS to request your objects, and even automatically redirect users from an HTTP endpoint to the HTTPS endpoint for your distribution. This results in connections between users and Amazon CloudFront being encrypted. You also can configure Amazon CloudFront to use HTTPS to retrieve objects from your origin so that connections are encrypted when Amazon CloudFront communicates with your origin from edge locations and Regional Edge Caches.

Here is the process that is followed when Amazon CloudFront receives a request for an object, and you require HTTPS to communicate with both your users and your origin:

1. A web client submits an HTTPS request to Amazon CloudFront. There is a Secure Sockets Layer (SSL)/Transport Layer Security (TLS) negotiation here between the user and Amazon CloudFront. The client submits the request in an encrypted format.
2. If the object is in the Amazon CloudFront Regional Edge Cache, Amazon CloudFront encrypts the response and returns it to the client. The client then decrypts it.
3. If the object is not in the Amazon CloudFront cache, Amazon CloudFront performs SSL/TLS negotiation with your origin and, when the negotiation is complete, forwards the request to your origin in an encrypted format.
4. The origin decrypts the request, encrypts the requested object, and returns the object to Amazon CloudFront.
5. Amazon CloudFront decrypts the response, re-encrypts it, and forwards the object to the client. Amazon CloudFront also saves the object in its cache so that the object is available the next time it is requested.
6. The client decrypts the response.

When a client makes an HTTP request that is redirected to an HTTPS request, Amazon CloudFront charges for both requests. For the HTTP request, the charge is only for the request and for the headers that Amazon CloudFront returns to the client. For the HTTPS request, the charge is for the request and for the headers and the objects that are returned by your origin.

You cannot use a self-signed certificate for HTTPS communication between Amazon CloudFront and your origin.

If the origin server returns an expired certificate, an invalid certificate, or a self-signed certificate, or returns the certificate chain in the wrong order, Amazon CloudFront drops the Transmission Control Protocol connection, returning HTTP status code 502 (Bad Gateway).

Amazon CloudFront and AWS Certificate Manager (ACM)

AWS Certificate Manager (ACM) is designed to simplify and automate many of the tasks that are traditionally associated with management of SSL/TLS certificates. ACM takes care of the complexity surrounding the provisioning, deployment, and renewal of digital certificates, with certificates being provided by Amazon's certificate authority (CA), Amazon Trust Services.

You can provision SSL/TLS certificates and associate them with Amazon CloudFront distributions. First, you provision a certificate using ACM and then deploy it to your Amazon CloudFront distribution. ACM also has the ability to manage certificate renewals for you. ACM allows you to provision, deploy, and manage the certificate with no additional charges. There are, however, additional charges when using Amazon CloudFront and HTTPS.

To use an ACM Certificate with Amazon CloudFront, you must request or import the certificate in the US East (N. Virginia) Region. ACM certificates in this region that are associated with an Amazon CloudFront distribution are disseminated to all the geographic locations configured for that distribution.

To use an ACM certificate with Amazon CloudFront, you must request or import the certificate in the US East (N. Virginia) Region.

Invalidating Objects (Web Distributions Only)

If you need to remove objects from an Amazon CloudFront Regional Edge Cache before they expire, you can *invalidate* the object from the Amazon CloudFront Regional Edge Caches. There is no charge for the first 1,000 invalidations per month; you pay for each invalidation over 1,000 in a month.

To invalidate objects, you can specify either the path for individual objects or a path that ends with the * wildcard, which might apply to one object or many objects. The following are examples of specific object and wildcard invalidations:

- `/images/image1.jpg`
- `/images/image*`
- `/images/*`

An alternative to invalidating objects is to use object versioning to serve a different version of the object that has a different fully-qualified name (name including path).

You can invalidate most types of objects that are served by a web distribution, but you cannot invalidate media files in the Microsoft Smooth Streaming format when you have enabled Smooth Streaming for the corresponding cache behavior. In addition, you cannot invalidate objects that are served by an RTMP distribution.

Access Logs

Amazon CloudFront can create log files that contain detailed information about every user request that Amazon CloudFront receives. Access logs are available for both web and RTMP distributions. When you enable logging for your distribution, you specify the Amazon S3 bucket in which you want Amazon CloudFront to store log files.

You can store the log files for multiple distributions in the same bucket. When you enable logging, you can specify an optional prefix for the file names so that you can keep track of which log files are associated with which distributions.

If you are using Amazon S3 as your origin, we recommend that you do not use the same bucket for your log files. Using a separate bucket simplifies maintenance.

Amazon CloudFront and AWS Lambda@Edge

AWS Lambda@Edge is an extension of AWS Lambda, a compute service that lets you execute functions that customize the content that is delivered through Amazon CloudFront. You can author functions in one region and execute them in AWS Regions and edge locations globally, without provisioning or managing servers. Just as with AWS Lambda, Lambda@Edge scales automatically, from a few requests per day to thousands per second. Lambda@Edge processes requests at edge locations instead of an origin server, which can significantly reduce latency and improve the user experience.

When you associate an Amazon CloudFront distribution with a Lambda@Edge function, Amazon CloudFront intercepts requests and responses at Edge locations. Lambda@Edge functions execute in response to Amazon CloudFront events in the region or edge location that is closest to your customer.

You can execute AWS Lambda functions when the following Amazon CloudFront events occur:

- When Amazon CloudFront receives a request from a viewer (viewer request)
- Before Amazon CloudFront forwards a request to the origin (origin request)
- When Amazon CloudFront receives a response from the origin (origin response)
- Before Amazon CloudFront returns the response to the viewer (viewer response)

The following are some example use cases for Lambda@Edge:

- You can write AWS Lambda functions that inspect cookies and rewrite URLs so that users see different versions of a site for A/B testing.
- You can use an AWS Lambda function to generate HTTP responses when Amazon CloudFront viewer request events or origin request events occur.
- An AWS Lambda function can inspect headers or authorization tokens and insert the applicable header to control access to your content before Amazon CloudFront forwards a request to the origin.
- An AWS Lambda function can add, drop, and modify headers and can rewrite URL paths so that Amazon CloudFront returns different objects.

Amazon CloudFront Field-Level Encryption

With Amazon CloudFront Field-Level Encryption, you can encrypt sensitive pieces of content at the edge before requests are forwarded to your origin servers. The data is encrypted using a public key that you supply. That data can then be decrypted inside your application using the associated private key. In an era of agile dev/ops teams developing large applications on the basis of a range of APIs and loosely-coupled micro-services, isolating sensitive data when it first enters the application, and only decrypted it at one or a few key points in its lifecycle, can significantly improve application security while enabling greater agility in secure application development.

You configure Amazon CloudFront field-level encryption by going through a series of steps that include uploading the private key, creating encryption profiles, setting up a configuration that makes use of those profiles, and then linking that configuration to cache behavior. You can specify up to 10 fields in an HTTP POST request that are to encrypted, and you can set it so that different profiles are applied to each request based on a query string within the request URL.

When all is properly configured, sensitive data fields coming from end users will be encrypted automatically at the edge, and then the body of the content including both encrypted and unencrypted data can flow to and throughout your application. Only at the point where the application—most likely, a particular micro-service carefully designed and managed to deal with the sensitive data—needs to read the original data, is data decrypted and utilized. Meanwhile, all other parts of the application, as well as general logging, monitoring, performance tracing facilities, will never inadvertently examine or record or expose the sensitive data elements that arrived from the user if configured correctly.

Summary

In this chapter, you learned about Amazon CloudFront, a global CDN service that integrates with other AWS products to give developers and organizations an easy way to distribute content to end users with low latency, high data transfer speeds, and no minimum usage commitments.

You learned about the different capabilities and features of Amazon CloudFront, including edge locations, Regional Edge Caches, web and RTMP distributions, origin servers, dynamic content delivery, access logs, Lambda@Edge and field-level encryption.

CDNs are one of the main ways to provide consistent performance to users who are geographically dispersed across the globe. They can also reduce load on your origin server and provide increased web application scalability, performance, and security.

Exam Essentials

Know the basic use cases for Amazon CloudFront. Know when to use Amazon CloudFront, such as for popular static and dynamic content with geographically-distributed users.

Know how Amazon CloudFront works. Amazon CloudFront optimizes downloads by using geolocation to identify the geographical location of users and then serving and caching content at the edge location closest to each user.

Know how to create an Amazon CloudFront distribution and what types of origins are supported. To create a distribution, you specify an origin and the type of distribution, and then Amazon CloudFront creates a new domain name for the distribution. Origins supported include Amazon S3 buckets or static Amazon S3 websites and HTTP servers located on Amazon EC2 or in your own data center.

Know how to use Amazon CloudFront for dynamic content and multiple origins. Understand how to specify multiple origins for different types of content and how to use cache behaviors and path strings to control what content is served by which origin.

Know what mechanisms are available to serve private content through Amazon CloudFront. Amazon CloudFront can serve private content using Amazon S3 OAIs, signed URLs, and signed cookies.

Know how access logs for Amazon CloudFront work. Amazon CloudFront can create log files that contain detailed information about every user request that Amazon CloudFront receives.

Know how and why you would invalidate objects from Amazon CloudFront. If you need to remove objects from an Amazon CloudFront edge location cache before the object expires, you can invalidate the object from the Amazon CloudFront edge location caches.

Know how Lambda@Edge works and the use cases where it would be useful. Lambda@Edge is an extension of AWS Lambda, a compute service that lets you execute functions that customize the content that is delivered through Amazon CloudFront. You can execute AWS Lambda functions when Amazon CloudFront events occur.

Know why and how you would use ACM. ACM is designed to simplify and automate many of the tasks that are traditionally associated with management of SSL/TLS certificates. To use an ACM certificate with Amazon CloudFront, you must request or import the certificate in the US East (N. Virginia) Region.

Know why and how you would use HTTPS with Amazon CloudFront. For web distributions, you can configure Amazon CloudFront to require that viewers use HTTPS to request your objects.

Test Taking Tip

Flashcards are a great way to recognize areas where you may have gaps in knowledge, reviewing these after reading a chapter can help you identify where you might need to go back and review content. To review content, re-reading that section for the topic you are reviewing, and then walking through the accompanying exercise can help. Flashcards can also help to review topics mentally in the lead up to an exam. You can use the cards provided with this book and even create some of your own.

Resources to Review

Amazon CloudFront:

`https://aws.amazon.com/cloudfront/`

Amazon CloudFront User Guide:

`https://aws.amazon.com/documentation/cloudfront/`

AWS re:Invent Presentations:

AWS re:Invent 2017: Amazon CloudFront Flash Talks: Best Practices on Configuring, Se security, caching, measuring performance using Real User Monitoring (RUM), and customizing content delivery with Lambda@Edge. (CTD301):

`https://www.youtube.com/watch?v=8U3QdNSFJDU`

AWS re:Invent 2017: Introduction to Amazon CloudFront and AWS Lambda@Edge (CTD201):

`https://www.youtube.com/watch?v=wRaPw1tx6LA`

Exercises

The best way to become familiar with Amazon CloudFront is to build your own Amazon CloudFront distribution, which is what you will be doing in this section.

For assistance completing these exercises, refer to the Amazon CloudFront user guide located at: `https://aws.amazon.com/documentation/cloudfront/`.

EXERCISE 7.1

Create an Amazon CloudFront Web Distribution

1. Sign in to the AWS Management Console as Administrator or Power User.
2. Upload your content to Amazon S3 and grant object permissions.
    a. Through the Amazon S3 console, create a bucket with the same name as your desired website hostname and Amazon CloudFront distribution.
    b. Upload the static files to the bucket. Make sure the files do not contain any sensitive data, since they will be readable by anyone on the Internet.
    c. Make all of the files public (world readable).
    d. Enable static website hosting for the bucket. This includes specifying an index document and an error document.
    e. Your website will now be available at the Amazon S3 website URL: `<bucket-name>.s3-website-<AWS-region>.amazonaws.com`
3. Create an Amazon CloudFront web distribution.
    a. Navigate to the Amazon CloudFront console.
    b. Choose Create Distribution and follow the required steps.
4. Test your links. After you have created your distribution, Amazon CloudFront knows the location of your Amazon S3 origin server, and you know the domain name associated with the distribution. You can create a link to your Amazon S3 bucket content with that domain name and have Amazon CloudFront serve it.

You have created your first Amazon CloudFront web distribution.

EXERCISE 7.2

Create an Amazon CloudFront RTMP Distribution

1. Sign in to the AWS Management Console as Administrator or Power User. Navigate to the Amazon CloudFront console.

2. Create an Amazon S3 bucket for your media files. If you are using a different Amazon S3 bucket for your media player, create an Amazon S3 bucket for the media player files too. The names of your buckets must be all lowercase and cannot contain spaces.
3. Upload the files for your media player to the origin that Amazon CloudFront should use to retrieve files. If you are using an Amazon S3 bucket as the origin for the media player, make the files (not the bucket) publicly readable.
4. Create a web distribution for your media player.
5. Upload your media files to the Amazon S3 bucket that you created for the media files. Make the content (not the bucket) publicly readable. Media files in a Flash Video container must include the `.flv` file name extension or the media will not stream. You can put media player files and media files in the same bucket.
6. Create an RTMP distribution for your media files.
7. Configure your media player. To play a media file, you must configure the media player with the correct path to the file. How you configure the media depends on which media player you are using and how you are using it.
8. After Amazon CloudFront creates your distribution, the value of the Status column for your distribution will change from InProgress to Deployed. If you chose to enable the distribution, it will then be ready to process requests. This should take less than 15 minutes.

You have created your first Amazon CloudFront RTMP distribution.

EXERCISE 7.3

Add an Alternate Domain Name to Your Amazon CloudFront Distribution

1. Sign in to the AWS Management Console as Administrator or Power User. Navigate to the Amazon CloudFront console.
2. Select your previously-created Amazon CloudFront web distribution.
3. Add the applicable alternate domain names.
4. Configure the DNS service for the domain to route traffic for the domain, such as `example.com`, to the Amazon CloudFront domain name for your distribution, such as `d111111abcdef8.cloudfront.net`. The method that you use will depend on whether you are using Amazon Route 53 as the DNS service provider for the domain, either with an Alias record set or by adding an appropriate CNAME resource record set for the hosted domain of your provider.

EXERCISE 7.3 *(continued)*

5. Using `dig` or a similar tool, confirm that the resource record set that you created in the previous step points to the domain name for your distribution. The following shows an example:

```
[prompt]--> dig images.example.com
; <<> DiG 9.3.3rc2 <<> images.example.com
;; global options: printcmd
;; Got answer:
;; ->>HEADER<<- opcode: QUERY, status: NOERROR, id: 15917
;; flags: qr rd ra; QUERY: 1, ANSWER: 9, AUTHORITY: 2, ADDITIONAL: 0
;; QUESTION SECTION:
;images.example.com. IN A
;; ANSWER SECTION:
images.example.com. 10800 IN CNAME d111111abcdef8.cloudfront.net.
...
...
```

You have added your first alternate domain name to your Amazon CloudFront distribution.

EXERCISE 7.4

Configure Amazon CloudFront to Require HTTPS Between Viewers and Amazon CloudFront

1. In the top pane of the Amazon CloudFront console, choose the ID for the distribution that you want to update.
2. On the Behaviors tab, choose the cache behavior that you want to update and then choose Edit.
3. Specify one of the following values for Viewer Protocol Policy:

   Redirect HTTP to HTTPS

   HTTPS Only

You have enabled Amazon CloudFront to require HTTPS between viewers and Amazon CloudFront.

EXERCISE 7.5

Delete a CloudFront Distribution

1. Sign in to the AWS Management Console as Administrator or Power User.
2. In the right pane of the Amazon CloudFront console, find the distribution that you want to delete. Review the value of the State column and its status.
   a. If the value of the State column is Disabled, skip to Step 6.
   b. If the value of State is Enabled and the value of Status is Deployed, continue to Step 3 to disable the distribution before deleting it.
   c. If the value of State is Enabled and the value of Status is InProgress, wait until Status changes to Deployed. After the Status is Deployed, continue to Step 3 to disable the distribution before deleting it.
3. In the right pane of the Amazon CloudFront console, select the checkbox for the distribution that you want to delete.
4. Click Disabled to disable the distribution. Click Yes, Disable to confirm. Click Close.
5. The value of the State column immediately changes to Disabled. Wait until the value of the Status column changes to Deployed.
6. Check the checkbox for the distribution that you want to delete.
7. Click Delete. Click Yes, Delete to confirm. Click Close.

You have deleted your first CloudFront distribution.

Review Questions

1. What is a Content Delivery Network (CDN)?
   - **A.** A managed Domain Name System (DNS) service
   - **B.** A type of load balancer
   - **C.** A distributed network of caches
   - **D.** A protocol for the distribution of traffic over the web

2. You are using Amazon CloudFront for your website. A user requests content, which is routed to a local edge location. What happens before the requested content is available at that edge location?
   - **A.** Amazon CloudFront will respond with an HTTP 404 error.
   - **B.** Amazon CloudFront will not send users to edge locations that do not contain the requested data.
   - **C.** Amazon CloudFront always pre-positions content in edge locations so that users never experience a cache miss.
   - **D.** The edge location sends a request to the origin server, serves the user the content, and then stores the content.

3. Amazon CloudFront can work with which of the following origin servers? (Choose three.)
   - **A.** Amazon Simple Storage Service (Amazon S3)
   - **B.** Elastic Load Balancing
   - **C.** On-premises servers
   - **D.** An Amazon Elastic Compute Cloud (Amazon EC2) Auto Scaling group
   - **E.** A Virtual Private Cloud (VPC) route table

4. What is the default expiry time for an Amazon CloudFront cache?
   - **A.** 300 seconds
   - **B.** 24 hours
   - **C.** 12 months
   - **D.** Objects never expire by default.

5. What does the Amazon CloudFront invalidation feature do?
   - **A.** Blocks users from flooding edge locations with requests.
   - **B.** Removes duplicate objects from the origin server.
   - **C.** Allows the override of origin server encryption.
   - **D.** Removes objects from the CloudFront cache.

6. What does an Amazon CloudFront cache behavior do?
   - **A.** Controls how requests are cached.
   - **B.** Applies rules to control selection of origins.

C. Enforces HTTPS encryption for all users.

D. Allows dynamic content caching.

7. What does Amazon CloudFront do when it uses HTTP Live Streaming (HLS), HTTP Dynamic Streaming (HDS), Smooth Streaming, and MPEG DASH formats for streaming video?

A. Uses the native Amazon CloudFront media player for improved performance.

B. Uses multiple edge locations for improved performance.

C. Sends parallel streams for improved performance.

D. Encapsulates video into pull (rather than push) formats that allow clients to adapt to changing conditions for improved performance.

8. When adding an alternate domain to your Amazon CloudFront distribution, the wildcard * can be used to do what?

A. Replace part of a subdomain name (for example, subdomain.`*.example.com`).

B. Replace part of a subdomain name (for example, `*domain.example.com`).

C. Act in the place of specifying subdomains individually.

D. Reference multiple files on your origin server.

9. When using AWS Certification Manager (ACM) and Amazon CloudFront, you configured your certificate within ACM. When you try to enable Amazon CloudFront, however, you do not see the certificate available for use. What could be the problem?

A. ACM does not support Amazon CloudFront.

B. You need to purchase a certificate from a third-party Certificate Authority (CA) and upload it to ACM.

C. You need to configure the preshared key for ACM.

D. You might not have created the ACM certificate in the right region.

10. How can you use the wildcard * when invalidating objects with Amazon CloudFront?

A. In place of specifying subdomains individually.

B. As a form of object versioning.

C. To allow access to your origin server.

D. To specify a path that applies to many objects.

11. What do Amazon CloudFront access logs do?

A. They are a way to monitor performance of your Amazon Simple Storage Service (Amazon S3) bucket.

B. They contain detailed information about every user request that Amazon CloudFront receives.

C. They enable you to capture information about the IP traffic going to and from network interfaces.

D. They enable governance, compliance, operational auditing, and risk auditing of your AWS account.

Network Security

THE AWS CERTIFIED ADVANCED NETWORKING – SPECIALTY EXAM OBJECTIVES COVERED IN THIS CHAPTER MAY INCLUDE, BUT ARE NOT LIMITED TO, THE FOLLOWING:

Domain 2.0: Design and Implement AWS Networks

- ✓ **2.2 Given customer requirements, define network architectures on AWS**
- ✓ **2.5 Derive an appropriate architecture based on customer and application requirements**

Domain 3.0: Automate AWS Tasks

- ✓ **3.2 Apply AWS networking concepts**

Domain 5.0: Design and Implement for Security and Compliance

- ✓ **5.1 Evaluate design requirements for alignment with security and compliance objectives**
- ✓ **5.2 Evaluate monitoring strategies in support of security and compliance objectives**
- ✓ **5.3 Evaluate AWS security features for managing network traffic**
- ✓ **5.4 Utilize encryption technologies to secure network communications**

There's a clear trend in the IT industry with respect to network security: the boundary is shrinking. Gone are the "hard on the outside, soft on the inside" days that focused a disproportionate amount of attention on network boundary protection. Pushing all traffic through a static, throughput-constrained edge security stack is no longer considered a complete security solution. Moreover, cloud architectures—with their virtually unlimited horizontal scalability—challenge these traditional notions of network security.

We now see the rise of micro-segmentation, zero trust networks, and software-defined perimeters. And while security in the cloud is still familiar to most network and security professionals, the principles translate into slightly different practices. *Defense in depth* continues as a guiding principle, and this chapter provides perspective on a range of capabilities that you can leverage in securing your environment.

When you think holistically about security in AWS, it is critical to remember that security is a shared responsibility between you and AWS. Make sure that you are clear where AWS responsibility ends and your responsibility begins; otherwise, you leave a threat vector open to malicious actors.

AWS provides a baseline of security for you. For example, AWS protects service Application Programming Interface (API) endpoints to ensure that they are continuously available. You have responsibilities regarding the protection of your workloads. AWS offers you many network security services and features, and you should understand when and how to use them. Additional capabilities are available as vendor products and services in the AWS Marketplace.

This chapter reviews the services and features that AWS provides to support confidentiality, integrity, and availability of your networks. After a brief section on the importance of cloud governance, the rest of the chapter is dedicated to the implementation of network security in three primary areas: data flow, AWS security services, and detection and response. Data flow security focuses on services like Amazon CloudFront, AWS Shield, and AWS WAF, which provide inline network security capabilities. AWS security services will cover Amazon GuardDuty, Amazon Macie, and Amazon Inspector. These services, when enabled, detect anomalies in your environment. The final portion of the chapter will discuss the ways that you can integrate AWS Cloud services and features to detect and respond to network security events. Key architectural patterns, such as the security of Amazon Virtual Private Cloud (Amazon VPC) and Elastic Load Balancing are covered in Chapter 16, "Scenarios and Reference Architectures." You should have a deep understanding across the breadth of network security offerings available from AWS to pass the AWS Certified Advanced Networking – Specialty Exam.

Governance

Your ability to protect, detect, and respond to network security events is predicated on your ability to identify assets and understand normal operational behaviors. When VPCs, AWS Identity and Access Management (IAM) principles, or sensitive datasets are created ad hoc without oversight or process, your workloads are exposed to significant risk. This reason, among others, is why an overall governance approach is so important to a holistic security approach in the cloud. AWS provides methodologies, including the *AWS Cloud Adoption Framework (CAF)*, to help you along your cloud journey.

A fundamental principle of security is automation. Chapter 10, "Automation," provides a deep dive on automation for the network. We cover a few key services in this chapter that take the human element out of the loop with respect to creating, operating, managing, and decommissioning your AWS environments. People make mistakes, people bend the rules, and people can act with malice. Your ability to automate processes will greatly contribute to the overall network security of your environments.

AWS Organizations

AWS Organizations provides centralized management of multiple AWS accounts. It delivers two important features in addition to consolidated billing. The first feature is the concept of a *Service Control Policy (SCP)*. The SCP allows the designated master account to define policies that restrict, at the account level, what services and actions member-account users, groups, and roles can take, including the account root user. SCPs are similar to IAM permission policies and use nearly identical syntax. The second feature is programmatic account creation. When you use AWS Organizations to create a new account within an organization, the new account is created with an administrative role, typically called `OrganizationAccountAccessRole`, which you assume to access the new account.

We'll explain why these two features are important for network security with the following example. Let's say that your organization allows each department to have its own individual AWS account in which to create one or more VPC enclaves. That is, each department may have VPCs that connect back to the organization using a Virtual Private Network (VPN) and a Virtual Private Gateway (VGW), but an Internet gateway is never allowed. Using the AWS Organizations account creation API, you can generate a new account, assume its administrative role, create a VPC in a specific region, connect the VPC to the organizational network over a VPN, and then apply an SCP to the account that prohibits the use of an Internet gateway.

For the exam, you should have general familiarity with AWS Organizations and IAM.

AWS CloudFormation

AWS CloudFormation is a service that allows you to define and manage your AWS environment. With AWS CloudFormation, you define your infrastructure as code using either JSON or YAML. This textual definition, called a *template*, describes exactly what resources to provision and their respective configurations. You manage the collection of resources in AWS CloudFormation as a single unit called a *stack*. A stack is the target of create, update, or delete actions that you take with a template. Figure 8.1 shows how you use templates and stacks with AWS CloudFormation.

FIGURE 8.1 Templates and stacks

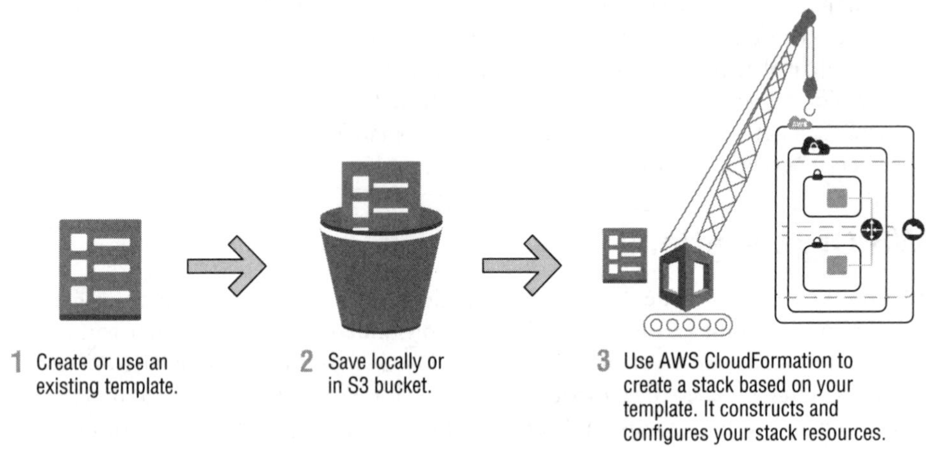
1 Create or use an existing template.
2 Save locally or in S3 bucket.
3 Use AWS CloudFormation to create a stack based on your template. It constructs and configures your stack resources.

When you operate a multi-region or multi-account environment, AWS CloudFormation StackSets is particularly useful. AWS CloudFormation StackSets extends the functionality of stacks by enabling you to create, update, or delete stacks across multiple accounts and regions with a single operation. Using an administrator account, you define and manage an AWS CloudFormation template and use the template as the basis for provisioning stacks into selected target accounts across specified regions.

In order to understand how AWS CloudFormation helps with network security, let's revisit our previous example. Instead of manually creating a VPC and a connection back to the organization using a VPN, you can define the VPC and VPN using an AWS CloudFormation template. When the cross-account, administrative role is assumed, your automation tooling can call AWS CloudFormation to create these resources in the new account. Because the template is a text file, you can add it to your change and version control systems. Using your Continuous Integration/Continuous Delivery (CI/CD) tool chain, you can scan the template for undesirable elements such as security groups that are open to the world. You can trigger alerts and initiate an investigation if unapproved changes are integrated into the template.

For the exam, you should have a thorough understanding of AWS CloudFormation.

AWS Service Catalog

AWS Service Catalog allows organizations to create and manage a curated *portfolio* of *products*. These products might be specific software, servers, or complete multi-tier architectures. AWS Service Catalog allows your organization to assert deployment consistency and governance. AWS Service Catalog uses a combination of IAM roles, termed *launch constraints*, and AWS CloudFormation templates to deliver fine-grained control of access and configuration during the provisioning process. Figure 8.2 demonstrates the overall workflow, from template creation to product launch.

FIGURE 8.2 AWS Service Catalog workflow

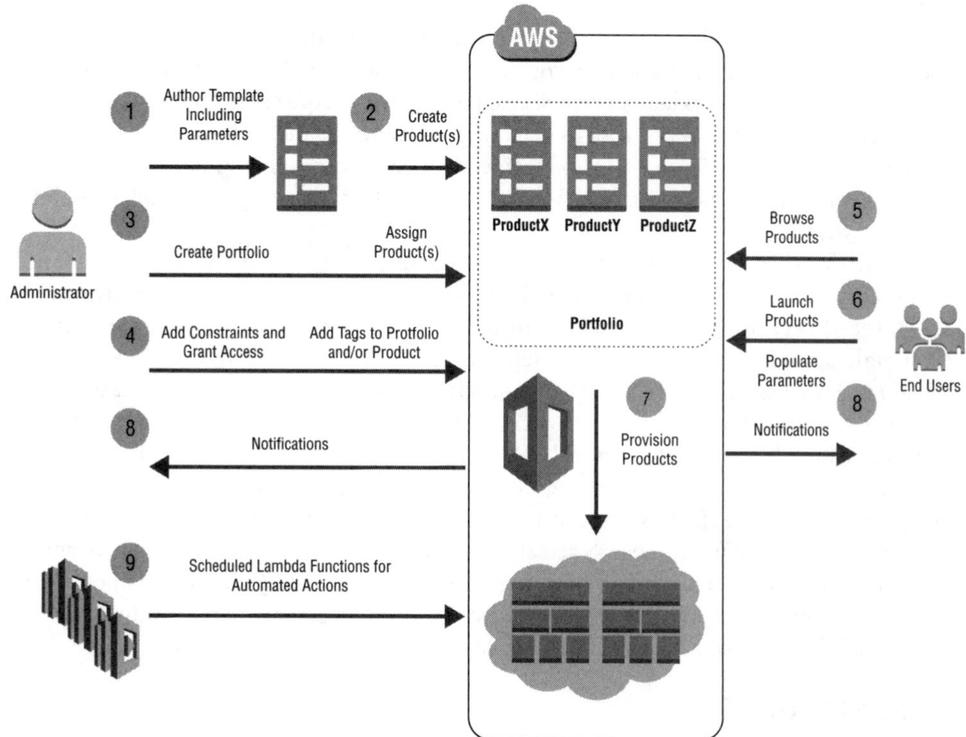

Let's revisit our example once more to demonstrate how you can continue to remove humans from the loop, improving your overall security posture. Instead of manually assuming the administrative role in the new account and launching the AWS CloudFormation template, you can instead bundle a new AWS CloudFormation template and launch constraints as a product available to the departments in an AWS Service Catalog. When this enclave VPC product is selected, AWS Service Catalog executes a template to generate the new AWS account, create the VPC enclave, build the VPN, and apply the restrictive SCP. With this approach, creation and configuration of a new account is completely automated. Moreover, the process is standardized, repeatable, and auditable.

Data Flow Security

In this section, we cover AWS Cloud services and features that operate directly on the flow of traffic in your AWS environment. AWS provides multiple options that you can use individually or in combination to achieve your required level of network security. The rest of this section describes each of the services and features, starting from edge locations and working inward to regional capabilities and Amazon Elastic Compute Cloud (Amazon EC2) instance capabilities.

Edge Locations

AWS delivers several services from a distributed network of edge locations across the globe. This edge infrastructure allows you to improve the overall throughput and latency characteristics of your workloads when servicing incoming requests from the Internet. This infrastructure is also a key tool in detecting, preventing, and mitigating the impact of *Distributed Denial of Service (DDoS)* attacks on your environment. For the exam, you should understand how edge locations impact the confidentiality, integrity, and availability of your networks.

All services that run in edge locations share a common set of network security characteristics. First, the edge locations all include built-in network layer (Layer 3) and transport layer (Layer 4) network mitigations. The infrastructure is continuously analyzing traffic for anomalies, and it provides built-in defense against common DDoS attacks such as SYN floods, User Datagram Protocol (UDP) floods, and reflection attacks. In the case of SYN floods, for example, SYN cookies are activated to avoid impact on legitimate traffic. As another example, only well-formed UDP or Transmission Control Protocol (TCP) packets are serviced by the edge locations. More generally, all traffic is scored across a set of dimensions to prioritize the flow of legitimate traffic. Second, the global scale of the edge infrastructure allows AWS to absorb attacks by diffusing the incoming traffic flows across multiple edge locations. Third, many services running in an edge location have the ability to apply geographic isolation and restriction; that is, both automated and manual whitelisting and blacklisting of source traffic is possible.

Amazon Route 53

Nearly all network communication starts with the process of translating a resource identifier into a network location. The Internet leverages the Domain Name System (DNS) to perform this task. As IPv6 adoption continues to accelerate, the notion of recalling or hard-coding IP addresses is fading away. Therefore, DNS is a critical network service. Disruption of DNS service can render your environment inaccessible and inoperable.

Amazon Route 53 is a highly-available and scalable DNS web service offered by AWS. Route 53 is covered in depth in Chapter 6, "Domain Name System and Load Balancing." In this section, we describe how Route 53 uses shuffle sharding and anycast striping to deliver continuous availability in the face of DDoS attacks and other events that impact availability. Route 53 is the only AWS Cloud service with a 100 percent availability Service Level Agreement (SLA).

Shuffle sharding is a technique designed to minimize correlated failures by simultaneously leveraging the traditional benefits of sharding (such as fault isolation and performance scaling) and the effects of randomized, or shuffled, assignment. Imagine for a moment that Amazon Route 53 uses ten instances to create 5 shards, with each shard having a pair of instances for internal redundancy (Amazon Route 53 has significantly more capacity). Further, each customer's hosted zones are placed on a single shard. If the placement of customers is evenly divided across the shards by customer ID, for example, it might always be the case that zones for Customer 1 and Customer 2 are served from the same shard. In that case, these two customers could have correlated failures. If, for example, Customer 2's DNS zones were under a DDoS attack, Customer 1 might experience an impact as well. Moreover, one-fifth of all customers might experience that same impact. If instead we took the 10 instances and randomly assigned customers to a pair of instances, the likelihood of correlated failures would significantly decrease. With this method, Customer 1 is on a shuffle shard composed of instances 3 and 5, for example, while Customer 2 is on a shuffle shard composed of instances 4 and 5. Even though the random allocation of shard instances yielded an overlap on instance 5, the failures are no longer necessarily correlated because client retry logic will mitigate the impact of an availability loss to instance 5. Figure 8.3 provides a visual depiction of this approach.

FIGURE 8.3 Shuffle sharding

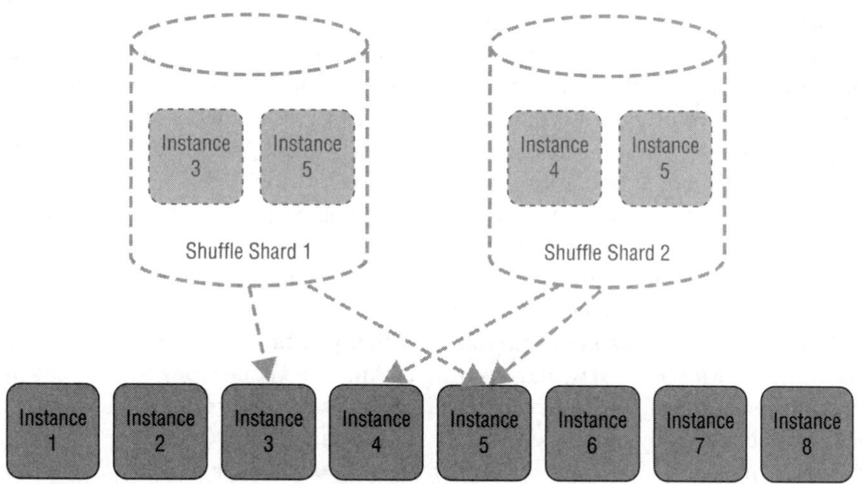

Anycast striping is another availability mechanism built into Amazon Route 53. Anycast is the notion that multiple systems respond to the same IP address. In practical terms, anycast means that when your DNS resolver initiates a connection to an Amazon Route 53 DNS server, the actual responder to which you connect could be in any of several locations across the globe advertising the same anycast address. For example, `example.aws` is a public hosted zone on Amazon Route 53. It is assigned the name server `ns-962.awsdns-56.net`, which has an IPv4 address of `192.0.2.194`. This IPv4 address is an anycast address, and AWS advertises the address to the Internet from multiple edge locations. Your request will route to the "closest" anycast server (from a Border Gateway Protocol [BGP] perspective).

Given that DNS uses an iterative lookup process, how will you resolve the name server's fully qualified domain name to an IP address if the `.net` Top Level Domain (TLD) servers are not responding? The answer: You won't. To address this failure mode, AWS stripes public hosted zones across Amazon Route 53 DNS servers in each of four TLDs. In this way, not only does Amazon Route 53 provide multiple anycast name server addresses, but the lookup process for the DNS servers themselves are also dispersed across multiple TLDs.

Amazon Route 53 also provides mechanisms to block invalid or unwanted requests. As part of the edge infrastructure, packet filters are applied that drop invalid DNS requests. If you wish to block requests further, Amazon Route 53 provides geolocation routing policies that give you control over the responses provided to DNS resolvers based on their source IP addresses. You can delineate responses by continent, country, or by state in the United States.

Amazon CloudFront

Amazon CloudFront is a global *Content Delivery Network (CDN)* operated through edge locations that provide regional and global edge caches. The service is designed to bring content closer to consumers on the Internet. Amazon CloudFront is covered in depth in Chapter 7, "Amazon CloudFront." In addition to overall edge acceleration capabilities, Amazon CloudFront provides several security features that promote availability of your environments and confidentiality of your content.

Because of its ability to mitigate the impact of DDoS attacks, Amazon CloudFront is frequently used to front both static and dynamic content. In order to effectively protect the content sources, called *origins*, it is important that the origins are accessible only by Amazon CloudFront. That is, if you use Amazon CloudFront to protect your infrastructure, it has little value if a malicious actor can simply bypass Amazon CloudFront and attack your origin directly. There are two common approaches to protecting origins: using an Origin Access Identity (OAI) with Amazon Simple Storage Service (Amazon S3) and using custom headers. Once direct access to your origins is restricted, you can leverage Amazon CloudFront security features like geo-restriction, signed URLs, and signed cookies.

An *OAI* is a special Amazon CloudFront user that you can associate with your distributions. A *distribution* is a particular instance of Amazon CloudFront with a defined set of configurations, origins, and behaviors. You grant permissions to the OAI on Amazon S3 objects and buckets. By requiring that access to Amazon S3 occur through Amazon CloudFront using the OAI, you preclude the bypassing of network security controls that you implement in Amazon CloudFront. For example, you might leverage the Amazon CloudFront geo-restriction feature to prevent IP addresses outside of your country from accessing Amazon S3 objects.

For custom origins, like Amazon EC2 and Elastic Load Balancing, you can extend the notion of an OAI to systems outside of Amazon S3 by using custom HTTP headers. Amazon CloudFront allows you to manipulate many of the headers that are passed to your origin. By configuring a custom header, you can restrict access to only those Amazon CloudFront distributions that you designate. A simple approach to protecting a custom origin is simply to limit access to only the known Amazon CloudFront IP addresses. While it is true that AWS publishes the IP addresses used by Amazon CloudFront, the naïve approach misses the fact that anyone with an AWS account can create their own Amazon CloudFront distribution and point it to your origin, bypassing any IP restrictions that you configured on your origin. To resolve this issue, you can add a custom header so that your origin can authenticate whether the incoming traffic originated from your Amazon CloudFront distribution.

With your origin protected from direct access, you can implement controls to ensure the confidentiality of your content. From a purely networking perspective, Amazon CloudFront allows you to enforce the use of particular protocols for transport and encryption. For communication from Amazon CloudFront to your origins, you can require the use of HTTPS and specify the particular version of Transport Layer Security (TLS). For communication from viewers to Amazon CloudFront, you can enforce the use of HTTPS and specify the versions of HTTP supported. You can further improve viewer security by selecting a pre-defined security policy that enforces TLS version 1.1 or 1.2 as the minimum protocol version. When HTTPS is used for viewers, you can leverage the default Amazon CloudFront certificate, use AWS Certificate Manager, or import your own custom certificate.

The use of encryption protects your data in transit, but you may also wish to exert fine-grained control over access to your content. To achieve this confidentiality, Amazon CloudFront allows you to require *signed URLs* or *signed cookies* for access to restricted content. When using either of these two methods, you are responsible for creating and distributing the signed tokens. When using signed URLs or signed cookies, you specify the date and time at which the content is no longer available to the consumer. You can optionally specify a starting date and time as well as a restricted set of consumer source IPs.

To provide finer-grained data protection, you can use a new Amazon CloudFront capability called *Field-Level Encryption* to further enhance the security of sensitive data, like credit card numbers or personally identifiable information (PII). CloudFront's field-level encryption further encrypts sensitive data in an HTTPS form using field-specific encryption keys before a POST request is forwarded to your origin. This ensures that sensitive data can only be decrypted and viewed by certain components or services in your origin application stack.

AWS Lambda@Edge

AWS Lambda@Edge allows you to run AWS Lambda functions inside of Amazon CloudFront. The service executes on the basis of Amazon CloudFront events, called *triggers*, that occur during the normal lifecycle of request/response interactions with viewers and origins. While AWS Lambda@Edge opens a broad range of opportunities for application enhancement, there are specific uses of the service that can materially improve the security of your origins.

In the previous section on Amazon CloudFront, we described the use of headers to authenticate a specific distribution to the origin. Historically, this header/value pair was static and slow-changing. Static values are more readily compromised over time. For example, imagine if you never changed your user name and password. With AWS Lambda@Edge, you can implement a programmatic method to populate the header value dynamically, making it more difficult to subvert your origin access enforcement mechanisms.

A similar use case involves validation of consumer-provided authorization tokens. You can use AWS Lambda@Edge to inspect headers and authorization tokens. For example, if you experienced an application layer attack (Layer 7), you could leverage AWS Lambda@Edge to validate the format and validity of the asserted session or authorization tokens to distinguish between accepting valid traffic and dropping malicious traffic. As a result, invalid requests would not reach the origin.

Edge Locations and Regions

Some AWS Cloud services provide network security capabilities both to edge locations and to AWS Regions. This section describes these services and the AWS resources that they can protect.

AWS Certificate Manager

AWS Certificate Manager is an AWS Cloud service for creating and managing TLS certificates for your AWS websites and applications. AWS Certificate Manager is supported on Amazon CloudFront, Elastic Load Balancing, AWS Elastic Beanstalk (using Elastic Load Balancing), and Amazon API Gateway. You can use certificates generated by AWS Certificate Manager, or you can import your own certificates into AWS Certificate Manager. The use of certificates supports the network security objectives of confidentiality and integrity.

When you use AWS Certificate Manager certificates, AWS provides you with a domain-validated RSA-2048, Secure Hash Algorithm (SHA)-256 certificate that is valid for 13 months. The service will attempt to auto-renew the certificate, typically 30 days before expiration, provided that the certificate is Internet accessible to the service. The certificate must include at least one Fully Qualified Domain Name (FQDN), and you can add additional names. You may also request wildcard names (such as `*.example.aws`). AWS Certificate Manager-generated certificates are free, and you cannot download the private key. The private key is encrypted at rest with AWS Key Management Service (AWS KMS).

Certificates in AWS Certificate Manager are regional resources. When you want to use the same FQDN in multiple regions, you'll need to request or import a certificate in each region. For Amazon CloudFront, you perform these tasks in the US East (N. Virginia) Region.

AWS WAF

AWS WAF is a web application firewall that allows you to protect specific AWS resources from common web exploits that could affect the confidentiality, integrity, and availability of your network and your data. AWS WAF integrates with Amazon CloudFront and the Application Load Balancer to monitor HTTP and HTTPS requests. Using custom rules and common, built-in attack patterns, you can prevent impact to your workloads.

With AWS WAF, you implement *Web Access Control Lists* (ACLs) to control your HTTP and HTTPS traffic. Web ACLs are composed of *rules*, and rules are composed of *conditions*. Figure 8.4 depicts these relationships. The rest of this section will describe each of these components in greater detail.

FIGURE 8.4 Web ACLs, rules, and conditions

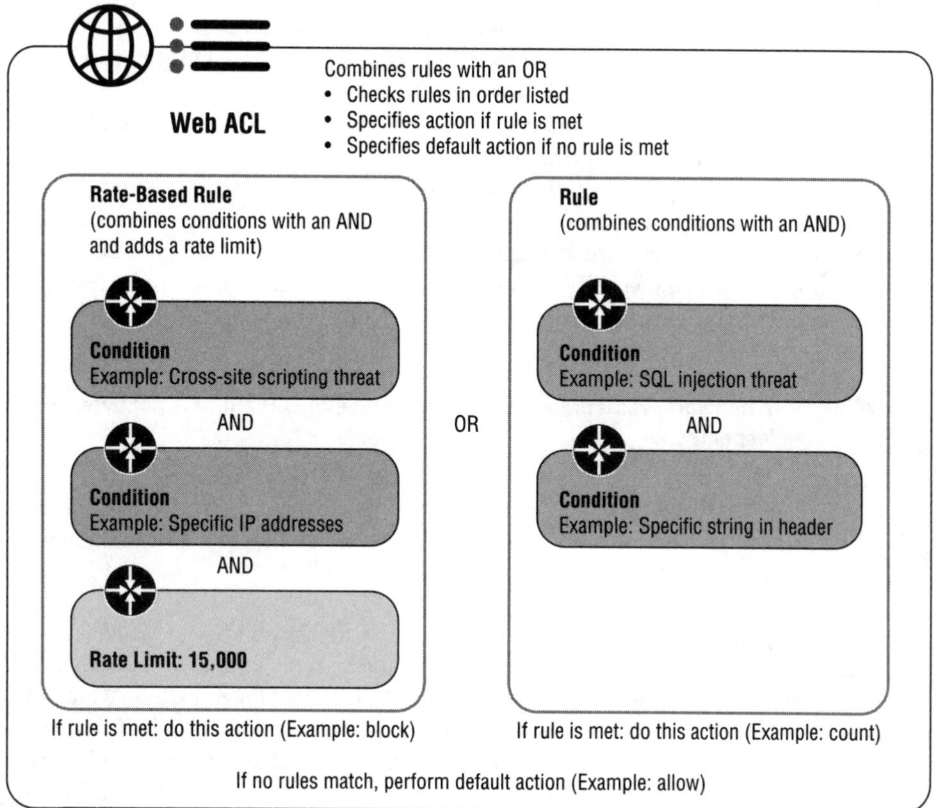

Conditions are the basic building blocks for AWS WAF. Six condition types are supported. When you create a condition with multiple filters, any given entry will satisfy the condition (that is, the filters are OR'ed). For example, one of the condition types is IP addresses. When you add multiple IP addresses to a single condition, the match of any single address makes the condition true. The conditions for AWS WAF are listed next.

The first condition, *Cross-Site Scripting (XSS)*, enables you to match web requests containing scripts that might exploit vulnerabilities in your applications. This condition allows you to search for XSS in common parts of the request data, including the HTTP method, header, query string, Uniform Resource Identifier (URI), or body. This condition also allows you to manipulate the request data, termed *transformation*, to facilitate matching. You can convert all of the data to lower case, decode HTML, decode the URI, normalize the whitespace, and simplify strings intended to represent command-line text.

The second condition, *IP addresses*, allows you to match on IPv4 and IPv6 addresses. For IPv4 addresses, AWS WAF will only filter /8, /16, /24, and /32. For IPv6 addresses, AWS WAF will only filter /24, /32, /48, /56, /64, and /128.

The third condition, *size constraints*, allows you to match requests on the basis of length. This condition will evaluate common parts of the request data, and it allows you to apply the same transformations available in XSS. With this condition, you specify the byte size and the comparison operator (for example, equals, not equals, greater than, or less than).

The fourth condition is *SQL injection (SQLi)*. Like XSS and size constraints, you filter on common parts of the request data and can apply transformations. This built-in attack pattern then evaluates the data for indicators of SQLi.

The fifth condition, *geographic match*, enables you to allow or block requests based on the country from which the request originates.

The last condition, *string match*, allows you to match based on string content. String match filters on the common parts of the request data, and it allows you to use the same transformations previously described. You select the match operator (for example, contains, starts with, or ends with) and specify the match value. This match value can be textual or base64 encoded. Regular expression (regex) matching is also supported.

When you evaluate the body of a request, only the first 8,192 bytes are inspected.

The maximum size of the value to match is 50 bytes. When using base64 encoding, the limit is 50 bytes before encoding.

Once the conditions are defined, you compose rules with the conditions. Each rule contains a name, an Amazon CloudWatch metric name, a rule type, and a condition list. The name of the rule is used later when creating the web ACL. The Amazon CloudWatch metric name is the name of the dimension that will appear in Amazon CloudWatch. The rule type can be either *regular rule* or *rate-based rule*. The distinction is that rate-based rules also take into account the number of matching requests that arrive from a given IP address in a five-minute interval. The rate limit must be greater than or equal to 2,000 requests per five-minute interval. For each condition you add to the rule, you can specify whether the evaluation should occur on the defined filters (for example, does match) or an inverse of the filters (for example, does not match). When you add multiple conditions to a rule, all conditions must match (that is, conditions are AND'ed).

If no conditions are specified for a rate-based rule, AWS WAF will match all incoming requests and apply the rate-based rule against all incoming IP addresses.

You can associate an AWS resource—either an Amazon CloudFront distribution or an Application Load Balancer—with a single web ACL. Multiple resources can use the same web ACL. Each web ACL has a name and an Amazon CloudWatch metrics name, similar to the rules definition. Web ACLs are composed of a list of rules, evaluated in order, and a default action that allows or blocks unmatched traffic. Regular rules allow you to specify whether the web application firewall should allow, block, or count the request. Rate-based rules allow you to block or count. When the count action is selected, AWS WAF increments a counter and then continues to process the next rule in the web ACL.

Once a web ACL is implemented, you can view request metrics from Amazon CloudWatch and retrieve sample match data. The sample data includes source IP, country, method, URI, request headers, matched rule, the action taken on the request, and the time the request was received.

AWS WAF with Amazon CloudFront metrics are only available when you use the US East (N. Virginia) Region.

You can use AWS WAF in a static configuration, a dynamic configuration, or as an integrated component with a third-party offering. Static configuration means that the configuration of your web ACLs is not automatically updated based on changes in the threat landscape of your environment. Dynamic configuration of AWS WAF is covered later in this chapter in the "Detection and Response" section. There are also third-party vendors that integrate with AWS WAF. You can find these third-party offerings in the AWS Marketplace.

AWS Shield

AWS Shield provides protection against DDoS attacks. AWS Shield offers two distinct levels of protection. The first, AWS Shield Standard, provides protection for all AWS customers against common and most frequently occurring attacks—like SYN/UDP floods, reflection attacks, and others—to support high availability of applications on AWS. It is a no-cost, always-on option that is designed to mitigate the majority of Layer 3 and Layer 4 attacks. AWS Shield Standard contains a continuously evolving rule base that is updated by AWS in response to changes in the Internet threat landscape. Customer visibility into the details of attacks is limited, however.

The second level, AWS Shield Advanced, provides additional DDoS attack protection for Amazon Route 53 hosted zones, Amazon CloudFront distributions, Elastic Load Balancing load balancers, and resources attached to Elastic IP addresses, like Amazon EC2 instances. In addition to network layer (Layer 3) and transport layer (Layer 4) detection and mitigation, AWS Shield Advanced also provides intelligent DDoS attack detection and mitigation for application layer (Layer 7) attacks. Information about ongoing attacks are provided in real time through detailed metric reporting, and customers receive attack forensic reports. Moreover, customers can contact a 24x7 DDoS Response Team (DRT) for assistance during an attack.

There is one last, important point about AWS Shield Advanced. With the move to the cloud and its virtually unlimited resources, many well-architected, horizontally-scalable applications can absorb a typical DDoS attack. That is, cloud architectures can often scale out to meet the surge demands of a typical DDoS attack. Customers pay for resources consumed in the cloud; as a result, we now see customers affected by Economic Denial of Sustainability (EDoS) attacks. The notion of EDoS is that, while a DDoS attack may not impact your availability, the financial cost of absorbing an attack itself becomes untenable. With AWS Shield Advanced, AWS offers some cost protection against billing spikes caused by a DDoS attack. This cost protection, however, is limited to Amazon Route 53 hosted zones, Amazon CloudFront distribution, Amazon EC2 instances, and Elastic Load Balancing load balancers.

When using AWS Shield Advanced, you mitigate application layer (Layer 7) attacks either with your own custom mitigations or through engagement of the DRT. When you create your own mitigations, you implement rules in AWS WAF, which is included for free with your AWS Shield Advanced subscription. When you engage the DRT, an AWS DDoS expert works with you to identify attack signatures and patterns. With your permission, the DRT creates and deploys the mitigations onto your AWS WAF. In order to allow the DRT to push these mitigations to your AWS WAF, you must first authorize the DRT by creating a cross-account IAM role.

Regions

AWS provides a series of region-based services that enable you to protect your environment. This section describes the services that act directly on data flows in the region and the AWS resources that they can protect.

Elastic Load Balancing

Elastic Load Balancing allows you to distribute incoming traffic across multiple resources, such as Amazon EC2 instances within an AWS Region. Load balancing is covered in depth in Chapter 6. In this section, we discuss features of Elastic Load Balancing that you can leverage to provide confidentiality, integrity, and availability to your workloads.

Because Elastic Load Balancing sits in front of your resources, it provides you with a level of protection. Elastic Load Balancing will automatically scale to meet the demands of the vast majority of use cases, contributing to the overall availability of your workload. With Elastic Load Balancing, you define the ports and protocols that it will accept, which are called *listeners*. Elastic Load Balancing only accepts incoming traffic on its listeners, minimizing the attack surface. Moreover, Elastic Load Balancing proxies connections to your VPC resources, so common attacks like SYN floods are not seen by your back-end resources because only well-formed TCP connections result in data flow to your resources.

When you use Application Load Balancer to provide access from the Internet to your VPC resources, the load balancer forwards traffic into your VPC using private IPv4 addresses from the subnet on which its network interfaces reside. Network Load Balancer, however, will propagate the originating, public source IPv4 address. While Internet-facing load balancers have public IP addresses, resources in your VPC are not required to use publicly-routable IP addresses. Without a publicly-routable IP address, traffic from resources in your VPC, like an Amazon EC2 instance, cannot reach the Internet directly.

Even when your Application Load Balancer is in dual-stack mode supporting IPv4 and IPv6, requests from the load balancer to your VPC resources are made over IPv4.

To support your confidentiality and integrity goals, Elastic Load Balancing has options for connections over Secure Sockets Layer (SSL)/TLS with Classic Load Balancers and HTTPS both for Classic Load Balancer and Application Load Balancer. As part of the configuration process, you provide a certificate, and you can use AWS Certificate Manager for this process. You also select the *security policies* used on incoming connections. Security policies allow you to select from a suite of ciphers for various SSL/TLS protocol versions.

A common approach, often termed the *Elastic Load Balancing sandwich*, leverages two tiers of load balancers to provide inline data flow analysis. In this architecture, a front-end set of Internet-facing load balancers receives incoming traffic. The traffic is load balanced to a fleet of Amazon EC2 instance running security processes of some type (such as web application firewall, content filters, or data loss prevention). In turn, this fleet of security devices forwards the traffic to a second set of load balancers. Finally, these internal load balancers forward the traffic to your workload's front end.

You can use a similar approach to provide inline data flow analysis for traffic leaving your VPC. In this architecture, you configure your workload's proxy setting to send requests through Elastic Load Balancing. The load balancer, in turn, forwards the traffic to a fleet of Amazon EC2 instances running proxy software and security processes. Finally, these security devices forward the permitted traffic onto the intended destination. Note that the second layer of load balancers is not used in this configuration.

Subnets and Route Tables

Route tables control the behavior of the implicit router on each subnet of a VPC. A *subnet* is a network segment within the Classless Inter-Domain Routing (CIDR) range of your VPC contained within a single Availability Zone. Route tables and subnets are covered in depth in Chapter 2, "Amazon Virtual Private Cloud (Amazon VPC) and Networking Fundamentals." From a network security perspective, you should understand how the allocation of subnets and route tables enables you to construct architectures that promote secure operation.

When you construct a VPC, it is important that you clearly demarcate the infrastructure based on intended routing behaviors. For example, it is common for customers to place Internet-facing load balancers into dedicated public subnets. This approach allows you to apply fine-grained controls on the routing within the subnet, implement network ACLs at the subnet boundary, configure security group rules on the load balancer's elastic network interfaces, and limit resources in the subnet with an IAM policy. With these four levers, you have precise control over the flow of traffic into and out of your infrastructure.

Route tables are particularly important when you want to keep traffic within the AWS infrastructure. Leveraging *gateway VPC endpoints*, you can create routes that, for example, provide a path directly between your VPC resources and Amazon S3. Moreover, with VPC endpoints for Amazon S3 and Amazon DynamoDB, you define policies that determine the degree of access granted through the endpoint. Another example is *VPC peering*. With peering, you create a relationship between VPCs, and the route table entries you supply cause traffic to flow directly between the two VPCs using only the AWS infrastructure. Finally, *AWS PrivateLink* offers another mechanism to consume services without leaving the AWS infrastructure. When you use PrivateLink, AWS places an elastic network interface into your VPC connected to a load balancer that sends traffic to a fleet in the provider's VPC. The effect is similar to peering, without the need to expose an entire VPC.

From an availability perspective, it is worth noting that AWS-provided gateways, endpoints, and peering are highly available. The Internet gateway, for example, is not a single device—it is a horizontally-scaled fleet of edge devices.

Customers often want to connect back to an on-premises environment as well. The two primary methods used are AWS Direct Connect, which was discussed in depth in Chapter 5, "AWS Direct Connect," and VPNs, which were discussed in depth in Chapter 4, "Virtual Private Networks." Availability approaches are also discussed in Chapters 4 and 5. To deliver confidentiality and integrity, you can leverage two common patterns to create an encrypted connection between your on-premises location and AWS using IP security (IPsec) over AWS Direct Connect.

The simplest pattern is to use an AWS managed VPN connection over a public Virtual Interface (VIF), configuring your edge router as the customer gateway. Traffic leaving your edge router would pass through the IPsec connection, running over your public VIF, and terminate on the VGW connected to your VPC. Subnets requiring access would add a route in their associated route table to the VGW. This pattern is shown in Figure 8.5.

FIGURE 8.5 VPN over Public VIF

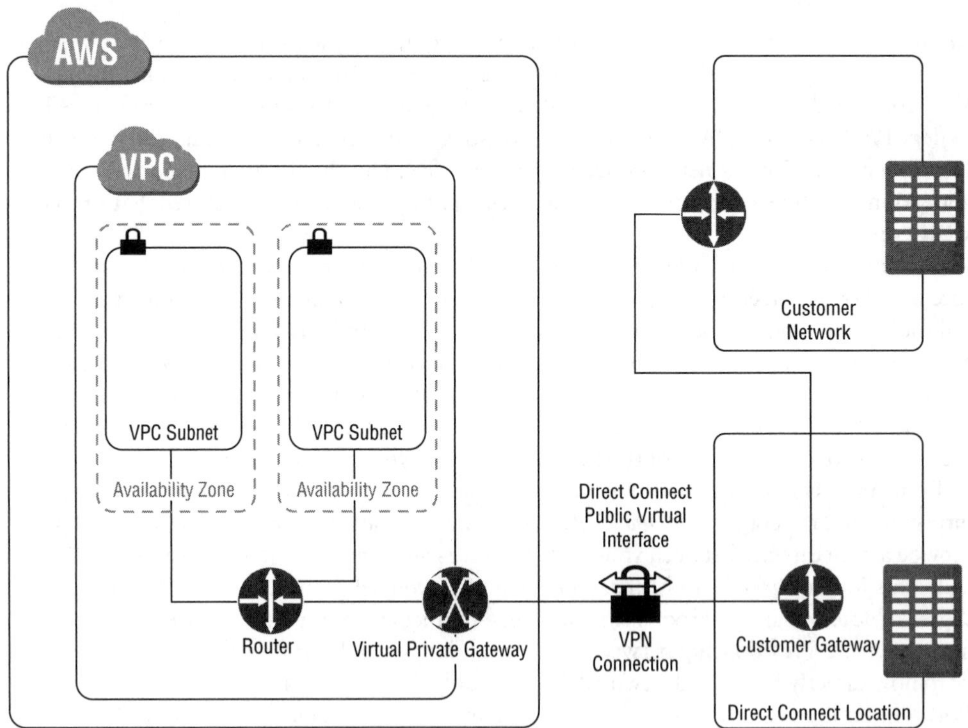

Another pattern uses *Virtual Routing and Forwarding (VFR)* on the customer gateway to create an IPsec connection over a private virtual interface, terminating on an Amazon EC2 instance in your VPC running VPN software. Subnets requiring access would add a route in their associated route table to the Amazon EC2 instance running the VPN software. This Amazon EC2 instance must have source/destination checking disabled. This pattern is shown in Figure 8.6.

FIGURE 8.6 VPN over Private Virtual Interface

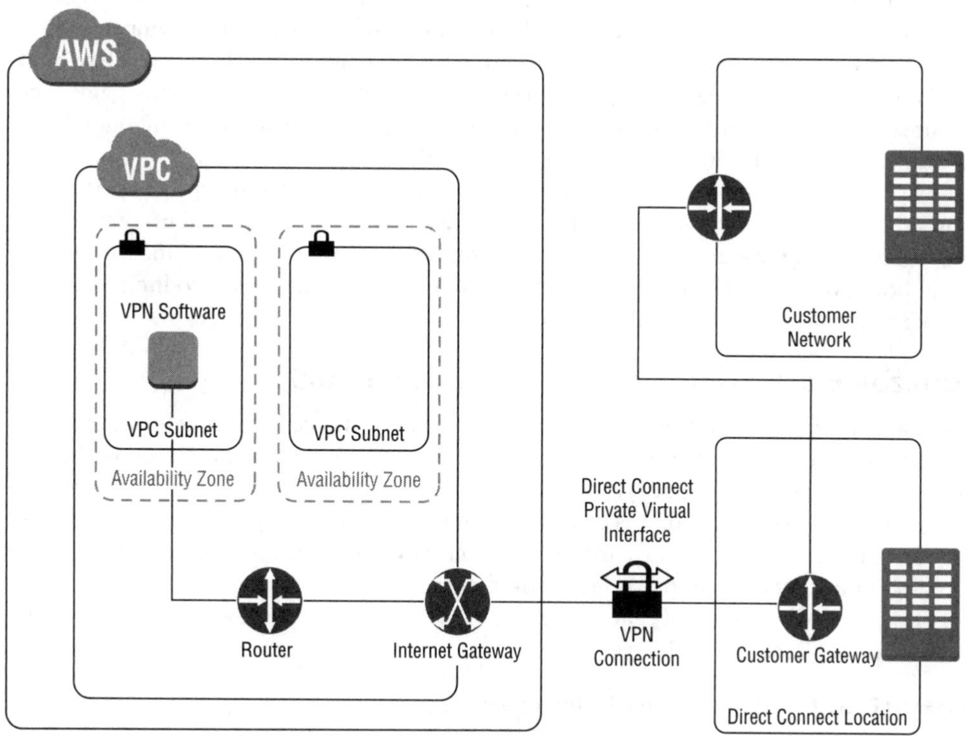

Security Groups and Network Access Control Lists (ACLs)

The most basic primitives for delivering network security on AWS are security groups and network ACLs. *Security groups* are stateful network layer (Layer 3)/transport layer (Layer 4) firewalls that you apply to network interfaces in your VPC. *Network ACLs* are stateless network layer (Layer 3)/transport layer (Layer 4) filters that you apply to subnets within your VPC. Both are covered in depth in Chapter 2.

Because cloud architectures scale elastically, there are typically changes in resources over time. Security groups allow you to abstract this complexity. For example, when using Auto Scaling, you specify a security group to use. As Amazon EC2 instances are added or removed from the Auto Scaling group, the set of IP addresses in use will change. The security group assigned to instances' network interfaces, however, will not. As a result, you can reference this security group in your Amazon Relational Database Service (Amazon RDS) security group, for example, to ensure that the database is continuously accessible by your Amazon EC2 instances.

Network ACLs provide another method for managing the flow of packets in your VPC. By default, the network ACL in your VPC allows all packets into and out of all subnets. Some customers use the fact that both security groups and network ACLs control packet flow to implement a type of separation of duties. That is, the workload owner is given control of the security group configuration, but the organization charged with network security retains control of the network ACLs. In this way, coordination between the two parties is required to allow new packet flows. Often, the network ACLs are configured on private subnets to permit only the transmission and receipt of traffic within the particular VPC. In this way, the workload owner can make needed changes to the security groups. If a malicious actor gains access to the security group configuration, however, any attempt to exfiltrate (transmit out without authorization) data directly to the Internet would fail.

As you compose your subnets, think through your anticipated and expected traffic flows. If you lay out your subnets such that you can summarize related subnets into an aggregate, you can create clean or simple network ACLs that are easier to understand. In addition, you should consider that network ACLs are a common way to limit inter-subnet traffic allowed by the VPC local route.

Amazon Elastic Compute Cloud (Amazon EC2)

From an Amazon VPC perspective, your Amazon EC2 instances are arguably the most important piece of the network security environment. Weak authentication, unpatched operating systems, and unmanaged Amazon EC2 instances are likely to fall victim to compromise. When an instance is compromised, it provides a launch pad from which malicious actors can attempt to move throughout your environment, even through AWS Direct Connect or a VPN connection. When thinking through network security, always be mindful of the shared responsibility model. Figure 8.7 provides an overview of the responsibility delineation for Amazon EC2.

FIGURE 8.7 Shared responsibility model

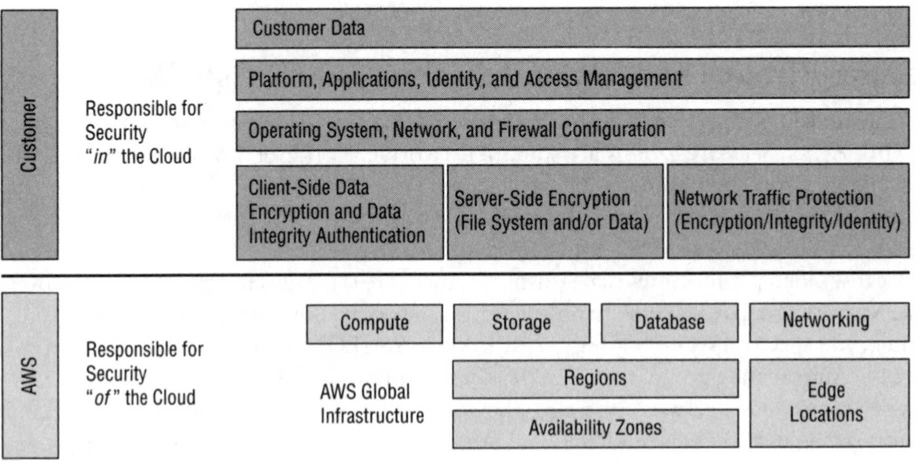

When reviewing Figure 8.7, note that network traffic protection, network configuration, and firewall configuration are all customer responsibilities. When traffic passes between Amazon EC2 instances in your VPC, for example, you have no visibility into how that traffic is routed in the underlying AWS infrastructure. Recall from Chapter 2 that an Availability Zone contains one or more data centers. Instances that you launch in a subnet might reside on physical hosts in separate data centers. As a result, traffic would flow on fiber-optic cables between buildings. If you want to ensure the confidentiality and integrity of data in transit, you should leverage encryption when communicating between VPC resources, including Amazon EC2 instances. You should also encrypt sessions that you initiate to Amazon EC2 instances using protocols like Secure Shell (SSH). You should use encryption throughout your environments.

Network configuration is another important aspect of network security. For example, an Amazon EC2 instance can have more than one network interface. This simple capability has dramatic implications on the configuration of the network in your VPC. By extension, it has a direct impact on network security.

Imagine for a moment that you have a public website that captures sensitive information. You leverage a common architecture, placing your Internet-facing Elastic Load Balancing load balancers in a dedicated public subnet, and you create a private subnet for the rest of your instances. Because you do not want data exfiltrated from the instances in your private subnet, you apply security groups that only permit traffic within the VPC; you configure network ACLs similarly. You ensure that the route table associated with your private subnet has only the local VPC CIDR route. Moreover, you apply an IAM policy that prevents anyone from changing the security groups, the network ACLs, and the route tables in the VPC. Is this a secure network configuration?

What if a malicious actor within your company launches an Amazon EC2 instance in the private subnet? He creates an elastic network interface in the public subnet and attaches it to the instance. With the primary interface in the private subnet and a second interface in the public subnet, he configures the instance for Network Address Translation (NAT). With a few routing changes on the instance, he confirms that he can reach the Internet. After logging on to one of the instances housing the sensitive data, he updates the default gateway in the operating system to point to his newly created NAT instance. With a few more clicks of the mouse, the malicious actor is exfiltrating sensitive data to the Internet.

Another consideration, one that could have helped in the previous example, is effective management of operating system firewalls. When these are centrally managed and enforced by policy, operating system firewalls can prevent unknown or unexpected data flows. Moreover, operating system firewalls often provide a mechanism to correlate the process or software receiving or transmitting data. If, for example, your Amazon EC2 instance were compromised by a virus of some sort, your firewall might block unexpected data flows or unknown processes, mitigating risk while you investigate.

In AWS, it is not possible to create a Switched Port Analyzer (SPAN) port, but you can use on-instance agents to achieve the same outcome. Using integrated operating system capabilities or offerings from the AWS Marketplace, it is possible to capture packet data from each Amazon EC2 instance and stream the data to a collector. Similarly, you can implement advanced network security features like Intrusion Detection or Prevention Systems (IDS/IPS) using on-instance agents.

Regional Services

AWS offers many regional services that operate outside of your VPC. Services like Amazon Kinesis and Amazon Simple Queue Service (Amazon SQS) are managed by AWS, and AWS assumes more responsibility for delivering them to you. Even so, you still have some responsibility for the confidentiality, integrity, and availability of your data over the network. For example, you should connect to these services using SSL/TLS. You should encrypt data at rest using client-side encryption or using AWS KMS server-side encryption. You should sanitize data inputs to these services to prevent failures of availability in downstream processing. Lastly, you should create AWS Organizations SCPs and/or IAM policies that set sensible restrictions on the actions users can take on the services.

AWS Security Services

AWS delivers several managed services that, when enabled, provide you with visibility into the security of your network. Each service employs an approach that is tailored for its specific usage to identify anomalies and notify you. The services are built and operated by the AWS Security organization and benefit from Amazon's experience operating security at scale.

Amazon GuardDuty

Amazon GuardDuty is a managed, intelligent threat detection service that provides you with a more accurate and easy way to continuously monitor and protect your AWS accounts and workloads. With a single-click in the AWS Management Console, GuardDuty immediately begins analyzing billions of events from AWS CloudTrail, VPC Flow Logs, and DNS Logs. There are no agents, sensors, or network appliances to deploy and absolutely no footprint in your AWS account, meaning that there is no risk of performance or availability impact to existing workloads. GuardDuty uses threat intelligence feeds, such as lists of malicious IPs and domains, and machine learning to detect threats more accurately. Unlike compliance and best practices services like AWS Config and AWS Trusted Advisor, Amazon GuardDuty is designed to identify active threats in your environment. Furthermore, Amazon GuardDuty has broad visibility going beyond protecting just virtual machines and the network to monitor and profile all AWS account behavior. For example, GuardDuty can detect compromised EC2 instances serving malware or mining Bitcoins. It can detect attackers scanning your web servers for known application vulnerabilities, or accessing AWS resources from an unusual geolocation. It also monitors AWS account access behavior for signs of compromise, such as unauthorized infrastructure deployments, like instances deployed in a region that has never been used, or unusual API calls, like a password policy change to reduce password strength. When a threat is detected, GuardDuty delivers a detailed security finding to the console and AWS CloudWatch Events, making alerts actionable and easy to integrate into existing event management or workflow systems. With GuardDuty, you get intelligent threat detection and actionable alerts in an easy-to-use, pay-as-you-go cloud security service.

Amazon Inspector

Amazon Inspector is a security service that allows you to analyze your VPC environment to identify potential security issues. With Amazon Inspector, you create assessment targets using Amazon EC2 instance tags, create an assessment template with a selected rules package, and then run the assessment. At the end of the assessment period, Amazon Inspector produces a set of findings and recommended steps to resolve potential security issues.

As discussed in the Data Flow Security section of this chapter, Amazon EC2 security failures can have a material impact on the overall network security of your environment. Amazon Inspector offers a straightforward approach to understanding the posture of your Amazon EC2 instances. This information is certainly important, but you also need to understand your overall network configuration.

Amazon Macie

Amazon Macie is a security service that uses machine learning to discover, classify, and protect sensitive data in AWS automatically. Amazon Macie recognizes sensitive data such as Personally Identifiable Information (PII) or intellectual property and provides you with dashboards and alerts that give visibility into how this data is being accessed or moved. Amazon Macie leverages User and Entity Behavioral Analytics (UEBA), a Support Vector Machine (SVM) classifier to automate document classification, predictive analytics to baseline user activity and identify risky accesses that could indicate targeted attack or unauthorized access to data stored in Amazon S3, and insider threats on data stored in Amazon S3.

Amazon Macie starts by identifying and protecting the data that malicious actors are likely to target. Amazon Macie automatically learns jargon and internal project names and estimates the business value for each object within your Amazon S3 buckets. Next, Amazon Macie learns how users interact with that data by examining historical access activity. When Amazon Macie detects anomalous activity, it generates alerts. These alerts are available in Amazon CloudWatch Events, and you can build automation with services like AWS Lambda to take action to protect your data.

Because Amazon Macie provides a fully customizable, proactive loss-prevention capability, it is an important part of your network security toolbox. Not only does Amazon Macie allow you to understand the relationship between your most sensitive data and user access patterns, it is also able to identify information stored in Amazon S3 that could undermine your network security posture.

When you consider network security in the cloud, you must also consider the methods by which changes are made to your environment. Unlike traditional, physical data centers, an API call will cause immediate changes to your AWS environment. As a result, the security of your network can change quickly. Amazon Macie can alert you when AWS API credentials or SSH keys appear in your Amazon S3 buckets.

Detection and Response

Up to this point, the chapter has focused on individual services and features related to network security. For the rest of the chapter, we provide a series of examples that demonstrate how you can integrate AWS Cloud services to enhance detection and response. The examples provided are not exhaustive. For the exam, you should understand the integration points that are available in AWS Cloud services for detection and response.

Secure Shell (SSH) Login Attempts

A series of failed login attempts often indicates an active intrusion threat. This example leverages several AWS Cloud services to detect and respond to these login failures. Once the failures are detected, action is taken to block the source of the attack.

AWS Cloud Services

The example integrates the following AWS Cloud services:

Amazon CloudWatch monitors your AWS resources and the applications that you run on AWS in real time. You can use Amazon CloudWatch to collect and track metrics, logs, and events. Amazon CloudWatch alarms send notifications or automatically makes changes to the resources that you are monitoring based on rules that you define.

AWS CloudTrail acts as a recorder, documenting the history of AWS API calls and related events in your account. AWS CloudTrail delivers these records in a log file to an Amazon S3 bucket that you specify. You can even have AWS CloudTrail logs from multiple accounts delivered to the same bucket. To provide confidentiality and integrity, you can configure AWS CloudTrail to encrypt logs and generate an integrity digest file.

IAM helps you securely control access to AWS resources. You use IAM to control who or what can use your AWS resources, what resources they can use, and the ways they can use them.

AWS Lambda lets you run code without provisioning or managing servers. AWS Lambda executes your code only when needed and it scales automatically. You can use AWS Lambda to run your code in response to events.

Amazon Simple Notification Services (Amazon SNS) coordinates and manages the delivery messages to subscribing endpoints. Amazon SNS facilitates communication between publishers and subscribers. Publishers, like Amazon CloudWatch alarms, communicate asynchronously with subscribers by producing and sending a message to a topic. Subscribers, like AWS Lambda functions, receive the message when they are subscribed to the topic.

Architecture Overview

The diagram in Figure 8.8 provides an overview of the components in this example.

FIGURE 8.8 SSH login attempts overview

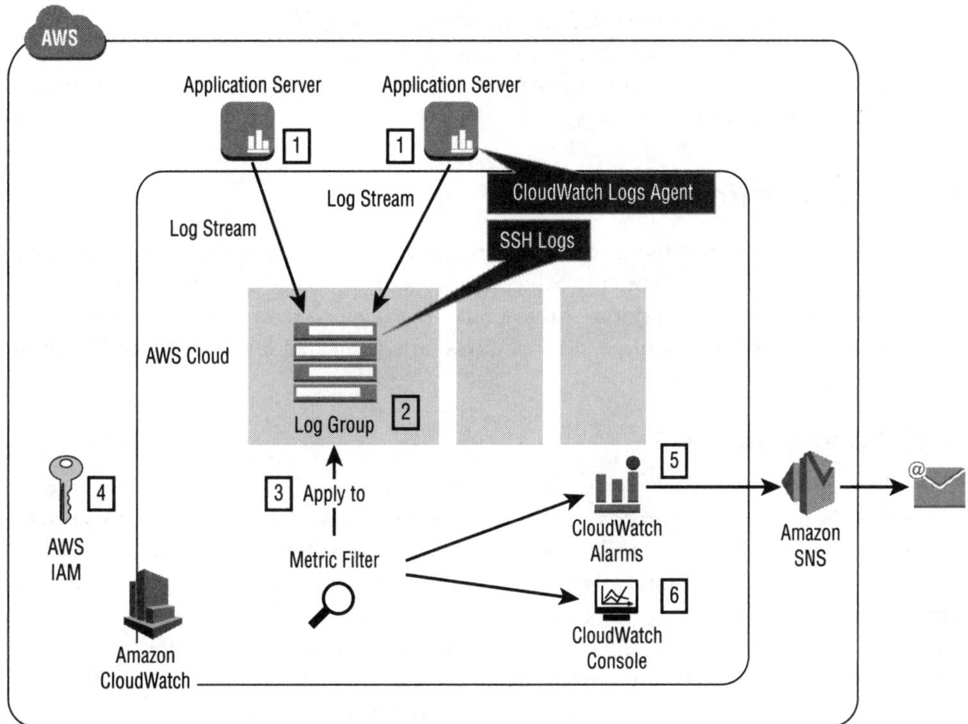

Solution Description

In this example, your application runs on Linux instances. SSH is the mechanism used to log in and manage the systems. Each instance on which you run the Amazon CloudWatch Logs agent also has an IAM instance role assigned to the Amazon EC2 instances to allow the agent to write to Amazon CloudWatch Logs. As the SSH daemon updates its logs, the information is sent from the instance to Amazon CloudWatch Logs. The logs for each instance are represented in Amazon CloudWatch Logs as a unique *log stream*. The instance log streams are aggregated into a *log group*.

With the log group in place, you can create a metric filter. *Metric filters* express how Amazon CloudWatch should extract observations from ingested logs and represent them as data points in an Amazon CloudWatch metric. Metric filters are assigned to log groups. You configure the metric filter to match the specific string sequence in the logs that indicate a login failure. You also specify an Amazon CloudWatch alarm to indicate when the allowed number of failed login attempts per unit time (for example, two failed attempts every five minutes) is exceeded. As part of the alarm configuration, you specify an Amazon SNS topic on which to publish the alarm.

In order to automate response, you subscribe an AWS Lambda function to the alarm topic in Amazon SNS. The subscribed AWS Lambda function contains your code for processing the source IP address of the failures and, using an IAM role for the AWS Lambda execution, updates the VPC network ACLs to deny incoming requests from the source. (Recall that network ACLs allow deny statements, but security groups do not.) You can also subscribe your email address to the AWS Lambda topic to receive an email when the alarm threshold is breached.

Network Traffic Analysis

One method for detecting network anomalies in your environment is to understand traffic flow patterns. Sudden changes in "top talkers," for example, could indicate an active data exfiltration. You might also find it useful to understand denied data flows or unused security groups and ports. This example demonstrates how you can gain visibility and analyze your flow data from your VPC.

AWS Cloud Services

The example integrates the following AWS Cloud services:

Amazon CloudWatch monitors your AWS resources and the applications that you run on AWS in real time. You can use Amazon CloudWatch to collect and track metrics, logs, and events. Amazon CloudWatch alarms send notifications or automatically makes changes to the resources you are monitoring based on rules that you define.

Amazon Elasticsearch Service makes it easy to create a domain and deploy, operate, and scale managed Elasticsearch clusters. Elasticsearch is a popular, open source search and analytics engine for use cases such as log analytics, real-time application monitoring, and clickstream analytics.

IAM helps you securely control access to AWS resources. You use IAM to control who or what can use your AWS resources, what resources they can use, and in what ways they can use them.

Kibana allows you to visualize data in Amazon Elasticsearch Service. Kibana is a popular open source visualization tool designed to work with Elasticsearch. Amazon Elasticsearch Service provides an installation of Kibana with every Amazon Elasticsearch Service domain. You can find a link to Kibana on your domain dashboard in the Amazon Elasticsearch Service console.

Amazon Kinesis Firehose delivers managed, real-time streaming data to destinations such as Amazon S3, Amazon Redshift, or Amazon Elasticsearch Service. You configure your data producers to send data to Amazon Kinesis Firehose, and it automatically delivers the data to the destination that you specified. You can also configure Amazon Kinesis Firehose to transform your data before data delivery.

AWS Lambda lets you run code without provisioning or managing servers. AWS Lambda executes your code only when needed, and it scales automatically. You can use AWS Lambda to run your code in response to events.

VPC Flow Logs enables you to capture information about the IP traffic going to and from network interfaces in your VPC. Flow log data is stored using Amazon CloudWatch Logs.

Architecture Overview

The diagram in Figure 8.9 provides an overview of the components in this example.

FIGURE 8.9 Network traffic analysis overview

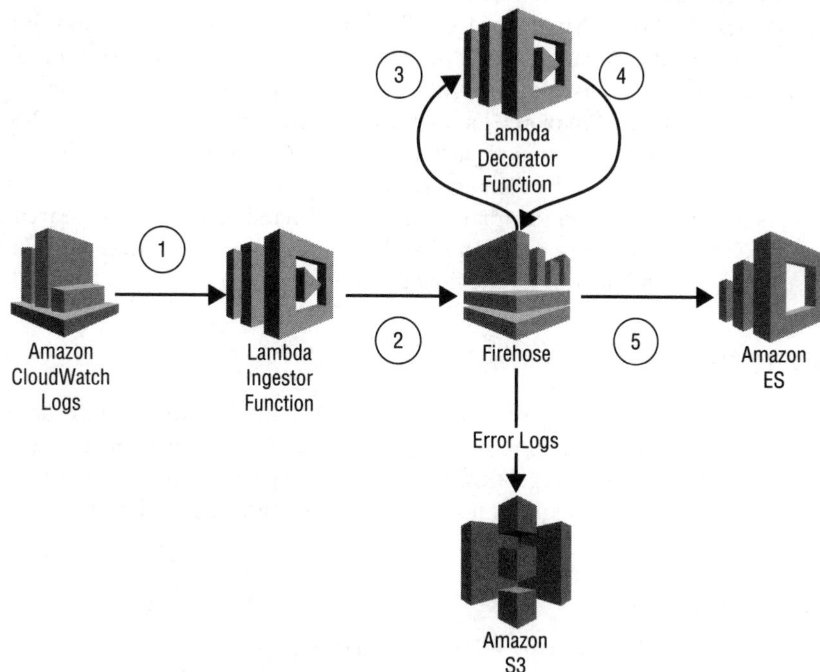

Solution Description

In order to analyze your network traffic, this example leverages the VPC Flow Logs features and Amazon Elasticsearch Service. To augment the analysis, flow data is correlated with information about the relevant security groups. The complete dataset is stored in Amazon Elasticsearch Service, allowing you to view flow data, analyze unused security groups, and identify unused security group rules with Kibana.

The heart of this solution is the Elasticsearch cluster. After you create an Amazon Elasticsearch Service domain, you need to populate the cluster with flow data. Amazon Kinesis Firehose provides a simple mechanism for pumping data into Amazon Elasticsearch Service. You can augment the information passed into Amazon Elasticsearch Service by using a Amazon Kinesis Firehose data transformation. With data transformations, you send Amazon Kinesis Firehose data through an AWS Lambda function that modifies the Amazon Kinesis Firehose output. For this solution, you create an AWS Lambda function that augments the VPC Flow Log data by adding information about direction of the traffic (that is, inbound or outbound), security groups associated with the traffic, and information about the IP address (for example, geolocation). When complete, you have a Amazon Kinesis Firehose delivery stream that takes input, transforms it, and delivers it to your Elasticsearch cluster.

The last piece of the solution is connecting VPC Flow Logs into the Amazon Kinesis Firehose delivery stream that you created. VPC Flow Logs are delivered to Amazon CloudWatch Logs. You can use AWS Lambda as an Amazon CloudWatch Logs streaming target to ingest data from Amazon CloudWatch Logs and push it into Amazon Kinesis Firehose. Once you enable Amazon CloudWatch Logs streaming to your AWS Lambda function, the end-to-end flow is complete. VPC Flow Logs periodically places data into Amazon CloudWatch Logs. Amazon CloudWatch Logs streams the data to an AWS Lambda function that you've written to push data into a Amazon Kinesis Firehose delivery stream. As the data is processed by Amazon Kinesis Firehose, another AWS Lambda function augments the flow data, and the final product is delivered to your Elasticsearch cluster.

With the VPC Flow Logs data augmented and delivered to your Elasticsearch cluster, you can use Kibana to run queries on the flow data.

IP Reputation

As discussed earlier in the chapter, AWS WAF integrates with Amazon CloudFront and Application Load Balancer and allows you to protect your AWS environments. Because AWS WAF is API-driven, you can gain tremendous value by automating configuration of web ACLs. This example demonstrates how you automate third-party detection data into your own response actions.

AWS Cloud Services

The example integrates the following AWS Cloud services:

Amazon CloudWatch monitors your AWS resources and the applications you run on AWS in real time. You can use Amazon CloudWatch to collect and track metrics, logs, and events. Amazon CloudWatch alarms send notifications or automatically makes changes to the resources that you are monitoring based on rules that you define.

IAM helps you securely control access to AWS resources. You use IAM to control who or what can use your AWS resources, what resources they can use, and the ways they can use them.

AWS Lambda lets you run code without provisioning or managing servers. AWS Lambda executes your code only when needed, and it scales automatically. You can use AWS Lambda to run your code in response to events.

AWS WAF lets you monitor the HTTP and HTTPS requests that are forwarded to Amazon CloudFront or an Application Load Balancer. AWS WAF also lets you control access to your content based on conditions that you specify, such as the IP addresses.

Architecture Overview

The diagram in Figure 8.10 provides an overview of the components in this example.

FIGURE 8.10 IP reputation overview

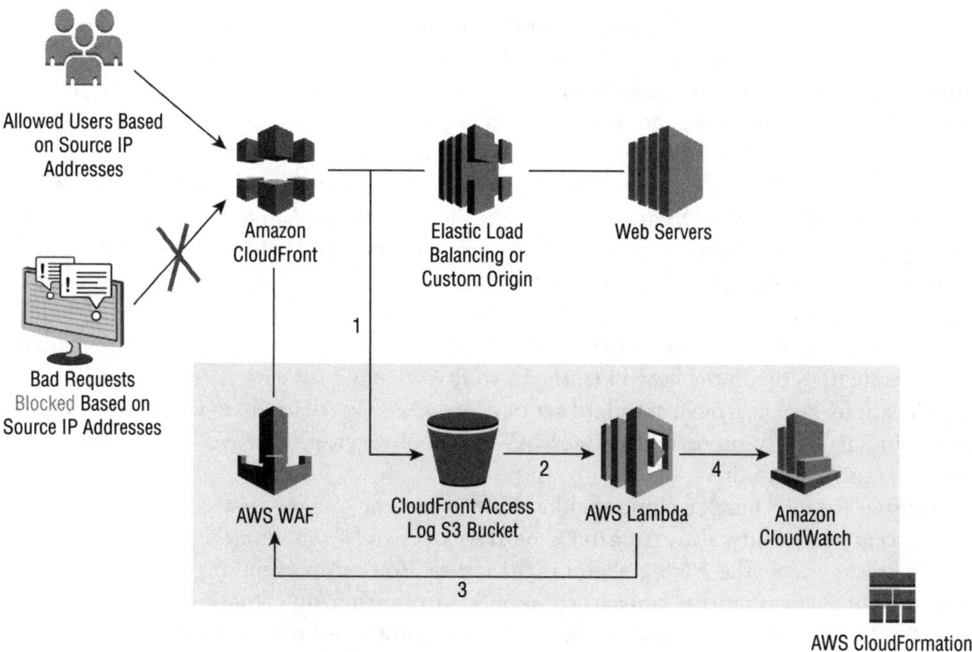

Solution Description

There are several publicly-available IP reputation lists that provide information about known bad IP address. You can protect your AWS environments by programmatically incorporating these IP addresses into AWS WAF web ACLs that block them. This solution provides a straightforward approach for using Amazon CloudWatch Events, AWS Lambda, and AWS WAF to generate and update a dynamic list of disallowed IP addresses.

The first step in the solution is to create a periodic event that triggers an AWS Lambda function. Amazon CloudWatch Events provides an event bus where actions across your AWS Cloud environment are seen. Amazon CloudWatch Events also has the capability to generate scheduled events. In order to process updates in the IP reputation lists, you configure a scheduled Amazon CloudWatch Event. The event calls an AWS Lambda function that you create to download and process one or more IP reputation lists. The AWS Lambda function uses an IAM role that allows it to call the AWS WAF APIs directly, updating the IP addresses condition used for blocking IPs. Once the AWS Lambda function completes, the current list of bad IPs is blocked from Amazon CloudFront distributions and Application Load Balancers.

Summary

In this chapter, you reviewed network security concepts, AWS Cloud services relevant to network security, and the integration of multiple AWS Cloud services to enable higher-level capabilities. The chapter discussed governance considerations, protecting data flow, managed AWS security services, and detection and response. The chapter is not exhaustive, but it does provide you with a solid foundation of network security for the exam.

In the section on governance, you learned about the importance of controlling your AWS accounts. Tools like AWS Organizations, AWS CloudFormation, and AWS Service Catalog allow you to control change in your environment, enforce standards, and implement guard rails. Moreover, these services allow you to automate, taking manual, human action out of the process. Automation can dramatically improve your overall security posture.

In the section on data flow security, you reviewed the edge location and region services that operate directly on the flow of traffic in your AWS environment. Services that run in edge locations benefit from a standard set of protections. Particular services have additional capabilities to withstand network attack. AWS designs services to deliver confidentiality, integrity, and availability.

Amazon Route 53 uses techniques like shuffle sharding and anycast striping to deliver a 100 percent availability SLA. Amazon CloudFront provides you with the ability to diffuse DDoS attacks across the AWS global infrastructure. You can prevent direct attacks on your origins by ensuring that they only accept requests from Amazon CloudFront. You can also use AWS Lambda@Edge to validate incoming Amazon CloudFront requests before they are passed to the origin, further protecting your environment.

AWS Certificate Manager facilitates the creation and management of SSL/TLS certificates for Amazon CloudFront and Elastic Load Balancing, delivering confidentiality and integrity to data in transit. When you use AWS Certificate Manager certificates, AWS provides you with a domain-validated RSA-2048, SHA-256 certificate that is valid for 13 months. The service will attempt to auto-renew the certificate, typically 30 days before expiration, provided that the certificate is Internet accessible to the service. You can use fully qualified domain names or wildcard names with AWS Certificate Manager. If you use a third-party certificate provider, you can upload your certificate into AWS Certificate Manager.

AWS WAF and AWS Shield provide protection for your Amazon CloudFront and Application Load Balancer resources. AWS WAF uses web ACLs that contain ordered rules to allow, block, or count incoming requests. Rules are either standard or rate based and contain match conditions. AWS WAF evaluates conditions on cross-site scripting, IP address, size, SQLi, geo-location, and string matches. AWS Shield Standard is available to all customers at no additional charge. AWS Shield Standard mitigates the majority of network layer (Layer 3) and transport layer (Layer 4) attacks. AWS Shield Advanced provides additional capabilities, including intelligent DDoS attack detection and mitigation for application layer (Layer 7) attacks. AWS Shield Advanced provides real-time, detailed metric reporting, and you have access to a 24x7 DRT. Lastly, AWS Shield Advanced offers some cost protection against billing spikes.

Elastic Load Balancing load balancers provide you with a level of protection when placed in front of your Internet-facing VPC resources. Elastic Load Balancing only accepts incoming traffic on its listeners, minimizing the attack surface. Elastic Load Balancing proxies connections to your VPC resources, mitigating common attacks like SYN floods because only well-formed TCP connections result in data flow to your resources. Using an Elastic Load Balancing sandwich, you can place security processes and appliances inline with traffic incoming to your VPC. You can use a load balancer with a proxy fleet to achieve similar inline security filtering for outbound traffic.

Subnets and route tables allow you to control the behavior of packet flows in your VPC. Leveraging VPC endpoints allows resources in your VPC to communicate with external services without attaching an Internet gateway or VGW. Similarly, you can communicate between VPCs using VPC peering. When you need to communicate with your on-premises environment, you can encrypt communications using an IPsec connection with an AWS managed VPN connection over the Internet or over an AWS Direct Connect public VIF. You can also establish an encrypted connection using an Amazon EC2 instance running VPN software and an AWS Direct Connect private VIF.

Security groups and network ACLs are primitives used within your VPC to control traffic flow. Security groups provide stateful firewall capabilities, and they allow you to use the security group as an abstraction to hide dynamic changes in your VPC. Network ACLs are typically coarser-grained, stateless rules. Some organizations use a separation of duties model, where security groups are controlled by one team and network ACLs are controlled by another.

You reviewed how the shared responsibility model applies to Amazon EC2 instances. Network communication protection and operating system patches are your responsibility. You should use the tools available within your instance's operating system to secure the network further. Without a deliberate, thoughtful approach to protection of your VPC, malicious actors can use your Amazon EC2 instances to bypass the network flow controls you establish.

Amazon offers a number of regional services beyond those described explicitly in the chapter. Each provides mechanisms to control access, enforce encryption, and emit log data for analysis. IAM and AWS KMS are important services for access control and encryption, respectively.

You also reviewed managed security offerings. Amazon GuardDuty detects and alerts on active threats in your environment. Amazon Inspector rationalizes the layers of security around applications running on your Amazon EC2 instances. Amazon Macie identifies threats with respect to data in Amazon S3.

The final section of the chapter provided examples of how you can integrate AWS Cloud services to provide higher-level capabilities for network security. Each example demonstrated how you can improve visibility and automate action to protect your environments. For the exam, you should understand the integration points available in AWS Cloud services for detection and response.

Resources to Review

For more information on the AWS Cloud services discussed in this chapter, visit the following URLs:

AWS Organizations:

`https://aws.amazon.com/documentation/organizations/`

AWS CloudFormation:

`https://aws.amazon.com/documentation/cloudformation/`

AWS Service Catalog:

`https://aws.amazon.com/documentation/servicecatalog/`

Amazon Route 53:

`https://aws.amazon.com/documentation/route53/`

Amazon CloudFront:

`https://aws.amazon.com/documentation/cloudfront/`

AWS Lambda:

`https://aws.amazon.com/documentation/lambda/`

AWS WAF:

`https://aws.amazon.com/documentation/waf/`

AWS Certificate Manager:

`https://aws.amazon.com/documentation/acm/`

Elastic Load Balancing:

`https://aws.amazon.com/documentation/elastic-load-balancing/`

Amazon Elastic Compute Cloud (Amazon EC2):

`https://aws.amazon.com/documentation/ec2/`

Amazon Virtual Private Cloud (Amazon VPC):

`https://aws.amazon.com/documentation/vpc/`

AWS Key Management Service (AWS KMS):

`https://aws.amazon.com/documentation/kms/`

AWS Identity and Access Management (IAM):

`https://aws.amazon.com/documentation/iam/`

Amazon CloudWatch:

`https://aws.amazon.com/documentation/cloudwatch/`

AWS CloudTrail:

https://aws.amazon.com/documentation/cloudtrail/

AWS Simple Notification Service (SNS):

https://aws.amazon.com/documentation/sns/

Amazon Elasticsearch Service (Amazon ES):

https://aws.amazon.com/documentation/elasticsearch-service/

Amazon Kinesis:

https://aws.amazon.com/documentation/kinesis/

Amazon Macie:

https://aws.amazon.com/documentation/macie/

For examples of service integration, visit the following URLs:

How to Monitor and Visualize Failed SSH Access Attempts to Amazon EC2 Linux Instances:

https://aws.amazon.com/blogs/security/how-to-monitor-and-visualize-failed-ssh-access-attempts-to-amazon-ec2-linux-instances/

How to Visualize and Refine Your Network's Security by Adding Security Group IDs to Your VPC Flow Logs:

https://aws.amazon.com/blogs/security/how-to-visualize-and-refine-your-networks-security-by-adding-security-group-ids-to-your-vpc-flow-logs/

AWS WAF Security Automations – AWS Implementation Guide:

https://s3.amazonaws.com/solutions-reference/aws-waf-security-automations/latest/aws-waf-security-automations.pdf

How to Detect and Automatically Remediate Unintended Permissions in Amazon S3 Object ACLs with CloudWatch Events:

https://aws.amazon.com/blogs/security/how-to-detect-and-automatically-remediate-unintended-permissions-in-amazon-s3-object-acls-with-cloudwatch-events/

How to Use AWS WAF to Block IP Addresses That Generate Bad Requests:

https://aws.amazon.com/blogs/security/how-to-use-aws-waf-to-block-ip-addresses-that-generate-bad-requests/

Use AWS WAF to Mitigate OWASP's Top 10 Web Application Vulnerabilities:

https://d0.awsstatic.com/whitepapers/Security/aws-waf-owasp.pdf

AWS Best Practice for DDoS Resiliency:

https://d0.awsstatic.com/whitepapers/Security/DDoS_White_Paper.pdf

Exam Essentials

Understand the shared responsibility model. While AWS manages security *of* the cloud, security *in* the cloud is your responsibility. You control what security you choose to implement to protect your content, platform, applications, systems, and networks. When using Amazon EC2, you are responsible for network traffic protection.

Understand how to automate security in your environment. Using AWS Cloud services like AWS Organizations, Amazon CloudFront, and AWS Service Catalog, you can automate the creation of known account baselines. When you automate, you can build in best practices, implement guard rails, and centralize logging to provide security visibility across your AWS accounts. People make mistakes, people bend the rules, and people can act with malice. Your ability to automate will greatly contribute to the overall network security of your environments.

Understand edge location capabilities that protect your environments from DDoS attacks. Edge locations all include built-in network layer (Layer 3) and transport layer (Layer 4) network mitigations. The edge location infrastructure is continuously analyzing traffic for anomalies, and it provides built-in defense against common DDoS attacks such as SYN floods, UDP floods, and reflection attacks. AWS can activate SYN cookies to avoid impact to legitimate traffic. Only well-formed UDP or TCP packets are serviced by the edge locations. All traffic is scored across a set of dimensions to prioritize the flow of legitimate traffic. The global scale of the edge infrastructure allows AWS to absorb attacks by diffusing the incoming traffic flows across multiple edge locations.

Understand the availability techniques for Amazon Route 53. Amazon Route 53 uses shuffle sharding and anycast striping to isolate availability challenges and mitigate impact to you. The service only responds to well-formed DNS requests.

Understand how to prevent malicious actors from bypassing Amazon CloudFront. You can use an Amazon S3 OAI to ensure that only Amazon CloudFront can access your Amazon S3 buckets. For other origins, you can insert HTTP headers to authenticate that the request originated from Amazon CloudFront. AWS Lambda@Edge can be used to generate these authenticators dynamically. You can use signed URLs and signed cookies to restrict access further to your origins.

Understand the capabilities offered by AWS WAF. AWS WAF can protect your Amazon CloudFront distributions, Application Load Balancers, and Amazon EC2 instances. AWS WAF uses web ACLs. Web ACLs contain an ordered list of rules that specify whether to allow, count, or drop traffic. Rules are either standard or rate-based and are composed of conditions. Conditions match on cross-site scripting, IP addresses, size, SQLi, geo-location, and string match.

Understand the details of AWS Certificate Manager certificates. AWS Certificate Manager certificates provide you with a domain-validated RSA-2048, SHA-256 certificate that is valid for 13 months. The service will attempt to auto-renew the certificate, typically 30 days before expiration, provided that the certificate is Internet accessible to the service.

The certificate includes at least one FQDN, and you can add additional names. You may also request wildcard names (for example, `*.example.com`). AWS Certificate Manager-generated certificates are free, and you cannot download the private key.

Understand how Elastic Load Balancing protects your VPC resources. Elastic Load Balancing automatically scales to meet the demands of the vast majority of use cases, contributing to the overall availability of your workload. With Elastic Load Balancing, you define the ports and protocols it will accept, minimizing the attack surface. Elastic Load Balancing proxies connections to your VPC resources; so, common attacks like SYN floods are not seen because only well-formed TCP connections result in data flow to your resources. When you wish to provide inline security processes for traffic inbound to your VPC, you can leverage an Elastic Load Balancing sandwich. When you want to provide inline security processes for traffic outbound from your VPC, you can leverage an internal load balancer and a proxy fleet of Amazon EC2 instances.

Understand how to protect traffic using route tables and subnets. Route tables allow you to control how traffic leaves your subnets. You can use VPC endpoints and VPC peering to keep traffic within the AWS infrastructure without attaching an Internet gateway or VGW to your VPC. When you do need to connect to your on-premises infrastructure, encrypt your traffic using IPsec connections. You can use an AWS managed VPN connection over the Internet or over an AWS Direct Connect public VIF. You can use your own VPN software on an Amazon EC2 instance over an AWS Direct Connect private VIF.

Understand how to secure your Amazon EC2 instances. AWS provides many services and features to assist you in securing your network. Even so, you should also secure your Amazon EC2 instances. Use tools to manage configurations, enforce policies, and detect anomalous behavior on your instances. Understand the risks posed to your environments by a compromised Amazon EC2 instance and devise mechanisms to detect and respond to anomalous behavior.

Understand the capabilities of each managed AWS security service. Amazon GuardDuty detects and alerts on active threats in your environment. Amazon Inspector rationalizes the layers of security around applications running on your Amazon EC2 instances. Amazon Macie identifies threats with respect to data in Amazon S3.

Understand how you can integrate various AWS Cloud services to deliver higher-level security capabilities. You can combine AWS Cloud services to provide detection and response capabilities. For the exam, you should understand the integration points available in AWS Cloud services for detection and response.

Test Taking Tip

When reviewing a question, make a mental note of what answer you expect before reviewing the responses. If none of the responses match your expectation, it is likely that you've misread or misunderstood the question.

Exercises

The best way to become familiar with the various network security services and features is through direct, hands-on experience. The following exercises provide you with the opportunity to experiment and learn. You should feel free to expand beyond the exercises.

For assistance completing these exercises, refer to the following Amazon User Guides:

Amazon Simple Storage Service (Amazon S3):

`https://aws.amazon.com/documentation/s3/`

Amazon Route 53:

`https://aws.amazon.com/documentation/route53/`

Amazon CloudFront:

`https://aws.amazon.com/documentation/cloudfront/`

AWS WAF:

`https://aws.amazon.com/documentation/waf/`

EXERCISE 8.1

Create a Static Amazon S3 Website

In this exercise, you will create a static Amazon S3 website.

1. Sign in to the AWS Management Console as Administrator or Power User.
2. Select the Amazon S3 icon to launch the Amazon S3 dashboard.
3. Create a bucket in US East (N. Virginia). Take note of your bucket name.
4. Upload a publicly readable object named `index.html` containing the text "Hello, World!"
5. Navigate to `https://s3.amazonaws.com/<bucketname>/index.html` and confirm that you see "Hello, World!"

You have created an Amazon S3 bucket with static content.

EXERCISE 8.2

Set Up an Amazon CloudFront Distribution

In this exercise, you will set up an Amazon CloudFront distribution in front of your Amazon S3 static website.

1. From the AWS Management Console, select the Amazon CloudFront icon to launch the Amazon CloudFront dashboard.

2. Create a web distribution.
3. For the Origin Domain Name, select `<bucketname>.s3.amazonaws.com` from the drop-down.
4. Accept the remaining defaults and create the distribution.
5. Navigate to the domain name of your distribution, appending `/index.html` to the end, and confirm that you see "Hello, World!"

You now have an Amazon CloudFront distribution for your Amazon S3 static website. Note that your website is accessible both through Amazon CloudFront and directly from Amazon S3.

EXERCISE 8.3

Use an Amazon CloudFront Origin Access Identity

In this exercise, you will use an Amazon CloudFront Origin Access Identity for your static Amazon S3 website.

1. From the AWS Management Console, select the Amazon CloudFront icon to launch the Amazon CloudFront dashboard.
2. Select the ID of the distribution that you created in Exercise 8.2.
3. Change to the Origins tab, select the origin and click Edit.
4. Toggle Restrict Bucket Access to Yes.
5. Confirm that Origin Access Identity is set to Create a New Identity.
6. Set Grant Read Permission on Bucket to Yes, Update Bucket Policy.
7. Click Yes, Edit.
8. Navigate to the Amazon S3 bucket, select the `index.html` object, and remove the public read permissions.
9. Confirm that the object is *not* directly accessible from the URL that you used in Exercise 8.1.
10. Confirm that the object *is* accessible from the URL that you used in Exercise 8.2.

You have now restricted access to your Amazon S3 bucket to requests that originate from your Amazon CloudFront distribution.

EXERCISE 8.4

Configure Amazon CloudFront to Block Requests

In this exercise, you will configure Amazon CloudFront to block requests based on geography of the source IP.

1. Select the Amazon CloudFront icon to launch the Amazon CloudFront dashboard.
2. Select the ID of the distribution that you created in Exercise 8.2.
3. Change to the Restrictions tab, select the origin, and click Edit.
4. Enable geo-restriction.
5. Blacklist your particular country.
6. Click Yes, Edit.
7. Navigate to the URL from Exercise 8.2. You should receive a distribution is configured to block access from your country error.
8. Change the geo-restriction to whitelist your particular country.
9. Navigate to the URL from Exercise 8.2. Confirm that you see "Hello, World!"

You have enabled geo-restriction on your Amazon CloudFront distribution.

EXERCISE 8.5

Deploy AWS WAF to Block a Specific IP Address

In this exercise, you will deploy AWS WAF to block a specific IP address.

1. Select the AWS WAF icon to launch the AWS WAF dashboard.
2. Create an IP match condition for Global (CloudFront) that matches your IPv4 or IPv6 address.
3. Create a regular rule for Global (CloudFront) that matches the IP address condition that you just created.
4. Create a web ACL for Global (CloudFront) associated with your Amazon CloudFront distribution.
5. Add a single block rule using the rule you created.
6. Set the default action to allow requests that don't match any rules.
7. Navigate to the URL from Exercise 8.2. You should receive a `Request Blocked` error.
8. Modify the web ACL to allow requests from the IP match rule, setting the default action to deny requests that don't match any rules.
9. Navigate to the URL from Exercise 8.2. Confirm that you see "Hello, World!"

You have created and associated a web ACL with your Amazon CloudFront distribution.

Review Questions

1. Which of the following allows you to create new AWS accounts programmatically?
   - A. AWS Identity and Access Management (IAM)
   - B. AWS Organizations
   - C. Amazon Simple Storage Service (Amazon S3)
   - D. AWS CloudTrail
2. AWS CloudFormation allows you to define your infrastructure as code in what artifact?
   - A. JSON
   - B. StackSets
   - C. Stacks
   - D. Templates
3. Which of the following is a security benefit of services such as AWS Service Catalog? (Choose two.)
   - A. Automation
   - B. Repeatability
   - C. Self-service
   - D. Curation
   - E. AWS Marketplace Integration
4. Amazon Route 53 uses several methods to deliver a 100 percent availability Service Level Agreement (SLA). Which method guards against failures of Top Level Domain (TLD) servers?
   - A. Shuffle sharding
   - B. Routing policies
   - C. Anycast striping
   - D. Latency routing
5. Which of the following allows you to restrict access to your Amazon Simple Storage Service (Amazon S3) bucket to Amazon CloudFront distributions that you control?
   - A. Custom HTTP header
   - B. Origin Access Identity (OAI)
   - C. AWS Lambda@Edge
   - D. Preshared keys

6. Private keys in AWS Certificate Manager are protected using which one of the following?
   - **A.** AWS CloudHSM
   - **B.** AWS Key Management Service
   - **C.** Client-side encryption
   - **D.** Amazon S3 server-side encryption

7. AWS WAF integrates with which one of the following AWS resources?
   - **A.** Amazon Simple Storage Service (Amazon S3)
   - **B.** Amazon DynamoDB
   - **C.** Amazon CloudFront
   - **D.** Amazon Route 53

8. AWS Shield Standard provides protection at which layers of the Open Systems Interconnection (OSI) model? (Choose two.)
   - **A.** Physical (Layer 1)
   - **B.** Data Link (Layer 2)
   - **C.** Network (Layer 3)
   - **D.** Transport (Layer 4)
   - **E.** Application (Layer 7)

9. Which Amazon Virtual Private Cloud (Amazon VPC) feature allows you to access AWS Cloud services without the use of an Internet gateway?
   - **A.** VPC endpoints
   - **B.** VPC peering
   - **C.** Customer-hosted endpoints
   - **D.** Network Address Translation (NAT) gateway

10. What aspect of an Amazon Virtual Private Cloud (Amazon VPC) is stateful?
    - **A.** Network Access Control Lists (ACLs)
    - **B.** Security groups
    - **C.** Amazon VPC Flow Logs
    - **D.** Prefix list

11. Which AWS Cloud service will help you identify sensitive account data, like access and secret keys, stored in an Amazon Simple Storage Service (Amazon S3) bucket?
    - **A.** Amazon Inspector
    - **B.** AWS Config
    - **C.** AWS CloudTrail
    - **D.** Amazon Macie

12. You are tasked with identifying unused security groups and ports in a Virtual Private Cloud (VPC). Which AWS capabilities should you use?
    A. Amazon CloudWatch metrics
    B. AWS CloudTrail
    C. AWS Config
    D. VPC Flow Logs

13. To protect its website, the organization directs you to implement known-attacker protection for the website. The website resides behind an Application Load Balancer. You have subscribed to a threat intelligence service that posts hourly IP reputation lists. What combination of AWS Cloud services will allow you to block traffic based on this threat intelligence?
    A. Amazon CloudWatch, AWS Lambda, AWS WAF
    B. Amazon CloudFront, AWS Lambda, AWS WAF
    C. AWS CloudTrail, AWS Lambda, AWS Config
    D. AWS CloudTrail, Amazon CloudWatch, AWS Lambda

Network Performance

THE AWS CERTIFIED ADVANCED NETWORKING – SPECIALTY EXAM OBJECTIVES COVERED IN THIS CHAPTER MAY INCLUDE, BUT ARE NOT LIMITED TO, THE FOLLOWING:

Domain 2.0: Design and Implement AWS Networks

- ✓ **2.4 Determine network requirements for a specialized workload**
- ✓ **2.5 Derive an appropriate architecture based on customer and application requirements**

Modern applications depend on the network for communication between services or between other application components. Since the network connects all application components, it can have major impacts, both positive and negative, on application performance and behavior. There are also applications that are heavily dependent on network performance, such as *High Performance Computing (HPC)*, where deep network understanding is important to increasing cluster performance.

This chapter focuses on network performance characteristics that are important to applications, examples of network-dependent applications, options to improve network performance, and how to optimize network performance on Amazon Elastic Compute Cloud (Amazon EC2).

Network Performance Basics

It's common for end users and developers simply to describe their network performance as fast or slow. The user experience of the network is a combination of several networking aspects that likely span multiple different networks and applications. For example, a user at a coffee shop accessing a website hosted on Amazon EC2 must pass through the local coffee shop wireless network, the service provider network, and the AWS network. The website application likely also has multiple dependencies within AWS. In this context, it's important to separate network performance into multiple, more accurate, and measurable terms.

Bandwidth

Bandwidth is the maximum rate of transfer over the network. Typically, this is defined in bits per second (abbreviated Bps), Mbps for one million bits per second, or Gbps for one billion bits per second. Network bandwidth defines the maximum bandwidth rate, but the actual user or application transfer rate will also be affected by latency, protocol, and packet loss. In comparison, throughput is the successful transfer rate over the network.

Pay attention to bits versus bytes for bandwidth. Metrics such as Amazon CloudWatch NetworkIn and NetworkOut are defined in bytes. Network speeds with AWS Direct Connect are defined in bits. Storage is typically defined in bytes, and network bandwidths are typically in bits.

Latency

Latency is the delay between two points in a network. Latency can be measured in one-way delay or Round-Trip Time (RTT) between two points. Ping is a common way to test RTT delay. Delays include propagation delays for signals to travel across different mediums such as copper or fiber optics, often at speeds close to the speed of light. There are also processing delays for packets to move through physical or virtual network devices, such as the Amazon Virtual Private Cloud (Amazon VPC) virtual router. Network drivers and operating systems can be optimized to minimize processing latency on the host system as well.

Jitter

Jitter is the variation in inter-packet delays. Jitter is caused by a variance in delay over time between two points in the network. Jitter is often caused by variations in processing delays and queueing delays in the network, which increase with higher network load. For example, if the one-way delay between two systems varies from 10 ms to 100 ms, then there is 90 ms of jitter. This type of varying delay causes issues with voice and real-time systems that process media because the systems have to decide to buffer data longer or continue without the data.

Throughput

Throughput is the rate of successful data transferred, measured in bits per second. Bandwidth, latency, and packet loss affect the throughput rate. The bandwidth will define the maximum rate possible. Latency affects the bandwidth of protocols like *Transmission Control Protocol (TCP)* with round-trip handshakes. TCP uses congestion windows to control throughput. One side of the TCP connection will send a single segment of data and then wait for confirmation from the other side before sending more data. If the handshake continues at the single-segment rate, the throughput will be heavily affected by the latency involved in the round-trip confirmation. This is why TCP uses scaling window sizes to increase throughput. Conversely, *User Datagram Protocol (UDP)* doesn't acknowledge packets with handshakes, though some applications built on top of UDP may implement RTT requirements. UDP will not adaptively throttle traffic rates when there is loss unless application logic decides to back off.

Packet Loss

Packet loss is typically stated in terms of the percentage of packets that are dropped in a flow or on a circuit. Packet loss will affect applications differently. TCP applications are generally sensitive to loss due to congestion control. For instance, TCP Reno, a common implementation of TCP, halves its congestion window on a single packet loss.

Packets per Second

Packets per second refers to how many packets are processed in one second. Packets per second are a common bottleneck in network performance testing. All processing points in the network must process each packet, requiring computing resources. Particularly for small packets, per-packet processing can limit throughput before bandwidth limits are reached. You can monitor the packets per second on AWS Direct Connect ports with Amazon CloudWatch metrics.

Maximum Transmission Unit

The *Maximum Transmission Unit (MTU)* defines the largest packet that can be sent over the network. The maximum on most Internet and Wide Area Networks (WANs) is 1,500 bytes. *Jumbo frames* are packets larger than 1,500 bytes. AWS supports 9,001 byte jumbo frames within a VPC. VPC peering and traffic leaving a VPC support up to 1,500 byte packets, including Internet and AWS Direct Connect traffic. Increasing the MTU increases throughput when the packet per second processing rate is the performance bottleneck.

Amazon Elastic Compute Cloud (Amazon EC2) Instance Networking Features

Amazon EC2 offers a set of networking features directly to instances in addition to the features available in Amazon VPC and Amazon Route 53. Amazon EC2 offers different networking capabilities by instance type and features such as placement groups, Amazon Elastic Block Store (Amazon EBS)-optimized instances, and enhanced networking.

Instance Networking

AWS offers instance families for different use cases, each with different network, computing, and memory resources.

Examples of Instance Families

- General Purpose (M4)
- Compute Optimized (C5)
- Memory Optimized (R4)
- Accelerated Computing (P2)

These families have different networking speeds and capabilities, such as enhanced networking and Amazon EBS-optimized networking. Each instance type's network performance is documented as low, medium, high, 10 Gigabit, up to 10 Gigabit, or 20 Gigabit. Larger instance types in a family have bandwidth that generally scales with the vCPU quantity within the family.

Placement Groups

A *placement group* is a logical grouping of instances within a single Availability Zone. Placement groups are recommended for applications that benefit from low network latency, high network throughput, or both. Use a placement group to provide the lowest latency and the highest packet-per-second network performance.

Placement groups enable higher bandwidths for instances. When instances are documented with 10 Gigabit network performance, those numbers refer to placement group performance. Newer instance types that have up to 10 Gigabit or 25 Gigabit network performance can achieve those bandwidths outside of a placement group, however. The instance and flow bandwidth capabilities are important for network-bound applications that require high network throughput to resources outside of the local VPC, such as Amazon Simple Storage Service (Amazon S3). A single flow inside a placement group is limited to 10 Gbps and flows outside a placement group are limited to 5 Gbps. Multiple flows can be used to achieve higher aggregate throughput.

Placement groups are ideal for distributed applications that require low latency, such as HPC. HPC cluster performance is dependent on network latency, and the communication is kept within the cluster.

We recommend launching all of the instances that you will need into a placement group at the time you provision them. When you add new instances to a placement group, there is a higher chance for insufficient capacity errors.

Placement groups are local to a single Availability Zone. If your application requires high availability, the application instances should be placed in multiple placement groups in different Availability Zones.

Amazon Elastic Block Store (Amazon EBS)-Optimized Instances

Amazon EBS provides persistent block storage volumes for use with Amazon EC2 instances. You can launch selected Amazon EC2 instance types as *Amazon EBS-optimized instances*. Amazon EBS input and output affect network performance because the storage is network-attached. Amazon EBS optimization enables Amazon EC2 instances to fully use the Input/Output Per Second (IOPS) provisioned on an Amazon EBS volume. Amazon EBS-optimized instances deliver dedicated throughput between Amazon EC2 and Amazon EBS, with options between 500 and 4,000 Mbps depending on the instance type. The dedicated throughput minimizes contention between Amazon EBS Input/Output (I/O) and other traffic from your Amazon EC2 instance, providing the best performance for your Amazon EBS volumes.

Amazon EBS-optimized instances are designed for use with both Standard and Provisioned IOPS Amazon EBS volumes. When attached to Amazon EBS-optimized instances, Provisioned IOPS volumes can achieve single-digit millisecond latencies. We recommend using Provisioned IOPS volumes with Amazon EBS-optimized instances or with instances that support cluster networking for applications with high storage I/O requirements and low latency.

Amazon EBS is network-attached storage, so there is a similar relationship between IOPS and throughput for storage. To maximize IOPS (similar to throughput), you may need to increase the block size (similar to MTU). In addition, larger disk sizes are capable of higher IOPS.

Network Address Translation (NAT) Gateways

You can use *Network Address Translation (NAT) gateways* to enable outbound access to the Internet while preventing inbound connectivity. NAT gateways offer better network performance than operating your own NAT instance. A NAT gateway is horizontally scalable within an Availability Zone and can forward up to 10 Gbps of traffic. NAT gateways increase availability and remove the bottleneck that a single NAT instance creates.

Enhanced Networking

Enhanced networking uses Single Root I/O Virtualization (SR-IOV) and Peripheral Component Interconnect (PCI) passthrough to provide high-performance networking capabilities on supported instance types for Linux, Windows, and FreeBSD. SR-IOV and PCI passthrough are methods of device virtualization that provide higher I/O performance and lower CPU utilization when compared to traditional virtualized network interfaces. Enhanced networking provides higher bandwidth—over one million packets per second performance—and consistently lower inter-instance latencies. Combined with placement groups, it provides full bi-section bandwidth without bandwidth oversubscription for the largest instance types. Enhanced networking requires both operating system driver support and for the Amazon Machine Image (AMI) or instance to be flagged for Enhanced networking.

Network Drivers

Depending on the instance type, enhanced networking can be enabled with one of two drivers: the *Intel 82599 Virtual Function interface* and the Amazon *Elastic Network Adapter (ENA)* driver. The ENA driver was built for newer instance families to support speeds up to 400 Gbps, with current instances using up to 25 Gbps. Each instance family supports either the Intel or the ENA driver but not both. In Linux, the `ixgbevf` module provides 82599 Virtual Function driver support.

Enabling Enhanced Networking

There are two methods to enable enhanced networking for an instance. The first method is to enable the enhanced networking attribute set on the AMI. The second method is to set the instance attribute to enable enhanced networking. The latest *Amazon Linux* Hardware Virtual Machine (HVM) AMI launches with enhanced networking support by default.

Operating System Support

Support for the Intel 82599 Virtual Function is available for Linux, Windows Server 2008 R2, Windows Server 2012, Windows Server 2016, and BSD. Enhanced networking is not available on Windows Server 2008 or Windows Server 2003.

Support for the ENA driver is available for Linux, Windows Server 2008 R2, Windows Server 2012, Windows Server 2016, and FreeBSD. The driver code is hosted on GitHub and is included in the Linux 4.9 kernel.

Additional Tuning and Driver Support

Enhanced networking is a fundamental component to increasing networking performance on AWS. We recommend enabling enhanced networking for all instances that support it. There are additional tuning and optimization techniques available for applications that require the highest performance available.

The Intel *Data Plane Development Kit (DPDK)* is a set of libraries and drivers for fast packet processing. It supports Linux, Windows, and a subset of features for FreeBSD. DPDK extends the packet processing capabilities of enhanced networking with support for both the Intel 82599 Virtual Interface and the ENA driver. This amount of control is application-specific, so DPDK has a different level of complexity to enable its benefits as compared to enhanced networking.

Enhanced networking and SR-IOV reduce the overhead of packet processing between an instance and the Hypervisor. DPDK reduces the overhead of packet processing inside the operating system, which provides applications with more control of network resources such as ring buffers, memory, and poll-mode drivers. Combining DPDK and enhanced networking provides higher packets per second, less latency, less jitter, and more control over packet queueing. This combination is most common in packet processing devices that are highly impacted by networking performance such as firewalls, real-time communication processing, HPC, and network appliances.

There are additional operating system-specific enhancements such as TCP settings, driver settings, and Non-Uniform Mapping Access (NUMA) that can further increase performance. Since these are not AWS-specific concepts, they are not covered in depth in this study guide.

Optimizing Performance

It's important to learn how to use the concepts just discussed to tune and optimize your network performance. This section reviews some of those concepts and methods.

Enhanced Networking

If your application requires high network performance, we suggest using an instance type that supports enhanced networking. This is a fundamental step in reducing latency, packet loss, and jitter and in increasing bandwidth for instances. Remember to have both operating system support and for the instance to be flagged for enhanced networking support.

Jumbo Frames

For applications that require high throughput, such as bulk data transfer, increasing the MTU can increase throughput. In scenarios where the performance bottleneck is packets per second, increasing the MTU can increase overall throughput by sending more data per packet.

The most common MTU found on the Internet is 1,500 bytes, which is what AWS supports across AWS Direct Connect and Internet gateways. Any Ethernet frame larger than 1,500 bytes is called a jumbo frame. Certain instance families support an MTU of 9,001 bytes within a VPC. If you have a cluster in a placement group, enabling jumbo MTUs can increase the cluster performance. To enable jumbo MTUs, you will need to change the operating system network parameters. For example, on Linux this is a parameter of the `ip` command.

Simply enabling jumbo MTUs on your instance does not guarantee that other parts of the network will use larger frames. Jumbo MTUs must be enabled on any instance that needs to use large frames. In addition, Internet traffic will be limited to 1,500 bytes. To assist with allowing other instances to discover the MTU limit, you should allow Destination Unreachable in a custom Internet Control Message Protocol (ICMP) rule in your security groups. This ICMP packet type is used in Path MTU Discovery (PMTUD) by many operating systems to detect MTU settings.

Network Credits

Instance families such as R4 and C5 use a *network I/O credit mechanism*. Most applications do not consistently need a high level of network performance, but can benefit from having access to increased bandwidth when they send or receive data. For example, the smaller R4 instance sizes offer peak throughput of 10 Gbps. These instances use a network I/O credit mechanism to allocate network bandwidth to instances based on average bandwidth utilization. These instances accrue credits when their network throughput is below their baseline limits and can then use these credits when they perform network data transfers.

If you plan on running performance baselines with instances that support network credits, we recommend accounting for built-up credits during the test. One approach is to test with freshly installed instances. You can also send a large amount of traffic until you get to a steady state of throughput after all credits have been exhausted. Currently, there is no metric to track network credits for instances.

Instance Bandwidth

Each instance type has a bandwidth definition ranging from low to 20 gigabit. Larger instance types have more bandwidth and packet per second capabilities. There are no explicit bandwidth limits for any single VPC, VPC peering connection, or Internet gateway. We suggest trying a larger instance type if your application has a bandwidth bottleneck. If you are not sure about your performance bottleneck, trying a larger instance size is the easiest method to determine whether bandwidth supported by the instance is your bottleneck. The instance's allowed bandwidth is roughly proportional to the size of the instance. Different instance families, such as C3 and C4, use different hardware and potentially networking implementations, so they may have slightly different performance characteristics as traffic gets closer to your networking limits. The Compute-Optimized (C family) and General-Purpose (M family) instances are common choices for network-bound applications.

Instance bandwidth is also dependent on the network driver in use. Instance types using the Intel 82599 interface with the `ixgbevf` module have both an aggregate and flow-based bandwidth limit of 5 Gbps. Instances with the AWS ENA driver have a 5 Gbps flow limit outside of a placement group but can achieve an aggregate bandwidth of 25 Gbps within a VPC or a peered VPC with multiple flows.

A practical tip is to baseline your application performance on instance types that are close to your needs in order to confirm that the performance meets the requirements.

Flow Performance

In addition to instance bandwidth, the quantity of flows that your application uses also affects throughput. In a placement group, any single flow will be limited to 10 Gbps. This is important to understand so that you can use the full bandwidth of any instance with greater than 10 Gbps performance.

Outside of a placement group, the maximum throughput for a single flow is 5 Gbps. Examples include traffic between Availability Zones in the same VPC, a flow between an Amazon EC2 instance and Amazon S3, and traffic between an instance and an on-premises resource.

Load Balancer Performance

If your application will be using Elastic Load Balancing, you have multiple choices for load balancing. The Application Load Balancer has many HTTP and Layer 7 features. The Network Load Balancer has more TCP and Layer 3 features. These options are covered in more depth in Chapter 6, "Domain Name System and Load Balancing."

The advantages of the Network Load Balancer are performance and scale. Since it is less computationally complex to forward packets without looking inside them, the Network Load Balancer scales faster and has lower latency. If your application does not require HTTP or Layer 7 features, you can improve performance with a Network Load Balancer. The additional latency is measured in microseconds for Network Load Balancer packet processing.

Virtual Private Network (VPN) Performance

The Virtual Private Gateway (VGW) is the AWS managed Virtual Private Network (VPN) service. When a VPN connection is created, AWS provides tunnels to two different VPN endpoints. These VPN endpoints are capable of approximately 1.25 Gbps per tunnel depending on packet size.

To increase bandwidth into AWS, you can forward traffic to both endpoints. This design requires that on-premises equipment support *Equal Cost Multipath (ECMP)* to load balance traffic across both links or to balance more preferred prefixes on each VPN endpoint. It is possible to set different route preferences so that traffic leaves from both VPN endpoints for egress diversity.

This design requires manual intervention with the default routing provided by the VGW. While it does allow you to double the default bandwidth, the complexity can be significant. In addition, if the prefixes aren't evenly balanced, which may change based on traffic flow, there will be uneven usage of the endpoints.

In addition to the AWS VGW, you can install a VPN endpoint on your own Amazon EC2 instances. This approach allows more options for routing, performance tuning, and encryption overhead. Note that AWS does not manage the availability of this option. You should either test the VPN endpoint performance in your own account or work with the software provider to obtain their performance evaluations.

AWS Direct Connect Performance

One of the primary reasons for using AWS Direct Connect is to obtain more predictable performance than can be obtained using a VPN. Using a dedicated circuit or existing network allows you to control the quality of the network between on-premises infrastructure and AWS. For example, you can use a dedicated fiber between your data center and the AWS Direct Connect facility to reduce latency.

Another advantage that AWS Direct Connect offers is high bandwidth. While the VGW service is multi-gigabit, it is not suitable for throughputs of 10 Gbps and higher. AWS Direct Connect allows for customers to provision multiple 10 Gbps connections and also aggregate those connections into a single 40 Gbps circuit.

Quality of Service (QoS) in a VPC

On-premises networks often support *Quality of Service (QoS)* with *Differentiated Services Code Point (DSCP)* in order to have more control over which traffic is prioritized in case of network congestion. All traffic is treated equally inside of a VPC. The DSCP is the seven bits in the IP header used to identify the priority of traffic. The DSCP is not used to modify traffic forwarding in AWS networks, but the header remains as it was received.

You can use AWS Direct Connect in conjunction with QoS to improve application performance and reliability. When packets leave on-premises and traverse any service provider networks that honor DSCP bits, QoS can be applied normally. The goal is to use service provider networks that honor QoS so that performance is improved from on-premises infrastructure to AWS. Even so, packets are not differentiated at the AWS edge of the connection. This is common for real-time communications packets and other flows that are sensitive to packet loss.

Example Applications

The majority of applications on AWS perform adequately without needing advanced tuning or involvement of optional networking features. This is a study guide for advanced networking, though, so this section will review some of AWS more complex networking configurations.

High Performance Computing

High Performance Computing (HPC) allows scientists and engineers to solve complex, compute-intensive, and data-intensive problems. HPC applications often require high network performance, fast storage, large amounts of memory, very high compute capabilities, or all of these. HPC performance can be bound by network latency, so it is important to minimize latency within a cluster.

Using placement groups with HPC enables access to a low-latency, high-bandwidth network for tightly coupled, IO-intensive, and storage-intensive workloads. For faster Amazon EBS IO, we recommend using Amazon EBS-optimized instances and Provisioned IOPS volumes for high performance.

Real-Time Media

Real-time media services include applications like *Voice over IP (VoIP)*, media streaming using the *Real-time Transport Protocol (RTP)* or *Real-time Messaging Protocol (RTMP)*, and other video and audio applications. Real-time media use cases include enterprise migrations of existing communications infrastructure as well as service provider telephony and video services.

Media streams can have different requirements on the network depending on the implementation and architecture. Video workloads can have varying bandwidth requirements during an existing flow, which can be dependent on the complexity of movement in the video. Audio flows may also change their bandwidth requirements if the audio stream supports redundancy or adaptive changes. In most cases, both audio and video streams are highly sensitive to packet loss and jitter. Packet loss and jitter can cause distortion and gaps in the media, which are easily detected by end users. We recommend taking steps to reduce loss and jitter.

The first step to reducing loss and jitter on AWS is to make sure that enhanced networking is enabled for real-time media applications. This feature provides a smoother packet delivery. If AWS Direct Connect is used, you can use QoS on the circuit if the provider or equipment supports it, reducing the chance of packet loss.

Detailed monitoring and proactive routing control can also mitigate network congestions and challenges. For highly sensitive media with multiple potential network paths, you can configure monitoring probes on Amazon EC2 instances to report on link health. That information can be used centrally to modify routes to alternative network paths that are healthy.

Some media applications support buffering traffic before the media is played to the user. This buffering can help guard against jitter and varying network latencies. For media streams that can buffer audio or video, decreasing jitter is more important than reducing the average latency.

Data Processing, Ingestion, and Backup

When you want to move, process, or back up terabytes of data in AWS, the network is an important consideration. Data transfer can occur from on premises or within a VPC. It may also include different storage services such as Amazon EBS and Amazon S3, which have different networking characteristics.

You should understand potential performance limitations for data transfers, particularly if the transfer rate is important for your operation. Data processing and transfer in AWS generally follows this flow:

1. Read data and potentially metadata from storage.
2. Encapsulate the data in a transfer protocol, such as File Transfer Protocol (FTP), Secure Copy (SCP), or HTTP.
3. Transfer the data over a network, such as VPN, the Internet, or AWS Direct Connect.
4. Decapsulate the data and perform validation or other processes.
5. Write the data to storage.

Network transfer is one part of the overall performance equation. The other performance components are storage IOPS, read performance, metadata processing, and write performance. It is possible for storage performance to be the primary bottleneck. You can try benchmarking different network configurations, test an entirely local transfer, and monitor storage performance rates to determine the relationship between the network and the storage transfer rate. If there are Amazon EC2 instances involved, such as VM Import/Export, you can also try using different instance sizes.

Remember that there is a relationship between latency and bandwidth to achieve throughput. If your file transfer is using TCP, higher latencies will reduce overall throughput. There are approaches to fix this with TCP tuning and optimized transfer protocols, some of which use UDP.

On-Premises Data Transfer

On-premises use cases may include migration to AWS, on-premises processing, or backup data. In addition to the storage components mentioned above, on-premises networking affects data movement performance.

One primary performance aspect is the existing Internet or private circuits available between transfer points. For Internet transfers, the existing Internet connection bandwidth and utilization can be a bottleneck. If there is a single 20 Mbps Internet connection that's 50 percent utilized, that provides 10 Mbps of available bandwidth. For large transfers, AWS Direct Connect can provide a dedicated circuit with less latency and more predictable throughput. Provisioning AWS Direct Connect takes more time than configuring a VPN, however, so timing is a consideration.

Security is an important factor for data transfer. If the data transfer is over insecure protocols, we suggest using encryption over any untrusted connections. The techniques for increasing performance through VPN mentioned in the VPN Performance section of this chapter can be used in this scenario. Note that IP Security (IPsec) can limit performance due to the encapsulation involved.

There are many additional services and concepts that are outside the scope of the AWS Certified Advanced Networking – Specialty Exam. Consider using services like AWS Snowball, AWS Snowmobile, or AWS Storage Gateway for transferring datasets larger than 1 TB. Amazon S3 has additional optimizations such as Transfer Acceleration and multipart uploads. There may also be additional optimizations at the operating system level to tune window scaling, interrupts, and Direct Memory Access (DMA) channels.

To get the highest performance of data transfer to Amazon EC2 or Amazon S3, we suggest splitting the data transfer and processing across many instances. Inside a VPC, any instance accessing data over the network (for example, Amazon S3) will be limited to 5 Gbps for a single flow. Instances that are ENA enabled can achieve higher bandwidth to S3 by using multiple flows, up to 25 Gbps. Some applications may be single-threaded, which will require more instances or threads to achieve higher performance.

Network Appliances

Routers, VPN appliances, NAT instances, firewalls, intrusion detection and prevention systems, web proxies, email proxies, and other network services have historically been hardware-based solutions in the network. On AWS, these solutions are implemented virtually on Amazon EC2. Since these solutions are deployed on operating systems on Amazon EC2, they begin to look like applications themselves, even if they participate in routing.

Some, or even all, of your VPC traffic can be forwarded through these instances, so it's important to improve performance. You should size the instance correctly by testing your required throughput on different instance types. Enhanced networking is highly important for performance as well. It's common for the network appliance to connect to external networks. If this is the case, placement groups will not increase performance to destinations outside of a placement group.

These network appliances may require multiple interfaces in different subnets to achieve different routing policies. You should understand that there are maximum interface counts and maximum amounts of IP addresses that you can apply per interface. As of this writing, a c4.8xlarge can have 8 interfaces with 30 IP addresses per interface. The quantity of network interfaces does not affect performance characteristics if the instance type supports enhanced networking. Remember, additional network interfaces do not change the networking performance.

For Amazon EC2 VPN instances, you should understand that the additional IPsec headers reduce the overall throughput because there is less data in each 1,500-byte frame. It's important to reduce the MTU to allow additional room for headers for protocols like IPsec. Most applications will have mixed packet sizes that are less than the MTU, so Amazon EC2 VPN endpoints are likely to be bound by packets per second rather than CPU, memory, or network bandwidth.

One of the benefits of operating on AWS is scalability and the ability to build fault-tolerant applications—this concept applies to network appliances. If possible, network appliances should be able to use Auto Scaling and interact with Elastic Load Balancing to scale and be fault tolerant. The Network Load Balancer supports long-lived sessions based on source IP address, destination IP address, source port, destination port, and protocol (5-tuple hash), making it well suited for network applications that use TCP.

You should understand that not every protocol can be load balanced, such as IPsec with Encapsulating Security Protocol (ESP) and Authentication Header (AH). ESP and AH are transport protocols that are not supported by Elastic Load Balancing.

Routing traffic through instances is accomplished by modifying the routing table of subnets. Each subnet can have a route for a certain prefix (for example, default route) to the elastic network interface of a network appliance instance. When routing traffic to an elastic network interface, remember that you are responsible for the fault tolerance and availability of that route. By default, this route or elastic network interface requires additional configuration to be fault tolerant. Some approaches include Amazon EC2 instances with AWS Identity and Access Management (IAM) roles that allow them to modify routes or attach the elastic network interface to a new instance when the instance detects a failure. AWS has published some example scripts to accomplish failover in NAT instances (see `https://aws.amazon.com/articles/2781451301784570`). Another approach could include using AWS Lambda to monitor and provide fault tolerance.

Performance Testing

Running performance tests and establishing a baseline is important for applications with high network performance requirements, as mentioned previously in this chapter.

Amazon CloudWatch Metrics

Amazon CloudWatch metrics make it easy to observe and collect data about your network's. Amazon CloudWatch metrics are available for many AWS Cloud services, including Amazon EC2. Amazon EC2 instances have a variety of CPU, memory, disk, and networking metrics available by default in five-minute increments. To receive one-minute metrics, detailed monitoring can be enabled for an additional cost. For the exam, you should understand which metrics are available, but you do not need to memorize specific details. Table 9.1 lists available instance networking metrics in Amazon CloudWatch.

TABLE 9.1 Instance Networking Amazon CloudWatch Metrics

Amazon CloudWatch Metric	Description
`NetworkIn`	The number of bytes received on all network interfaces by the instance. This metric identifies the volume of incoming network traffic to a single instance.
`NetworkOut`	The number of bytes sent out on all network interfaces by the instance. This metric identifies the volume of outgoing network traffic from a single instance.
`NetworkPacketsIn`	The number of packets received on all network interfaces by the instance.
`NetworkPacketsOut`	The number of packets sent out on all network interfaces by the instance.

In addition to instance metrics, Amazon CloudWatch metrics is available for Amazon VPN. Table 9.2 lists available Amazon EC2 VPN metrics in Amazon CloudWatch.

TABLE 9.2 Amazon EC2 VPN Amazon CloudWatch Metrics

Amazon CloudWatch Metric	Description
`TunnelState`	The state of the tunnel. 0 indicates DOWN and 1 indicates UP.
`TunnelDataIn`	The bytes received through the VPN tunnel.
`TunnelDataOut`	The bytes sent through the VPN tunnel.

You should remember that Amazon CloudWatch metrics for instances and VPN are in bytes. If you are interested in measuring bits per second, you'll need to do some math. For example, to calculate bits per second for 10,920,000 NetworkIn bytes over 5 minutes, the math is 10,920,000 divided by 8 to account for bits, divided by 300 to account for seconds, resulting in 4,550 Bps (or 4.55 Kbps).

Table 9.3 lists available AWS Direct Connect metrics in Amazon CloudWatch.

TABLE 9.3 AWS Direct Connect Amazon CloudWatch Metrics

Amazon CloudWatch Metric	Description
`TunnelState`	The state of the tunnel. 0 indicates DOWN and 1 indicates UP.
`ConnectionBpsEgress`	The bit rate for outbound data from the AWS side of the connection.
`ConnectionBpsIngress`	The bit rate for inbound data to the AWS side of the connection.
`ConnectionPpsEgress`	The packet rate for outbound data from the AWS side of the connection.
`ConnectionPpsIngress`	The packet rate for inbound data to the AWS side of the connection.
`ConnectionCRCErrorCount`	The number of times Cyclic Redundancy Check (CRC) errors are observed for the data received at the connection.
`ConnectionLightLevelTx`	Indicates the health of the fiber connection for egress (outbound) traffic from the AWS side of the connection.
`ConnectionLightLevelRx`	Indicates the health of the fiber connection for ingress (inbound) traffic to the AWS side of the connection.

Testing Methodology

Application performance is a combination of memory, CPU, networking, storage, application architecture, latency, and other factors. Testing different configurations and settings is a cost-effective way to determine how to increase performance. There are a wide array of tools and methods available, so this section will focus on testing as it relates to AWS networking.

Throughput Testing

It is possible to baseline network performance for an instance type so that you know where the performance boundaries are. Here are some considerations for testing network throughput on AWS.

- The instance type and size will largely determine maximum throughput and packets per second.
- Test the right scenario. If your application will be communicating between Availability Zones or outside of the VPC, test that flow. Testing traffic within an Availability Zone or placement group will provide different performance than between Availability Zones.

- Enable enhanced networking for optimal performance.
- Test over multiple flows, test over multiple copies of the application, and distribute the test over multiple instances. Tools that are single-threaded or use a single TCP flow are not likely to maximize network throughput.
- Test with jumbo MTUs within your VPC to maximize throughput.
- TCP and UDP will react differently to congestion and latency, so test the protocols that your application will be using.
- With high-latency connections, you can try tuning different TCP parameters, such as TCP implementation, congestion window sizes, and timers.

To create latency or simulate an on-premises workload, test using multiple AWS Regions and send traffic over the Internet or VPN.

Solution Testing

Testing network throughput and connectivity is helpful, but ultimately you care about the application's performance over the network. We suggest performing end-to-end testing of metrics for the application. This may involve using tools to simulate web requests, transactions, or data processing. With the data from your network tests, you can identify network bottlenecks using Amazon CloudWatch reports and operating system statistics. This is where trying different approaches such as placement groups, larger instance sizes, and more distributed systems increases application performance. There are tools like Bees with Machine Guns that can run a distributed load test.

One helpful tool to investigate further is a *packet capture* on the network. A packet capture is a raw dump of the traffic sent or received over the network. The easiest way to do this in a VPC is to run a packet capture locally on the instance with tools such as tcpdump. External tools can run packet loss analysis, or you can look for TCP retransmissions that indicate packet loss. These actions are also an effective way to determine if the network has latency or if it is the application. The packet timing can determine when the host receives network packets and how quickly the application responds.

Summary

In this chapter, you learned about the different aspects of network performance in AWS networks. Each application and network topology can interact differently, so understanding the relationship between features, instances, technologies, and applications is core to improving performance. Every modern application is dependent on the network for performance, so every improvement can make many applications more responsive, run faster, or be more reliable.

It is important to understand core concepts such as bandwidth, latency, packet loss, jitter, and throughput. After you understand core performance as a concept, the next step is to understand what features AWS offers to increase performance. In addition to the available features, it is important to understand the differences between instances and enhanced networking support. With that knowledge, you can start to apply AWS features to different types of specialized applications and networking scenarios. To validate the concepts, you should run both networking and application performance tests to further tweak and tune networking configuration.

To provide higher network performance, AWS offers a variety of features such as placement groups, Provisioned IOPS, enhanced networking, and jumbo frames. We reviewed the network performance characteristics that instances can have, such as enhanced networking, which reduces jitter, increases throughput, and improves reliability.

Network performance is a critical component of applications for HPC, high-throughput data processing, and real-time media, as well as for network appliances. Each of these use cases has differing requirements for latency, jitter, packet loss, and throughput. Those differences will change the outcome of the network architecture and networking features required for optimal performance.

Theory and features are helpful, but ensuring that performance is achieved for your applications to function in an efficient manner is paramount. It is important to know how to test your network and understand the baseline and peak capabilities of your environment. Experiencing a full deployment and testing it will drive further validation and opportunities for tweaks and improvements.

Resources to Review

For further review, check out the following URLs:

Performance Testing:

`https://aws.amazon.com/premiumsupport/knowledge-center/network-throughput-benchmark-linux-ec2/`

Network Credits:

`http://docs.aws.amazon.com/AWSEC2/latest/UserGuide/memory-optimized-instances.html#memory-network-perf`

Instance Types:

`https://aws.amazon.com/ec2/instance-types/`

Exam Essentials

Understand latency, jitter, bandwidth, and packets per second. Latency is the time delay between two points of the network. Jitter is the variance in delay between two points of the network. Bandwidth is the maximum amount of data that can be transferred at one point of the network. Packets per seconds is the rate of packets that a point of the network is transmitting or receiving.

Understand throughput and the relationship to latency. Throughput is the successful transfer rate between two points in a network. This is different from bandwidth, which is simply the maximum possible transfer rate. Throughput is affected by packet loss, protocol, latency, MTU, and other components such as storage and application processing.

Know the relevance of the MTU and jumbo frames. The MTU is the largest Ethernet frame that can be sent on a network. Most networks, including the Internet, use a 1,500-byte MTU. This is the maximum in AWS, except within a VPC where the MTU is 9,001 bytes. Any MTU over 1,500 bytes is considered a jumbo frame. The MTU increases throughput because each packet can carry more data while maintaining the same packets per second.

Understand the relationship between instance size and bandwidth. Each instance is given a certain bandwidth, ranging from low to 25 Gigabit. As you increase the instance size within a family, you generally get higher bandwidths.

Understand Amazon EBS-optimized instances. Amazon EBS-optimized instances have provisioned network bandwidth that allows instances to fully utilize the IOPS available on the network-attached storage.

Understand when and why to use a placement group. A placement group is a logical grouping of instances within an Availability Zone that is designed to provide instances with the highest bandwidth, lowest latency, and highest packets per second. Placement groups are useful for high-performance applications that communicate within a single Availability Zone.

Understand what enhanced networking offers and what is required to support it. Enhanced networking enables instances to use SR-IOV to provide lower latency, more reliability, and higher packet per second performance for instances. Instances must support either the Intel 82599 Virtual Function driver or the ENA driver on a variety of Linux, Windows, and FreeBSD operating systems. In addition to driver support, the AMI or instance must be flagged for enhanced networking support.

Understand some of the steps required to optimize performance for an instance. Important steps include enabling enhanced networking, configuring the operating system for jumbo MTUs, and trying larger instance types. You should also understand the benefits of using multiple instances and flows for performance.

Understand the limitations of instances, placement groups, and flows. Instances will have bandwidth and packets per second limitations that differ based on enhanced networking support, the instance family, the instance size, whether the traffic flow is within a placement group, and how many flows are used. Any single instance or flow leaving an Availability Zone is limited to 5 Gbps for instances using the `ixgbevf` driver and 25 Gbps for ENA enabled instances. Any single flow inside a placement group is limited to 10 Gbps, even for 20 Gigabit instance types.

Understand network credits and the benefit they offer. Certain instance families, such as the Memory-Optimized R4 and Compute-Optimized C5, have network I/O credits. This feature allows instances to utilize higher network bandwidths if they have accrued credits.

They accrue more credits the longer they run while remaining under their bandwidth allocation. You should understand that this network credit may cause variance in load testing, depending on how long the instance has been running and its throughput.

Understand the impact that AWS Direct Connect can have on performance. AWS Direct Connect allows for control over network paths, which can decrease latency, reduce jitter, increase bandwidth, and increase reliability. Bandwidth is only limited by the port speeds. Even though traffic is treated equally on AWS, it is possible to use QoS on networks connected to AWS Direct Connect that support QoS.

Understand the performance advantages of the Network Load Balancer. The Network Load Balancer is a Layer 3 and Layer 4 load balancer that can reduce latency and scale for incoming traffic. It has lower latency than other Elastic Load Balancing options, measured in microseconds.

Understand how to apply networking features to specialized workloads. HPC requires low latency and high bandwidth, so we recommend using placement groups. Enabling enhanced networking and reducing jitter are important for applications like real-time media. Applications that require heavy data processing should spread flows over multiple instances for higher throughput. Network appliances like proxies should support enhanced networking and have an appropriate instance size for their required bandwidth.

Learn how to investigate network performance through testing. You should understand the Amazon CloudWatch metrics that are available for both Amazon EC2 and VPN. End-to-end system testing differs from load testing the networking capacity of a single instance because applications have many other dependencies such as storage, application logic, and latency that will affect overall performance.

Test Taking Tip

Generally speaking, larger instance types will provide higher networking throughput. This is helpful for increasing the performance of traffic flows through a NAT instance or proxy instance. Enhanced networking has no real drawbacks, but it may not always be the answer that the exam question is seeking. Placement groups increase performance for specific types of applications, but they have limited use for certain applications and scenarios.

Exercises

Increasing network performance requires both understanding concepts and putting them into practice. The best way to grasp these concepts and interconnected relationships is to measure performance, change settings, and measure again.

For assistance completing these exercises, refer to the Amazon VPC User Guide located at `http://aws.amazon.com/documentation/vpc/` and `https://aws.amazon.com/documentation/ec2/`.

Note that using the same instance type for the following exercises can better help you compare network performance in different scenarios.

EXERCISE 9.1

Test Performance Across Availability Zones

Create a new Amazon VPC or use an existing VPC with at least two subnets in different Availability Zones. For the following exercises, the instances need access to the Internet through an Internet gateway.

1. Launch two Amazon Linux (or any Red Hat Enterprise Linux [RHEL]-based distribution) instances that support enhanced networking in different Availability Zones. The instance types that support enhanced networking are listed in the Amazon EC2 User Guide at `http://docs.aws.amazon.com/AWSEC2/latest/UserGuide/enhanced-networking.html#supported_instances`.
2. Choose one instance to be an iperf server and one to be a client. Use tags or modify the instance name to make them easier to identify.
3. Modify the security group to allow TCP port 5201 incoming and outgoing security group on the client and server.

Technically, you only need outbound TCP 5201 on the client and incoming TCP 5201 on the server, but enabling it in both directions on both servers provides more flexibility if you change the testing or confuse the client and server.

4. Run these commands on the server instance:

```
$ wget http://downloads.es.net/pub/iperf/iperf-3.0.6.tar.gz
$ tar zxvf iperf-3.0.6.tar.gz
$ sudo yum install gcc -y
$ cd iperf-3.0.6
$ ./configure
$ make
$ sudo make install
$ cd src
$ iperf3 -s
```

EXERCISE 9.1 *(continued)*

5. Run these commands on the client instance:

```
$ wget http://downloads.es.net/pub/iperf/iperf-3.0.6.tar.gz
$ tar zxvf iperf-3.0.6.tar.gz
$ sudo yum install gcc -y
$ cd iperf-3.0.6
$ ./configure
$ make
$ sudo make install
$ cd src
$ iperf3 -t 10 -c x.x.x.x #replace x.x.x.x with your server IP
```

You should see a bandwidth test run over port TCP 5201 ten times, followed by a summary of the data transfer and averaged throughput numbers.

If you are running on burstable instances or instances that support network credits, you may see varying network results. You may not see exact bandwidths. Data transfers are throughput tests, and TCP doesn't use all the available bandwidth.

Check the latency between the hosts by running the following command:

```
$ ping x.x.x.x #replace x.x.x.x with the other instance's IP address
```

Terminate the instances, unless you want to run other performance tests. You may want to test other tools like MTR.

EXERCISE 9.2

Inside a Placement Group

Now let's run a similar experiment, but this time in a placement group. For assistance with steps in this exercise, refer to the documentation on placement groups in the Amazon EC2 User Guide at `http://docs.aws.amazon.com/AWSEC2/latest/UserGuide/placement-groups.html`. The instance types that support placement groups are also listed on that page.

1. Create a placement group. This step may take a few minutes to complete.
2. Create two new instances that support enhanced networking, and provision them in the placement group. There is a drop-down to select a placement group in the

Configure Instance Details step of the Amazon EC2 Console. If the drop-down is not there, the instance type does not support placement groups.

3. Choose one instance to be an iperf server and one to be a client. Use tags or modify the instance name to make them easier to identify.

4. Modify the security group to allow TCP port 5201 incoming and outgoing security group on the client and server.

5. Run these commands on the server instance:

```
$ wget http://downloads.es.net/pub/iperf/iperf-3.0.6.tar.gz
$ tar zxvf iperf-3.0.6.tar.gz
$ sudo yum install gcc -y
$ cd iperf-3.0.6
$ ./configure
$ make
$ sudo make install
$ cd src
$ iperf3 -s
```

6. Run these commands on the client instance:

```
$ wget http://downloads.es.net/pub/iperf/iperf-3.0.6.tar.gz
$ tar zxvf iperf-3.0.6.tar.gz
$ sudo yum install gcc -y
$ cd iperf-3.0.6
$ ./configure
$ make
$ sudo make install
$ cd src
$ iperf3 -t 10 -c x.x.x.x #replace x.x.x.x with your server IP
```

You should see a bandwidth test run over port TCP 5201 ten times, followed by a summary of the data transfer and averaged throughput numbers.

If you used the same instance type in the two exercises, what were the differences in the summary data? Larger instances types will generally have larger additional bandwidth in a placement group.

Check the latency between the hosts again using the following command:

```
$ ping x.x.x.x #replace x.x.x.x with the other instance's IP address
```

Is there a difference in latency? You should see lower latency here.

You may wish to keep one instance for Exercise 9.4. Otherwise, you can terminate both instances.

EXERCISE 9.3

Jumbo Frames

If you want to see higher performance in the placement group, enable jumbo frames on both of the instances you created in the previous exercise.

This will be effective for instances that are listed with a 10 or 20 gigabit network. The costs of these instances are higher than most, so be sure to terminate instances after use.

A VPC is already enabled for jumbo frames. To enable it on your instance, you can use the following command. Remember to do this on both instances. These commands assume Amazon Linux.

```
$ sudo ip link set dev eth0 mtu 9001
```

Check that the change was made on both instances by running the following command:

```
$ ip link show eth0 | grep mtu
```

(Optional) To persist your MTU change through a reboot, add the following lines to your `/etc/dhcp/dhclient-eth0.conf` file:

```
interface "eth0" {
supersede interface-mtu 1500;
}
```

Run this command on the server instance:

```
$ iperf3 -s #if the server isn't still running
```

Run this command on the client instance:

```
$ iperf3 -t 10 -c x.x.x.x #replace x.x.x.x with your server IP
```

If you're running an instance with a 10 gigabit or higher network, you should see larger bandwidths than the previous exercises.

You can use these instances for the next exercises or previous instances that may be smaller.

EXERCISE 9.4

Performance Between Regions

In the previous exercises, we tested bandwidth between Availability Zones and in a placement group within one Availability Zone. Let's test the bandwidth with more latency. To do this, we'll use two different regions.

You can use one of the instances used in the previous exercises. Otherwise, create two instances in different regions. For the biggest difference in performance, choose two regions that are very far apart such as US East (Ohio) and Asia Pacific (Tokyo).

Choose one instance to be an iperf server and one to be a client.

Modify the security group to allow TCP port 5201 incoming and outgoing security group on the client and server.

Run these commands on the server instance:

```
$ wget http://downloads.es.net/pub/iperf/iperf-3.0.6.tar.gz
$ tar zxvf iperf-3.0.6.tar.gz
$ sudo yum install gcc -y
$ cd iperf-3.0.6
$ ./configure
$ make
$ sudo make install
$ cd src
$ iperf3 -s
```

Run these commands on the client instance:

```
$ wget http://downloads.es.net/pub/iperf/iperf-3.0.6.tar.gz
$ tar zxvf iperf-3.0.6.tar.gz
$ sudo yum install gcc -y
$ cd iperf-3.0.6
$ ./configure
$ make
$ sudo make install
$ cd src
$ iperf3 -t 10 -c x.x.x.x #replace x.x.x.x with your server IP
```

You should see lower bandwidth than you had received in previous exercises. If you have been using the same instance types for these tests, you can see that the additional latency has an effect on throughput, even with the same hardware and bandwidth capacity. You can repeat the steps to make another client and server in a third region that is somewhere closer or further from the server instance's region. This will give you an even better understanding of the relationship between latency and throughput.

There are additional methods that you can use to mitigate latency, such as performing manual congestion window tuning, trying different TCP implementations, or using network performance appliances. These methods are out of the scope of this study guide, though we encourage you to explore them to broaden your understanding of network operations and performance. Jumbo frames would increase throughput, but you are limited at 1,500 bytes due to being outside of the VPC.

EXERCISE 9.5

Use Amazon CloudWatch Metrics

In this exercise, we'll confirm network bandwidth with Amazon CloudWatch Metrics with detailed monitoring. This exercise will use the same server and client instances from the previous exercise.

For more information on enabling detailed monitoring for instances, refer to the Amazon EC2 User Guide at `http://docs.aws.amazon.com/AWSEC2/latest/UserGuide/using-cloudwatch-new.html`.

Enable detailed monitoring in the Monitoring tab of your instances, which will change the intervals for metrics to one minute.

To reduce data transfer costs, you can run this performance test within one Availability Zone.

Run this command on the server instance:

```
$ iperf3 -s
```

Run this command on the client instance:

```
$ iperf3 -t 180 -c x.x.x.x #replace x.x.x.x with your server IP
```

We've extended the time of our transfer to three minutes so that we can monitor a steady bandwidth. It is possible to perform this test without detailed monitoring, but it would require running longer tests.

After running the transfer command, navigate to the Amazon EC2 Console. In the Monitoring tab, you can view network statistics such as Network In and Network Out, measured in bytes. After a few minutes, you should see the bandwidth even out.

To calculate Megabits per second (one million bits per second), we need to do some math. Network In and Network Out are in bytes, so we'll first need to divide by eight. We can further divide by one million to determine Mbps.

Does this math confirm the bandwidth that `iperf` has given you?

It is okay if your math differs slightly because there is additional traffic on your instance (for example, your active Secure Shell [SSH] session).

Now that you have tested a number of networking scenarios, you should have a better understanding of AWS networking features, relationships between performance concepts, and some basic performance testing techniques.

Review Questions

1. In order to decrease the number of instances that have inbound web access, your team has recently placed a Network Address Translation (NAT) instance on Amazon Linux in the public subnet. The private subnet has a 0.0.0.0/0 route to the elastic network interface of the NAT instance. Users are complaining that web responses are slower than normal. What are practical steps to fix this issue? (Choose two.)

   A. Replace the NAT instance with a NAT gateway.

   B. Enable enhanced networking on the NAT instance.

   C. Create another NAT instance and add another 0.0.0.0/0 route in the private subnet.

   D. Try a larger instance type for the NAT instance.

2. Voice calls to international numbers from inside your company must go through an open-source Session Border Controller (SBC) installed on a custom Linux Amazon Machine Image (AMI) in your Virtual Private Cloud (VPC) public subnet. The SBC handles the real-time media and voice signaling. International calls often have garbled voice, and it is difficult to understand what people are saying. What may increase the quality of international voice calls?

   A. Place the SBC in a placement group to reduce latency.

   B. Add additional network interfaces to the instance.

   C. Use an Application Load Balancer to distribute load to multiple SBCs.

   D. Enable enhanced networking on the instance.

3. Your big data team is trying to determine why their proof of concept is running slowly. For the demo, they are trying to ingest 1 TB of data from Amazon Simple Storage Service (Amazon S3) on their c4.8xl instance. They have already enabled enhanced networking. What should they do to increase Amazon S3 ingest rates?

   A. Run the demo on-premises and access Amazon S3 from AWS Direct Connect to reduce latency.

   B. Split the data ingest on more than one instance, such as two c4.4xl instances.

   C. Place the instance in a placement group and use an Amazon S3 endpoint.

   D. Place a Network Load Balancer between the instance and Amazon S3 for more efficient load balancing and better performance.

4. Your database instance running on an r4.large instance seems to be dropping Transmission Control Protocol (TCP) packets based on a packet capture from a host with which it was communicating. During initial performance baseline tests, the instance was able to handle peak load twice as high as its current load. What could be the issue? (Choose two.)

   A. The r4.large instance may have accumulated network credits before load testing, which would allow higher peak values.

   B. There may be additional database processing errors causing connection timeouts.

   C. The read replica database should be placed in a separate Availability Zone.

   D. The Virtual Private Network (VPN) session should be configured for dynamic Border Gateway Protocol (BGP) routing for higher availability.

5. Your development team is testing the performance of a new application using enhanced networking. They have updated the kernel to the latest version that supports the Elastic Network Adapter (ENA) driver. What are the other two requirements for support? (Choose two.)

   A. Use an instance that supports the ENA driver.

   B. Support the Intel Virtual Function driver in addition to the ENA driver.

   C. Flag the Amazon Machine Image (AMI) for enhanced networking support.

   D. Enable enhanced networking on the elastic network interface.

6. The new architecture for your application involves replicating your stateful application data from your Virtual Private Cloud (VPC) in US East (Ohio) to Asia Pacific (Tokyo). The replication instances are in public subnets in each region and communicate with public addresses over Transport Layer Security (TLS). Your team is seeing much lower replication throughput than they see within a single VPC. Which steps can you take to improve throughput?

   A. Increase the application's packets per second.

   B. Configure the Maximum Transmission Unit (MTU) to 9,001 bytes on each instance's eth0 to support jumbo frames.

   C. Create a Virtual Private Network (VPN) connection between the regions and enable jumbo frames on each instance.

   D. None of the above

7. Which networking feature will provide the most benefits to support a clustered computing application that requires very low latency and high network throughput?

   A. Enhanced networking

   B. Network Input/Output (I/O) credits

   C. Placement groups

   D. Amazon Route 53 performance groups

8. What would you recommend to make a scalable architecture for performing very high throughput data transfers?

   A. Use enhanced networking.

   B. Configure the Amazon Virtual Private Cloud (Amazon VPC) routing table to have a single hop between every instance in the VPC.

   C. Distribute the flows across many instances.

   D. Advertise routes to external networks with Border Gateway Protocol (BGP) to increase routing scale.

9. One of the applications that you want to migrate to AWS has high disk performance requirements. You need to guarantee certain baseline performance with low latency. Which feature can help meet the performance requirements of this application?

   A. Amazon Elastic Block Store (Amazon EBS) Provisioned Input/Output Per Second (IOPS)

   B. Amazon Elastic File System (Amazon EFS)

C. Dedicated network bandwidth

D. Quality of Service (QoS)

10. Your application developers are facing a challenge relating to network performance. Their application creates a buffer to accept network data so that it can be analyzed and displayed in real time. It seems that packets have delays of between 2 milliseconds and 120 milliseconds, however. Which network characteristic do you need to improve?

A. Bandwidth

B. Latency

C. Jitter

D. Maximum Transmission Unit (MTU)

11. The operations group at your company has migrated one of your application components from R3 instances to R4 instances. The networking performance is not as high as expected, however. What could be this issue? (Choose two.)

A. Instance routes have become more specific, creating network latency.

B. The operating system does not have the ixgbevf module installed.

C. The instance type does not support the Elastic Network Adapter (ENA) driver.

D. The instance or Amazon Machine Image (AMI) is no longer flagged for enhanced networking.

12. Your application is having a slower than expected transfer rate between application tiers. What is the best option for increasing throughput?

A. Use a single Network Load Balancer in front of each instance.

B. Enable Quality of Service (QoS).

C. Reduce the jitter in the network.

D. Increase the Maximum Transmission Unit (MTU).

13. Your company has an application that it would like to share with a business partner, but the performance of the application is business-critical. The network architects are discussing using AWS Direct Connect to increase performance. Which of the following are performance advantages of AWS Direct Connect compared to a Virtual Private Network (VPN) or Internet connectivity? (Choose three.)

A. Lower latency

B. Ability to use jumbo frames

C. Ability to configure Quality of Service (QoS) on the AWS Direct Connect provider's circuits

D. Lower egress costs

E. Ability to perform detailed monitoring of the AWS Direct Connect connections

14. What information is most efficient to determine whether a workload is CPU bound, bandwidth bound, or packets per second bound? (Choose four.)

    A. Amazon CloudWatch CPU metrics

    B. Packet captures

    C. Elastic network interface count

    D. Amazon CloudWatch network bytes metrics

    E. Amazon CloudWatch packets per second metrics

    F. Kernel version

    G. Host CPU information

15. Your organization is planning on connecting to AWS. The organization has decided to use a specific Virtual Private Network (VPN) technology for the first phase of the project. You are tasked with implementing the VPN server in a Virtual Private Cloud (VPC) and optimizing it for performance. What are important considerations for Amazon Elastic Compute Cloud (Amazon EC2) VPN performance? (Choose two.)

    A. The VPN instance should support enhanced networking.

    B. Because all VPN connections use the Virtual Private Gateway (VGW), it's important to scale the VGW horizontally.

    C. IP Security (IPsec) VPNs should use a Network Load Balancer to create a more scalable VPN service.

    D. Investigate packet per second limitations and bandwidth limitations.

16. Your research and development organization has created a mission-critical application that requires low latency and high bandwidth. The application needs to support AWS best practices for high availability. Which of the following is not a best practice for this application?

    A. Deploy the application behind a Network Load Balancer for scale and availability.

    B. Use a placement group for the application to guarantee the lowest latency possible.

    C. Enable enhanced networking on all instances.

    D. Deploy the application across multiple Availability Zones.

17. Your security department has mandated that all traffic leaving a Virtual Private Cloud (VPC) must go through a specialized security appliance. This security appliance runs on a bespoke operating system that users cannot access. What considerations are the most important for this operating system performance on AWS? (Choose two.)

    A. Driver support for the Intel Virtual Function and Elastic Network Adapter (ENA)

    B. Support for Amazon Linux

    C. Instance family and size support

    D. Domain Name System (DNS) resolution speed

18. Your company has deployed a bursty web application to AWS and would like to improve the user experience. It is important for only the web host to have the private key for Transport Layer Security (TLS), so the Classic Load Balancer has a listener on Transmission Control Protocol (TCP) port 443. What are some approaches that you can use to reduce latency and improve the scale-out process for the application?

    A. Use an Application Load Balancer in front of the application, enabling better utilization of multiple target groups with different HTTP paths and hosts.

    B. Configure enhanced networking on the Classic Load Balancer for lower latency load balancing.

    C. Use Amazon Certificate Manager (ACM) to distribute new certificates to Amazon CloudFront to accomplish handling content at the edge.

    D. Use a Network Load Balancer in front of your application to increase network performance.

19. You are in charge of creating a network architecture for a development group that is interested in running a real-time exchange on AWS. The participants of the exchange expect very low latency but do not operate on AWS. Which description most accurately describes the networking and security tradeoffs for potential network designs?

    A. Use AWS Direct Connect to connect to the exchange application. This allows for lower latency and native encryption but requires additional configuration to support multi-tenancy and agreements from participants.

    B. Configure a separate Virtual Private Network (VPN) connection on the Virtual Private Gateway (VGW) for each participant. This will allow individual scaling per participant and the lowest latency but requires customers to support VPN devices.

    C. Use AWS Direct Connect to connect to the exchange application. This allows for more control of the latency, but it requires organizing connectivity to each of the participants and provides no security guarantees.

    D. Allow participants to connect directly via the Internet. This allows for customers to come in freely but does not guarantee security. Latency can be managed with Transmission Control Protocol (TCP) tuning and network performance appliances.

20. Which statement about Maximum Transmission Units (MTUs) on AWS is true?

    A. MTUs define the maximum throughput on AWS.

    B. You must configure a Virtual Private Cloud (VPC) to support jumbo frames.

    C. You must configure a placement group to support jumbo frames.

    D. Increasing the MTU is most beneficial for applications limited by packets per second.

21. What is the advantage of the Data Plane Development Kit (DPDK) over enhanced networking?

    A. DPDK decreases the overhead of Hypervisor networking.

    B. Enhanced networking only increases bursting capacity, whereas DPDK increases steady-state performance.

    C. DPDK decreases operating system overhead for networking.

    D. DPDK allows deeper access to AWS infrastructure to enable new networking features that enhanced networking does not provide.

22. What is the optimal performance configuration to enable high-performance networking for an Amazon Elastic Compute Cloud (Amazon EC2) instance operating as a firewall?

    A. One elastic network interface for all traffic.

    B. One elastic network interface for management traffic and one elastic network interface for each subnet the firewall operates in.

    C. Configure as many elastic network interfaces as possible and use operating system routing to split traffic over all interfaces.

    D. None of the above.

23. Your team uses an application to receive information quickly from other parts of your infrastructure. It leverages low-latency multicast feeds to receive information from other applications and displays analysis. Which approach could help satisfy the application's low latency requirements in AWS?

    A. Maintain the same multicast groups in AWS because the application will work in a Virtual Private Cloud (VPC).

    B. Work with the application owners to find another delivery system such as a message queue or broker. Place the applications in a placement group for low latency.

    C. Move the multicast application to AWS and enable enhanced networking. Configure the other applications to send their multicast feed to the application over AWS Direct Connect.

    D. Use the VPC routing table to route 224.0.0.0/8 traffic to the instance elastic network interface. Enable enhanced networking and jumbo frames for low latency and high throughput.

24. What is bandwidth?

    A. Bandwidth is the number of bits that an instance can store in memory over a network.

    B. Bandwidth is the amount of data transferred from one point in the network to another point.

    C. Bandwidth is a measurement of the largest capacity of handling network traffic in any given path in a network.

    D. Bandwidth is the maximum data transfer rate at any point in the network.

25. Why does User Datagram Protocol (UDP) react to performance characteristics differently than Transmission Control Protocol (TCP)?

    A. UDP requires more packet overhead than TCP.

    B. UDP supports less resilient applications.

    C. UDP is not a stateful protocol, so it reacts differently to latency and jitter.

    D. UDP lacks traffic congestion awareness.

Chapter 10

Automation

THE AWS CERTIFIED ADVANCED NETWORKING – SPECIALTY EXAM OBJECTIVES COVERED IN THIS CHAPTER MAY INCLUDE, BUT ARE NOT LIMITED TO, THE FOLLOWING:

Domain 2.0: Design and Implement AWS Networks

- ✓ **2.1 Apply AWS networking concepts**
- ✓ **2.2 Given customer requirements, define network architectures on AWS**
- ✓ **2.3 Propose optimized designs based on the evaluation of an existing implementation**
- ✓ **2.5 Derive an appropriate architecture based on customer and application requirements**

Domain 3.0: Automate AWS Tasks

- ✓ **3.1 Evaluate automation alternatives within AWS for network deployments**
- ✓ **3.2 Evaluate tool-based alternatives within AWS for network operations and management**

Introduction to Network Automation

Making a change in a physical network requires human effort: coordinating the schedules of multiple individuals, interrupting other business activities, and generally slowing down the pace of innovation in an organization. Doing this repeatedly, at scale, becomes a tedious exercise, and human errors become increasingly likely. Moreover, when you want to test out a new idea, the best practice is to use a test environment that mirrors the production environment as closely as possible, but replicating a physical network is an expensive proposition.

An *Amazon Virtual Private Cloud (Amazon VPC)*, however, is a flexible, software-defined network. Creating a subnet, changing routing rules on an existing subnet, adding and removing gateways, and more are all programmatic actions without human involvement. Tasks that were once infeasible suddenly become tractable: You can go from making a few changes each month to a few changes each day. That said, it is important to make the process repeatable and testable; otherwise, because each change carries risk with it, your network infrastructure will quickly become chaotic.

This chapter covers the services needed to automate the deployment, management, and monitoring of your network infrastructure within AWS.

Infrastructure as Code

An increasingly common practice for creating reusable infrastructure is to describe it in a programmatic document. This document can be stored in a source control system and deployed through a *continuous delivery* pipeline.

AWS CloudFormation provides an easy way to create and manage a collection of related AWS resources. An *AWS CloudFormation template* is a text document in JavaScript Object Notation (JSON) or Yet Another Markup Language (YAML) format that provides a blueprint that can be used and reused to instantiate one or more *stacks*.

Unlike traditional programming or scripting languages, an AWS CloudFormation template specifies the end state of a stack—not the actions needed to get to that state. You specify what resources are required and properties for each resource instead of Application Programming Interface (API) calls like `CreateVPC` or `ModifySubnetAttribute`. Resources can depend on other resources; for example, a subnet can reside within a VPC that is specified in the same template. AWS CloudFormation rationalizes the proper order for creating or deleting these automatically.

These templates can be stored in a repository such as *AWS CodeCommit* or GitHub. These are managed Git repositories that provide backups, visual displays of code changes, and strong authentication and authorization controls. These also provide the hooks required for an *AWS CodePipeline* to deploy the changes automatically to your environments. Typically, you will set up a pipeline to watch your repository, initiate a stack update to a test environment, run tests on the test environment, and then, if everything passes, send the stack update through to the production environment, perhaps with an approval step to allow a human to review or schedule the changes. This helps improve the agility of your organization by keeping the code, test environment, and production environment synchronized, and it helps improve the quality of the infrastructure by running automated tests.

Templates and Stacks

To get started, you will create a minimal template that describes just a VPC in the us-west-2 region with a Classless Inter-Domain Routing (CIDR) range of 10.17.0.0/16. This template might look like the following using the YAML format:

```
AWSTemplateFormatVersion: "2010-09-09"
Description: VPC in Oregon
Resources:
  MyVPC:
    Type: AWS::EC2::VPC
    Properties:
      CidrBlock: "10.17.0.0/16"
      InstanceTenancy: default
      Tags:
        - Key: Name
          Value: MyVPC
        - Key: Environment
          Value: Testing
```

There are a few elements to call out in this example:

- `AWSTemplateFormatVersion` specifies which version of the template language was used. Currently, `"2010-09-09"` is the only valid value. Should the language ever require a backward-incompatible change, this field would be used to disambiguate how to interpret your template.
- All resources go into the `Resources` section of the template.
- In YAML, structure is identified by indentation. For example, `MyVPC` is a block within the Resources block, while `Resources` and `Description` are sibling blocks. If a block contains `key: value` pairs, it is a mapping; if it contains `- value` items (that is, values prefixed with a dash and space), it is a list.

- Each resource has a *logical name*. In this case, we gave the VPC the logical name of `MyVPC`.
- The type of the resource is specified within the `Type` field. `AWS::EC2::VPC` specifies a VPC. The *AWS CloudFormation User Guide* lists the valid resource types here:

  `https://docs.aws.amazon.com/AWSCloudFormation/latest/UserGuide/aws-template-resource-type-ref.html`
- The resource-specific properties are always within the `Properties` block.
  - `CidrBlock` is required and specifies the CIDR block for MyVPC.
  - `InstanceTenancy` specifies the tenancy (default or dedicated) for new Amazon Elastic Compute Cloud (Amazon EC2) instances launched within MyVPC. This parameter is optional.
  - `Tags` is a list of tags to apply to the VPC. Each tag is a mapping with `Key` specifying the tag name and `Value` specifying the tag value. In this example, tags have been specified for `Name` and `Environment` keys.
  - We have omitted the other optional properties—`EnableDnsSupport`, `EnableDnsHostnames`, and `Tags`.

The template can be saved locally or to an Amazon Simple Storage Service (Amazon S3) bucket. In this example, you will save it locally with the filename `my-network-template.yaml`.

Templates can be up to 450 KB in size. However, templates larger than 50 KB must be uploaded to Amazon S3.

To instantiate the template, create a stack using either the AWS CloudFormation console or AWS Command Line Interface (CLI). Using the CLI, the process would be as follows:

```
> aws cloudformation create-stack --stack-name MyNetworkStack --template-body
file://my-network-template.yaml
{
    "StackId": "arn:aws:cloudformation:us-west-
2:123456789012:stack/MyNetworkStack/4af622f0-8a24-11e7-8692-503ac9ec2435"
}
```

AWS CloudFormation will start creating your stack. You can watch its progress by calling the `DescribeStack` API. While it is being created, the output will look like this:

```
> aws cloudformation describe-stack --stack-name MyNetworkStack
{
    "Stacks": [
        {
            "StackId": "arn:aws:cloudformation:us-west-
2:123456789012:stack/MyNetworkStack/4af622f0-8a24-11e7-8692-503ac9ec2435",
```

```
            "Description": "VPC in Oregon",
            "Tags": [],
            "CreationTime": "2012-09-18T12:00:00.102Z",
            "StackName": "MyNetworkStack",
            "NotificationARNs": [],
            "StackStatus": "CREATE_IN_PROGRESS",
            "DisableRollback": false
        }
    ]
}
```

When the stack creation process has finished, CREATE_IN_PROGRESS will change to CREATE_COMPLETE. You can verify that the VPC has been created by calling DescribeVpcs:

```
> aws ec2 describe-vpcs --filters "Name=tag:Name,Values=MyVPC"
{
    "Vpcs": [
        {
            "VpcId": "vpc-1a2b3c4d",
            "InstanceTenancy": "default",
            "Tags": [
                {
                    "Value": "arn:aws:cloudformation:us-west-
2:123456789012:stack/MyNetworkStack/4af622f0-8a24-11e7-8692-503ac9ec2435",
                    "Key": "aws:cloudformation:stack-id"
                },
                {
                    "Value": "MyVPC",
                    "Key": "aws:cloudformation:logical-id"
                },
                {
                    "Value": "MyVPC",
                    "Key": "Name"
                },
                {
                    "Value": "MyNetworkStack",
                    "Key": "aws:cloudformation:stack-name"
                },
                {
                    "Value": "Environment",
                    "Key": "Testing"
```

```
                }
            ],
            "State": "available",
            "DhcpOptionsId": "dopt-5e6f7a8b",
            "CidrBlock": "10.17.0.0/16",
            "IsDefault": false
        }
    ]
}
```

Note that AWS CloudFormation automatically applied three additional AWS-specific tags to the resource in addition to the `Name` tag. This can be useful for identifying resources in your account that are being managed by AWS CloudFormation. While you may be able to modify or delete these resources outside of AWS CloudFormation, this may impede the ability of AWS CloudFormation to manage these resources.

Stack Dependencies

The previous example does not create a usable VPC: It lacks subnets, a gateway, and routes that allow access to Amazon EC2 resources in the Amazon VPC. A minimally functional example is shown in Figure 10.1.

FIGURE 10.1 Minimal VPC with a single public subnet

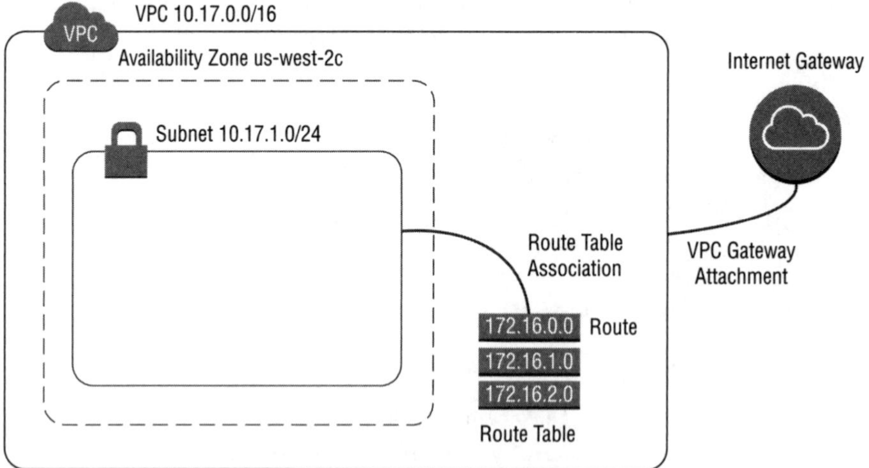

To create the subnet, you need to specify the Availability Zone, CIDR block, and VPC ID. The VPC is created elsewhere in the template, however, so you won't know the ID beforehand. You can use the `Ref` *intrinsic function* to obtain the value.

```
Resources:
  # VPC definition omitted
  MySubnet2c:
    Type: AWS::EC2::Subnet
    Properties:
      AvailabilityZone: us-west-2c
      CidrBlock: "10.17.1.0/24"
      Tags:
        - Key: Name
          Value: MySubnet2c
      VpcId: !Ref MyVPC
```

Because the subnet resource references a property from the VPC, AWS CloudFormation automatically recognizes the dependency and will not start creating the subnet until the VPC has been created.

The syntax for calling intrinsic functions in JSON is `{ "`*`function`*`": `*`value`*` }`. YAML, being a superset of JSON, can use this syntax as well; however, the shorthand directive syntax, `!`*`function value`*, is more common.

The route table also requires the VPC ID. Associating it with the subnet is done though a separate association resource that requires the subnet ID:

```
Resources:
  # Other resources omitted
  MyRouteTable:
    Type: AWS::EC2::RouteTable
    Properties:
      VpcId: !Ref MyVPC
  MySubnet2cRouteTableAssociation:
    Type: AWS::EC2::SubnetRouteTableAssociation
    Properties:
      RouteTableId: !Ref MyRouteTable
      SubnetId: !Ref MySubnet2c
```

The Internet gateway follows a similar pattern. Internet gateways are created and then attached to a VPC:

```
Resources:
  # Other resources omitted
  MyInternetGateway:
    Type: AWS::EC2::InternetGateway
```

```
  MyGatewayAttachment:
    Type: AWS::EC2::VPCGatewayAttachment
    Properties:
      InternetGatewayId: !Ref MyInternetGateway
      VpcId: !Ref MyVPC
```

Lastly, you need to create the default route through the Internet gateway.

```
Resources:
  # Other resources omitted
  MyDefaultRoute:
    Type: AWS::EC2::Route
    DependsOn: MyGatewayAttachment
    Properties:
      DestinationCidrBlock: "0.0.0.0/0"
      GatewayId: !Ref MyInternetGateway
      RouteTableId: !Ref MyRouteTable
```

Note the use of the DependsOn attribute. This instructs AWS CloudFormation to wait until the gateway has been attached to the VPC before creating this route. Without this attribute, AWS CloudFormation may attempt to create the route before the Internet gateway has been attached to the VPC, creating a race condition. Routes cannot refer to gateways that are not attached to the same VPC in which the route table resides.

The `Ref` function returns the physical resource ID for a resource, such as a VPC or subnet ID. You may want to use other attributes of a resource, however, such as the default network Access Control List (ACL) for a VPC. For these attributes, use the `GetAtt` intrinsic function: `!GetAtt MyVPC.DefaultNetworkAcl`. A list of the available attributes can be found in the Intrinsic Function Reference section of the AWS CloudFormation User Guide.

The full template is shown here.

```
AWSTemplateFormatVersion: "2010-09-09"
Description: VPC in Oregon
Resources:
  MyVPC:
    Type: AWS::EC2::VPC
    Properties:
      CidrBlock: "10.17.0.0/16"
      InstanceTenancy: default
      Tags:
        - Key: Name
          Value: MyVPC
```

```
        - Key: Environment
          Value: Testing
  MySubnet2c:
    Type: AWS::EC2::Subnet
    Properties:
      AvailabilityZone: us-west-2c
      CidrBlock: "10.17.1.0/24"
      Tags:
        - Key: Name
          Value: MySubnet2c
      VpcId: !Ref MyVPC
  MyRouteTable:
    Type: AWS::EC2::RouteTable
    Properties:
      VpcId: !Ref MyVPC
  MySubnet2cRouteTableAssociation:
    Type: AWS::EC2::SubnetRouteTableAssociation
    Properties:
      RouteTableId: !Ref MyRouteTable
      SubnetId: !Ref MySubnet2c
  MyInternetGateway:
    Type: AWS::EC2::InternetGateway
  MyGatewayAttachment:
    Type: AWS::EC2::VPCGatewayAttachment
    Properties:
      InternetGatewayId: !Ref MyInternetGateway
      VpcId: !Ref MyVPC
  MyDefaultRoute:
    Type: AWS::EC2::Route
    DependsOn: MyGatewayAttachment
    Properties:
      DestinationCidrBlock: "0.0.0.0/0"
      GatewayId: !Ref MyInternetGateway
      RouteTableId: !Ref MyRouteTable
```

To add these new resources to the existing stack, you call the `UpdateStack` API:

```
> aws cloudformation update-stack --stack-name MyNetworkStack --template-body
file://my-network-template.yaml
{
    "StackId": "arn:aws:cloudformation:us-west-
2:123456789012:stack/MyNetworkStack/4af622f0-8a24-11e7-8692-503ac9ec2435"
}
```

Errors and Rollbacks

There are two classes of errors that can occur in a template: validation errors and semantic errors. A *validation error* is when AWS CloudFormation cannot parse the template. Forgetting a closing quotation mark, misspelling `Resources` as `Resuorces`, specifying an Amazon S3 URL that you do not have permission to access, and incorrectly indenting a YAML file are all examples of validation errors. AWS CloudFormation immediately returns an error when you attempt to call `CreateStack` or `UpdateStack` in the presence of a validation error, and the call is aborted before any operations proceed:

```
> aws cloudformation create-stack --stack-name MyNetworkStack --template-body
file://my-network-template.yaml

An error occurred (ValidationError) when calling the CreateStack operation:
Invalid template property or properties [Resuorces]
```

A *semantic error*, on the other hand, is not detected until the resource is created or updated. This happens when AWS CloudFormation attempts to invoke an underlying API on your behalf, but that API call returns an error. When this happens, AWS CloudFormation stops the creation or update process and (by default) attempts to roll back the stack to the previous state. For example, when you omit the `DependsOn` attribute for the route resource in the previous example, you can see the stack go through the `UPDATE_IN_PROGRESS`, `UPDATE_ROLLBACK_IN_PROGRESS`, and finally the `UPDATE_ROLLBACK_COMPLETE` states by using either the AWS Management Console (as shown in Figure 10.2) or by calling the `DescribeStacks` API from the command line.

FIGURE 10.2 The stack state in the AWS Management Console when the stack has been rolled back

	Stack Name	Created Time	Updated Time	Status
▢	MyNetworkStack	2017-08-27 14	2017-08-27	UPDATE_ROLLBACK_COMPLETE

```
> aws cloudformation update-stack --stack-name MyNetworkStack --template-body
file://bad-network-template.yaml
{
    "StackId": "arn:aws:cloudformation:us-west-
2:1234567890:stack/MyNetworkStack/48b718d0-8b6b-11e7-a582-503f20f2ade6"
}

> aws cloudformation describe-stacks --stack-name MyNetworkStack
{
    "Stacks": [
        {
```

```
            lines omitted for brevity
            "StackStatusReason": "The following resource(s) failed to create:
[MyDefaultRoute, MyGatewayAttachment, MySubnet2cRouteTableAssociation]. ",
            "StackStatus": "UPDATE_ROLLBACK_IN_PROGRESS",
            "DisableRollback": false,
        }
    ]
}
```

To find the reason for the failure, you would look at the stack events. This would typically be done by going to the AWS CloudFormation console, selecting the stack, and clicking on the events tab to view the errors, as shown in Figure 10.3.

FIGURE 10.3 The stack events showing the route failed to create because it could not reference the Internet gateway

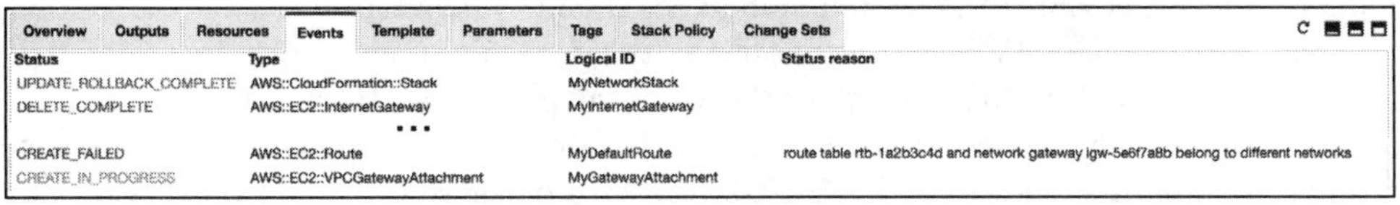

Overview | Outputs | Resources | Events | Template | Parameters | Tags | Stack Policy | Change Sets

Status	Type	Logical ID	Status reason
UPDATE_ROLLBACK_COMPLETE	AWS::CloudFormation::Stack	MyNetworkStack	
DELETE_COMPLETE	AWS::EC2::InternetGateway	MyInternetGateway	
	...		
CREATE_FAILED	AWS::EC2::Route	MyDefaultRoute	route table rtb-1a2b3c4d and network gateway igw-5e6f7a8b belong to different networks
CREATE_IN_PROGRESS	AWS::EC2::VPCGatewayAttachment	MyGatewayAttachment	

For programmatic use, the `DescribeStackEvents` API can also be used.

Template Parameters

The template that you have designed hard codes all of the values for your resources. To be able to reuse the template, you will want to customize resource properties such as the subnet Availability Zone and CIDR ranges. While you could edit the template for each stack that you create, this kind of customization makes it difficult to roll out new changes from a centralized team because each customized template must have the patches applied manually.

Template *parameters* allow users to specify values at stack creation or update time. They are provided in a `Parameters` block.

```
Parameters:
  VPCCIDR:
    Type: String
    Default: "10.17.0.0/16"
    Description: The CIDR range to assign to the VPC.
    AllowedPattern: "[0-9]{1,3}\\.[0-9]{1,3}\\.[0-9]{1,3}\\.[0-9]{1,3}/[0-9]
{1,2}"
    ConstraintDescription: An IPv4 block in CIDR notation is required, e.g.
10.17.0.0/16
```

```
  SubnetAZ:
    Type: AWS::EC2::AvailabilityZone::Name
    Default: us-west-2c
    Description: The availability zone to assign to the subnet.
  SubnetCIDR:
    Type: String
    Default: "10.17.0.0/16"
    Description: The CIDR range to assign to the subnet.
    AllowedPattern: "[0-9]{1,3}\\.[0-9]{1,3}\\.[0-9]{1,3}\\.[0-9]{1,3}/[0-9]
{1,2}"
    ConstraintDescription: An IPv4 block in CIDR notation is required, e.g.
10.17.1.0/24
```

Each parameter must specify a type. Basic types are `String`, `Number` (which can be an integer or floating-point number), `CommaDelimitedList` (a list of strings separated by commas), and `List<Number>` (a list of numbers separated by commas).

In addition, there are AWS-specific parameter types, such as the `AWS::EC2::AvailabilityZone::Name` for the `SubnetAZ` parameter. In the AWS CloudFormation user interface, these are rendered as drop-down menus to make it easier to specify valid inputs, as shown in Figure 10.4. A full list of the valid AWS-specific types can be found in the AWS CloudFormation User Guide.

FIGURE 10.4 Parameters for the single public subnet template with the Availability Zone drop-down menu

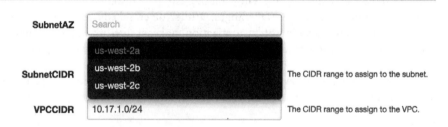

The `Description` field is optional but highly recommended; it is displayed alongside the parameter to help guide the user. `Default` is also optional; having reasonable default values assists new users who are trying your template for the first time.

There are additional fields that allow you to verify user input before changes to the stack are made. The previous example uses `AllowedPattern`, which specifies a regular expression against which the user input is matched. `ConstraintDescription` is text that is displayed to the user if the verification fails. Other verification fields are `MinLength` and `MaxLength` for strings and `MinValue` and `MaxValue` for numbers. Without these validations, the user must wait for a stack creation or update operation to fail and attempt to find the issue in the events.

A detailed discussion of the valid regular expression syntax is available in the Java API documentation on the Pattern class at:

`https://docs.oracle.com/javase/7/docs/api/java/util/regex/Pattern.html`

Note that backslashes in both JSON and YAML must be doubled because they interpret a backslash as an escape sequence. The `\.` is regular expression syntax for a literal period, whereas the `\\.` is how this is specified in JSON or YAML.

To use the parameters user interface for the first time, upload the template from the AWS CloudFormation console.

Using parameters within the template uses the `Ref` intrinsic function introduced earlier. Using parameters for the VPC and subnet resource properties would look like the following listing:

```
MyVPC:
    Type: AWS::EC2::VPC
    Properties:
      CidrBlock: !Ref VPCCIDR
      InstanceTenancy: default
      Tags:
        - Key: Name
          Value: MyVPC
        - Key: Environment
          Value: Testing
  MySubnet2c:
    Type: AWS::EC2::Subnet
    Properties:
      AvailabilityZone: !Ref SubnetAZ
      CidrBlock: !Ref SubnetCIDR
      Tags:
        - Key: Name
          Value: MySubnet2c
      VpcId: !Ref MyVPC
```

It is also possible to specify parameters through the API. This is useful for programmatically specifying the parameters. When updating a stack, you have the option of specifying a new value or instructing AWS CloudFormation to use the previous value. For example, the following would update the Availability Zone and CIDR range of the subnet while keeping the VPC CIDR range intact:

```
> aws cloudformation update-stack --stack-name MyNetworkStack --use-previous-
template --parameters ParameterKey=VPCCIDR,UsePreviousValue=true
ParameterKey=SubnetCIDR,ParameterValue=10.17.2.0/24
ParameterKey=SubnetAZ,ParameterValue=us-west-2b
```

```
{
    "StackId": "arn:aws:cloudformation:us-west-
2:123456789012:stack/MyNetworkStack/48b718d0-8b6b-11e7-a582-503f20f2ade6"
}
```

Verifying Changes with Change Sets

Manually calculating the changes being made when a stack is updated can be difficult. For example, VPC and subnet CIDR ranges are immutable. What might seem like a small change, such as narrowing a CIDR range from /24 to /26, would actually require building a new subnet, re-creating any Amazon EC2 instances in the new subnet, terminating the instances from the old subnet, and deleting the old subnet—a potentially disruptive change. The AWS CloudFormation User Guide lists the impact of each parameter change, but it can be easy to miss a detail in a larger template.

Change sets allow you to visualize and approve a proposed change to a stack before it is updated. From the AWS CloudFormation console, select the stack and then click on Actions and Create Change Set for Current Stack, as shown in Figure 10.5.

FIGURE 10.5 Creating a change set for an existing stack

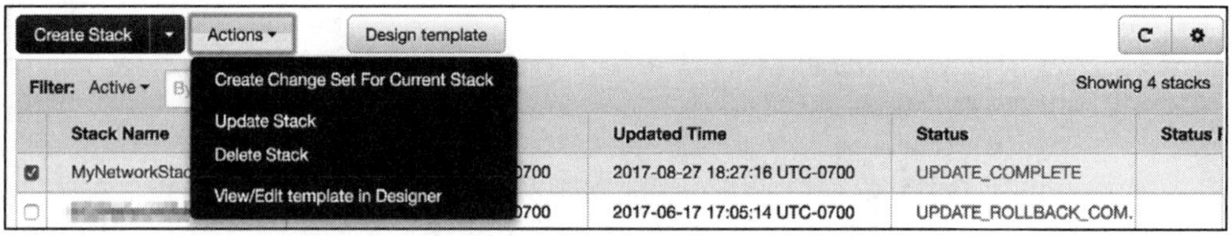

After specifying a change set name and giving a new value for the subnet CIDR range, you can examine the changes, as shown in Figure 10.6. Note that the Replacement value for the subnet resource is True, indicating that a new subnet will be created and the old one deleted.

FIGURE 10.6 Examining the changes that would result by narrowing the CIDR range

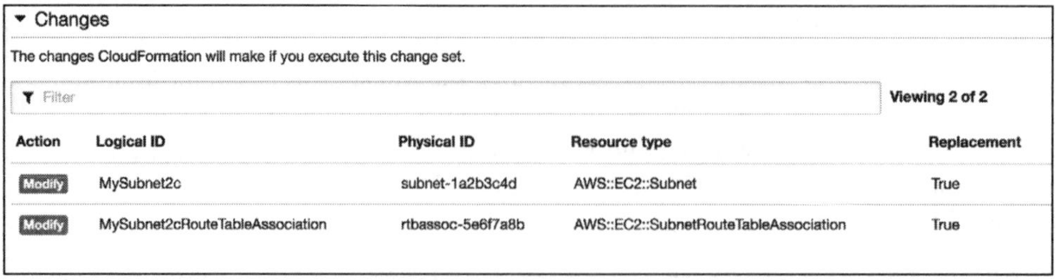

▾ Changes

The changes CloudFormation will make if you execute this change set.

Filter — Viewing 2 of 2

Action	Logical ID	Physical ID	Resource type	Replacement
Modify	MySubnet2c	subnet-1a2b3c4d	AWS::EC2::Subnet	True
Modify	MySubnet2cRouteTableAssociation	rtbassoc-5e6f7a8b	AWS::EC2::SubnetRouteTableAssociation	True

To execute the change set, you can click on the Execute button in the upper-right corner. On the other hand, if you elect not to accept the changes, you can delete the change set by clicking on Other Actions and then Delete.

When updating a stack using the AWS CloudFormation user interface, the review screen automatically creates and displays a change set for the update operation.

Retaining Resources

When you delete a stack, AWS CloudFormation deletes all associated resources by default. You might prefer to retain the resources instead, however. For example, you might instruct a new user to create a stack from a template for a new account to ensure that all networking resources are created. After this is done, the user might want to remove the stack so that it is no longer visible in the AWS Management Console. You have to be able to remove the stack but keep the resulting network configuration.

In the template, you can specify which resources to retain by adding a `DeletionPolicy` attribute with a value of `Retain`. This must be applied to each resource. For example, the following would retain the VPC created by the template.

```
Resources:
  MyVPC:
    Type: AWS::EC2::VPC
    DeletionPolicy: Retain
    Properties:
      CidrBlock: !Ref VPCCIDR
      InstanceTenancy: default
      Tags:
        - Key: Name
          Value: MyVPC
        - Key: Environment
          Value: Testing
```

Configuring Non-AWS Resources

AWS CloudFormation supports almost all AWS Cloud services available. You may also want to configure non-AWS resources when creating or updating a stack.

For example, consider the case of setting up a VPC with only a private subnet connected back to an on-premises network through a VPN, as shown in Figure 10.7. You can configure the VPN gateway, customer gateway, and VPN connection directly through AWS CloudFormation. The on-premises router will require custom configuration that AWS CloudFormation cannot perform natively, however.

FIGURE 10.7 A VPC with a private subnet connected to an on-premises network via a VPN.

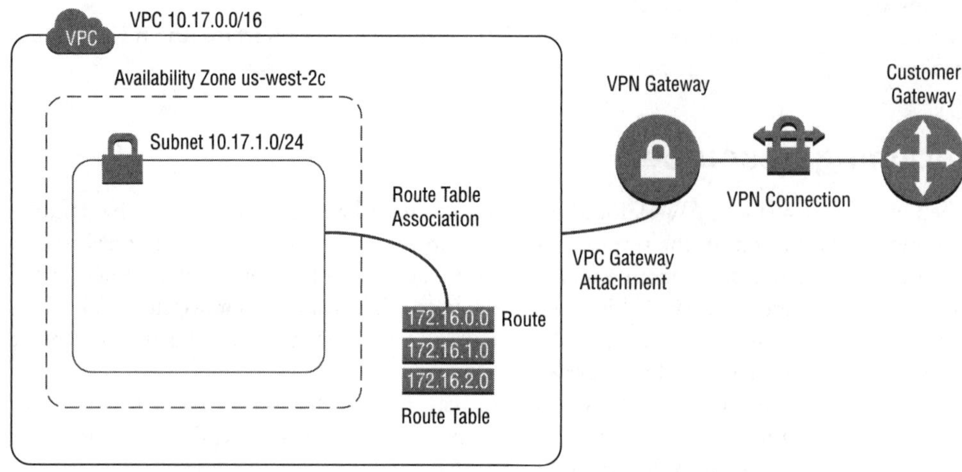

Custom resources allow us to bridge this gap. Within a template, a custom resource is a resource of type `AWS::CloudFormation::CustomResource` or any type in the form `Custom::`*ResourceType*. When a custom resource is created, updated, or deleted, AWS CloudFormation sends a notification to an Amazon Simple Notification Service (Amazon SNS) topic or invokes an AWS Lambda function. Within the event, AWS CloudFormation provides the following properties:

- `LogicalResourceId`: The name of the resource in the stack (for example, MyVPC for the VPC in the previous example).
- `OldResourceProperties`: The previous user-specified properties during an update operation.
- `PhysicalResourceId`: The physical resource ID returned by an earlier invocation of your function. This is provided for update and delete requests only.
- `RequestId`: A unique ID for the request.
- `RequestType`: `Create`, `Update`, or `Delete`.
- `ResourceType`: The type specified for the resource.
- `ResourceProperties`: The user-specified properties for the resource.
- `ResponseURL`: A pre-signed Amazon S3 URL to which your code must write output.
- `StackId`: The AWS CloudFormation stack Amazon Resource Name (ARN).

AWS CloudFormation then waits for your code to `PUT` output to the pre-signed Amazon S3 URL. The body of this object is a JSON mapping object with the following attributes:

- `LogicalResourceId: The LogicalResourceId from the request event.`
- `Status`: Whether the custom resource operation was successful (`SUCCESS`) or if it failed (`FAILED`)

- `Reason`: If the request failed, this describes the reason for the failure.
- `PhysicalResourceId`: If the request was successful, this is an identifier specific to your function.
- `RequestId`: The `RequestId` from the request event.
- `StackId`: The `StackId` from the request event.
- `Data`: If the request was successful, this property contains a mapping of arbitrary key-value attributes that can be retrieved using the `GetAtt` intrinsic function.

To configure a VPN for a router, for example, you could use an AWS Lambda function written in Python that uses the Paramiko library `http://www.paramiko.org/` to use Secure Shell (SSH) to access the router and execute router commands.

Security Best Practices

In the previous examples, we have not specified what permissions AWS CloudFormation should have when performing operations. In this case, AWS CloudFormation uses a temporary session created from your credentials when you create or update the stack. If you have administrative permissions, for example, then AWS CloudFormation will also have administrative permissions when executing a stack operation.

A better practice is to limit the permissions to the least privilege necessary for stack management. To do this, you can create an AWS Identity and Access Management (IAM) *service role* that specifies the calls that AWS CloudFormation can make. This role remains associated with the stack for all future operations. This can be used to avoid granting excessive permissions to end users. For example, a user may not have the expertise required to set up a VPN for a VPC; having them attempt this directly may cause disruption to your organization's network operations. Instead, you can allow them to use and update an AWS CloudFormation stack from a template using the service role.

If a template includes certain IAM resources, AWS CloudFormation requires you to acknowledge this when creating or updating the stack. You do this by passing the *capabilities* flag `CAPABILITIES_IAM` or `CAPABILITIES_NAMED_IAM` (if the resources have custom names).

To prevent a stack from accidental deletion, stack termination protection can be enabled. To prevent specific resources within a stack from accidentally being replaced, modified, or deleted, you can designate them as protected resources by attaching a stack policy to the stack. For example, the following *stack policy* prevents the VPC and subnet from the earlier example from being replaced.

```
{
    "Statement": [
        {
            "Effect": "Allow",
            "Action": "*",
            "Principal": "*",
```

```
            "Resource": "*"
        },
        {
            "Effect": "Deny",
            "Action": "Update:Replace",
            "Principal": "*",
            "Resource": ["LogicalResourceId/MyVPC",
                         "LogicalResourceId/MySubnet"]
        }
    ]
}
```

For the exam, you should be familiar with AWS CloudFormation concepts, including templates, stacks, native AWS resources types related to networking, custom resources, and change sets.

Configuration Management

Using a local file system to store templates might work for a small organization with a single administrator, but it quickly stops scaling beyond that point. A *version control system* for checking in the resulting templates is a must. Modern systems such as Git (`https://git-scm.com/`) are robust yet lightweight enough for even a single administrator to use.

If your organization already has a version control system in place, this can be used to store your AWS CloudFormation templates. Otherwise, you can use AWS CodeCommit to create a Git repository for your template. The AWS CodeCommit User Guide at `http://docs.aws.amazon.com/codecommit/latest/userguide/welcome.html` has tutorials at `http://docs.aws.amazon.com/codecommit/latest/userguide/getting-started-topnode.html`, which guide you through creating a repository and using basic Git commands to interact with it.

Branches allow you and your collaborators to organize your code to avoid conflicts. For most infrastructure template projects, there will just be a single default branch named `master` by convention. If you were testing something risky such as upgrading an existing VPC to IPv6, you might create a separate `ipv6` branch, switch your development there, and create test stacks from it. When you are confident that the changes are correct, you can merge the `ipv6` branch back into the `master` branch.

Continuous Delivery

Keeping AWS CloudFormation templates and test and production stacks in sync is a tedious task if done manually. Many organizations require human review and approval before changes are applied to a production environment, but manually computing these changes is an error-prone process. AWS CodePipeline provides a way to automate the synchronization and change computation steps.

Pipeline Stages, Actions, and Artifacts

A *pipeline* is composed of *stages*. Each stage in a pipeline operates on a single revision at a time and performs one or more *actions*. Actions within a stage can execute sequentially or in parallel; all actions must complete successfully before the stage is considered complete. An output produced by an action is called an *artifact*. Some actions require inputs. These are artifacts from previous actions in the pipeline. Stages, actions, and artifacts are all named.

Actions belong to one of six categories: source, build, approval, deploy, invoke, or test. Following are brief explanations of these categories:

- Source actions watch a repository for new *revisions* and are the first actions in the pipeline. When a change is detected, AWS CodePipeline downloads the latest version of the source and initiates the remaining stages in the pipeline.
- Build actions compile source files into output files. You will not be using build actions in this guide.
- Approval actions send a message to an Amazon SNS topic and wait for a response before continuing.
- Deploy actions perform a deployment action. AWS CodePipeline supports a number of different deployment providers. We will focus exclusively on the AWS CloudFormation provider in this chapter.
- Invoke actions allow you to execute an AWS Lambda function to perform a custom action not otherwise shown. We will not be using invoke actions in this guide.
- Test actions allow you to execute a test against a deployed system using third-party test frameworks. We will not be using test actions in this guide.

A simple pipeline that watches an AWS CodeCommit repository for changes and then deploys them to AWS CloudFormation test and production stacks is shown in Figure 10.8. Note that there are three files in the repository: `template.yml`, containing the template itself, and two parameter files, `test-params.json` and `prod-params.json`, for the test and production stacks, respectively.

Approvals

Before deploying to production, your organization may require human review of the necessary changes. Typically, you will want to be able to see the actual changes that will be deployed before making an approval decision.

To do this, you typically separate the deployment into three separate actions. The first action is a deployment action that computes an AWS CloudFormation change set but does not execute it. The second action is an approval action, which sends a notification using *Amazon SNS*, and then waits for an approval signal. The third action is another deployment action that executes the AWS CloudFormation change set created by the first action.

FIGURE 10.8 AWS CodePipeline continuous deployment example

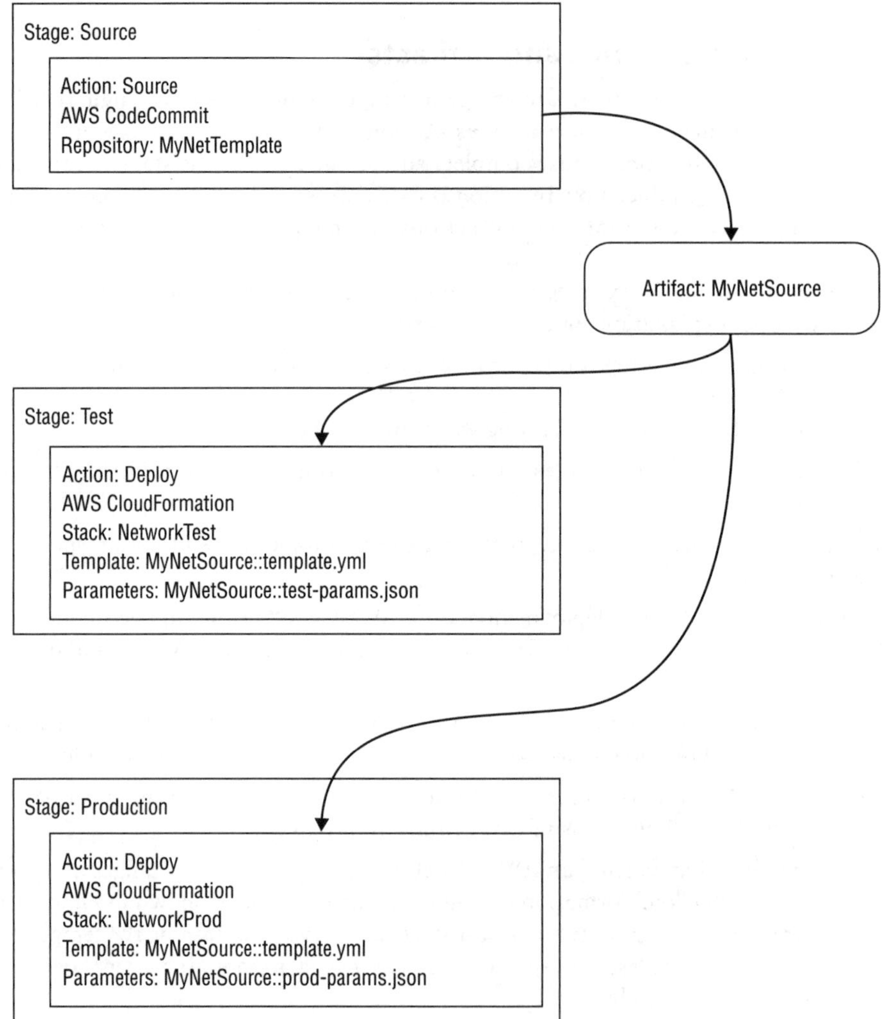

An Amazon SNS *topic* is a communications channel used to send messages and subscribe to notifications. It provides an access point for publishers and subscribers to communicate with each other. For manual approvals, the subscriber will be one or more email addresses that receive notifications from AWS CodePipeline that a pipeline change is ready to be approved or rejected.

Approvals can also be performed programmatically. This is useful, for example, if deployments are required to be performed during specified time windows or synchronized with other external events. In this case, the subscriber will typically be an application listening on an HTTP endpoint. When the conditions allow for the deployment to proceed, the application invokes the AWS CodePipeline `PutApprovalResult` API.

For the exam, you should be familiar with AWS CodePipeline, including configuring the source stage, deployment stages, and approval stages. You should also be familiar with the basics of version control; AWS CodeCommit is not required, but it can be helpful here.

Network Monitoring Tools

The network is a critical service that underlies practically every modern operation. Having reliable health metrics is essential to providing a robust, reliable service. When an issue does arise, tools and automation are key components in restoring normal operations.

Monitoring Network Health Metrics

Amazon CloudWatch allows you to collect *metrics* and log files, set alarms, and invoke actions in response to these alarms. Many of the metrics of interest are collected automatically. For example, you can view the state of VPN tunnels and connections by going to the Amazon CloudWatch console, clicking on Metrics, and browsing through the VPN service options. In Figure 10.9, we've plotted the state of a VPN connection and the two tunnels. After bringing the connection up, we briefly interrupted one of the tunnels on the connection and then restored it.

FIGURE 10.9 Amazon CloudWatch graph showing standard VPN metrics

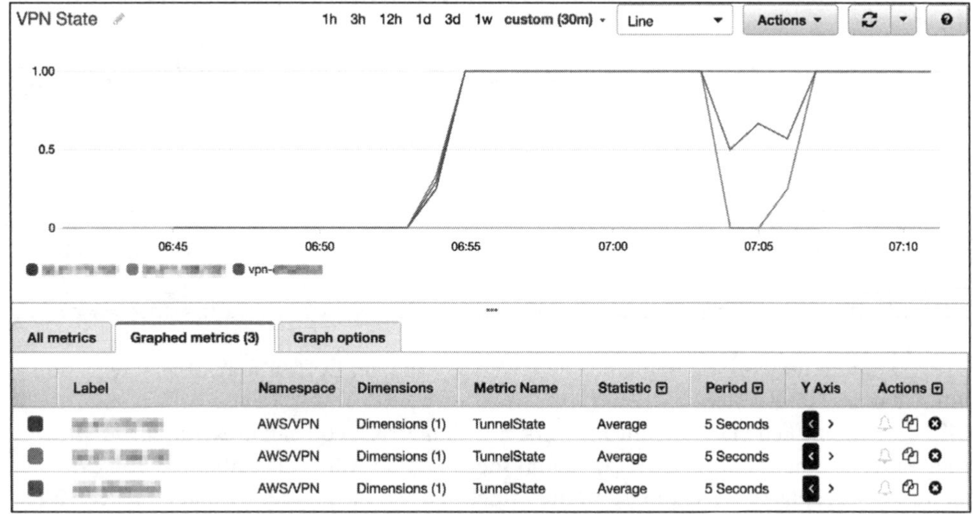

When graphing a metric, you can view different *statistics*, including minimum, maximum, average, and various percentile values. The sum statistic is all of the values submitted over a time period added together. This is typically used for calculating the total volume of a metric—for example, the number of bytes over a VPN tunnel.

You can also create custom metrics using either the AWS CLI or a Software Development Kit (SDK) for a programming language. Metrics belong to a *namespace*, which can be used to collect related metrics. Metrics are further subdivided by *dimensions*: up to 10 key/value pairs that contain additional information to identify the metric uniquely. For example, if you wanted to record the packet loss to a given host every 60 seconds, you might run this loop on a Linux host:

```
#!/bin/sh
remote_ip=192.0.2.17
ping_count=5

while true; do
  packet_loss=$(ping -c $ping_count $remote_ip | grep 'packet loss' | \
              sed -e 's/^.*received, //' -e 's/% packet loss.*//')
  Amazon CloudWatch put-metric-data --namespace NetOps \
    --metric-name PacketLoss --unit Percent --value "$packet_loss" \
    --dimensions RemoteIp="$remote_ip";
  sleep 60;
done;
```

From the Amazon CloudWatch console, you can then view graphs for these metrics. For example, Figure 10.10 shows the plot of packet loss to three hosts.

FIGURE 10.10 Amazon CloudWatch custom metrics showing packet loss to three different hosts

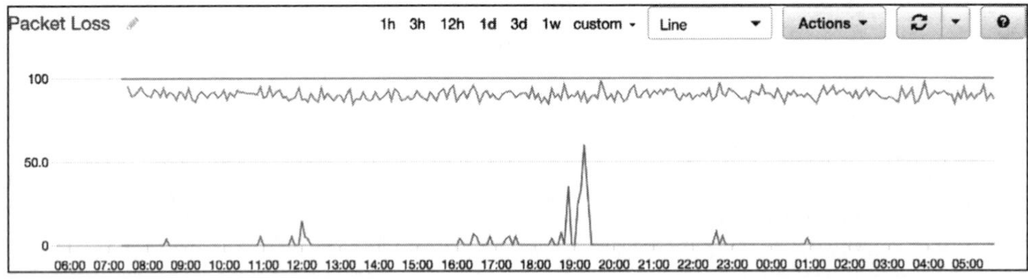

If you have a networking appliance deployed to Amazon EC2, it may offer integration with Amazon CloudWatch.

To create a unified view of your network health metrics, you can create a *dashboard*. From a metric graph, selection Actions, and then click on Add to Dashboard. You can add multiple graphs to a dashboard in line, stacked area, or number formats. Figure 10.11 shows a network health dashboard containing metrics about your VPN connection and the Amazon EC2 instances it serves within your VPC.

FIGURE 10.11 Amazon CloudWatch dashboard for a VPN connection

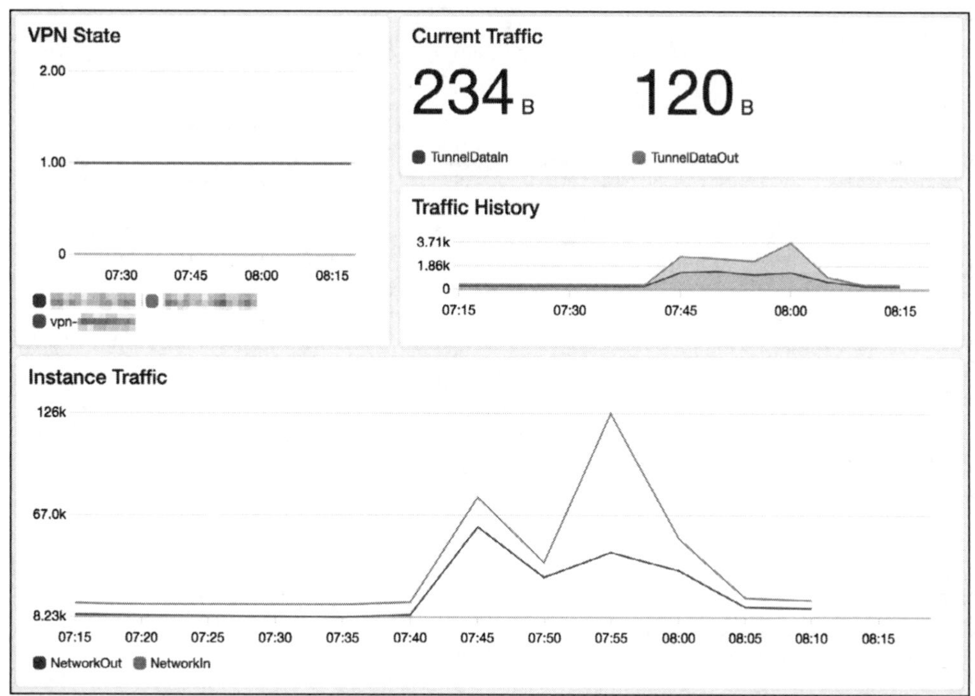

Creating Alarms for Unusual Events

While dashboards provide you with a view into the health of your network, you don't want to rely on someone monitoring the dashboard to maintain high availability. Amazon CloudWatch metrics can be used to create *alarms* that send alerts to an Amazon SNS topic. A topic can send notifications to subscribed email addresses, mobile phones (via SMS or mobile push), HTTP endpoints, AWS Lambda functions, and Amazon Simple Queue Service (Amazon SQS) queues.

To create an alarm, select the alarm bell icon next to a metric graph. You will see a wizard like the one shown in Figure 10.12. In this example, we've created a packet loss alarm to one of the endpoints and subscribed the PacketLoss topic to it.

The format of the alarm will vary in a way that is appropriate for the receiver. For example, Figure 10.13 shows the same alarm received over SMS and email for the packet loss metric.

FIGURE 10.12 Creating an alarm for a custom packet loss metric

Create Alarm
1. Select Metric
2. Define Alarm
Alarm Threshold
Provide the details and threshold for your alarm. Use the graph on the right to help set the appropriate threshold.
Name: PacketLoss
Description: Excessive packet loss detected
Whenever: PacketLoss
is: >= 35
for: 1 consecutive period(s)
Additional settings
Provide additional configuration for your alarm.
Treat missing data as: bad (breaching threshold)
Actions
Define what actions are taken when your alarm changes state.
Notification
Delete
Whenever this alarm: State is ALARM
Send notification to: PacketLoss
New list Enter list
This notification list is managed in the SNS console.
+ Notification
+ AutoScaling Action
+ EC2 Action
Alarm Preview
This alarm will trigger when the blue line goes up to or above the red line for a duration of 5 minutes
PacketLoss >= 35
40
30
20
10
0
9/14 05:00
9/14 06:00
9/14 07:00
9/14 08:00
Namespace: NetOps
RemoteIp: 192.0.2.20
Metric Name: PacketLoss
Period: 5 Minutes
Statistic: Standard Custom
Average
Cancel
Previous
Next
Create Alarm

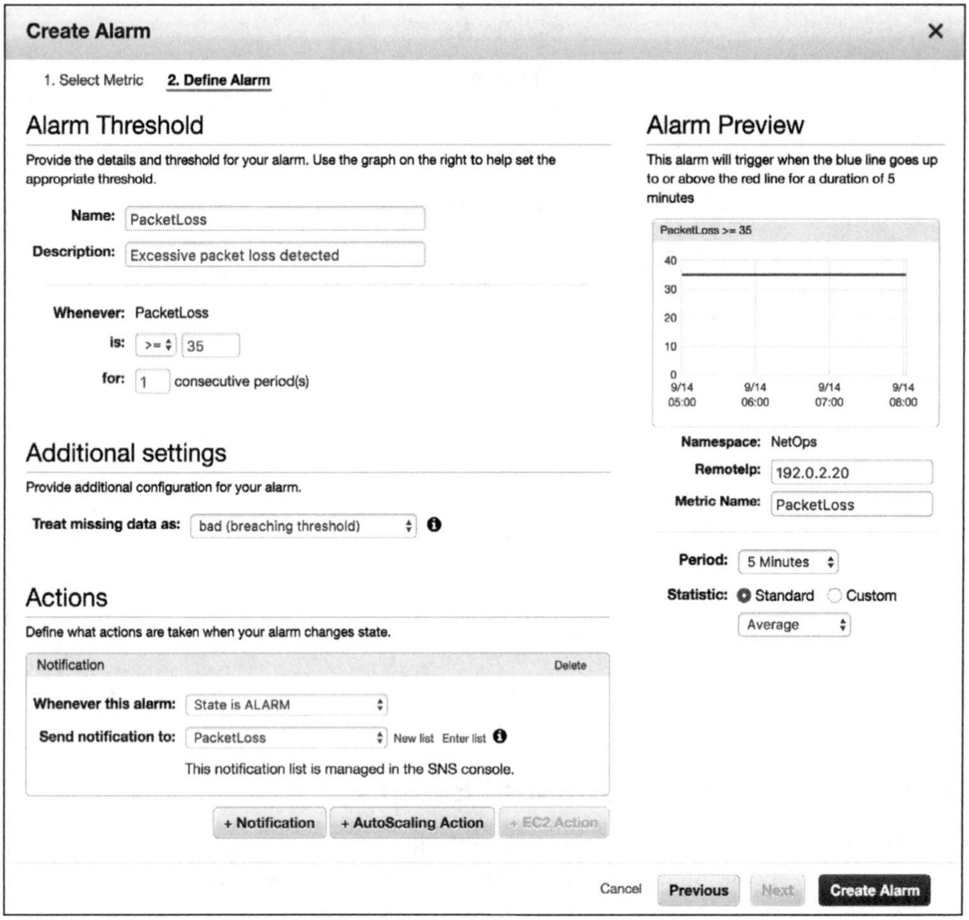

FIGURE 10.13 The format of the received alarm over SMS (left) and email (right)

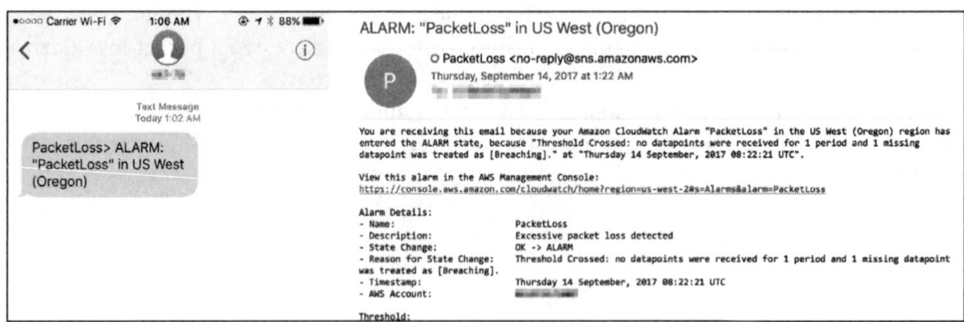

Carrier Wi-Fi
1:06 AM
88%
Text Message
Today 1:02 AM
PacketLoss> ALARM: "PacketLoss" in US West (Oregon)
ALARM: "PacketLoss" in US West (Oregon)
PacketLoss <no-reply@sns.amazonaws.com>
Thursday, September 14, 2017 at 1:22 AM
You are receiving this email because your Amazon CloudWatch Alarm "PacketLoss" in the US West (Oregon) region has entered the ALARM state, because "Threshold Crossed: no datapoints were received for 1 period and 1 missing datapoint was treated as [Breaching]." at "Thursday 14 September, 2017 08:22:21 UTC".
View this alarm in the AWS Management Console:
https://console.aws.amazon.com/cloudwatch/home?region=us-west-2#s=Alarms&alarm=PacketLoss
Alarm Details:
- Name: PacketLoss
- Description: Excessive packet loss detected
- State Change: OK -> ALARM
- Reason for State Change: Threshold Crossed: no datapoints were received for 1 period and 1 missing datapoint was treated as [Breaching].
- Timestamp: Thursday 14 September, 2017 08:22:21 UTC
- AWS Account:
Threshold:

Collecting Text Logs

Having a central repository such as *Amazon CloudWatch Logs* for collecting human-readable logs generated by applications and networking devices helps correlate events and can help reduce the time to recovery if a system failure occurs. Each *log event* is a record of some activity. Sequences of log events from the same source are stored in a *log stream*. Each log stream belongs to a *log group* that defines retention, monitoring, and access control policies.

For example, when you enable flow logs for a VPC, you specify a log group to which to send events. Within the log group, a log stream is created for each elastic network interface within the VPC. Here is a sample of a flow logs log stream.

```
2 123456789012 eni-a1b2c3d4 192.0.2.139 172.31.0.5 43160 1433 6 1 40 1504769338
1504769393 REJECT OK
2 123456789012 eni-a1b2c3d4 172.31.0.5 192.0.2.30 123 123 17 1 76 1504769338
1504769393 ACCEPT OK
2 123456789012 eni-a1b2c3d4 192.0.2.109 172.31.0.5 42481 1433 6 1 40 1504769399
1504769453 REJECT OK
2 123456789012 eni-a1b2c3d4 192.0.2.229 172.31.0.5 6000 1433 6 1 40 1504769399
1504769453 REJECT OK
2 123456789012 eni-a1b2c3d4 172.31.0.5 192.0.2.139 0 0 1 1 32 1504769399
1504769453 ACCEPT OK
2 123456789012 eni-a1b2c3d4 192.0.2.139 172.31.0.5 0 0 1 1 32 1504769399
1504769453 ACCEPT OK
```

The AWS CLI can be used to send log events to a log stream directly. For example, if you have a routing appliance running in Amazon EC2, you could use a script to write your own flow logs using a command such as this:

```
> aws logs create-log-stream --log-group-name FlowLogs \
  --log-stream-name router-1
> aws logs put-log-events --log-group-name FlowLogs \
  --log-stream-name router-1 \
  --log-events timestamp=1483228800000,message="2 123456789012 router-1
192.0.2.254 172.31.0.10 44178 80 6 1 1718 1483228800 1483228860 REJECT OK"
{
    "nextSequenceToken":
"49576537118627494925011401022786533057489097985223586498"
}
```

It's more likely that you will want to send an existing log file on the host directly to Amazon CloudWatch Logs, however. The CloudWatch Logs agent provides this functionality. On an Amazon EC2 instance running Amazon Linux, you can install this directly from the package repository.

```
> sudo yum install -y awslogs
Loaded plugins: priorities, update-motd, upgrade-helper
```

```
Resolving Dependencies
--> Running transaction check
---> Package awslogs.noarch 0:1.1.2-1.10.amzn1 will be installed
--> Finished Dependency Resolution
...
Installed:
  awslogs.noarch 0:1.1.2-1.10.amzn1

Complete!
> # Configure files to send to Amazon CloudWatch Logs
> sudo nano /etc/awslogs/awslogs.conf
> sudo service awslogs start
Starting awslogs:                                          [  OK  ]
> sudo chkconfig awslogs on
```

The default configuration file sends the `/var/log/messages` file to a log group also named `/var/log/messages` and uses the Amazon EC2 instance ID as the log stream name.

Converting Logs to Metrics

The text logs captured by Amazon CloudWatch Logs can be filtered and sent to another service for processing or storage. Services capable of receiving these logs are Amazon CloudWatch metrics, AWS Lambda, Amazon Kinesis Streams, and Amazon Elasticsearch.

For example, the following *metric filter* could be used to match all `REJECT` entries from a flow log.

```
[version, account_id, eni_id, src_ip, dst_ip, src_port, dst_port, protocol,
packets, bytes, start_time, end_time, action="REJECT", status]
```

Next, you can send this to Amazon CloudWatch as a metric. The fields that make sense would be either packets or bytes. Specify `$bytes` as the metric value when creating the metric filter.

When graphing the values, it's important to keep in mind how the values are being sent to Amazon CloudWatch as data points. For example, in the following abbreviated log stream (with byte values highlighted), there are six individual entries:

```
2 ... eni-a1b2c3d4 192.0.2.139 172.31.0.5 43160 443 6 2 80 ... REJECT OK
2 ... eni-a1b2c3d4 192.0.2.220 172.31.0.5 44792 443 6 1 40 ... REJECT OK
2 ... eni-a1b2c3d4 192.0.2.109 172.31.0.5 51482 443 6 1 40 ... REJECT OK
2 ... eni-a1b2c3d4 192.0.2.229 172.31.0.5 64809 443 6 1 40 ... REJECT OK
2 ... eni-a1b2c3d4 192.0.2.174 172.31.0.5 37829 443 6 1 40 ... REJECT OK
2 ... eni-a1b2c3d4 192.0.2.139 172.31.0.5 43161 443 6 2 80 ... REJECT OK
```

The total number of bytes transmitted in this window is 320. A common mistake is to try to graph the maximum value here (80), which just happens to be a host that attempted connections quickly enough to have two packets captured in a single entry. Instead, you need to graph the sum of the data points.

For the exam, you should know how to configure Amazon CloudWatch Logs filters and Amazon CloudWatch metrics. Knowledge of other subscribing services is helpful but not required.

Summary

In this chapter, you learned about the services needed to automate the deployment, management, and monitoring of AWS network components and infrastructure.

AWS CloudFormation allows you to create templates to deploy infrastructure as code. Templates can have parameters that allow them to be reused without hard coding values to create one or more stacks. You learned how AWS CloudFormation handles dependencies between resources within a template and how it rolls back a stack when errors are encountered during an update.

Custom resources allow you to manage non-AWS resources within a stack. A custom resource can invoke an AWS Lambda function to reconfigure an on-premises VPN acting as a customer gateway, for example.

Rather than computing stack changes manually, change sets provide an exact description of the actions AWS CloudFormation will take when creating or updating a stack. After being reviewed, change sets can be executed, ensuring that the actions taken are exactly those reviewed. If a stack has changed since the review, the change set will be rejected, ensuring updates never collide.

Continuous delivery is a methodology through which changes are automatically built, tested, and deployed to production. You learned how to create a pipeline within AWS CodePipeline to orchestrate a continuous delivery system. Within the pipeline, you configure actions within stages to deploy changes, compute change sets, or wait for change sets to be reviewed.

Amazon CloudWatch allows you to collect, visualize, and set alarm metrics on your network infrastructure. A metric can be viewed over various time periods and have statistics applied to it. Custom metrics can be used to show the health and performance of non-AWS resources or other details that are unique to your environment. Dashboards create a unified view of metrics to simplify operations.

Text logs can be collected by Amazon CloudWatch Logs. Beyond being a central log repository, log events can have metric filters applied and converted to metrics so that they can be graphed and trigger an alarm.

Exam Essentials

Understand AWS CloudFormation templates and stacks. An AWS CloudFormation template is a text document in JSON or YAML format that provides a blueprint for creating resources. Parameters can be supplied to make templates reusable. Templates are used to create or update stacks.

Understand how AWS CloudFormation handles dependencies and errors. An AWS CloudFormation template describes the end state of a stack. If resource A references resource B, AWS CloudFormation infers that A depends on B and will create it only after B has been created. You do not specify individual actions needed to get to this state.

If the template contains syntax errors, AWS CloudFormation will not create or update a stack with it, immediately failing these operations. If the errors are semantic, however, these are only detected by the underlying service when the resource is created or modified. When AWS CloudFormation encounters such an error, it rolls the stack back to its previous state.

Identify the purpose of AWS CloudFormation change sets and how they can improve change management. An AWS CloudFormation change set describes the actions that will be taken when a stack is created or updated. Computing these changes manually can be error-prone; using manual descriptions in a change management process may result in the actual change being different from what was approved. Change sets describe exactly what AWS CloudFormation will do and can be used to better understand the changes being deployed.

Know the purpose of custom resources. Custom resources in an AWS CloudFormation template allow you to configure non-AWS resources or resources not supported by AWS CloudFormation. In a networking context, these will typically be used to configure customer gateways for VPNs or an AWS Direct Connect virtual interface. You can also use custom resources to make calls to an IP Address Management (IPAM) service to allocate a CIDR block for a VPC.

Know how to retain essential resources after a stack is deleted. When an AWS CloudFormation stack is deleted, by default, all of the resources managed by it are also deleted. Resources that should not be deleted can override this behavior by having a `DeletionPolicy` property set to `Retain`.

Understand how to apply the principles of least privilege in the context of AWS CloudFormation stacks. AWS CloudFormation can use either the caller's permissions or an IAM service role to execute the actions necessary to perform stack actions. By using a service role, users can manipulate AWS CloudFormation stacks that require elevated privileges without granting these privileges to the users directly. Conversely, the service role can also restrict the actions that AWS CloudFormation can perform, preventing resources from being unexpectedly created, deleted, or modified if a template change was missed when being reviewed.

Understand the basic concepts of version control systems. You should be familiar with how to check out, edit, commit, and view the history of files being managed by a version control system. You should also understand how branches can allow you to make a series of experimental changes without affecting others.

Know how to implement a continuous delivery system for network infrastructure using AWS CodePipeline. AWS CodePipeline automatically detects changes to source files and can orchestrate infrastructure as code deployments with AWS CloudFormation.

Manual reviews can be improved and enforced by creating approval stages with AWS CloudFormation change sets to review.

Know how to graph metrics using Amazon CloudWatch and how to get different views of the underlying data. You should know how to use Amazon CloudWatch metrics to visualize the health and performance of your network infrastructure. You should understand the differences between sum, max, percentile, and average statistics for metrics.

Understand how Amazon CloudWatch can be used to centralize network operations. Amazon CloudWatch provides dashboards that can be used to visualize the state and health of a network. Alarms can be created for individual metrics that can notify an operations team when performance has deviated from normal.

Understand how to store and get basic metrics from text logs using Amazon CloudWatch Logs. Text logs, such as those from Amazon EC2 instances or VPC Flow Logs, can be stored in Amazon CloudWatch Logs. Log groups can have metric filters attached to them that allow metrics to be extracted and graphed using Amazon CloudWatch.

Test Taking Tip

Each question on the exam is independent of the others. When a question presents you with a detailed scenario, mark your response (and flag for review, if necessary) and clear your mind as you move on to the next question. You will not need to refer back to scenarios from previous questions.

Resources to Review

For further information, refer to the following pages on the AWS website.

AWS CloudFormation:

`https://aws.amazon.com/documentation/cloudformation/`

AWS CodePipeline:

`https://aws.amazon.com/documentation/codepipeline/`

Amazon CloudWatch and Amazon CloudWatch Logs:

`https://aws.amazon.com/documentation/cloudwatch/`

AWS Lambda FAQs:

`https://aws.amazon.com/lambda/faqs/`

AWS CodeCommit FAQs:

`https://aws.amazon.com/codecommit/faqs/`

Exercises

The best way to become familiar with automation is to configure your own templates, continuous delivery pipelines, and monitoring. For assistance completing these exercises, refer to the guides in the previous sections.

EXERCISE 10.1

Create a Template

In this exercise, you will create a basic AWS CloudFormation template for deploying a VPC. The goal of this exercise is to become familiar with the basic syntax of AWS CloudFormation templates and the service console.

1. Using a text editor, create an AWS CloudFormation template containing just a single VPC with a CIDR range of 10.0.0.0/16. Save this file locally as `netauto.yml`.
2. Sign in to the AWS Management Console as an Administrator or Power User.
3. Select the AWS CloudFormation icon to reach the AWS CloudFormation welcome page (or dashboard if stacks already exist).
4. Click on Create New Stack (or Create Stack if stacks already exist).
5. Upload the template that you created earlier. Click Next.
6. On the Specify Details page, type NetAutomation for the stack name. Click Next.
7. On the Options page, click Next.
8. On the Review page, click Create.
9. Wait for the stack to finish creating.
10. Switch to the Amazon VPC console. The VPC you specified in the template should now be visible.

EXERCISE 10.2

Update a Stack

In this exercise, you will change a template and apply this to an existing stack. The goal of this exercise is to become familiar with how AWS CloudFormation handles updates.

1. Using your `netauto.yml` template from Exercise 10.1, add a subnet within the VPC with a CIDR range of 10.0.0.0/24.
2. Sign in to the AWS Management Console as an Administrator or Power User.
3. Select the AWS CloudFormation icon to reach the AWS CloudFormation dashboard.

4. Toggle the checkbox next to the stack you created in Exercise 10.1. Click on Actions and then Update Stack.
   a. Upload the revised template. Click Next.
   b. On the Specify Details page, click Next.
   c. On the Options page, click Next.
   d. On the Review page, click Update.
   e. Wait for the stack to finish updating.
5. Switch to the Amazon VPC console. The VPC should now have a subnet with a CIDR range of 10.0.0.0/24. Your template change has updated the existing VPC resource.

EXERCISE 10.3

Parameterize Templates

In this exercise, you will parameterize the hard-coded values in an existing template. The goal of this exercise is to become familiar with AWS CloudFormation template parameters and creating reusable templates.

1. Using your template from Exercise 10.2, add a Parameters section that allows you to specify the following parameters:
   - VPCCIDRRange
   - SubnetCIDRRange
2. Alter the VPC and subnet resources to refer to these parameters.
3. Sign in to the AWS Management Console as an Administrator or Power User.
4. Select the AWS CloudFormation icon to reach the AWS CloudFormation dashboard.
5. Toggle the checkbox next to the stack that you created in Exercise 10.1. Click on Actions and then Update Stack.
6. Upload the revised template. Click Next.
7. On the Specify Details page, supply the following parameter values (note that these are different from Exercise 10.1 and Exercise 10.2):
   - VPCCIDRRange: 10.1.0.0/16
   - SubnetCIDRRange: 10.1.0.0/24
8. Click Next.
9. On the Options page, click Next.
10. On the Review page, click Update.

EXERCISE 10.3 ***(continued)***

11. Wait for the stack to finish updating. Note that a new VPC and new subnet were created and the old ones were deleted.
12. Switch to the Amazon VPC console. You should now have a new VPC with a CIDR range of 10.1.0.0/16 and a subnet within the VPC with a CIDR range of 10.1.0.0/24. The old VPC with a CIDR range of 10.0.0.0/16 should have been deleted. You have now replaced hard-coded values in the template with parameters.

EXERCISE 10.4

Rollbacks

In this exercise, you will add a semantic error to an AWS CloudFormation template. The goal of this exercise is to gain familiarity with how AWS CloudFormation handles these kinds of errors by rolling back stack updates.

1. Sign in to the AWS Management Console as an Administrator or Power User.
2. Select the AWS CloudFormation icon to reach the AWS CloudFormation dashboard.
3. Toggle the checkbox next to the stack that you created in Exercise 10.1. Click on Actions and then Update Stack.
4. Make sure Use Current Template is selected. Click Next.
5. On the Specify Details page, supply the following parameter values:
   - VPCCIDRRange: 10.1.0.0/16
   - SubnetCIDRRange: 10.2.0.0/24
6. Note that the subnet CIDR range is not within the VPC CIDR range. Click Next.
7. On the Options page, click Next.
8. On the Review page, click Update.
9. Note that AWS CloudFormation is unable to create the new subnet and rolls back the stack to its previous state.
10. Switch to the Amazon VPC console. The existing VPC and subnet should be unchanged. You have now seen how rollbacks do not affect existing AWS CloudFormation resources.

EXERCISE 10.5

Version Control

In this exercise, you will check a template into a Git repository, make edits, and view the changes and history of the template. The goal of this exercise is to gain familiarity with the basic concepts of version control.

1. Sign in to the AWS Management Console as an Administrator or Power User.
2. Select the AWS CodeCommit icon to reach the AWS CodeCommit welcome page (or dashboard if repositories already exist).
3. Click on Get Started (or Create Repository).
4. Type **`NetAuto`** for the repository name. Click on Create Repository.
5. Follow the instructions on the Connect to Your Repository dialog box. You should have an empty directory named `NetAuto`.
6. Copy the `netauto.yml` template into the `NetAuto` directory.
7. Stage the file for commit: `git add netauto.yml`.
8. Commit the change locally, supplying a commit description such as "Initial commit" in the text editor: `git commit`.
9. Push your change to the remote (AWS CodeCommit) repository: `git push`.
10. Check the status of your local repository: `git status`. Note that it is in sync with the remote repository.
11. Edit the template by adding a comment to the file:

    ```
    # Sample comment for exercise 10.5
    ```

12. Check the status of your local repository: `git status`. Note that it is in sync with the remote repository but it has local edits.
13. View the differences from the current version of the file versus what has been committed: `git diff`.
14. Commit the revised version locally, supplying a commit description such as "Testing changes": `git commit -a`.
15. Check the status of your local repository: `git status`. Note that it is no longer in sync with the remote repository as a result of the previous commit, but it no longer has local edits.
16. View the log of changes made: `git log`. Make a note of the first few characters of the latest commit ID (a long hex string, for example, `7fdeaa504da4114950e3aa2ce816ff3f8728776f`).
17. Verify that there are no local edits: `git diff`.

EXERCISE 10.5 *(continued)*

18. View the differences between the latest commit and the previous commit (replace `7fdeaa` with your actual commit ID): `git diff 7fdeaa^ 7fdeaa`. You should see your comment being added.

Git allows you to shorten the commit ID as long as it is still unique. In the `diff` command, you typed two commit IDs. The first is the old commit ID; the caret (^) at the end of the commit ID means "the commit previous to," so that you are looking at the differences between the commit previous to `7fdeaa` and commit `7fdeaa`.

You could also omit the second `7fdeaa`; Git will then show the differences from the commit to the latest commit (`7fdeaa` itself), also called `HEAD`. You could have shortened this command to: `git diff HEAD^`.

19. Push your change to the remote repository: `git push`.
20. Lastly, verify that everything is again in sync with no local edits: `git status`.
21. You have successfully placed your template under version control.

EXERCISE 10.6

Pipeline Integration

In this exercise, you will create a pipeline in AWS CodePipeline that automatically deploys an AWS CloudFormation template. The goal of this exercise is to gain familiarity with the basic concepts of continuous delivery.

1. Sign in to the AWS Management Console as an Administrator or Power User.
2. Before getting started with AWS CodePipeline, you will need to create two service roles. If you are unfamiliar with this process, refer to the Creating a Role for an AWS Service section of the AWS Identity and Access Management User Guide at:

   `http://docs.aws.amazon.com/IAM/latest/UserGuide/id_roles_create_for-service.html`

   a. Create a service role for AWS CloudFormation named `CloudFormation-NetAuto`. Attach the `PowerUserAccess` managed policy to it.

   b. Create a service role for AWS CodePipeline named `CodePipeline-NetAuto`. Attach the `PowerUserAccess` managed policy to it.
3. Select the AWS CodePipeline icon to reach the AWS CodePipeline welcome page (or dashboard if pipelines already exist).

4. Click on Get Started (or Create Pipeline) to enter the pipeline creation wizard.

Step 1— **Name:** Type **`NetAuto`** for the pipeline name. Click Next Step.

Step 2— **Source:** Select AWS CodeCommit for the source provider. Select the `NetAuto` repository and the `master` branch. Click Next Step.

Step 3— **Build:** Select No Build. You will not be using a build provider for this exercise. Click Next Step.

Step 4— **Deploy:** Select AWS CloudFormation as the deployment provider. Set the properties as follows and click Next Step.

Action mode: Create or update a stack.

Stack name: `NetAuto`

Template file: `netauto.yml`

Configuration file: Leave blank.

Capabilities: Leave blank.

Role name: `CloudFormation-MyNetAuto`

Step 5— **Service Role:** Enter `CodePipeline-NetAuto`. Click Next Step.

Step 6— **Review:** Check over the details and click Create Pipeline.

You have now created a continuous delivery pipeline for your template.

EXERCISE 10.7

Monitor Network Health

In this exercise, you will create a dashboard to monitor the health of an AWS-managed VPN. The goal of this exercise is to become familiar with automating network operations using Amazon CloudWatch.

1. Sign in to the AWS Management Console as an Administrator or Power User.
2. Create an AWS-managed VPN following the steps outlined in Chapter 4, "Virtual Private Networks," Exercise 4.1. Make note of the VPN ID and the IP addresses of the Virtual Private Gateway (VGW) endpoints.
3. Select the Amazon CloudWatch icon to reach the Amazon CloudWatch console.
4. In the left pane, click on Metrics.
5. In the bottom-right pane, under AWS Namespaces, click on VPN and then on VPN Connection Metrics.
6. Find your VPN ID and select the checkboxes for the `TunnelDataIn`, `TunnelDataOut`, and `TunnelState` metrics. You should now see three lines in the graph in the upper-right pane.

EXERCISE 10.7 *(continued)*

`TunnelState` is a binary metric (either 0 or 1, indicating that the VPN is unhealthy or healthy, respectively), while the `TunnelData` metrics are measured in bytes (with values that may go into the billions). You need to plot these on different y-axes to make them readable. In the bottom-right pane, click on the Graphed Metrics tab. Find the `TunnelState` metric and plot it against the right-side axis by clicking on the > symbol under the Y Axis column.

Your graph shows the overall state of the entire VPN connection. You also want to monitor the state of the individual tunnels in the VPN connection. In the bottom-right pane, click on the All Metrics tab, then click on VPN in the guide labeled "All > VPN > VPN Connection Metrics." This time, click on VPN Tunnel Metrics. Find the IP addresses of your VGW endpoints and select the checkboxes next to the six metrics (`TunnelDataIn`, `TunnelDataOut`, and `TunnelState` for each of the two endpoints).

7. Click on the Graphed Metrics tab again. Change the `TunnelState` metrics for the VGW endpoints so that they plot against the right y-axis.

8. You will want to give your graph a more meaningful name. In the upper-right pane, click on the pencil icon next to the "Untitled Graph" text. Type **Exercise 10.7 VPN Health** and press Enter.

9. Lastly, you will save this graph to a dashboard for future reference. In the upper-right pane, click on the Actions drop-down and select Add to Dashboard. In the dialog box that appears, do the following:

   a. Under the Select a Dashboard section, click on Create New. Type **Exercise-10-7** for the dashboard name and then click on the checkmark next to the name field.

   b. Under the Select a Widget Type section, explore the different plot options: Line, Stacked area, and Number. The Preview pane will display how this will appear in the final dashboard. When you are done, click on Line again.

   c. Click on Add to Dashboard.

10. In the dashboard window, resize the graph by hovering over the bottom-right corner and then clicking and dragging the graph.

11. Experiment with plotting different time periods for the dashboard by clicking on the 1h, 3h, 12h, 1d, 3d, and 1w options in the upper-right corner.

12. Make the dashboard automatically refresh by clicking on the drop-down menu next to the refresh symbol. Select the Autorefresh checkbox, and then change the refresh interval to 10 seconds.

13. You have now created an Amazon CloudWatch dashboard to monitor network operations.

Review Questions

1. In an AWS CloudFormation template, you attempt to create a Virtual Private Cloud (VPC) with a Classless Inter-Domain Routing (CIDR) range of 10.0.0.0/16 and a subnet within the VPC with a CIDR range of 10.1.0.0/24. What happens when you initiate a `CreateStack` operation with this template?

   A. AWS CloudFormation detects the conflict and returns an error immediately.

   B. AWS CloudFormation attempts to create the subnet. When this fails, it skips this step and creates the remaining resources.

   C. AWS CloudFormation attempts to create the subnet. When this fails, it rolls back all other resources.

   D. AWS CloudFormation attempts to create the subnet. When this fails, it calls a custom resource handler to handle the error.

2. You have created a large AWS CloudFormation template so that users in your company can create a Virtual Private Cloud (VPC) with a Virtual Private Network (VPN) connection back to the company's on-premises network. This template sometimes fails, with an error message about routes not being able to use the Virtual Private Gateway (VGW) because it is not attached to the VPC. What is the best way to solve this issue?

   A. Add a `DependsOn` attribute to the route resource and make it depend on the gateway attachment resource.

   B. Reorder the resources in the template so that the route resource comes after the VGW.

   C. Use a custom resource to create the route. In the code for the custom resource, have the code sleep for two minutes to allow the VGW time to attach to the VPC.

   D. Add a `DependsOn` attribute to the gateway attachment resource and make it depend on the route resource.

3. When an AWS CloudFormation stack is deleted, what happens to the resources it created?

   A. They are deleted unless their `aws:cloudformation:stack-id` tag has been removed.

   B. They are retained unless they have a `DeletionPolicy` attribute set to `Delete`.

   C. They are deleted unless AWS CloudFormation detects whether they are still in use.

   D. They are deleted unless they have a `DeletionPolicy` attribute set to `Retain`.

4. You are building an AWS CloudFormation template that will be deployed using a continuous delivery model. Which of the following sources can AWS CodePipeline monitor directly? (Choose two.)

   A. AWS CodeCommit

   B. A Git repository on an Amazon Elastic Compute Cloud (Amazon EC2) instance

   C. An on-premises GitHub Enterprise repository

   D. A Git repository in Amazon Elastic File System (Amazon EFS)

   E. Amazon Simple Storage Service (Amazon S3)

5. What tool or service is needed to aggregate log files from multiple routing appliances running on Amazon Elastic Compute Cloud (Amazon EC2) instances?
   A. AWS Lambda
   B. Amazon Inspector agent
   C. Amazon CloudWatch Logs agent
   D. AWS Shield

6. You are creating a pipeline in AWS CodePipeline that will deploy to an AWS CloudFormation test stack. If the deployment is successful, then AWS CodePipeline will deploy a production stack. The Virtual Private Cloud (VPC) Classless Inter-Domain Routing (CIDR) ranges used by the two stacks are different. What is the best way to proceed?
   A. Create two templates, `test.yml` and `prod.yml`, containing different CIDR ranges.
   B. Use a custom resource for creating the VPC that configures the VPCs appropriately.
   C. Use an AWS CloudFormation intrinsic function that detects which stack it is deploying to and sets the value accordingly.
   D. Create a single template with parameters. Create two parameter files, `test.json` and `prod.json`, containing different CIDR ranges.

7. Your organization requires human review of changes to a production AWS CloudFormation stack. A recent change to a Virtual Private Cloud (VPC) caused an outage when the changes unexpectedly deleted a subnet. What is the best way to prevent a similar occurrence in the future?
   A. Use the AWS CloudFormation `ValidateTemplate` Application Programming Interface (API) to verify the correctness of the template.
   B. Add an approval action to AWS CloudFormation that displays the pending changes and waits for approval.
   C. Create a change set in AWS CloudFormation for review. If the changes are approved, then execute the change set.
   D. Create a change set in AWS CloudFormation for review. If the changes are approved, then deploy the new template.

8. You are starting a new networking deployment that will leverage the infrastructure as code model. What is the best way to track and visualize changes to the source code?
   A. Create a Git repository using GitHub.
   B. Set up an Amazon Simple Storage Service (Amazon S3) bucket with versioning enabled as a repository.
   C. Record changes using AWS CloudFormation change sets.
   D. Use AWS CodePipeline stages to track code state.

9. You have an AWS CloudFormation stack that contains a Virtual Private Cloud (VPC) with a Classless Inter-Domain Routing (CIDR) range of 10.0.0.0/16. You change the template to add two subnets to the VPC, SubnetA and SubnetB, both with CIDR ranges of 10.0.0.0/24. What happens when you update the stack?

   A. AWS CloudFormation detects the error and does not perform any actions.

   B. AWS CloudFormation creates SubnetA and then attempts to create SubnetB; when this fails, it stops.

   C. AWS CloudFormation creates SubnetA and SubnetB in an indeterminate order; when one fails, it stops.

   D. AWS CloudFormation creates SubnetA and SubnetB in an indeterminate order; when one fails, it rolls back both subnets.

10. An AWS CloudFormation stack contains a subnet that is critical to your infrastructure and should never be deleted, even if the stack is updated with a template that requires this. What is the best way to protect the subnet in this situation?

    A. Add a stack policy that denies the `Update:Delete` and `Update:Replace` actions on this resource.

    B. Use an AWS Identity and Access Management (IAM) service role that prohibits calls to `ec2:DeleteSubnet`.

    C. Add a `DeletionPolicy` property to the subnet resource with a value of `Retain`.

    D. Delete the `aws:cloudformation` tags attached to the subnet.

Chapter 11

Service Requirements

THE AWS CERTIFIED ADVANCED NETWORKING – SPECIALTY EXAM OBJECTIVES COVERED IN THIS CHAPTER MAY INCLUDE, BUT ARE NOT LIMITED TO, THE FOLLOWING:

Domain 4.0: Configure Network Integration with Application Services

✓ 4.6 Reconcile AWS Cloud service requirements with network requirements

Introduction to Service Requirements

The AWS Cloud platform offers over 90 services that customers can leverage. A number of these services either reside within a Virtual Private Cloud (VPC) or have the option to do so. Understanding how the service and networking interactions work, both in general and for each service, is critical for planning and operating networking within AWS. By understanding service requirements and mapping them to network requirements, you can allocate resources appropriately and ensure that AWS Cloud services will operate correctly within your VPC environment.

The Elastic Network Interface

An *elastic network interface* is a virtual network interface that you can attach to an instance in a VPC. It is more simply referred to as a network interface. Many AWS managed services can be launched with network interfaces to allow them to reside within a VPC, while still having the ability to be managed by AWS. For more information on network interfaces, refer to Chapter 2, "Amazon Virtual Private Cloud (Amazon VPC) and Networking Fundamentals."

AWS Cloud Services and Their Network Requirements

This section covers AWS Cloud services that have specific network requirements. A description of each service is provided along with the network requirements.

Amazon WorkSpaces

Amazon WorkSpaces is a managed, secure Desktop as a Service (DaaS) solution that runs on AWS. With Amazon WorkSpaces, you can easily provision virtual, cloud-based

Microsoft Windows desktops for your users, providing them with access to the documents, applications, and resources they need—anywhere, any time, and from any supported device.

Each WorkSpace desktop is provisioned with two network interfaces. One interface resides in a customer-specified VPC and another resides in an AWS management VPC, which allows for external connectivity from the Amazon WorkSpaces client. The management VPC has a private Classless Inter-Domain Routing (CIDR) of one of the following: 172.31.0.0/16, 192.168.0.0/16, or 198.19.0.0/16. The CIDR is automatically chosen so as not to conflict with the VPC CIDR.

If the AWS management VPC CIDR range is in use elsewhere in your architecture, you will encounter routing issues.

Amazon WorkSpaces Requirements

Amazon WorkSpaces has the following network requirements:

Amazon WorkSpaces client application You'll need an Amazon WorkSpaces-supported client device. You can also use Personal Computer over Internet Protocol (PCoIP) zero clients to connect to Amazon WorkSpaces. Zero-client connectivity will also require a PCoIP connection manger running in the customer VPC.

A VPC in which to run your WorkSpace You will need a minimum of two subnets for an Amazon WorkSpaces deployment because each AWS Directory Service construct requires two subnets in a Multi-AZ deployment. Each subnet should have sufficient capacity for future growth. Each WorkSpace will have a network interface in one of the VPC subnets.

A directory service to authenticate users and provide access to their WorkSpaces Amazon WorkSpaces currently works with AWS Directory Service and Active Directory. You can use your on-premises Active Directory server with AWS Directory Service to support your existing enterprise user credentials with Amazon WorkSpaces.

Security group(s) to control access for Amazon WorkSpaces Network access to and from the Amazon WorkSpaces customer-specified VPC network interface is controlled by security groups.

Amazon AppStream 2.0

Amazon AppStream 2.0 is a managed, secure application streaming service that allows you to stream desktop applications from AWS to any device running a web browser without rewriting them. Amazon AppStream 2.0 provides users instant-on access to the applications they need and a responsive, fluid user experience on the device of their choice.

A set of applications is run from an Amazon AppStream 2.0 instance, which is dedicated to a single user. A configurable fleet of instances can be created that automatically scales to meet user demand. Each Amazon AppStream 2.0 instance is provisioned with two network interfaces. One interface resides in a customer-specified VPC, and another resides in an AWS management VPC, which allows for external connectivity to the Amazon AppStream 2.0 applications.

Amazon AppStream 2.0 Requirements

Amazon AppStream 2.0 has the following network requirements:

An HTML5-compatible web browser Amazon AppStream 2.0 delivers applications through any modern HTML5-compatible web browser.

A VPC in which to run your Amazon AppStream 2.0 applications You will need at least one subnet for Amazon AppStream 2.0. You should use two subnets for high availability. Each Amazon AppStream 2.0 instance in the fleet will have a network interface in a VPC subnet. A new instance is used for each unique user connection.

Security group(s) to control access for Amazon AppStream 2.0 Network access to/from the Amazon AppStream 2.0 customer-specified VPC network interface is controlled by security groups.

AWS Lambda (Within a VPC)

AWS Lambda is a compute service that lets you run code without provisioning or managing servers. AWS Lambda executes your code only when needed and scales automatically, from a few requests per day to thousands per second. You pay only for the compute time you consume—there is no charge when your code is not running. With AWS Lambda, you can run code for virtually any type of application or back-end service, all with zero administration. AWS Lambda runs your code on a high-availability compute infrastructure and performs all of the administration of the compute resources, including server and operating system maintenance, capacity provisioning and automatic scaling, code monitoring, and logging. All you need to do is supply your code in one of the languages that AWS Lambda supports (Node.js, Java, C#, and Python at the time of this writing).

AWS Lambda runs in a managed network by default, where the networking requirements and scaling are managed by AWS. AWS provides the option to run AWS Lambda functions from within a customer VPC, the requirements for which are discussed in the following subsection.

When using AWS Lambda within a VPC, there is a "cold start" time when ramping up additional AWS Lambda function execution to provision additional elastic network interfaces.

AWS Lambda Requirements

AWS Lambda (running within a VPC) has the following network requirements:

VPC subnet(s) with sufficient capacity AWS Lambda functions are executed on demand, so the IP address requirement will vary with invocation count. In the most extreme case, this could be up to 1,000 (the current per-region soft limit of concurrent AWS Lambda function executions). For an estimate of the required IP addresses needed, the following calculation can be used:

Projected peak concurrent executions × (Memory in GB/1.5GB)

You should use multiple subnets that span Availability Zones for availability.

Security group(s) to allow access from AWS Lambda AWS Lambda leverages security groups to control network access to each AWS Lambda function. Note that there is limited inbound access built into the AWS Lambda service for security reasons.

Network Address Translation (NAT) for Internet access AWS Lambda functions cannot be assigned public IPs. A NAT gateway or customer-managed NAT instance is required for Internet connectivity.

For address separation and security group hardening, you can create dedicated subnets for running your AWS Lambda functions.

Amazon EC2 Container Service (Amazon ECS)

Amazon EC2 Container Service (Amazon ECS) is a highly scalable, high-performance container management service that supports Docker containers and allows you to run applications easily. Amazon ECS works in one of two ways: as a managed cluster of *Amazon Elastic Compute Cloud (Amazon EC2)* instances or as *AWS Fargate*, a technology for deploying and managing containers without having to manage any of the underlying infrastructure. Amazon ECS eliminates the need for you to install, operate, and scale your own cluster management infrastructure. With simple Application Programming Interface (API) calls, you can launch and stop Docker-enabled applications, query the complete state of your cluster, and access many familiar features like security groups, Elastic Load Balancing, Amazon Elastic Block Store (Amazon EBS) volumes, and AWS Identity and Access Management (IAM) roles.

The default setup in the AWS Management Console will create a new Virtual Private Cloud (VPC) and subnets for your Amazon ECS cluster; however, an existing VPC can be used. Amazon ECS running on managed Amazon EC2 instances uses AWS CloudFormation to create clusters and Amazon EC2 instances, which can all be tracked in the AWS Management Console. These types of containers run within the provisioned Amazon EC2 instances. Amazon ECS running on AWS Fargate, on the other hand, makes use of an AWS-managed container infrastructure. The Application Load Balancer and Network Load Balancer integrate with Amazon ECS, and they can perform mapping of ports to the backend containers.

Each container can either share the networking stack with the underlying Amazon ECS instance or operate with a dedicated network interface. There are four modes for container network connectivity:

Bridge This is the default option, and it works by "bridging" from a container's internal network into a common Docker network.

Host With this option, containers are directly mapped into the host network.

Awsvpc This option lets you attach an elastic network interface directly to each container. This is the only option for containers running on AWS Fargate.

None This option disables external networking for a container.

Amazon ECS Requirements

Amazon ECS has the following network requirements:

A VPC in which to run Amazon ECS You will need at least one subnet in which to run Amazon ECS. For availability, multiple subnets in different Availability Zones are recommended. For instance-based Amazon ECS, each instance in the cluster will need an IP in the subnet. If awsvpc mode is used, then each container will need an IP address in the subnet. You should plan ahead so that each subnet has enough available IP addresses.

Security group to control access for Amazon ECS Network access to and from each Amazon ECS instance is controlled by a security group. The security group will need to allow traffic to ports on the containers that are running.

Access to the Internet to reach the Amazon ECS service endpoint Container instances need external network access to communicate with the Amazon ECS service endpoint. If your container instances do not have public IP addresses, then they must use NAT or an HTTP proxy to provide this access.

Amazon EMR

Amazon EMR provides a managed Hadoop framework that makes it easy, fast, and cost effective to process vast amounts of data across dynamically-scalable Amazon EC2 instances. *Hadoop* is an open source Java software framework that supports data-intensive distributed applications running on large clusters of commodity hardware. You can also run other popular distributed frameworks such as Apache Spark, HBase, Presto, and Flink in Amazon EMR and interact with data in other AWS data stores such as Amazon Simple Storage Service (Amazon S3) and Amazon DynamoDB.

Amazon EMR can be launched in either a public or private subnet. Given the high throughput requirement of the Hadoop framework, an Amazon EMR cluster is launched within a single Availability Zone for performance and cost optimization.

Amazon EMR Requirements

Amazon EMR has the following network requirements:

Domain Name System (DNS) hostnames enabled on your VPC Amazon EMR requires that hostnames be enabled on the VPC for proper hostname-to-address resolution.

Private CIDR for your VPC To ensure that name resolution works correctly, only private IP ranges (10.0.0.0/8, 172.16.0.0/12, and 192.168.0.0/16) should be used. Using public IPs for the VPC CIDR could cause name resolution issues.

Connectivity to AWS Cloud services At a minimum, access to Amazon S3 is required for logging (an Amazon S3 VPC endpoint can be used for connectivity). Access to Amazon Simple Queue Service (Amazon SQS) is required for debugging support. Amazon DynamoDB connectivity is required if Amazon EMR will interact with Amazon DynamoDB tables (a VPC endpoint can be used).

Amazon Relational Database Service (Amazon RDS)

Amazon Relational Database Service (Amazon RDS) makes it easy to set up, operate, and scale a relational database in the cloud. It provides cost-efficient and resizable capacity while automating time-consuming administration tasks such as hardware provisioning, database setup, patching, and backups. It allows you to focus on your applications so that you can give them the fast performance, high availability, security, and compatibility they need. Amazon RDS is available for six popular data engines: Amazon Aurora, PostgreSQL, MySQL, MariaDB, Oracle, and Microsoft SQL Server.

Amazon RDS provides high availability and failover support for DB instances using Multi-AZ deployments. Amazon RDS uses several different technologies to provide failover support. Multi-AZ deployments for Oracle, PostgreSQL, MySQL, and MariaDB DB instances use Amazon's failover technology. SQL Server DB instances use SQL Server Mirroring. Amazon Aurora instances store copies of the data in a DB cluster across multiple Availability Zones in a single region, regardless of whether the instances in the DB cluster span multiple Availability Zones. Read replicas are also available in Amazon RDS for MySQL, MariaDB, and PostgreSQL.

Amazon RDS Requirements

Amazon RDS has the following network requirements:

A VPC in which to run Amazon RDS You will need one subnet in which to run Amazon RDS. If you choose a Multi-AZ deployment, then you will need at least two subnets in differing Availability Zones. If Amazon RDS read replicas are used, then a subnet is required. Amazon RDS subnet groups are used to specify which subnets in a VPC are used for Amazon RDS.

Security group(s) to allow access to Amazon RDS Amazon RDS leverages security groups to control inbound and outbound access to the database.

AWS Database Migration Service (AWS DMS)

AWS Database Migration Service (AWS DMS) helps you migrate databases to AWS quickly and securely. The source database remains fully operational during the migration, minimizing downtime to applications that rely on the database. AWS DMS can migrate your data to and from most widely-used commercial and open source databases.

AWS DMS Requirements

AWS DMS has the following network requirements:

A VPC in which to run AWS DMS You will need at least one subnet in which to run AWS DMS. If you choose a Multi-AZ deployment, then you will need at least two subnets in different Availability Zones. Multi-AZ deployment is recommended for high availability. If Internet connectivity is required, then the AWS DMS instance(s) should reside in either a public subnet with a public IP or in a private subnet with a NAT gateway or NAT instance. Private connectivity to AWS DMS is recommended.

Security group(s) to allow access for AWS DMS AWS DMS leverages security groups to control inbound and outbound access to databases. Security groups will need to be configured to allow outbound access to each database that the service will use as either a source or target.

Amazon Redshift

Amazon Redshift is a fast, managed data warehouse that makes it simple and cost effective to analyze all of your data using standard SQL and your existing Business Intelligence (BI) tools. It allows you to run complex analytic queries against petabytes of structured data, using sophisticated query optimization, columnar storage on high-performance local disks, and massively parallel query execution. Most results come back within seconds.

With Amazon Redshift, there is a leader node and one or more compute nodes. Compute nodes store data and execute your queries. The leader node is the access point for Open Database Connectivity (ODBC)/Java Database Connectivity (JDBC) and generates the query plans executed on the compute nodes. Users do not interact directly with the compute nodes.

Amazon Redshift can be deployed in either a standard or enhanced routing configuration. With enhanced VPC, all traffic is forced to flow through the VPC. Enhanced VPC routing affects the way that Amazon Redshift accesses other resources, so `COPY` and `UNLOAD` commands might fail unless you configure your VPC correctly. You must specifically create a network path between your cluster's VPC and your data resources.

Amazon Redshift Requirements

Amazon Redshift has the following network requirements:

A VPC in which to run Amazon Redshift You will need a subnet in which to run Amazon Redshift. The subnet must have enough IP addresses for each node plus an additional IP address for the leader node. AWS provides the option to allow public IPs. If public connectivity is required, then a public subnet should be used.

Security group(s) for cluster access At least one security group is required to control access to the cluster.

DNS hostnames enabled on your VPC Amazon Redshift requires that hostnames be enabled on the VPC for proper hostname-to-address resolution.

If enhanced routing is configured:

Connectivity to Amazon S3 Connectivity to Amazon S3 buckets in the same region can be accomplished through an Amazon S3 VPC endpoint. Connectivity to Amazon S3 in another region or to public AWS Cloud services will require either a public IP and an Internet gateway, NAT gateway, or NAT instance.

AWS Glue

AWS Glue is a managed Extract, Transform, and Load (ETL) service that makes it easy for customers to prepare and load their data for analytics. You can create and run an ETL job with a few clicks in the AWS Management Console. You simply point AWS Glue to your data stored on AWS, and AWS Glue discovers your data and stores the associated metadata (for example, table definition and schema) in the AWS Glue Data Catalog. Once cataloged, your data is immediately searchable, queryable, and available for ETL. AWS Glue generates the code to execute your data transformations and data loading processes.

AWS Glue Requirements

AWS Glue has the following network requirements:

A VPC in which to run AWS Glue Each AWS Glue connection to a data source requires network interfaces within a subnet in a VPC.

Security group(s) to allow access from Glue Glue leverages security groups to control access to data sources. At least one security group with access to the data source is required. AWS Glue also requires one or more security groups with an inbound source rule that allows AWS Glue to connect (a self-referencing rule allowing all inbound traffic to the security group).

NAT for Internet access AWS Glue network interface functions cannot be assigned public IPs. If AWS Glue will be accessing data sources over public IP addresses, then a NAT gateway or customer-managed NAT instance is required for Internet connectivity.

AWS Elastic Beanstalk

AWS Elastic Beanstalk is an easy-to-use service for deploying and scaling web applications and services developed with Java, .NET, PHP, Node.js, Python, Ruby, Go, and Docker on familiar servers such as Apache, Nginx, Passenger, and IIS.

You can simply upload your code, and AWS Elastic Beanstalk automatically handles the deployment, from capacity provisioning, load balancing, and automatic scaling to application health monitoring. At the same time, you retain full control over the AWS resources powering your application and can access the underlying resources at any time.

AWS Elastic Beanstalk can be configured to scale and load balance an application automatically through a simple web Graphical User Interface (GUI) without the need for manual configuration of resources. AWS CloudFormation is used to create and manage an AWS Elastic Beanstalk application environment. The status of the deployment can be tracked from the AWS CloudFormation section of the AWS Management Console. Amazon EC2 resources that are created can be viewed from the Amazon EC2 console.

AWS Elastic Beanstalk Requirements

AWS Elastic Beanstalk has the following network requirements:

A VPC in which to run AWS Elastic Beanstalk If no customization is made, the default VPC is selected for use with AWS Elastic Beanstalk. If custom networking is configured, then a VPC (with subnets and an Internet gateway), security groups, network Access Control Lists (ACLs), and routing must be properly configured for the applications to be accessible. The architecture will vary based on the connectivity needs of the application being deployed and public versus private deployment.

Security group(s) to allow access AWS Elastic Beanstalk leverages security groups to control access to Amazon EC2 instances. Inbound rules for the Amazon EC2 instances, or a load balancer if load balancing is used, is required for connectivity to the AWS Elastic Beanstalk application. Outbound access to User Datagram Protocol (UDP) port 123 is required to allow Network Time Protocol (NTP) traffic for time synchronization.

Internet connectivity AWS Elastic Beanstalk requires Internet connectivity either directly through the assignment of public IP addresses or through NAT. Note that using a proxy server is not supported for Linux instances.

Summary

In this chapter, you reviewed AWS Cloud services and their network requirements.

Amazon WorkSpaces is a virtual desktop solution delivered through the Amazon WorkSpaces client application or zero-client hardware. At least two subnets are required to allow connectivity of virtual desktops to other resources running within a VPC. A directory service running within the VPC is required for user authentication.

Amazon AppStream 2.0 is an application streaming service that works with a standard HTML5-compatible web browser. One or two subnets are used to allow connectivity of applications to other resources running within a VPC. (Multiple subnets should be used for availability.)

AWS Lambda is a serverless code execution service. AWS Lambda can run without a VPC or can be placed in a VPC to allow for access to resources within a VPC. (Multiple subnets should be used for availability.) If Internet access is required for AWS Lambda running within a VPC, then NAT must be used.

Amazon ECS is a container management service. Amazon ECS manages Amazon EC2 instances that are used to run containers. The container instance requires at least one subnet, and multiple subnets in different Availability Zones are recommended for high availability.

Amazon EMR is a managed Hadoop framework. Amazon EMR requires a subnet in which to run. Private IP addresses are required for the VPC CIDR along with DNS hostnames enabled. Connectivity to Amazon S3 is required for logging. Access to Amazon SQS is required for debugging, and access to Amazon DynamoDB is required if working with data in Amazon DynamoDB tables.

Amazon RDS is a service that provides managed relational databases with support for Amazon Aurora, PostgreSQL, MySQL, MariaDB, Oracle, and Microsoft SQL Server. The service requires at least one subnet (two or more for Multi-AZ).

AWS DMS facilitates the migration of data between databases of the same or differing types. AWS DMS requires at least one subnet, and two are required for a Multi-AZ deployment.

Amazon Redshift is managed data warehouse. An Amazon Redshift cluster requires a subnet and can either be public or private. It requires that DNS hostnames be enabled on the VPC. You have the option to enable enhanced VPC routing to force all traffic to go through the VPC. If enhanced VPC routing is enabled, then connectivity to Amazon S3 must be provided.

AWS Glue is a managed ETL service. A connection to a data source requires network interfaces that reside in a subnet. AWS Glue also requires one or more security groups with an inbound source rule that allows AWS Glue to connect (a self-referencing rule allowing all inbound traffic to the security group).

AWS Elastic Beanstalk is an easy-to-use service for deploying and scaling web applications and services. The default option selects the default VPC for deployment. Optionally, a custom VPC can be used. Security groups need to be configured to allow outbound connectivity to NTP and inbound connectivity from the AWS Elastic Beanstalk application clients. Internet connectivity is required for the Amazon EC2 instances that are launched, either through direct public IP assignment or NAT.

Understanding the requirements of each service will greatly assist in mapping to network requirements and help you effectively design for the appropriate network access. This knowledge will contribute to your ability to design and identify appropriate network architectures for the exam.

Exam Essentials

Understand what an elastic network interface in an Amazon VPC subnet is and how it is used. Many AWS Cloud services can reside within a VPC. An elastic network interface connected to a VPC subnet facilitates this connectivity.

Understand the Internet connectivity requirements for each service. Some services and deployment options will require Internet connectivity. This connectivity can be accomplished through the use of NAT, public IP address, or proxy. The appropriate type of connectivity will vary with each service. In general, NAT can be used with most services.

Understand the VPC architecture for each service. At least two subnets in differing Availability Zones should be used for each AWS service. Many services, like AWS Lambda and Amazon ECS, support the use of more than two Availability Zones for additional redundancy and scale.

Understand the interconnectivity requirements between services. The AWS ecosystem of services often work hand-in-hand to provide capabilities. For example, AWS Glue can perform ETL across varying on-premises and AWS resources and Amazon WorkSpaces can use several AWS services for authentication. Understanding these requirements and interconnection points is key to designing an appropriate network architecture.

Test Taking Tip

Make sure that you know the network requirements of each AWS service and how to design the network appropriately to support them.

Resources to Review

For further information, refer to the following pages on the AWS website.

Amazon WorkSpaces:

`https://aws.amazon.com/workspaces/`

Amazon AppStream 2.0:

`https://aws.amazon.com/appstream2/`

Amazon RDS:

`https://aws.amazon.com/rds/`

AWS DMS:

`https://aws.amazon.com/dms/`

Amazon EMR:

`https://aws.amazon.com/emr/`

Amazon Redshift:

`https://aws.amazon.com/redshift/`

AWS Glue:

`https://aws.amazon.com/glue/`

AWS Elastic Beanstalk:

`https://aws.amazon.com/elasticbeanstalk/`

AWS Lambda:

`https://aws.amazon.com/lambda/`

Exercises

The best way to become familiar with AWS Cloud services and their requirements is to experiment with them through the AWS Management Console. There is no substitute for the experience that comes from working with the AWS environment and becoming familiar with networking requirements.

When you are done with each exercise, be sure to delete the resources you created to avoid usage fees.

EXERCISE 11.1

Set Up Amazon WorkSpaces

In this exercise, you will deploy an Amazon WorkSpace.

1. Sign in to the AWS Management Console as Administrator or Power User.
2. Navigate to Amazon WorkSpaces in the console.
3. Select Launch WorkSpaces.
4. Create a new directory. Select Simple AD and fill in the required field. Select the default VPC for network settings. It will take a few minutes for the directory to build.
5. After the directory has a status of Active, navigate to the Amazon WorkSpaces tab on the left side of the AWS Management Console.
6. Click on the Launch WorkSpaces button.
7. Select the directory that you just created and select next.
8. Create a new user and add an email address. Select the next step. Credentials to log in will be emailed to the address you provide.
9. Choose a bundle to launch. Be sure to select one that is AWS Free Tier eligible.
10. Select the next step and then Launch WorkSpace.
11. Connect to the WorkSpace using the Amazon WorkSpaces client. Try to launch other services with the VPC and connect to them from the WorkSpace.
12. Navigate to the Amazon EC2 section of the AWS Management Console and select Network Interfaces on the left side. Look through the descriptions to identify one that says WorkSpaces. This is the interface that the WorkSpace is using in the default VPC.

You have successfully deployed an Amazon WorkSpace and connected to it with the WorkSpace client.

EXERCISE 11.2

Set Up Amazon RDS

In this exercise, you will deploy an Amazon RDS instance.

1. Sign in to the AWS Management Console as Administrator or Power User.
2. Navigate to Amazon RDS in the console and click the Launch a DB Instance button.
3. Select Amazon Aurora. Select db.t2.small as the DB Instance Class. Complete the required setting fields on the form and click Next Step.
4. Accept the default settings of using the default VPC and then select Launch DB Instance.
5. Navigate to the Amazon EC2 section of the AWS Management Console and select Network Interfaces on the left side. Look through the descriptions to identify the elastic network interface that says Amazon RDS. This is the interface that the Amazon RDS instances are using within the default VPC.

You have successfully deployed an Amazon RDS database.

EXERCISE 11.3

Create an AWS Elastic Beanstalk Application

In this exercise, you will deploy an AWS Elastic Beanstlak application.

1. Sign in to the AWS Management Console as Administrator or Power User.
2. Navigate to AWS Elastic Beanstalk in the console and click the Get Started button.
3. Enter an application name and select Node.js as the platform. Click the Create Application button. This will create a simple AWS Elastic Beanstalk application. It will take a few minutes for the application to complete.
4. Navigate to AWS CloudFormation in the AWS Management Console. From there you can track the status of the AWS CloudFormation script that is running to provision the AWS Elastic Beanstalk infrastructure.
5. Navigate to Amazon EC2 in the AWS Management Console, where you can see that an Amazon EC2 instance has been created. If you place the instance's elastic IP address into a web browser, you will see that the sample application is running.

You have now deployed a simple web application using AWS Elastic Beanstalk.

EXERCISE 11.4

Create an Amazon EMR Cluster

In this exercise, you will launch an Amazon EMR cluster.

1. Sign in to the AWS Management Console as Administrator or Power User.
2. Navigate to Amazon EMR in the console and click the Create Cluster button.
3. Under Amazon EC2 key pair, choose the Proceed Without an Amazon EC2 Key Pair option and click Create Cluster.
4. Navigate to the Amazon EC2 section of the AWS Management Console and select Network Interfaces on the left side. Look through the security groups to identify one that includes the text ElasticMapReduce. These are the interfaces that the Amazon EMR nodes are using.

You have now launched an Amazon EMR cluster.

EXERCISE 11.5

Create an Amazon Redshift Cluster

In this exercise, you will launch an Amazon Redshift cluster in the default VPC.

1. Sign in to the AWS Management Console as Administrator or Power User.
2. Navigate to Amazon Redshift in the console, and click the Launch Cluster button.
3. Fill in the required fields for cluster name and password. Then click Continue.
4. Leave the default single node cluster settings and click Continue.
5. Leave the default network settings and click Continue.
6. Review the configuration and then click Launch Cluster.
7. Navigate to the Amazon EC2 section of the AWS Management Console and select Network Interfaces on the left side. Look through the descriptions to identify one that says Amazon Redshift. This is the interface that the Amazon Redshift node is using in the default VPC.

You have successfully launch an Amazon Redshift cluster.

Review Questions

1. Which AWS Cloud service provides end-user connectivity to applications running within a Virtual Private Cloud (VPC)? (Choose two.)
   - **A.** Remote Desktop Protocol
   - **B.** PCoIP
   - **C.** Amazon AppStream 2.0
   - **D.** Amazon WorkSpaces

2. How many network adapters are attached to a WorkSpace instance?
   - **A.** 1
   - **B.** 2
   - **C.** 3
   - **D.** 4

3. How can AWS Lambda connect to the Internet when running in a Virtual Private Cloud (VPC)? (Choose two.)
   - **A.** Internet gateway
   - **B.** NAT Instance
   - **C.** NAT gateway
   - **D.** Public IP

4. Amazon EMR requires which of the following? (Choose three.)
   - **A.** DNS hostnames enabled on a VPC
   - **B.** Private IP addresses
   - **C.** Internet connectivity
   - **D.** Amazon S3 connectivity

5. What AWS Cloud service allows for serverless code execution?
   - **A.** Amazon EC2
   - **B.** Amazon RDS
   - **C.** Amazon EMR
   - **D.** AWS Lambda

6. How can users reach the Internet through Amazon WorkSpaces? (Choose two.)
   - **A.** No action is required; this is enabled by default.
   - **B.** Through a public IP address assigned to each instance with an Internet gateway attached to the VPC
   - **C.** Through a NAT gateway
   - **D.** Specify Internet connectivity in the WorkSpace configuration.

7. Which service provides managed database instances?
   - A. Amazon ECS
   - B. Amazon RDS
   - C. AWS Lambda
   - D. Amazon SQS
8. What is required for Amazon RDS high availability?
   - A. Multi-AZ deployment with two subnets
   - B. Amazon RDS snapshots
   - C. Multi-AZ deployment with one subnet
   - D. High availability is provided by default
9. Which service will automatically provision and scale an application infrastructure with a user only needing to provide application code?
   - A. Amazon ECS
   - B. Elastic Load Balancing
   - C. AWS Elastic Beanstalk
   - D. AWS CloudFormation
10. A developer wants to create a simple application to run on AWS using AWS Elastic Beanstalk. What must the network administrator set up?
    - A. Load balancers
    - B. Amazon EC2
    - C. Security groups
    - D. None of the above
11. An application developer wants to replicate data automatically between an on-premises database and Amazon RDS asynchronously between different database engines. What steps will allow this? (Choose two.)
    - A. Create an AWS DMS instance.
    - B. Allow access to the database server on-premises from with a VPC.
    - C. Open all database servers up for Internet connectivity.
    - D. Create a security group to allow connectivity between the Amazon RDS and the on-premises databases.
12. Your team is going to provision a 10-node Amazon Redshift cluster. How many IP addresses should be available in the subnet?
    - A. 9
    - B. 10
    - C. 11
    - D. 12

13. Your team has created a Multi-AZ Amazon RDS instance. The front-end application tier connects to the database through a custom DNS A record. After the primary database fails, the front-end application server can no longer reach the database. What change needs to be made to ensure availability in the event of a failover?

    A. The A name needs to be updated.

    B. The primary Amazon RDS instance needs to be restored.

    C. The application needs to use the IP address of the secondary Amazon RDS instance.

    D. The application needs to use the Amazon RDS hostname to connect to the database.

Hybrid Architectures

THE AWS CERTIFIED ADVANCED NETWORKING – SPECIALTY EXAM OBJECTIVES COVERED IN THIS CHAPTER MAY INCLUDE, BUT ARE NOT LIMITED TO, THE FOLLOWING:

Domain 1.0: Design and Implement Hybrid IT Network Architectures at Scale

- ✓ **1.1 Apply procedural concepts for the implementation of connectivity for hybrid IT architecture**
- ✓ **1.2 Given a scenario, derive an appropriate hybrid IT architecture connectivity solution**
- ✓ **1.4 Evaluate design alternatives leveraging AWS Direct Connect**
- ✓ **1.5 Define routing policies for hybrid IT architectures**

Domain 4.0: Configure Network Integration with Application Services

- ✓ **4.2 Evaluate Domain Name System (DNS) solutions in a hybrid IT architecture**

Domain 5.0: Design and Implement for Security and Compliance

- ✓ **5.4 Use encryption technologies to secure network communications**

Introduction to Hybrid Architectures

The goal of this chapter is to provide you with an understanding of how to design hybrid architectures using the technologies and AWS Cloud services discussed so far in this Study Guide. We go into details of how AWS Direct Connect and Virtual Private Networks (VPNs) can be leveraged to enable common hybrid IT application architectures. In our discussion, *hybrid* refers to the scenario where on-premises applications communicate with AWS resources in the cloud. We focus on the connectivity aspects of these scenarios.

At their cores, AWS VPN connections and AWS Direct Connect enable communication between on-premises applications and AWS resources. They vary in their characteristics, and one may be preferable over the other for certain types of applications. Some hybrid applications might require the use of both. We cover these scenarios in this chapter.

We look at several application architectures, like a Three-Tier web application, Active Directory, voice applications, and remote desktops (Amazon Workspaces). We examine the connectivity requirements of these applications when running in a hybrid mode and how AWS VPN connections or AWS Direct Connect can help fulfill these requirements. We also dive deeper into how to design for special routing scenarios, such as transitive routing.

Choices for Connectivity

In a hybrid deployment, you will have on-premises servers and clients that require connectivity to and from Amazon Elastic Compute Cloud (Amazon EC2) instances that reside in a Virtual Private Cloud (VPC) environment. There are three ways to establish this connectivity.

Accessing AWS resources using public IPs over the public Internet You can assign Amazon EC2 instances with public IP addresses. The on-premises applications can then access these instances using the assigned public IP. This is the easiest option to implement but might not be the most preferable from a security and network performance perspective. From a security standpoint, you can protect the Amazon EC2 instances using security groups and network Access Control Lists (ACLs) to restrict traffic only from on-premises server IPs. You can also whitelist the elastic IPv4 addresses or IPv6 addresses on the on-premises firewalls. You can achieve traffic encryption by using Transport Layer Security

(TLS) at the transport layer or using an encryption library at the application layer. The bandwidth and network performance will depend on your on-premises Internet connectivity, as well as the type and size of the Amazon EC2 instance.

Accessing AWS resources using private IPs leveraging site-to-site IP Security (IPsec) VPN over the public Internet Using the public Internet, you can set up an encrypted tunnel between your on-premises environment and your VPC. This tunnel will be responsible for transporting all traffic between the two environments in a secure, encrypted fashion. You can terminate this VPN on a Virtual Private Gateway (VGW) or on an Amazon EC2 instance. When terminating VPNs on the VGW, AWS takes care of IPsec and Border Gateway Protocol (BGP) configuration and is responsible for uptime, availability, and patching/maintenance of the VGW. You are responsible for configuring IPsec and routing at your end. When terminating a VPN on an Amazon EC2 instance, you are responsible for deploying the software, IPsec configuration, routing, high availability, and scaling. For more details, refer to Chapter 4, "Virtual Private Networks." As VPN connections traverse the Internet, they are usually quick and easy to set up and often leverage existing network equipment and connectivity. Note that these connections are also subject to jitter and bandwidth variability, depending on the path that your traffic takes on the Internet. There are several applications that can use VPN to run efficiently. For other hybrid applications that require more consistent network performance or high network bandwidth, AWS Direct Connect will be the more suitable option.

Accessing AWS resources over a private circuit leveraging the AWS Direct Connect service The best way to remove the uncertainty of the public Internet when it comes to performance, latency, and security is to set up a dedicated circuit between a VPC and your on-premises data center. AWS Direct Connect lets you establish a dedicated network connection between your network and one of the AWS Direct Connect locations. For more details refer to Chapter 5, "AWS Direct Connect."

Application Architectures

Now that you have a clearer understanding of the connectivity options, let's examine various application types that require hybrid IT connectivity and how these connectivity options can be leveraged for each use case.

Three-Tier Web Application

A Three-Tier web application is commonly referred to as a *web application stack*. This type of application consists of multiple layers, each of which performs a specific function and is isolated in its own networking boundary. Typically, the stack consists of a web layer, which is responsible for accepting all incoming end-user requests, followed by an application layer, which is responsible for implementing the business logic of the application, and lastly followed by a database storage layer, which is responsible for storing the application data.

Usually, you would want all the three layers to be either on-premises or in AWS for minimal latency between layers, but there are scenarios where a hybrid solution is more suitable. For example, you may be in the transition phase of an application migration to AWS, or you want to use AWS to augment on-premises resources with Amazon EC2 instances, such as to distribute application traffic across both your AWS and on-premises resources. In such scenarios, the application stack spans both AWS and on-premises, and a crucial component to the success of such deployment is the connectivity between your on-premises data center and your VPC.

During this phased migration, you can start by deploying the web layer in AWS, while the application and database layers remain on-premises. Initially, you can have the web servers both in AWS and on-premises, using Application Load Balancer or Network Load Balancer to spread traffic across both of these stacks. Application Load Balancer and Network Load Balancer can route traffic directly to on-premises IP addresses that reside on the other end of the VPN or AWS Direct Connect connection. You need to make sure that the load balancer is in a subnet that has a route back to the on-premises network. We recommend testing this scenario for latency and user experience before deployment. Figure 12.1 depicts this hybrid use case.

FIGURE 12.1 Hybrid web application using AWS Load Balancing

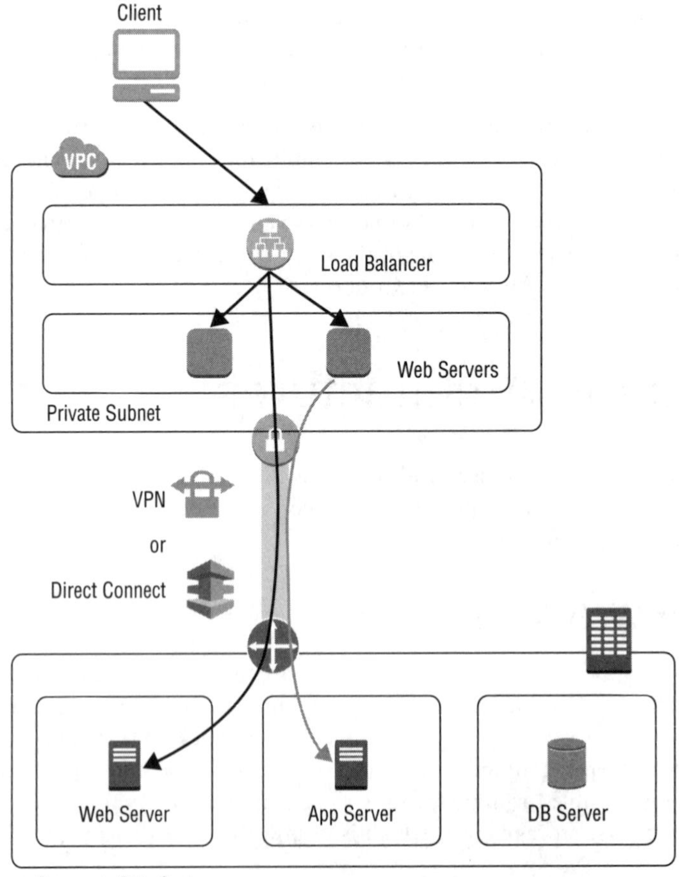

Another way to load-balance traffic between multiple environments is to use DNS-based load balancing. In this scenario, you would use a Network Load Balancer in AWS to load-balance traffic to your web layer. You would create a DNS record mapping to your domain name that contains the IP of both the Network Load Balancer and the on-premises load balancer. If you're using Amazon Route 53 as your DNS provider, you can choose any of the seven routing policies that are supported to load balance traffic across Network Load Balancer and an on-premises load balancer. An example would be using the weighted routing policy, with which you would create two records, one for an on-premises server and another for Network Load Balancer, and assign each record a relative weight that corresponds to how much traffic you want to send to each resource. For more details on Amazon Route 53 routing policies, refer to Chapter 6, "Domain Name System and Load Balancing." This scenario is shown in Figure 12.2.

FIGURE 12.2 Hybrid web application using DNS and AWS load balancing

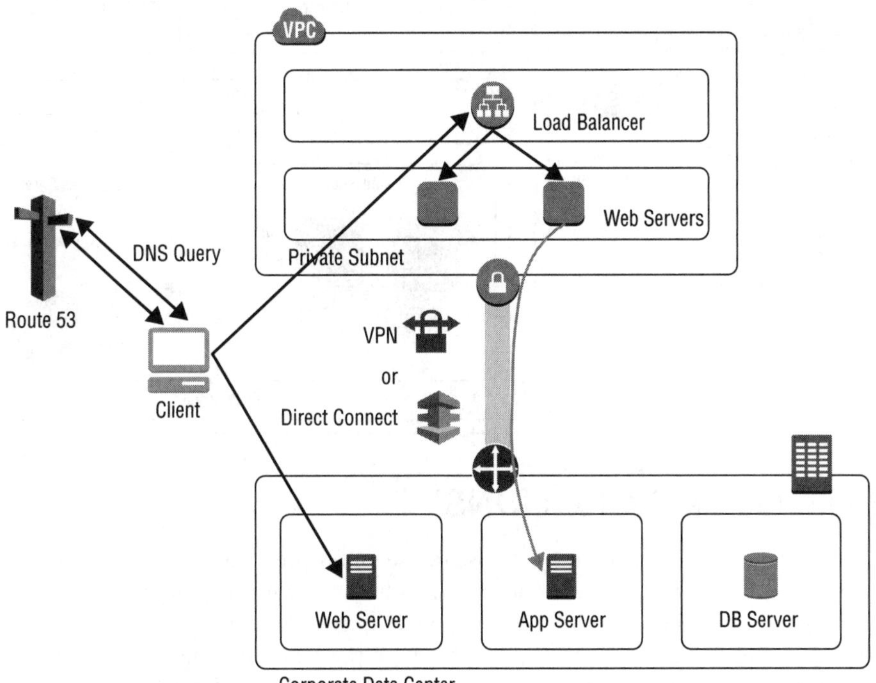

Active Directory

Active Directory is essential for Windows and/or Linux workloads in the cloud. When deploying application servers on AWS, you may choose to use the on-premises Active Directory servers and connect them to your VPC environment. You may also choose to deploy Active Directory servers in the VPC, which will act as a local copy of the on-premises Active Directory. This can be achieved by using AWS Directory Service for

Microsoft Active Directory (Enterprise Edition) and establishing a trust relationship with on-premises Active Directory servers. In either scenario, you will require a VPN or an AWS Direct Connect private Virtual Interface (VIF) between your on-premises data center and AWS. Figure 12.3 depicts this hybrid use case.

FIGURE 12.3 Hybrid Active Directory setup

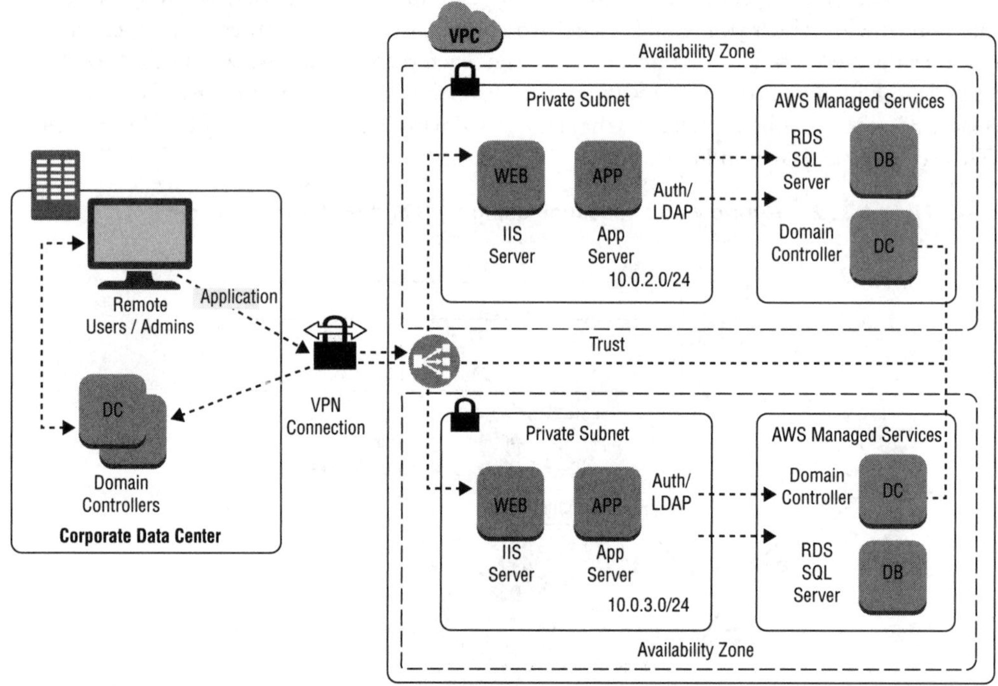

Domain Name System (DNS)

Similar to Active Directory, you may choose to use an on-premises server (colocated with the Active Directory Domain controller or otherwise) for assigning DNS names to your Amazon EC2 instances and/or resolving DNS queries for on-premises server names. In either case, you will require connectivity between the VPC and your on-premises data center. Typically, you will have one or more (for high availability) DNS forwarders sitting inside the VPC, which are responsible for forwarding DNS queries for VPC services to the VPC DNS and forwarding DNS queries for on-premises resources to the on-premises DNS server. Proper connectivity using AWS Direct Connect or VPN is required between the forwarder and the on-premises DNS server.

Applications Requiring Consistent Network Performance

Certain applications require a specific level of network consistency to ensure a proper end-user experience. This requires particular attention because traffic is often flowing from an on-premises environment to AWS when using a hybrid architecture. Customers usually architect hybrid IT connectivity such that all applications share the same Direct Connect port and so contend for the port bandwidth. A high-bandwidth-consuming application like data archiving can saturate the circuit, affecting the performance of other applications.

When looking at how application degradation can be avoided, you can consider reserving a separate AWS Direct Connect connection solely for any application traffic that requires Quality of Service (QoS). Essentially, if the shared connection cannot be policed, then it is best to have separate connections. A sub-1 Gbps or 1 Gbps connection can be dedicated to this application traffic, which will provide the application with the required bandwidth it needs to function properly. In Figure 12.4, Application 1 has been given a dedicated 1 Gbps AWS Direct Connect connection, while the rest of the production environment shares a 10 Gbps AWS Direct Connect connection. The two Apps can be located in two different VPC subnets within the same VPC if they communicate with different subnets on-premises. You can use as-path prepends to make the 1Gbps link primary for one on-premises subnet while the 10Gbps primary for the other. If the two Apps communicate with the same on-premises subnet, place them in different VPC's. Make sure that the VPC's are attached to different AWS Direct Connect Gateways. Private VIF over the 1Gbps link should be attached to the AWS Direct Connect Gateway of the App 1 VPC and respectively for 10Gbps link on App 2.

FIGURE 12.4 Quality of Service implementation

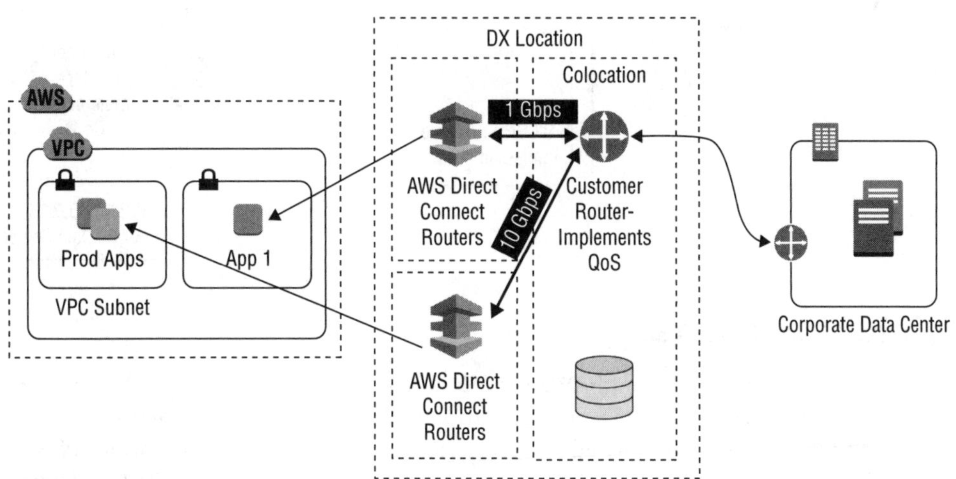

Within AWS Direct Connect routers, all traffic on a given port is shared. Certain traffic cannot be given priority over others. You can, however, use QoS markings within your networks and network devices. When packets leave on-premises network boundaries and traverse through your service provider networks that should honor Differentiated Services Code Point (DSCP) bits, QoS can be applied normally. When the traffic reaches AWS, DSCP is not used to modify traffic forwarding in AWS networks, but the header remains as it was received. This ensures that the return traffic has the QoS markings required for the intermediary service provider and your on-premises devices to police traffic.

If you are using VPN (over the Internet or AWS Direct Connect), the QoS configuration varies based on where you are terminating the VPN on the AWS end. When terminating VPN on the VGW, as well as in the case of AWS Direct Connect, QoS markings are not acted upon by the VGW. When you are terminating VPN on an Amazon EC2 instance, you can honor the QoS markings and/or implement policy-based forwarding to prioritize certain traffic flow over others. This should be supported by your VPN software loaded on the Amazon EC2 instance with appropriate configuration as required. Using advanced libraries like Data Plane Development Kit (DPDK), you can get complete visibility into the packet markings and can implement a custom packet forwarding logic.

QoS is not acted on by the AWS networking plane after the packet leaves the Amazon EC2 instance (terminating VPN) toward the final Application 1 server. QoS is only used by an Amazon EC2 instance at the operating system level to make its to make its forwarding decision, prioritizing Application 1 traffic over Production traffic coming over the VPN tunnel.

FIGURE 12.5 AWS CodeDeploy endpoint access over public VIF

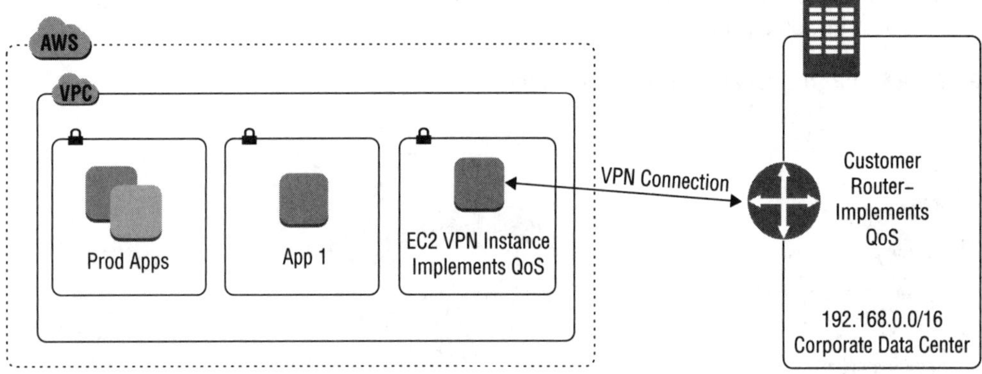

Hybrid Operations

You can use AWS CodeDeploy and AWS OpsWorks to deploy code and launch infrastructure, both on-premises and in AWS. You can also use Amazon EC2 Run Command to remotely and securely manage virtual machines running in your data center or on AWS. Amazon EC2 Run Command provides a simple way of automating common administrative tasks, like executing Shell scripts and commands on Linux, running PowerShell commands on Windows, installing software or patches, and more. Together, these tools let you build a unified operational plane for virtual machines, both on-premises and on AWS.

For these tools to work, you need to enable access to AWS public endpoints from within the on-premises environment. This access can be over the public Internet or can be through AWS Direct Connect. By creating an AWS Direct Connect public VIF, you can enable access to all AWS endpoints in the Amazon public IP space. All traffic to and from the Amazon EC2, AWS CodeDeploy, and AWS OpsWorks endpoints will be sent over the AWS Direct Connect circuit. An example of this traffic flow is shown in Figure 12.5.

Remote Desktop Application: Amazon Workspaces

Amazon WorkSpaces is a managed, secure Desktop as a Service (DaaS) solution that runs on AWS. The networking requirements of Amazon Workspaces were briefly covered in Chapter 11, "Service Requirements." In this section, we look at how you can leverage hybrid connectivity while using Amazon WorkSpaces. One common use case is for the connectivity of your on-premises Active Directory server with AWS Directory Service to enable using your existing enterprise user credentials with Amazon WorkSpaces. We covered how you can use AWS Direct Connect private VIF or VPN to enable this same capability in the previous section.

Another use case is for providing Amazon WorkSpaces users access to internal systems hosted in your data center, such as internal websites, human resources applications, and internal tools. You can connect your Amazon WorkSpaces VPC to your on-premises data center using an AWS Direct Connect private VIF or VPN. You would create a private VIF to the VPC in which Amazon WorkSpaces is hosted.

A third use case is for access to Amazon WorkSpaces from end-user clients. The Amazon WorkSpaces clients connect to a set of Amazon WorkSpaces PC over IP (PCoIP) proxy endpoints. The clients also require access to several other endpoints, such as update services, connectivity check services, registration, and CAPTCHA. These endpoints sit outside the VPC in the Amazon public IP range. You can use an AWS Direct Connect public VIF to enable connectivity to these IP ranges from your on-premises network to AWS. This connectivity option is depicted in Figure 12.6.

FIGURE 12.6 Using AWS Direct Connect and VPN for Amazon WorkSpaces connectivity

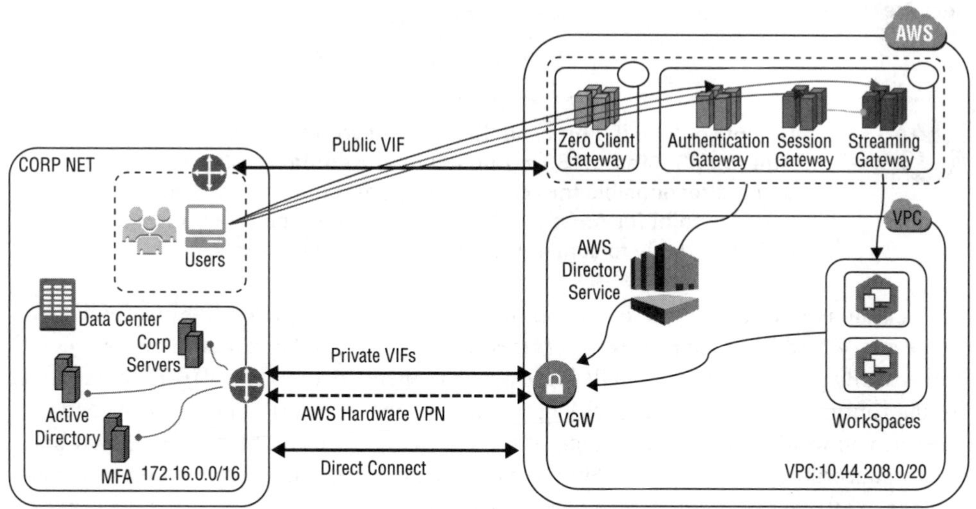

Application Storage Access

The two most commonly used AWS storage services in hybrid application architectures are Amazon Simple Storage Service (Amazon S3) and Amazon Elastic File System (Amazon EFS). In this section, we review how these storage classes can be accessed using an AWS Direct Connect VPN connection.

Amazon Simple Storage Service (Amazon S3)

Accessing Amazon S3 from on-premises networks is one of the most common hybrid IT use cases. Whether you have applications that use Amazon S3 as their primary storage layer, or you want to archive data to Amazon S3, low-latency and high-bandwidth access to the service is desirable.

Amazon S3 endpoints sit in the Amazon public IP space. You can easily access Amazon S3 endpoints using an AWS Direct Connect public VIF. If Amazon S3 is the only AWS Cloud service for which you want to use the public VIF, you can configure your on-premises router to route only to the Amazon S3 IP range and ignore all of the other routes advertised by AWS over the public VIF. You can determine the exact IP range of Amazon S3 in each AWS Region by programmatically calling the ec2 describe-prefix-lists Application Programming Interface (API). This API call describes the available AWS Cloud services in a prefix list format, which includes the prefix list name and prefix list ID of the service and the IP address range for the service.

Another way to get access to this same data is via the `ip-ranges.json` document located in the AWS documentation under the AWS General Reference, AWS IP Address Ranges section. The Amazon S3 IP range can be located by parsing the JSON file (manually or programmatically) and looking for all entries where the value of service is `S3`. The following is an example of an Amazon S3 entry:

```
{
"ip_prefix": "52.92.16.0/20",
"region": "us-east-1",
"service": "S3"
}
```

Do not confuse the Amazon S3 endpoint with the VPC private endpoint for Amazon S3. Amazon S3 endpoints refer to Amazon S3 service endpoints that are responsible for accepting all Amazon S3-bound traffic. A VPC private endpoint for Amazon S3 is a gateway endpoint for your VPC to send traffic privately to actual Amazon S3 service endpoints.

Note that as AWS continues to expand our services, the advertised IP ranges will change as AWS adds public ranges to services such as Amazon S3. These changes are automatically propagated using BGP route advertisements over public VIF. If you are filtering routes or putting static entries based on an Amazon S3 IP range as mentioned, however, you would want to keep track of these changes. You can be notified if that happens by subscribing to an Amazon Simple Notification Service (Amazon SNS) topic that we make available for this purpose. The Amazon Resource Name (ARN) for this topic is `arn:aws:sns:us-east-1:806199016981:AmazonIpSpaceChanged`. This notification will be generated anytime there is a change to the `ip-ranges.json` document. Upon receiving a notification change, you will have to check whether the Amazon S3 range is changed. This can be automated with an Amazon SNS-triggered AWS Lambda function.

Another way to access Amazon S3 from an on-premises network is to proxy all traffic via a fleet of Amazon EC2 instances that reside inside your application VPC. The idea is to use AWS Direct Connect private VIF to send Amazon S3-bound traffic to a fleet of Amazon EC2 instances sitting behind a Network Load Balancer in the VPC. These Amazon EC2 instances are running Squid and will proxy all traffic to Amazon S3 using the VPC private endpoint for Amazon S3. This solution is depicted in Figure 12.7.

You can also leverage the transit VPC architecture, which is discussed in greater detail later in this chapter, to access Amazon S3 over AWS Direct Connect. In this method, you will have to rely on the Amazon S3 IP range to send traffic to the transit hub. The same consideration regarding IP range changes and subscribing to an Amazon SNS topic applies.

FIGURE 12.7 Accessing Amazon S3 over AWS Direct Connect private VIF

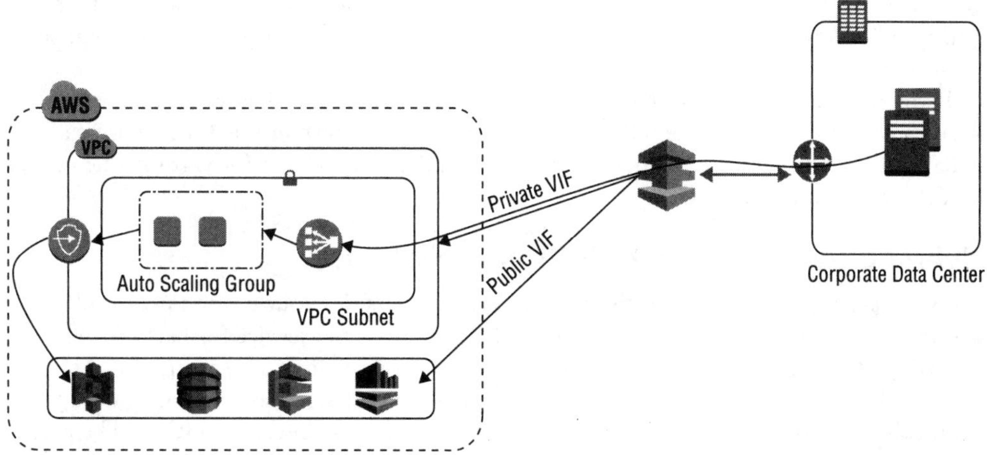

Make sure that the subnets in which the proxy servers are running have route tables that direct Amazon S3 traffic to a VPC endpoint.

You will have to configure the end clients to use a proxy and enter the Network Load Balancer DNS name as the proxy server in the client proxy settings.

From a throughput and latency point of view, leveraging public VIF (the first option discussed) should work the best. You should be able to get the full bandwidth to Amazon S3, as determined by your AWS Direct Connect port speed. The option involving the transit VPC architecture, is limited by the throughput of the transit Amazon EC2 instances. You will also have additional latency involved with IPsec packet processing. You also pay for Amazon EC2 transit instances compute costs and any software licensing for VPN software.

The option involving the use of an Amazon EC2-based proxy layer over private VIF supports horizontal scaling, so it can provide full bandwidth to Amazon S3, as determined by your AWS Direct Connect port speed. There is, however, additional latency involved with proxying traffic to intermediary hosts and the associated cost of running those hosts (Amazon EC2 compute cost plus proxy software licensing, if applicable).

Amazon Elastic File System (Amazon EFS)

Using AWS Direct Connect private VIF, you can simply attach an Amazon EFS file system to your on-premises servers, copy your data to it, and then process it in the cloud as desired, leaving your data in AWS for the long term.

After you create the file system, you can reference the mount targets by their IP addresses (which will be part of the VPC IP range), Network File System (NFS)-mount them on-premises, and start copying files. You need to add a rule to the mount target's security group in order to allow inbound Transmission Control Protocol (TCP) and User Datagram Protocol (UDP) traffic to port 2049 (NFS) from your on-premises servers.

If you want to use the DNS names of the Amazon EFS mount, then you will have to set up a DNS forwarder in the VPC. This forwarder will be responsible for accepting all Amazon EFS DNS resolution requests from on-premises servers and forwarding them to the VPC DNS for actual resolution.

Hybrid Cloud Storage: AWS Storage Gateway

AWS Storage Gateway is a hybrid storage service that enables your on-premises applications to seamlessly use AWS Cloud storage. You can use the service for backup and archiving, disaster recovery, cloud bursting, multiple storage tiers, and migration. Your applications connect to the service through a gateway appliance using standard storage protocols, such as NFS and Internet Small Computer Systems Interface (iSCSI). The gateway connects to AWS storage services, such as Amazon S3, Amazon Glacier, and Amazon Elastic Block Store (Amazon EBS), providing storage for files, volumes, and virtual tapes in AWS.

In order for AWS Storage Gateway to be able to push data to AWS, it needs access to the AWS Storage Gateway service API endpoints and the Amazon S3 and Amazon CloudFront service API endpoints. These endpoints are in Amazon's public IP space and can be accessed over the public Internet or by using AWS Direct Connect public VIF.

If you have vast amounts of data to be transferred and are concerned about high network costs and long transfer times, you can use AWS Snowball. AWS Snowball uses secure appliances and the AWS Snowball client to accelerate petabyte-scale data transfers into and out of AWS without the need for hybrid IT connectivity.

Application Internet Access

Applications that require Internet access use an Internet gateway in the VPC as the default gateway. For some sensitive applications, you may choose to deploy an Amazon EC2 instance-based firewall capable of advanced threat protection as the default gateway. Another option is to route all Internet-bound traffic back to your on-premises location and then send it via your on-premises Internet connection. Packet inspection of the traffic can be performed using an existing on-premises security stack. You may also choose to bring all Internet traffic on-premises if you want to source all traffic from the IPv4 address range that you own.

In order to bring all traffic back on-premises, whether it be over VPN or AWS Direct Connect, you need to advertise a default route to the VGW attached to the VPC. Making appropriate bandwidth estimations is recommended before enabling this traffic flow to ensure that Internet-bound traffic is not saturating the link, which would otherwise be used for hybrid IT traffic.

Access VPC Endpoints and Customer-Hosted Endpoints over AWS Direct Connect

Gateway VPC endpoints and interface VPC endpoints allow you to access AWS Cloud services without the need to send traffic via an Internet gateway or Network Address Translation (NAT) device in your VPC. Customer-hosted endpoints allow you to expose your own service behind a Network Load Balancer as an endpoint to another VPC. For more details on how these endpoints work, refer to Chapter 3, "Advanced Amazon Virtual Private Cloud (Amazon VPC)." In this section, we focus on how these endpoints can be reached over AWS Direct Connect or VPN.

Gateway VPC endpoints use the AWS route table and DNS to route traffic privately to AWS Cloud services. These mechanisms prevent access to gateway endpoints from outside the VPC, i.e., over AWS Direct connect, AWS managed VPN. Connections that come from VPN and AWS Direct Connect through the VGW cannot natively access gateway endpoints. You can, however, build a self-managed proxy layer (as described in the Amazon S3 section of this chapter) to enable access to gateway VPC endpoints over AWS Direct Connect private VIF or VPN.

Interface VPC endpoints and customer-hosted endpoints, both powered by Private Link, can be accessed over AWS Direct Connect. When the interface endpoint or customer-hosted endpoint is created, the AWS Cloud service has a regional and zonal DNS name that resolves to the local IP addresses within your VPC. This IP address will be reachable over AWS Direct Connect private VIF. Accessing interface VPC endpoints or customer-hosted endpoints over AWS managed VPN or VPC peering, however, is not supported.

If you want to access interface VPC endpoints, customer-hosted endpoints over VPN, you have to set up VPN termination on an Amazon EC2 instance and apply NAT for all incoming traffic to the IP address of the Amazon EC2 instance. This hides the source IP and makes the traffic look as if it was being initiated from within the VPC. This method is valid for accessing Gateway VPC endpoints as well. For more details on Amazon EC2 instance-based VPN termination, refer to Chapter 4.

Encryption on AWS Direct Connect

In Chapter 5, we briefly discussed how you can use IPsec site-to-site VPN over AWS Direct Connect to enable encryption. In this section, we examine the finer details of setting this up and the various options available.

If you want to encrypt all application traffic, ideally you should use TLS at the application layer. This approach is more scalable and does not impose challenges regarding high availability and throughput scalability, which inline encryption gateways impose. If your application is not able to encrypt data using TLS (or some other encryption library), or if you want to encrypt Layer 3 traffic (like Internet Control Message Protocol [ICMP]), you can set up site-to-site IPsec VPN over AWS Direct Connect.

The easiest way to set up IPsec VPN over AWS Direct Connect is to terminate VPN on the AWS-managed VPN endpoint, VGW. As discussed in Chapter 4, when setting up a VPN connection, VGW provides two public IP-based endpoints for terminating VPN. These public IPs can be accessed over an AWS Direct Connect public VIF. If required, you can configure your on-premises router to filter routes received from the AWS router over public VIF and allow only routing to the VPN endpoints. This will block the use of AWS Direct Connect for any other traffic destined to AWS public IP space. Figure 12.8 depicts this option.

FIGURE 12.8 VPN to VGW over AWS Direct Connect public VIF

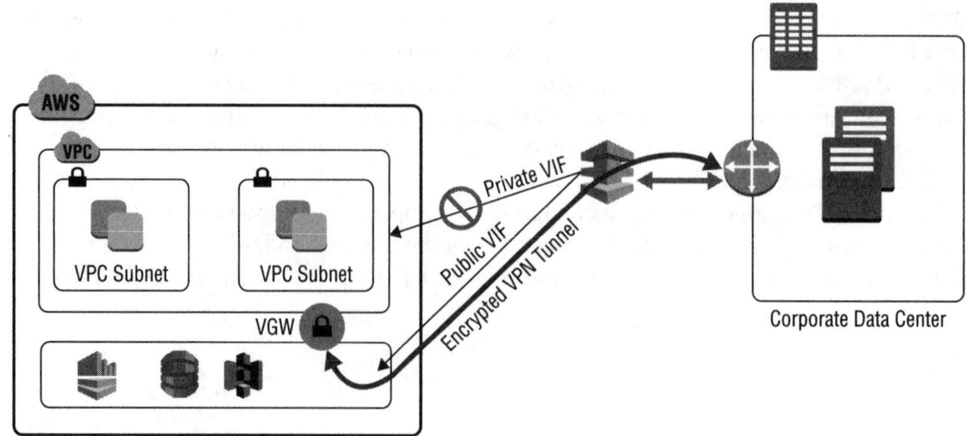

Another way to encrypt traffic over AWS Direct Connect is to set up site-to-site VPN to an Amazon EC2 instance inside a VPC. The details for setting a site-to-site IPsec VPN to an Amazon EC2 instance from an on-premises environment is explained in Chapter 4. When setting up AWS Direct Connect, instead of using the Amazon EC2 instance's elastic IP, you can use its private IP for VPN termination. You will set up private VIF to the VPC that contains the Amazon EC2 instance. You will use this private VIF to access the private IP of the Amazon EC2 instance. Figure 12.9 depicts this option.

FIGURE 12.9 VPN to Amazon EC2 instance over AWS Direct Connect private VIF

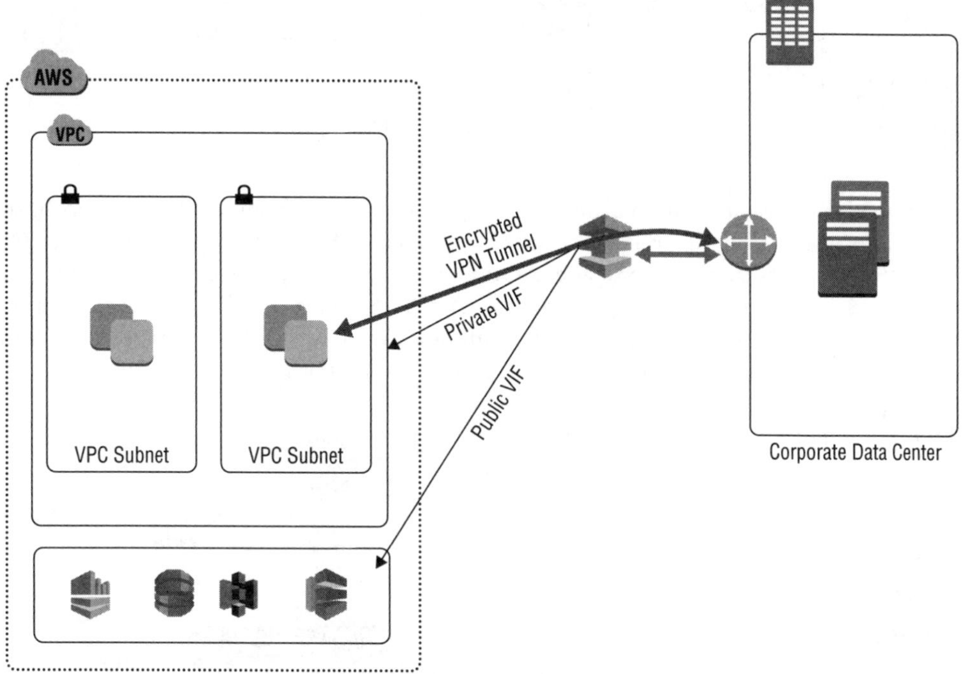

Note that the VPC IP range will be advertised over the private VIF. You want to use this routing domain to reach the Amazon EC2 instance responsible for VPN termination. All of the other traffic destined to other resources in the VPC should go through the VPN tunnel interface. You can leverage any router features/techniques to achieve this. One way to do this is by leveraging Virtual Routing and Forwarding (VRF) where the BGP peering to the VGW over private VIF is handled in a separate VRF in the router. VPN is set up to the Amazon EC2 instance leveraging VRF. Outside the VRF, the next hop to reach the VPC IP range will be the tunnel interface. An example of this is shown in Figure 12.10, where the customer router has a direct connection to AWS. It is using private VIF to connect to a VPC with Classless Inter-Domain Routing (CIDR) 172.31.0.0/16. The native access to this VPC is restricted to the VRF. A VPN tunnel is set up to an Amazon EC2 instance in the VPC. The tunnel interface on the customer router becomes the next hop to reach the VPC CIDR in the main routing table to the router.

FIGURE 12.10 Isolating routing domains using VRF

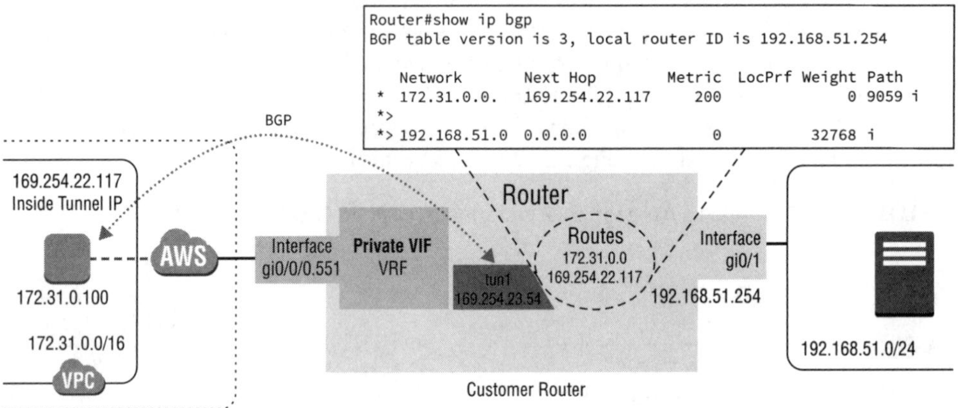

```
Router#show ip bgp
BGP table version is 3, local router ID is 192.168.51.254

   Network          Next Hop            Metric  LocPrf Weight Path
 * 172.31.0.0.      169.254.22.117        200                0 9059 i
 *>
 *> 192.168.51.0    0.0.0.0                 0            32768 i
```

BGP
169.254.22.117
Inside Tunnel IP
AWS
172.31.0.100
172.31.0.0/16
VPC
Interface
gi0/0/0.551
Private VIF
VRF
Router
tun1
169.254.23.54
Routes
172.31.0.0
169.254.22.117
192.168.51.254
Interface
gi0/1
192.168.51.0/24
Customer Router

Another way to set this up to avoid receiving the same route from VGW and the Amazon EC2 instance is by assigning the Amazon EC2 instance an Elastic IP address and using public VIF to access that Elastic IP address. As mentioned before, you can configure your on-premises router to filter routes received from an AWS router over public VIF and allow only routing to this Elastic IP address. This will block the usage of AWS Direct Connect for any other traffic destined to AWS public IP space. This setup is depicted in Figure 12.11.

FIGURE 12.11 VPN to Amazon EC2 over AWS Direct Connect public VIF

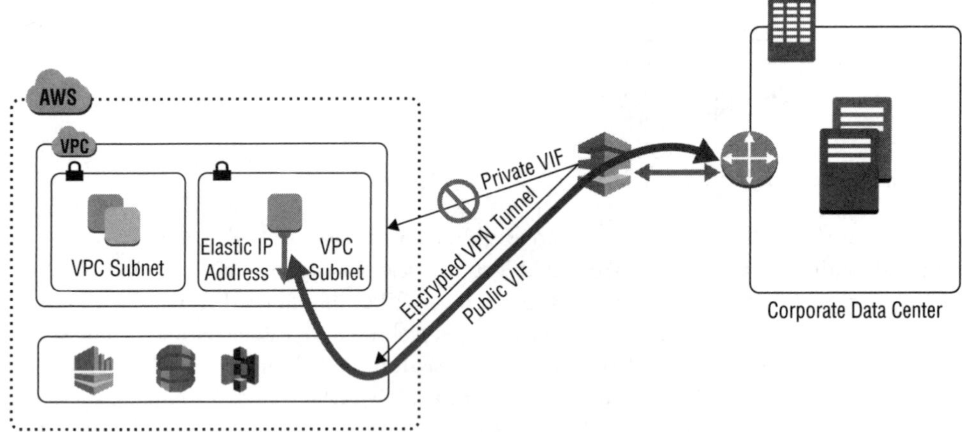

For high availability, you should have two Amazon EC2 instances in different Availability Zones for VPN termination.

You should also implement this setup with Internet as a backup in case the AWS Direct Connect connectivity is interrupted. For the first method where we created tunnels to VGW endpoints over public VIF, your router will have to use the Internet to access the same endpoints in the event of a failure. The IPsec tunnels and routing will have to be reestablished upon failure, resulting in minor downtime. If you want to have an active-active setup, you will have to set up a secondary active VPN connection with a different source IP at your end—VGW cannot create two VPN connections to the same customer gateway IP at the same time.

In the case of terminating VPN over private VIF to an Amazon EC2 instance using its private IP, Internet failover cannot be achieved to the same IP because RFC 1918 IP ranges are publicly non-routable. You will have to assign an Elastic IP address to the Amazon EC2 instance and set up a VPN tunnel to it using the Elastic IP address over the Internet. You can configure this through the BGP AS path prepend and local preference parameters, making the VPN tunnel over the private VIF the primary VPN tunnel and the Internet-based VPN tunnel the backup.

Use of Transitive Routing in Hybrid IT

Chapter 3 and Chapter 4 discussed what transitive routing is and some of the limitations around establishing it natively on AWS. Those chapters also discussed how you can leverage Amazon EC2 instances to enable transitive routing by setting up VPN tunnels. Further, in Chapter 5, you saw how transit VPC architecture can be connected to AWS Direct Connect. In this section, we dive deeper into the transit VPC architecture.

In the context of hybrid connectivity, a transit VPC architecture allows on-premises environments to access AWS resources while transiting all traffic through a pair of Amazon EC2 instances. This is depicted in the architecture shown in Figure 12.12.

FIGURE 12.12 Transit VPC architecture

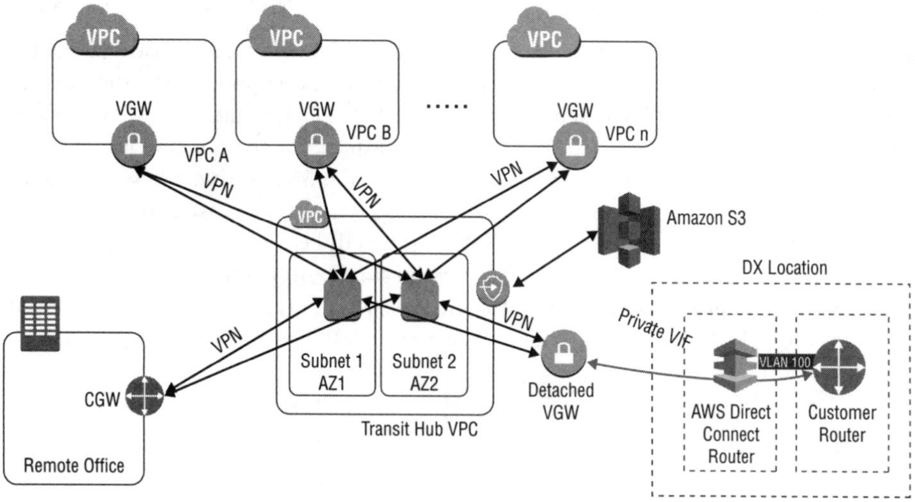

In this architecture, we have the transit hub VPC, which consists of Amazon EC2 instances with VPN termination software loaded on them. These Amazon EC2 instances are present in different Availability Zones for high availability and act as a transit point for all remote networks. Spoke VPCs use VGW as their VPN termination endpoint. There are pairs of VPN tunnels from each spoke VPC to the hub Amazon EC2 instances. Remote networks connect to the transit VPC using redundant, dynamically-routed VPN connections set up between your on-premises VPN termination equipment and the Amazon EC2 instances in the transit hub. This design supports BGP dynamic routing protocol, which you can use to route traffic automatically around potential network failures and to propagate network routes to remote networks.

All communication from the Amazon EC2 instances, including the VPN connections between corporate data centers or other provider networks and the transit VPC, uses the transit VPC Internet gateway and the instances' Elastic IP addresses.

AWS Direct Connect can most easily be used with the transit VPC solution by using a detached VGW. This is a VGW that has been created but not attached to a specific VPC. Within the VGW, AWS VPN CloudHub provides the ability to receive routes via BGP from both VPN and AWS Direct Connect and then re-advertise/reflect them back to each other. This enables the VGW to form the hub for your connectivity.

Transit VPC Architecture Considerations

Using VPC peering vs. transit VPC for spoke-VPC-to-spoke-VPC communication For some inter-spoke VPC communication, VPC peering can be used instead of sending traffic via the Amazon EC2 instance in the transit hub VPC. This is a common scenario when you have two (or more) security zones: one trusted zone and other non-trusted zones. You would use the transit VPC to communicate between VPCs belonging to trusted and non-trusted zones. For VPCs that belong to the same trusted zone, you can bypass the transit VPC and directly use VPC peering. Using direct VPC peering provides better throughput and availability and also reduces traffic load on the transit VPC Amazon EC2 instances.

In order for this scenario to work, you will set up a VPC peering connection to the target VPC and add an entry in the spoke VPC subnet route table pointing to the peering connection as the next hop for reaching the remote VPC. Note that both of the spoke VPCs are still connected to the transit VPC. No architectural change is required for this to work, apart from creating the VPC peering connection and adding a new static entry in the route tables. Assuming that the routes from the transit VPC are propagated in the spoke VPC subnet route tables from the VGW, there will be a route to reach the target VPC with the next hop as VGW, in addition to the static entry pointing to the peering connection that you just created. The static route entry will take priority. If you remove this static route, all traffic will fall back to the transit VPC path. This scenario is depicted in Figure 12.13.

FIGURE 12.13 VPC peering vs. transit VPC for spoke-to-spoke communication

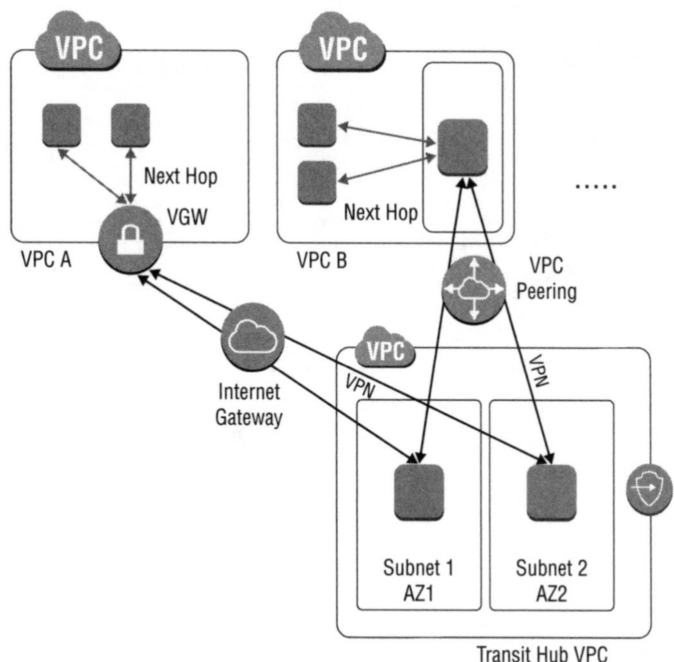

Using AWS Direct Connect gateway vs. transit VPC infrastructure for on-premises environment to spoke VPC communication Similar to the rationale for spoke-VPC-to-spoke-VPC communication, if you want to access a trusted VPC from an on-premises environment, you can leverage AWS Direct Connect to send traffic directly to the VPC instead of sending traffic to the transit VPC. In this scenario, your on-premises router will get two routes for the spoke VPC CIDR: one from the detached VGW and the other from the spoke VPC VGW. The spoke BGP route advertisement from the spoke VPC VGW will have a shorter AS path and will be preferred. This scenario is depicted in Figure 12.14.

Using VGW vs. Amazon EC2 instances over VPC peering for connecting spoke VPC to hub In our architecture, spoke VPC leverages VGW capabilities for routing and failover in order to maintain highly-available network connections to the transit VPC instances. VPC peering is not used to connect to the hub because VGW endpoints are not accessible over VPC peering. You can choose to deploy Amazon EC2 instances in spoke VPC for VPN termination instead of using VGW. In this architecture, you can leverage VPC peering for the VPN connection between the Amazon EC2 instance in spoke and hub. This is not the recommended approach, however, because you have to maintain and manage additional Amazon EC2 VPN instances in every spoke VPC, which is potentially more expensive, less highly available, and more difficult to manage and operate. One benefit of choosing this route would be to receive more hub-to-spoke VPN bandwidth than what VGW can support. This scenario is depicted in Figure 12.15.

FIGURE 12.14 Transit VPC vs. AWS Direct Connect Gateway for hybrid traffic

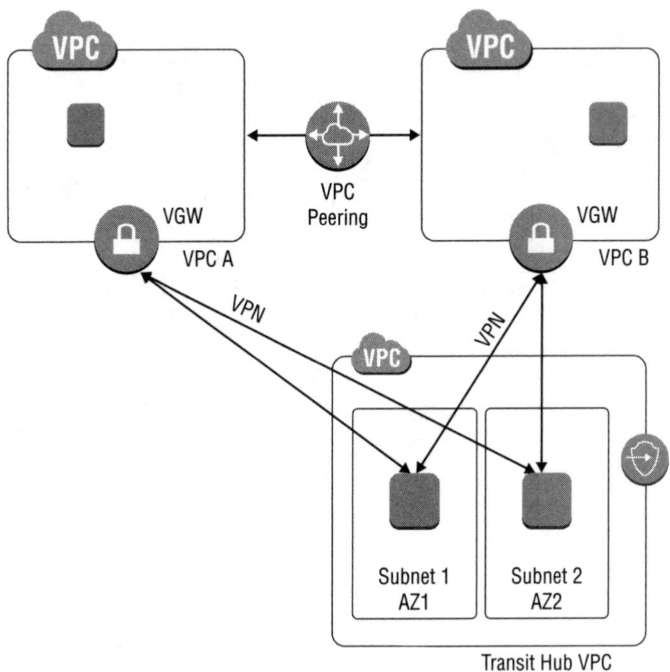

FIGURE 12.15 Transit VPC vs. AWS Direct Connect Gateway for hybrid traffic

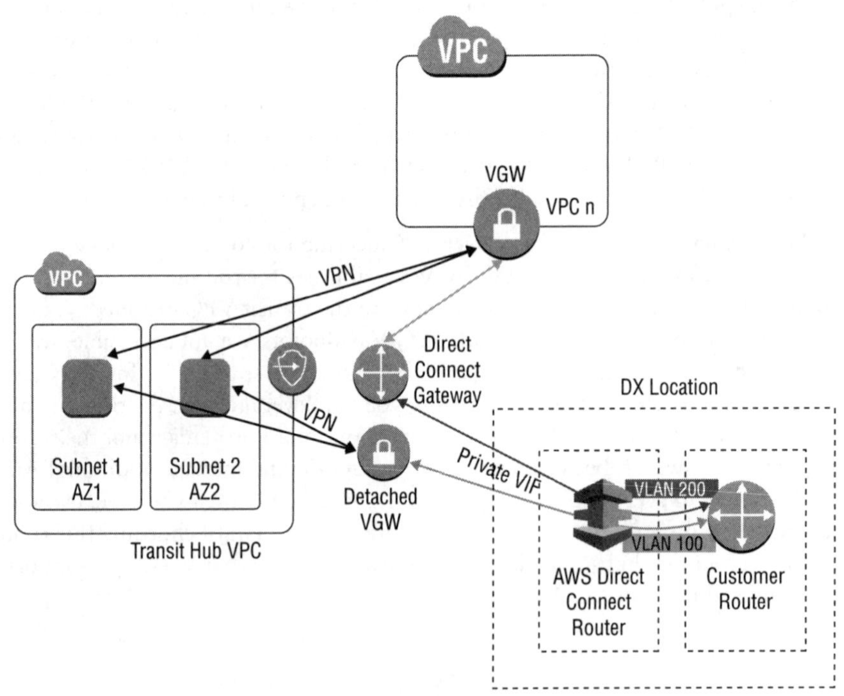

Using detached VGW vs. VPN from an on-premises VPN device to Amazon EC2 instances in transit VPC In our architecture, we leverage a detached VGW as a bridging point between the AWS Direct Connect circuit and the transit VPC infrastructure. The AWS Direct Connect private VIF is set up to this detached VGW. Alternatively, you can also set up private VIF to a VGW attached to the transit VPC and set up VPN from an on-premises VPN termination device to the Amazon EC2 instances in the transit VPC. This setup is similar to setting up VPN over AWS Direct Connect, as discussed in the previous section. We did not choose that route in our architecture by default because you have to manage the VPN on-premises, which results in extra overhead. One reason for choosing this route would be to receive high VPN throughout, which can be achieved by scaling transit Amazon EC2 instances (assuming that your on-premises VPN infrastructure can support high VPN throughput over what VGW VPN supports). For more information on scaling the VPN throughput of Amazon EC2 instance-based VPN termination, refer to Chapter 4. This is a more viable option if you have a 10 Gbps AWS Direct Connect connection. This scenario is depicted in Figure 12.16.

FIGURE 12.16 Detached VGW vs. on-premises initiated VPN

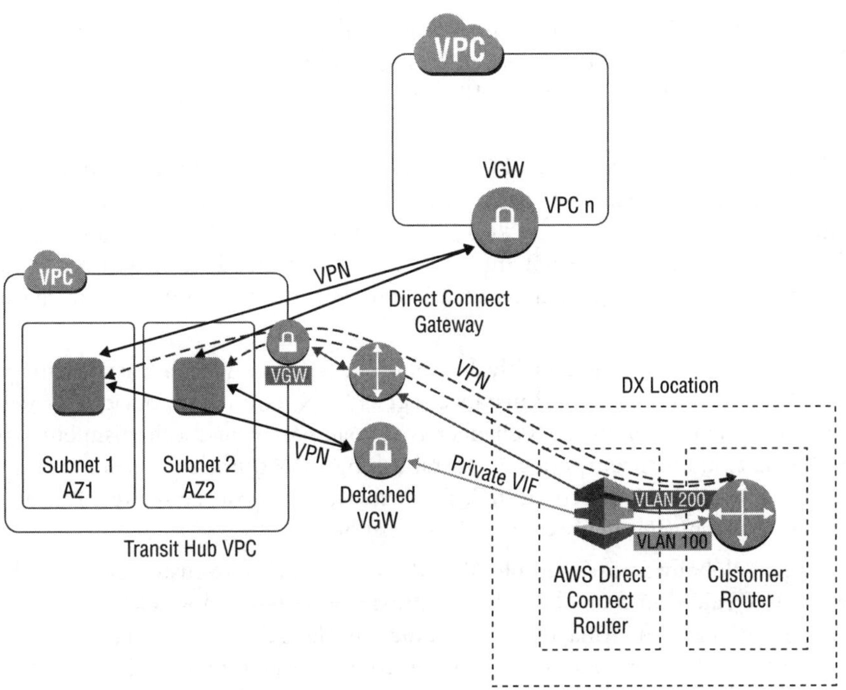

Using BGP routing vs. static routes between hub and spokes In our architecture, we used BGP for exchanging routes. Alternatively, you can also set up static routes between spoke VPCs and the transit Amazon EC2 instances. While this is a valid way of networking, it is recommended to use BGP because it makes recovery from failure and traffic rerouting seamless and automatic.

Transit VPC Scenarios

Transit VPC design can be leveraged in several scenarios:

- It can be used as a mechanism to reduce the number of tunnels required to establish VPN connectivity to a large number of VPCs. In this scenario, the transit point (that is, a pair of Amazon EC2 instances in transit VPC) becomes the middleman between the on-premises VPN termination endpoint and the VPCs. You only need to set up a pair of VPN tunnels to the transit point once from your on-premises device. As new VPCs are created, VPN tunnels can be set up between the transit point and the VGW of the VPCs without requiring any change in configuration on the on-premises devices. This is a desirable pattern because VPN tunnel creation in AWS can be automated, but VPN configuration changes on on-premises devices require manual effort with a potentially long approval process.
- It can be used to build a security layer for all hybrid traffic. Because the transit point has visibility into all hybrid traffic, you can also build an advanced threat protection layer at this point to inspect all inbound and outbound traffic. This is useful if you have untrusted remote networks connecting into your transit VPC hub.
- It can also be useful when you want to connect an on-premises/remote network to a VPC when both have the same, overlapping IP address range. The transit point becomes the NAT layer, translating IP to a different range to enable communication between the two networks.
- It also allows remote access to VPC endpoints and customer-hosted endpoints. Similar to the previous scenario, the transit point will be responsible for performing a source NAT for all incoming packets. Note that only endpoints hosted in the hub VPC will be accessible to remote networks. Spoke VPC endpoints will not be accessible unless you are using Amazon EC2 instances for VPN termination in the spoke VPCs as well.
- It can also be used to build a highly-available client-to-site VPN infrastructure on AWS. The transit Amazon EC2 instances act as VPN termination devices for remote clients. Usually the remote VPN clients have a load balancing mechanism built-in, which results in them connecting and establishing VPN tunnels to one of the Amazon EC2 VPN instances. Once connected, they can access any of the spoke VPCs and on-premises environments connected to the transit hub.
- It can span globally across multiple AWS Regions and remote customer sites, allowing you to create your own global VPN infrastructure leveraging AWS. Both the VGW in spoke VPCs and the Amazon EC2 instances in the hub VPC leverage public IP addresses for VPN termination, so they can connect even if they are in different AWS Regions. In addition, as long as a remote customer network has Internet connectivity or an AWS Direct Connect connection, it can reach the hub and join the VPN infrastructure irrespective of its location in the world. An example of this architecture is shown in Figure 12.17.

FIGURE 12.17 Global transit VPC

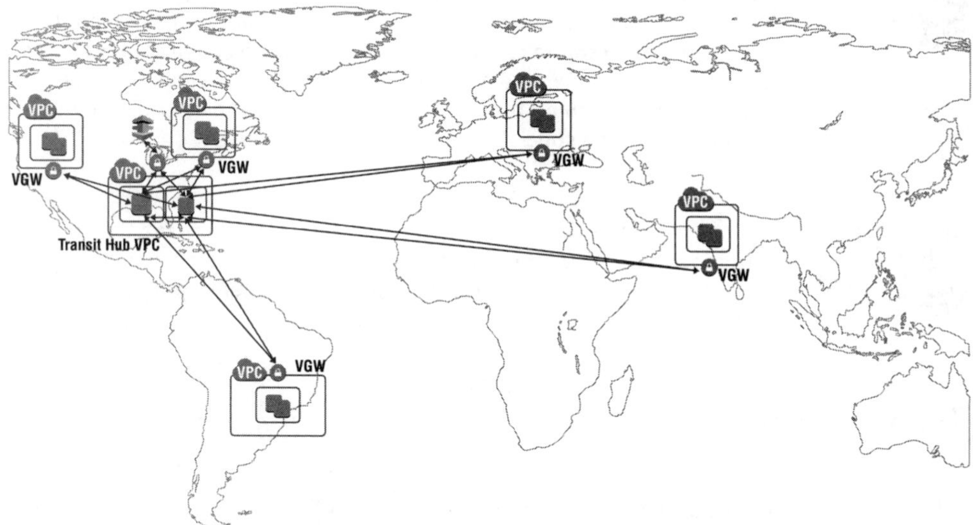

Based on your traffic access patterns, you can deploy one transit hub per AWS Region and bridge those transit hubs in mesh using IPsec or Generic Routing Encapsulation (GRE) VPNs over cross-region VPC peering. This is desirable if you have a lot of communication between the spoke networks within the local regions. This scenario is depicted in Figure 12.18.

FIGURE 12.18 Global transit VPC with regional transit hub

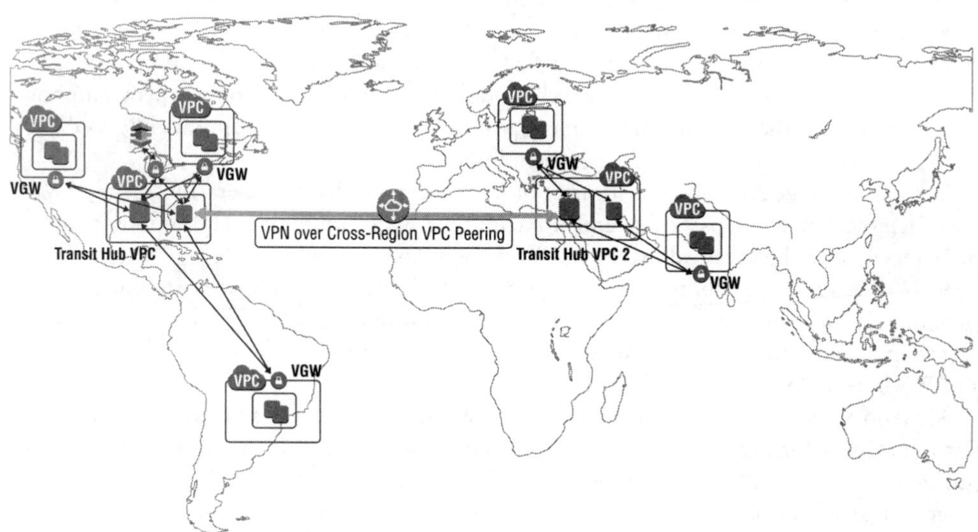

Transit VPC is not the default architecture that you should be implementing for native access to AWS resources. If your requirement is meant to access a VPC in a remote region from an on-premises environment, then you should access it using AWS Direct Connect Gateway over Private VIF rather than designing transit VPC architecture. Transit VPC should be implemented for the special use cases listed previously.

As cross-region VPC peering is encrypted by default, you can use GRE VPN to connect the transit hubs to increase performance and reduce network latency.

Summary

In this chapter, we looked at how AWS Direct Connect and VPN can be leveraged to build hybrid IT architectures. You can leverage these technologies to run applications in hybrid mode.

If you are in the process of migrating a Three-Tier web application to AWS, you can distribute the web layer across AWS and your on-premises data center using Application Load Balancer or DNS load balancing. You can also have the web layer only in AWS while the application and database layers are on-premises. You can leverage an AWS Direct Connect private VIF to connect the web layer in AWS to the application layer on-premises. You can also use AWS Direct Connect or VPN to make your on-premises Active Directory and DNS servers accessible to the resources inside your VPC.

For applications that require QoS, you have the option of using a separate AWS Direct Connect connection for isolating this traffic from other application traffic. If you are using Amazon EC2 instance-based VPN over the Internet or AWS Direct Connect, you can honor QoS markings on the VPN termination endpoints. Note that AWS endpoints like VGW do not honor QoS markings but will keep them intact.

You can leverage AWS Direct Connect or VPN to enable hybrid operations using AWS CodeDeploy, Amazon OpsWorks, and Amazon EC2 Run Command. The endpoints for these services can be accessed using an AWS Direct Connect public VIF.

VPN or AWS Direct Connect are crucial parts of Amazon WorkSpaces architectures, enabling access to on-premises Active Directory and several other internal servers. End users can also use their Amazon WorkSpaces clients to connect to their WorkSpace using an AWS Direct Connect public VIF.

Amazon S3 is one of the most widely-used AWS storage services across various applications, including for hybrid IT applications. Applications that reside on-premises can access Amazon S3 over an AWS Direct Connect public VIF. You can also use the Amazon S3 IP range to restrict traffic on your routers to access only Amazon S3. This is possible because AWS will advertise the entire Amazon public IP range by default over an AWS Direct

Connect public VIF. You can also set up a proxy layer consisting of a fleet of Amazon EC2 instances in your VPC and use that as an intermediary point to access Amazon S3. All traffic will be proxied to this layer, which then will use VPC private endpoints to send traffic to Amazon S3. You can set this up in a transparent mode or non-transparent mode.

Another commonly accessed storage service in a hybrid IT setup is Amazon EFS. You can access Amazon EFS by referencing the Amazon EFS mount targets by their IP addresses. These IP addresses belong to the VPC IP range and so can be reached over AWS Direct Connect private VIF.

You can also use AWS Direct Connect to access interface VPC endpoints and customer-hosted endpoints, both powered by Private Link. AWS VPN connections do not support access to these gateways, but you can leverage Amazon EC2 instance-based VPN termination along with source NAT to enable this access. Gateway VPC endpoints are not natively accessible over AWS Direct Connect or VPN. You can, however, use a fleet of proxy instances or Amazon EC2 instance-based VPN termination with source NAT, similar to the Amazon S3 setup discussed earlier.

We looked at how you can achieve encryption over AWS Direct Connect by setting up an IPsec VPN overlay. You can terminate a VPN connection on the VGW, which leverages the AWS Direct Connect public VIF. You can also set up a tunnel to an Amazon EC2 instance inside the VPC over an AWS Direct Connect private VIF using its private IP or over public VIF using its Elastic IP address. You should also consider an Internet-based VPN connection as a backup in case there is a failure on your AWS Direct Connect links.

We discussed how transitive routing challenges can be solved using the transit VPC architecture. In this architecture, we have the transit hub VPC that comprises a pair of Amazon EC2 instances with VPN termination software installed. These Amazon EC2 instances act as a transit point for all remote networks. All spoke VPCs connect to the pair of Amazon EC2 instances using IPsec VPN, leveraging VGW as the VPN termination endpoint at their end. AWS Direct Connect is integrated with this architecture using a detached VGW, which bridges the AWS Direct Connect routing domain with VPN infrastructure. When creating the transit VPC architecture, you have several architecture choices to make. In our example, we decided to use VGW in the spoke VPCs for VPN termination instead of a pair of Amazon EC2 instances. This allows us to leverage the inherent active-standby high availability of VGW and reduced maintenance overhead. For similar reasons, we leveraged a detached VGW instead of setting up a VPN from on-premises directly to the Amazon EC2 instances over an AWS Direct Connect private VIF. This section reviewed the considerations of using one option versus the other.

We also explored how we can leverage VPC peering for some use cases, thereby bypassing the transit hub. Similarly, we can directly access VPCs from on-premises using AWS Direct Connect gateway instead of using the transit hub. The transit VPC architecture has several use cases, including reducing the number of VPN tunnels required to connect your on-premises environment to large numbers of VPCs and implementing a security layer at the transit point. Transit VPC can also be useful when you want to connect an on-premises/remote network to a VPC when both have the same, overlapping IP address range. Transit VPC also allows remote access to VPC endpoints and customer-hosted endpoints. Lastly, transit VPC can be used to build a global VPN infrastructure.

Exam Essentials

Understand how AWS Direct Connect and VPN can be leveraged to enable several hybrid applications. You can leverage AWS Direct Connect and VPN to enable access to VPCs and other AWS resources from on-premises environments. This connectivity enablement is crucial for many hybrid applications, like the Three-Tier web application, Active Directory, DNS, and hybrid operations using AWS CodeDeploy, AWS OpsWorks, and Amazon EC2 Run Command. Each of these applications has certain requirements from a connectivity standpoint, and it is important to understand how these requirements can be fulfilled using AWS Direct Connect and VPN.

Understand how storage services like Amazon S3 and Amazon EFS can be accessed over AWS Direct Connect and VPN. Applications that are on-premises can use AWS Cloud services for their storage and archiving. It is important to understand how Amazon S3 and Amazon EFS can be accessed using AWS Direct Connect and VPN. Applications can access Amazon S3 using an AWS Direct Connect public VIF or via a proxy layer in a VPC over an AWS Direct Connect private VIF. Amazon EFS shares can be mounted using their private IPs over the private VIF.

Understand how VPC gateway endpoints and Private Link endpoints can be accessed over AWS Direct Connect and VPN. Both interface endpoints and customer-hosted endpoints can be accessed over AWS Direct Connect private VIF. VPN does not allow access to these endpoints, but you can use Amazon EC2-based VPN termination along with source NAT to allow this connectivity. VPC gateway endpoints cannot be accessed natively over AWS Direct Connect. You can, however, build a proxy layer in the VPC or use Amazon EC2 instance-based VPN termination with source NAT to access the endpoint.

Understand how encryption can be achieved over AWS Direct Connect. You can set up IPsec VPN connections over AWS Direct Connect to achieve encryption. You can terminate VPN connections on the VGW by leveraging an AWS Direct Connect public VIF or by setting up an Amazon EC2 instance inside the VPC over an AWS Direct Connect private VIF using its private IP. You can set up the VPN over a public VIF using its Elastic IP address as well. Internet backup to this infrastructure is an option for added redundancy.

Understand how transit VPC architectures work and the rationale behind various design decisions. Transit VPC architectures leverage a pair of Amazon EC2 instances to act as the transit point for remote networks. This is implemented in a hub-and-spoke model: The Amazon EC2 instances sit in the hub VPC, and the spoke VPCs use VGW at their end to set up IPsec VPN tunnels to the hub. Remote, on-premises networks can leverage AWS Direct Connect or IPsec VPN to connect to the hub.

Understand the various use cases for implementing transit VPC architectures. Transit VPC architectures can be leveraged to fulfill several requirements, such as reducing the number of VPN tunnels required to connect an on-premises environment to a large number of VPCs, implementing a security layer at the transit point, overcoming overlapping IP address ranges between VPC and on-premises networks, establishing remote access to VPC endpoints and customer-hosted endpoints, and building a global VPN infrastructure.

Test Taking Tip

There may be questions that task you to choose the right connectivity solution based on a given scenario on the exam. Carefully identify the parameters for which the scenario is testing (for example, High Availability, Performance, Cost...and so on), and evaluate the connectivity options mentioned in this chapter against those parameters to deduce the right answer.

Resources to Review

Global transit VPC solution brief:

`https://aws.amazon.com/answers/networking/aws-global-transit-network/`

Transit VPC implementation guide:

`http://docs.aws.amazon.com/solutions/latest/cisco-based-transit-vpc/welcome.html`

AWS Answers – Networking Section:

`https://aws.amazon.com/answers/networking/`

AWS re:Invent 2017: Networking Many VPCs: Transit and Shared Architectures (NET404):

`https://www.youtube.com/watch?v=KGKrVO9xlqI`

AWS re:Invent 2017: Extending Data Centers to the Cloud: Connectivity Options and Co (NET301):

`https://www.youtube.com/watch?v=lN2RybC9Vbk`

Exercises

The best way to understand how hybrid IT connectivity works is to set it up and use it to access various AWS Cloud services, which is the goal of the exercises in this chapter.

EXERCISE 12.1

Set Up a Hybrid Three-Tier Web Application Using Network Load Balancer

In this exercise, you will set up a Three-Tier web application consisting of a web layer, application layer, and database layer. The web layer will be in the VPC and on-premises. Network Load Balancer will distribute traffic to the web layer in the VPC and on-premises. You will use AWS Direct Connect for connectivity between the VPC and the on-premises data center.

EXERCISE 12.1 *(continued)*

Before beginning the exercise, make sure that you have an existing VPC set up with multiple subnets. You should also have a web application that can be deployed in a VPC and on-premises. If you do not have one, you can either install an open source Apache HTTP web server or browse AWS Marketplace for a web server software and create a simple web application.

1. Set up an AWS Direct Connect connection between your on-premises data center and AWS. Create a private VIF to the VPC that you will be using for this exercise. Configure routing to enable traffic flow between VPC and the on-premises network. If you do not have access to an AWS Direct Connect circuit, you can perform this exercise by creating a VPN connection to the VPC. You must use an Amazon EC2 instance for VPN termination over VGW for this exercise to work.
2. Launch your web application stack on-premises and test that it is functioning properly. Note the IP addresses of the web layer instances that are on-premises.
3. Launch the web layer of your application stack on an Amazon EC2 instance. Note its IP addresses.
4. Test connectivity between the web layer in AWS and the application layer on-premises.
5. Within the AWS Management Console dashboard, navigate to the Amazon EC2 dashboard and then to the Load Balancer configuration page.
6. Create a new Network Load Balancer. Create a new target group with target type as IP. Choose the correct port number based on your application.
7. Register the web layer IP addresses that you noted in Step 2 and the Amazon EC2 instance IP address from Step 3 with the load balancer.
8. Send dummy traffic to the Network Load Balancer endpoint. You should see traffic hitting both the on-premises web servers and the web layer in AWS.

You have now successfully deployed and tested a hybrid web application. You learned how you can use a load balancer to distribute traffic across AWS and on-premises using Network Load Balancer and AWS Direct Connect. You also observed how servers in a VPC can communicate with servers on-premises.

EXERCISE 12.2

Access Amazon S3 over AWS Direct Connect

In this exercise, you will set up the infrastructure required to access Amazon S3 objects from on-premises using a high-speed AWS Direct Connect connection.

1. Set up an AWS Direct Connect connection between your on-premises data center and AWS.

2. Create a public VIF. Configure your router with the parameters that you specified while creating the public VIF.
3. Make sure that BGP peering is up and that your router is receiving the AWS routes.
4. Configure your on-premises servers to point to your router as the default gateway.
5. Configure your router to apply NAT for all packets to a public IP before sending it over AWS Direct Connect.

The public IP you use to apply NAT should be in the IP range that your router advertises over AWS Direct Connect.

6. Log in to one of your servers and try downloading an object from Amazon S3.

You have successfully set up connectivity for your applications to access Amazon S3.

EXERCISE 12.3

Set Up Encryption over AWS Direct Connect

In this exercise, you will set up an encrypted IPsec tunnel over AWS Direct Connect. This encrypted tunnel will be used to access your VPC.

1. Set up an AWS Direct Connect connection between your on-premises data center and AWS.
2. Create a public VIF. Configure your router with the parameters that you specified while creating the public VIF.
3. Make sure that BGP peering is up and that your router is receiving the AWS routes.
4. Navigate to the Amazon VPC console and create a new VPN connection. Select the VGW attached to the VPC and customer gateway IP representing your on-premises VPN termination device.

The public IP you use as a customer gateway IP should be part of the IP range that your router advertises over AWS Direct Connect. You can also terminate VPN on your router if it has the functionality without requiring a separate device.

5. Download the VPN configuration file from the AWS Management Console and use it to configure your on-premises VPN termination device.

EXERCISE 12.3 *(continued)*

6. The VPN termination device should use your router as the default gateway, or it should have a route to reach the VGW IPs with the next hop as your router.
7. When the VPN is up, verify that you are receiving the VPC IP range as route advertisements inside the VPN tunnel.
8. Your VPN device should be the next hop for your internal servers to reach the VPC IP range.
9. Test ping connectivity to an Amazon EC2 instance from an internal server.

You have successfully set up an encrypted tunnel over AWS Direct Connect.

EXERCISE 12.4

Create a Transit VPC Global Infrastructure

In this exercise, you will learn how to set up a transit VPC infrastructure that spans multiple AWS Regions. You will also connect this transit VPC infrastructure to on-premises infrastructure using AWS Direct Connect. You will be leveraging existing automation for this exercise.

Before beginning this exercise, familiarize yourself with the transit VPC architecture and components explained here:

```
http://docs.aws.amazon.com/solutions/latest/cisco-based-transit-vpc/
appendix-a.html
```

The artifacts are available here:

```
https://github.com/awslabs/aws-transit-vpc
```

If you are looking for steps that are more detailed than those listed here, follow this guide:

```
https://s3.amazonaws.com/solutions-reference/transit-vpc/
latest/cisco-based-transit-vpc.pdf
```

1. Create a VPC in any AWS Region with two public subnets and an attached Internet gateway. This VPC will act as the transit hub VPC.
2. Create several spoke VPCs with private subnets in multiple AWS Regions. Launch a t2.nano Amazon EC2 instance in these VPCs that you can ping for reachability testing. Make sure that you have a VGW attached to the VPCs.

Avoid overlapping IP addresses in spoke VPCs for this exercise.

3. Launch the AWS CloudFormation template listed here:

   `http://docs.aws.amazon.com/solutions/latest/cisco-based-transit-vpc/appendix-b.html`

   Take note of the parameters entered while launching the AWS CloudFormation template.

4. If you do not have a license, you can choose Bring Your Own License (BYOL) for the Cisco Cloud Service Router (CSR). Enter the transit VPC ID and the public subnets when prompted in the template launch wizard. Make note of two parameters: "Spoke VPC Tag Name" and "Spoke VPC Tag Value."

5. After the AWS CloudFormation template has finished deploying, navigate to the Output tab. The tab will show details about the resources created by the AWS CloudFormation template, such as the IP addresses of the CSR instances.

6. Navigate to the Amazon VPC dashboard. Tag the VGW of the spoke VPCs that you created in Step 2 with the parameters from Step 3 (that is, "Spoke VPC Tag Name" and "Spoke VPC Tag Value"). This tag will be detected by the AWS Lambda function, which will use API calls to establish a VPN connection between the Spoke VPC and the CSR instances.

7. You will now connect the on-premises data center to the transit VPC infrastructure using AWS Direct Connect. Navigate to the AWS Management Console and create a new VGW. Do not attach this VGW to any VPC. Tag this VGW with the parameters noted in Step 3. This will create a VPN connection from the VGW to the transit CSR instances.

8. Set up an AWS Direct Connect connection between your on-premises data center and AWS. Create a private VIF to the VGW created in Step 6. Configure routing to enable traffic flow between the VPC and the on-premises network. You should now see routes of all spoke VPCs being advertised to your on-premises router by the VGW over the private VIF BGP peering.

9. Test ping connectivity from an on-premises server to a server in the spoke VPC.

You have now successfully built a global transit VPC architecture.

Review Questions

1. You have an on-premises application that requires access to Amazon Simple Storage Service (Amazon S3) storage. How do you enable this connectivity while designing for high-bandwidth access with low jitter, high availability, and high scalability?

   A. Set up an AWS Direct Connect public Virtual Interface (VIF).

   B. Set up public Internet access to Amazon Simple Storage Service (Amazon S3).

   C. Set up an AWS Direct Connect private VIF.

   D. Set up an IP Security (IPsec) Virtual Private Network (VPN) to a Virtual Private Gateway (VGW).

2. You have two Virtual Private Clouds (VPCs) set up in AWS for different projects. AWS Direct Connect has been set up for hybrid IT connectivity. Your security team requires that all traffic going to these VPCs be inspected using a Layer 7 Intrusion Prevention System (IPS)/Intrusion Detection System (IDS). How will you architect this while considering cost optimization, scalability, and high availability?

   A. Set up a transit VPC architecture with a pair of Amazon Elastic Compute Cloud (Amazon EC2) instances acting as a transit point for all traffic. These transit instances will host Layer 7 IPS/IDS software.

   B. Use host-based IPS/IDS inspection on the end servers.

   C. Deploy an inline IPS/IDS instance in each VPC and add an entry in the route table to point to the Amazon EC2 instance as the default gateway.

   D. Use AWS WAF as an inline gateway for all hybrid traffic.

3. You have set up a transit Virtual Private Cloud (VPC) architecture and want to connect the spoke VPCs to the hub VPC. What termination endpoint should you choose on the spokes, considering the least management overhead?

   A. Virtual Private Gateway (VGW)

   B. Amazon Elastic Compute Cloud (Amazon EC2) instance

   C. VPC peering gateway

   D. Internet gateway

4. You are tasked with setting up IP Security (IPsec) Virtual Private Network (VPN) connectivity between your on-premises data center and AWS. You have an application on-premises that will exchange sensitive control information to an Amazon Elastic Compute Cloud (Amazon EC2) instance in the Virtual Private Cloud (VPC). This traffic should take priority in the VPN tunnel over all other traffic. How will you design this solution, considering the least management overhead?

   A. Terminate a VPN connection on an Amazon EC2 instance loaded with a software supporting Quality of Service (QoS) and use Differentiated Services Code Point (DSCP) markings to give priority to the application traffic as it sent and received over the VPN tunnel.

   B. Terminate VPN on a Virtual Private Gateway (VGW) and use DSCP markings to give priority to the application traffic as it is sent and received over the VPN tunnel.

C. Terminate a VPN connection on two Amazon EC2 instances. Use one instance for sensitive control information and the other instance for the rest of the traffic.

D. Move the sensitive application to a separate VPC. Create separate VPN tunnels to these VPCs.

5. Which of the following endpoints can be accessed over AWS Direct Connect?

   A. Network Address Translation (NAT) gateway

   B. Internet gateway

   C. Gateway Virtual Private Cloud (VPC) endpoints

   D. Interface VPC endpoints

6. You have to set up an AWS Storage Gateway appliance on-premises to archive all of your data to Amazon Simple Storage Service (Amazon S3) using the file gateway mode. You have AWS Direct Connect connectivity between your data center and AWS. You have set up a private Virtual Interface (VIF) to a Virtual Private Cloud (VPC), and you want to use that for sending all traffic to AWS. How will you architect this?

   A. Set up a Squid HTTP proxy on an Amazon Elastic Compute Cloud (Amazon EC2) instance in the VPC. Configure the storage gateway to use this proxy.

   B. Set up a storage gateway appliance in the VPC and use that as a gateway.

   C. Create an IP Security (IPSec) Virtual Private Network (VPN) tunnel between the storage gateway and the VPC over a private VIF.

   D. Configure the storage gateway to use a VPC private endpoint on the VPC.

7. You have a hybrid IT application that requires access to Amazon DynamoDB. You have set up AWS Direct Connect between your data center and AWS. All data written to Amazon DynamoDB should be encrypted as it is written to the database. How will you enable connectivity from the on-premises application to Amazon DynamoDB?

   A. Set up a public Virtual Interface (VIF).

   B. Set up a private VIF.

   C. Set up IP Security (IPsec) Virtual Private Network (VPN) over public VIF.

   D. Set up IPSec VPN over private VIF.

8. You have a transit Virtual Private Cloud (VPC) set up with the hub VPC in us-east-1 and the spoke VPCs spread across multiple AWS Regions. Servers in the VPCs in Mumbai and Singapore are suffering huge latencies when connecting with each other. How do you re-architect your VPCs to maintain the transit VPC architecture and reduce the latencies in the overall architecture?

   A. Set up a local transit hub VPC in the Mumbai region. Connect the VPCs in Mumbai and Singapore to this hub. Set up an IP Security (IPsec) Virtual Private Network (VPN) over cross-region VPC peering between the two hubs.

   B. Set up a local transit hub in the Singapore region. Connect the VPCs in Mumbai and Singapore to this hub VPC. Set up a Generic Routing Encapsulation (GRE) VPN over cross-region VPC peering between the two hubs.

   C. Add transit Amazon Elastic Compute Cloud (Amazon EC2) instances in the us-east-1 hub VPC dedicated to the traffic coming from the Mumbai and Singapore regions.

   D. Add a transit VPC hub in us-east-1. Connect the VPCs in Mumbai and Singapore to this new hub and then connect the two hubs using VPC peering.

9. You have an application in a Virtual Private Cloud (VPC) that requires access to on-premises Active Directory servers for joining the company domain. How will you enable this setup, considering low latency for domain join requests?
   A. Set up a Virtual Private Network (VPN) terminating on a Virtual Private Gateway (VGW) attached to the VPC.
   B. Set up an AWS Direct Connect public Virtual Interface (VIF).
   C. Set up an AWS Direct Connect private VIF.
   D. Set up a VPN terminating on an Amazon Elastic Compute Cloud (Amazon EC2) instance in the VPC.

10. Which of the following is a good use case for leveraging the transit Virtual Private Cloud (VPC) architecture?
    A. Allow on-premises resources access to any VPC globally in AWS.
    B. Allow on-premises resources access to Amazon Simple Storage Service (Amazon S3).
    C. Allow on-premises resources access to AWS resources while inspecting all traffic for compliance reasons.
    D. Allow on-premises resources access to other remote networks.

Network Troubleshooting

THE AWS CERTIFIED ADVANCED NETWORKING – SPECIALTY EXAM OBJECTIVES COVERED IN THIS CHAPTER MAY INCLUDE, BUT ARE NOT LIMITED TO, THE FOLLOWING:

Domain 2.0: Design and Implement AWS Networks

✓ **2.1 Apply AWS networking concepts**

Domain 6.0: Manage, Optimize, and Troubleshoot the Network

✓ **6.1 Troubleshoot and resolve a network issue**

Introduction to Network Troubleshooting

AWS provides a number of networking features to connect within the AWS Cloud, outside the AWS Cloud to the Internet, and in a hybrid manner to an on-premises environment. This chapter discusses tools and techniques for troubleshooting networking issues that can arise with these connections. In addition, the chapter discusses a number of common troubleshooting scenarios. Knowledge of AWS troubleshooting tools and how to troubleshoot common scenarios are both required skills for the exam, which are highlighted in this chapter.

Methodology for Troubleshooting

Troubleshooting can follow either a bottom-up approach (traversing through the Open Systems Interconnection [OSI] model one by one) or a top-down approach (working through likely areas that can cause issues). There are scenarios where each has its own merits, and they can be used in combination to help resolve issues quickly. The approach can also change based on the environment in which the troubleshooting is occurring.

Traversing through the OSI model systematically from Layer 1 through Layer 7 is often a useful way to pinpoint issues. Such a method can be optimized by taking into account the environment. For example, there is implicit routing for all subnets by default within a Virtual Private Cloud (VPC). This can rule out Layer 2 and Layer 3 communication issues within a VPC; thus, troubleshooting should start at Layer 4. In another example, when custom routing is set up through Amazon Elastic Compute Cloud (Amazon EC2) instances, Layer 3 troubleshooting may be required to ensure that routing is occurring as expected.

Stepping back and taking a top-down approach to pinpointing potential areas for network issues is also a valuable way to troubleshoot. Knowing service limits, for example, can help resolve otherwise difficult issues to fix. Being able to recognize security group and network Access Control List (ACL) issues without having to dig through the network stack layer-by-layer is also another example of how this approach can be helpful.

Network Troubleshooting Tools

AWS offers a rich set of tools that can be combined with traditional tools to help troubleshoot networking connectivity issues. Both traditional tools and AWS-native tools are discussed in this section.

Traditional Tools

In this section, we discuss traditional network troubleshooting tools, many of which you may be already familiar with.

Packet Captures

For troubleshooting when deep packet inspection is necessary, *packet captures* can be useful. Packet capture tools like Wireshark (Windows/Linux) and tcpdump (Linux) can be run on an Amazon EC2 instance. By listening at the interface level, these tools are able to view the packets as they are sent to and received from the network, revealing both packet header and payload.

ping

ping is a utility that records network round trip times using the Internet Control Message Protocol (ICMP). It is commonly used to test if a host is up and responsive on a network. ping can be useful for troubleshooting within AWS. It is important to note that network ACLs, security groups, and operating system firewalls must all be configured to allow ICMP traffic for this tool to be useful. Note that ICMP traffic is typically not enabled by default on many network devices and operating systems.

traceroute

traceroute is a utility that discovers the path to a destination IP or hostname. This tool can be helpful in verifying the route that traffic is following through a network. It works by sending out an ICMP packet with increasing Time-To-Live (TTL) values. Note that not all devices in a network path will respond to the ICMP request, so there may not be a value for all hops in the route. In addition, this tool will not provide meaningful results within a VPC or across VPC peering links because each is only one network hop away.

Telnet

Telnet is a text-based TCP utility. While the default telnet port is 23, telnet can be set to initiate a TCP connection on any user-specified port. This can be very helpful for troubleshooting if a service is running on a port and responding to traffic.

nslookup

nslookup is a command-line utility that resolves hostnames into IP addresses. It can be useful in network troubleshooting to confirm your Domain Name System (DNS) server settings and determine to what IP address a hostname is being resolved.

AWS-Native Tools

In this section, we discuss AWS-native tools for troubleshooting, which provide additional insight to augment traditional troubleshooting tools.

Amazon CloudWatch

Amazon CloudWatch is a monitoring service for AWS Cloud resources and the applications that you run on AWS. You can use Amazon CloudWatch to collect and track metrics, collect and monitor log files, set alarms, and automatically react to changes in your AWS resources.

The services shown in Table 13.1 send network metrics to Amazon CloudWatch that can be useful in troubleshooting.

TABLE 13.1 Amazon CloudWatch Metrics

Amazon CloudWatch Metric	Description
Amazon EC2	Sends metrics to Amazon CloudWatch recording the number of bytes and packets in and out of each Amazon EC2 instance
Amazon VPC Virtual Private Network (VPN)	Sends metrics to Amazon CloudWatch recording tunnel state and bytes in and out
AWS Direct Connect	Sends metrics to Amazon CloudWatch recording connection state, bits per second egress and ingress, packets per second egress and ingress, Cyclic Redundancy Check (CRC) error count, and connection-light level egress and ingress (only for 10 Gbps port speeds)
Amazon Route 53	Sends metrics to Amazon CloudWatch recording health check count, connection time, health check percentage, health check status, Secure Sockets Layer (SSL) handshake time, and time to first byte
Amazon CloudFront	Sends metrics to Amazon CloudWatch recording requests, bytes downloaded and uploaded, bytes uploaded, total error rate, 4xx error rate, and 5xx error rate
Elastic Load Balancing	Sends metrics to Amazon CloudWatch recording healthy host count, 4xx and 5xx load balancer error count, back-end/target error count (2xx, 3xx, 4xxx, and 5xx), and a number of additional metrics
Amazon Relational Database Service (Amazon RDS)	Sends metrics to Amazon CloudWatch recording network receive and transmit throughput
Amazon Redshift	Sends metrics to Amazon CloudWatch recording network receive and transmit throughput

Note: There are many more Amazon CloudWatch metrics that are recorded.

Amazon VPC Flow Logs

Amazon VPC Flow Logs is a feature that enables you to capture information about the IP traffic going to and from network interfaces in your VPC. Flow log data is stored using Amazon CloudWatch Logs. After you have created a flow log, you can view and retrieve its data in Amazon CloudWatch Logs.

Flow logs can help you with a number of tasks, such as troubleshooting why specific traffic is not reaching an instance. If you see that the traffic is logged in flow logs, then you know it is reaching the VPC. In turn, if you notice that there is a DENY entry, then it points to a permission issue and can help you diagnose overly restrictive security group rules or network ACLs. You can also use flow logs as a security tool to monitor the traffic that is reaching your instance. Flow logs can also be exported to other services like the Amazon Elasticsearch Service to gain insight into traffic and to enable visualizations.

AWS Config

With *AWS Config*, you can capture a comprehensive history of your AWS resource configuration changes to simplify troubleshooting of your operational issues. AWS Config can be used to help identify AWS resource changes that may have caused operational issues. AWS Config leverages AWS CloudTrail records to correlate configuration changes to particular events in your account. You can obtain the details of the event Application Programming Interface (API) call that invoked the change (for example, who made the request, at what time, and from which IP address) from the AWS CloudTrail logs.

AWS Trusted Advisor

AWS Trusted Advisor is an online resource to help you reduce cost, increase performance, and improve security by optimizing your AWS environment. AWS Trusted Advisor provides real-time guidance to help you provision your resources following AWS best practices. Part of the metrics and recommendations that are reported are network-related service limits around VPCs, elastic IPs, and load balancers. These service limit metrics can help quickly identify whether a service limit has been reached, and they allow you to request limit increases proactively.

AWS Identity and Access Management (IAM) Policy Simulator

The *AWS Identity and Access Management (IAM) Policy Simulator* is a very useful tool in troubleshooting IAM permissions. The simulator evaluates the policies that you choose and determines the effective permissions for each of the actions that you specify. The simulator uses the same policy evaluation engine that is used during real requests to AWS Cloud services.

Troubleshooting Common Scenarios

There are some common scenarios and technologies that can experience network connectivity issues. A description of each, situations in which they occur, and key points to consider in troubleshooting are discussed in this section.

Internet Connectivity

New VPCs do not have public Internet connectivity by default. User action is required to set up the appropriate requirements for Internet connectivity.

There are five requirements for connectivity to the Internet from an Amazon EC2 instance:

- A public IP address is assigned to an instance (note that for IPv6, all addresses are assigned by AWS and are public) or a Network Address Translation (NAT) gateway with a public IP in a public subnet.
- An Internet gateway is attached to the VPC.
- There is a default route to an Internet gateway in the route table on the public subnet. If a NAT gateway is used, then the default route on private subnets should be the NAT gateway instance.
- Outbound ports are open in the instance security group (80 and 443 for web traffic).
- Inbound and outbound ports are open in the subnet network ACL (80 and 443 outbound and ephemeral port range inbound).

Virtual Private Network

AWS provides a managed Virtual Private Network (VPN) service to allow for easy connectivity between on-premises environments and VPCs. After you have created your VPN, you can download the IP Security (IPsec) VPN configuration from the VPC console to configure the firewall or device in your local network that will connect to the VPN.

The following should be checked if there are issues with traffic over a VPN tunnel:

1. Verify that the VPN tunnels are connected. (See the following section for more details on Internet Key Exchange [IKE] phase 1 and phase 2 troubleshooting.)
2. Verify that the proper VPC is attached to the Virtual Private Gateway (VGW).
3. Verify that there are either propagated or static routes to the VPN subnets, with the VGW as the destination, in each subnet route table.
4. Verify that the subnet network ACLs and instance security groups are set to allow the traffic that you would like to flow over the VPN.

These steps can be optimized using a top-down approach. For example, if some traffic is traversing a VPN connection and other traffic is not, then you can skip the steps on troubleshooting the VPN tunnel connectivity and start looking at routing and security groups/network ACLs.

Note that the VPN tunnel may go down if there is no traffic traversing it. If there is not any traffic going across a VPN tunnel, then it can be helpful to initiate a continuous ping to ensure the tunnel stays up.

Internet Key Exchange (IKE) Phase 1 and Phase 2 Troubleshooting

In the event that the VPN tunnels are not established, IKE phase 1 followed by IKE phase 2 of the IPsec tunnel should be investigated.

If there are issues establishing an IKE phase 1 connection, then the following should be checked:

1. Verify that IKEv1 is being used instead of IKEv2; AWS only supports IKEv1.
2. Verify that Diffie-Hellman (DH) group 2 is being used.
3. Verify that the phase 1 lifetime is set to 28,800 seconds (480 minutes or 8 hours).
4. Verify that phase 1 is using the Secure Hash Algorithm (SHA) 1 hashing algorithm.
5. Verify that phase 1 is using Advanced Encryption Standard (AES) 128 as the encryption algorithm.
6. Verify that the customer gateway device is configured with the correct Preshared Key (PSK) specified in the downloaded AWS VPN configuration for the tunnels.
7. If the customer gateway endpoint is behind a NAT device, verify that IKE traffic leaving the customer on-premises network is sourced from the configured customer gateway IP address and on User Datagram Protocol (UDP) port 500. Also test by disabling NAT traversal on the customer gateway device.
8. Verify that UDP packets on port 500 (and port 4500 if using NAT traversal) are allowed to pass to and from your network to the AWS VPN endpoints. Ensure that there is no device in place between your customer gateway and the VGW that could be blocking UDP port 500; this includes checking Internet Service Providers (ISPs) that could be blocking UDP port 500.

If there are issues establishing an IKE phase 2 connection, then the following should be checked:

1. Verify that Encapsulating Security Payload (ESP) protocol 50 is not blocked inbound or outbound.
2. Verify that the security association lifetime is 3,600 seconds (60 minutes).
3. Verify that there are no firewall ACLs interfering with IPsec traffic.
4. Verify that phase 2 is using the SHA-1 hashing algorithm.
5. Verify that phase 2 is using AES-128 as the encryption algorithm.
6. Verify that Perfect Forward Secrecy (PFS) is enabled and that DH group 2 is being used for key generation.
7. Enhanced AWS VPN endpoints support some additional advanced encryption and hashing algorithms, such as AES 256; SHA-2(256); and DH groups 5, 14–18, 22, 23, and 24 for phase 2. If your VPN connection requires any of these additional features, contact AWS to verify that you are using the enhanced VPN endpoints. Typically, you must re-create the VGW of your VPC to move to the enhanced VPN endpoints.
8. If you are using policy-based routing, verify that you have correctly defined the source and destination networks in your encryption domain.

AWS Direct Connect

AWS Direct Connect lets you establish a dedicated network connection between your network and one of the AWS Direct Connect locations. Using industry standard 802.1q Virtual Local Area Networks (VLANs), this dedicated connection can be partitioned into multiple Virtual Interfaces (VIFs). This allows you to use the same connection to access public resources, such as objects stored in Amazon Simple Storage Service (Amazon S3) using public IP address space and private resources such as Amazon EC2 instances running within a VPC using private IP space, all while maintaining network separation between the public and private environments. VIFs can be reconfigured at any time to meet your changing needs.

An AWS Direct Connect connection can either be established directly within an AWS Direct Connect location or extended to your location through an AWS Partner Network (APN) partner. Some APN partners also offer hosted VIFs at sub-1 Gbps speeds. Note that these hosted VIFs are not full AWS Direct Connect connections and only support a single VIF.

The following are items to consider when troubleshooting an AWS Direct Connect connection:

- AWS Direct Connect requires single mode fiber.
- A VIF must have a public or private Border Gateway Protocol (BGP) Autonomous System Number (ASN). If you are using a public ASN, you must own it.
- For a public VIF, you must specify public IPv4 addresses (/30) that you own.
- For IPv6, regardless of the type of VIF, AWS automatically allocates a /125 IPv6 Classless Inter-Domain Routing (CIDR) for you. You cannot specify your own peer IPv6 addresses.
- There is a limit of 50 VIFs per AWS Direct Connect connection.
- There is a limit of 100 routes per BGP session. Advertising more routes than this can cause port flapping.
- AWS Direct Connect supports a Maximum Transmission Unit (MTU) up to 1,522 bytes at the physical connection layer. If your network path does not support this, then you should set an MTU value below 1,500 bytes on your router to avoid issues.
- Security groups and network ACLs must be configured to allow access.
- Route propagation needs to be enabled on each subnet route table for the routes learned through BGP to show up.

Security Groups

Security groups are implicit DENY. Unless a rule allowing incoming or outgoing traffic is created, traffic will not flow. This means that even if two instances are in the same subnet, they will not be able to communicate with each other unless there is a rule created allowing such traffic. Security groups are also stateful, meaning that if an inbound or outbound rule is created, it will allow the return traffic.

The following are items to consider when troubleshooting security groups:

- There is a limit on the number of inbound and outbound rules of 50.
- Up to five security groups can be added per network interface.
- Only ALLOW rules can be added to a security group.

Amazon VPC Flow Logs can be useful for troubleshooting security group-related issues. Traffic will be recorded as a rejected packet if there is not a rule in place to allow it.

Network Access Control Lists

By default, the network access control list (ACL) on a VPC is set to allow all inbound and outbound traffic. If network ACLs are set to be more restrictive, care must be taken to allow all required traffic. Note that network ACLs are not stateful like security groups—return traffic to an outbound port must be explicitly permitted with an ALLOW rule. For example, locking down outbound to port 80 and port 443 only in a subnet would also require an inbound ALLOW rule for ephemeral ports (1024-65535). A good understanding of network traffic flows and ports and protocols in use should be established prior to implementing network ACLs on a subnet.

The following are items to consider when troubleshooting network ACLs:

- Network ACLs are not stateful like security groups.
- Return traffic may need the entire ephemeral port range of 1024-65535 to be open.
- There is a limit of 20 inbound and outbound rules per ACL.
- By default, each custom network ACL denies all inbound and outbound traffic until you add rules.
- Rules are evaluated starting with the lowest numbered rule. As soon as a rule matches traffic, it is applied regardless of any higher-numbered rule that may contradict it.

Applications commonly communicate over a number of ports and often require an inbound rule for return traffic. Amazon VPC Flow Logs can be useful for troubleshooting network ACL-related issues. Traffic will be recorded as a rejected packet if there is not a rule to allow it or there is an explicit rule to block it.

Routing

Routing within a VPC is controlled by a route table attached to each subnet. Note that unless a route table is explicitly associated with a subnet, the main route table for the VPC will be used for each subnet. Knowing the caveats of routing and how routing within VPC works is beneficial to troubleshooting. The following are some common considerations when troubleshooting route tables:

- The most specific route that matches traffic in a route table is used.
- IPv4 and IPv6 routes are handled separately.

- The default local route of the VPC CIDR cannot be modified.
- When you add an Internet gateway, an egress-only Internet gateway (for IPv6), a VGW, a NAT device, a peering connection, or a VPC endpoint in your VPC, you must update the route table for any subnet that uses these gateways or connections.
- There is a limit of 50 non-propagated routes that you can have in a route table.
- There is a hard limit of 100 routes that can be propagated to a VPC route table. More general routes or a default route should be used if this limit is reached.
- If a custom Amazon EC2 instance is used as a router, then its elastic network interface needs to be added in the route table as a destination. Note that the instance must also be set to disable source/destination checking for traffic to flow.

Route propagation is not enabled by default on a route table. It must explicitly be enabled for a route table to receive routes advertised by BGP or statically assigned to the VGW.

Virtual Private Cloud (VPC) Peering Connections

A *VPC peering connection* is a networking connection between two VPCs that enables you to route traffic between them using private IPv4 addresses or IPv6 addresses. Instances in either VPC can communicate with each other as if they are within the same network. You can create a VPC peering connection between your own VPCs or with a VPC in another AWS account. In both cases, the VPCs must be in the same AWS Region.

AWS uses the existing infrastructure of a VPC to create a VPC peering connection; it is neither a gateway nor a VPN connection, and it does not rely on a separate piece of physical hardware. There is no single point of failure for communication or a bandwidth bottleneck.

The following are items to consider when troubleshooting VPC peering connections:

- VPC peering connections are not transitive. Traffic not in a destination VPC CIDR will not flow over a peering link.
- A VPC peering connection cannot be used to reach out to the Internet or to a VPN connection.
- A route needs to be added to each subnet route table with the remote VPC CIDR and the peering connection as the destination. This needs to be done on both sides of the VPC peering connection.
- There cannot be conflicting or overlapping VPC CIDR ranges.
- There is a limit of 50 VPC peering connections per VPC. This limit can be increased to maximum of 125 by opening an AWS Support ticket.
- Security groups and network ACLs need to be set to allow traffic to flow on the source and destination instances and subnets.

Connectivity to AWS Cloud Services

AWS Cloud services that reside outside of a VPC require a public IP address for access. This can be accomplished through a NAT gateway, public IP address, proxy server, or by setting up an endpoint on a VPC (if an endpoint is available for the service).

The following considerations should be checked when there are issues accessing AWS Cloud services:

1. There should be an Internet gateway, proxy, or VPC endpoint that enables connectivity from private IP addresses with the VPC.
2. If a VPC endpoint is used, there should be a route in the route table that has the VPC endpoint as the destination.
3. Security groups and network ACLs should be checked to confirm they are properly set to allow the instances and services to communicate.
4. IAM roles (if in use) allow communication with the service. If a VPC endpoint is used, then the IAM policy on the endpoint must be set to allow access. The IAM Policy Simulator tool is helpful in troubleshooting permissions issues.

Amazon CloudFront Connectivity

Amazon CloudFront is a global Content Delivery Network (CDN) service that securely delivers data, videos, applications, and APIs to viewers with low latency and high transfer speeds. Amazon CloudFront is integrated with AWS—both physical locations which are directly connected to the AWS global infrastructure, as well as software that works seamlessly with services including AWS Shield for Distributed Denial of Service (DDoS) mitigation, Amazon S3, Elastic Load Balancing, or Amazon EC2 as origins for your applications, and AWS Lambda to run custom code close to your viewers.

The following are some common items to consider when troubleshooting Amazon CloudFront connectivity problems:

- If you are using a custom DNS entry, then it must be a CNAME that points to your Amazon CloudFront distribution's domain name.
- If the Amazon CloudFront origin is an Amazon S3 bucket, the objects must either be publically readable or have an Origin Access Identity (OAI) created and attached to the distribution with permissions assigned to the Amazon S3 objects.
- HTTP 502 status codes (Bad Gateway) indicates that Amazon CloudFront was not able to serve the requested object because it could not connect to the origin server. If 502 errors are seen, connectivity to the origin server should be confirmed.
- HTTP 503 Status Codes (Service Unavailable) status code typically indicates a lack of capacity on the origin server. If 503 errors are seen, capacity at the origin server should be confirmed.

Elastic Load Balancing Functionality

Elastic Load Balancing automatically distributes incoming application traffic across multiple Amazon EC2 instances. It enables you to achieve fault tolerance in your applications, seamlessly providing the required amount of load balancing capacity needed to route application traffic.

Due to the scalable nature of Elastic Load Balancing, the fleet of AWS-managed Elastic Load Balancing instances will grow and shrink to meet demand. This scaling requires allocating a sufficient amount of available IP addresses to the Elastic Load Balancing subnet. Failure to account for the scaling of an Elastic Load Balancing fleet can result in errors and the inability of the load balancer to balance traffic.

The following are some common considerations to take into account when troubleshooting Elastic Load Balancing:

- Verify that a public load balancer resides only in public subnets.
- Verify that the load balancer security group and network ACLs allow inbound traffic from the clients and outbound traffic to the clients.
- Verify that the load balancer targets security groups and network ACLs allow inbound traffic from the load balancer subnet and outbound traffic to the load balancer subnet.
- Verify that the default success code for a health check is 200. (This should be modified if your application uses an alternate success code.)
- Verify that sticky sessions are enabled on the load balancer; stateful connections will not work correctly otherwise.

Domain Name System

Domain Name System (DNS) provides hostname to IP resolution. AWS creates a DNS server by default within a VPC. (This option can be disabled.) AWS has a managed DNS service called Amazon Route 53 that provides the ability to create public and private hosted zones. Private hosted zones are only available within a VPC, while public hosted zones are globally accessible throughout the world.

DNS entries have a TTL value for each DNS record within a domain that specifies how long a client can cache the values of a DNS query. These TTL values are only a suggestion, and they can be ignored by caching at intermediary DNS servers, operating systems, and individual applications. For this reason, DNS queries may take some time to resolve to the correct values, even after the TTL period has expired.

The following are items to consider when troubleshooting DNS issues:

- AWS allocates the second IP address in a VPC CIDR as a DNS server. If a custom DNS server is needed, then an alternate Dynamic Host Configuration Protocol (DHCP) option set can be created.
- If a DNS entry is not resolving properly after an entry update, then the TTL of a DNS entry may not have expired.

- DNS values can be cached by ISPs, operating systems, and applications, and they can return incorrect values even after a TTL has expired.
- Only CNAME records should be used to point to AWS Cloud services. Using A records can cause errors.
- `EnableDnsHostnames` and `enableDnsSupport` must be set to true for Amazon Route 53 private hosted zones.

The `nslookup` command is a useful tool for troubleshooting DNS issues to determine to which IP address a hostname resolves.

Hitting Service Limits

Every AWS Cloud service has some type of limit. There are hard limits, which cannot be increased, and soft limits, which can be increased with an AWS Support ticket. It is very important to understand these limits. A lot of troubleshooting time can be saved by recognizing when a service limit is the root cause of an issue. Each service's page on the AWS website lists the limits. A subset of network limits can also be seen in AWS Trusted Advisor:

- Elastic IP address
- Amazon VPC
- Subnets per security group
- Internet gateway
- Active load balancers

Many services will show an error in the API response or AWS Management Console when trying to create or allocate resources once a limit has been reached.

Summary

In this chapter, you reviewed core concepts of troubleshooting connectivity within AWS and connectivity from AWS to on-premises networks.

Core troubleshooting tools consist of the following:

- Traditional Tools
  - Packet captures
  - ping
  - traceroute
  - Telnet
  - nslookup

- AWS Native Tools
  - Amazon CloudWatch
  - Amazon VPC Flow Logs
  - AWS Config
  - AWS Trusted Advisor
  - IAM Policy Simulator

In this chapter, you also reviewed some common troubleshooting scenarios. The best way to get experience in troubleshooting is to use the tools and address common issues that may arise. It is recommended that you complete the exercises at the end of this chapter in order to gain hands-on experience with network troubleshooting in AWS.

Exam Essentials

Understand methodologies for troubleshooting. It is important to understand how to troubleshoot common network anomalies that occur and how doing so in a cloud or hybrid environment can be different from on-premises networking.

Understand tools for troubleshooting. In addition to traditional troubleshooting tools, there are a number of AWS tools discussed in this chapter with which you should be familiar.

Understand the conditions required for Internet connectivity. There are five conditions that must be met for connectivity to the Internet from an Amazon EC2 instance:

- A public IP is assigned to an instance (note for IPv6 that all addresses are assigned by AWS and are public) or a NAT gateway with a public IP in a public subnet.
- An Internet gateway is attached to the VPC.
- There is a default route to an Internet gateway in the route table on the public subnet. If a NAT gateway is used, then the default route on private subnets should be the NAT gateway instance.
- Outbound ports are open in the instance security group (ports 80 and 443 for web traffic).
- Inbound and outbound ports are open in the subnet network ACL (ports 80 and 443 outbound and ephemeral port range inbound).

Understand network ACLs vs. security groups. Security groups are stateful, whereas network ACLs are not. There is an implicit DENY with security groups. Rules must be added to allow network traffic. If network ACLs are used, then care must be taken to ensure that return traffic (whether inbound or outbound) is allowed.

Understand how routing works with Amazon VPC. There is an implicit route within a VPC for its CIDR. All other routes to destinations outside of the CIDR need to be added to the route table. There is a master route table for all subnets when a VPC is initially created, and additional route tables can be added. There is a one-to-one mapping of route table to subnet; however, multiple subnets can share the same route table. More specific routes have a higher preference.

Understand VPN IPsec and how to troubleshoot. There are two phases to IPsec to establish a VPN tunnel. You should know the requirements for each phase and how to troubleshoot when one or both fail to complete. You should also understand how routing works with VPN tunnels and how it works as a standby if an AWS Direct Connect is also in use.

Understand AWS Direct Connect and how to troubleshoot. There are a number of requirements that must be completed before traffic can flow over an AWS Direct Connect connection. There is also a difference between a private VIF (connectivity to a VPC) and public VIF (connectivity to public AWS Cloud services). In the case of a hosted VIF, there is only one VIF that can be created with each.

Understand VPC peering and valid versus invalid configurations. VPC peering will not be established if there are overlapping or conflicting CIDR addresses. Peering connections are not transitive. Any traffic that is not in the CIDR range of the VPC peer will not flow over the peering connection.

Understand how DNS and Amazon Route 53 work and how to troubleshoot. DNS resolution is provided by default within a VPC by an AWS-managed endpoint. Amazon Route 53 can be used for hosting private zones within a VPC and public zones outside of a VPC. CNAMEs should be used to point to AWS-provided endpoint hostnames.

Test Taking Tip

Be familiar with AWS network troubleshooting tools and when each is most appropriate to use.

Resources to Review

For further information, refer to the following pages on the AWS website:

AWS Troubleshooting Amazon VPC Connectivity:

`https://aws.amazon.com/premiumsupport/knowledge-center/connect-vpc/`

AWS VPN Troubleshooting:

`https://aws.amazon.com/premiumsupport/knowledge-center/vpn-tunnel-troubleshooting/`

AWS Direct Connect Troubleshooting:

`http://docs.aws.amazon.com/directconnect/latest/UserGuide/Troubleshooting.html`

AWS CloudFront Troubleshooting:

`http://docs.aws.amazon.com/AmazonCloudFront/latest/DeveloperGuide/Troubleshooting.html`

AWS Instance SSH Connectivity Troubleshooting:

`https://aws.amazon.com/premiumsupport/knowledge-center/instance-vpc-troubleshoot/`

Exercises

The best way to become familiar with troubleshooting is to install and leverage the tools mentioned in this chapter. There is no substitute for the experience that comes from working within the AWS environment, becoming familiar with how networking works, and learning how to work through common troubleshooting situations.

EXERCISE 13.1

Set Up Flow Logs

Complete the Exercises in Chapter 2 if you have not already done so.

1. Sign in to the AWS Management Console as Administrator or Power User.
2. Create an Amazon CloudWatch log group under the Amazon CloudWatch section of the AWS Management Console.
3. Navigate to the Amazon VPC section of the AWS Management Console and select the Amazon VPC called *My First VPC*.
4. Select Flow Logs and click Create New Flow Logs. Fill in the required fields. An IAM role is required; there is a wizard to create the required role and permissions automatically. Make sure that you select the options to log both ACCEPT and REJECT traffic logging.

You have now enabled flow logs on your custom VPC.

EXERCISE 13.2

Test Instance-to-Instance Connectivity with ping

In this exercise, you will test the ability of two instances within the same subnet to communicate using the ping tool.

1. Open up a Secure Shell (SSH) connection to your instance in the public subnet.
2. Use the `ping` command to try to reach the instance in the private subnet.
3. You will notice that the ICMP traffic fails unless you have already modified the security groups.
4. Under the Amazon VPC section of the AWS Management Console, navigate to Security Groups.
5. Create a new security group that allows inbound and outbound ICMP traffic from the subnets of which each instance is a part.
6. Under the Amazon EC2 section of the AWS Management Console, select each instance and attach the newly-created security group. This option is available within the sections Actions, Networking, and then Security Groups.

The instances will now be able to ping each other.

EXERCISE 13.3

Inspect Amazon VPC Flow Logs

In this exercise, you will use Amazon VPC Flow Logs to view network traffic.

1. Navigate to the Amazon CloudWatch section of the AWS Management Console and click on Logs. Wait at least 10 minutes to ensure that the flow logs have been reported to Amazon CloudWatch.
2. Click on the name of the flow log that you created.
3. Click on the flow log associated with the private instance elastic network interface.
4. Scroll through the logs. You will see REJECT entries for the initial public subnet to private subnet ping.
5. Continue to scroll through the logs. You will see ACCEPT entries for the time after you created the security group to enable ICMP traffic.

You have successfully used Amazon VPC Flow logs to view network traffic.

EXERCISE 13.4

Using traceroute

In this exercise, you will use the traceroute tool to determine the route of network traffic.

1. Create a new VPC. Peer the new VPC with your existing VPC.
2. Create a `t2.micro` instance in the new VPC and enable inbound ICMP traffic.
3. Use SSH to access your public Amazon EC2 instance. Run traceroute from an IP address in your VPC peer.
4. You will notice that the traffic goes out over the default route to the Internet and that traceroute will eventually time out.
5. Add a route to the route table that is attached to the public subnet using the CIDR of the new VPC that you created and a destination of the VPC peering connection.
6. Run traceroute again. You will notice that traffic will not traverse the VPC peering connection; however, it will still fail to complete.
7. Add a route to the route table in the new VPC using the CIDR of the existing VPC and a destination of the VPC peering connection.
8. Run traceroute again. This time it will complete and return a response.

Using the traceroute tool, you were able to identify a routing issue and correct it by adding a route to the route table.

EXERCISE 13.5

Use AWS Trusted Advisor to Troubleshoot Service Limits

In this exercise, you will use AWS Trusted Advisor to check on networking service limits.

1. Sign in to the AWS Management Console as Administrator or Power User.
2. Navigate to the Amazon VPC console and create three additional VPCs. You will receive an error.
3. Navigate to the AWS Trusted Advisor dashboard and select Performance. Scroll down and expand Service Limits.
4. Navigate through the windows to Amazon VPC Limit. You will see that you have reached the limit of five VPCs in the AWS Region that you are using for this exercise. You may need to refresh the service limit checks to see this.

If you would like your VPC limit increased, you can submit a service ticket with the request.

Review Questions

1. You place an application load balancer in front of two web servers that are stateful. Users begin to report intermittent connectivity issues when accessing the website. Why is the site not responding?
   A. The website needs to have port 443 open.
   B. Sticky sessions must be enabled on the application load balancer.
   C. The web servers need to have their security group set to allow all Transmission Control Protocol (TCP) traffic from 0.0.0.0/0.
   D. The network Access Control List (ACL) on the subnet needs to allow a stateful connection.

2. You create a new instance, and you are able to connect over Secure Shell (SSH) to its private IP address from your corporate network. The instance does not have Internet access, however. Your internal policies forbid direct access to the Internet. What is required to enable access to the Internet?
   A. Assign a public IP address to the instance.
   B. Ensure that port 80 and port 443 are not set to DENY in the instance security group.
   C. Deploy a Network Address Translation (NAT) gateway in the private subnet.
   D. Ensure that there is a default route in the subnet route table that goes to your on-premises network.

3. You create a Network Address Translation (NAT) gateway in a private subnet. Your instances cannot communicate with the Internet. What action must you take?
   A. Add a default route out to the Internet gateway.
   B. Ensure that outbound traffic is allowed on port 80 and port 443.
   C. Delete the NAT gateway and deploy it in a public subnet.
   D. Place the instances in a public subnet.

4. What is *not* required for Internet connectivity from a public subnet?
   A. Public IP
   B. Network Address Translation (NAT) gateway
   C. Outbound rule in a security group
   D. Inbound rule in the network Access Control List (ACL)
   E. Outbound rule in the network ACL
   F. An Internet gateway
   G. A default route to an Internet gateway

5. You are trying to add two new Virtual Private Cloud (VPC) peering connections to a VPC with 24 existing peering connections. The first connection works fine, but the second connection returns an error message. What should you do?
   A. Submit a request to AWS Support to have your VPC peer limit increased.
   B. Select another AWS Region to set up the VPC peering connection.
   C. Retry the request again; the error may go away.
   D. Deploy a Virtual Private Network (VPN) instance to connect the VPC.
6. You created a new endpoint for your Virtual Private Cloud (VPC) that does not have Internet connectivity. Your instance cannot connect to Amazon Simple Storage Service (Amazon S3). What could be the problem?
   A. There is no route in your route table to the Amazon S3 VPC endpoint.
   B. The Amazon S3 bucket is in another region.
   C. Your bucket access list is not properly configured.
   D. The VPC endpoint does not have the proper AWS Identity and Access Management (IAM) policy attached to it.
   E. All of the above
7. You recently set up Amazon Route 53 for a private hosted zone for a highly-available application hosted on AWS. After adding a few A records, you notice that the instance hostnames are not resolving within the Virtual Private Cloud (VPC). What actions should be taken? (Choose two.)
   A. Allow port 53 on the instance security group.
   B. Create a Dynamic Host Configuration Protocol (DHCP) option set.
   C. Set `enableDnsHostnames` to true on the VPC.
   D. Set `enableDnsSupport` to true on the VPC.
8. You discover that the default Virtual Private Cloud (VPC) has been deleted from region us-east-1 by a coworker in the morning. You will be deploying a lot of new services during the afternoon. What should you do?
   A. It's not important, so no action is required.
   B. Designate a VPC that you create as the default VPC.
   C. Create an AWS Support ticket to have your VPC re-created.
   D. Perform an Application Programming Interface (API) call or go through the AWS Management Console to create a new default VPC.

9. You are responsible for your company's AWS resources. You notice a significant amount of traffic from an IP address range in a foreign country where your company does not have customers. Further investigation of the traffic indicates that the source of the traffic is scanning for open ports on your Amazon Elastic Compute Cloud (Amazon EC2) instances. Which one of the following resources can prevent the IP address from reaching the instances?

    A. Security group

    B. Network Address Translation (NAT) gateway

    C. Network Access Control List (ACL)

    D. A Virtual Private Cloud (VPC) endpoint

10. Which of the following tools can be used to record the source and destination IP addresses of traffic? (Choose two.)

    A. Flow logs

    B. Packet capture on an instance

    C. AWS CloudTrail

    D. AWS Identity and Access Management (IAM)

Chapter 14

Billing

THE AWS CERTIFIED ADVANCED NETWORKING – SPECIALTY EXAM OBJECTIVES COVERED IN THIS CHAPTER MAY INCLUDE, BUT ARE NOT LIMITED TO, THE FOLLOWING:

Domain 2.0: Design and Implement AWS Networks

✓ **2.6 Evaluate and optimize cost allocations given a network design and application data flow**

Content may include the following:

- Data transfer charges within a Virtual Private Cloud (VPC)
- Data transfer charges with AWS Cloud services outside an Amazon VPC
- Data transfer charges when using AWS Direct Connect
- Data transfer charges over the Internet

Billing Overview

Billing for AWS networking-related services can often be complex and initially confusing. In this chapter, we examine the elements used to evaluate which charges apply to a particular flow of data to or from services hosted within AWS.

There are three elements for network-related charges:

- A service or port-hour fee
- A data processing fee
- Data transfer

Service or port-hour fees can include services such as Virtual Private Networks (VPNs), AWS Direct Connect, and Network Address Translation (NAT) gateways, where an hourly charge is applied once the service has been configured. Other service charges can reflect an inclusive data transfer element where it is not charged separately.

Data processing fees are applied on services such as NAT gateway and Elastic Load Balancing.

Data transfer costs are the fees charged by AWS when data is moved over a network where at least one end of the traffic flow is located within an AWS Region.

In this chapter, pricing for the us-east-1 (N. Virginia) region at the time of writing is used for all examples. You should check for the latest pricing on the AWS website, noting that different AWS Regions may use different pricing. Where tiered pricing exists for a service, the chapter uses the first non-free rate.

Service and Port-Hour Fees

The following network-specific services incur service or port-hour fees in addition to data transfer (which is covered in the section that follows).

Virtual Private Network (VPN) Connections

VPN connections are charged per connection hour. This means that the connection-hour fee applies once you provision an AWS-managed VPN and it becomes available for use. An AWS-managed VPN connects a Virtual Private Gateway (VGW) on a Virtual

Private Cloud (VPC) to a customer gateway. Deleting the VPN connection ceases the connection-hour charge. In addition to the connection-hour fee, there is a charge for data transfer that can vary depending on the location of the customer gateway. For most architectures, the customer gateway is located within a customer's network and data transfer is charged at Internet rates. Using the us-east-1 region as an example, this is $0.09 per GB outbound from AWS. You are not charged for inbound data transfer in this scenario.

AWS Direct Connect

AWS Direct Connect connections are charged per port-hour. This means that the port-hour charge applies after you are provisioned with an AWS Direct Connect connection and either its status becomes "available" for the first time or 90 days pass (whichever occurs first). In the case of a hosted connection, which is provided by an AWS Direct Connect partner, the port-hour charge applies once the receiving account accepts the connection. In both situations, the account that has the connection is charged the port-hour fee.

AWS Direct Connect cannot be used effectively until a *Virtual Interface (VIF)* has been created. A VIF establishes the Border Gateway Protocol (BGP) session and enables traffic to flow. After creating a VIF, AWS Direct Connect data transfer charges then apply and are charged to the account that owns the VIF. The account that owns the VIF can be different from the account that owns the AWS Direct Connect connection. AWS Direct Connect data transfer rates then also apply and are different for each region and AWS Direct Connect location. AWS Direct Connect data transfer rates are, however, consistently lower than standard Internet-out rates.

AWS PrivateLink

If you choose to create an interface type VPC endpoint in your VPC, you are charged for each hour that your VPC endpoint is provisioned in each Availability Zone. Data processing charges apply for each gigabyte processed through the VPC endpoint, regardless of the traffic's source or destination. Each partial VPC endpoint-hour consumed is billed as a full hour.

NAT Gateway

A NAT gateway is charged based on NAT gateway hours from the moment that the gateway is provisioned and available. These charges stop when the NAT gateway is deleted. As the NAT gateway processes traffic and performs the NAT, there is a charge for the volume of data processed regardless of the traffic's source or destination. In addition, standard data transfer charges apply for the traffic flowing through the NAT gateway. In most architectures, this will be Internet-out rates.

Elastic Load Balancing

Elastic Load Balancing has three different types of load balancers.

Application Load Balancer You are charged for each hour or partial hour that an Application Load Balancer is running and for the number of *Load Balancer Capacity Units (LCUs)* used by the load balancer per hour.

Network Load Balancer You are charged for each hour or partial hour that a Network Load Balancer is running and for the number of LCUs used by the load balancer per hour.

Classic Load Balancer You are charged for each hour or partial hour that a Classic Load Balancer is running and for each GB of data transferred through your load balancer.

For Application Load Balancers and Network Load Balancers, the variable component is based on the number of LCUs. An LCU measures the dimensions on which the load balancer processes your traffic (averaged over an hour).

The dimensions measured are as follows:

New connections or flows Number of newly-established connections per second. Many technologies (for example, HTTP or WebSockets) reuse Transmission Control Protocol (TCP) connections for efficiency. The number of new connections is typically lower than your request or message count.

Active connections or flows. Number of active connections per minute.

Bandwidth. The amount of traffic processed by the load balancer in Mbps.

Rule evaluations (only for Application Load Balancer). The product of number of rules processed by your load balancer and the request rate. You are not charged for the first 10 processed rules:

Rule evaluations = Request rate × [Number of rules processed – 10 rules]

You are charged only on the one dimension that has the highest usage for the hour.

An LCU for the Application Load Balancer contains the following:

- 25 new connections per second
- 3,000 active connections per minute
- 2.22 Mbps (which translates to 1 GB per hour)
- 1,000 rule evaluations per second

If you have 10 or fewer rules configured, the rule evaluations dimension is ignored in the LCU computation.

An LCU for the Network Load Balancer contains the following:

- 800 new non-Secure Sockets Layer (SSL) connections or flows per second
- 100,000 active connections or flows (sampled per minute)
- 2.22 Mbps (which translates to 1 GB per hour)

Types of Data Transfer

AWS data transfer is generally metered at the resource or service interface. The source and destination for an associated traffic flow is identified and then charged at the appropriate rate. There can be an exception when a private VIF is used on AWS Direct Connect. If the traffic flow is identified as having a target that is reachable via the VIF, then data transfer is charged at the appropriate rate attributed to the Direct Connect location and the specific AWS Region as identified on the AWS Direct Connect pricing web page outbound from AWS.

Data Transfer: Internet

The definition of Internet with regard to data transfer is when traffic flows between an AWS-owned public IP address and a non-AWS-owned public IP address. This definition excludes traffic between two AWS Regions or traffic between public IPs in the same AWS Region.

Data transfer in from the Internet to an AWS public IP is not charged. Data transfer out to the Internet from an AWS public IP is charged at $0.09 per GB up to the first 10TB.

Data Transfer: Region to Region

When traffic flows between AWS public IP addresses in different AWS Regions, then the traffic incurs the region-to-region rate of $0.02 per GB. This charge applies for traffic flow in the outbound direction from a region. For bi-directional data transfer between two different AWS Regions, each flow is only charged once in each direction (on egress). Due to the bi-directional flow, however, each flow is actually charged separately.

Whether the AWS public IP being used is associated with an Amazon Elastic Compute Cloud (Amazon EC2) instance or an AWS Cloud service (such as Amazon Simple Storage Service [Amazon S3]) does not make a difference on data transfer charges.

Amazon CloudFront

Amazon CloudFront has a range of charges for data transfer outbound from edge locations to end users/viewers of content.

When the origin being used for an Amazon CloudFront distribution is hosted in an AWS Region (for example, on Amazon S3 or an Amazon EC2 instance), there is no outbound data transfer charge from that resource. If Amazon CloudFront is also being used for uploading content, however, that inbound data transfer is charged at the inter-region rate of $0.02 per GB uploaded to the region.

Data Transfer: Same Region via Public IP

There is no charge for traffic flows to and from an AWS regional service (such as Amazon S3, Amazon Simple Queue Service [Amazon SQS], or Amazon Simple Email Service [Amazon SES]) in the same region as the source. Whether the service/resource is owned by the same account does not make a difference.

An exception is that if the traffic flow is between two Amazon EC2 instances (in the same or different AWS accounts) using their public IP, then the data transfer is charged at $0.01 per GB in both directions. It does not matter whether the traffic remains in the Availability Zone—it is still charged the same rate.

Data Transfer: Inter-Availability Zone

Traffic flow between two Amazon EC2 instances in the same VPC but in different Availability Zones is charged at $0.01 per GB in each direction. This traffic flow also includes access to services that are provided inside that VPC (such as Amazon Relational Database Service [Amazon RDS] and Amazon Redshift).

Data Transfer: VPC Peering

Traffic flow between two Amazon EC2 instances in different VPCs is charged at $0.01 per GB in each direction. This also includes access to services that are provided inside the peered VPC (for example, Amazon RDS and Amazon Redshift). The Availability Zone and customer account for the peered VPC do not affect this charge.

Data Transfer: Intra-Availability Zone

There are no charges for data transfer between Amazon EC2 instances within the same Availability Zone if they are in the same VPC.

Virtual Private Network (VPN) Endpoints (Virtual Private Gateways [VGWs])

The VGW IP addresses used by the AWS managed VPN solution for IP Security (IPsec) VPN endpoints are included in the definition of AWS public IPs for a region. Therefore, if you build a software VPN from an Amazon EC2 instance in another region acting as the customer gateway, you will be charged at the $0.02 per-GB rate for the flow in each direction rather than the Internet rate of $0.09 per GB that you may assume.

AWS Direct Connect Public Virtual Interfaces (VIFs)

When you transfer data over an AWS Direct Connect public VIF, the AWS billing system validates whether the destination IPs for a traffic flow are listed for use with an account associated with your AWS organization/billing family. These IP addresses are defined when creating the public VIF. If the IP addresses are associated with one of your accounts and the VIF has a BGP status of "up" advertising those prefixes, data transfer from resources owned by the organization is charged at the reduced AWS Direct Connect rate (as calculated based on the AWS Direct Connect location and the AWS Region being used).

If these conditions are not met, then the traffic may still flow via AWS Direct Connect; however, it will be charged at Internet rates to the owner of the resource.

Scenarios

The following section provides common examples of elements seen within application architectures and how the networking elements are charged.

Scenario 1

This scenario shows regular data transfer between two different AWS customers using Amazon EC2 instances in two different regions (see Figure 14.1).

Scenario 2

This scenario is a highly-available application replicating data between Amazon EC2 instances, both within one AWS Region and a different region chosen for disaster recovery purposes (see Figure 14.2).

FIGURE 14.1 Scenario 1

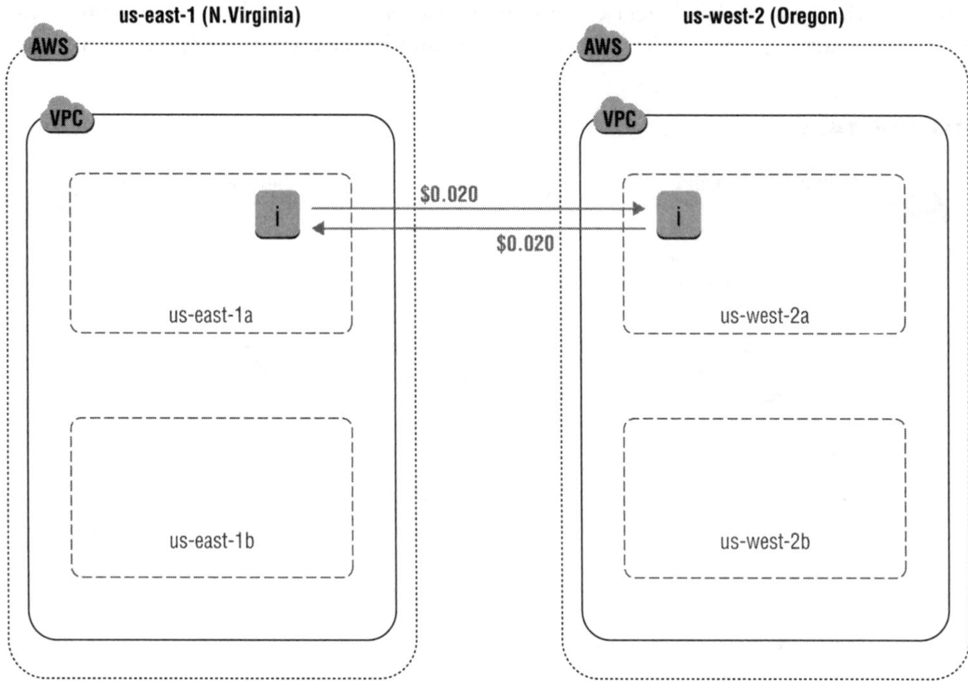

FIGURE 14.2 Scenario 2

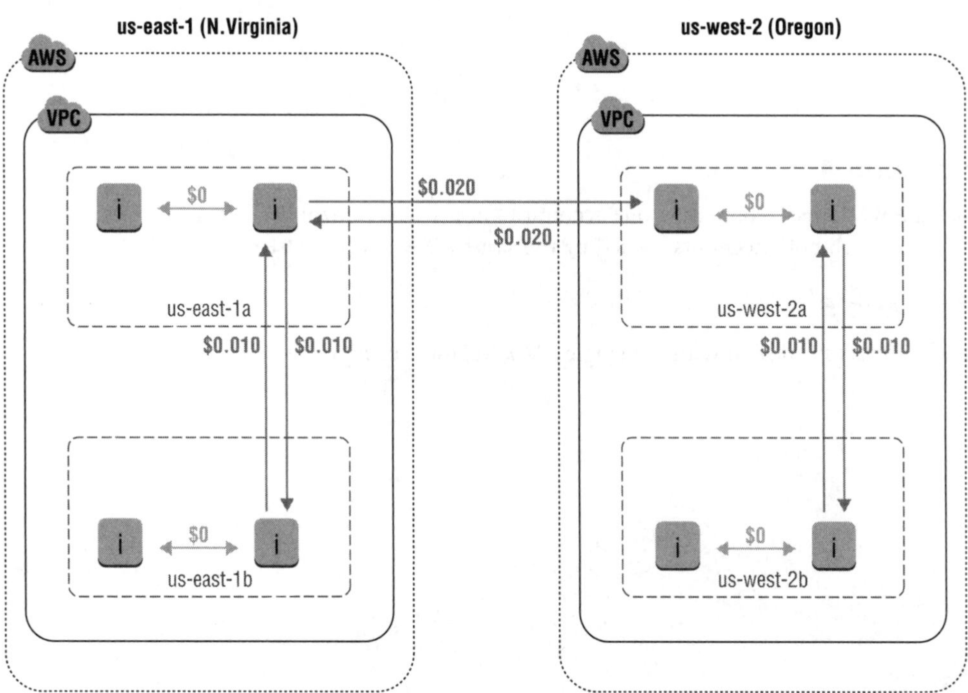

Scenario 3

This scenario is using AWS Direct Connect to access an Amazon S3 bucket owned by your organization and an Amazon S3 bucket owned by another customer (see Figure 14.3).

FIGURE 14.3 Scenario 3

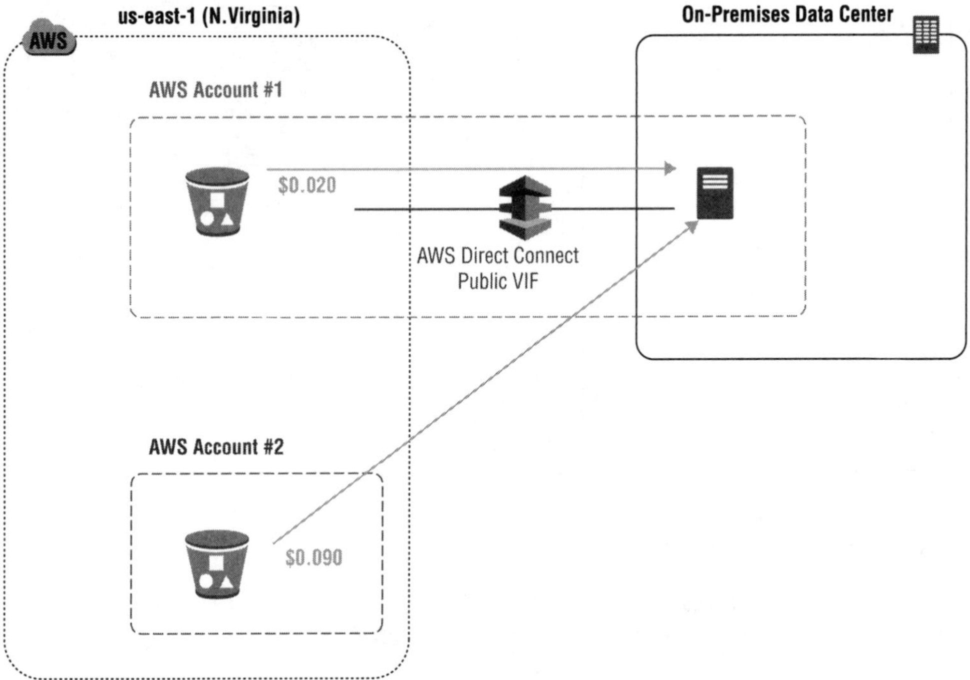

Scenario 4

Using AWS Direct Connect in one account to access an Amazon EC2 instance in another account, with both accounts owned by the same AWS customer (see Figure 14.4).

Scenario 5

The transit VPC design within a single AWS Region (see Figure 14.5).

FIGURE 14.4 Scenario 4

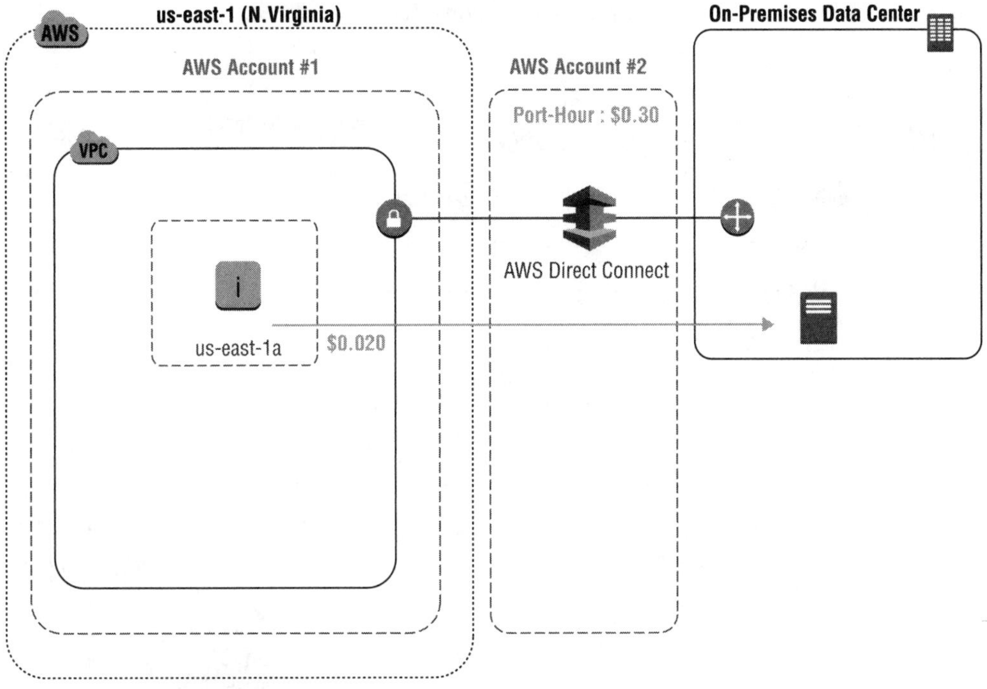

FIGURE 14.5 Scenario 5

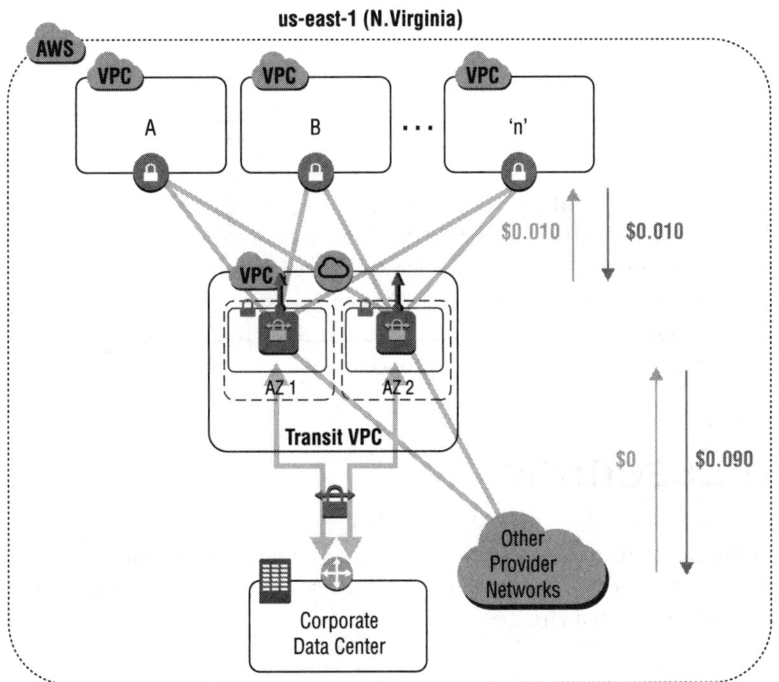

Scenario 6

The transit VPC design over multiple AWS Regions (see Figure 14.6).

FIGURE 14.6 Scenario 6

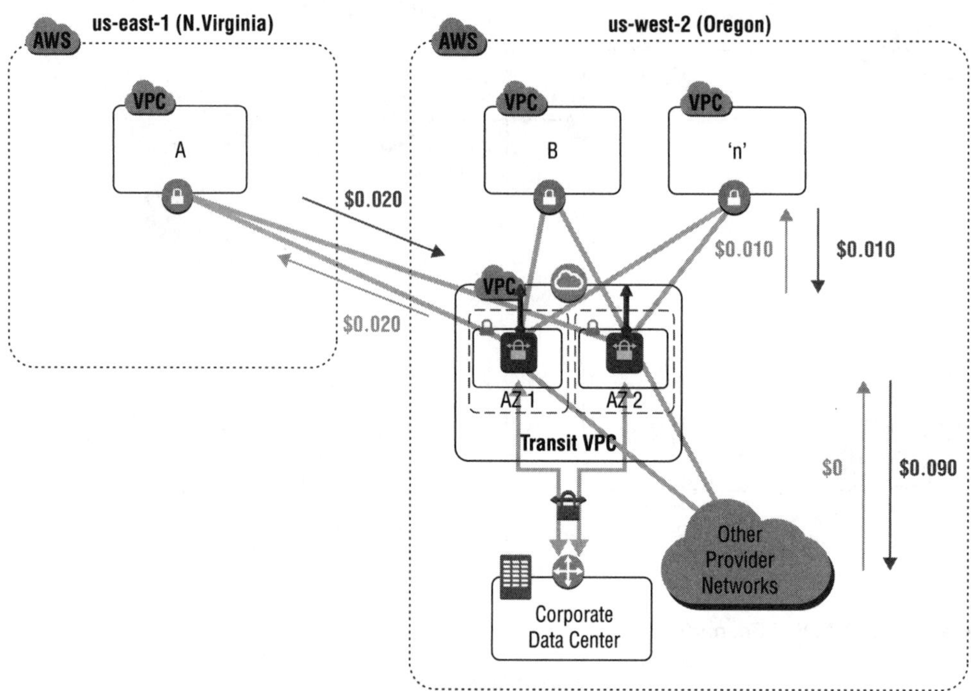

Summary

Understanding networking billing within AWS requires you to have a clear understanding of the source and destination for a specific traffic flow. You can use that information to attribute each end of the flow to one of the service and port-hour fee categories mentioned in this chapter and the AWS documentation. This then enables you to establish which of the various data transfer categories applies to that particular flow. Regardless of the categories, it's important to understand if you are charged once or twice for each flow in each direction.

Exam Essentials

Understand the key elements used for billing related to networking on AWS. Port-hour/service charges, data transfer, and data processing are the three key elements used to calculate networking-related charges.

Understand how AWS Direct Connect affects billing. Private VIFs simply reduce the outbound data transfer rates from Internet ($0.09 per GB) to AWS Direct Connect rates ($0.020 per GB).

Public VIFs have multiple factors to consider before the reduced rate applies, specifically ownership of the resource, ownership of the VIF, relationship of the VIFs within the AWS organization, whitelisted IP prefixes, BGP status, and whether the prefix is being advertised.

Understand how to combine relevant components to derive a cost for an architecture. The VGW IPsec VPN endpoints are within an AWS Region. There may be two elements to the data transfer charge, depending on where a traffic flow restarts due to a VPN appliance or similar mechanism. You will be charged twice for a traffic flow in certain situations, such as between two Availability Zones.

Test Taking Tip

Remembering specific charges for services is not relevant to the certification; however, understanding how they are applied for different traffic flow scenarios is very important.

Resources to Review

AWS Account Billing Documentation:

`https://aws.amazon.com/documentation/account-billing/`

Amazon Virtual Private Cloud (Amazon VPC) Pricing:

`http://aws.amazon.com/vpc/pricing`

AWS Direct Connect Pricing:

`https://aws.amazon.com/directconnect/pricing/`

Amazon CloudFront Pricing:

`https://aws.amazon.com/cloudfront/pricing/`

Amazon EC2 Pricing:

`https://aws.amazon.com/ec2/pricing/`

Exercises

The best way to become familiar with the AWS billing model and associated charges is to configure your own architecture and then use available resources (for example, AWS Cost and Usage reports) to understand the charges for each component.

For assistance completing these exercises, refer to the AWS Documentation located at `https://aws.amazon.com/documentation/account-billing/` and the individual service pricing pages on the AWS website.

EXERCISE 14.1

Create a Billing Alarm

In this exercise, you will create a billing alarm that notifies you when your account usage exceeds the specified limit.

1. Sign in to the AWS Management Console as Administrator or Power User.
2. Navigate to Preferences. Check the Receive Billing Alerts box.
3. Navigate to the Amazon CloudWatch Console. Choose Alarms and then Billing.
4. Create an alarm when your total AWS charges for the month exceed $20 and send a notification to your email.

If you completed this exercise successfully, you will receive an email when your charges exceed $20.

EXERCISE 14.2

Configure a Budget

In this exercise, you will use AWS Budgets to configure a budget that will notify you by email if you are forecasted to exceed a particular monthly cost threshold.

1. Sign in to the AWS Management Console as Administrator or Power User.
2. Navigate to Budgets. Choose Create Budget.
3. Fill in the Name field, select a cost amount, and set the Period as Monthly.
4. Set "Notify Me When" to Forecasted, Greater Than 100.
5. Add your email address to the contacts list.
6. Click Create.

Completing this exercise successfully will result in a notification when your forecasted spending exceeds $100.

EXERCISE 14.3

Enable Cost and Usage Report

In this exercise, you will enable the Cost and Usage report and retrieve it from Amazon S3.

1. Sign in to the AWS Management Console as Administrator or Power User.
2. Navigate to Reports. Choose Create a Report.
3. Name the report and set the time unit to Hourly.
4. Enter the IDs of all relevant resources. Choose the Amazon S3 bucket and prefix to save the reports to.
5. After 24 hours, download a report.

Completing this exercise successfully will result in reports being created at regular intervals in your Amazon S3 bucket.

Review Questions

1. You have two Amazon Elastic Compute Cloud (Amazon EC2) instances in two different Virtual Private Clouds (VPCs) that have a peering connection. Both VPCs are in the same Availability Zone. What charge will you see on your bill for data transfer between those two instances?

   A. $0.00 per GB in each direction

   B. $0.01 per GB in each direction

   C. $0.02 per GB in each direction

   D. $0.04 per GB in each direction

2. Which of the following statements regarding data transfer into Amazon Simple Storage Service (Amazon S3) is not true?

   A. Data transfer from a non-AWS public IP to Amazon S3 is not charged.

   B. Data transfer from Amazon Elastic Compute Cloud (Amazon EC2) in us-west-2 to an Amazon S3 bucket in eu-west-1 is not charged.

   C. Data transfer from Amazon EC2 to Amazon S3 in the same region is not charged.

   D. Data transfer from Amazon S3 to an Amazon CloudFront edge location is not charged.

3. You elect to use an AWS Direct Connect public Virtual Interface (VIF) to carry an IP Security (IPsec) Virtual Private Network (VPN) from your Virtual Private Cloud (VPC) Virtual Private Gateway (VGW) to your customer gateway. What rate is charged for all of the data transfer over the VPN?

   A. $0.00 per GB

   B. $0.020 per GB

   C. $0.05 per GB

   D. $0.09 per GB

4. Which of the following types of data transfer is not charged?

   A. From Amazon Elastic Compute Cloud (Amazon EC2) in eu-west-1 to Amazon Simple Storage Service (Amazon S3) in us-east-1

   B. From your on-premises data center to Amazon S3 in us-east-1

   C. From Amazon EC2 in eu-west-1 to your on-premises data center

   D. From Amazon S3 in us-east-1 to Amazon EC2 in eu-west-1

5. You want to receive an email in advance if it is likely that your monthly charge will exceed $200. Which is the most appropriate mechanism to generate this notification?

   A. Create a billing alarm in Amazon CloudWatch.

   B. Create a budget.

   C. Enable Cost and Usage reporting.

   D. Access your billing console.

6. After creating an AWS Direct Connect connection, what is the earliest point in time that you start receiving port-hour charges?
   A. 90 days from creation
   B. When the connection becomes available for the first time
   C. Once you have transferred 100 MB of data
   D. When a Virtual Interface (VIF) is created

7. Which of the following is not used for billing of the Network Address Translation (NAT) gateway?
   A. NAT gateway hourly charge
   B. NAT gateway data processing charge
   C. Active session charge
   D. Data transfer charge

8. Which of the following is the charge for data transfer out from Amazon Simple Storage Service (Amazon S3) to Amazon CloudFront?
   A. $0.000 per GB
   B. $0.010 per GB
   C. $0.020 per GB
   D. Varies by edge location

9. When using a public Virtual Interface (VIF) on AWS Direct Connect, you access an Amazon Simple Storage Service (Amazon S3) bucket owned by someone who is not part of your organization. Who pays for data transfer from that bucket?
   A. The owner of the AWS Direct Connect connection
   B. The Amazon S3 bucket owner
   C. The owner of the public VIF
   D. No one; it is not charged.

10. You make a connection from an Amazon Elastic Compute Cloud (Amazon EC2) instance that you own to the public IP address for another Amazon EC2 instance in your account. Both instances are in the same Availability Zone. How much does this cost in us-east-1?
    A. Nothing; data transfer is not charged within the same Availability Zone
    B. $0.010 per GB in each direction
    C. $0.090 per GB in each direction
    D. Nothing in one direction; $0.090 per GB in the other direction

Risk and Compliance

THE AWS CERTIFIED ADVANCED NETWORKING – SPECIALTY EXAM OBJECTIVES COVERED IN THIS CHAPTER MAY INCLUDE, BUT ARE NOT LIMITED TO, THE FOLLOWING:

Domain 5.0: Design and Implement for Security and Compliance

- ✓ **5.1 Evaluate design requirements for alignment with security and compliance objectives**
- ✓ **5.2 Evaluate monitoring strategies in support of security and compliance objectives**
- ✓ **5.3 Evaluate AWS security features for managing network traffic**
- ✓ **5.4 Utilize encryption technologies to secure network communications**

It All Begins with Threat Modeling

Before building any kind of workload-bearing environment on AWS (or anywhere else), it is vitally important to consider the nature of the data you want to process from the perspective of regulatory, classification, and attendant requirements—usually in the context of Confidentiality, Integrity, and Availability—and determine whether the proposed environment is suitable. The human mind is poor at assessing risk objectively, so you should use or extend one of the numerous risk characterization and assessment frameworks that are available.

AWS has its own threat model for the environment on the AWS side of the shared responsibility model demarcation line, which drives many design decisions for the underlying AWS environment. For example, while AWS Application Programming Interface (API) endpoints are Internet-facing, they are highly scaled and tightly monitored, and their inbound network connections are traffic-shaped. All Internet-connected AWS production networks also have packet scoring and filtering capabilities that are invisible to customers. These capabilities are in place to protect the AWS infrastructure, and all customers benefit from them by processing their data on AWS. These packet-scoring and filtering capabilities form a significant part of the AWS Shield service, which is described in more detail later in this chapter.

Some of the ways in which AWS addresses its threat model, which we recommend that you use, include the following:

Separation of duty This is used in the context of specific, security-sensitive operations, and requires multiple individuals to work together in concert in order perform an operation. Actions that require such collaboration between people are sometimes referred to as being subject to "multi-eyes rules."

Least privilege This involves only giving permissions to people and system processes necessary to perform the actions they need to perform and at the time they need to perform them. In the context of AWS Identity and Access Management (IAM), this typically involves granting users and processes a minimal default set of permissions and requiring them to authenticate to a role in order to perform more privileged operations only when they need to do so.

Need to know This can be considered an extension of separation of duty. If you only need to interact with environments in certain ways to do your job, you only need to know enough about those environments to interact with them successfully in those ways, while having an escalation path in the event that something goes wrong. AWS Cloud services are driven by APIs, so for abstract services, you only need to know the API calls, their responses, and logging and alerting events to use them successfully, rather than needing the full details of "what goes on behind the scenes."

Compliance and Scoping

After you have determined that your workload is broadly suitable for deployment on AWS, the next step is to determine which services may be used and how they may be used in order to meet the requirements of any legislative or regulatory frameworks that pertain to the workload. AWS maintains compliance with a number of external standards for many services. A matrix of which services are audited and in scope for which standards is maintained at `https://aws.amazon.com/compliance/services-in-scope/`. In this context, Amazon Virtual Private Cloud (Amazon VPC) elements such as security groups, network Access Control Lists (NACLs), subnets, Virtual Private Gateways (VGWs), Internet gateways, Network Address Translation (NAT) Gateways, VPC private endpoints, and the Domain Name System (DNS) service are all subsumed under Amazon VPC.

If a service is not in scope for a particular standard, this does not necessarily mean that it must be excluded from an environment that needs to be compliant with the standard. Rather, it cannot be used to process data that the standard defines as being sensitive. A common and recommended approach is to isolate environments that are in scope for specific compliance requirements from environments that are not, not only by containing them in separate VPCs, but also in separate AWS accounts. Accounts and VPCs also serve as clearly defined technical scope boundaries for your auditor to consider.

If you have been involved in compliance for any length of time, you understand that if you have compliant thing A and connect it to compliant thing B, the result will not necessarily be a compliant thing. While AWS has individual services certified by third-party auditors against a number of external compliance standards, it remains possible to build non-compliant environments out of compliant parts. To make it easier to build environments that your auditor is more likely to approve, AWS provides assets under the Enterprise Accelerator program. These comprise a spreadsheet mapping of the controls specified in the standard to the means of achieving and enforcing them in AWS, a modular set of AWS CloudFormation templates that can be plugged together to reasonably reflect your intended network design and accompanying documentation.

If you are required to meet other compliance standards, the National Institute of Standards and Technology (NIST)-focused asset set in particular is worth examining, because the large number of technical controls in NIST 800-53 means that it is likely to have a reasonable overlap with the controls in the standard(s) you require.

Audit Reports and Other Papers

Ultimately, the arbiter of whether or not your environment meets compliance requirements is your auditor. To help understand AWS environments, we provide a free online training course, access to which can be requested by emailing `awsaudittraining@amazon.com`. This is in addition to numerous guidance whitepapers and assets in our Enterprise Accelerator program.

Available assets include the following:

AWS Overview of Security Processes whitepaper This covers human factors such as separation of duty, need to know, and service maintenance:

`https://d0.awsstatic.com/whitepapers/aws-security-whitepaper.pdf`

AWS Security Best Practices whitepaper This covers configuration recommendations, data deletion processes, and physical security:

`https://d0.awsstatic.com/whitepapers/Security/AWS_Security_Best_Practices.pdf`

AWS Risk and Compliance whitepaper This provides answers to questions commonly found in customer compliance questionnaires; this also contains a completed copy of the Cloud Security Alliance CAIQ questionnaire and an Information Security Registered Assessors Program (IRAP) assessment:

`https://d0.awsstatic.com/whitepapers/compliance/AWS_Risk_and_Compliance_Whitepaper.pdf`

AWS also makes a number of reports from external auditors available online. These reports enable you to gain third-party-vetted details on AWS technologies, organization, environments, and operational practices. They can also help your auditors determine whether the whole environment you are deploying, on both your and AWS's side of the shared responsibility model demarcation, meets compliance requirements.

These audit reports are available for free via the AWS Artifact service (`https://aws.amazon.com/artifact/`), which presents the reports via an AWS Management Console-based portal and API. Note that a number of the reports and scoping documents require a separate click-through Non-Disclosure Agreement (NDA) before you download them. Even if you do not need to be Payment Card Industry Data Security Standard (PCI DSS)-compliant, the PCI DSS audit report contains information on AWS's approach to assisting with forensic investigations and guest-to-guest separation in our hypervisor. If the PCI DSS guest-to-guest separation assurance is insufficient for your own threat model, Amazon Elastic Compute Cloud (Amazon EC2) Dedicated Instances are also available. These instances use a different placement algorithm to ensure that your guests are only launched on physical servers hosting guest instances belonging to you, rather than to any other customer.

Ownership Model and the Role of Network Management

As discussed in Chapter 8, "Network Security," management of the underlying AWS network is AWS's responsibility. Even though an Availability Zone comprises one or more data centers, the network for each Availability Zone is part of a contiguous Open Systems Interconnection (OSI) Layer 2 space in the Amazon EC2 network for that Availability Zone. This layer can be separated into VPCs and connected with Internet gateways to the Amazon border network, which links all public AWS Regions (except China) and houses AWS API endpoints.

The Amazon VPC environment is designed to reflect the most common ways of organizing traditional data center environments and access permissions over them. As such, it makes sense for network permissions to be assignable to different teams on your workforce. Separation of duty is a key mechanism within AWS for maintaining human security. You can use IAM policies to assign permissions over security groups, network ACLs, and more to different IAM roles. You can also consider moving to a complete DevOps/DevSecOps model to remove humans from the data and system management process as much as possible.

Controlling Access to AWS

All access to AWS APIs for non-root users is controlled by IAM, which can now be augmented with AWS Organizations *Service Control Policies (SCPs)*. SCPs are discussed further in Chapter 8.

An *IAM policy* is a JSON document that follows a Principal, Action, Resource, Condition (PARC) model. An IAM policy contains the following components:

Effect The effect can be Allow or Deny. By default, IAM users do not have permission to use resources and API actions, so all requests are denied. An explicit Allow overrides the default. An explicit Deny overrides any number of Allows; this can be useful as policies grow in complexity.

Principal The entity or service associated with the policy. Most often, the IAM principal is the entity (for example, user, group, or role) against which the policy is applied.

Action The action is the specific API action for which you are granting or denying permission.

Resource The resource is what is affected by the action. Some Amazon EC2 API actions allow you to include specific resources in your policy that can be created or modified by the action. To specify a resource in the statement, you need to use its Amazon Resource Name (ARN). If the API action does not support ARNs, use the * wildcard to specify that all resources can be affected by the action.

Condition Conditions are optional. They can be used to control when your policy is in effect.

Each service has its own set of actions, details of which are typically found in that service's developer guide.

Figure 15.1 shows the decision tree used when evaluating policies.

FIGURE 15.1 Policy evaluation decision flow

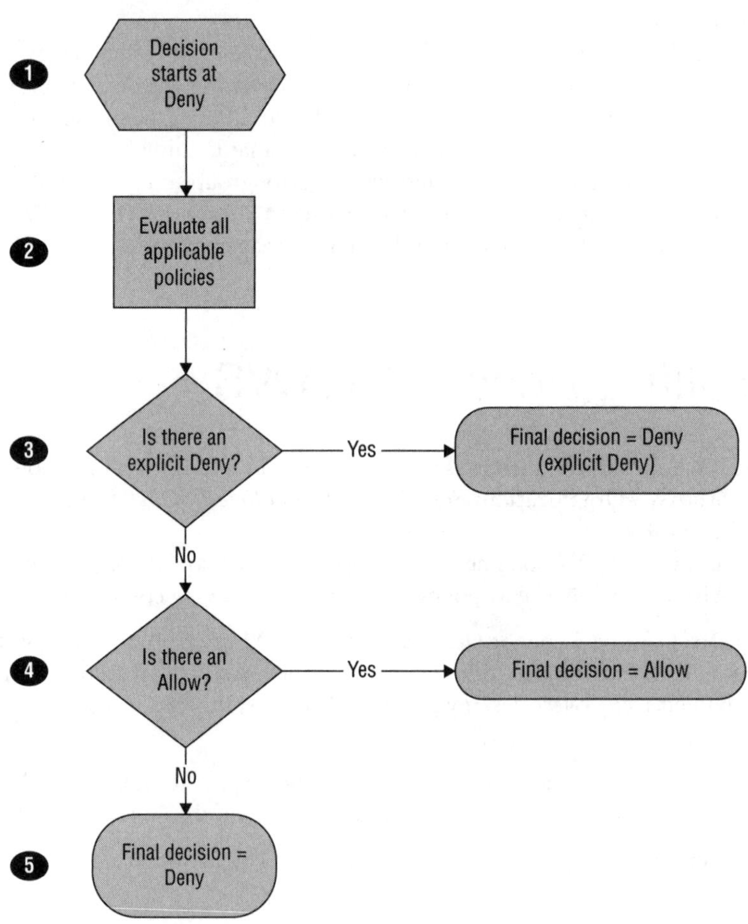

IAM policies can also be used with the `SourceIp` condition, which can in many cases restrict the source IP addresses from which API calls can be made with the `SourceIp` condition. Multiple IP ranges can be specified on the condition, which are evaluated using `OR`. For example:

```
"IpAddress" : {
"aws:SourceIp" : ["192.0.2.0/24", "203.0.113.0/24"]
}
```

The *aws:SourceIp condition* key works only in an IAM policy if you are calling the tested API directly as a user. If you instead use a service to call the target service on your behalf, the target service sees the IP address of the calling service rather than the IP address of the originating user. This can happen, for example, if you use AWS CloudFormation to call Amazon EC2 to construct instances for you. There is currently no way to pass the originating IP address through a calling service to the target service for evaluation in an IAM policy. For these types of service API calls, do not use the `aws:SourceIp` condition key.

AWS Organizations

Until the introduction of AWS Organizations, the root user in an AWS account was a very traditional omnipotent user, such that IAM policy constraints did not apply to it. With *AWS Organizations*, an SCP can be applied to a child account such that the root user (and all other IAM users) in that child account is not only subject to the constraints imposed by the SCP, but also cannot read or alter it.

SCPs closely resemble IAM policies but do not currently support IAM Conditions or fine-grained Resource elements. While the most common approach is to use SCPs at account creation to deny access to AWS Cloud services that are not required or desirable to use, you can also use them with the same granularity as IAM policy at any time in the account lifecycle to deny access to specific API calls.

For a networking example, an SCP that denies the ability to attach an Internet gateway, attach a VGW, or peer a VPC would enforce isolation from the Internet of any VPCs created while the SCP is in force.

SCPs can be assigned to individual child accounts in an organization or to accounts grouped into an Organizational Unit (OU). An AWS Organization's master account cannot apply an SCP to itself that affects the root user, so the root user continues to behave like a classic omnipotent user in an AWS Organization's master account only.

Amazon CloudFront Distributions

Amazon CloudFront has built-in support for IP-based georestriction if you need to restrict access to services that you host in AWS based on client geographical location (for example, to comply with denied and restricted parties lists). While mapping location by IP address is an inexact science, especially if the client is using a proxy, it is still a control that can be used as an argument in demonstrating compliance.

While Amazon CloudFront distributions are paid for based on anticipated geographical usage, data can potentially be cached in and emitted from any Amazon CloudFront Point of Presence (PoP), irrespective of distribution configured. This is done in part so that, in the event of Distributed Denial of Service (DDoS) attacks, Amazon Route 53 sharding can be used to balance load across PoPs transparently, which are not within scope of the attack.

Encryption Options

AWS uses encryption, transaction authentication, and IAM authorization for the API call system, and we recommend that customers encrypt data at rest by default, where supported. Encryption in transit is more nuanced and is covered in greater detail in the following sections.

AWS API Calls and Internet API Endpoints

API calls are made using *AWS's Signature Version 4 (Sigv4) algorithm*, which provides authentication and integrity of each transaction over an encrypted communications channel that has unidirectional cryptographic trust based on an API endpoint-side certificate/key pair. Cryptographic services on the API endpoint side are provided by AWS's own s2n implementation of Transport Layer Security (TLS), a minimal, formally-proven implementation written from scratch in C, which is open source and available for use and analysis at: `https://github.com/awslabs/`. API endpoint certificates are signed using Amazon Trust Services, which is a global root Certificate Authority (CA) and is also used by AWS Certificate Manager.

Rather than authenticate your API-calling endpoint with a bidirectional cryptographic handshake (like TLS mutual authentication), AWS uses the Sigv4 algorithm to authenticate each individual transaction. All AWS Software Development Kits (SDKs) implement Sigv4, as does the AWS Command Line Interface (CLI), which uses boto3, the Python SDK. Currently, the only AWS Cloud service that performs a more traditional bidirectional cryptographic handshake between client and AWS-side API endpoint is the AWS Internet of Things (IoT) service.

s2n (as well as Elastic Load Balancing, Application Load Balancer, Amazon Relational Database Service [Amazon RDS], and Amazon CloudFront cipher suites, which are covered later) offers Secure Sockets Layer (SSL) 3.0 and all versions of TLS up to and including 1.2, with Diffie-Hellman Encryption (DHE) and Elliptic-Curve Diffie-Hellman Encryption (ECDHE). While SSL has been deprecated following the uncovering of the Padding Oracle On Downgraded Legacy Encryption (POODLE) vulnerability, there are still a significant number of active customers working with devices that require it, which is why it is still offered for AWS API endpoints. If you are concerned about the choice of cipher used to establish the HTTPS connection to the AWS API endpoints, we recommend configuring your client to accept only offers to use protocols and ciphers of your choice.

Selecting Cipher Suites

As already discussed, API endpoints and AWS IoT offer a range of cipher options that are client-side selectable. These options are also available for Elastic Load Balancing, Application Load Balancer, and Amazon CloudFront, though server-side control is offered for these as well. Cipher suites for each load balancer and Amazon CloudFront distribution can be selected as part of their configuration. The AWS recommendation is always to choose the most recent cipher suite unless you have a compelling business need not to do so.

In the event of a cryptographic algorithm, key length, or mode being deprecated by AWS Security, a new cipher suite will be made available that removes the deprecated combination of algorithm, key length, and mode(s). In the case of POODLE, for example, Amazon CloudFront and Elastic Load Balancing were issued with a new TLS-only cipher suite within 24 hours. When such deprecation events occur, however, you should check your configurations to ensure that an appropriate cipher suite is in place for your needs.

Encryption in Transit Inside AWS Environments

Amazon CloudFront, Elastic Load Balancing, Amazon API Gateway, and AWS IoT all normally terminate connections at their network interfaces. It is normal to terminate encryption there too, although Elastic Load Balancing can be also configured in a pass-through mode that allows ciphertext to be proxied through for termination in (typically) an Amazon EC2 instance. Pass-through is typically used when protocols other than HTTPS are involved or when unconventional combinations of algorithm, key length, and mode are involved.

Amazon CloudFront has no pass-through mechanism; the principal purpose of a Content Distribution Network (CDN) is to cache content as close to the consumer as possible, so there is no practical purpose in caching ciphertext. In addition, in order to perform deep-packet inspection, *AWS Web Application Firewall (AWS WAF)* must be able to see cleartext.

Both the Application Load Balancer and Amazon CloudFront are able to use keys presented to them using AWS Certificate Manager. Domain-validated (DV) certificates generated by AWS Certificate Manager are provisioned with a 13-month validity and are automatically renewed approximately 30 days before expiration. Certificate/key pairs generated in AWS Certificate Manager are usable in Application Load Balancer and Amazon CloudFront, but the private keys are not available for you to download into, for example, an Amazon EC2 instance. Alternatively, if you need to use extended-validation (EV) keys, you should obtain these according to your normal process from your usual CA and upload them into AWS Certificate Manager.

Both Application Load Balancer and Amazon CloudFront can also re-encrypt data for transfer into your VPC and to your origin, respectively, using different keys if desired.

You have the option to encrypt all data in transit inside your VPC if your security policy or external regulatory requirements require it. It is worth considering, however, if encryption in transit is a compliance requirement, or if it is actually necessary according to your own threat model. A VPC is defined as being a private network at OSI Layer 2 and is asserted as being such in the Service Organization Controls (SOC) 1 and PCI DSS audit reports. Many customers encrypt all communication within the VPC; however, you may have no strict requirement to do so. When you make a decision on intra-VPC traffic encryption, make sure that you consult your threat model, review the relevant information assurance or compliance frameworks, and assess your organizational risk profile.

Encryption in Load Balancers and Amazon CloudFront PoPs

Application Load Balancer and Amazon CloudFront can use keys generated by, or imported into, AWS Certificate Manager to terminate TLS and SSL for inbound connections. AWS load balancers can only engage in unidirectional-trust connections; there is no means at the network level of mutually authenticating connections between client and load balancer using asymmetric cryptographic keys bound to each party. If this kind of mutual authentication is needed, you should examine third-party load balancers in the AWS Marketplace for suitable options.

Network Activity Monitoring

One of the strengths of a cloud environment is the fact that all asset creation and modification operations must be performed via an API. There is no mechanism for you or your colleagues to change the disposition of assets in an AWS environment at an AWS level without executing AWS API calls. This makes the API a single point of control, visibility, and audit. In a cloud environment, there are no virtual desks under which you can hide your virtual servers.

AWS provides a number of logging capabilities for the APIs themselves (AWS CloudTrail), the effects that API calls produce (AWS Config), network traffic (Amazon VPC Flow Logs), Amazon EC2 instance statistics (Amazon CloudWatch and Amazon CloudWatch Logs), and sessions processed by load balancers (Elastic Load Balancing logs), among others. When considering a management, monitoring, and alerting capability, remember that such a capability needs to be at least as robust, responsive, scalable, and secure as the live service environment that it is managing, monitoring, and alerting on. With all of the logging capabilities listed, AWS transparently handles the scaling of the services involved. AWS CloudTrail, AWS Config, Elastic Load Balancing, and Amazon CloudFront logs are sent to Amazon Simple Storage Service (Amazon S3) by default (AWS Config logs can also be sent to an Amazon Simple Notification Service [Amazon SNS] topic), and Amazon S3 bucket capacity expands to accommodate the data involved. Amazon CloudWatch, Amazon CloudWatch Logs, and Amazon VPC Flow Logs log to a separate stream mechanism.

Different log mechanisms have different delivery latencies. Currently Amazon CloudWatch has the lowest delivery latency, varying from milliseconds to seconds. For automated event analysis and response using AWS Lambda, Amazon CloudWatch Events is currently the preferred AWS Lambda triggering mechanism.

Each of these logging sources needs to be enabled in every region, Amazon VPC Flow Logs needs to be configured in each VPC, and the Amazon CloudWatch Logs agent needs to be installed and configured on each Amazon EC2 instance, unless you choose to use agents native to your preferred Security Information and Event Management (SIEM) to scrape operating system- and application-level logs instead.

AWS CloudTrail

AWS CloudTrail's data sources are the API calls to AWS Cloud services that have AWS CloudTrail support. Mature production services that have an API will support AWS CloudTrail. Not all services have AWS CloudTrail support when they are in preview mode; some only integrate AWS CloudTrail when they move into production. The current list of supported services is available at:

```
http://docs.aws.amazon.com/awscloudtrail/latest/userguide/
cloudtrail-supported-services.html
```

The Amazon S3 bucket to which AWS CloudTrail logs are sent can be encrypted using your preferred Amazon S3 encryption mechanism—we recommend server-side encryption with AWS KMS–managed keys (SSE-KMS). Uniquely among AWS logging services, AWS CloudTrail can also deliver a digest of a log record to the same bucket; if you use a bucket policy that partitions access grants on key prefix, you can use these digests as an integrity check for your actual AWS CloudTrail records. Digests are delivered hourly and contain SHA-256 digests of each object written during the hour. In the manner of a blockchain, digests also contain the digest of the previous digest record so that tampering with the digest objects can be detected over time. An empty digest file is delivered if there have been no objects written during the hour.

If you disable log file integrity validation, the chain of digest files is broken after one hour. AWS CloudTrail will not create digest files for log files that were delivered during a period in which log file integrity validation was disabled. The same applies whenever you stop AWS CloudTrail logging or delete a trail.

If logging is stopped or the trail is deleted, AWS CloudTrail will deliver a final digest file. This digest file can contain information for any remaining log files that cover events up, to and including the `StopLogging` event.

AWS CloudTrail records are delivered to Amazon S3 between 5 and 15 minutes after the API call is executed. AWS is continually working to reduce this delivery latency.

AWS Config

AWS Config can be viewed as a logical complement to AWS CloudTrail. While AWS CloudTrail records API calls, AWS Config records the changes that those API calls affect for AWS assets. If you work with an Information Technology Infrastructure Library (ITIL) model, AWS Config serves as your Configuration Management Database (CMDB) for services in scope at an AWS asset level.

The set of AWS Cloud services and assets within them that are enabled for AWS Config is available at:

`http://docs.aws.amazon.com/config/latest/developerguide/resource-config-reference.html#supported-resources`

AWS Config tracks changes in the configuration of your AWS resources, and it regularly sends updated configuration details to an Amazon S3 bucket that you specify. For each resource type that AWS Config records, it sends a configuration history file every six hours. Each configuration history file contains details about the resources that changed in that six-hour period. Each file includes resources of one type, such as Amazon EC2 instances or Amazon Elastic Block Store (Amazon EBS) volumes. If no configuration changes occur, AWS Config does not send a file.

Amazon SNS notifications for AWS Config changes are typically ready for delivery in less than one minute and are delivered in this time plus the latency associated with the delivery mechanism that you chose.

AWS Config sends a configuration snapshot to your Amazon S3 bucket when you use the `deliver-config-snapshot` command with the AWS CLI or when you use the `DeliverConfigSnapshot` action with the AWS Config API. A *configuration snapshot* contains configuration details for the resources that AWS Config records in your AWS account. The configuration history file and configuration snapshot are in JSON format.

AWS Config has its own AWS Lambda trigger; AWS Lambda functions that trigger on it are referred to as *AWS Config Rules*. In addition to enabling you to trigger your own functions to analyze and potentially act in response to changes, AWS curates a set of more than 20 functions—Managed Config Rules—that are popular with a broad range of customers. These functions can be used to analyze individual configuration items commonly involved in compliance and report issues to an Amazon SNS topic that you choose. Source code for these functions is available at: `https://github.com/awslabs/aws-config-rules`, and AWS welcomes contributions of new rules.

AWS Config Rules functions are normally triggered a few seconds after the change being recorded is made, but latencies of a few minutes between change event and log write are possible.

The AWS Management Console enables you to set up AWS Config data for consumption in one of three ways:

Timeline For each asset, you can view the history of its configuration since the time AWS Config was enabled, provided that AWS Config been operating continuously.

Snapshot For the whole of your in-scope AWS assets within an account and a region, you can obtain a description of their disposition at any point in time since AWS Config was enabled, provided that AWS Config has been operating continuously.

Stream If you (and your SIEM) prefer to consume AWS Config records via a stream mechanism rather than by retrieving them from an Amazon S3 bucket, you have that option.

Amazon CloudWatch

You can use *Amazon CloudWatch* to gain system-wide visibility into resource utilization, application performance, and operational health. You can use these insights to react and keep your application running smoothly.

Amazon CloudWatch was originally created to make Hypervisor-based statistics available as generally applicable performance metrics, perform statistical analysis on them, and provide an alarm system that could trigger Auto Scaling and other actions. In addition to monitoring and alerting on metrics specific to services, Amazon CloudWatch is also commonly used to monitor and alert on AWS account billing.

Amazon CloudWatch provides standard metrics for AWS services at various intervals, depending on the service. Some services, such as Amazon EC2, provide detailed metrics, typically at a one-minute interval. Amazon CloudWatch stores data about a metric as a series of data points. Each data point has an associated time stamp.

You can also publish your own metrics to Amazon CloudWatch using the AWS CLI or an API. A statistical graph of this information is published in the AWS Management Console. Custom metrics have a standard resolution of one-minute granularity. For custom metrics you may also use a one-second, high resolution granularity.

Amazon CloudWatch includes an alarm capability. You can use an alarm to initiate actions automatically on your behalf. An alarm watches a single metric over a specified time period and performs one or more specified actions based on the value of the metric relative to a threshold over time. The action is a notification sent to an Amazon SNS topic or an Auto Scaling policy. You can also add alarms to dashboards.

Alarms invoke actions for sustained state changes only. Amazon CloudWatch alarms do not invoke actions simply because they are in a particular state. The state must have changed and been maintained for a specified number of periods.

When creating an alarm, select a period that is greater than or equal to the frequency of the metric to be monitored. For example, basic monitoring for Amazon EC2 provides metrics for your instances every five minutes. When setting an alarm on a basic monitoring metric, select a period of at least 300 seconds (five minutes). Detailed monitoring for Amazon EC2 provides metrics for your instances every one minute. When setting an alarm on a detailed monitoring metric, select a period of at least 60 seconds (one minute).

If you set an alarm on a high-resolution metric, you can specify a high-resolution alarm with a period of 10 seconds or 30 seconds, or you can set a regular alarm with a period of any multiple of 60 seconds. A maximum of five actions can be configured per alarm.

Amazon CloudWatch Logs

Amazon CloudWatch processes AWS-originated and customer-originated textual log data. Amazon EC2 instance logs (which use the Amazon CloudWatch Logs agent), Amazon VPC Flow Logs, and AWS CloudTrail records (where redirection is set up) can all send records to *Amazon CloudWatch Logs*. AWS Lambda functions can also use the `print()` function to send arbitrary output to Amazon CloudWatch Logs; this is often used for debugging and logging.

The Amazon CloudWatch Logs agent will send log data every five seconds by default and is configurable by the user. Other Amazon CloudWatch Logs records are delivered in milliseconds to seconds.

The Amazon CloudWatch Logs agent invokes AWS API calls in order to submit log records. As Amazon CloudWatch Logs does not have a VPC private endpoint, this means that security groups, network ACLs, and routing require instances using the agent to have HTTPS access to the relevant API endpoint in the Amazon boundary network.

Amazon CloudWatch handles storage of all metrics for customers from the previous 14 days to 15 months. Amazon CloudWatch retains metric data as follows:

- Data points with a period of less than 60 seconds are available for three hours. These data points are high-resolution custom metrics.
- Data points with a period of 60 seconds (one minute) are available for 15 days.
- Data points with a period of 300 seconds (five minutes) are available for 63 days.
- Data points with a period of 3,600 seconds (one hour) are available for 455 days (15 months).

Amazon VPC Flow Logs

Amazon VPC Flow Logs are enabled on a per-VPC, per-subnet, or per-interface basis. They deliver NetFlow-like records of network data flows (potentially throughout the VPC), taken over a sample time window and from each elastic network interface in scope. Amazon VPC Flow Logs are delivered to an Amazon CloudWatch Logs-based log group comprising a linked list of records per elastic network interface.

Amazon VPC Flow Logs do not record traffic to and from VPC-native DNS services, the Amazon EC2 metadata service, Dynamic Host Configuration Protocol (DHCP) services, or the Windows license activation server.

Like other Amazon CloudWatch Logs records, Amazon VPC Flow Logs data is delivered a matter of seconds after the end of the sample time window. The exception to this delivery schedule is if Amazon CloudWatch Logs rate limiting has been applied and the delivery rate of aggregate data, including Amazon VPC Flow Log data, exceeds this.

As with other Amazon CloudWatch Logs, AWS Lambda functions can be triggered by new log data arriving as Amazon CloudWatch Events both to analyze and respond to log records at arrival time. Amazon CloudWatch Logs, while also being a stream into which AWS CloudTrail can be piped, can themselves be piped into Amazon Elasticsearch Service (for more information, refer to `http://docs.aws.amazon.com/AmazonCloudWatch/latest/logs/CWL_ES_Stream.html`). However, depending on your compliance requirements, you may need to perform some pre-processing on your log data before you commit it to long-term storage. For example, some legislation considers a tuple of a source IP address and a timestamp to constitute Personally Identifiable Information (PII).

One of the most popular uses of Amazon CloudWatch Logs Metric Filters is to scan Amazon VPC Flow Logs records for `REJECT` flags in the penultimate field. The principle here is that, after you have your security groups and network ACLs set up suitably for your environment, a `REJECT` in an Amazon VPC Flow Log record indicates that traffic is trying to get to or from somewhere it should not be. This trigger marks the instances associated with the source and destination IP addresses in the log record as being worthy of further investigation. While Amazon VPC Flow Logs records do not perform full-packet capture, the Amazon VPC Flow Logs ➢ Amazon CloudWatch Metric Filter ➢ Amazon CloudWatch Alarms ➢ Amazon SNS architecture is a simple approach to a basic Network Intrusion Detection System (NIDS). This approach scales inline with workloads without you needing to perform any operations for it to do so because AWS handles those operations. More information on Amazon CloudWatch Log Metric Filters is available at:

`http://docs.aws.amazon.com/AmazonCloudWatch/latest/logs/FilterAndPatternSyntax.html`

Amazon CloudFront

You can configure *Amazon CloudFront* to create log files that contain detailed information about every user request that Amazon CloudFront receives. These access logs are available for both web and Real-Time Messaging Protocol (RTMP) distributions. If you enable logging, you can also specify the Amazon S3 bucket in which you want Amazon CloudFront to save files.

Amazon CloudFront's data sources are the Amazon CloudFront endpoint PoPs and the HTTP, HTTPS, and RTMP connections that they serve.

Amazon CloudFront delivers access logs for a distribution up to several times an hour. In general, a log file contains information about the requests that Amazon CloudFront received during a given time period. Amazon CloudFront usually delivers the log file for that time period to your Amazon S3 bucket within an hour of the events that appear in the log. Note, however, that some or all of the log file entries for a time period can be delayed by up to 24 hours. When log entries are delayed, Amazon CloudFront saves them in a log file with a file name that includes the date and time of the period in which the requests occurred, rather than the date and time when the file was delivered.

As you can receive multiple access logs an hour, we recommend that you combine all of the log files that you receive for a given period into one file. You can then analyze the data for that period more quickly and accurately.

Other Log Sources

Most other AWS Cloud services have their own logging mechanisms. In the particular context of networking, Elastic Load Balancing can generate logs that are sent to an Amazon S3 bucket.

Malicious Activity Detection

AWS uses a variety of technologies to monitor and protect core infrastructure from attack as part of AWS's side of the shared responsibility model. All AWS customers benefit from these technologies when they use the AWS Cloud. Be sure review Chapter 8, as well, which covers additional AWS Cloud services like Amazon Macie and Amazon GuardDuty.

AWS Shield and Anti-DDoS Measures

Customers have the option to use AWS Cloud services such as AWS WAF, Amazon CloudFront, and Amazon Route 53 to protect environments. AWS also provides protection services that are enabled by default, such as the (customer-transparent) Blackwatch traffic-scoring system and AWS Shield. AWS Shield comes in two forms: Standard and Advanced.

AWS Shield Advanced provides expanded protection against many types of attacks, including:

User Datagram Protocol (UDP) reflection attacks An attacker can spoof the source of a request and use UDP to elicit a large response from the server. The extra network traffic directed toward the spoofed, attacked IP address can slow the targeted server and prevent legitimate users from accessing needed resources.

SYN flood The intent of an SYN flood attack is to exhaust the available resources of a system by leaving connections in a half-open state. When a user connects to a TCP service like a web server, the client sends a SYN packet. The server returns an acknowledgment, and the client returns its own acknowledgement, completing the three-way handshake. In an SYN flood, the third acknowledgment is never returned, and the server is left waiting for a response. This can prevent other users from connecting to the server.

DNS query flood In a DNS query flood, an attacker uses multiple DNS queries to exhaust the resources of a DNS server. AWS Shield Advanced can help provide protection against DNS query flood attacks on Amazon Route 53 DNS servers.

HTTP flood/cache-busting (Layer 7) attacks With an HTTP flood, including `GET` and `POST` floods, an attacker sends multiple HTTP requests that appear to be from a real user of the web application. Cache-busting attacks are a type of HTTP flood that uses variations in the HTTP request's query string that prevent use of edge-located cached content and forces the content to be served from the origin web server, causing additional and potentially damaging strain on the origin web server.

With AWS Shield Advanced, complex DDoS events can be escalated to the *AWS DDoS Response Team (DRT)*, which has deep experience in protecting AWS, `Amazon.com`, and its subsidiaries.

For Layer 3 and Layer 4 attacks, AWS provides automatic attack detection and proactively applies mitigations on your behalf. For Layer 7 DDoS attacks, AWS attempts to detect and notify AWS Shield Advanced customers through Amazon CloudWatch alarms, but it does not apply mitigations proactively. This is to avoid inadvertently dropping valid user traffic.

AWS Shield Advanced customers have two options to mitigate Layer 7 attacks:

Provide your own mitigations AWS WAF is included with AWS Shield Advanced at no extra cost. You can create your own AWS WAF rules to mitigate DDoS attacks. AWS provides preconfigured templates to get you started quickly. The templates include a set of AWS WAF rules that are designed to block common web-based attacks. You can customize the templates to fit your business needs. For more information, see AWS WAF Security Automations:

`https://aws.amazon.com/answers/security/aws-waf-security-automations/`

In this case, the DRT is not involved. You can, however, engage the DRT for guidance on implementing best practices, such as AWS WAF common protections.

Engage the DRT If you want additional support in addressing an attack, you can contact the AWS Support Center. Critical and urgent cases are routed directly to DDoS experts. With AWS Shield Advanced, complex cases can be escalated to the DRT. If you are an AWS Shield Advanced customer, you also can request special handling instructions for high-severity cases.

The response time for your case depends on the severity that you select and the response times, which are documented on the AWS Support Plans page.

The DRT helps you triage the DDoS attack to identify attack signatures and patterns. With your consent, the DRT creates and deploys AWS WAF rules to mitigate the attack.

When AWS Shield Advanced detects a large Layer 7 attack against one of your applications, the DRT might proactively contact you. The DRT triages the DDoS incident and creates AWS WAF mitigations. The DRT then contacts you for consent to apply the AWS WAF rules.

Amazon VPC Flow Logs Analysis

Flow log data is statistical in nature from being averaged across a time window. Even so, it can still be used to derive insight not only about top talkers (from the combination of timestamp and source IP address, filtered to exclude the addresses used by your Amazon EC2 and Amazon RDS instances), but also whether there are attacks in progress. We have already discussed the use of Amazon CloudWatch filter metrics to look for REJECTs in flow log records, and further interesting information can be derived from plotting the data.

The cube in Figure 15.2 is from internal research, where a heavily hardened and minimized Amazon EC2 Linux instance was stood up on an Elastic IP address directly exposed to the Internet. Using gnuplot to graph time against destination port against activity, some rotation reveals a number of sets of points that form distinct lines across the space.

FIGURE 15.2 Rotated plot of Amazon VPC flow logs: time/destination port/activity

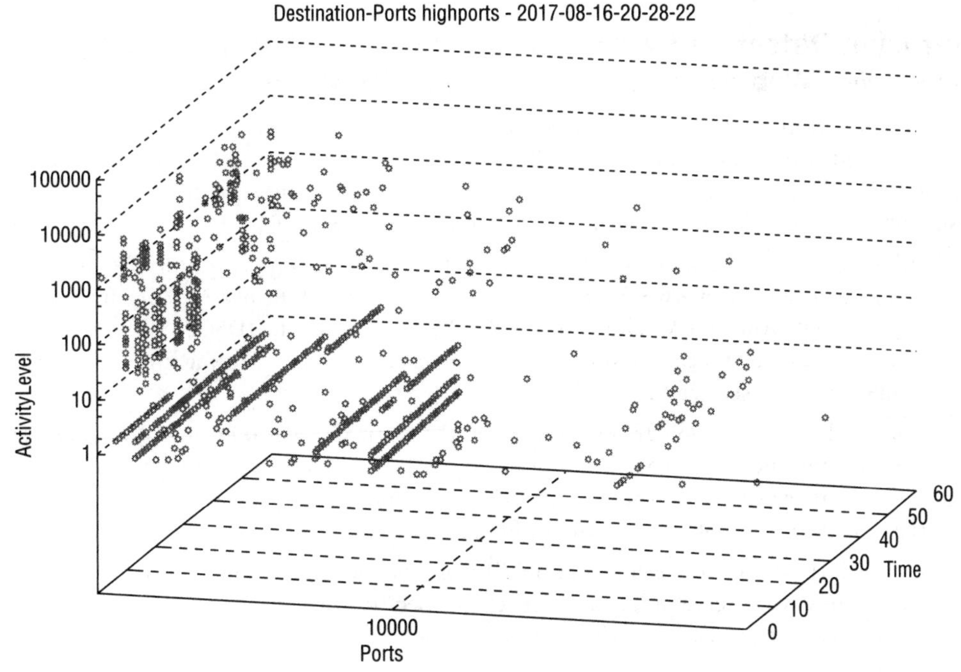

As these lines are invariant in the ActivityLevel axis and proceed up the Ports range as Time progresses, it is reasonable to assume that they represent simple port scans without any of the stealth or randomization options enabled.

Amazon CloudWatch Alerting and AWS Lambda

Amazon CloudWatch can also be used to generate statistical information and trigger alarms based on thresholding. A common example is raising an alarm if logs from an Amazon EC2 instance show there to be more than 10 unsuccessful Secure Shell (SSH) login attempts in a minute—such logs are a sound indication that an instance is under sustained probing. Amazon CloudWatch Events, another feature of Amazon CloudWatch, are the lowest-latency means of triggering AWS Lambda functions from another service.

AWS Marketplace and Other Third-Party Offerings

The AWS Marketplace contains a large number of security tools from third parties. A description of some of the capabilities they provide follows.

Security Information and Event Management (SIEM)

If you want to manage your *Security Information and Event Management (SIEM)* capability in-house, take particular note of which AWS log sources the SIEMs that you are considering can ingest and parse, based on the services you intend to use.

Intrusion Detection System (IDS)/Intrusion Prevention System (IPS)/AWS Web Application Firewall (AWS WAF)

Unless it is part of your organizational structure or policy to have a hard separation between the team maintaining your IDS/Intrusion Prevention System (IPS) and the team maintaining the Amazon EC2 instances providing the service, there are three advantages in using on-instance rather than in-network IDS/IPS within your VPC.

1. While some network-based IDS/IPS systems have Auto Scaling capability by virtue of being deployed out of AWS Marketplace as an AWS CloudFormation template rather than a simple Amazon Machine Image (AMI), if you run your IDS/IPS on your front-end servers, then you can be sure that your protection is Auto Scaling up and down inline with your service capability.
2. You can be sure that you are going to be on the cleartext side of any crypto boundary when on-instance. If you are performing your IDS/IPS "in transit" with a separate box, you may need to decrypt and potentially re-encrypt for forwarding in the event that you need encryption in transit inside your VPC.
3. More subtly, if you are performing IDS/IPS on-instance, then you can get a privileged view of how your server application reacts to specific requests in terms of logs, load, and more. If an attacker is trying to enact application/semantic-level breaks against

your environment, then an inline network AWS WAF would recognize questionable activity because your serving instances would return 404 errors in response to a lot of deliberately-malformed probing queries. It would not, however, be able to see whether the processing of these bad URLs would have other adverse effects, such as generating excessive server-side load. An on-instance WAF would have a better opportunity to identify those additional adverse effects.

The downside is that WAF is computationally expensive, so if you are running small front-end instances, you may need to move up a size.

Amazon Inspector

Penetration testing involves connecting to network listeners presented by service environments and determining and attempting to provoke the services binding the listeners to behave in a manner outside their design specification. However, it is possible using *Amazon Inspector* to have a much more comprehensive and privileged view of the behavior of an Amazon EC2 instance, both when it is being attacked in a penetration testing context and when not.

Amazon Inspector involves an agent, installed on an Amazon EC2 instance, that communicates outbound over HTTPS with an Internet-facing service endpoint in the AWS Regions where Amazon Inspector is available. The agent features a kernel module, which instruments the instance. Amazon Inspector provides a number of precompiled test suites to assess the configuration and behavior of the instance and application set running on it to identify issues based on the selected rules package.

In contrast to tools that are run sequentially as a point-in-time evaluation of configuration and status, the Amazon Inspector agent captures configuration data for periods of time up to 24 hours. This feature enables Amazon Inspector to identify and record transient issues, as well as persistent ones. Amazon Inspector is often used to instrument Amazon EC2 instances in a dev/test Continuous Integration (CI)/Continuous Delivery (CD) chain so that security issues can be found and characterized when release candidate code is exercised by its test harness. Amazon EC2 instances instrumented with Amazon Inspector must be able to communicate outbound over HTTPS with the Internet in order to reach the API endpoint. This communication can be directed via an Elastic IP address, a NAT Gateway, or a proxy such as Squid.

Other Compliance Tools

In addition to traditional SIEM capabilities, a number of companies are producing tools whose purpose goes beyond monitoring to near-real-time automated mitigation. It is possible to integrate your own detection and response system using Amazon CloudWatch Events and AWS Lambda, as detailed in the "Automating Security Event Response, from Idea to Code to Execution" presentation from AWS re:Invent 2016, available at: `https://www.youtube.com/watch?v=x4GkAGe65vE`. The AWS Trusted Advisor tool implements various triggerable environment checks, which can input into compliance capabilities.

Penetration Testing and Vulnerability Assessment

AWS recognizes the importance of *penetration testing*, both to meet your potential regulatory requirements and as general good security practice. AWS performs and commissions thousands of penetration tests a year in order to maintain standards compliance and test services both in production and development. As network traffic associated with penetration testing is indistinguishable from network traffic associated with an actual attack, it is necessary to apply to AWS for authorization to perform your own penetration testing to or from AWS environments, subject to a few exceptions.

Penetration Test Authorization Scope and Exceptions

You can conduct and manage penetration testing against the following, subject to authorization:

- Amazon EC2, except t1.micro, m1.small, and nano instance types
- Amazon RDS, except micro, small, and nano instance types
- AWS Lambda functions
- Amazon CloudFront distributions
- Amazon API Gateway gateways
- Amazon Lightsail

For tests restricted to OSI Layer 4 and above, you can test "through" an Elastic Load Balancing load balancer, subject to authorization.

You can also test environments outside AWS from AWS environments (that is, traffic outbound from AWS rather than inbound to AWS), subject to the same authorization process.

The exception where testing can be conducted without express authorization from AWS is when testing traffic originates from an Amazon EC2 instance running a pre-approved AMI from the AWS Marketplace.

AWS has worked with a number of AWS Marketplace vendors to vet and pre-authorize a select set of AWS Marketplace AMIs, such that testing traffic from Amazon EC2 instances built using these AMIs will not trigger abuse alarms. Use the search term "pre-authorized" in the AWS Marketplace to find these offerings.

You are prohibited from performing Denial of Service (DoS) attacks, or simulations of such, to or from any AWS asset. Other types of testing to investigate the security of a service or assets deployed in it, including fuzzing, are permitted.

Targets for testing must be resources you own (such as Amazon EC2 or on-premises instances). AWS-owned resources (such as Amazon S3 or the AWS Management Console) are prohibited from being tested by customers.

Applying for and Receiving Penetration Test Authorization

Penetration testing can be authorized for a time window of up to 90 days. AWS recognizes that for many customers, particularly those performing Continuous Deployment, penetration testing also needs to be a continuous process triggered by deployment events. Therefore, a penetration test authorization request can be made for a new time window while an existing time window is in effect. This enables multiple time windows to be "rolled together" into a contiguous and ongoing block. Penetration test authorization has a Service Level Agreement (SLA) of 48 working hours. AWS recommends applying for a new authorization at the start of the last full week of an existing time window, if the two windows are to be rolled together.

To apply for a penetration test authorization, use the web-based application form or send an email. Email allows applications to be submitted by users who do not have access to the root user in the AWS account, whereas the web-based form currently requires root access.

If you are an IAM user in an account, complete the following fields and send the information to `aws-security-cust-pen-test@amazon.com`.

Account Name:

Account Number:

Email Address:

Additional Email address to cc:

Third Party Contact information (if any):

IPs to be Scanned:

Target or Source:

Amazon EC2/Amazon RDS Instance IDs:

Source IPs:

Region:

Time Zone:

Expected Peak Bandwidth in Gigabits per Second (Gbps):

Start Date/Time:

End Date/Time:

If you will be testing Amazon API Gateway/AWS Lambda or Amazon CloudFront, provide the following additional information.

API or Amazon CloudFront Distribution ID:

Region:

Source IPs (if a private IP is provided, clarify whether it is an AWS IP, include account if different, or an on-premises IP):

Penetration Test Duration:

Do you have an NDA with AWS?

If a third party is performing the testing (source), does AWS have an NDA with this entity?

What is your expected peak traffic (e.g., 10 rps, 100,000 rps)?

What is your expected peak bandwidth (e.g., 0.1 Mbps, 1 Mbps)?

Test Details/Strategy:

What criteria/metrics will you monitor to ensure the success of the pen-test?

Do you have a way to immediately stop the traffic if we/you discover any issues?

Phone and Email of Two Emergency Contacts:

When authorization requests are couched in terms of Classless Inter-Domain Routing (CIDR) blocks rather than individual IP addresses, IPv4 ranges must be no larger than /24, and IPv6 ranges must be no larger than /120.

Response from the Penetration Test Authorization team should be expected by email within 48 business hours. Approval will include a request approval number. Non-approval will include one or more requests for clarification regarding the information submitted in the request. Testing should proceed only if you get an authorization number.

Summary

AWS has a threat model and mitigating controls on the AWS side of the shared responsibility model demarcation line; you also need to take the same approach for your side of the demarcation.

Many of the mitigating controls AWS uses are described in the audit reports we publish free of charge and under click-through NDA, via the AWS Artifact service.

The human brain is notoriously poor at objectively assessing risk, so formal models and frameworks are necessary.

Compliance frameworks have scopes. If a service isn't in scope for your compliance requirements, it doesn't mean that you can't use it, but you need to isolate it from the sensitive data signal path using mechanisms that satisfy your auditor. Building an environment from compliant services does not necessarily result in a compliant environment, but AWS provides materials to assist in designing and building for compliance.

The ability to implement separation of duty between your network management team and your server and serverless infrastructure management teams is designed into AWS services.

IAM has fine-grained action permissions and flexible principal, resource, and condition elements that you can use to give fine-grained scope to the actions you choose to allow and deny.

AWS Organizations' SCPs can be used to implement Mandatory Access Control on the child accounts in an organization.

Amazon CloudFront and Amazon Route 53 should be used together when implementing effective DDoS mitigation. The AWS Shield service enables further useful DDoS mitigation capabilities.

AWS API calls are encrypted by default. Cipher suites for AWS services are updated promptly when cryptographic algorithms are deprecated. AWS Certificate Manager can provision, manage, and automatically renew domain-validated certificate/key pairs for use with Amazon CloudFront and AWS load balancers. Encryption of data at rest should be considered a default position. CloudHSM is available if you have regulatory requirements that mandate the use of an HSM; otherwise, AWS KMS is the recommended option. Encryption in transit within your VPCs is often a matter of individual risk appetite, and many external standards do not mandate it.

Most AWS services can generate logs. The scaling of log generation and storage is in line with the scalability of the services themselves. Different log sources have different latencies between event occurrence and log record delivery. These logs are useful for purposes as diverse as maintaining ITIL compliance and performing simple network-based intrusion detection, as well as being consumable by code triggered in response to the event of a log record being written, where the code can act automatically to address issues reflected in the log record content.

The AWS Marketplace contains many security-focused products from vendors with whom you are likely to be familiar, so it is often straightforward to deploy the same third-party security technologies you use in your data centers in AWS.

When used to instrument EC2 instances, Amazon Inspector can reveal both persistent and transient software misbehaviors and misconfigurations that are contrary to AWS recommendations and/or which have records in the public CVE database.

Penetration testing is permitted against certain AWS services, subject to AWS approval and the meeting of specific conditions.

Exam Essentials

Understand the compliance documentation AWS makes available. Review the Risk and Compliance whitepaper, and other AWS whitepapers, available from `https://aws.amazon.com/security/security-resources/`, including those which focus on designing for specific compliance standards such as HIPAA. Examine the set of audit reports available via the AWS Artifact service at `https://aws.amazon.com/artifact/`, and the NIST 800-53 and PCI-DSS documents available via the Enterprise Accelerator initiative.

Understand the compliance standards and certifications that AWS meets and understand scoping. Understand the information at `https://aws.amazon.com/compliance` and identify which services are in scope for at least one external standard. Know the circumstances in which it is likely to be appropriate to use a service that is not in scope for a specific standard in the context of supporting an environment that needs to maintain compliance against that standard. Also, be aware of the need to satisfy an auditor that circumstances cannot arise where such a service will come into contact [with data] that the standard defines as sensitive.

Understand Threat Modeling. Threat modeling is fundamental to the understanding of risk. Control frameworks are based on compliance requirements plus mechanisms needed to mitigate the items on your own risk register in order to meet your own risk appetite. There are many standards and frameworks for doing threat modeling, some of which have free public documentation; read a selection of them.

Understand what logs can be generated by which AWS services, what AWS logging services aggregate them, what tools exist to analyze them and alert you, and know how to act on events of interest. AWS has a number of presentations, as well as papers and service documentation, on log gathering, aggregation, monitoring, analysis, and remediation. Start with the service documentation, and also be aware of what the latencies are between event and record for each logging service.

Understand how the AWS Shield service works in concert with other AWS services to mitigate and manage different kinds of DoS attacks. In addition to reading the service documentation, `https://www.youtube.com/watch?v=w9fSW6qMktA` demonstrates how the different aspects of the service work in concert to reduce the volume of attack traffic.

Understand the requirements and scoping for penetration testing on AWS. This encompasses what services can and can't be penetration tested, the duration of a test window, how to apply for initial testing authorization and authorization renewal, and how to know when authorization has been granted.

Resources to Review

The AWS Shared Security Responsibility Model in practice:

`https://youtu.be/RwUSPklR24M`

IAM recommended practices:

`https://youtu.be/R-PyVnhxx-U`

Encryption options on AWS:

`https://youtu.be/DXqDStJ4epE`

Compliance, logging, analysis, and alerting:

`https://www.brighttalk.com/webcast/9019/261915`

Getting started with AWS Security:

`https://www.brighttalk.com/webcast/9019/256391`

AWS Security checklist:

`https://www.brighttalk.com/webcast/9019/257297`

Automating security event response:

`https://www.brighttalk.com/webcast/9019/258547`

Compliance with AWS – Verifying AWS Security:

`https://www.brighttalk.com/webcast/9019/260695`

Securing Enterprise Big Data workloads:

`https://www.brighttalk.com/webcast/9019/261911`

Architecting security across multi-account architectures:

`https://www.brighttalk.com/webcast/9019/261915`

AWS Security best practices:

`https://www.brighttalk.com/webcast/9019/264011`

Software Security and best practices:

`https://www.brighttalk.com/webcast/9019/264917`

AWS Risk and Compliance whitepaper:

`https://d0.awsstatic.com/whitepapers/compliance/AWS_Risk_and_Compliance_Whitepaper.pdf`

Exercises

For assistance completing these exercises, refer to the User Guides and related documentation for each of the relevant AWS services below. These are located at:

Exercise 15.1:

`https://aws.amazon.com/documentation/inspector/`

Exercise 15.2:

`https://aws.amazon.com/documentation/artifact/`

Exercise 15.3:

`https://aws.amazon.com/premiumsupport/trustedadvisor/`

Exercise 15.4:

`https://aws.amazon.com/documentation/cloudtrail/`

Exercise 15.5:

`https://aws.amazon.com/documentation/config/`

EXERCISE 15.1

Use Amazon Inspector

In this exercise, you will use Amazon Inspector to identify static and dynamic security issues in an Amazon EC2 instance.

1. Provision an Amazon Linux EC2 Linux instance in a region where Amazon Inspector is available. Do not patch the instance.
2. Make sure that the instance can access the Internet, either via an Elastic network interface on a public subnet or via a NAT Gateway.
3. Install the Amazon Inspector agent.
4. Create an assessment target.
5. Create an assessment template using the Common Vulnerabilities and Exposures rules package.
6. Choose Create. Run the assessment for a 15-minute duration.
7. When the assessment has finished, examine its findings.
8. Generate and view an Assessment Report.

You now have an Assessment Report for your instance against the current CVE database. You can look into each of the findings to see information on the nature of each issue and details of how to mitigate it. You can run further assessments and graph their findings over time to see how effective your security monitoring and management program is. Running Assessment Reports with all rules packages enabled while your instance and the applications it is running are being penetration tested can often give further insight into the behavior of your applications than the tester's report alone.

EXERCISE 15.2

Use AWS Artifact

In this exercise, you will use AWS Artifact to review the current AWS SOC 1 report.

1. Log in to the AWS Management Console.
2. Select AWS Artifact.
3. Under Reports, navigate to the current SOC 1 report. Select Get This Artifact.
4. Review the terms and conditions.
5. Download and open the report using Adobe Acrobat.

You now have copy of an audit report describing in detail the physical and logical controls AWS uses to secure the services in-scope, and the means to obtain copy of the audit reports and other materials published via the AWS Artifact service. This includes not only the current and previous versions of SOC reports, but also ISO certificates, the PCI-DSS audit report, workbooks on meeting compliance requirements of various regional standards such as iRAP, MTCS, and so forth. Artifact also contains a continuity letter for assurance that, subsequent to the publication of the current SOC report and at the current date, a new SOC report is in preparation.

EXERCISE 15.3

Use AWS Trusted Advisor

In this exercise, you will use AWS Trusted Advisor to identify network configuration weaknesses.

1. Log in to the AWS Management Console.
2. Identify the security group associated with your running instance from Exercise 15.2.
3. Add an inbound security group rule allowing TCP port 3389 from 0.0.0.0/0.
4. Select AWS Trusted Advisor from the AWS Management Console. Select Security.
5. Review the findings, which should now include a security group finding for an unrestricted port. You may need to refresh the security checks.
6. Remove the inbound security group rule from Step 3.

You have just used one of the features of Trusted Advisor to identify and report on a security weakness in your environment's configuration. You can invoke this test and others that Trusted Advisor offers (the tests available vary by your AWS support contract level) whenever you make changes to your AWS infrastructure's configuration, or periodically and programmatically using mechanisms such as CloudWatch Events and Lambda, as a simple means of checking that your configuration has not changed to include specific weaknesses.

EXERCISE 15.4

Enable AWS CloudTrail Encryption and Log File Validation

In this exercise, you will enable AWS CloudTrail, log file encryption, and log file validation.

1. Log in to the AWS Management Console.
2. Select AWS CloudTrail from the service list.

EXERCISE 15.4 *(continued)*

3. Create a trail that captures all management events and all Amazon S3 data events from all regions.
4. Specify an Amazon S3 bucket for log storage.
5. Enable log file encryption validation.
6. When the next AWS CloudTrail log file is delivered to Amazon S3, confirm that the file encryption is AWS KMS by viewing the Overview tab for the object in the Amazon S3 console.
7. Use the AWS CLI to validate the log files using the `aws cloudtrail validate-logs` command.

You have just set up the AWS-native mechanism for capturing logs of all API calls to an AWS account and configured options to encrypt them at rest (providing confidentiality and, as only you have access to the encryption key unless you extend the AWS KMS key grant or give others permission to do so in IAM, nonrepudiation beyond what the API itself provides). You can use this as a log data source for a SIEM system, or trigger Lambda functions when logs are written to scan and analyze your new logs using your own code—either can then trigger actions to alert on or address issues arising. To enable your SIEM or Lambda function to read the log records, it not only needs read access to the Amazon S3 bucket, but a decrypt grant on the KMS key.

EXERCISE 15.5

Enable AWS Config

In this exercise, you will enable AWS Config.

1. Log in to the AWS Management Console.
2. Turn on recording on all resources, including global resources.
3. Log data to an Amazon S3 bucket.
4. Launch an Amazon EC2 instance.
5. After you have logged in to the instance, terminate it.
6. Wait 15 minutes.
7. Proceed to the Resources section of the AWS Config console.
8. Look up Amazon EC2: Instance resources, including deleted resources.
9. Click on the AWS Config timeline to review the instance history.

You have just enabled the AWS Config service, which gives you a configuration management database for your in-scope AWS assets, and you used a timeline view to examine some of the first records the service has made. Your AWS Config database will go on to record changes in services as they are made in response to the API calls you make; these will be reflected in the timelines for the assets involved, and you can also get a snapshot view which gives you details of the disposition of all in-scope AWS assets in your account at any time since you set the service up. If you need to, you can also use the EC2 System Manager agent and use the Inventory tool within that service to integrate EC2 instance package management information into your instances' timelines.

Review Questions

1. Amazon Virtual Private Cloud (Amazon VPC) Flow Logs reports accept and reject data based on which VPC features? (Choose two.)
   - **A.** Security groups
   - **B.** Elastic network interfaces
   - **C.** Network Access Control Lists (ACLs)
   - **D.** Virtual routers
   - **E.** Amazon Simple Storage Service (Amazon S3)

2. What is the minimum runtime for Amazon Inspector when initiated from the AWS Console?
   - **A.** 1 minute
   - **B.** 5 minutes
   - **C.** 10 minutes
   - **D.** 15 minutes

3. Compliance documents are available from which of the following?
   - **A.** AWS Artifact on the AWS Management Console
   - **B.** Compliance portal on the AWS website
   - **C.** Services in Scope page on the AWS website
   - **D.** AWS Trusted Advisor on the AWS Management Console

4. AWS Identity and Access Management (IAM) uses which access model?
   - **A.** Principal, Action, Resource, Condition (PARC)
   - **B.** Effect, Action, Resource, Condition (EARC)
   - **C.** Principal, Effect, Resource, Condition (PERC)
   - **D.** Resource, Effect, Action, Condition, Time (REACT)

5. Which hash algorithm is used for AWS CloudTrail record digests?
   - **A.** SHA-256
   - **B.** MD5
   - **C.** RIPEMD-160
   - **D.** SHA-3

6. Penetration requests may be submitted to AWS by which means?
   - **A.** Postal mail
   - **B.** Email
   - **C.** Social media
   - **D.** AWS Support

7. What is the maximum duration of an AWS penetration testing authorization?
   A. 24 hours
   B. 48 hours
   C. 30 days
   D. 90 days

8. Who is responsible for network traffic protection in Amazon Virtual Private Cloud (Amazon VPC)?
   A. AWS
   B. The customer
   C. It is a shared responsibility.
   D. The network provider

9. What authorization feature can restrict the actions of an account's root user?
   A. AWS Identity and Access Management (IAM) policy
   B. Bucket policy
   C. Service Control Policy (SCP)
   D. Lifecycle policy

10. Which AWS Cloud service provides information regarding common vulnerabilities and exposures?
   A. AWS CloudTrail
   B. AWS Config
   C. AWS Artifact
   D. Amazon Inspector

Scenarios and Reference Architectures

THE AWS CERTIFIED ADVANCED NETWORKING – SPECIALTY EXAM OBJECTIVES COVERED IN THIS CHAPTER MAY INCLUDE, BUT ARE NOT LIMITED TO, THE FOLLOWING:

Domain 1.0: Design and Implement Hybrid IT Network Architectures at Scale

✓ **1.2 Given a scenario, derive an appropriate hybrid IT architecture connectivity solution**

Domain 2.0: Design and Implement AWS Networks

✓ **2.2 Given customer requirements, define network architectures on AWS**

✓ **2.3 Propose optimized designs based on the evaluation of an existing implementation**

Introduction to Scenarios and Reference Architectures

As you have seen throughout this guide, AWS provides many network services and features to help you build highly available, robust, scalable, and secure networks in the cloud. This chapter covers scenarios and reference architectures for combining many of these network components to meet common customer requirements. These scenarios include implementing network patterns that create hybrid networks and span multiple regions and locations. The exercises at the end of this chapter will help you design appropriate network architectures on AWS. Understanding how to architect networks to meet customer requirements is required to pass the exam, and we highly recommend that you complete the exercises in this chapter.

Hybrid Networking Scenario

Imagine that you work for a company that is looking to expand a flagship application from a company data center onto AWS. The application has been successfully serving your customers in Europe, and you have been asked to extend application functionality quickly into the eu-central-1 region. Your application's current design is depicted in Figure 16.1.

As you can see, the application implements a traditional "N-tier" architecture with web, application, and database tiers. All user data is stored in a relational database. Your initial task is to scale the web and application tiers to support increased demand for web and application server resources. As a result, you propose the network architecture depicted in Figure 16.2.

FIGURE 16.1 Current application network design

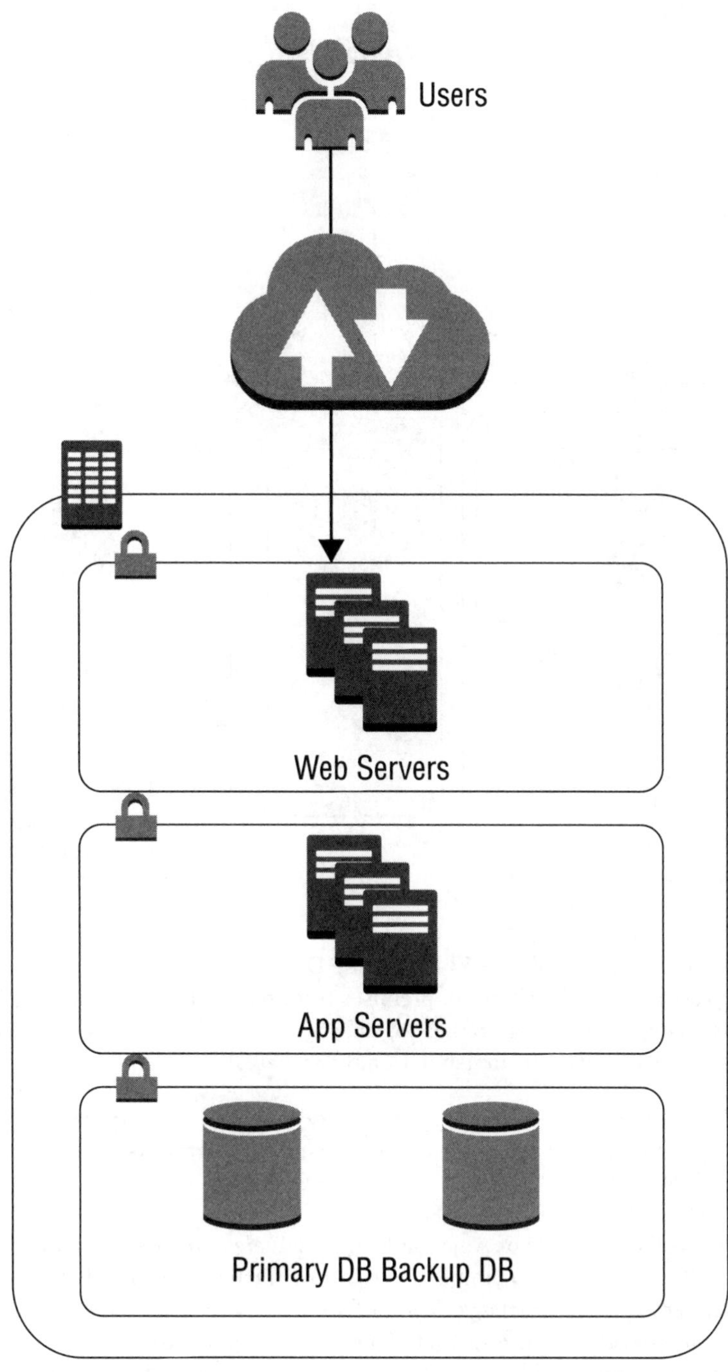

FIGURE 16.2 Web and application server network design

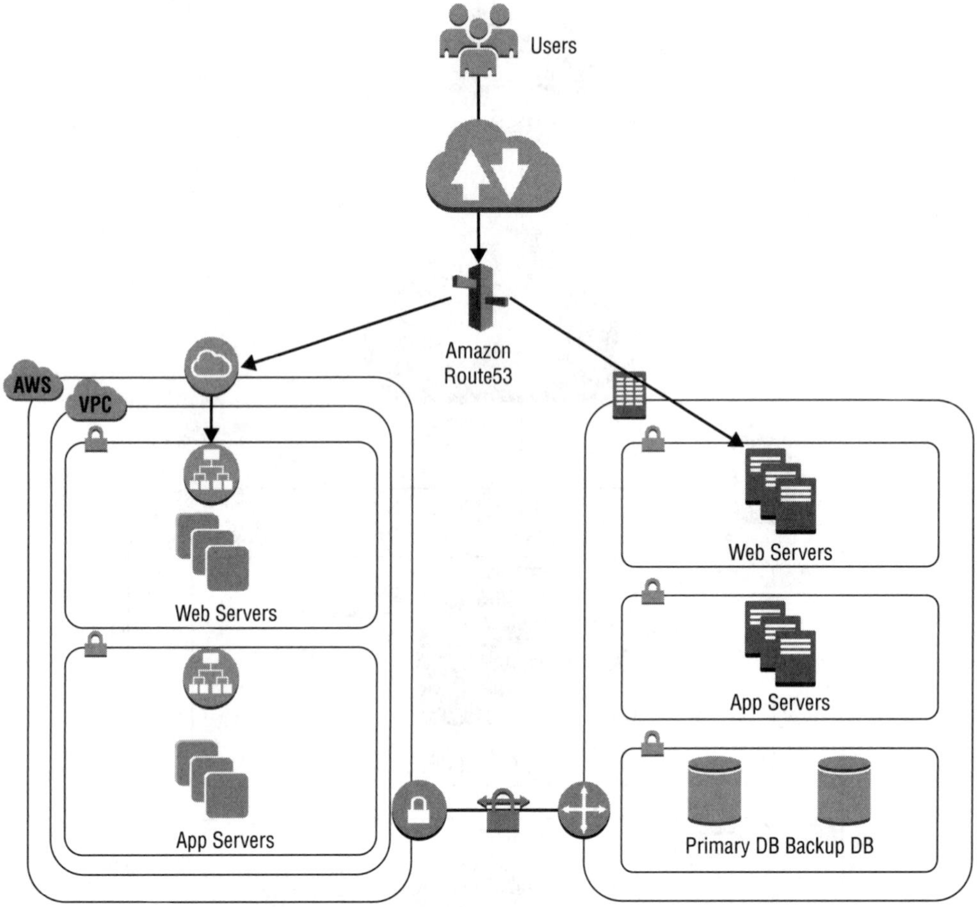

This design adds Amazon Route 53 to provide Domain Name System (DNS)-based routing between AWS and your existing on-premises resources. It hosts web and application tiers, with associated Elastic Load Balancing. Lastly, it provides back-end connectivity for the application to access data from its relational database.

Understand the implications of using different Amazon Route 53 routing policies.

For this network design, use of Amazon Route 53 *Weighted Round Robin (WRR) routing* and health checks are recommended to allow traffic to be dialed up and down based on what percentage of traffic you would like to send to AWS versus your on-premises resources. The use of other Amazon Route 53 routing options (for example, latency-based routing) are not recommended because they do not provide as much control over how much traffic will be sent to AWS versus your on-premises resources. This lack of control could lead to several undesirable scenarios, such as the following:

- Excess traffic still getting directed to and overloading on-premises resources.
- Too much traffic getting directed to AWS and overloading your AWS resources. Ideally, your application teams will have properly implemented AWS scaling features like Auto Scaling to take advantage of elasticity in the cloud. Hybrid networking scenarios such as this, however, often require higher degrees of network traffic control to ensure that network and application teams are aligned on scaling expectations.
- Too much traffic getting directed to AWS and overloading your provisioned back-end network connectivity between AWS and the on-premises network.

The design shown in Figure 16.2 retains application data on-premises, and therefore it requires careful back-end connectivity consideration. Many customers start with a Virtual Private Network (VPN) connection because VPN connections can often be set up more quickly than can AWS Direct Connect connections. VPN connections can be useful for experimenting with cloud bursting, as a bridge for establishing AWS Direct Connect connections, or when back-end connectivity bandwidth is relatively low and can tolerate Internet-influenced variable latency and jitter. AWS Direct Connect connections should be leveraged for high bandwidth needs, such as when multiple 10 Gbps connections are required or for being able to provide consistent network latency with minimal network jitter to your applications.

Understand the implications of implementing different types of back-end connectivity and look for the most appropriate connectivity option to meet your network requirements.

This design could also be augmented in a number of different ways, depending on application requirements, including:

- For simplicity, the diagram in Figure 16.2 does not depict the use of multiple Availability Zones and their associated subnets. It is an AWS best practice to leverage multiple Availability Zones for each application tier.
- The database tier could be moved to AWS. This is especially useful if you would like to move to a managed database service such as Amazon Relational Database Service (Amazon RDS) or when an application is running into on-premises scaling challenges that could be addressed by migrating to a more scalable database such as Amazon Aurora.
- A read replica of the database tier could be replicated between AWS and the on-premises network. Replicating the database could potentially reduce back-end network traffic or latency for application database read operations. Similarly, a database caching layer such as Amazon ElastiCache could be leveraged to improve application read performance.
- Amazon CloudFront could be included to reduce latency for serving content to your users and offload requests to your application resources either in AWS or on-premises.
- AWS WAF could be included to provide an additional layer of security to your application both in AWS and on-premises.

Multi-Location Resiliency

For this next scenario, consider a company that is looking to implement multi-location resiliency for a flagship application. The application must be able to scale up and down gracefully based on user demand, and it must be capable of surviving the failure of multiple data centers, including the loss of an entire region. In the event of a multi-region disaster, the company still wants to be able to serve a static version of the website to users. To accomplish this goal, we will break down the requirements by regional, multi-regional, and disaster recovery components.

Figure 16.3 depicts a highly available regional design. Users are directed by Amazon Route 53 to an Application Load Balancer configured with web application firewall rules, cross-zone load balancing, connection draining, and instance health checks. This load balancer is responsible for applying security rules to user traffic while also distributing valid request load evenly across all healthy instances in multiple Availability Zones. It also integrates with a Multi-AZ Auto Scaling group to ensure that in-flight requests are handled gracefully before an Amazon Elastic Compute Cloud (Amazon EC2) instance is removed from the load balancer. This combination protects the application from Availability Zone outages, ensures that a minimal number of Amazon EC2 instances are running, and can respond to load changes by scaling each group's Amazon EC2 instances up or down as needed.

Understand how features from multiple services can be used together to monitor the health of your applications.

Lastly, the Amazon EC2 instances are configured to connect to a Multi-AZ Amazon RDS database. Amazon RDS creates a master database and synchronously replicates all data to a slave database instance in another Availability Zone. Amazon RDS monitors the health of the master instance and will automatically fail over to the slave instance in the event of a failure.

Figure 16.4 expands this application's network architecture to another region. In this example, the first region's network infrastructure is replicated into a second region, including the application's Virtual Private Cloud (VPC), subnets, Application Load Balancer and web application firewall rules, Amazon EC2 instances, and Auto Scaling configuration. Additionally, the Amazon Route 53-managed alias record for this domain is updated to include both load balancers with a health check and failover routing policy to reroute traffic from the primary region to a secondary region in the event of a regional failure. Additionally, the Amazon RDS configuration is updated to create an asynchronous read replica of the application's database in the new region. In the event of a regional failure, the Amazon RDS read replica could be promoted to become the master database instance.

FIGURE 16.3 Regional availability

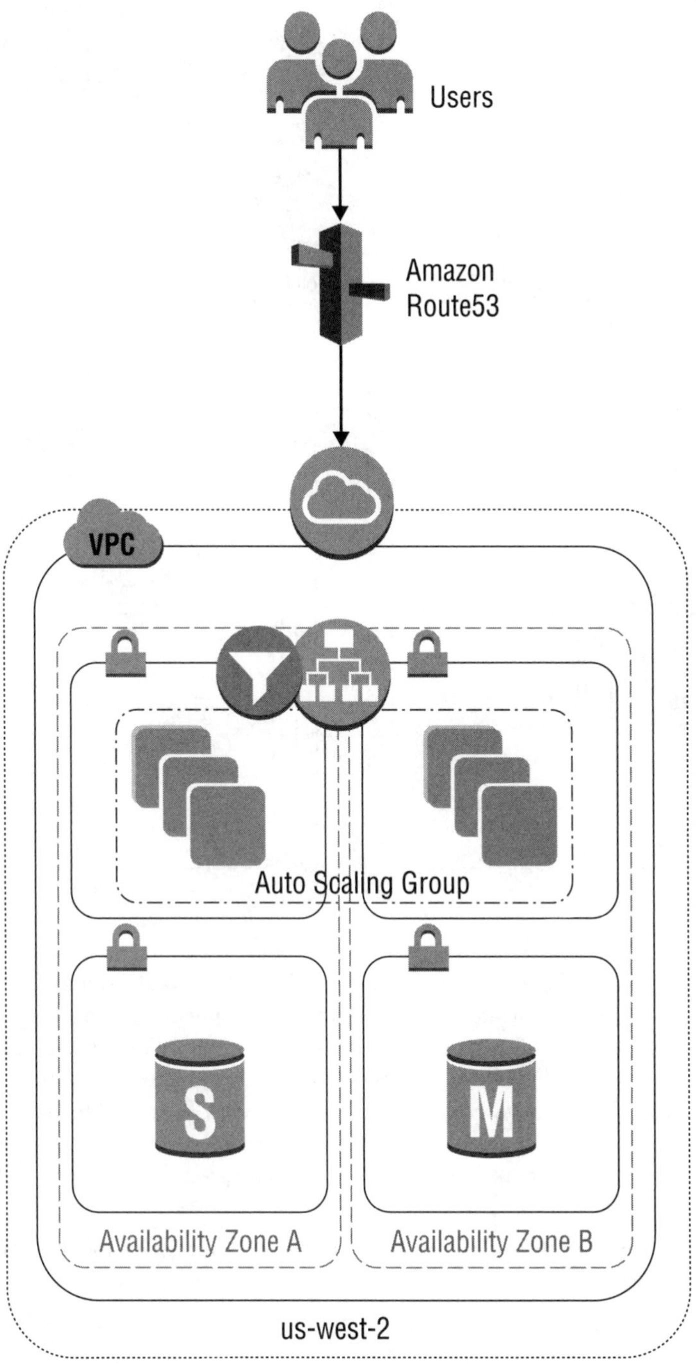

FIGURE 16.4 Multi-regional resiliency

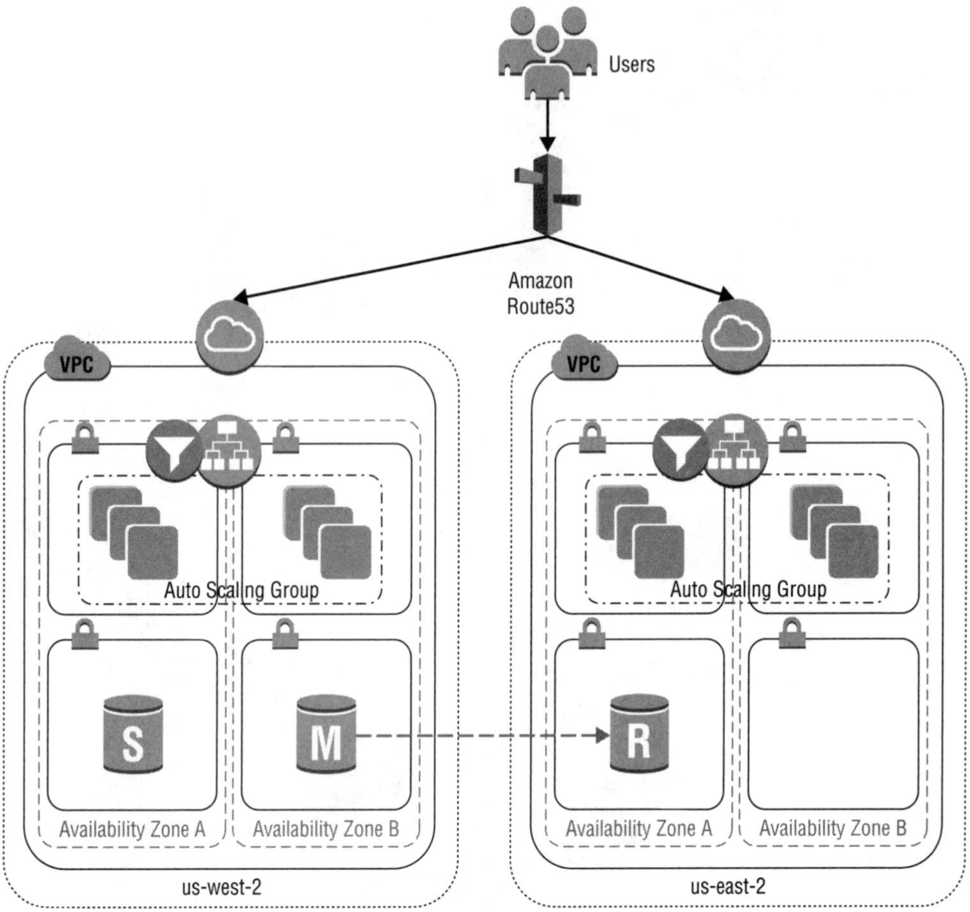

A variation of this design could include adding Amazon CloudFront and AWS WAF to manage centrally web application firewall rules for the application. Another variation could include creating an Amazon Route 53 latency-based routing policy instead of a failover policy. This approach would create an active-active environment that routes requests to the closest healthy load balancer based on minimizing network latency. This scenario requires tight coordination with the application team to ensure that additional database network connectivity requirements are met. Approaches for managing database connectivity include the following:

- Configuring the application in the second region to leverage its local database replica for read operations.

- Implementing cross-region network connectivity between your VPCs to allow Amazon EC2 instances in the second region to connect to the master database to perform writes. Refer to the following chapters for additional information.
  - VPC Peering in Chapter 2, "Amazon Virtual Private Cloud (Amazon VPC) and Networking Fundamentals"
  - VPN connections with Amazon EC2 instances in Chapter 4, "Virtual Private Networks (VPN)"
  - Transit VPC in Chapter 12, "Hybrid Architectures"
- Implementing a write Application Programming Interface (API) that leverages an Amazon Route 53 failover routing policy to direct user writes to the region hosting the master database instance.

Figure 16.5 expands this architecture to include a final multi-region disaster recovery failover environment. In this example, two additional Amazon Route 53 aliases are created for the application. Users are directed to the application's user-friendly domain name (such as `www.domain.com`), which is configured by Amazon Route 53 with a failover alias record pointing to the application's production domain name (for example, `prod.domain.com`) as primary and the application's static application domain name (such as `static-app.domain.com`) for failover.

FIGURE 16.5 Multi-region disaster planning

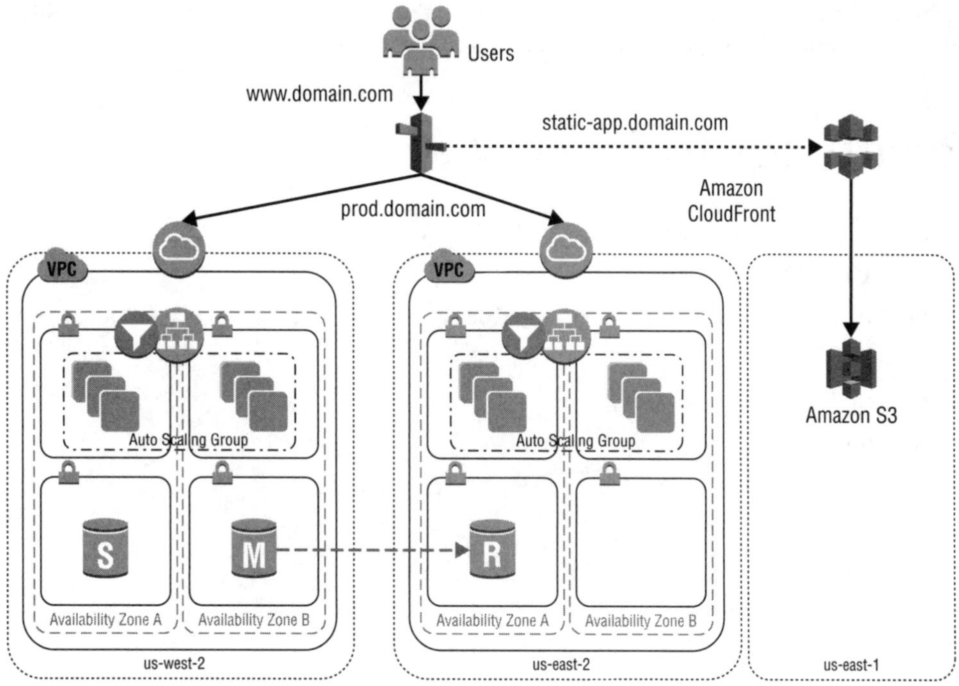

The production domain name maintains the previous configuration, which includes records pointing to each regional Application Load Balancer and health checks. The static domain name is configured with a CName record pointing to an Amazon CloudFront distribution with an Amazon Simple Storage Service (Amazon S3) bucket origin hosting a static version of the application. In this scenario, the application's user-friendly domain name will direct traffic to the application's production load balancers as long as at least one of them is healthy. In the event that all resources across multiple Availability Zones and regions are unhealthy, Amazon Route 53 will direct users to an Amazon CloudFront distribution and Amazon S3 bucket in yet another region.

Additionally, Amazon CloudFront could be used to serve both static and dynamic content to your customers. Using Amazon CloudFront allows your content to be delivered to users from edge locations distributed across the world, can reduce the load on your back-end resources, and provides many additional benefits. More details are available in Chapter 7, "Amazon CloudFront."

Summary

In this chapter, you learned about some additional scenarios where multiple AWS network services and features can be combined to build highly available, robust, scalable, and secure networks in the cloud to meet common customer requirements. These scenarios included creating hybrid networks to support application scaling to AWS and implementing highly robust applications that span multiple regions and locations.

Resources to Review

For further learning, review the following URLs:

AWS Global Infrastructure:

`https://aws.amazon.com/about-aws/global-infrastructure/`

Amazon EC2:

`https://aws.amazon.com/ec2/`

Amazon VPC:

`https://aws.amazon.com/vpc/`

AWS Direct Connect:

`https://aws.amazon.com/directconnect/`

Elastic Load Balancing:

`https://aws.amazon.com/elasticloadbalancing/`

Amazon Route 53:

`https://aws.amazon.com/route53/`

Amazon CloudFront:

`https://aws.amazon.com/cloudfront/`

AWS WAF:

`https://aws.amazon.com/waf/`

AWS Shield:

`https://aws.amazon.com/shield/`

AWS Organizations:

`https://aws.amazon.com/organizations/`

AWS Config:

`https://aws.amazon.com/config/`

AWS CloudTrail:

`https://aws.amazon.com/cloudtrail/`

AWS CloudFormation:

`https://aws.amazon.com/cloudformation/`

AWS Service Catalog:

`https://aws.amazon.com/servicecatalog/`

AWS Guard Duty:

`https://aws.amazon.com/guardduty/`

Amazon Macie:

`https://aws.amazon.com/macie/`

Amazon Inspector:

`https://aws.amazon.com/inspector/`

Exam Essentials

Understand the different types of Amazon Route 53 routing and know when you would use each one. Amazon Route 53 provides a number of different routing policies. These routing policies affect how network traffic is sent to your applications. Make sure that you understand the implications of each option so that you are able to map the most appropriate routing feature to different application requirements. Review Chapter 6, “Domain Name System and Load Balancing” for more information about Amazon Route 53 features.

Understand the different types of on-premises network connectivity requirements and know when you would use each one. AWS provides both VPN and AWS Direct Connect for connecting on-premises networks with AWS. Make sure that you are familiar with the implications of each option and can apply the appropriate solution to meet application connectivity requirements. Review Chapter 4, and Chapter 5, "AWS Direct Connect," for details about each of these options.

Understand the health check capabilities for services such as Amazon Route 53 and Elastic Load Balancing. AWS provides many features for monitoring the health of your application. Make sure that you are familiar with not only these features, but also how they can be used together to provide end-to-end application health monitoring and dynamic routing around failed application components. Review Chapter 6 for more information about Amazon Route 53 features.

Test Taking Tip

Carefully note requirements called out in test questions. These requirements are often the key to determining the correct answer from otherwise very similar answers.

Exercises

You should have performed the exercises in previous chapters for all of the services covered in this chapter. Take the time to go back and review previous chapters and their associated exercises to make sure that you are familiar with the implications of using each individual service or feature. The following exercises are designed to help you think about additional scenarios and determine how you would architect network connectivity solutions.

EXERCISE 16.1

Enterprise Shared Services

Consider the common network scenario of creating a shared services network for your applications on AWS.

1. Think about the types of services that reside in a typical shared services network. Shared services could include Lightweight Directory Access Protocol (LDAP) or Active Directory, DNS, network time, source code repositories, or code build systems.
2. Think through the different requirements of these services and different ways that these services could be exposed from a shared services VPC to other accounts.
3. Review Chapter 2 and think about which services could be shared using VPC peering connections.

4. Review Chapter 3, "Advanced Amazon Virtual Private Cloud" and think about which services could be shared using Private Link.
5. Review Chapters 4 and 5 and think about the implications of accessing shared services over VPN or AWS Direct Connect connections.

After completing this exercise, you will have reviewed pertinent chapters in the context of leveraging multiple AWS networking services to support enterprise shared service use cases.

EXERCISE 16.2

Network Security

Consider the common network scenario of controlling network traffic in and out of a network.

1. Think about the types of controls that are often implemented to monitor and control network traffic. These could include controls such as network and web application firewalls and access control lists, network monitoring, and intrusion detection and prevention.
2. Review Chapters 2 and 3 and think about how each Amazon VPC feature could be used to control or monitor network traffic. Specifically, review the following:
   - Security Groups
   - Network Access Control Lists (ACLs)
   - Route Tables
   - Different types of gateways
   - Network Address Translation (NAT) instances
   - Amazon VCP Flow Logs
   - Different types of VPC endpoints
   - AWS PrivateLink
3. Review Chapter 8, "Network Security," and think about the various services and features that help implement security governance, protect data in motion and at rest, protect your AWS accounts, and assist with network detection and response. Specifically, review the following services.

Governance Services

- AWS Organizations
- AWS Config
- AWS CloudTrail

EXERCISE 16.2 *(continued)*

- AWS CloudFormation
- AWS Service Catalog

Services for Controlling Data Flows

- AWS Shield
- Amazon Route 53
- Amazon CloudFront
- AWS WAF
- Security Groups
- Network ACLs

AWS Account Services

- Amazon GuardDuty
- Amazon Macie
- Amazon Inspector

Network Detection and Response Services

- Amazon VPC Flow Logs
- Amazon CloudWatch

After completing this exercise, you will have reviewed pertinent chapters in the context of leveraging multiple AWS networking services to support enterprise shared service use cases.

Review Questions

1. Which Amazon Route 53 routing policy would be the most appropriate for gradually migrating an application to AWS?
   - **A.** Weighted
   - **B.** Latency-based
   - **C.** Failover
   - **D.** Geolocation
2. When connecting an on-premises network to AWS, which option reuses existing network equipment and Internet connections?
   - **A.** VPN connection
   - **B.** AWS Direct Connect
   - **C.** VPC Private Endpoints
   - **D.** Network Load Balancer
3. Which Amazon Route 53 routing policy would be the most appropriate for directing users to application resources that offer payment in their local currency?
   - **A.** Weighted
   - **B.** Latency-based
   - **C.** Failover
   - **D.** Geolocation
4. Your current web application's network security architecture includes an Application Load Balancer, locked down Security Groups, and restrictive VPC route tables. You have been asked to implement additional controls for temporarily blocking hundreds of noncontiguous, malicious IP addresses. Which AWS service or features should you add to this architecture?
   - **A.** AWS WAF
   - **B.** Network ACLs
   - **C.** AWS Shield
   - **D.** Amazon VPC Private Link
5. A previous network administrator implemented a transit VPC architecture using Amazon EC2 instances with 10 GB networking to facilitate communication between multiple AWS VPCs in various regions and on-premises resources. Over time, the transit VPC Amazon EC2 instance network bandwidth has become saturated with on-premises traffic, causing application requests to fail. What design recommendations can you make to reduce application failures?
   - **A.** Implement AWS Direct Connect and migrate to a AWS Direct Connect gateway.
   - **B.** Enable SR-IOV on your transit VPC instance ENIs.
   - **C.** Offload network traffic to Private Link to facilitate connectivity with on-premises resources.
   - **D.** Upgrade from 10 GB Amazon EC2 instances to 25 GB instances with ENA.

6. A previous network administrator implemented a transit VPC architecture to facilitate communication between multiple AWS networks and on-premises resources. Over time, the transit VPC Amazon EC2 instance network bandwidth has become saturated with cross-region traffic. What highly available design change should you recommend for this network?
   A. Migrate cross-region traffic to a point-to-point VPN connection between an Amazon EC2 instance in each VPC.
   B. Disable route propagation on your VPC route tables to disable cross-region traffic.
   C. Leverage VPC Peering connections between VPCs across regions.
   D. Implement network ACLs to rate limit cross-region traffic.

7. You support an application that is hosted in ap-northeast-1 and eu-central-1. Users from around the word sometimes complain about long page-load times. Which Amazon Route 53 routing policy would provide the best user experience?
   A. Weighted
   B. Latency-based
   C. Failover
   D. Geolocation

8. When connecting an on-premises network to AWS APIs, which option provides the least amount of network jitter and latency?
   A. VPN connection
   B. AWS Direct Connect private VIF
   C. AWS Direct Connect public VIF
   D. VPC Endpoints

9. Which combination of Amazon Route 53 policies provide location-specific services with redundant, backup connections? (Choose two.)
   A. Weighted
   B. Latency-based
   C. Failover
   D. Geolocation
   E. Simple

10. What is a scalable way to provide Amazon EC2 instances in a private subnet with IPv4 egress access to the Internet with no need for network administration?
   A. Create a transit VPC with network address translation for all your VPCs.
   B. Create an egress-only Internet Gateway.
   C. Create multiple Amazon EC2 NAT instances in each Availability Zone.
   D. Create NAT Gateways.

11. Your users have started to complain about poor application performance. You determine that your on-premises VPN connection is saturated with authentication and authorization traffic to the on-premises Microsoft Active Directory (AD) environment. Which option will reduce on-premises network traffic?

    A. Replicate Microsoft AD to Amazon EC2 instances in a shared service network and migrate to VPC Peering connections.

    B. Migrate from a VPN connection to multiple AWS Direct Connect connections.

    C. Create a trust relationship between AWS Directory Service and your on-premises Microsoft AD and migrate to VPC Peering connections.

    D. Offload network traffic to Private Link to facilitate connectivity with Microsoft AD on-premises.

Answers to Review Questions

Chapter 1: Introduction to Advanced Networking

1. B. AWS Direct Connect provides private connectivity between customer environments and AWS.
2. C. Amazon CloudFront is a Content Distribution Network (CDN) that operates from AWS edge locations.
3. D. AWS Regions contain two or more Availability Zones. Availability Zones contain one or more data centers. Edge locations are located throughout the Internet.
4. D. AWS Regions contain two or more Availability Zones. Availability Zones contain one or more data centers. A region contains a cluster of two or more data centers.
5. A. AWS Regions contain two or more Availability Zones. Availability Zones contain one or more data centers. If you distribute your instances across multiple Availability Zones and one instance fails, you can design your application so that an instance in another zone can handle requests.
6. C. Amazon Virtual Private Cloud (Amazon VPC) allows customers to create a logically-isolated network within an AWS Region.
7. A. AWS Shield provides DDoS mitigation. AWS Shield Standard is available to all customers at no additional charge.
8. A. The AWS global infrastructure is operated by a single company, Amazon.
9. B. Amazon VPC is an isolated, logical portion of an AWS Region that you define.
10. B. The mapping service maintains topology information about every resource in a VPC.
11. D. When you create an Amazon VPC, you choose the IPv4 address range to use. You may optionally enable IPv6 on your Amazon VPC.
12. B. Amazon Route 53 is a managed Domain Name System (DNS) service. You may register domains using Amazon Route 53.
13. A. AWS Direct Connect lets you create a dedicated network connection between your location and AWS. AWS Direct Connect provides a more consistent network experience than the Internet.
14. C. AWS WAF allows you to create web Access Control Lists (ACLs) to protect your Amazon CloudFront and Elastic Load Balancing (for example, Application Load Balancer) environments.
15. B. Elastic Load Balancing provides application traffic distribution among healthy Amazon EC2 instances in your Amazon Virtual Private Cloud (Amazon VPC).

Chapter 2: Amazon Virtual Private Cloud (Amazon VPC) and Networking Fundamentals

1. C. You need two public subnets (one for each Availability Zone) and two private subnets (one for each Availability Zone). Therefore, you need four subnets.

2. B. The NAT gateway uses an IPv4 Elastic IP address when it performs many-to-one address translation. In order for the traffic to route to the Internet, the NAT gateway must be placed in a public subnet with a route to an Internet gateway.

3. D. Placement groups are designed to provide the highest performance network between Amazon Elastic Compute Cloud (Amazon EC2) instances.

4. A. When you create an Amazon VPC, a route table is created by default. You must manually create subnets and an Internet gateway.

5. A. You may only have one Internet gateway for each Amazon VPC.

6. B. Security groups are stateful, whereas network ACLs are stateless.

7. D. A customer gateway is the customer side of a VPN connection, and an Internet gateway connects a network to the Internet. A Virtual Private Gateway (VGW) is the Amazon side of a VPN connection.

8. D. Attaching an elastic network interface associated with a different subnet to an instance can make the instance dual-homed.

9. C. Each Amazon VPN connection provides two IPsec tunnel endpoints.

Chapter 3: Advanced Amazon Virtual Private Cloud (Amazon VPC)

1. D. VPC endpoints are private access to otherwise public services. This access method does not decrease performance or increase availability. In addition, the services are still available through public APIs unless service-specific configurations, such as Amazon Simple Storage Service (Amazon S3) bucket policies, have been configured to limit access to VPC endpoints.

2. D. This is expected behavior when you limit access to a VPC endpoint. It is possible that a proxy also blocks access. The objects are still there. The VPC endpoint policy does not have a condition that applies specifically to the console, and endpoint policies do not restrict which resources can access buckets. In order to enable access to Amazon S3 buckets through the AWS Management Console, you must allow public access.

3. C, D. AWS PrivateLink applies source Network Address Translation (NAT), so the source IP will not be natively available. VPC peering allows bidirectional communication, but it does not allow better performance or scalability. AWS PrivateLink is unidirectional only. AWS PrivateLink does support more spoke VPCs than VPC peering. AWS PrivateLink will not increase the performance; that only comes from adding more resources.

4. A, B. AWS PrivateLink only supports TCP traffic. It is possible to use the IPv4 address of an AWS PrivateLink endpoint as opposed to the DNS name. There is no inherit authentication for VPC endpoints, other than what is defined at an application level. You cannot create a VPN through an AWS PrivateLink because it does not support IPsec.

5. A, D. DNS must be enabled for Amazon S3 endpoints to function. Amazon S3 endpoints do not require IP addresses. Endpoints also are not affected by private or public subnets. Amazon S3 endpoints do require a route in the routing table.

6. B, E. Inbound security groups do not define outbound policy. In addition, the NAT instance could have an iptables rule or similar firewall rule for 8080. It is possible for NAT instances to run out of ports, but it is nearly impossible for multiple instances to simultaneously run out of ports for 8080 because they support 65,000 ports. Network ACLs inbound block inbound ports, not outbound ports in this case. It is also possible for the server to be blocking the addresses or method you are using to access port 8080.

7. C. Transitive routing prevents instances from communicating across transitively peered VPCs. If instances are configured to use a proxy, then the destination IP on each hop is an instance in the peered VPC. You cannot define a route to a network interface in a peered VPC.

8. C, D. AWS PrivateLink does not use prefix lists. Instances do not need additional interfaces to use VPC endpoints. Instances do need to support DNS and to use the correct entry. Security groups can block access to private services. A route table with AWS PrivateLink will not have IP addresses.

9. A, D. You cannot create new CIDR ranges if you are at the maximum allowed routes. Subnets and VPCs do not affect new CIDR ranges. There are limitations on valid CIDR ranges based on the original CIDR range defined. Other VPCs do not create dependencies on adding. The VPC is new and so would not be peered with any other VPCs.

10. D. The routing, subnets, and new CIDR range are valid. New CIDR ranges must be more specific than existing routes, which is the case here. CIDR ranges do not need to be contiguous.

11. C, D. AWS PrivateLink can scale to this use case, as well as provide central services. Another option is to access these services over the Internet, provided that authentication and encryption are strong. VPC peering does not work with thousands of VPCs. Security groups cannot be referenced without an associated peering connection. You cannot create a VPN between two VGWs because neither will initiate a connection.

12. C. You cannot add different RFC1918 CIDR ranges to an existing VPC, and you also cannot use new CIDR ranges on existing subnets. In addition, NAT Gateways will not support custom NAT. The only option presented that works is peering to a new VPC.

13. B. This is a test of transitive routing rules. The only connection that has an external source from the perspective of VPC routing and an external destination is the virus scan. Traffic within the VPN stays on the instance and can route. The API request is sourced from

an instance in the peered VPC and the destination is an instance. While the web request appears to be an external source and destination, the packet is tunneled, so VPC sees it as a new flow, where the source is the network interface of the VPN server.

14. A, D. The Network Load Balancer and interface VPC endpoints are accessible over AWS Direct Connect. Gateway VPC endpoints require a proxy. The AWS metadata service isn't a network interface, so it could work through a proxy but would return results specific to the proxy.

15. C. The one large VPC approach and the replication approach do not meet the organizational requirements. Cross-account network interfaces will not scale, and you do not route code. This leaves AWS PrivateLink, which provides scalability and meets the requirements.

16. A, C. Auto-assigned addresses are not eligible for recall. You can only recall Elastic IP addresses the account has owned. Tagging is not necessary. It is possible to recall Elastic IP addresses in some scenarios. The Elastic IP address is not related to an instance number because it won't be automatically associated with an instance but rather returned to the account.

Chapter 4: Virtual Private Networks

1. A, E. VGW is the managed VPN endpoint for your Amazon VPC. Alternatively, you can terminate VPN on an Amazon EC2 instance.

2. B. Two tunnels are required: one to each of the Virtual Private Gateway's (VGW) endpoints.

3. B, C. When you create a dynamic tunnel, BGP is used. When you create a static tunnel, static routes are used.

4. D. In an Amazon EC2-based VPN termination option, you are responsible for maintaining all infrastructure from the operating system level up. AWS is responsible for maintaining the underlying hardware and Hypervisor.

5. A. The Source/Destination Check attribute controls whether source destination checking is enabled on the instance. Disabling this attribute enables an instance to handle network traffic that isn't specifically destined for the instance. Because this Amazon EC2 instance will handle and route traffic to all Amazon EC2 instances in the VPC in this case, this check has to be disabled.

6. B. Unlike site-to-site VPN, AWS currently doesn't offer a managed gateway endpoint for this type of VPN setup. You will have to use an Amazon EC2 instance as a client-to-site VPN gateway.

7. C. SSL or Transport Layer Security (TLS) works at the application layer and encrypts all TCP traffic. SSL is a more efficient algorithm than IPsec and is easier to deploy/use. By using SSL, you can also encrypt only the traffic for the application that requires it, whereas with IPsec all traffic is encrypted. Option D is incorrect as it covers encryption at rest while the question is about achieving encryption in motion.

8. A. The IP addresses of the VGW endpoints are automatically generated. These IP addresses are used to terminate the VPN connections.

Chapter 5: AWS Direct Connect

1. C. The VGW provides connectivity to your Amazon VPC. The Internet gateway provides access to the Internet. VPC endpoints are for specific AWS Cloud services. A peering connection is used to connect to other VPCs.

2. A. AWS Direct Connect requires the use of BGP to exchange routing information.

3. D. One is the minimum number of connections in a LAG.

4. D. AWS Direct Connect supports public and private VIFs.

5. A. Each AWS Direct Connect location has a minimum of two devices for resilience, meaning that a resilient connection can be established at a single location if desired.

6. C. One hundred prefixes can be announced over a private VIF.

7. A. A LAG behaves as a single Layer 2 connection. Each provisioned (VIF) spans the LAG but requires only a single BGP session.

8. B. Local routes to the VPC are always the highest priority route. Amazon VPC does not allow you to have more specific routing than the VPC Classless Inter-Domain Routing (CIDR) range.

9. B. A customer can define and allocate a VIF to another AWS account. This configuration is a hosted VIF.

10. D. The only mechanism to stop billing on an AWS Direct Connect connection is to delete the connection itself. Even with all the VIFs deleted, you are still charged the port-hour fees for the connection.

Chapter 6: Domain Name System and Load Balancing

1. A, E. There are two types of hosted zones: private and public. A private hosted zone is a container that holds information about how you want to route traffic for a domain and its subdomains within one or more Amazon VPCs. A public hosted zone is a container that holds information about how you want to route traffic on the Internet for a domain.

2. D. Amazon Route 53 can route queries to a variety of AWS resources. It is important to know what resources are not applicable, such as AWS CloudFormation and AWS OpsWorks.

3. C. If you want to stop sending traffic to a resource, you can change the weight for that record to 0.

4. A. If you associate a health check with a multivalue answer record, Amazon Route53 responds to Domain Name System (DNS) queries with the corresponding IP address only when the health check is healthy. If you do not associate a health check with a multivalue answer record, Amazon Route53 always considers the record to be healthy.

5. D. You get access to Amazon Route 53 traffic flow through the AWS Management Console. The console provides you with a visual editor that helps you create complex decision trees.

6. D. You can enable this function using a multivalue answer routing policy.

7. A. Classic Load Balancer and Application Load Balancer IP addresses may change as the load balancers scale. Referencing them by their IP addresses instead of DNS names may result in some load balancer endpoints being underutilized or sending traffic to incorrect endpoints.

8. B. When the `enableDnsHostname` attribute is set to true, Amazon will auto-assign DNS hostnames to Amazon EC2 instances.

9. D. `enableDnsHostnames` indicates whether the instances launched in the VPC will receive a public DNS hostname. `enableDnsSupport` indicates whether the DNS resolution is supported for the VPC. Both must be set to true for your Amazon EC2 instances to receive DNS hostnames within your VPC.

10. B. Network Load Balancer has support for static IP addresses for the load balancer. You can also assign one Elastic IP address per Availability Zone enabled for the load balancer.

Chapter 7: Amazon CloudFront

1. C. A CDN is a globally distributed network of caching servers that speed up the downloading of web pages and other content. CDNs use DNS geolocation to determine the geographic location of each request for a web page or other content.

2. D. If the content is already in the edge location with the lowest latency, Amazon CloudFront delivers it immediately. If the content is not currently in that edge location, Amazon CloudFront retrieves it from the origin server to deliver.

3. A, B, C. Amazon CloudFront is optimized to work with other AWS Cloud services as the origin server, including Amazon S3 buckets, Amazon S3 static websites, Amazon EC2 instances, and Elastic Load Balancing load balancers. Amazon CloudFront also works seamlessly with any non-AWS origin server, such as an existing on-premises web server.

4. B. Objects expire from the cache after 24 hours by default.

5. D. This feature removes the object from every Amazon CloudFront edge location regardless of the expiration period that you set for that object on your origin server.

6. A. You control which requests are served by which origin and how requests are cached using a feature called cache behaviors.

7. D. When streaming with Amazon CloudFront and using either of those protocols, Amazon CloudFront will break video into smaller chunks that are cached in the Amazon CloudFront network for improved performance and scalability.

8. C. When you add alternate domain names, you can use the wildcard * at the beginning of a domain name instead of specifying subdomains individually.

9. D. To use an ACM certificate with Amazon CloudFront, you must request or import the certificate in the US East (N. Virginia) Region.

10. D. To invalidate objects, you can specify either the path for individual objects or a path that ends with the * wildcard, which might apply to one object or many objects.

11. B. Amazon CloudFront can create log files that contain detailed information about every user request that Amazon CloudFront receives. Access logs are available for both web and Real-Time Messaging Protocol (RTMP) distributions. When you enable logging for your distribution, you specify the Amazon S3 bucket in which you want Amazon CloudFront to store log files.

Chapter 8: Network Security

1. B. AWS Organizations includes an account creation Application Programming Interface (API) that adds new accounts to the organization.

2. D. An AWS CloudFormation template contains the textual definition of your environment in JSON or YAML format. When you instantiate a template, it is called a stack.

3. A, B. Removing the human element with respect to creating, operating, managing, and decommissioning your AWS environment significantly contributes to overall security. People make mistakes, people bend the rules, and people can act with malice.

4. C. Amazon Route 53 stripes its Name Servers across four TLD servers to mitigate the impact of a TLD failure.

5. B. Origin Access Identity (OAI) is a special Amazon CloudFront user that you can associate with your Amazon S3 bucket to restrict access.

6. B. AWS Certificate Manager uses AWS KMS to help protect the private key.

7. C. AWS WAF integrates with Amazon CloudFront, Application Load Balancer, and Amazon Elastic Compute Cloud (Amazon EC2).

8. C, D. AWS Shield Standard provides protection for all AWS customers against the most common and frequently occurring infrastructure (Layer 3 and Layer 4) attacks, like SYN/User Datagram Protocol (UDP) floods, reflection attacks, and others, to support high availability of your applications on AWS.

9. A. A VPC endpoint enables you to create a private connection between your Amazon VPC and another AWS Cloud service without requiring access over the Internet, through a NAT device, a VPN connection, or AWS Direct Connect.

10. B. Security groups are stateful, whereas network ACLs are stateless.

11. D. Amazon Macie is a security service that uses machine learning to automatically discover, classify, and protect sensitive data in AWS.

12. D. Amazon VPC Flow Logs is a feature that enables you to capture information about the IP traffic going to and from network interfaces in your VPC.

13. A. Configure an Amazon CloudWatch scheduled event to call an AWS Lambda function each hour. The AWS Lambda function processes the threat intelligence data and populates an AWS WAF condition. The AWS WAF is associated with the Application Load Balancer.

Chapter 9: Network Performance

1. A, D. NAT gateways are capable of higher performance than NAT instances. Trying a larger instance type can increase bandwidth capacity to the private subnet instances. Amazon Linux has enhanced networking enabled by default. Only one route can exist for any given prefix.

2. D. Enhanced networking can help reduce jitter and network performance. Placement groups and lower latency will not assist with flows leaving the VPC. Network interfaces do not affect network performance. An Application Load Balancer will not assist with performance issues.

3. B. Using more than one instance will increase the performance because any given flow to Amazon S3 will be limited to 5 Gbps. Moving the instance will not increase Amazon S3 bandwidth. Placement groups will not increase Amazon S3 bandwidth either. Amazon S3 cannot be natively placed behind a Network Load Balancer.

4. A, B. R4 instances use network Input/Output (I/O) credits that allow higher bandwidths when credits are available, which may affect baseline performance tests. In addition, the database may have other application-level impacts on the performance of the TCP stream.

5. A, C. Operating systems must support the appropriate network driver for the correct instance type. The AMI or instance must be flagged for enhanced networking support in addition to having driver support.

6. D. Jumbo frames are not supported over the Internet, and VPN will not increase throughput. Increasing the packets per second will most likely reduce throughput. There are additional measures that could be taken instead, such as tweaking operating system Transmission Control Protocol (TCP) stacks, using network accelerators, or changing application mechanics.

7. C. Placement groups will provide more benefit than other features for applications such as High Performance Computing (HPC) that are extremely sensitive to latency and throughput.

8. C. Distribute flows across many instances to ensure that the bandwidth of any given flow or instance does not limit overall performance. Enhanced networking can assist with performance, but does not increase scale. BGP and VPC routing also do not increase the scale of data transfer.

9. A. Amazon EBS Provisioned IOPS will help reduce latency and create more consistent disk performance.

10. C. Jitter is the variance in delay between packets. You can reduce jitter by making delay more consistent. Enhanced networking and eliminating CPU or disk bottlenecks can help reduce jitter.

11. C, D. C4 instances support the Intel Virtual Function driver, and C5 instances support the ENA driver. In addition, the instance must be flagged for enhanced networking. There are no specific instance routes in an Amazon Virtual Private Cloud (Amazon VPC).

12. D. If your throughput is lower, increasing the MTU in your Amazon Virtual Private Cloud (Amazon VPC) can increase performance. Unless there are application issues, using the largest MTU available (9,001 bytes) will help increase performance. Jitter is not typically an issue for throughput. Amazon VPC will treat all packets fairly, without QoS. Using a Network Load Balancer per instance would be inefficient and reduce performance.

13. A, C, E. AWS Direct Connect offers lower latency and more control over monitoring than VPN or Internet connections offer. QoS can be configured on the circuit connected to AWS Direct Connect, but not within the AWS networks. This typically means that the service provider network will honor Differentiated Services Code Point (DSCP) bits, but any egress packets from AWS will be dropped equally. Similarly, jumbo frames can be configured, but this would not offer any performance benefit because jumbo frames are only supported within an Amazon Virtual Private Cloud (Amazon VPC).

14. A, D, E, G. Amazon CloudWatch metrics and host metrics will be the most efficient way to determine bottlenecks. Packet captures and the other options can help in some situations, but they are not the most efficient. Elastic network interfaces do not affect whether a workload is network bound.

15. A, D. VPN instances should support enhanced networking for the highest performance possible. IPsec as a protocol can reduce throughput, putting more pressure on both packets per second and bandwidth. The VGW is managed by AWS. IPsec as a protocol doesn't function through a Network Load Balancer due to non-Transmission Control Protocol (TCP) protocols like Encapsulating Security Protocol (ESP) and User Datagram Protocol (UDP).

16. B. A single placement group is specific to one Availability Zone, which would reduce availability.

17. A, C. It is important to support enhanced networking for instances with networking requirements. In addition, the instance sizes and families that the operating system supports will largely define its maximum throughput and bandwidth.

18. D. The Network Load Balancer will be able to provide lower latency and faster scaling for TCP traffic than the Classic Load Balancer. Both the Application Load Balancer and Amazon CloudFront options require sharing the private key with others. You cannot configure enhanced networking on Elastic Load Balancing.

19. C. Using AWS Direct Connect is the most accurate answer. AWS Direct Connect does not provide native encryption. VPN connections do not scale individually per connection. Latency is not something you can manage reliably with TCP tuning or network appliances.

20. D. MTUs allow for applications to send more data per packet, which can increase throughput. Jumbo frames are enabled in a VPC by default and work outside of placement groups.

21. C. DPDK is a set of libraries and tools used to reduce networking overhead in the operating system.

22. D. Elastic network interfaces do not have an effect on network performance for any instance that supports enhanced networking.

23. B. Multicast traffic requires Layer 2 switching and routing infrastructure that are not present in a VPC. It is best to redesign the application components and provide low latency with a placement group.

24. C. Bandwidth is the maximum data transfer rate at any point in the network.

25. D. TCP has congestion management protocols built-in and will adapt to traffic changes. UDP does not, so it will not natively adapt to changing network conditions.

Chapter 10: Automation

1. C. AWS CloudFormation can detect syntax errors but not semantic errors. If a service call it makes returns an error, then the stack creation or update process stops. By default, AWS CloudFormation rolls back the stack to the previous state.

2. A. AWS CloudFormation is not aware that the route must wait for the gateway attachment to finish first, so this dependency must be explicitly stated. The order of resources is irrelevant in a template. Waiting may help reduce the errors, but it does not provide a guarantee and may make create or update operations unnecessarily slower.

3. D. AWS CloudFormation deletes every resource except those that have a `DeletionPolicy` of `Retain`. It does not have a way to detect whether resources are in use (this may prevent a resource from being deleted, but AWS CloudFormation will still attempt to do so). Tags beginning with `aws:` cannot be altered by users.

4. A, E. AWS CodePipeline can monitor AWS CodeCommit, public GitHub repositories, and ZIP file bundles on Amazon S3. Repositories stored elsewhere must be published to Amazon S3 as a ZIP bundle.

5. C. The Amazon CloudWatch Logs agent can be installed on an instance to monitor log files. When data is added to a log file, the agent sends them to Amazon CloudWatch Logs where they can be aggregated into a single log group.

6. D. Parameters are the most straightforward way to make a template reusable. The other solutions can be made to work, but they introduce unnecessary complexity into the template.

7. C. Creating a change set will show how a new template differs from the current stack state. Executing the change set ensures that only those changes are executed. The execution will be rejected if the stack changed since the change set was generated. Executing the template instead may overwrite intermediate changes. The `ValidateTemplate` API only verifies the syntactic correctness of the template. Approval actions are used with AWS CodePipeline—not AWS CloudFormation.

8. A. A version control system such as Git provides a history of changes made to the source code and allows you to create branches for experimental development. Amazon S3 versioning only allows linear changes and does not provide visualization capabilities. AWS CloudFormation and AWS CodePipeline do not record history.

9. D. AWS CloudFormation cannot detect this semantic error. Resource creation is unordered except when there is a dependency, so the order in which the subnets are created is indeterminate. When an error is encountered, AWS CloudFormation attempts to roll back the update.

10. A. The stack policy can prevent resources from being modified, deleted, or replaced when a stack is updated. The IAM service role will also effectively do this, but it will also prohibit other subnets from being deleted. `DeletionPolicy` only applies when the AWS CloudFormation stack is being deleted—not the resource itself. Tags starting with `aws:` cannot be modified.

Chapter 11: Service Requirements

1. C, D. Amazon AppStream 2.0 and Amazon WorkSpaces are both AWS Cloud services that support end-user connectivity into applications running within a VPC.

2. B. There are two adapters connected to each WorkSpace instance: one in a customer Virtual Private Cloud (VPC) and another in an AWS-managed VPC.

3. B, C. AWS Lambda requires NAT to connect to the Internet. Public IP addresses cannot be assigned to an AWS Lambda function.

4. A, B, D. Internet connectivity is not a requirement for Amazon EMR; however, Amazon S3 connectivity, DNS hostnames, and private IP addresses are required.

5. D. AWS Lambda is an AWS Cloud service that allows for serverless code execution.

6. B, C. A NAT gateway or public IP with an Internet gateway attached to the VPC is required for Internet connectivity within Amazon WorkSpaces. Both options require user configuration and are not set up by default.

7. B. Amazon RDS is the AWS service that provides managed database instances.

8. A. A Multi-AZ deployment requires two subnets in order to provide high availability for Amazon RDS.

9. C. AWS Elastic Beanstalk can automatically provision and scale an infrastructure on behalf of a user.

10. D. AWS Elastic Beanstalk deploys the infrastructure automatically. Custom Virtual Private Clouds (VPCs) and security groups can be used but are not required.

11. A, B. AWS Database Migration Service (AWS DMS) facilitates replication between different database engines. Direct connectivity between the databases is not required.

12. C. Amazon Redshift requires an IP for each node in the cluster, plus one additional IP for the leader node.

13. D. Only the Amazon RDS hostname (or a CNAME to it) should be used to connect. It will be updated in the event of a failover.

Chapter 12: Hybrid Architectures

1. A. An AWS Direct Connect public VIF allows private connectivity from on-premises to AWS Cloud services.

2. B. Host-based IPS/IDS is a more scalable solution and does not impose challenges regarding high availability and throughput scalability that inline IPS/IDS gateways impose. It is also more cost effective because it does not require inline gateways to be run.

3. A. VGW is a managed endpoint.

4. A. You can use a VPN/routing software on the Amazon EC2 instance that supports packet manipulation based on QoS markings. Using separate Amazon EC2 VPN instances will not help because the traffic from the VPC to on-premises can only use one Amazon EC2 instance as a gateway. Using two VPCs will not work because the traffic from the VPC to the on-premises gateway will not have QoS and so will contend for the same router resources.

5. D. Only interface VPC endpoints can be accessed over AWS Direct Connect.

6. A. To send all traffic via a VPC, you will have to proxy all traffic via Amazon EC2 instances. AWS Storage Gateway supports HTTP proxy in the file gateway mode.

7. A. You can use a public VIF to access Amazon DynamoDB. You can use Amazon DynamoDB client libraries to encrypt traffic as it is being written to the database. VPN is not required.

8. B. You can reduce latency by setting up a local hub in the Singapore region. Traffic would then flow from the spoke VPC in the Mumbai region to the hub in the Singapore region and then to the spoke in the Singapore region. GRE should be used over IPsec for reduced latencies because GRE does not encrypt data, resulting in faster packet processing.

9. C. AWS Direct Connect private VIF will enable connectivity from on-premises Amazon EC2 instances to the on-premises Active Directory server.

10. C. Transit VPC should not be used for basic hybrid IT connectivity. It should be leveraged only for special scenarios, such as inline packet inspection.

Chapter 13: Network Troubleshooting

1. B. Sticky sessions will enable a session to be kept with the same web server to facilitate stateful connections.
2. D. Because you can access the instance but not the Internet, there is not a default route to the Internet through the on-premises network.
3. C. NAT gateways need to be in a public subnet to enable communication with the Internet.
4. B. All but a NAT gateway is required for Internet connectivity from a public subnet.
5. A. There is a limit of 25 VPC peering connections per VPC by default.
6. E. Answers A through D are all possible misconfigurations.
7. C, D. Both Domain Name System (DNS) settings must be enabled on a VPC for a private hosted zone to work correctly.
8. D. Some AWS Cloud services rely on the existence of a default VPC. There is an option to create a new default VPC.
9. C. Network ACL rules can deny traffic.
10. A, B. Flow logs and packet captures are two ways to record the source and destination IP addresses of traffic.

Chapter 14: Billing

1. C. Peering carries a \$0.01 per-GB charge for traffic leaving or entering a VPC; therefore, a single flow would cost \$0.02 in each direction. Being in the same Availability Zone does not affect pricing.
2. B. Because the data transfer is to another region, you will be charged for egress from the source region.
3. B. The VGW IPsec endpoints are considered AWS public IPs, and the resource is owned by you. The reduced AWS Direct Connect rate applies because of these factors.
4. B. Your on-premises data center is not within AWS public IP address range, so data transfer is metered as Internet-in, which is not charged.
5. B. Budgets enable forecasting and allow you to set alarms to trigger on current billing.
6. B. Charges start when the connection becomes available for the first time, or 90 days from creation, whichever occurs first.
7. C. Active session charge is used as a component of Load Balancer Capacity Units (LCUs) in Elastic Load Balancing, not NAT gateway.

8. A. Data transfer from Amazon S3 to Amazon CloudFront is not charged.
9. B. The bucket owner always pays for data transfer from their bucket. In this particular example, they pay Internet-out rates.
10. B. The Availability Zone does not affect the pricing when communicating via public IP, so the charge is at the regional data transfer rate.

Chapter 15: Risk and Compliance

1. B, D. Security groups and network ACLs permit or deny traffic. These determinations are reflected in Amazon VPC Flow Log data.
2. D. Amazon Inspector supports evaluation durations between 15 minutes and 24 hours.
3. A. AWS Artifact provides on-demand access to AWS security and compliance documents, also known as audit artifacts.
4. A. IAM uses a PARC access model.
5. A. The AWS CloudTrail record digest uses SHA-256 for hashing.
6. B. AWS accepts requests via an authenticated, online web form and via email.
7. D. Authorization may be requested for a maximum of 90 days per request.
8. C. AWS is responsible for maintaining Amazon VPC separation assurance; however, the customer is responsible for configuring subnets, security groups, NACLs, and other application-layer mechanisms appropriately.
9. C. The AWS Organizations SCP is applied to member account root users in addition to IAM users.
10. D. Amazon Inspector is an automated security assessment service that helps improve the security and compliance of applications deployed on AWS.

Chapter 16: Scenarios and Reference Architectures

1. A. Amazon Route 53 weighted policies provide the most control over how much traffic is directed to specific application resources. Failover policies would not support a gradual migration, and latency-based and geolocation policies offer limited administrative control about which requests get directed at specific application resources.

2. A. VPN connections typically reuse existing on-premises VPN equipment and Internet connections. AWS Direct Connect requires a new circuit to be provisioned. Options C and D are options for providing access to individual applications or AWS services, not for connecting networks.

3. D. Amazon Route 53 geolocation policies provide the ability to direct users based on their geographic location, and are therefore the only way to direct customers to applications based on their locality. Weighted and failover policies are indiscriminate of location. Latency-based policies operate based on end-user latency, which often is correlated to end-user location, but not always.

4. A. AWS WAF can be integrated with Application Load Balancer for blocking IP addresses at scale. Network ACLs can deny traffic but not to the required scale. AWS Shield and Amazon VPC Private Link do not provide capabilities for denying network traffic.

5. A. In this scenario, the network requirements for on-premises network connectivity are exceeding the network capacity of Amazon EC2 instances operating outside of a placement group. This requirement eliminates Options B and D. Option C provides a different interface for interacting with on-premises resources, but it does not reduce the amount of traffic that must traverse the network. AWS Direct Connect connections will allow on-premises connectivity to scale beyond individual Amazon EC2 instance network limitations, and AWS Direct Connect gateway will provide a similar experience as a transit VPC for all attached VPCs.

6. C. Option A is not highly available. Option B disables cross-region traffic, which is not the desired outcome. Option D is not possible. This leaves option C as the best answer.

7. B. Amazon Route 53 latency-based policies will route a request to the closest location based on client latency. Weighted and failover policies are indiscriminate of location. Geolocation is indiscriminate of end-user latency.

8. C. AWS Direct Connect public Virtual Interfaces (VIF) support on-premises access to AWS APIs. All of the other options require additional infrastructure and configuration, which can introduce additional complexity and variability into the network design.

9. C, D. Amazon Route 53 geolocation policies are suited for directing user traffic to location-specific services. Failover policies are useful for sending requests to a redundant, backup location in the event that the primary site fails its health checks.

10. D. NAT Gateways provide a highly-scalable network egress option for Amazon EC2 instances in private networks. Egress-only Internet Gateways provide IPv6 egress traffic. Neither transit VPCs nor Amazon EC2 NAT instances are as scalable as NAT Gateways.

11. A. Replicating your users and permissions to a VPC peered shared services network is the only option that will reduce on-premises network traffic. All of the other options continue to send all authentication and authorization traffic to on-premises resources.

Index

A

B

C

D

E

F

G

H

I

J

K

L

M

N

O

P

R

S

T

U

V

W-Z

Comprehensive Online Learning Environment

Register to gain one year of FREE access to the comprehensive online interactive learning environment and test bank to help you study for your AWS Certified Advanced Networking - Specialty exam.

The online test bank includes:

- **Assessment Test** to help you focus your study to specific objectives
- **Chapter Tests** to reinforce what you've learned
- **Practice Exams** to test your knowledge of the material
- **Digital Flashcards** to reinforce your learning and provide last-minute test prep before the exam
- **Searchable Glossary** to define the key terms you'll need to know for the exam

Go to `http://www.wiley.com/go/sybextestprep` to register and gain access to this comprehensive study tool package.